The Routledge Companion to Creativity

Creativity can be as difficult to define as it is to achieve. This is a complex and compelling area of study and this volume is perfectly poised to explore how creativity can be better understood, and used, in a range of contexts. The book not only centres on creativity in wider organizational theory, but also defines the conditions in which creativity can flourish, and assesses how the contemporary business environment has an impact on creative solutions.

The volume grounds concepts of creativity in sound theoretical frameworks and explores issues of practical and theoretical consequence covering a range of themes, including:

- innovation and entrepreneurship
- creativity and design
- environmental influences
- knowledge management
- meta-theories of creativity
- personal creativity
- structured interventions

Comprising articles written by an unusually wide array of leading creativity scholars, *The Routledge Companion to Creativity* is an insightful resource text and is an essential purchase for anyone with an interest in creativity from a business, psychology or design perspective.

Tudor Rickards is Professor of Creativity at Manchester Business School, UK. He is founding co-editor (with Susan Moger) of the journal *Creativity and Innovation Management*. His extensive publications include *Dilemmas of Leadership*, published by Routledge in 2006.

Mark A. Runco is E. Paul Torrance Professor of Creative Studies at the University of Georgia, USA. He is also a Professor at the Norwegian School of Economics and Business. He has published extensively and is editor of the *Creativity Research Journal*.

Susan Moger is a Senior Fellow in Leadership at Manchester Business School, UK. She is founding co-editor of the journal *Creativity and Innovation Management* and has written and edited a number of books, including the *Handbook for Creative Team Leaders*, published by Gower in 1999.

The Routledge Companion to Creativity

Edited by Tudor Rickards, Mark A. Runco and Susan Moger

LONDON AND NEW YORK

First published 2009
by Routledge
2 Park Square, Milton Park, Abingdon, Oxon OX14 4RN

Simultaneously published in the USA and Canada
by Routledge
270 Madison Avenue, New York NY 10016

Routledge is an imprint of the Taylor and Francis Group, an informa business

© 2009 Tudor Rickards, Mark A. Runco and Susan Moger

Typeset in Bembo by Swales & Willis Ltd, Exeter, Devon
Printed and bound in Great Britain by
The Cromwell Press, Trowbridge, Wiltshire

British Library Cataloguing in Publication Data
A catalogue record for this book is available from the British Library

Library of Congress Cataloging-in-Publication Data
The Routledge companion to creativity / edited by Tudor Rickards, Mark A. Runco, and
Susan Moger.
p. cm.
Includes bibliographical references and index.
1. Creative ability in business.   I. Rickards, Tudor.   II. Runco, Mark A.   III. Moger, Susan.
HD53.R687 2008
658.3′14—dc22   2008021055

ISBN 10: 0–415–77317–2 (hbk)
ISBN 10: 0–203–88884–7 (ebk)

ISBN 13: 978–0–415–77317–1 (hbk)
ISBN 13: 978–0–203–88884–1 (ebk)

Contents

List of figures and tables   viii
List of contributors   x
Acknowledgements   xiii

Part 1: Introduction   1

1   *The Companion to Creativity*: a synoptic overview   3
    Tudor Rickards, Mark A. Runco and Susan Moger

Part 2: Creativity and design   11

Theme 1 Creativity and design

2   Creativity, improvisation and organizations   13
    Colin M. Fisher and Teresa Amabile

3   Creativity and sound: the agony of the senses   25
    Richard Coyne

4   Unleashing the creative potential of design in business   37
    Margaret Bruce

5   Space to adapt: workplaces, creative behaviour and
    organizational memetics   46
    Ilfryn Price

Part 3: Environmental actors and influences   59

Theme 2 Environmental influences

6 Creating or destroying business value: understanding the opportunities
and the limits of a win–win collaboration   61
Andrew Cox

7 The style/involvement model of consumer innovation   71
Gordon Foxall and Victoria James

8 Creativity and knowledge relationships in the creative industries   88
Paul Jeffcutt

9 Leading for renewal: the value of positive turbulence   99
Stanley S. Gryskiewicz

Theme 3 Innovation and entrepreneurship

10 Evolutionary models of innovation and creativity   109
Colin Martindale

11 Creativity and entrepreneurship   119
Mathew Manimala

12 Social networks and creativity: combining expertise in complex innovations   132
Arent Greve

Part 4: Creativity and knowledge   147

Theme 4 Knowledge management

13 Knowledge management and the management of creativity   149
Geir Kaufmann and Mark A. Runco

14 Creating organizational knowledge dialogically: an outline of a theory   160
Haridimos Tsoukas

Theme 5 Meta-theories of creativity

15 Computers and creativity: models and applications   179
Margaret Boden

16 Relationship creativity in collectives at multiple levels   189
Subrata Chakrabarty and Richard W. Woodman

17 Creativity and economics: current perspectives   206
Isaac Getz and Todd Lubart

18 Deconstructing creativity   222
Alf Rehn and Christian De Cock

19 Idea activity in our nations and workplaces   232
    Glenn Rothberg

Part 5: The creative individual   245

Theme 6 Personal creativity

20 Genius, creativity and leadership   247
    Dean Keith Simonton

21 Intellectual styles and creativity   256
    Li-fang Zhang and Robert J. Sternberg

22 Creativity and personality   267
    Stephen J. Guastello

23 The thinking of creative leaders: outward focus, inward focus and integration 279
    Michael D. Mumford, Cristina L. Byrne and Amanda S. Shipman

24 Creativity: a systems perspective   292
    Seana Moran

25 Change-oriented leadership behaviour: a consequence of
    post-bureauratic organisations?   302
    Jouko Arvonen

Theme 7 Structured interventions

26 Prototyping processes that affect organizational creativity   317
    Cameron Ford

27 Creative problem solving: past, present and future   327
    Gerard Puccio and John Cabra

28 Thinking outside the box: Edward de Bono's lateral thinking   338
    Sandra Dingli

29 Computer-supported idea generation   351
    Rene Ziegler and Michael Diehl

Part 6: Integration   361

30 Integration: prospects for future journeys   363
    Mark A. Runco, Tudor Rickards and Susan Moger

Index   371

List of figures and tables

Figures

2.1 Realms of individual and collective action in organizations   17
2.2 Proposed model of improvisational creativity on organizations   20
4.1 Linking creativity and design to business performance   40
6.1 Objective outcomes in inter-organizational exchange between buyers suppliers   64
8.1 CI ecosystem: key features   93
11.1 Creativity and entrepreneurship: a conceptual model   127
14.1 The dialogical and quasi-dialogical creation of knowledge in organizations   168
14.2 Petra's architectural drawings   170
16.1 The 'How' of the role of relationships for creativity   193
16.2 Framework: three creativity outcomes at three levels of analysis   197
19.1 Workplace perspective on idea activity   237
23.1 Key processes involved in leader creative thought   289
27.1 Creative problem solving: the Thinking Skills Model   330

Tables

7.1 Summary of research findings   76
16.1 Overall process leading to creativity in collectives   194
16.2 Creative action process   194
19.1 Average growth in real GDP and innovation among OECD countries, 1985–2004   238
19.2 Average of annual growth rates estimated factor contributions to OECD economic growth, selected countries 1985–2004   239
21.1 Intellectual styles   258

22.1 Validity coefficients for 16PF and CPS creativity indices based on
      profiles of incumbents in creative occupations and creative behavior   270
22.2 Correlations between source traits and creative behavior   273
25.1 Factor analyses of the CPE measures from the five studies   306
25.2 CPE dimensions and effectiveness assessments   309
27.1 Creative problem-solving models: developments and spin-offs   329
28.1 Summary of lateral thinking and related methodologies   342

List of contributors

Teresa Amabile is Edsel Bryant Ford Professor of Business Administration at Harvard Business School, USA.

Jouko Arvonen is a Senior Consultant and owner of the FaraxGroup in Stockholm and Helsinki.

Margaret A. Boden is Research Professor of Cognitive Science in the Centre for Research in Cognitive Science at the University of Sussex, Brighton, UK

Margaret Bruce is Professor of Design Management and Marketing at the Manchester Business School, University of Manchester, UK, Professor of Strategic Management of Design, ICN Ecole de Management, Université de Nancy 2, France, and Professor of Design and Fashion Retailing, University of the Arts, London, UK

Cristina L. Byrne is a Doctoral Student in Industrial and Organizational Psychology at the University of Oklahoma, USA.

John Cabra is Assistant Professor of Creativity at the International Center for Studies in Creativity, Buffalo State – State University of New York.

Subrata Chakrabarty is a PhD candidate in the Department of Management at Mays Business School, Texas A&M University, USA.

Andrew Cox is Chairman of Robertson Cox Limited, UK.

Richard Coyne is Professor of Architectural Computing and Head of the School of Arts, Culture and Environment at the University of Edinburgh, UK.

Christian De Cock is Professor of Organizations Studies at Swansea University, UK.

Michael Diehl is Professor of Personality and Social Psychology in the Department of Psychology at the Eberhard-Karls-University in Tuebingen, Germany.

Sandra Dingli is Director of the Edward de Bono Institute for the Design and Development of Thinking, University of Malta, Malta.

Colin M. Fisher is a Doctoral Candidate in Organizational Behavior at Harvard University, USA.

Cameron Ford is an Associate Professor of Organization Management at the University of Central Florida, and Director of the UCF Center for Entrepreneurship and Innovation.

Gordon Foxall is Distinguished Research Professor, Cardiff Business School, Cardiff University, Wales, UK.

Isaac Getz is Professor, Idea, Involvement, Innovation Management at ESCP-EAP European School of Management, Paris, France

Arent Greve is Dr. oecon, Professor in the Department of Strategy and Management at the Norwegian School of Economics and Business Administration.

Stan Gryskiewicz is President of Positive Turbulence LLC in Alexandra, Virginia and Senior Fellow at the Center for Creative Leadership, USA.

Stephen J. Guastello is Professor of Industrial Organizational Psychology and Human Factors Engineering at Marquette University, Milwaukee, USA.

Victoria James is a Lecturer in Marketing and Strategy at Cardiff Business School, Cardiff University, Wales, UK.

Paul Jeffcutt is Professor of Management Knowledge at Queen's University School of Management, Belfast, UK.

Geir Kaufmann is Professor of Psychology in the Lillehammer University College, Lillehammer, Norway.

Todd Lubart is Professor of Psychology at University of Paris Descartes, France.

Mathew J. Manimala is Professor of Organizational Behaviour at the Indian Institute of Management, Bangalore, India.

Colin Martindale is Professor Emeritus at the University of Maine, USA and Honorary Professor of Psychology and Art, Perm State Institute of Arts and Culture, Perm, Russia.

Susan Moger is a Senior Fellow in Leadership, Manchester Business School, University of Manchester, UK.

Seana Moran is a Research Associate for the Youth Purpose Project at the Center for Adolescence, Stanford University, California, USA.

Michael D. Mumford is George Lynn Cross Distinguished Research Professor at the University of Oklahoma, USA.

Ilfryn Price is Professor of Innovation and Facilities Management in the Faculty of Organisation and Management at Sheffield Hallam University, UK.

Gerard J. Puccio is Professor of Creativity and Department Chair at the International Center for Studies in Creativity, Buffalo State – State University of New York.

Alf Rehn is Professor of Innovation and Entrepreneurship at the Royal Institute of Technology, Stockholm, Sweden and Chair of Management and Organization at Abo Akademi University in Finland.

Tudor Rickards is Professor of Creativity and Organisational Change, Manchester Business School, University of Manchester, UK.

Glenn Rothberg is Managing Director of Intrepid Group, Melbourne, Australia.

Mark A. Runco is the E. Paul Torrance Professor of Creative Studies at the University of Georgia, Athens, USA, and Professor at the Norwegian School of Economics and Business Administration.

Amanda S. Shipman is a Doctoral Student in Industrial and Organizational Psychology at the University of Oklahoma, USA.

Dean Keith Simonton is Distinguished Professor of Psychology at the University of California, Davis, USA.

Robert J. Sternberg is Dean of the School of Arts and Sciences and Professor of Psychology at Tufts University in Medford, MA, USA.

Haridimos Tsoukas is the George D. Mavros Research Professor of Organization Theory, ALBA, Greece, and Professor of Organization Studies, University of Warwick, UK.

Richard W. Woodman is Fouraker Professor of Business and Professor of Management, Mays Business School, Texas A&M University, USA.

Li-fang Zhang is Associate Dean for Research Higher Degrees in the Faculty of Education at the University of Hong Kong.

Rene Ziegler is Senior Lecturer (Social and Organisational Psychology) in the Department of Psychology at the Eberhard-Karls-University in Tuebingen, Germany.

Acknowledgements

We would like to thank our colleagues and friends in the creativity community for their encouragement and support in the production of this book. John Arnold gave encouragement and support when it was greatly needed. Jonathan Guiliano, Alex Hough and Andy Timming made contributions to manuscripts at critical stages, and all our authors responded to our invitation to contribute with enthusiasm and commitment. The editors gratefully acknowledge the support given by their academic institutes for the work carried out during the editing process. We also thank the editorial and production teams at Routledge for the opportunity to produce this volume.

A special thanks to Margaret Cannon, editorial coordinator *extraordinaire*, without whose professional expertise and dedication this book would not have been possible.

Tudor Rickards, Mark A. Runco and Susan Moger
April 2008

Part 1

Introduction

The Companion to Creativity: a synoptic overview

Tudor Rickards, Mark A. Runco and Susan Moger

A companion is literally someone who accompanies you on your journeys. This book is a metaphoric companion to accompany you on your journeys into the realms of creativity. Experienced guides into such journeys have provided the contents.

Each traveler will be on a unique personal journey. It may be part of an examined course of study or it may be for development of creative understanding and potential in your professional life. The companion offers a wide range of information and suggestions in support of your leadership goals whatever they may be.

This edited book was conceived as of primary concern to researchers, teachers, postgraduates, masters and possibly undergraduate students of creativity within the organizational and professional domains seeking authoritative and critical perspectives.

Its contents are planned as short commissioned articles organized thematically rather than in A to Z format. Each chapter by an invited expert offers insights into cutting edge research and relevant implications for creative action

Themes of the *Companion*

In planning the book, the editors carried out a comprehensive review of contemporary works on creativity. Many of the authors of the chapters in the *Companion* figured prominently in that review. We were also able to draw on the contents of leading creativity journals. Rickards and Moger (2006) provided a classification framework of themes, which were able to adapt for the *Companion*. Runco and Pritzker's *Encyclopedia of Creativity* (1999) offered a comprehensive account of historical and contemporary issues. Other earlier texts to which we are indebted include Sternberg (1999), Glover *et al.* (1989), Runco and Albert (1980) and Boden (1994).

Each theme provides a focus around which issues of practical and theoretical consequence are explored. Our sequencing of themes has the merit of coherence, although we considered various other possibilities and other labels before reaching the final design decision. Furthermore, readers may conclude with us that some of the chapters could have fitted adequately into themes other than the ones allocated by the editorial choice.

We are particularly pleased with the international perspectives provided by the contributors who demonstrate the global nature of contemporary research into creativity. Their work extends, as suggested by Runco and Pritzker (1999), in domains as diverse as education, design, innovation, economics, problem solving, artificial intelligence, cognition and aesthetics. The chapters offer something of value to a readership in such fields including researchers, teachers, postgraduate, executive masters and possibly undergraduate students of creativity.

Theme 1: Creativity and design

Colin M. Fisher and Teresa Amabile – 'Creativity, improvisation and organizations'

Colin Fisher and Teresa Amabile suggest that there is a standard or dominant perspective, which presents organizational creativity as a series of bounded stages. The chapter offers improvisational processes as occurring in a way that cannot be confined within specific components of a linear characterization. Acts of organizational creativity (in common with acts of artistic or scientific creativity) are executed according to plan. However, expertise will have been acquired and skills developed through relevant experiences, which serve as prior rehearsals to acts of improvisation.

Richard Coyne – 'Creativity and sound: the agony of the senses'

Richard Coyne examines how creativity in design is mediated by the relationship between the senses, and the nature of engagement with the sensory experience. He helps position creativity as situated cognition. While vision and creativity are easily associated, creativity and sound are less so. He notes a Lacanian breach through which voice is denied, unless the creator/designer is able to reclaim it as embodied creativity.

Margaret Bruce – 'Unleashing the creative potential of design in business'

Margaret Bruce presents design as the purposive application of creativity throughout the process, which results in organizational innovation and competitiveness. She offers illustrative examples of organizations, which compete through design creativity. She illustrates how Fisher and Amabile's improvisation model matches the process of design creativity as well.

Ilfryn Price – 'Space to adapt: workplaces, creative behaviour and organizational memetics'

Ilfryn Price picks up the theme of situated creativity, and the significance of space or place, taking an evolutionary perspective. He notes the significance of language as a symbol system (cf. Coyne's treatment of sound and voice). Here, the focus is on the non-transparent nature of space within processes of creativity and design.

Theme 2: Environmental influences

Andrew Cox – 'Creating or destroying business value: understanding the opportunities and the limits of win–win collaboration'

Creativity has been frequently associated with synergy or integration of divergent perspectives through association, or bisociation. Win–win resolution of individual differences has attractive rhetorical possibilities. Andrew Cox shows that collaboration can create value, but can also destroy it according to context.

Gordon Foxall and Victoria James – 'The style/involvement model of consumer innovation'

Foxall and James examine an important issue in consumer research regarding consumer innovativeness. They offer a clarification of terminology regarding innovativeness. They report a series of studies demonstrating that consumers' innovation orientation will be situationally influenced.

Paul Jeffcutt – 'Creativity in the creative industries'

Paul Jeffcutt maintains that to understand creativity in the so-called creative industries, a key research challenge will be to overcome existing problems in the availability and sharing of detailed research knowledge on particular cultural economies and establish a generic framework for knowledge building

Stanley S. Gryskiewicz – 'Positive turbulence'

Stan Gyskiewicz confronts the increasingly significant environment of uncontrollable turbulence. His contribution is to examine the environment for means of responding effectively (positively) to such environments as a means of organizational renewal.

Theme 3: Innovation and entrepreneurship

Three chapters connect this theme to issues central to creativity.

Colin Martindale – 'Evolutionary models of innovation and creativity'

Colin Martindale reviews evolutionary models of innovation and creativity, revealing pre-Darwinian and non-Darwinian origins. He warns against simplistic metaphoric treatments of creativity, such as random variation within idea search and selection, or environmental adaptation.

Matthew Manimala – 'Creativity and entrepreneurship'

Matthew Manimala focuses on the creativity of entrepreneurs. Drawing on empirical and conceptual evidence, he proposes a framework for exploring the process through which entrepreneurs generate and gain acceptance for their ideas in their search for competitive advantage.

Arent Greve – 'Social networks and creativity'

Arent Greve offers case evidence of complex technological innovations in support of a multi-level analysis to understand how individual entrepreneurial efforts interact within networks of organizations and industries. Entrepreneurs are advised to understand the importance of building and maintaining social networks.

Theme 4: Knowledge management

Geir Kaufmann and Mark A. Runco – 'Knowledge management and the management of creativity'

Kaufman and Runco take on the challenge of exploring the role of creativity in knowledge management. They argue that learning, retention, thinking and creativity are 'in the same loop' and should not be regarded as separate, distinct and encapsulated processes.

Haridimos Tsoukas – 'Creating organizational knowledge dialogically: an outline of a theory'

Haridimos Tsoukas argues that an individual gains knowledge from the exercise of judgement involving dialogical relationships with real and imagined others and with artifacts. His contribution also adds to the theme of design creativity by drawing on the work of Donald Schön (1983).

Theme 5: Meta-theories of creativity

Margaret Boden – 'Computers and creativity: models and applications'

Margaret Boden provides a concise account of important themes in her extensive studies of computers and creativity. She shows how some of the ambiguities in creativity literature have arisen, and how they might be clarified. Her focus is on psychological (C) creativity, which she believes can be better understood through artificial intelligence studies.

Subrata Chakrabarty and Richard W. Woodman – 'Relationship creativity at multiple levels'

Chakrabarty and Woodman develop the well-known multi-level of creativity proposed in Woodman *et al.* (1993). In this chapter, the authors provide a framework of relationships at team, organization and sectoral levels, illustrating the significance of individual and collective creative actions.

Isaac Getz and Todd Lubart – 'Creativity and economics: current perspectives'

Getz and Lubart show how creativity theory has drawn on and been enriched through concepts from the economic domain. They further explore the investment theory of creativity (Sternberg and Lubart 1991, 1995).

Alf Rehn and Christian de Cock – 'De-constructing creativity'

Alf Rehn and Christian de Cock take on one of the precepts in traditional treatments of creativity. They apply a deconstructive technique to challenge assumptions about the nature, significance and centrality of novelty within the creative process.

Glenn Rothberg – 'Idea activity in our nations and workplaces'

Glenn Rothberg is in search of an alternative to current methods (such as patent counts) of assessing an economy's innovativeness. His treatment proposes a dynamic means of examining idea activity, applicable at organizational and macro-economic levels.

Theme 6: Personal creativity

Dean Keith Simonton – 'Genius, creativity and leadership'

Dean Simonton heads for one of the celebrated and most ancient themes of creativity, the nature of outstanding talent. Drawing on his extensive contributions to this subject and applying the methods of differential and developmental psychology, he argues for considerable convergence in the nature of exceptionally creative individuals and leaders.

Li-fang Zhang and Robert J. Sternberg – 'Intellectual styles and creativity'

Zhang and Sternberg provide us with their threefold model of intellectual styles to guide us through the thickets of the style territories, and in doing so explore the question of how creativity may be fostered through addressing intellectual styles.

Stephen J. Guastello – 'Creativity and personality'

Stephen Guestello guides us through the complexities of relationships between personality traits, creative behaviours, and occupations. In so doing, he engages with the issues of psychoticism, mood disorders, and emotional intelligence.

Michael D. Mumford, Cristina L. Byrne and Amanda S. Shipman – 'The thinking of creative leaders: outward focus, inward focus and integration'

Mumford, Byrne and Shipman address the important yet under-theorized construct of creative leaders and their conceptual processes. In an imaginative revision of bisociative models of creativity, they suggest that the process fundamentally concerns inward and outward foci and integration between the two components.

Seana Moran – 'Creativity: a systems perspective'

Seana Moran reviews systems perspectives on creativity, and applying role theory, presents literature as an exemplary case. She argues that confusion has followed a conflation of the social and symbolic aspects of work roles. The distinction helps scholars and educators address issues of personal and career development, and of motivational dynamics.

Juoko Arvonen – 'Change-oriented leadership'

Juoko Arvonen presents substantial evidence to suggest that the dominant two-factor model of leadership requires adjustments in contemporary circumstances to include a third factor of change-centred leadership, which incorporates creative behaviours supporting transformational change.

Theme 7: Structured interventions

Cameron Ford – 'Prototyping processes that affect organizational creativity'

Cameron Ford examines the significance of thought experiments as prototyping processes in the development of creative work proposals. Designing and sharing prototypes is a visualization strategy that can play a part in individual and organizational creativity.

Gerard Puccio and John Cabra – 'Creative problem solving: past, present and future'

Puccio and Cabra trace the origins and evolution of the Creative Problem Solving (CPS) system developed from the pioneering work of Osborn and Parnes. They look ahead to future applications, while proposing that regardless of changes to context, the fundamental principle that will be retained is a means of separating critical and creative thinking.

Sandra Dingli – 'Thinking outside the box: Edward de Bono's lateral thinking'

Sandra Dingli examines and reviews Lateral Thinking, arguably the best-known system for stimulating individual creativity. She provides a much-needed critique of evidence of its extensive practical applications and its rationale as a means of supporting the brain's self-structuring operations. Sandra also distinguishes between Lateral Thinking and Edward de Bono's other considerable contributions to cognitive studies.

Rene Ziegler and Michael Diehl – 'Computer-supported idea generation'

Zeigler and Diehl review the claims of computer-supported idea generation activities. They show the evidence that such approaches can weaken problems of production blocking and cognitive interference. They approach issues in the emerging web-based communications systems.

Integration

Mark A. Runco, Tudor Rickards and Susan Moger – 'Prospects for future journeys'

Runco, Rickards and Moger offer an integrative perspective emerging from the contributions of the *Companion to Creativity*.

References

Boden, M.A. (ed.) (1994) *Dimensions of Creativity*, Cambridge, MA: MIT Press.
Glover, J.A., Ronning, R.R. and Reynolds, C.R. (eds) (1989) *Handbook of Creativity: Perspectives on Individual Differences*, New York: Plenum Press.
Rickards, T. and Moger, S. (2006) Creative leaders: a decade of contributions from *Creativity and Innovations Management Journal, Creativity and Innovation Management*, 18(1): 4–18.
Runco, M.A. and Albert, R.S. (eds) (1990) *Theories of Creativity*, Newbury Park, CA: Sage.
Runco, M.A. and Pritzker, S.R. (1999) *Encyclopedia of Creativity*, San Diego, CA: Academic Press.

Schön, D. (1983) *The Reflective Practitioner*, New York: Basic Books.

Sternberg, R.J. (1999) *Handbook of Creativity*, New York: Cambridge University Press.

Sternberg, R.J. and Lubart, T. (1995) *Defying the crowd: Cultivating creativity in a culture of conformity*, New York: Free Press.

Woodman, R.W., Sawyer, J.E. and Griffin, R.W. (1993) Toward a theory of organizational creativity, *Academy of Management Review*, 18(2): 293–321.

Part 2

Creativity and design

Theme 1 Creativity and design

2

Creativity, improvisation and organizations

Colin M. Fisher and Teresa Amabile

Introduction

Although the literatures on both organizational creativity and organizational improvisation have been expanding in recent years, the links between these literatures have not been deeply explored. This chapter explores those links to create a conceptualization of improvisational creativity in organizations. After reviewing existing theory on the creative process in organizations, and existing theory on organizational improvisation, we synthesize the two, fill in some conceptual gaps, and propose a preliminary model. The chapter ends with research questions suggested by our analysis.

The creative process in organizations

As the world moves more deeply into the twenty-first century, more and more of the important new ideas seem to emerge from organizations. Lone creators appear increasingly anachronistic, as teams and larger groups in organizations become the dominant mode through which progress is made in much of the world. Appropriately, then, organizational scholars have been turning their attention increasingly to organizational creativity over the past several years.

The term 'organizational creativity' has been variously used to refer to the creativity of an organization's new products, services, processes, or strategies (e.g. Amabile 1988, 1996; Ford 1996; Woodman *et al.* 1993); the creativity of members of an organization (e.g. Guilford 1950; Nicholls 1972); and the processes undertaken by members of an organization (e.g. Drazin *et al.* 1999). In this chapter, we adopt the widely accepted definition of organizational creativity as the production of ideas for novel and appropriate (useful or valuable) products, services, processes or strategies in an organization (Amabile 1996; Rothenberg 1990; Stein 1953). However, we focus here not on those ideas but on the process by which they are produced.

Scholarly research on creativity began in the psychological domain, and the traditional view of the creative process in psychology stems from Wallas' (1926) seminal work. Wallas proposed four distinct stages: (1) Preparation, in which the problem to be solved is detected, and relevant data are identified; (2) Incubation, in which the problem is 'left alone' for a time while the unconscious mind works on it; (3) Illumination, in which the idea or solution suddenly appears; and (4) Verification, in which the idea or solution is tested against criteria of acceptability. Subsequent psychological theories of the creative process have presented variations on these ideas. In some (e.g. Simonton 1999), incubation plays a prominent role; in others (e.g. Amabile 1996), it is combined with illumination in an idea-generation step. Generally, however, psychological theories addressing the creative process include distinct stages, in sequence, moving from understanding the problem, to developing creative solutions, to selecting among the alternative solutions (Kaufmann 1988).

We refer to this standard view as *compositional creativity*, and it seems to adequately capture many instances of creativity in organizations, such as the creation of new products through carefully planned and rigorously followed stage-gate processes. However, there is another form of creative process, in which there is little evidence of distinct stages across time. Following Sawyer (2000), we refer to this as *improvisational creativity*. Although we will offer a formal definition later, we begin by offering examples of improvisational creativity in three primary organizational situations that are likely to evoke such a process: responses to emergent crises, responses to unexpected opportunities, and responses generated as part of a more compositional creativity process.

First, emergent crises can evoke improvisational creativity. Weick (1993) analyzed the Mann Gulch disaster, in which some fire fighters were able to go beyond the scope of their training and survive by lying in the ashes of a small fire they created as the larger fire passed around them. Serious crises arise suddenly within organizations, as well. In 1982, three people died after taking the over-the-counter medication Tylenol that had traces of poison in it. James Burke, CEO of Johnson and Johnson, which manufactured and sold Tylenol, had to react quickly and decisively to this crisis, with incomplete knowledge about the source of the poison (possibly introduced during the manufacturing process) and with considerable conflicting advice (Tedlow and Smith 1989). Burke's decision, made under extreme time pressure and with national attention, was to recall all Tylenol products from all stores immediately. At the time, many analysts predicted that this decision would mean the demise of the product. Nonetheless, Burke's decision and subsequent immediate actions (after the discovery that the products had been tampered with in stores by a private citizen) are now credited with restoring the public's trust in the brand and saving the company.

Second, unexpected opportunities call for improvisational creativity. In 1970, PhD engineer and entrepreneur George Hatsopoulos was trying to start an instrument business within his modestly successful young company. He had some ideas for industrial measurement instruments he might design, but no such products. At a lunch meeting, a Ford Motor Company executive complained that the US Congress had just passed the Clean Air Act of 1970, requiring all new vehicles to monitor and control oxides of nitrogen to an accuracy of one part per million, but there were currently no instruments available to fulfill this requirement. On the spot, Hatsopoulos promised that, if Ford placed an order with him, he would deliver an instrument in three months that would fulfill their requirements. Hatsopoulos had no product (nor even a prototype) but, after his fateful lunch meeting, he received orders not only from Ford, but from Toyota and Mercedes as well. He found that price was no object to them, because they knew his was the only instrument that would soon be available. Hatsopoulos' improvised response to this unexpected opportunity was the beginning of a great corporate success story: Thermo-Electron Corporation, an industrial powerhouse for several decades (Kahalas and Suchon 1995).

Third, improvisational creativity can be embedded within a larger process of compositional creativity. Some organizational scholars have recognized this possibility. Eisenhardt and Tabrizi

(1995) found that improvisation helped accelerate innovation processes in computer product development. Sutton and Hargadon (1996), in their ethnography of the celebrated design firm IDEO, described the central importance of highly improvisational, time-constrained brainstorming practices within the entire process of designing new products – a process that can, in total, take several weeks or months.

Organizational theorists have recently begun to consider the role of improvisation within organizations (e.g. Moorman and Miner 1998; Vera and Crossan 2005), sometimes drawing on improvisational performing arts such as jazz for conceptual inspiration (e.g. Barrett 1998). However, few have made explicit links to the more established literature on organizational creativity. In this chapter, we aim to make those links. After reviewing the literature on compositional creativity and the literature on organizational improvisation, we propose a synthetic model of creative improvisation in organizations. We end by sketching some research questions provoked by our analysis.

Compositional creativity in organizations: the traditional approach

Comprehensive theories of organizational creativity were proposed by Amabile (1988, 1996), Ford (1996) and Woodman *et al.* (1993). To the extent that they address the creative process at all, these theories view it according to defined stages similar to those specified in the psychological literature. For example, the componential theory of organizational creativity (Amabile 1988, 1996) proposes five stages similar to Wallas' (1926): (1) Problem presentation (or task identification), based on either an *internal* or an *external* stimulus; (2) Preparation: building up and/or reactivating a store of relevant information and response algorithms; (3) Response generation (or idea generation): searching memory and the immediate environment to generate response possibilities; (4) Response execution (validation and communication): testing response possibilities against factual knowledge and other criteria; and (5) Outcome: success, failure, or progress toward the goal. Although the theory includes caveats that the stages do not always happen in strict sequence, and that there is often an iterative cycling from later stages back to earlier ones, the underlying assumption is that the process happens in a more or less ordered fashion, over a considerable period of time. This view extends to empirical work. Most psychological and organizational research on creativity investigates situations in which individuals are given a problem or task, have some time to prepare themselves to carry it out, generate response possibilities, and choose an idea to communicate from among those possibilities that seem most promising. Depending on the context (laboratory or field research), the time period can range from an hour or less, to several days, weeks or months.

The componential theory (Amabile 1996) also outlines the four necessary components for an individual to carry out such a process. The theory includes three intra-individual components – task motivation, domain-relevant skills, and creativity-relevant processes. It also includes the environment in which the individual works. The source of task motivation can be primarily external, wherein a person is motivated through rewards and punishments, or internal, wherein a person wants to do a task for its own sake. Task motivation is affected by the social environment and the success (or failure) of previous work on the task or in the domain. Domain-relevant skills include the technical knowledge and skills necessary to perform the task. Creativity-relevant processes include thinking styles, heuristics, and working styles. The ability to increase domain-relevant skills and creativity-relevant processes through learning is influenced by task motivation.

According to this theory, the components described above have differential effects on the stages of the creative process. Problem presentation (Stage 1) is primarily affected by task motivation – a person is more likely to find a problem and engage the creative process if he/she finds the task interesting. Preparation (Stage 2) is affected by the domain-relevant skills an individual brings to bear on the task; at times, a person may have to build up domain-relevant skills in order to begin work. Response generation (Stage 3) is affected again by task motivation and also by creativity-relevant processes. Creativity-relevant processes determine how flexibly a person uses cognitive and physical resources and how many responses can be generated. Further, task motivation influences the likelihood that creativity-relevant processes will be engaged enough to generate novel and multiple options. In response execution (Stage 4), domain-relevant skills again come in to play; how well someone performs the task and assesses the appropriateness of the generated novel responses depends on his/her skill in the domain. After a response is selected, the goal is either attained or not (Stage 5), or some progress is made, often resulting in a return to an earlier stage. Success (or failure) in achieving (or progressing toward) the goal subsequently affects task motivation to continue the task or to participate in the future.

Unlike traditional stage models of creativity, however, improvisation condenses many of the traditional stages of creativity. To improvise, actors must simultaneously identify new challenges and generate responses, with little or no time to prepare or activate relevant information. In fact, the process of improvising is one single step: a response is generated and executed as the task is presented. Preparation must happen previously, outside of the frame of action. Although it is clear that there are significant differences between compositional and improvisational processes, we must first clearly delineate the two processes to illuminate these differences.

Improvisation and composition in organizations

In the literature on musical creativity, there is an accepted distinction between composing and improvising music (i.e. Nettl 1998). Well-known jazz saxophonist Steve Lacy provides a succinct explanation of the difference between improvisation and composition:

> In 1968 I ran into [improviser/composer] Steve Lacy on the street in Rome. I took out my pocket tape recorder and asked him to describe in fifteen seconds the difference between composition and improvisation. He answered: 'In fifteen seconds the difference between composition and improvisation is that in composition you have all the time you want to decide what to say in fifteen seconds, while in improvisation you have fifteen seconds.' His answer lasted exactly fifteen seconds and is still the best formulation of the question I know.
>
> (Bailey 1993: 140–141)

As Lacy pointed out, the main difference between improvisation and composition is the time available for response generation and the simultaneity of response generation and execution in improvisation. This distinction is echoed in Sawyer's (2000) descriptions of improvisational creativity and 'product creativity' as separate processes in the arts.

Organizational scholars have also distinguished improvisation from other types of action on several dimensions, including temporal separation of response generation and response execution. Moorman and Miner (1998) define improvisation as 'the degree to which the composition and execution of an action converge in time' (p. 698). Vera and Crossan (2005) define team improvisation as 'the creative and spontaneous process of trying to achieve an objective in a new way' (p. 205), building on the same principle from Crossan and Sorrenti's (1997) definition of improvisation as 'intuition guiding action in a spontaneous way' (p. 156). From their review of the literature on organizational improvisation, Cunha *et al.* (1999) define organizational improvisation as 'the conception of action as it unfolds, by an organization and/or its members, drawing on available cognitive, affective and social resources' (p. 302).

In all these definitions, we see the central role of two concepts: novelty and time. Moorman and Miner (1998) explained that improvisation must involve novelty and diverge in some way from prior plans or designs (p. 702). In fact, 'conception of action as it unfolds' (Cunha *et al.* 1999: 302) can only be claimed if response execution diverges in some way from prior plans and habits; if one is using a plan or a habit, then the action was conceived of before it unfolded, and the process is not improvisational. Vera and Crossan (2005) call improvisation 'creative,' in the sense of a process that is intended to generate novelty, but may succeed or fail. Equally central to definitions of improvisation is the role of time – all of these definitions propose that *conceiving of what to do* (response generation) and *doing it* (response execution) must be simultaneous or convergent in time. If we array organizational action on these two dimensions, we can summarize organizational action using the four categories depicted in Figure 2.1.

Highly novel actions are arrayed in the top two quadrants and are often referred to as creative processes.[1] Indeed, both improvisation and composition can generate novel products or outcomes; what differentiates the two is the time between the moment when the action is conceived and the moment when that action is executed. In composition, there is clear temporal separation between when a response is generated and when it is executed. In improvisation, there is little such separation – responses are generated and executed simultaneously. For example, in musical composition, composers often outline every detail of a symphony – not only the notes and rhythms, but the dynamics (loudness), the tempo, and many expressive considerations – long before a symphony orchestra ever plays any of it. In contrast, a jazz musician chooses notes, rhythms, dynamics, and all expressive considerations at the same time the music is being performed.

The bottom two quadrants (III and IV) represent actions low in novelty. When one is forced

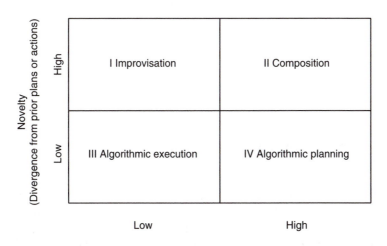

Figure 2.1 Realms of individual and collective action in organizations

to act in the moment, with little time for planning, but responds in planned or habitual ways, we see quadrant III – algorithmic execution. Ruscio and Amabile (1999) use the term 'algorithmic' to describe those instructions that specify each step of an action and are learned by rote. Similarly, actions low in novelty that are configured on the spur of the moment must rely on elements that are commonly used or were learned by rote at an earlier time. In contrast to improvisation, algorithmic execution is either the execution of a composed plan, like a computer running code, or a habitual response. For example, operators in a nuclear power plant follow detailed written procedures in almost every aspect of their work, specifying which buttons to push, where each button is located, how to assess if pushing the button generated the desired outcome, what page to proceed to if pushing the button does not result in that outcome, and so on (Wieringa and Farkas 1991). Habitual responses, which must compete with novel responses (Ford 1996), are also examples of algorithmic execution.

When novelty is low and temporal separation is high, we see algorithmic planning (quadrant IV). Algorithmic planning is like creating the list of procedures for the nuclear power plant operators to follow – the procedures to be written down are known (and often legislated) and the job of the actor is to record them as accurately as possible so that others may execute those instructions; their only concern is to express the plan so that it is executed without errors or violations (Wieringa and Farkas 1991). Because both quadrants III and IV are low in novelty, and thus, not creative, they lie outside the scope of the remainder of this chapter and will not be discussed further.

Clearly, these four types of action rarely occur in their pure forms; in practice, improvisation generally involves the execution of parts of previously composed material, and many compositions come about partially through moments of improvisation. Furthermore, both improvisation and composition often rely on a 'vocabulary' of pre-existing small chunks of action – called 'ready-mades' in improvisational theatre (Vera and Crossan 2004) or 'licks' in jazz (Bailey 1993) – which introduce many elements that are not, by themselves, novel. However, despite these grey areas, thinking about improvisation and composition as relatively distinct processes has interesting implications for research on creativity.

If we situate improvisation within the stages outlined in the componential theory of creativity, we find that improvisation is characterized by the way it combines some aspects of the compositional process. Improvisation describes actions in which there is a high divergence from prior actions or plans, combined with a low temporal separation of problem identification, idea generation, and idea execution. Thus, we define improvisation as actions with high novelty (divergence from prior actions) and low temporal separation of conception and execution. Improvisational actions are arrayed on a continuum, depending on the degree of novelty and the degree of temporal separation. When such actions occur in an organizational context, they are considered to be instances of *organizational improvisation*.

Creative improvisation in organizations: a synthesis and proposed model

The relationship between improvisation and creativity is unclear in the existing literature. Some theorize that improvisation and creativity are two overlapping but distinct concepts because many creative products are not improvised (e.g. Moorman and Miner 1998). Others argue that improvisation is a 'creative process' that is intended to generate creative products, but may or may not succeed in generating a creative (novel and appropriate) outcome (e.g. Vera and Crossan 2004). We propose that improvisation is one process by which creative products or actions can be generated, but that not all improvisation results in true creativity – appropriate novelty. Figure 2.1 specifies the elements that are necessary for improvisation: high novelty (divergence from prior actions), and low temporal separation of conception and execution. But improvisation requires one additional element to achieve the status of creativity. The action must not only be spontaneous and novel, it must also be appropriate, in order to meet the definition of creativity.

As noted earlier, there are two different types of creativity. A key difference between the two, improvisational and compositional creativity, is that process and product cannot be separated in improvisation. In composition, the process of composing results in some sort of product, service, or design. This resultant product is then assessed for creativity. For example, a Picasso painting that hangs in a gallery is creative to the extent that viewers find it novel and appropriate – expressive or aesthetically appealing – regardless of the process behind it. In contrast, in impro-visation, the unit of assessment is the act of creating; the improvisation is both the process of action and the product that is judged as creative or uncreative. For instance, when we call Hatsopoulos's behaviour at that fateful lunch 'creative,' we are characterizing *what he did* as both novel (because it was far from the typical or expected response) and appropriate (because it responded perfectly to the demands of the situation in which he found himself). Because his improvised actions responded to situational demands appropriately, they can be considered creative.

Thus, we propose that all improvisational creativity includes one key element that has not been specified by improvisation theorists: *responsiveness to temporally proximate stimuli*. Temporally proximate stimuli consist of whatever relevant situational factors are observable at or immedi-ately before the moment of action. In a jazz band, those stimuli are usually what other group members are playing and what the individual himself just played. Jazz bands are creative *as a group* to the extent that they are responsive to and adjust to what the other members of the group play. Even if the individual contributions of group members were novel and appropriate when heard individually, the group would not be considered a creative improvising unit unless group members were responsive to each other.

Drawing on prior conceptions of organizational creativity (especially the componential theory of creativity (Amabile 1988, 1996) prior conceptions of improvisation in organizations, and the new idea of responsiveness to temporally proximate stimuli, we propose a preliminary model of creative improvisation in organizations. (See Figure 2.2.)

In this model, we define creative improvisation as actions responsive to temporally proximate stimuli, where the actions contain both a high degree of novelty and a low temporal separation of problem presentation, idea generation, and idea execution. Such actions are arrayed on a continuum, depending on the degree of novelty, the degree of temporal separation, and the degree of responsiveness to temporally proximate stimuli. When such actions occur in an organizational context, they are considered to be instances of organizational improvisational creativity.

In contrast to traditional models of compositional creativity, our model contains two dis-tinguishing features: (a) preparation precedes the improvisational process, and (b) the stages are 'fluid', with problem presentation, response generation, and response execution happening virtually simultaneously. In compositional creativity, preparation might include learning rele-vant skills and obtaining information necessary to perform the task. For example, when an advertising agency team is developing a campaign for a new client, it often researches previous advertising campaigns, learns about the industry, and compares the client to its competitors before beginning to generate responses. In improvisational creativity, however, such preparation cannot occur because immediate action is needed; individuals must instead build up a store of

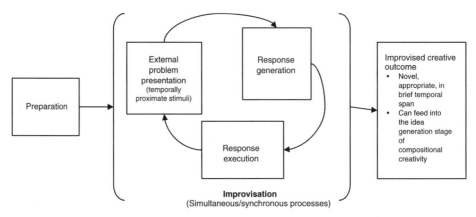

Figure 2.2 Proposed model of improvisational creativity on organizations

Note: This figure is based on the prior literature on organizational creativity and organizational improvisation. It is a modification of Amabile, 1996, p. 113.

knowledge and routines that are both quickly accessible and flexible to various situational demands. Jazz musicians, for example, learn common patterns and theory before knowing what song they will play at a jam session; the ideas used in a solo are generated and executed as they are performed. Similarly, Hatsopoulos did not prepare a response to his lunch partner's complaints after contemplating them; he told the Ford executive of his ideas as they came into his head, based on his extensive prior research, training and experience.

After preparation comes the actual process of improvisation. As we described earlier, improvisation is defined by the temporal convergence of response generation and execution. Response generation and execution are prompted and shaped by the temporally proximate stimuli, which constantly inform and shape the problem at hand – the problem presented by the external environment. Crises, such as Burke's case at Johnson and Johnson, are instigated by external stimuli that can change over time. As events unfold and data becomes available, actions are shaped accordingly, and the nature of the problem itself can change. In this way, temporally proximate stimuli not only present the problem but also shift as responses are generated and executed. The resultant improvised creative outcomes are novel (by being divergent) and appropriate (by responding to temporally proximate stimuli). As we mentioned earlier, these outcomes might be the final result, as in a jazz improvisation, or they might represent possible responses in a compositional process, as in the structured brainstorming used at IDEO (Sutton and Hargadon 1996).

The components that influence improvisational creativity also differ somewhat from those in the componential model of creativity (Amabile 1996). In improvisational creativity, a large number of well-learned facts and routines that are both readily accessible and flexibly organized are important prior to action. Unlike in compositional creativity, such expertise cannot be obtained after a problem is presented. Because improvisation often occurs in response to crises or unexpected opportunities, it is likely that a person or group with less expertise would improvise less creatively in such situations.

Further, we propose that the creativity-relevant processes of risk-orientation (Barrett 1998; Cunha *et al.* 1999) and responsiveness to temporally proximate stimuli are especially important for improvisational creativity. Risk-orientation is often essential for an individual to engage in improvisation instead of pursuing a more known, if less creative, path during turbulent times.

Similar to its role in compositional creativity, intrinsic motivation is important for engaging in and persisting with improvisation. An intrinsically motivated person who is improvising can focus more on the problem presenting itself, instead of focusing on evaluation and its impact on rewards and punishments. Furthermore, because improvisation is often used instead of algorithmic execution in times of crisis, several theorists have proposed that internal motivation will increase not only from the success of the process, but from the increased autonomy that improvisation offers members of an organization (e.g. Barrett 1998).

We propose that several aspects of the work environment that have been identified in the improvisation literature also facilitate improvisational creativity in organizations. Cunha *et al.* (1999) identified an experimental culture and minimal structures as important environmental conditions for improvisation. An experimental culture is one that tolerates or promotes mistakes as a source of learning, promotes action, and has a sense of urgency. It is likely that a culture that tolerates mistakes and promotes action will facilitate improvisational creativity. Minimal structures mean that there are only loose procedures in place in domains where improvisation is likely; having more detailed policies would make people likely to follow them and execute algorithmically. Finally, Crossan and colleagues (2005) have proposed that the availability of real-time information is crucial. Having access to real-time information and structures that facilitate its communication increases the resources that improvisers have available to them, multiplying the sources of ideas and solutions.

Overall, this model highlights certain contrasts to traditional models of compositional creativity. Specifically, the role of preparation and the synchronous nature of problem presentation, response generation and response execution are starkly contrasted with linear ideas of the creative process. Furthermore, we propose a number of elements that facilitate improvisational creativity. However, there is a great deal of research that must be done in the future to fully understand what facilitates improvisational creativity and to fully explicate the nature of its differences from compositional creativity.

Future research

At the intersection of research on creativity and improvisation in organizations, there is still much to be explored. Much of what is known about creativity has been drawn from studies of compositional creativity and may not apply to improvisational creativity. For example, many creativity-relevant processes, such as the ability to generate alternatives, divergent thinking, concentration and using effective heuristics (Amabile 1988), might apply equally to improvisation and composition. However, Amabile (1996), Campbell (1960) and Simonton (1999) proposed that accurate memory is a creativity-relevant process, but different types of memory may not play an equal role in improvised and composed creativity. Moorman and Miner (1998) posited that procedural memory (memory for how to do things) and declarative memory (memory for facts) affect improvised outcomes differentially. They propose that higher levels of declarative memory result in more creative (both novel and coherent) improvisation, and that higher levels of procedural memory result in more coherent, but less novel, improvisations.

Although it is possible that creativity-relevant processes like procedural memory affect improvisational and compositional creativity differentially, researchers should also examine the extent to which such previous work on improvisation in organizations might apply to compositional creativity. For instance, procedural memory is thought to inhibit novelty in improvisation because having high procedural memory habituates responses, making them more likely to arise in the course of action. However, Ford (1996) makes a very similar argument about creative action in general, positing that creative actions will only be selected when individual, social and environmental pressures push actors away from habitual responses. It may be that this phenomenon is not unique to improvisation, but is true of all creativity. Indeed, research on compositional creativity has found dampening effects of reliance on algorithmic learning (Ruscio and Amabile 1999), and future research could examine the relationship between algorithmic learning and procedural memory.

There are, though, many crucial differences between the factors that facilitate and inhibit improvisational and compositional creativity. The main contrast, as might be expected, is likely to be the role of urgency in improvisation and composition. Time pressure has been shown to be largely detrimental to compositional creativity (Amabile *et al.* 2002), whereas such time pressure is often what produces improvisation in the first place. However, there is an important difference between feeling pressured and working in a real-time environment. Crossan and colleagues (2005) proposed that, even in a time-pressured environment, team-level improvisation is facilitated by real-time information and communication, likely in a way that compositional creativity is not.

Our model suggests a number of questions that are yet to be investigated. For instance, little is known about the forms of preparation that are best suited to improvisational creativity. As Barrett (1998) points out, jazz musicians rely on 'minimal structures for maximal flexibility'; meaning that they rely on a skeletal harmonic and rhythmic structure that increases coordination and focuses attention. However, jazz musicians devote years of intense practice to being able to work with these structures on the fly. Further, in addition to the high costs of preparation, several scholars have argued that expertise itself involves costs to creativity because of the increased rigidity that comes from experience and becoming part of the status quo in a particular domain (i.e. Runco *et al.* 2007). To facilitate improvisational creativity, one must acquire the expertise to operate fluently in a domain without also acquiring the lack of novelty that often accompanies increased expertise. Can organizations use similar structures to facilitate creativity if the cost of preparation is as high? How high is the cost of preparation for improvisation in organizations, and what contextual factors influence this cost? What would the organizational equivalent of such 'practice' look like? What tradeoffs and costs to creativity might occur through fostering the fluency necessary to improvise?

Additionally, because of the prior research focus on compositional creativity, there is a dearth of research on the necessary expertise, creativity-relevant processes, intrinsic motivation and organizational work environments most conducive to improvisational creativity. For example, is there a distinct creativity-relevant skill of being responsive to temporally proximate stimuli and, if so, is it stable across domains? Some researchers (e.g. Amabile 1996) have argued that aspects of creative thinking transcend domain. Could such responsiveness be a similar skill? To what extent, and under what conditions, can it be learned?

Finally, in pointing out the intersections and divergences of the organizational creativity and improvisation literatures, we hope to stimulate synergy between the two. Indeed, there is little reason to research improvisation as a path to creativity unless doing so will bring us beyond what we already know about composition. One possible explanation for the separateness of these literatures is that composition is an intentional, often deliberate process most often found when organizations look for new ideas. Improvisation, on the other hand, is often forced upon members of an organization and getting through the situation, not creativity, is the goal. However, organizations that do not build a capacity to respond in novel and appropriate ways to emergent crises, unexpected opportunities, and dynamic environments are at a competitive disadvantage just as much as organizations that do not produce novel ideas and products. We believe that exploring the similarities and differences between improvisational and compositional creativity in organizations will yield a greater understanding of creativity in general.

Note

1 It should be noted that creative processes do not always result in creative products or actions (Vera and Crossan 2004), as the success of that product or action also depends on its appropriateness.

References

Amabile, T.M. (1988) A model of creativity and innovation in organizations, in: B. M. Staw and L.L. Cummings (eds), *Research in Organizational Behavior*, Greenwich, CT: JAI Press.

Amabile, T.M. (1996) *Creativity in Context*, Boulder, CO: Westview Press.

Amabile, T.M., Hadley, C.N. and Kramer, S.J. (2002) Creativity under the gun, *Harvard Business Review*, 80: 52–61.

Bailey, D. (1993) *Improvisation: Its Nature and Practice in Music*, New York: Da Capo Press.

Barrett, F.J. (1998) Creativity and improvisation in jazz and organizations: implications for organizational learning, *Organization Science*, 9: 605–622.

Campbell, D.T. (1960) Blind variation and selective retention in creative thought as in other knowledge processes, *Psychological Review*, 67: 380–400.

Crossan, M., Cunha, M.P.E., Vera, D. and Cunha, O. (2005) Time and organizational improvisation, *Academy of Management Review*, 30: 129–145.

Crossan, M. and Sorrenti, M. (1997) Making sense of improvisation, *Advances in Strategic Management*, 14: 155–180.

Cunha, M.P., Cunha, J.V. and Kamoche, K. (1999) Organizational improvisation: what, when, how and why, *International Journal of Management Review*, 1: 299–341.

Drazin, R., Glynn, M.A. and Kazanjian, R.K. (1999) Multilevel theorizing about creativity in organizations: a sensemaking perspective, *Academy of Management Review*, 24: 286–307.

Eisenhardt, K. and Tabrizi, B.N. (1995) Accelerating adaptive processes: product innovation in the global computer industry, *Administrative Science Quarterly*, 40: 84–110.

Ford, C.M. (1996) A theory of individual creative action in multiple social domains, *Academy of Management Review*, 21: 1112–1142.

Guilford, J.P. (1950) Creativity, *American Psychologist*, 5: 444–454.

Kahalas, H. and Suchon, K. (1995) Managing a perpetual idea machine: inside the creator's mind, *Academy of Management Executive*, 9: 57–66.

Kaufmann, G. (1988). Problem solving and creativity, in: K. Gronhaug and G. Kaufmann (eds), *Innovation: A Cross-Disciplinary Perspective*, Oslo, Norway: Norwegian University Press.

Moorman, C. and Miner, A.S. (1998) Organizational improvisation and organizational memory, *Academy of Management Review*, 23: 698–723.

Nettl, B. (1998) Introduction: an art neglected in scholarship, in: B. Nettl and M. Russell (eds), *In the Course of Performance: Studies in the World of Musical Improvisation*, Chicago: University of Chicago Press.

Nicholls, J.G. (1972) Creativity in the person who will never produce anything original and useful: the concept of creativity as a normally distributed trait, *American Psychologist*, 27: 717–727.

Rothenberg, A. (1990) *Creativity and Madness: New Findings and Old Stereotypes*, Baltimore: Johns Hopkins University Press.

Runco, M.A., Lubart, T.I. and Getz, I. (2007) Creativity in economics, in: M.A. Runco (ed.), *Handbook of Creativity*, Cresskill, NJ: Hampton Press.

Ruscio, A.M. and Amabile, T.M. (1999) Effects of instructional style on problem-solving creativity, *Creativity Research Journal*, 12: 251–266.

Sawyer, R.K. (2000) Improvisation and the creative process: Dewey, Collingwood, and the aesthetics of spontaneity, *Journal of Aesthetics and Art Criticism*, 58: 149–161.

Simonton, D.K. (1999) *Origins of Genius: Darwinian Perspectives on Creativity*, New York: Oxford University Press.

Stein, M.I. (1953) Creativity and culture, *Journal of Psychology*, 36: 311–322.

Sutton, R.I. and Hargadon, A. (1996) Brainstorming groups in context: effectiveness in a product design firm, *Administrative Science Quarterly*, 41: 685–718.

Tedlow, R. and Smith, W.K. (1989) James Burke: a career in American business (A). Harvard Business School Case #389177, Boston, MA: Harvard Business School Publishing.

Vera, D. and Crossan, M. (2004) Theatrical improvisation: lessons for organizations, *Organization Studies*, 25: 727–749.

Vera, D. and Crossan, M. (2005) Improvisation and innovative performance in teams, *Organization Science*, 16: 203–224.

Wallas, G. (1926) *The Art of Thought*, New York: Harcourt, Brace and Company.

Weick, K.E. (1993) The collapse of sensemaking in organizations: the Mann Gulch disaster. *Administrative Science Quarterly*, 38: 628–652.

Wieringa, D.R. and Farkas, D.K. (1991) Procedure writing across domains: nuclear power plant procedures and computer documentation. Proceedings of the Ninth Annual International Conference on Systems Documentation, Chicago: ACM Press.

Woodman, R.W., Sawyer, J.E. and Griffin, R.W. (1993) Toward a Theory of Organizational Creativity, *Academy of Management Review*, 18: 293–321.

3

Creativity and sound: the agony of the senses

Richard Coyne

People create with sound, music providing the obvious example. The growing fields of sound design in film, video games, installation works, multimedia interactives and other audio environments provide further evidence of a vibrant sonic creativity (Bull 2000; Kahn and Whitehead 1992; LaBelle 2006; Schafer 1993). There is much to be said about the tools of creation in sound; their temporal and spatial aspects, issues of notation, technology and performance, and not least the longstanding relationship between music and architecture (Blesser and Salter 2006; Wittkower 1998). But in this chapter I will focus on the relationship between sound and vision, and what this troubled relationship says about creativity. I marshal evidence to the claim that creativity emerges at the thresholds (Coyne 2005), the boundaries between conditions, and as such belongs within the ludic realms of *agon* (Caillois 1961), the assembly for contest, the place of competition between the senses.

Designers readily identify creative people as those with a strong orientation to the senses (Waterworth 1997). Francis Galton asserted that geniuses 'have the utmost delight in the exercise of [their] senses and affections' (Galton 1972: 279). In his 'incubation model' of creativity, Torrance identifies an open phase where the creator defers judgement, 'making use of all the senses, opening up new doors' (Torrance 1993: 233), and sensitivity as a creative attribute seems to derive from an acute engagement with sensory experience (Razik 1966: 164). The Romantic tradition (Albert and Runco 1999: 23) relates creativity to an enthusiasm for sensation, as evident in the appetite for the Continental grand tour amongst intellectuals and artists in the eighteenth and nineteenth centuries. John Ruskin offers a sonic, kinaesthetic, visual and tactile account of the experience of encountering St Mark's Square in Venice, in which he progressed from the narrow alleyways of the city 'resonant with the cries of itinerant salesmen' to the spectacle of glittering pinnacles and the confusion of delight, 'the flashes and wreaths of sculptured spray' (Ruskin and Links 1960: 149). Mathematical invention has also been described in terms that presuppose the ability to visualise, feel or hear relationships. Poincaré's famous description of his processes of mathematical discovery draws on concepts of combination, unconscious filtering, 'aesthetic feeling' and 'emotional sensibility,' but also implicate an unfolding narrative over time peppered with everyday sensuality: putting his foot on a step, taking his seat on the bus, and tripping to the seaside (Poincaré 2000). In so far as creativity involves detecting and exploring relationships, these seem to cross over the different senses. In fact the psychological condition known as synesthesia (Cytowic 1989: 269; 1995), in which individuals exhibit the capability to hear colours and see smells, has become emblematic of an aptitude within any of the arts to contemplate and seek out crossovers of the senses, well illustrated in the common association between musical tones, chords, keys and colours (Newton 2003). So in the realms of creativity the full range of the senses are open to scrutiny as are the ways human societies have identified and carved up the sensorium (Classen 1993). In this chapter I will concentrate on hearing and seeing, the antagonism between which has something to say about the spectrum of the senses. I argue that the troubled relationship between sound and sight has a bearing on creativity.

Unity and coherence

The classical tradition relates sound to vision as issues of harmony, unity and order. Architecture joins with music in giving expression to, or enabling participation in, the universe's yearning towards completeness. Hence the mathematician Poincaré appeals to the 'harmony of numbers and forms' and their 'geometrical elegance' (Poincaré 2000: 92). Under this Platonic model all modes of creation are subservient to the residence of the truly beautiful and complete in the realm of ideas, the perfect mind of the divine creator, a state that transcends the everyday. Music and architecture are thus thought to provide access to this ideal, the union of which constitutes a major narrative in the traditions of art and design explicit in various treatises, from Roman antiquity (Vitruvius and Morgan 1960) to the Renaissance.

Palladio's villas were said to be designed in accordance with principles of harmony, to the extent that room dimensions corresponded to harmonic triads (Palladio 1965; Wittkower 1998). Even the practicalities of sound are related to improvement, correction and movement towards an ideal. Vitruvius makes mention of the practical issues pertaining to sound isolation and transmission (Vitruvius and Morgan 1960: 136). The senate house was to be constructed with surface mouldings at the lower levels to assist the passage of the voices of the senators to the balcony above (p. 137). Theatres were to be configured as a series of concentric tiers to match the circular waves of the voice (p. 139) (Vovolis 2003). Vitruvius explains how the clarity of the voice is enhanced by the careful positioning of large bronze sounding vessels in the theatre, a functional schema elaborated by Alberti (Alberti 1996: 276; Naguib and Wiley 2001). The modernist tradition reconstructs the Ideal, and disengages function from transcendence and formalist cosmologies (Perez-Gomez 1985). But the tradition equating harmonization and beauty persists where creativity is at the service of the coherent, the ideal, the beautiful and the functional (Corbusier 1931).

The pursuit of beauty and coherence are now at the margins of contemporary creative practice. It is difficult to identify and agree on what constitutes the ideal. The tradition that seeks to conserve an ideal plays down the role of individual preference, cultural difference, the everyday, and the inevitability, role and productive value of interesting deviations. This challenge to the ideal is brought into sharp relief by contemporary composers, sound designers, performers, theorists, critics and audiences for whom contemporary compositions and sound works would not have been possible were the conventional canons of beauty adhered to, or regarded as, immutable (Kahn and Whitehead 1992). This challenge to the ideal is echoed in contemporary architectural theory (Koolhaas 1994).

Echo and Narcissus

Contrary to the tradition aligning sound, music, form, architecture and vision through concepts of coherence, a further tradition grasps the oppositional character of the senses, though the references are oblique, less obvious and require a kind of psychoanalysis of myths and texts. Much has been made of the myth of Oedipus in this regard: the story of the son who ostensibly kills his father and weds his mother. Freud (1991) uses this classical narrative to illustrate his theories about psychological repression. By various readings the mother represents some desirable, complete and primal condition (arguably a condition resonant with the ideal coherence championed by the classical tradition). The father represents a more tyrannical state, the oppressive rule of law. The story implicates concepts of creativity in that the mother, after whom supposedly Oedipus longs secretly, is enveloping, nurturing, generative and creative. The father, from whom he ostensibly retreats, is restricting, rule bound and unproductive. This mythic structure is obliquely connected with sound and vision, not least in the conclusion of the story, where Oedipus punishes himself by piercing his own eyes with broach pins. For Freud blinding is a symbol for castration, and encapsulates something about primal fears of retribution, feelings of guilt for seeking a return to primal bliss.

In his account of the early life of Leonardo da Vinci, Freud (1953) attributes much of da Vinci's putative genius and sustained creative production to the transference of erotic energy from unresolved feelings for his mother. Freud thus attributes creativity either to the condition of longing for some kind of wholeness and completeness, or as a symptom of unresolved sexual repression. I need not resolve here his precise attributions of creativity. It is sufficient to note that Freud's identification of various domestic and psychic complexes implicates vision, sound and creativity, and through a set of relationships that can be described as agonistic.

The myth of Echo and Narcissus (Ovid 1986) illuminates the tensions between the senses even more clearly, or at least demonstrates the power of the different senses to bring psychic conflicts into sharp relief. Echo was a nymph, whose name and circumstance clearly relate to sound. Narcissus was a youth enchanted by the beauty of his own reflection in a pool of water, a story suggestive of the seductions of the visual image. Echo had already been consigned to lingering in caves and groves, and could only repeat faintly what she heard. So she could not communicate her affections for Narcissus, and languished in a condition of unrequited love. Whatever the interpretations of this story, and there are many (Gildenhard and Zissos 2000), the antagonisms implicate two protagonists, one pertaining to sound, the other to vision. Both involve reproduction and repetition (sound reflection and visual reflection); both protagonists wasted away, one in pursuit of the other (Echo following Narcissus). The story suggests various interesting alignments: harmonising sound with a spontaneous mode of creation and vision with a kind of ordered coherence.

So sound and vision are implicated in various conflicts. Any storyteller who wishes to construct a narrative about dispute (father and son, mother and father, country and city, travellers and settlers, the proletariat and the bourgeoisie, creatives and bureaucrats) can do worse than deploy the vexed relationship between the ear and the eye to add emphasis. Odysseus and the Sirens, the Cyclops, Hermes and the lyre serve similar functions as stories invoking exaggerated or diminished sensory capability, and the increase or reduction of powers (Homer 1980: Hyde 1998).

Aural cultures

The myth of Echo and Narcissus can be taken as a reference to a lament over the replacement of one order by another. The idyllic, nomadic life in the countryside is supplanted by settled living in towns. Echo is all over the place, unconstrained, and of the earth. Narcissus is out hunting initially, a leisure pursuit of the settled rich (Veblen 1998). The youthful male is on the side of refinement and sophistication; the nymph is a rustic agent, free to roam, but with diminished sensory capability, consigned to repeating only what she has heard, and in muted tones. Sound and sight are assumed to be related along several lines: sound comes before vision chronologically, vision is superior to sound in providing us with greater control over our environment, sound is supplanted by vision, sound carries with it a kind of innocence, and a dependence on vision breeds a nostalgia for innocence.

Marshall McLuhan (1994) gave potent expression to this identification in his account of the emergence of the electronic age, and its potential for creativity. For McLuhan, the Narcissus story highlights the human capacity to be numbed by technologies (my reflection as an extension of myself). His account invokes three great epochs. In the primal era of sound the ear held sway as the dominant organ in human society. Human beings were immersed in sound. There was a lack of distinction between people, things and environments. People communicated through the voice, or at least, there was the persistent chatter of voices, in which humankind participated. Eventually people discovered, or invented, the power of visual symbols and made marks, pictures and inscribed texts. The transition to vision was complete with the invention of the printing press and the mass production of texts. The modern era is characterised by the pervasiveness of this capacity for pictorial representation, the ability to stand back and to observe. If the aural sense is about immersion and lack of distinctions, then the ascendancy of the visual sense enables detachment and a scientific sensibility. For McLuhan, thinking no doubt of the incessant noise of transistor radios, the multiplication of communication channels and the broadcasting of everyday street talk that crossed social, age and class barriers, the electronic age restores something of the babble of voices. Human kind is in a global condition, a global village, a restoration of the tribe, and one in which we wear all of humankind 'as our skin' (ibid.: 47).

McLuhan's account is romantic, utopian and over-determines the relationship between technology and the human condition (Coyne 1999; Ferguson 1991), but it taps into the power of the myth of primal conflict, between sound and vision. McLuhan (1968) was not alone in making such assertions, but he delivered them in a climate of celebrity, and deployed the very media he was justifying, in digestible sound bytes, and during the heyday of the baby boomers. His projections influenced a generation of computer systems developers (Kay 1990). His view of media reinforced the conflict between sound and vision, implicating creativity. In the electronic age (the digital age), creativity is distributed, or has the potential to be shared, whereas the culture of vision elevated the role of the individual as creative genius. It is aural culture that gives us initial access to creation, and provides the model for distributed, hypertextual creativity currently being attributed to peer-to-peer mass media, ubiquitous communications and the Internet (Rheingold 2002). Neither sense though has a hold on creativity. It is in the tension between them, or in the tensions that they exemplify, that creativity resides.

Textuality

The conflictual relationship between sound and vision is also prominent in language theory (Havelock 1986; Ong 1962). Speaking and listening both pertain to sound. On the other hand, to write something down is to resort to vision. Speech and writing are the polar equivalents of sound and vision in the realm of language. In the same way that McLuhan claimed a kind of privileging of sound over vision, there seems to be an asymmetry in the relationship between speech and writing. Writing is undeniably a major development, but it is nonetheless derived from speech. We write down what we hear or say. Speech is contingent, of the moment, open-ended as evident in the play of conversation. Things written down are fixed and assume authority. Whereas we require the evidence of the written word, speech, communication by voice and sound alone, can be vague and evasive. In so far as we think of language as caught up in these conflicts, we enter into the tradition of Hermes, the messenger god, whose name has carried over into the study of hermeneutics, the art of interpretation (Gadamer 1975; Snodgrass and Coyne 2006). Hermes was a thief, having stolen his brother Apollo's cattle then concealed the theft by trickery (Hyde 1998). According to Plato 'the name "Hermes" seems to have something to do with speech: he is an interpreter (hermeneus), a messenger, a thief and a deceiver in words, a wheeler-dealer – and all these activities involve the power of speech' (Plato 1997: 126). Theorists of language, such as Derrida (1976), seek to confuse the distinctions and priorities between speech and writing, and show that any conception we have of speaking as a primal condition is already imbued with the paraphernalia of writing. Even without examining these arguments in detail we can concede that the relationship between speech and writing is presented as an agonistic one, a concept close to Derrida's concept of the *aporia* (Derrida 1993).

Sound cuts

Returning to psychoanalysis and cultural theory, in the case of the visual image, according to Lacan (1977), there is a defining moment when a child first sees itself in a mirror and recognises itself as other than its mother and the world around it. For Lacanian psychoanalysis, this is the symbolic moment of the cut, or breach. In terms of the mythopoetics of sound and vision I have been discussing, the stage prior to the mirror phase equates to the immersive character of the sonic field. That the visual image is separate from me does not constitute the defining moment. Rather, the reflected image confirms that I am separate from everything else. Narcissus' image is not preserved, and few adults would think that the appearance of a person has a separate existence to that person. The artifice of painting and sculpture would have been required to preserve the image. But the mythos of sound provides one of the earliest indications that there is something about ourselves that can be separated and preserved without artifice. Echo dies, but her vocal renderings are preserved. Faint though it may be, the sound of the voice can be thought to persist independently of the originator, as if an emanation or secretion.

Human societies thought of this separation long before technologies existed for the preservation and transmission of the voice. Other bodily emanations can be preserved, but the voice is unlike bodily discharges (fluids, waste), in that the voice carries something of the originator, and life (the discharge of the breath). Rabelais plays with this independent existence of the voice in his sixteenth-century satire, *Gargantua and Pantagruel* (1955). While sailing in foreign seas, the sailors encounter voices hovering visibly and tangibly in space. Pantagruel grasps some words that are not yet thawed: 'Then he threw on the deck before us whole handfuls of frozen words, which looked like crystallized sweets of different colours. [. . .] When we warmed them a little between our hands, they melted like snow, and we actually heard them' (p. 569). Technologies for recording and transmitting sound make the separation and independence of the voice palpable.

Concepts of the cut may direct us to classical theories of soul and transcendence. Like the sound of the voice, the soul, the breath, can live outside, and outlive, the body. But the cut itself, as excision, rift, threshold, gap and disjunction, resonates throughout contemporary theories of literature, art and creation (Serres 1982; Tschumi 1994) and in ways that directly implicate sound (Augoyard and Torgue 2005; Connor 2004). Being cut off, cut up or cut open may be the direct result of violence, and provide a literal source of agony, but the agonistics of relationships are also negotiated across a cut or gap. There needs to be separation before there is anything to traverse. The cut also relates to anxiety. Because it is 'cut off', sound requires visual confirmation of its source. For Connor, sound 'is experienced as enigmatic or anxiously incomplete until its source can be identified, which is usually to say, visualised' (2000: 20), a requirement that is not necessarily reciprocated in the case of the visual sense. Whereas we appear to be adept at visual closure, completing an image consisting of four L-shaped marks such that we infer a square, our language for replacing sonic deficit seems to call for entities outside the experience of sound. In many ways sound speaks of incompleteness and the cut.

Adrian Snodgrass and I have explored at some length the importance of the gap, which resides at the core of design as a hermeneutical activity (Snodgrass and Coyne 2006). To design is to interpret, and common theories of interpretation point to the role of 'distanciation'. This is where something in the text confronts the interpreter as alien or unfamiliar (Gadamer 1975). The interpretive act is a negotiation across this distance. Distanciation can be introduced deliberately into the creative situation, as when a designer, composer, artist, problem-solver or experimenter seeks to adopt an unusual orientation to a task: thinking of a carbon chain as a snake, a churchyard as a nightclub, a musical refrain as an extreme sport. Another way of looking at the negotiation across the cut is through the play of interpretation, and creation, as rendering the familiar strange and the strange familiar in various ways (Gallagher 1992: 129), a role that gives space to the productive play of metaphor (Ricoeur 1977). Playing across the senses also operates as a distanciation, a play of metaphors that contributes to creative imagining: treating spaces as if white noise, columns as drum beats, stained glass as birdsong.

We don't only need sound to draw attention to the role of the cut, gap, rift, distance and creation, but such attentions bring productive conflict into sharp relief. Ardrey describes sound as having this agonistic character in any case, as articulating a non-dangerous social agonistics he calls 'nayou':

> Noise, naturally is a prominent characteristic of noyau. You can hear one from a long way off. There is not only the screeching, the yowling, and the hammered insults of the peripheries, but decibels rise like chimney smoke from the heartland too.
>
> (Ardrey 1967: 184)

He describes a husband returning home, as if 'to leave no neighbor in doubt that the master is at home and in charge of the situation'. As well as arguing with his wife, he starts up his car engine at four o'clock in the morning. Not to do so would imply 'a public humiliation, an announcement that he did not own a car' (op. cit.). Sounds provide a social purpose other than communicating lexical meanings. In many cases it matters less what is said than that something is said, that a noise is made, and that it is delivered agonistically.

The most gentle of sounds is borne of a benign violence: vibrations set in motion by impacts between solid, liquid and gaseous bodies. In so far as 'nayou' or *agon* implicate creativity, we could assert that sound is creative in any case. An even bolder claim would be to assert that the impulse to create actually derives from sound. To prove this it would be necessary to demonstrate that metaphors of creation, involving generation, source, emanation and propagation, are sonic before they are visual. Creation as a tendency towards the ideal commonly invokes illumination, but creation as agonistic arguably invokes sonic metaphors: chaos, eruption, explosion, bursting.

Deleuze and Guattari (1988: 311) offer a model of creativity that provides some support for this contention of the priority of sound in creation, of a breaking forth, a transition across a gap, that is both hermeneutical and sonic. They explain their model through three phases of the refrain. The first stage is characterised by the child who feels insecure and comforts herself with a familiar tune sung under the breath. As a second stage, this establishes a home:

> For sublime deeds like the foundation of a city or the fabrication of a golem, one draws a circle, or better yet walks in circles as in a children's dance, combining rhythmic vowels and consonants that correspond to the interior forces of creation as to the differentiated parts of an organism. A mistake in speed, rhythm or harmony would be catastrophic because it would bring back the forces of chaos, destroying both creator and creation.

In the third stage, one allows cracks in the circle:

> One launches forth, hazards an improvisation. . . . One ventures from home on the thread of a tune. Along sonorous, gestural, motor lines . . .
>
> (op. cit.)

Here, sound provides a suggestive language for articulating the creative propensity to celebrate the breach, negotiate the cut, to cross boundaries. These three phases are evident in terms of the mythic conflict between sound and vision. The human subject begins with sounds under the breath, a primal comfort in a condition of mobility, then progresses to a centre, a sense of home, articulated in architectural, geometrical and visual terms, which pertains to articulating space in terms of boundaries, as in Vitruvius' account of the laying out of a town through the constructions of the sacred gnomon, uniting heaven, earth and man (Snodgrass 1990; Vitruvius and Morgan 1960: 26). The breaking out, the quintessentially creative moment, is equated with sound, gesture and movement. It is achieved sonically, and presents as a return to an aural condition.

Everyday creativity

As part of our research into the relationships between sound and creativity, some colleagues and myself conducted a series of studies that focused on people's ability to arrange sound sources in a room. The initial task was for participants to listen to three fixed sound sources and provide diagrammatic representations of what they heard. They were then to arrange physically the sound sources in a defined space, represent and comment on what they had done and why.

We used mundane sound sources: an auctioneer, someone reading the stock market report for the FTSE100 and someone buying a rail ticket using an automated telesales service.

We avoided music, poetic recitations, radio announcements and uses of sound that carried suggestions of professional performance. We also provided some rudimentary props and a series of compact mobile speakers. The props included plastic storage boxes and lengths of fabric. We hoped the components of the installation would draw participants away from relying on common visual criteria for arranging objects in space: beauty, theatricality and the picturesque (as one might for example in flower arranging). The sounds were looped, and subjects could adjust the sound volume. We then replayed some of these experiments and some of our findings at cross-disciplinary focus group sessions for comment.

When confronted with tasks that appear unconstrained by purpose and sense, participants defaulted readily to arrangements that are symmetrical or follow some conventional ordering system. This seems to be a default condition pertaining to the spatial uncertainties of sound, as noise, cacophony and chaos. Domes and tubes featured prominently in people's verbal descriptions of the spatial qualities of sounds they were listening to. Certain of the voice recordings had the capacity to aggravate. Covering and occluding featured prominently as strategies for dealing with these sounds. There was ambivalence: respect for the sounds, the unusual process and the intentions of the research team. The sounds were never turned off. Hiding the sound sources was addressed covertly by keeping them audible, but in one case placing the auctioneer's sound source in a box, covered with fabric and under a table.

There is some accord here with Deleuze's second phase of the refrain, a kind of repression, bounding, layering and ordering. The process is spatial. According to one participant, 'I wanted the experience of moving around into these separate and overlapping sound spaces.' Participants also exhibited a propensity to break out of the constraints of the system, to 'break the unity of repetition with a story, a specific place'. The spatial implications of sound were also suggestive of leakage and flows. Deleuze and Guattari's concepts of anxiety, containment and breaking out were all in evidence, and each contributed to the creative moment, the agonistics of design with sound.

Embodied creativity

Much research into creativity focuses on cognitive functioning, as a product of the organ of the human brain – subject to influences, but as if isolated and autonomous (Boden 1990; Galton 1972; Sternberg and Lubart 1999; Torrance 1975). There are three arguments in favour of a revision of this hypothesis.

First: creativity is not only manifested in isolated, cognitive acts of introspective thought that can be tested by paper-based tasks; where creativity is construed as a text-based, numerical or visual activity, it is also manifested in dance, performance, and gesture, including movements of the hands, as in drawing and music-making. In his nineteenth-century survey of 'genius', Galton includes chapters on oarsmanship and wrestling, not as demonstrations of creative intelligence, but presented by way of contrast with intellectual virtuosity in science, poetry and statesmanship. Yet skills and outcomes in sports, performance, gesture and voice have equal purchase in the realms of creativity, not only in their tactics, choreography and design but also in their implementation and improvisation. Spontaneous and reflective creation involving limb, rhythm, movement, sound and response are the primary media of invention in many fields, and the neglect of the body in favour of classical views of cognition in creativity research constitutes a major shortcoming (Martindale 1999).

Our simple study described above indicates that where the diagrammatic representation of the spatial aspects of sound falters, people are adept at the embodied task of moving around loudspeakers, listening and re-positioning, to whatever purpose. Whereas people soon reach their limitations in talking about sounds in the abstract, they are adept at constructing narratives about actions that they have just performed, i.e. configuring sound sources. Their creativity is revealed in both physical action and reflection (Schön 1982).

Second: creativity is highly contextual. Societies and groups can exhibit creative behaviours without recourse to individual celebrity. The social construction of creativity requires some actions and individuals to be received as creative and acknowledged as such by some community or other, in a community of practice (Rickards and Moger 2006). The supposed genius of the moment may in fact be ahead of its time, in the wrong place at the right time, in the wrong circuit, or in last season's disciplinary matrix (Kuhn 1970). By a radical reading, it is social, cultural, legal and technological contexts that are the engines of creativity, elevating certain events and people as originators, heroes, geniuses and holders of intellectual property to a social or political end and there will always be those content to create in silence while others suffer the limelight. Our highly constrained experiment illustrates the complex relationship between context and agent. Were the experimenters the creative ones for inventing such an experiment, or were the participants for producing interesting outcomes? The question of the source of creativity is soon diffused as we think of the hardware, the intellectual climate and the circumstance.

Third: certain contemporary theories of cognition place thought beyond the brain in any case, as embodied, social, contextual and contingent (Anderson *et al.* 2000; Clark 1997, 2003; Coyne 2007). According to theories of situated cognition, brain function is incremental and timely, making maximum use of opportunity and context. We are not as isolated from our environment as we often think, or as suggested by our visually-oriented culture. Nor is the environment as mute. The cues are already there for individual cognitive apparatus to make its connections, born of generations over which personal and community practices and norms are bedded down. The social and material environment *thinks*, with creative events completed at any moment by the presence of the right individual or group at the appropriate time.

Were one to assert that creativity is in fact an action of the tribe, then it would be an easy slip into the endorsement of the creative power of the sonic field, of McLuhan's non-individuating aural primitivism. In our experiment, according to situated cognition, the thinking of the participants was already in place by virtue of the hardware, the room and the sounds. This is not to dispense with designer agency, but to situate it. In the world of abstract creativity studies, the brain of the individual is burdened with the necessity to imagine and take into account a whole context. For the designer on the case, working with the materials, the project is already at hand.

These assertions about creativity are further animated by concepts of *agon*. In so far as creativity is subjected to psychometric analysis it seems to rely on text and vision, and enters into conflict with aural and other sensory modalities. Failing to recognise or appropriate the conflict between the senses also ignores important aspects of creativity. The cut is after all a gesture. Like clapping (Connor 2003), it signals both the reward and the impetus to create. The contextual nature of creative achievement implicates competition and presents as the driver of creation. In so far as thought occurs in an extended environment with the brain as the organ of opportunity, then it operates at the margins, the incremental shifts, the micro-thresholds of existence, the minor cuts and agonies of human experience. Attending to sound amplifies the creative potential of *agon*.

Acknowledgements

I am grateful to co-investigators Martin Parker and Peter Nelson, and especially to Raymond Lucas for his input into the project and conducting the studies. This research is supported by a grant from the Arts and Humanities Research Council.

References

Albert, R. S. and M. A. Runco (1999). A history of research on creativity. In R. J. Sternberg, *Handbook of Creativity*. Cambridge, Cambridge University Press: 16–31.

Alberti, L. B. (1996). *On the Art of Building in Ten Books*. Cambridge, MA, MIT Press.

Anderson, J. R. *et al.* (2000). Perspectives on learning, thinking, and activity. *Educational Researcher*, 29(4): 11–13.

Ardrey, R. (1967). *The Territorial Imperative: A Personal Inquiry into the Animal Origins of Property and Nations*. London, Collins.

Augoyard, J.-F. and H. Torgue (2005). *Sonic Experience: A Guide to Everyday Sounds*. Montreal, McGill-Queens University Press.

Blesser, B. and L.-R. Salter (2006). *Spaces Speak; Are You Listening? Experiencing Aural Architecture*. Cambridge, MA, MIT Press.

Boden, M. (1990). *The Creative Mind: Myths and Mechanisms*. London, Abacus.

Bull, M. (2000). *Sounding Out the City: Personal Stereos and the Management of Everyday Life*. Oxford, Berg.

Caillois, R. (1961). *Man, Play, and Games*. New York, Free Press of Glencoe.

Clark, A. (1997). *Being There: Putting Brain, Body and World Together Again*. Cambridge, MA, MIT Press.

Clark, A. (2003). *Natural-Born Cyborgs: Minds, Technologies, and the Future of Human Intelligence*. Oxford, Oxford University Press.

Classen, C. (1993). *Worlds of Sense: Exploring the Senses in History and across Cultures*. London, Routledge.

Connor, S. (2000). *Dumbstruck: A Cultural History of Ventriloquism*. Oxford, Oxford University Press.

Connor, S. (2003). The help of your good hands: reports on clapping. In M. Bull and L. Back, *The Auditory Culture Reader*. Oxford, Berg: 67–76.

Connor, S. (2004). Edison's teeth: touching hearing. In V. Erlmann, *Hearing Cultures: Essays on Sound, Listening and Modernity*. Oxford, Berg: 153–172.

Corbusier, L. (1931) *Towards a New Architecture*. New York, Dover.

Coyne, R. (1999). *Technoromanticism: Digital Narrative, Holism, and the Romance of the Real*. Cambridge, MA, MIT Press.

Coyne, R. (2005) *Cornucopia Limited: Design and Dissent on the Internet*, Cambridge, MA, MIT Press.

Coyne, R. (2007) Thinking through virtual reality: place, non-place, and situated cognition. *Techné: Research in Philosophy and Technology, Special Issue: Real and Virtual Places*, 10(3): 26–38, at: http://scholar.lib.vt.edu/ejournals/SPT/v10n3/pdf/.

Cytowic, R. E. (1989). *Synesthesis: A Union of the Senses*. New York, Springer-Verlag.

Cytowic, R. E. (1995). Synesthesia: phenomenology and neuropsychology – a review of current knowledge. *PSYCHE* 2(10): http://psyche.csse.monash.edu.au/v2/psyche-2-10-cytowic.html.

Deleuze, G. and F. Guattari (1988). 1837: Of the refrain. *A Thousand Plateaus: Capitalism and Schizophrenia*. London, Athlone Press: 310–350.

Derrida, J. (1976). *Of Grammatology*. Baltimore, Maryland, Johns Hopkins University Press.

Derrida, J. (1993). *Aporias*. Stanford, CA, Stanford University Press.

Ferguson, M. (1991). Marshall McLuhan revisited: the 1960s zeitgeist victim or pioneer postmodernist. *Media, Culture and Society*, 13: 71–90.

Freud, S. (1953). Leonardo da Vinci and a memory of his childhood. In *Art and Literature, Jensens Gradiva, Leonardo da Vinci and Other Works*, Volume 14. London, Penguin: 151–231.

Freud, S. (1991). The dissolution of the Oedipus complex. In A. Richards, *The Penguin Freud Library, Volume 7: On Sexuality*. Harmondsworth, Penguin: 315–322.

Gadamer, H.-G. (1975). *Truth and Method*. New York, Seabury Press.

Gallagher, S. (1992). *Hermeneutics and Education*. Albany, NY, SUNY Press.

Galton, F. (1972). *Hereditary Genius: An Inquiry into Its Laws and Consequences*. Gloucester, MA, Peter Smith.

Gildenhard, I. and A. Zissos (2000). Ovid's Narcissus (Met. 3.339–510): echoes of Oedipus. *American Journal of Philology*, 121(1): 129–147.

Havelock, E. A. (1986). *The Muse Learns to Write: Reflections on Orality and Literacy from Antiquity to the Present*. New Haven, Yale University Press.

Homer (1980). *The Odyssey*. Oxford, Oxford University Press.

Hyde, L. (1998). *Trickster Makes This World: Mischief, Myth and Art*. New York, North Point Press.

Kahn, D. and G. Whitehead (eds) (1992). *Wireless Imagination: Sound, Radio, and the Avant-Garde*. Cambridge, MA, MIT Press.

Kay, A. (1990). User interface: a personal view. In B. Laurel, *The Art of Human–Computer Interface Design*. Reading, MA, Addison Wesley: 191–207.

Koolhaas, R. (1994). *Delirious New York*. New York, Monacelli Press.

Kuhn, T. (1970). *The Structure of Scientific Revolutions*. Chicago, University of Chicago Press.

LaBelle, B. (2006). *Background Noise: Perspectives on Sound Art*. New York, Continuum.

Lacan, J. (1977). *The Mirror Stage as Formative of the Function of the I*. London, Routledge: 1–7.

Martindale, C. (1999). Biological bases of creativity. In R. J. Sternberg, *Handbook of Creativity*. Cambridge, Cambridge University Press: 137–152.

McLuhan, M. (1968). The Medium is the Massage (long playing record). CS 9501, CL2701, Columbia Records.

McLuhan, M. (1994). *Understanding Media: The Extensions of Man*. Cambridge, MA, MIT Press.

Naguib, M. and R. H. Wiley (2001). Estimating the distance to a source of sound: mechanisms and adaptations for long-range communication. *Animal Behaviour*, 62(5): 825–837.

Newton, I. (2003). *Opticks: Or a Treatise of the Reflections, Inflections, and Colors of Light*. New York, Prometheus.

Ong, W. J. (1962). *The Barbarian Within, and Other Fugitive Essays*. New York, Macmillan.

Ovid, E. J. K. (1986). *Metamorphoses*. London, Oxford University Press.

Palladio, A. (1965). *The Four Books of Architecture*. New York, Dover.

Perez-Gomez, A. (1985). *Architecture and the Crisis of Modern Science*. Cambridge, MA, MIT Press.

Plato (1997). Cratylus. In J. M. Cooper, *Complete Works*. Indianapolis, ILL, Hackett: 101–156.

Poincarè, H. (2000). Mathematical creation. *Resonance: Journal of Science Education*, 5(2): 85–94.

Rabelais, F. (1955). *Gargantua and Pantagruel*. London, Penguin.

Razik, T. (1966). Recent findings and developments in creativity studies. *Theory into Practice*, 5(4): 160–165.

Rheingold, H. (2002). *Smart Mobs: The Next Social Revolution*. Cambridge, MA, Basic Books.

Rickards, T. and S. Moger (2006). Creative leaders: a decade of contributions from the *Creativity and Innovation Management* journal. *Creativity and Innovation Management*, 15(1): 4–18.

Ricoeur, P. (1977). *The Rule of Metaphor*. London, Routledge and Kegan Paul.

Ruskin, J. and J. G. Links (eds) (1960). *The Stones of Venice*. New York, Da Capo Press.

Schafer, R. M. (1993). *The Soundscape: Our Sonic Environment and the Tuning of the World*. Rochester, VT, Destiny.

Schön, D. (1982). *The Reflective Practitioner*. Cambridge, MA, MIT Press.

Serres, M. (1982). *The Parasite*. Baltimore, MD, John Hopkins University Press.

Snodgrass, A. B. (1990). *Architecture, Time and Eternity: Studies in the Stellar and Temporal Symbolism of Traditional Buildings*, Volumes I and II. New Delhi, Aditya Prakashan.

Snodgrass, A. B. and R. Coyne (2006). *Interpretation in Architecture: Design as a Way of Thinking*. London, Routledge.

Sternberg, R. J. and T. I. Lubart (1999). The concept of creativity: prospects and paradigms. In R. J. Sternberg, *Handbook of Creativity*. Cambridge, Cambridge University Press: 3–15.

Torrance, E. P. (1975). *Torrance Tests of Creative Thinking: Norms-technical Manual*. Lexington, MA, Ginn.

Torrance, E. P. (1993). Understanding creativity: where to start? *Psychological Inquiry*, 4(3): 232–234.

Tschumi, B. (1994). *Architecture and Disjunction*. Cambridge, MA, MIT Press.

35

Veblen, T. (1998). *The Theory of the Leisure Class*. Amherst, NY, Promethius.

Vitruvius, P. and M. H. Morgan (1960). *Vitruvius: The Ten Books on Architecture*. New York, Dover Publications.

Vovolis, T. (2003). The voice and the mask in ancient Greek tragedy. In L. Sider, D. Freeman and J. Sider, *Soundscape: The School of Sound Lectures 1998–2001*. London, Wallflower Press: 73–82.

Waterworth, J. A. (1997). Creativity and sensation: the case for synaesthetic media. *Leonardo*, 30(4): 327–330.

Wittkower, R. (1998). *Architectural Principles in the Age of Humanism*. Chichester, Academy Editions.

4

Unleashing the creative potential of design in business

Margaret Bruce

Introduction

Market leading businesses understand the connection between design, creativity and innovation. They develop and direct a core competence and capability in design and innovation, which is embedded in the know-how and culture of the company, and thus, becomes a proprietory competence and difficult to imitate. BMW, Apple, Sony, Electrolux and Paul Smith exhibit this ability.

Where consumers have increasing choice about what they buy and from whom, what makes them choose one product or service over another? In a crowded and global marketplace, why do some companies succeed whilst others fail? Design differentiates the winners from the losers. People choose things because of a combination of factors – quality, perceived value for money, aesthetic appeal, different and novel features, convenience and, of course, price.

Evidence from a variety of research studies and from the experiences of countless firms suggests that design contributes to business success. Attention to design can lead to superior products, inject life into mature markets or introduce new or adapted products to allow the company to diversify into more profitable markets (DTI 2005; Veryzer 2005).

The worldwide growth of the creative industries indicates the rising demand for creative people, for a different perspective or creative leadership in business (Florida 2002; NESTA 2003). In this chapter, we focus on the connection between creativity and design for innovation. We explore how designers work in practice and how design is managed in the innovation process. Often, the contribution of design to innovation is ignored, or taken for granted and has been referred to as 'hidden innovation' (Miles and Green 2007). Measurement of design's role is not easy to separate out from other factors to determine its direct impact on innovation and so becomes a 'hidden' activity in the innovation process. It is assumed that creative approaches to innovation through design simply happen because of the presence of talented individuals, rather than a process that can be managed. Once it is understood that design connects with creativity and innovation and can be managed, this then opens up a capability and competence, which can be managed, built upon and directed. In fact, businesses that harness design and realise its potential become market leaders, for example Apple, Caterpillar, BMW, and so on.

Design, creativity and innovation

As Bruce and Bessant (2002) suggest: 'Design is essentially the application of human creativity to a purpose – to create products, services, buildings, organisations and environments which meet people's needs. It is the systematic transformation of ideas into reality' and creative problem-solving capabilities are applied to deal with a particular challenge in a new way. For example, Apple's iPod is an ingenious product, which allows people to make a personal music selection and listen to this on the move, wherever they are located.

Design decisions are made about the shape, form, colour and choice of materials for all these items. In a broad sense, design is the conception and planning of man-made objects and as such, design encompasses three-dimensional objects, graphic communications and integrated systems from information technology to urban environments – furniture, textiles, cars and computers.

Design concerns problem solving. Changing patterns of consumption, taste and commercial imperatives all serve as design drivers. The need to create competitive products has driven the diversity of design. Design is not only a process linked with production, but is a means of conveying persuasive ideas, attitudes and values – such as experiencing fun in an amusement park, or the enjoyment of a superb meal in the relaxed environment of a well run restaurant. Such experiences do not emerge by accident but by a conscious and planned activity, that of design.

Freeman (1982) regards design as crucial to innovation in that it is the domain of creativity where ideas are devised; but where 'coupling' occurs, that is where technical possibilities are linked with market needs. Designers can translate technical ideas for the market; each technical idea is likely to generate an extensive array of possible design configurations and modifications. These may involve little or no technical change, but may result in a product with a different form, style, pattern or decoration, for example a new chair design (Walsh *et al.* 1991).

Design is not always about creating something totally new. Innovation may be about discovering new approaches, using new materials, etc. Consider how many different designs of chairs exist, all apparently being 'fit for purpose.' Sometimes the *demand* may be very clear, but the particular solution to meet the need is no available. Apple's iPod met a need for personalised music systems and made product affordable.

The availability of new knowledge – technology – may need to find a use. Examples of such 'solutions looking for a problem' include social networking technology, etc.

How designers think and work

Design is about doing things consciously and not because they have always been done in a certain way, it is about comparing alternatives to select the best possible solutions, it is about exploring and experimenting. Fisher and Amabile (see Chapter 2) explore improvisation and its links with creative play, which is integral to the creative process of design.

Indeed, designers deal with projects that involve unfamiliar concepts, are predominately visual, and entail ambiguity, subjectivity, gut feel and intuition. In particular, visual imagination is a crucial aspect of design because it enables mental pictures to be constructed of what has never been experienced. Drawing, model-making and visual sensitivity enable alternative forms, details and ideas to be explored, discussed and considered before time and capital are invested in making the design. Schön (1988) describes designing as 'relative chaos' and he explores 'how they reason', 'what they 'know' and their 'tacit knowledge', which he suggests is encased in 'rules, types and worlds'. He develops the notion of 'design worlds' and refers to these as: 'environments entered into and inhabited by designers when designing. They contain particular configurations of things, relations and qualities and they act as holding environments for design knowledge.'

Experimentation, play and doing are central to the creativity element of design to assess the consequences and implications of a drawing or a model. At the heart of the sophisticated and complex process of designing a car, clay models are constructed and used by the multi-disciplinary team of designers, engineers, project planners, marketers, etc. to view the car in three dimensions, to see its shape and the flow of lines and to understand the concept in reality. This helps to move from concept to reality and to underpin the decisions resulting in the final composition of the car. This is akin to the notion of 'positive turbulence' (see Gryskiewicz, Chapter 9), whereby creativity occurs through exposures to 'new worlds'. Electrolux has a futures lab where prototypes are produced and 'played with' to help in the thinking process leading to the generation of new and improved products and to close the gap between concept and reality. House robots, fridges fuelled by carbon-friendly energy sources and new materials are used to enhance familiar domestic technologies.

As well as experimenting, improvisation is another creative approach used by designers. Poolton and Ismail (1999) argue that 'second movers' or followers into a market take advantage of this. In the market for solid detergents, Lever's Persil Tablets was a first mover in the UK market, taking ten per cent of this segment immediately on entering this category. Twelve months later, its rival P and G came into the market with a higher-priced product that had significant benefits. Through test-marketing, P and G discovered a major weakness in the market leader's product; they improved on this, and entered the market.

Designers can create innovative products or services as well as translate innovative ideas to the marketplace. By extending the designer's role beyond the product design process, design sensibilities can be integrated with other functions and so widen its impact. Design skills and knowledge can contribute to many aspects and activities of a business, including research, marketing, promotion, branding, product augmentation, flexibility, competitor intelligence, integrating technology, spotting new opportunities, trend predictions, product improvements and cost reductions. This is forcefully expressed by Leonard-Barton (1995) in her comment that:

> But in practical terms the important point is not so much where the ideas come from as the way in which they become reality. In essence this involves some creative link between needs and means, which is then worked on to move the good idea to a successful artefact, which is accepted and widely used. 'Successful adaptation seems to involve the thoughtful, incremental redirection of skills and knowledge bases so that today's expertise is reshaped into tomorrow's capabilities.'

The important point in all of this is the need to recognise that success is likely to come from developing the skills and knowledge that enable a company to adjust and respond to change. New challenges need new ways of thinking, which may break conventional rules but offer a plan for future growth. Companies can act more creatively and learn to improve and innovate in all aspects of business. Indeed, 'design can play a crucial role in making businesses of all sorts more creative, more responsive and above all more competitive' (Design Council 1999).

Connecting creativity, design and innovation

Creativity, design and innovation are linked concepts, as Bruce and Bessant (2002) show:

'Creativity is the ability to combine ideas in new ways to solve problems and exploit opportunities.

Innovation is the successful application of new ideas in practice in the form of new or improved products, services or processes.

Design is the purposive application of creativity throughout the process of innovation'.

How these are connected is shown in Figure 4.1.

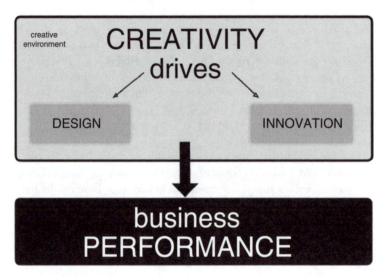

Figure 4.1 Linking creativity and design to business performance

Essentially, creativity is a way of thinking differently and allowing for novel ideas to come to the fore. Designers have an aptitude and have been trained to think 'out of the box'. Typically, they seek a solution to a problem, which may entail a redefinition of the problem to get to the optimum solution. They may apply techniques to stimulate creative thoughts, such as brain-storming, user trips, breaking down a product or service into its key elements and then rebuild-ing with different materials, functions and users in mind, or different cost parameters. Using tools like visualising, sketching, drawing and model-making they start to conceptualise and develop the idea. Then, by putting the concept into reality but testing, talking to users, etc., the concept may become a prototype ripe for further development.

In the product development process, other experts may be needed to carry the concept forward, such as engineers, material scientists, marketers, etc., who may also contribute to the creative process underpinning design and innovation. The multi-disciplinary team will revise, reform and refresh the concept to meet user and market needs. The designer will be involved at different stages to check that the novelty of the original idea is translated in some way in the final product and may check that the form of the product meets with the intended use and functionality. In some cases, time and effort to move from the creative phase through design to the finished outcome may be accomplished speedily and without mishaps. In others, the process will be complex and protracted and need a range of skills to bring the concept to fruition and design may only form a small part of the total enterprise. In the latter case, the creative idea could have arisen during RandD and been the outcome of research scientists working on a particular problem and design may not have been involved directly. It has been argued (Miles and Green 2007) that innovation in 'softer' industries, such as gaming, furniture, etc., may not require RandD and that such design-led innovation is an example of 'hidden innovation'. However, regardless of the scale and complexity of the task, the concept will have been borne from creativity – a thought, a novel idea, a different way of thinking through a problem. In this way, creativity is fundamental to innovation.

With this in mind, it is imperative that organisations have a culture appropriate to foster and encourage creativity, so that they can be constantly innovative and remain at the forefront of their sphere of expertise. Creative leadership (Mumford, Chapter 23, Cox Review 2006) is one issue that needs to be considered by modern organisations to enable them to flourish.

Inevitably the process of moving from a half-formed idea, however creative, to a successfully implemented product is one full of risks and failures. There may be many false starts, or recursions back to the drawing board, and there may be difficult technical problems to solve, which can slow down the project or put the costs up. Indeed, Boden (Chapter 15) focuses on the role of computers in creative production and the design process that has undergone fundamental changes over the last twenty years with the adoption of computers for design activities. Designers use computers to capture their ideas, to formulate these and to share them with other members of the design and production team. Software is so sophisticated that technical experts are needed to work alongside designers to translate the designs into realisable, tested concepts. The concepts can be stored, reproduced and changed online. The concepts can be made into models and prototypes from computer systems. The need of the model-maker and craft-based design associated activities have virtually disappeared and been replaced by programmers with an empathy for design. The speed of production has reduced as team members can check concepts online, amend, discuss, test and reject ideas in a virtual world.

There is the constant need to make sure that technical development of the idea does not take place in isolation from the end-users, otherwise there is the risk that the beautiful artefact which emerges at the end of the process is actually something no one wants. Indeed, researchers have argued that effective innovation involves users, or follows a 'customer active paradigm' (von Hippel 2005). Making the link between creativity and design, Leonard-Barton (1995) suggests that designers are empathetic to user needs and a design–oriented approach to innovation employs market research tools and techniques that elicit both overt and latent user needs. Open Innovation is an approach that encourages collaboration in the design and innovation process. With virtual working, an open platform can be powerful in enabling the participation of different sets of knowledge and ways of doing things.

Research aimed at understanding creativity process by Van de Ven and colleagues (1989) explored the limitations of simple models of turing new product ideas into adopted products. They found that:

- Shocks trigger innovations – change happens when people or organisations reach a threshold of opportunity or dissatisfaction.
- Ideas proliferate – after starting out in a single direction, the process proliferates into multiple, divergent progressions.

- Setbacks frequently arise – plans are over-optimistic, commitments escalate, mistakes accumulate and vicious cycles can develop.
- Restructuring of the innovating unit often occurs through external intervention, personnel changes or other unexpected events.
- Top management plays a key role in sponsoring, but also in criticising and shaping, the process and its outcome.
- Success criteria shift over time, differ between groups and make design and innovation a political process.
- The process involves learning, but many of its outcomes are due to other events that occur as the new idea develops, thus making learning often 'superstitious' in nature.

They indicate that the underlying structure of innovation can be represented by four key phases, which may be applied differently according to context. These styles are:

- initiation
- development
- implementation
- termination

Design Management

Design is connected with the four phases of initiation, development, implementation and termination. Design is concerned with how well the ideas are formulated, how clear the concept is, whether it meets or fits the needs or expectations of potential users, how well the project is managed and translating the initial idea into acceptable reality. These affect the final outcome of the process, in terms of delivering 'good' or 'bad' designs.

The design process translates ideas, opportunities or triggers into a final artefact through creativity. Take an example. Where does a new kettle come into from? It begins with some form of trigger – perhaps a new technological possibility, which has been developed in a research lab somewhere – maybe a new type of material or energy saving device. Alternatively, the idea may have come from marketing, where a particular target segment has been identified with a particular need – perhaps combining a water filter to clean the water prior to boiling to serve the health conscious market. Whatever the source of the idea, creativity is concerned with finding a solution to the problem. This may be a radically new idea or, more likely, it will be a combination of old and established ideas with some new elements.

As Bruce and Bessant (2002) suggest: 'even at this stage, the process can be influenced strongly by the ways in which the activities of identifying the trigger are carried out. How well and widely does the firm scan for signals about new technological opportunities? Does it keep track of what others are doing – for example, in university research labs, in other countries and especially amongst their competitors? Does it "reverse engineer" their products to find out what new technological ideas they are using? Does it look ahead to try to get a feel for how novel technological developments – perhaps through some form of technology foresight or forecasting?'

Market dynamics stimulate change and how effectively are these monitored ? Are forecasting and other techniques to track social and economic trends used? Are ideas tested out with potential customers to understand what they might like, dislike or value?

After idea generation is the process moves of refinement and problem solving – dealing with the technical issues (shape, form or materials) and with the market requirements (aesthetics, functionality, performance). Key issues are addressed, such as costs, quality, features and presentation for the marketplace. This is part of a broader cycle of invention and development, which continues after product launch.

The underlying process operates for different types of design and innovation – fashion, mobile phone, building, etc. It is a core process with a recognisable set of stages and connects creativity to design and innovation.

Creativity underpins design

The design process involves many inputs at different times and from different perspectives. But, the major driver is that of creative problem solving to successfully achieve the initial idea. What is the concept of creativity from the perspective of design and innovation and its contribution to these activities?

Creativity is not the domain of especially gifted individuals, but is generic and most people are capable of creativity. A useful approach to creativity is 'the generation of novel ideas' and novelty may occur from looking at things in a different way. Creativity can be inhibited by evaluating ideas too soon, or too rigorously.

Many great ideas arise through lucky accidental discoveries – for example, the adhesive behind Post-it notes. But as Louis Pasteur observed, 'chance favours the prepared mind', so it may be useful to understand how to set up the conditions within which such 'accidents' can take place.

Relevant to this is to recognise that creativity is an attribute most people possess – but they will have different predispositions and preferences. Some people are comfortable with big ideas, whilst others prefer smaller increments of change, such as ideas about how to improve their working environment.

This has implications for managing creativity within the organisation. Firstly, innovation the widespread use of a new artefact. Whilst the initial idea may require a significant creative leap, the following process entails hundreds of small problem-finding and -solving exercises – each involving creative input. And though the former may need the skills or inspiration of a particular individual, the latter requires the input of many different people over a sustained period of time. Developing Google or the iPod, or any successful innovation entails the combined creative endeavour of many individuals.

Secondly, creativity is not an entirely conscious or rational process. Bruce and Bessant (2002) suggest that creative behaviour follows a pattern:

- First insight – identifying and defining or redefining the problem.
- Preparation – mental groundwork, looking for information and prior experiences that might help solve it.
- Incubation – letting the unconscious work on the problem, often by sleeping on it.
- Illumination – the apparent flash of insight, the 'aha!' experience.
- Verification – testing and implementing the idea (Wallas 1926).

In other words, creativity is the result of interplay between conscious and rational thought and unconscious and apparently random or dream-like association and activity. For people to be creative, they need the space and time to undertake activities that enable both conscious and unconscious modes of thinking.

Many companies recognise that they need to create physical, temporal and mental space if they want their employees to be creative. And attempt to provide an environment, conditions and stimulating tools and techniques to encourage creativity.

Research shows that group creativity is a more powerful resource, than that of individuals because of the interplay and mutual stimulation of ideas produced from the mix of people of different backgrounds, experience and personality. They see a problem in different ways, approach its solution from different angles, and often open up new and unexpected lines of enquiry to others in the group.

Rickards and Moger (1999) distinguish between three types of creative teams – Dream Teams, Standard Teams and Teams from Hell. They identify seven factors that characterise creative teams: a platform of understanding, vision, climate, ideas, response to setbacks, network skills and response to evidence. Creative leadership is emphasised by Rickards and Moger (1999). These types of leaders believe in 'win–win', have a leadership style that is empowering and motivating, develop strategies and techniques which encourage members of the team to solve problems, and they align individual needs to the tasks in hand and responsibilities of the team.

The extent to which firms develop effective networks influences its ability to be creative. Sources of innovation do not just reside within the boundaries of a company, but partnering or working with suppliers and customers can yield novel ideas (Bruce and Jevnaker 1998)

Companies which underestimate the value of creativity do not appreciate the strategic contribution of design. Companies often associate design with high risk and fail to acknowledge its potential benefits for strategy and growth. Efforts are being made to convince such companies, small and medium-sized enterprises (SMEs) in particular, to adopt a design strategy to aid future growth (Cox 2006).

Conclusion

Design is the purposive application of creativity throughout the process of innovation. Creativity is the ability to combine ideas in new ways to solve problems and exploit opportunities. Innovation is the successful application of new ideas in practice, as new or improved products, services or processes. Recognition of the inter-connectedness of creativity, design and innovation, and providing a supportive culture that encourages this inter-connectedness, is central to an organisation's well-being and effectiveness.

Acknowledgement

The author wishes to thank Professor John Bessant, Tonaka Business School, Imperial College, London for his insights into the role of creativity in the innovation process.

References

Bayley, S. (2000). *General Knowledge*. London, Booth-Clibborn Editions.
Bruce, M. and Bessant, J. (2002). *Design in Business: Strategic Innovation through Design*. Englewood Cliffs, NJ, Prentice Hall.
Bruce, M. and Jevnaker, B.H. (1998). *Management of Design Alliances*. Chichester, Wiley.

Chee, L.S. and Phuong, T.H. (1996). Managing diverse groups for creativity. *Managing Diversity*, 5(2): 93–98.

Cox, G. (2006). Cox review of creativity in business: building on the UK's strengths, at: www.hm-treasury.gov.uk/cox.

Design Council (1999). *Design in Britain*. London, The Design Council.

DTI (2005). Creativity, design and business performance, DTI Economics Paper, no. 15.

Freeman, C. (1982). *The Economics of Industrial Innovation*. London, Frances Pinter.

Florida, R. (2002). *The Rise of the Creative Class*. New York, Basic Books.

Leonard-Barton, D. (1995). *Wellsprings of Knowledge: Building and Sustaining the Sources of Innovation*. Boston, MA, Harvard Business School Press.

Miles, I. and Green, L. (2007). *Hidden Innovation*, London, NESTA.

NESTA (2003) *Forward Thinking, New Solutions to Old Problems: Investing in the Creative Industries*. London, NESTA.

Poolton, J. and Ismail, H.S. (1999). The role of improvisation in new product development. *International Journal of New Product Development and Innovation Management,* 1(4): 321–331.

Rickards, T. and Moger, S. (1999). *Headbook for Creative Team Leaders*. Aldershot, Gower.

Schön, D. (1988). Designing: rules, types and worlds. *Design Studies*, 9(3): 181–190

Van de Ven, A. *et al.* (1989). *Research on the Management of Innovation.* New York, Harper and Row.

Veryzer, R.W. (2005). The roles of marketing and industrial design in discontinuous new product development. *Journal of Product Innovation Management*, 22(1): 22–41.

von Hippel, E. (2005) *Democratising Innovation*. Cambridge, MA: MIT Press.

Wallas, G. (1926). *The Art of Thought*. New York, Franklin-Watts.

Walsh, V., Roy, R., Bruce, M. and Potter, S. (1992). *Winning by Design: Technology, Product Design and International Competitiveness*. Oxford, Basil Blackwell.

5

Space to adapt: workplaces, creative behaviour and organizational memetics

Ilfryn Price

> As a matter of fact, most of natural selection is concerned with preventing evolutionary change rather than with driving it.
>
> (Dawkins 1986: 125)

Introduction: Why physical space and organizational evolution?

By 1837, according to his introduction to *The Origin of Species*, Charles Darwin had conceived what history would come to see as one of the most creative and original insights on record. Aware of potential controversy, he then all but shut his manuscript away for 21 years. Publication was forced in 1858 after Wallace independently conceived the same idea. The incident exemplifies the power of Waddington's (1977) 'conventional wisdom of the dominant group',[1] or Csikszentmihalyi's (1988) proposition that what is considered creative is subject to the prevailing mental models of what he termed the field (the influential individuals) and domain (the symbol system influenced) that contextualizes an individual's creative insight. Darwin, of course, conceived his theory after visiting the Galapagos Islands, now recognized as a shining example of the power of natural selection in small, reproductively isolated populations; 'peripheral isolates' in the domain of modern biology. Various ancestral species that flew or floated from South America evolved to fill new niches and possibility spaces, open to them in the islands.

This chapter examines the power of new spaces, mental but especially physical, in interrupting prevailing conventional wisdom and facilitating organizational adaptation. The theoretical underpinning will draw, like Csikszentmihalyi, on insights offered by understanding organizations in terms of evolving 'conventional wisdoms', memes, replicated by, among other factors, physical symbols. The practical basis of the chapter is, however, the power of physical space as, 'the most important and least appreciated tool of contemporary knowledge management' (attributed to Tom Peters). Empirical research now provides a mounting body of both case and survey evidence concerning the way in which some creative workspaces have catalysed changes of organizational culture, including greater innovation and cross-professional working (Price 2007). Chapter length and commercial constraints prevent a full treatment here, but examples include:

Thirteen record quarters in a row after a new CEO dynamited the 'sacred' HQ building.

'The best Christmas ever' after an MD we worked with used a change of physical space to catalyze a more 'agile and innovative' organization.

A reduction in the time to implement complex interdisciplinary solutions to new challenges from three months to 24 hours after a similar change in another knowledge organization.

The evidence in each case is business results and the perceptions of senior managers involved. What they and other examples have in common are changes to the physical geography and symbolism of workplaces. The ancestor's of Darwin's finches had no choice. They evolved to a physical terrain dictated by the quirks of climates and plate tectonics. Organizations, and their managers, are less circumscribed. Their physical space can be modified, sometimes dramatically, so as to, borrowing another geological metaphor, punctuate the equilibrium of an organization. All too often it is not. It becomes an unconscious contribution to the organizational status quo.

Where occupants have been surveyed (Haynes and Price 2004; Price 2007), the largest beneficial influences on perceived productivity always arise from the chances and spaces for informal interactions and conversations. Successful changes to workplace geography appear to encourage and enable such interactions. There is no universal recipe, and the informal interaction does not, in some contexts, preclude enclosed offices for concentrated work. What many of the successful designs do however share is a greater emphasis on common areas that attract people into them and enhance the opportunity for such interaction. They also tend to avoid straight, regimented lines of desks, cubicles or offices along a corridor. They emphasize 'public' spaces more than formal areas for scheduled meetings.[2] People, as agents of the organizational system, become more connected. In essence, and anticipating a concept from complexity theory (see below), the space is closer to the edge of chaos. A similar emphasis on social spaces and interaction can be found in designs for many modern learning spaces on university campuses (Marmot and Associates 2006) and the traditional common room may contribute more to a department's research output than its detractors realize.[3]

To this one might add the experience of innovative teachers and developers, who use a variety of physical and virtual spaces to encourage social networking and learning. Yet space remains off most MBA curricula and figures too rarely in managerial and HR discourses. Why? The possible answer, explored below, lies in the prevailing power of conventional wisdoms.

Organizational ecologies

Practice

The 'knowledge economy' and the increasing 'clock rate' of technological change are widely accepted. Organizations of many kinds see a need, or express an aspiration, to create cultures that are described by terms such as flexible, agile, innovative or networked. One I have worked with even spoke of increasing organizational velocity. Whatever the metaphor, there is a common concern to increase innovation and creativity.

Runaway increase also has a prospective downside. Jared Diamond (2004) has provided vivid examples of civilizations collapsing even as they struggled to keep perpetuating their status quo. The statue builders of Easter Island are well known. Less so are the Greenland Norse, using what small economic surplus their settlements afforded them to replicate the buildings and artifacts of European Christianity while refusing to learn from the Inuit whose technology was to prove more versatile in the face of a harsher climate. Both can be advanced as examples of fields (sensu Csikszentmihalyi) devoting an ever-greater share of their dwindling resources to replicating a prevailing domain of symbols. Current commercial systems are arguably doing the same. Greater creativity and agility may actually be hastening the moment when our economy reaches its limit to growth. On the other hand, if we are becoming victims of a runaway evolutionary spiral,[4] appreciating the process might aid the achievement of a creative but sustainable solution.

The statues of Easter Island or the churches of the Greenland settlements also serve to illustrate the influence of artifacts in general and buildings in particular. They not only express a dominant conventional wisdom, they also reinforce or replicate it. 'First we shape our buildings and thereafter they shape us,' as Churchill put it. More creative, non-traditional offices, often lumped under the generic title open plans, can shape greater flexibility (Price 2007), yet conventional wisdoms deny the evidence, much as the Greenland Norse appear to have refused to countenance Inuit technology.

Memetic immune systems?

We react to words. The emphasis on 'open plan' in the previous paragraph was deliberate. It permits an example of rhetorical selection in action. An academic reader might, by now, be horrified by an apparent endorsement of rows of tightly packed workstations. There is a high probability that the academic reader will, if they are tenured faculty, have their own office. The word 'open plan' is interpreted as a threat to this status quo. Their institution will have, though its power will vary, an estates department or facilities directorate that may well appear bent on enforcing ever more stringent 'space standards'. Academic staff tend, perhaps rightly I hasten to add, to interpret such rhetoric as a threat especially when it is justified by reference to cost savings rather than business benefits. Here, in a microcosm, are two fields of discourse each subject to misunderstandings and assertions about the other that serve to re-enforce and preserve the fields concerned (Matzdorf and Price 1999). Each tends to react to the other's discourse with an almost automatic rejection, hence the metaphor, which introduces the section.

The generalization is not universal. Some Deans' use of physical space in their schools or faculties could be added to the empirical cases cited earlier. They are though the exception. Simplistic as it is, the example does illustrate the proposition advanced in this chapter; the emergence and maintenance of self-referential, autopoetic communities (Csikszentmihalyi's fields) of discourse, which may not correspond, to the formal boundaries of an organization. Such fields are enabled by their shared discourse as it shapes, but also perpetuates their shared conventional wisdom. In the process the discourse and wisdom is replicated. Language is the predominant, but not the only symbol system involved. Physical spaces are a symbol system of their own. The example also provides a plausible explanation of the absence of consideration of space in most MBA curricula. The topic generates a negative reaction in the communities who generate those curricula. Again the status quo is preserved. Surprisingly the process can be interpreted as evolution.

The evolutionary dynamic

As a popular metaphor, evolution is frequently interpreted as steady state change; the antithesis of revolution. In fact Natural Selection is also a process that can resist change. Selection in biota illuminates an equivalent process in a separate domain, labeled here simply as the abiotic.[5] Evolution requires a source of variation in the properties of an organism upon which selection can act. Those marginally more suited to a particular environment (be it physical or ecological) are presumed to have an advantage when reproducing; i.e. their properties are more likely to be inherited in the next generation. It is their genotype, which enables inheritance and is replicated in the process. The phenotype is the organic body and behavioural set which a particular genotype enables or encodes. Phenotypes can, in theory, be traced through patterns of descent with modification, their phylogeny, or classified according to current properties to infer descent (cladistics).

The environment in which an organism is selected consists of other organisms' phenotypes. In a large interbreeding population the prevailing genotypes, the codes that we might express – metaphorically – as the conventional wisdom of species, can be a force for stability; hence speciation in reproductively isolated populations and the quotation that began this chapter.

The biotic domain is a classical open system. It has adapted over some 3.5 billion years to the vicissitudes of the physical environment, climate and sporadic impacts from large rocks. Yet complex ordered forms have emerged and are maintained, over the life cycle of individual organic entities and over the much longer life cycle of individual species. The system depends on genes that have even longer life spans.[6]

Conventional biotic selection is now interpreted in terms of the replicating properties of those genes, a result in turn of the chemical structure of DNA.[7] The most widely acknowledged lay explanation of the 'modern synthesis' is probably Richard Dawkins' *The Selfish Gene* (1976).[8] That book also introduced the concept of memes, cultural replicators. The term stuck, proved a successful meme, and earned a niche in various discourse systems, despite debate (see below), as to what a meme might be and whether the concept is useful or correct. I follow Csikszentmihalyi (and others) in arguing for 'conventional wisdoms' as, in effect, complexes of selfish memes, enabling social systems that assist those memes' replication. Despite the starting quote Dawkins is, in general, more ambivalent in his treatment of Punctuated Equilibrium, the concept paleontology brought to evolutionary theory (Eldredge and Gould 1972) – even if, for geologists, the evidence is now overwhelming (e.g. Benton 2003) that the history of life on earth shows (Ager 1973) 'long periods of boredom' interspersed with 'brief moments of terror'. Benton brings home the still recent displacement of traditional 'uniformitarianism' in the earth sciences by a renewed acceptance of the evidence for sudden, infrequent but catastrophic, influences on planetary history; another punctuation of a conventional wisdom.

The human species is prone to interpret the world through the lens of acquired ideas and mental models. My early professional years were spent as a geologist. For technical reasons[9] those of us concerned with the exploration of offshore basins were among the first to encounter the punctuated nature of the physical stratigraphic record.

Later, as first a manager and then a researcher into organizational behaviour, I was struck by the fact that innovation in large organizations appeared to be easier in small isolated populations (Tom Peter's skunk works) and that social/corporate history appeared to show longer periods of stability punctuated by periods of change. Kuhn's scientific revolutions provide an obvious example.[10] That apparent similarity underpinned an argument that organizational change and learning might be a selection process; one operating not on genes but on organizational paradigms (Price 1995).

Evolution by selection has a history in scholarship on social or organizational systems, either as a metaphor (Morgan's *Images of Organizations*) or a postulated real process (Aldrich 1999). In economics, an evolutionary perspective (e.g. Hodgson 1993) appears to be becoming at least legitimate as a field of inquiry. In psychology, the evolutionary label tends to have been claimed by advocates of a fiercely debated, genetically 'hard-wired', basis for human behaviour. Rather than such a position, I am exploring memes as a metaphor or explanation for the phenomena of social or cognitive psychology. In Csikszentmihalyi's (1988: 333) words:

> A domain is a system of related memes that change through time and what changes them is the process of creativity.

Others have made a similar claim; hence Lloyd (1990) used a memetic position to consider companies as creations of replicating strategies. For Price (1995) and Price and Shaw (1998), strategies were but an expression of organizational 'patterns of thought' transmitted through conversations and artefacts. Weeks and Galunic (2003) placed less emphasis on organizational boundaries when they claimed a new theory of the firm as 'an intra-organizational ecology of memes'. An ecology implies multiple species co-existing in various symbiotic or predatory relationships and the theory cautions against expecting an automatic correspondence between organic species and discreet organizations.

Interestingly, and perhaps at first counter-intuitively, there is a conceptual link here to physical space and Facilities (or Facility) Management (FM). The term today, especially in the UK, carries connotations of the management of buildings and the services which sustain them, but also the design and provision of physical working environments. In the USA, where the term was first coined (Price 2002), space still dominates academic thinking in the discipline. Research groups into physical environments are typically located within departments of human ecology. Some authorities, notably Franklin Becker (e.g. 1990), have argued for a view of physical workplaces as the environment in which the organizational ecology operates. The logic is explored in the remainder of this chapter. Does a memetic perspective yield insights (at a metaphoric level) or explanations (to an ontological realist) into organizational behaviour and the conditions that encourage or block creativity? Does it explain the empirical evidence of the power of the physical environment as a managerial lever to encourage or restrain innovation?

The evolution of evolutionary perspectives

To explore that question requires considering whether the organization is seen as a 'species' or an ecology. The literature on organizational evolution has focused, perhaps excessively, on the former, the firm or organization as a distinct, bounded entity; Aldrich's (1999) boundary maintaining, goal directed 'community'. Firms are conveyed as vehicles competing for resources and hence selected in the market place. As part of systems of production firm boundaries are, however, at least partially permeable. Firms exist in webs of relationships with competitors and/or collaborators and are themselves, if they grow, systems of similar relationships between – for example – departments, business units, professional groups, political factions and brands. They are (Weeks and Galunic 2003) more akin to ecosystems in which selection processes occur between different discourse systems; even if in any one firm certain dominant conventional wisdoms might exist. The phenomenon of sub-groups with their own discourse system is not unique to universities!

Firms, or more generally organizations, may not then be the prime candidates for the prospective role of memetic phenotypes. It is probably more enlightening to think, as Csikszentmihalyi did, of domains or communities who share a common conventional wisdom shaped by a shared set of symbols, be they languages, paradigms, artifacts or behaviours. Individuals may, indeed almost certainly will, belong to more than one community and different communities may find expression within a particular organization.

To return again to the higher education example, the members of various academic departments will belong to the community of a particular area of scholarship, and to varieties within a general field. The members of the estates department will also identify with their own professional community and groups therein. Hull (1988) has drawn a detailed account of the persistence of particular schools of thought within scientific paradigms, taking among his examples the biases displayed by various institutions (scientific societies, departments and journals) within the broadly cohesive field of biology.

Biology separates two forms of information transmission conventionally distinguished as vertical, inheritance between generations, and horizontal, replication of behaviour by imitation.[11] The memetic literature, and indeed Dawkins' original examples, concentrates largely on the latter: horizontal replication through imitation of fashions, tunes, cultural artifacts and behaviours. However, memetic domains also replicate vertically. Traditions, beliefs and symbol systems outlive individuals or a particular organization. Certain forms, such as religious groupings, are replicated over centuries and many generations.

Management fads, or fashions, provide a potentially illuminating example of a transition from horizontal to vertical. Their spread and decline can be documented by the frequency of citations in professional literature (Abrahamson and Fairchild 1999). They appear to displace each other by selective survival in managerial discourse as, for example, Scarborough and Swan's (1999) demonstration of the decline of the term 'Organizational Learning' and the rise of 'Knowledge Management' through the 1990s. The spread of a particular fashion, the replication of the term, is advanced by the actions of a community (Csikszentmihalyi's field) of individuals with an interest in its spread, be they researchers, educators, consultants, journalists or particular managers. In the process (Price in press), there may be wide variation in what a particular fashion is held to be, or how exactly it should be represented. The signifier that identifies a fashion, 'learning organization', say, or 'FM', does not have to signify the same set of practices and processes even to members of the community who use the term, let alone to others who hear or read it. Some fashions succeed in becoming institutionalized and transmitted vertically from generation to generation. FM has survived forty-nine years since the term was first coined. Some still older fashions have become fully institutionalized as professional bodies through accepted codes of practice and membership rites of particular groups. The actual utility of the fashion concerned to an organization that deploys it may reduce, as with Johnson and Kaplan's *Relevance Lost* for management accounting.

Complex evolving systems

A fashion that survives to become a professional community illustrates the property of emergent order, a phenomenon that has come in recent years to be associated with the behaviour of Complex Adaptive, or Evolving Systems. For complexity theorists, emergent and maintained order arises from the interactions of many individual agents acting according to simple rules or schemata. Waldrop's (1992) summary of the work of the Santa Fe institute is the standard introduction, though Waddington (1977) anticipated many of the ideas. Word limits prevent a full review but the avowed science of such systems has been embraced by some as a metaphor for holistic behaviour and even an antidote to what are seen as unnecessarily reductionist, or positivist, messages from neo-Darwinism.[12] More rational voices have emphasized that the

51

schemata are in effect the replicators of the more orthodox neo-Darwinian consensus, hence Gell-Mann (1996), in an address to the US National Defence University:

> In the case of societal evolution, the schemata consist of laws, customs, myths, traditions, and so forth. The pieces of such a schema are often called 'memes'.

Complex Evolving Systems[13] are believed, from computer simulations in particular to be at their most generative or adaptive at the so called 'edge-of-chaos'; a metaphor used to denote a critical zone where the influence on agents' behavior of each other reaches a critical density of connectedness (Waldrop 1992). Systems at the edge of chaos are claimed to have more rugged 'fitness landscapes.' They have more evolutionary possibilities open to them as the surrounding environment changes in contrast to 'single-peak', highly ordered landscapes; systems where one or a few dominant agents set the behavioral rules. Translated to the theme of creativity and innovation the proposition would be that human systems at or close to the 'edge-of-chaos' have a greater tendency to creativity. The answer to Csikszentmihalyi's question 'where is creativity?' might be at the 'edge-of-chaos'.

Stacey (1996) makes a similar point but seems to believe in a natural tendency for a CAS to reach such a position: an assumption that may be unduly optimistic. Organizations may not naturally seek the edge of chaos any more than ecosystems do. As argued above, both biotic and abiotic systems tend to preserve order on various timescales.[14] Such behaviour, even if it puzzles some writers on complexity, is perfectly compatible with the concept of selfish replicators. The basis of replicator success in this view of the world is the ability to pass on more copies, be they genes or cultural replicators, which for the sake of argument and precedence we are here calling memes. Purely rhetorically, and without implying any intentionality or consciousness to the replicator, from its point of view success is more copies. In normal times success equates with stability or at least bounded stability: fluctuation within limits.

There are also abnormal times. An external catastrophe may wipe out much of a system, as may an internally generated scarcity of resources or feedback between the biota and the global climate. Chance events may open up new opportunities (finches on the Galapagos) or introduce new competitor species (human beings among them). Both biotic and abiotic systems can get locked in to forms of 'arms race', where two competitors, firms, countries or species evolve their strategies, armaments and capabilities in tandem. When the environment changes, the power of particular replicators and their inherent tendency to copy themselves, may cease to enable and become a limit or even a terminal flaw, as for example Diamond's case of the Greenland Norse community. Either whole memetic traditions or local carriers of them can face extinction.[15]

The memetic perspective: tests and benefits

If the above is a correct or useful view, it raises the question as to what is actually replicating. Some advocates of cultural evolution have advocated specific aspects, technologies, routines and processes, paradigms or conventions. Others (Weeks and Galunic 2003) have adopted an approach similar to that of Gell-Mann (1996) and seen replicators embodied in all the paraphernalia of culture. Price and Shaw's (1998) 'patterns' took a similar stance while suggesting memes as being primarily transmitted by and manifested in languages and cultural artifacts. The conventional wisdom is 'languaged into existence'.

Memetic theorists from fields outside organizational studies have debated or advocated, largely it must be admitted without empirical evidence, the rival cases of the internal thoughts or neuronal assemblage, versus the external spoken/written word, behaviour or artifact. Dawkins, having opted for external examples in first proposing the meme, later apologized and opted for memes residing primarily in brains or artificial memory repositories such as books.

In contrast, Distin (2005), in what is arguably the most in-depth review yet published, makes a case for that which is replicated as systems of representation, either natural languages or symbolic ones such as mathematical notations, specialized professional usage, or cultural representation systems such as culture or music. This perspective appears to me to offer more promising lines of empirical inquiry, and to resonate more powerfully with observations on actual organizations and on the sociology and psychology of discourse and cognition. To return again, to the deliberately trivial example, the representation or signifier 'open-plan' conjures up different interpretations for different groups. Language and symbolic representations are the process by which ideas and meaning expressed by one individual are either interpreted in the minds of others or at the opposite extreme immediately rejected by the metaphorical memetic immune system.

There is no automatic requirement that the representation is interpreted, received, with the sense of meaning attached to its delivery. In terms of structuralist and post-structuralist theory, the signifier is replicated but the signified can vary. From a rhetorical selfish meme's perspective, a lack of clarity of meaning, an imprecise 'signified', can be a useful property when it comes to getting replicated. The signifier 'meme' is replicated every time new people enter a debate as to precisely what is signified; a 'strategy' that can of course be, or become, counterproductive if the signifier becomes so general that it ceases to be useful and fails to secure an enduring niche in a particular ecology of discourses. Equally within one particular community a particular shared signified might help construct a conventional wisdom as witnessed by the manner in which a pejorative sense of 'positivism' contributes to the unity of particular groups of organizational scholars. Similar communities may be found propagating particular management fashions, styles or technologies while denying the validity of others.

Other tests of this stance are possible. The evolutionary, or quasi-evolutionary, similarity of languages and other symbol systems can be tracked, as in theory could the relative contributions of genes and culture/language to national identities. Nations and cultures, religions, organizations and communities of practice are all, in this view, emergent phenomena enabled by the linguistic and other representations that replicate within them. Such systems are in theory at least capable of being analyzed and the theory presented here would suggest that a correct cladistic classification of a current population should illustrate a history of cultural speciation. If, for example, it proved impossible to infer the history of religious denominations from the similarity or otherwise of their current symbols and rituals, the theory might be said to be falsified. Lord (2002) showed that such a reconstruction was at least possible; in the process documented, an evolutionary bloom (cf. Galapagos finches) as various protestant groups expanded into the new, to them, physical spaces of North America. Another radiation appears to have followed after a religious 'clade' (Non-Episcopal churches) diversified once freed of the dominant influence of the bishop meme or as Csikszentmihalyi's model might put it, the field of bishops. In CES terms, the system became more chaotic once fewer individuals no longer exerted a dominant influence on the rules for all the other agents.

Other empirical studies grounded in such a memetic approach are possible. One current project is examining the degree to which traditional rituals and assumptions have hampered endeavours to change teachers in India faced with post-globalization challenges to their professional identity from new cultural 'species'. Another is examining the degree to which belief systems, embedded in and re-enforced by linguistic assertions, affect inter-organizational, contractual complexity between the UK's National Health Service and private contractors financing and building new hospital facilities. A third, which also examined that service, interpreted innovative and successful cleaning regimes as examples of conversational networks evolving in isolation from the dominant service discourse (Macdonald 2007).

None of these examples can necessarily prove the truth of cultural evolution as a process of memetic selection. Either could potentially refute it. At present, rather as was in its own infancy the theory of natural selection by descent with modification, all that can be said is that as a theory, or arguably a metaphor, it has great exploratory and explanatory power.

The theory is also capable of critical attack from a number of competing domains of conventional wisdom. To various religious fundamentalists wedded to creationism or intelligent design, the theory will be an anathema. For them sorrow is the only answer permitted within the word count of this chapter. I can do no better than offer Andrew Lord's metaphor of 'a human being who would fail the Turing Test', coined after online encounters with such individuals while endeavouring to research the finer points of various sects. A similar blighted fundamentalism, an attempt to discount all science, can be encountered in the arguably equally unthinking domains of extreme post-modernism. A third critique, which can itself in extremis veer towards uncritical fundamentalism, is mounted by the evolutionary psychologists who would like to interpret all, or much more, of human behaviour as hard wired in genes. At best, and without intending a moral value judgement, they perhaps present a case that has to be answered. The boundaries of nature and nurture are at least in theory capable of examination and I would side with those who say nurture offers the best hope of escape from the tyrannies of extreme genetic determinism.

Hence we arrive at a fourth, and for me, a more serious and valid critique that might be made by critical realists and liberal humanists generally. They might say that a theory of memetics is itself unduly deterministic: Rose's (1998) fallacy of self-centred selection. If memes do explain consciousness, does that not logically deny an ability to influence them? I disagree. A memetic theory can explain, and hence open up to scrutiny, the insidious influence of Waddington's COWDUNG to maintain false systems of understanding and the elites which thrive on them. Memetics surely re-enforces and justifies rather than denies the liberating power of reflective questioning. It can help tame the excesses of replicating ideologies. If we understand the barriers to creativity, we surely enable greater recognition of those barriers and the ability to do something about them. We can create metaphorical mental space for different conversations (cf. Stacey 1996). We may also use physical settings to enable greater creativity, especially in offices occupied by 'knowledge workers'.

Postscript: putting space into practice

To recap, the hypothesis of organizations as ecologies of selfish signifiers implies replication primarily through conversations and symbolic representations of conversations. Conventional wisdoms emerge from, and then stabilize, systems of conversation. There is now a body of empirical evidence that different physical spaces can catalyze different conversations, at scales from the small group to the whole organization. These spaces can be a tool through which creativity can be encouraged or constrained. The physical geography of the office can enable new ideas to emerge and evolve.

Buildings and office spaces do however tend to be fitted out then left. Designs reflect the conventional wisdoms and power structures, the memes, extant at the time of construction. The physical space then re-enforces that particular set of memes. It is common to see organizations expressing a desire for greater 'empowerment' (say) while signaling the opposite through the relics of their past space. Equally it is possible, if space has been changed but conventional wisdom has not, to see the old culture re-emerging as those who can recreate the symbols they are comfortable with. Watch those who can recreate subtle hierarchical symbolism in the supposedly non-territorial open plan. Look at your own workplace with the eyes of an outsider. What message is being conveyed?

Acknowledgements

I am grateful for comments by Kate Distin and Andrew Lord, and research ideas generated in conversations with Pete Andrews, Geetha Narayan, John Flowers and Rachel Macdonald.

Notes

1 Or, as he abbreviated it, COWDUNG.
2 And some organizations which have succeeded with their newer designs report a decrease in the time occupied by meetings, and the demand for meeting room spaces.
3 A theory capable of empirical test by comparing office designs and RAE scores.
4 There are probably other examples in the history of life on earth where the success of the dominant biota has been terminated in an atmospheric or climatic crisis.
5 To avoid having to distinguish different nuances of sociology, anthropology and culture.
6 Dawkins (2004) is as ever at the forefront of lay exposition.
7 Space is limited. See below for a brief diversion into considerations of ontological relativism.
8 In which, contra some philosophical interpretations of the 'selfish' metaphor, the author is absolutely clear firstly that genes operate in the context of complex systems of other genes and secondly that they do not have foresight. See the second (1989) edition or the preface to the recent thirtieth anniversary edition.
9 New seismic technology from circa the mid-1970s onwards.
10 Until the mid-1960s, continental drift was deeply unfashionable and its study was largely confined to two peripherally isolated groups in Cape Town and Hobart. Today, the largest collection of evolutionary economic researchers is likewise concentrated in an isolate, this time in Brisbane.
11 Some theorists are starting to argue a role for imitation in initiating selection pressure (Dawkins 1976).
12 It is to my mind another example of the behaviour of emergent systems of memetic discourse that these terms have become rallying calls for certain schools of social philosophy. Attaching such a label to an assertion engenders almost automatic acceptance of the advocated viewpoint.
13 The term is Mitleton Kelly's and is arguably a more precise description than the more widespread label of adaptive systems. Evolving systems do not necessarily adapt.
14 In technical terms, the magnitude of events in such systems departs from the perfect power law distribution believed to characterize self-organized criticality (SOC). Ball (2004) provides an accessible description and cites evidence that stock markets also show a departure, on shorter scales, from pure SOC behaviour.
15 As the first draft is in preparation (30 November 2006), the financial news headlines concern Ford offering half its North American workforce voluntary severance because of the continuing competition from 'Lean' as opposed to 'Mass' manufacturers.

References

Abrahamson, E. and Fairchild, G. Management fashions: lifecycles, triggers and collective learning processes, *Administrative Science Quarterly*, 40 1999, 708–40.

Ager, D. V. *The Nature of the Stratigraphical Record*, London: Macmillan Press 1973.

Aldrich, H. *Organizations Evolving*, London: Sage 1999.

Ball, P. *Critical Mass: How One Thing Leads to Another*, London: Arrow Books 2004.

Becker, F. *The Total Workplace: Facilities Management and Elastic* Organization, New York: Praeger 1990.

Benton, M. E. *When Life Nearly Died: The Greatest Mass Extinction of All Time*, London: Thames and Hudson 2003.

Csikszentmihalyi, M. Society, culture, and person: a systems view of creativity, in R. J. Sternberg (ed.), *The Nature of Creativity: Contemporary Psychological Perspectives*, New York: Cambridge University Press 1988, 325–39.

Dawkins, R. *The Selfish Gene*, Oxford: Oxford University Press 1976.

Dawkins, R. *The Blind Watchmaker*, London: Longman 1986.

Dawkins, R. *The Ancestor's Tale: A Pilgrimage to the Dawn of Life*, London: Wiedenfield and Nicolson 2004.

Diamond, J. *Collapse: How Societies Choose to Fail or Succeed*, New York: Viking 2004.

Distin, K. *The Selfish Meme: A Critical Reassessment*, Cambridge: Cambridge University Press 2005.

Eldredge, N. and Gould, S. J. Punctuated equilibrium: an alternative to phyletic gradualism, in T. J. M. Schopf (ed.), *Models in Paleobiology*, San Francisco: Freeman Cooper 1972, 82–115.

Gell-Mann, M. *Address to the US National Defence University* 1996, at: http://www.dodccrp.org/comch01.html.

Haynes, B. and Price, I. Quantifying the complex adaptive workplace, *Facilities*, 22 2004, 8–18.

Hodgson, G. M. *Economics and Evolution: Bringing Life Back into Economics*, Cambridge: Polity Press 1993.

Hull, D. L. *Science as a Process: An Evolutionary Account of the Social and Conceptual Development of Science*, Chicago: University of Chicago Press 1988.

Johnson, H. T. and Kaplan, R. S. *Relevance Lost: The Rise and Fall of Management Accounting*, Boston: Harvard Business School Press 1987.

Lloyd, T. *The Nice Company*, London: Bloomsbury 1990.

Lord, A. S. Organizational phylogenesis: developing and evaluating a memetic methodology, Sheffield Hallam University, PhD thesis 2002.

Macdonald, R. Excellent patient environments within acute NHS trusts: the leaders who enable them, Sheffield Hallam University, DBA thesis 2007.

Marmot, A. and Associates, *Spaces for Learning*, Edinburgh: Scottish Funding Council 2006, at: http://www.sfc.ac.uk/information/information_learning/Spaces_for_Learning_report.pdf.

Matzdorf, F. and Price, I. Benchmarking space utilisation and space charging ii: the qualitative side, Sheffield, Unpublished report, available on request 1999.

Price, I. Organizational memetics? Organizational learning as a selection process, *Management Learning*, 26 1995, 299–318.

Price, I. Chapter 3, Facility management as an emerging discipline; Chapter 4, The development of facility management, in R. Best, C. Langston and G. de Valence (eds.), *Workplace Strategies and Facilities Management*, Oxford: Butterworth-Heinemann 2002, 30–66.

Price, I. The lean asset: new language for new workplaces, *California Management Review*, 49(2) 2007, 102–118.

Price, I. The selfish signifier: mutation of meaning in management fashions, *Journal of Memetics* 2007, in press.

Price, I. and Shaw, R. *Shifting the Patterns: Breaching the Memetic Codes of Corporate Performance*, Chalfont: Management Books 1998.

Rose, N. Controversies in meme theory, *Journal of Memetics – Evolutionary Models of Information Transmission*, 2 1998, at: http://jom-emit.cfpm.org/1998/vol2/rose_n.html.

Scarbrough, H. and Swan, J. Knowledge management and the management fashion perspective, Manchester: British Academy of Management Refereed Conference, 'Managing Diversity' 1999.

Stacey, R. D. *Complexity and Creativity in Organizations*, San Francisco: Berret-Koehler 1996.

Waddington, C. H. *Tools for Thought: How To Understand and Apply the Latest Scientific Techniques of Problem Solving*, New York: Basic Books 1977.

Waldrop, M. M. *Complexity: The Emerging Science at the Edge of Order and Chaos*, New York: Simon and Schuster 1992.

Weeks, J. and Galunic, C. A theory of the cultural evolution of the firm: the intra-organizational ecology of memes, *Organization Studies*, 24 2003, 1309–1352.

Part 3

Environmental actors and influences

Theme 2 Environmental influences

6

Creating or destroying business value: understanding the opportunities and the limits of a win–win collaboration

Andrew Cox

Introduction: the meaning of value in business

This chapter focuses on the opportunities for, and the limits on, value creation for buying and selling organisations involved in collaborative relationships. Current thinking about the optimal way to manage inter-organisational relationships often recommends the collaborative search for win–win outcomes. It is argued that this thinking fails to fully understand the elusive nature of win–win as a concept, and the complex trade-offs over value and interests that organisations have to make, and especially when they interact as buyers and sellers. The search for win–win outcomes from collaboration can create value but it can also destroy it – especially if the unwary do not fully understand the rules of the game of transactional exchange.

In general, social science thinking has developed impressive insights into the benefits that can be achieved from longer-term collaborative relationships (Christopher and Towill 2002; Contractor and Lorange 1988; Hines *et al.* 2000). Most writers assume, however, that the best way to manage exchange relationships (whether at the dyadic or network levels) is to seek win–win outcomes based on the principles of mutuality (Lee 2004; Narayanan and Raman 2004). It can be argued, however, that current thinking does not fully specify what value means operationally and commercially from the perspective of organisations when they act as buyers or sellers.

Writers on transactional exchange argue that for relationships to be sustainable both parties must perceive that they are receiving something they value (Lamming 2001; Wilkinson and Young 2002; Williamson 1996). Despite a general agreement about the need for mutual benefit, there have been few systematic attempts to specify clearly what value means for organisations when they interact (Cousins 2002; MacNeil 1983; Ramsay 2005; Zajac and Olsen 1993). As a result, current thinking does not provide a clear conceptualisation of the *commercial and operational trade-offs over value* that organisations make when they enter into exchange relationships.

Since, the purpose of business is to make money, so the primary commercial value for any business organisation must be the ability to *improve profitability*. Once this is achieved, companies normally seek to *increase their share of market revenue*. Business organisations also normally try to create *differentiated products and/or services* in order to establish *sustainable isolating mechanisms* (Rumelt 1987). Finally, in order to reduce the overall costs of sales relative to revenue earned, companies normally seek a *constant reduction in the total costs of ownership of the internal and external processes and relationships* that deliver their products and/or services.

Operationally, companies value activities or outcomes that improve the efficiency and/or effectiveness of the processes and systems through which products and/or services are provided. Companies, therefore, normally value *improvements in capacity utilization* and *improvements in process cycle time*, as well as *improvements in product and service quality*. Companies also normally highly value *improvements in customer responsiveness* and *improvements in supplier and/or supply chain responsiveness*. Taking these value characteristics together, it is possible to understand the commercial and operational trade-offs that can occur in exchange relationships. Sometimes there are circumstances of *high commercial and operational value*. Conversely, there can be circumstances of *low commercial and operational value*. In between these two extremes are *high commercial but low operational value*, and *low commercial but high operational value*.

Creating and destroying value: understanding the range of potential outcomes in exchange relationships

When organisations interact, commercial and operational outcomes occur that can have a differential impact on what the two organisations value. If buyer and supplier views about high and low value from operational and commercial exchange are conjoined, then sixteen possible buyer and supplier value trade-offs from exchange could theoretically occur. Only when both parties simultaneously perceive that they achieve high commercial and operational gain, is it possible to argue that business relationships are fully aligned, with win–win (positive-sum) outcomes occurring. This does not mean, however, that exchange relationships cannot be conducted even if this outcome does not occur. Sustainable collaborative relationships can be conducted when there are non zero-sum outcomes – i.e. when both parties gain some but not all of the things they value operationally and commercially.

More interesting, perhaps, are the zero-sum outcomes that can occur when one party appropriates value while the other does not. In such circumstances, the loser is destroying value by entering into relationships that provide no commercial or operational gain. While it may be argued that this is unlikely to be a sustainable basis for collaboration, paradoxically win–lose outcomes can be sustained in some circumstances (Cox 2004b). This implies that only in the lose–lose outcome, where there is no commercial or operational gain, is exchange likely to be completely pointless for both parties.

What this discussion demonstrates is that one must be careful about assuming that a win–win (or positive-sum) outcome is a requirement for sustaining collaborative exchange relationships. This is because non zero-sum and some zero-sum outcomes may also be sustainable over time. The means that the concept of mutuality (mutual benefit from exchange) is much more complex than one may at first assume. Mutuality is not an absolute unless one defines it narrowly in terms of win–win (or positive-sum) outcomes. This is because it is possible for relationships to provide benefit for both of the exchange parties, without each party achieving exactly the same valued outcome as the other. In this sense, mutuality must be seen as a variable concept, especially because organisations (and the human beings working within them) can subjectively value different things, and sustain relationships because they believe they are receiving things that they value, even though another party is achieving more of what they value.

If this way of thinking is correct, then it opens up the possibility that collaborative relationships can be sustained with asymmetric outcomes, in which one party gains more than the other. If this is so, then excellence in relationship management may not be found in ensuring that both parties achieve a win–win (desirable though this may be as a theoretical ideal for sustainability), but in understanding how to ensure that one party achieves the maximum benefits feasible, while ensuring that the other receives sufficient to make the relationship work over time. Thus, while avoiding 'lose' outcomes in which no value is appropriated is a must for all organisations, avoiding over-generosity – in the form of a loss of value to the other exchange party that could have been appropriated for oneself – must be the hallmark of competence in relationship management. This becomes extremely important when one understands that in some types of exchange, win–win (positive-sum) outcomes are not feasible because of the non-commensurability of the interests of the parties to the exchange (Cox 2004a).

Managing different types of business relationships

Space does not provide for a full discussion of all of the types of business relationships that exist between individuals and organisations. It is important to recognise, however, that in general there are two broad types of business relationship – horizontal and vertical (Cox 2004b). Horizontal business relationships are those in which both parties to the exchange pursue the same business interests. Horizontal business relationships normally are those that occur when investors (individuals or organisations) and employees (with shares or share options) work together to create a separate organisation to market and sell products and/or services to others. When revenue is received by the organisation, the appropriation of value is shared (although not always equally) between the investors, employees or organisations owning the company. In these types of business relationships it is possible for win–win outcomes to be achieved by all parties involved in the exchange. The investors can earn above normal returns (rents) from the relationships and so can the employee (especially if they are share owners or have share options). These types of win–win outcome can also be achieved by organisations in strategic alliances. A strategic alliance here is defined as an agreement between individuals or organisations to work together to create a common product and/or service, from which it is possible for both to earn above normal returns (although this may not always occur).

These are not, however, the only types of business relationship that occur between individuals and organisations. Individuals and organisations also interact vertically as buyers and suppliers, and in such circumstances the interests of the two parties to the exchange are never the same (Cox 2004a, 2004b). The non-commensurability of the interests of buyers and suppliers can be understood quite simply. The ideal outcome for a buyer is to have continuous improvement in the commercial and operational outcomes from an exchange – and the same is true for the supplier. At this level it might appear that their interests are the same. The problem is that if the buyer maximises their interests, this can only be done at the expense of the supplier, and vice versa.

The reason for this tension in buyer and supplier exchange arises because the buyer normally seeks a continuous improvement in operational effectiveness from the supplier, i.e. improvements beyond x-efficiency, with a continuous reduction in the total costs of ownership commercially. This means that, since the profits of the supplier are part of the costs of ownership of the buyer, then the ideal situation is for the supplier to operate either with 'loss-leaders', at break even, or with only normal returns that tend to zero.

The supplier, on the other hand, has very different goals operationally and commercially. While the supplier wishes to differentiate their products and services operationally, this is normally only done in order to close the market to competitors so that above normal returns are made commercially. Thus, while the buyer and the supplier do not necessarily have any

63

conflict of interests when it comes to seeking an improvement in x-efficiency, there is an irreconcilable objective tension and conflict over the appropriation of commercial value from the relationship. The supplier seeks market closure in order to earn rents and, if this is achieved, the buyer can never achieve their ideal of continuous improvement in the commercial costs of ownership with suppliers making no better than normal returns that tend to zero.

In such circumstances, there is an inevitable objective tension between the interests of buyers and suppliers over value appropriation in vertical business exchange relationships, even though there is not between actors in horizontal business relationships. As Figure 6.1 demonstrates, while positive-sum outcomes are feasible in horizontal exchange, in vertical exchange between buyers and suppliers a win–win outcome is not feasible when an objective and economically rational view is taken of exchange. This means that buyer and supplier exchange must operate with either non zero-sum, zero-sum and negative-sum outcomes. Tension and conflicts of interest are therefore inevitable in buyer and supplier exchange, whatever individuals may desire or believe subjectively.

This implies that there must be more or less appropriate ways to manage horizontal or vertical exchange relationships. In horizontal exchange – since win–win outcomes are feasible – the use of transparency and trust in business relationships has much to commend itself. Unfortunately, in vertical business relationships the use of trust and transparency by one party when the other party has non-commensurable interests can be a recipe for operational and commercial disaster. The problem of managing so that value is not lost when it could have been appropriated in vertical business relationships between buyers and suppliers is discussed in what follows.

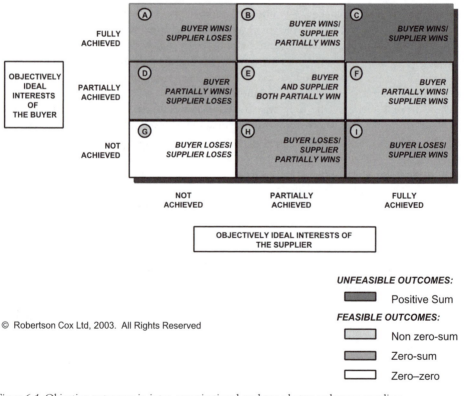

Figure 6.1 Objective outcomes in inter-organizational exchange between buyers suppliers

Creating or destroying value: aligning relationship management approaches appropriately

The problem for buyers and sellers when they interact is that, while it is unlikely that an exchange between a buyer and a supplier can occur unless there is an anticipation by both sides that they will receive value from the exchange, buyers and sellers do not pursue the same type of value from a relationship. Thus, even though there are occasions when buyers and sellers can interact to increase the size of what can be shared, there is always an objective commercial tension between both parties to any transaction. This is a particular problem in vertical business relationships because of the need for both the buyer and seller to understand which type of operational relationship approach – arm's length or collaborative – and which type of commercial management style – adversarial or non-adversarial – should be adopted to maximise operational and commercial value (Cox *et al.* 2004).

Given that there is a need to work together operationally, buyers and sellers have to decide whether they should work together at arm's length. This means that exchange occurs in the absence of close operational linkages. It is possible, however, for one or both parties to seek to establish very close working relationships operationally. In these circumstances there will normally be the establishment of dedicated investments, relationship specific adaptations, technical bonds and the creation of cultural norms about the ways of working together (Cannon and Perrault 1999).

Neither of these approaches – arm's length or collaborative – is necessarily superior for creating value. Rather, each is an appropriate way of managing relationships for buyers and sellers depending on the circumstances – sometimes a seller may need to collaborate with a buyer to improve x-efficiency; sometimes they can do it on their own, and vice versa. While buyers and sellers may be agnostic about which operational way of working is the most appropriate, they ought not to be when it comes to commercial exchange. There are two broad commercial choices. When a buyer or seller is commercially adversarial, this means that they are seeking to maximise their ideal – the lowest total cost of ownership for the buyer, with returns for the supplier tending to zero (or worse); or striving to close markets to competitors and to achieve above normal returns (rents) for the supplier. When a buyer or seller is commercially non-adversarial, this means that they are not in a position to maximise their ideals. In the case of the buyer, this means they will be a price and/or quality receiver from the supplier; in the case of the supplier, this means that they must constantly innovate in terms of quality and reduce price, while making only low returns that tend to zero (or worse).

It follows, therefore, that there are four broad choices for buyers and sellers when they manage relationships. They can be adversarial commercially and operate at arm's length operationally, or they can be adversarial but collaborate operationally. Conversely, they can be commercially non-adversarial but pursue arm's length or collaborative operational ways of working. While all four choices are available, only two of them are ideal for appropriating value. This is because it is normally a superior relationship management choice – given the non-commensurability of interests in vertical exchange – to adopt an adversarial commercial approach, with the other party pursuing a non-adversarial commercial approach, whichever operational way of working (arm's length or collaborative) is selected.

Whether one can pursue an adversarial approach, and force the other party in the relationship to be non-adversarial, depends of course on whether or not either party has the power resources to leverage this commercially ideal outcome. To understand how to appropriate value rather than to destroy it in vertical exchange relationships, one must understand the resources that are available to buyers and sellers to create this commercially ideal outcome. One way of thinking about this is to focus on the relative power and leverage resources available to buyers and sellers.

Power and leverage between buyers and suppliers can be understood primarily as a function of *the relative utility* and *the relative scarcity* of the resources that are exchanged between the two parties, and *the information advantages* that arise in exchange transactions for buyers and suppliers. Using this methodology each party in an exchange can be located in one of four basic power positions: *buyer dominance*; *interdependence*; *independence*; and *supplier dominance* (Cox *et al.* 2000, 2002, 2003).

These four power positions affect the ability of the buyer and seller to leverage their respective commercial ideals. In *buyer dominance*, the buyer has the potential to be commercially adversarial, with the supplier forced to accept a more subservient and non-adversarial commercial approach. Conversely, in *supplier dominance*, the supplier has the potential to be adversarial, with the buyer becoming a non-adversarial price and quality receiver. In *interdependence* power positions, neither party has the power resources to pursue adversarial commercial approaches and both parties normally have to adopt a non-adversarial approach commercially. In these circumstances value is normally shared relatively equally, with neither party maximising their goals. In *independence* power situations, both parties normally have to be non-adversarial because they both lack the power resources to impose their commercial interests on the other – although the supplier often suffers more than the buyer in this power position because this power situation normally arises in highly contested markets with relatively perfect information, ensuring that suppliers can only survive by constantly innovating and passing value to buyers in general. This means that all buyers gain, but no more so than every other buyer in the market.

To understand appropriateness in relationship management, it is possible to link these power situations and the relationship management approaches to understand the six broad options available for appropriately aligning business relationships. It is important to understand, however, that these options do not ensure that both parties to an exchange simultaneously achieve their commercial and operational ideals. In *buyer dominant collaboration*, an aligned relationship means that the adversarial buyer will appropriate a higher share of value from the relationship than the non-adversarial supplier when they collaborate operationally. Indeed, the buyer has the opportunity to achieve their ideal commercial goal while the seller does not. In *buyer dominant arm's length*, the same outcome occurs, although there is absence operationally of collaboration. In *supplier dominant collaboration* and *supplier dominant arm's length* relationships, the situation is reversed, with the supplier adversarially appropriating the lion's share of value rather than the non-adversarial buyer. The supplier here may also have the opportunity to achieve their commercial ideal but the buyer does not.

In *reciprocal collaboration*, both parties share value non-adversarially and collaborate operationally, but neither party is able to achieve the ideal commercial outcome that one party might have achieved in *buyer dominant collaboration* or in *supplier dominant collaboration*. This is because the power situation is one of *interdependence* – this means that value has to be shared and both parties have to satisfice one another rather than one party having the scope to maximise their interests because they are in a dominant power position. The final aligned relationship approach occurs in *reciprocal arm's length*, where the *independence* power position ensures that neither party can maximise, and that they must both accept the currently prevailing outcome operating as a result of market competition. In this approach, value is neither shared nor maximised; it is endured because neither party has the resources to impose its will on the other.

The problem with win–win collaboration in buyer and supplier exchange

Having discussed the six relationship management options available for aligning relationships between buyers and suppliers, a number of conclusions can be drawn. The first is that alignment does not mean that any one of the six options is always the most appropriate choice for buyers and sellers to adopt when they enter into relationships. On the contrary, the discussion shows that – given the power resources available and the scope for more or less collaborative ways of working – all six options may be sensible for a buyer or seller to adopt.

That said, some options are clearly more desirable than others. For both the buyer and supplier dominant collaboration or dominant arm's length relationship management options are more desirable than any of the other four options available. This is because these two options are the only ones that provide the opportunity to maximise commercial value for either party. This raises an interesting point because a great deal of recent writing in business management has argued the case for win–win collaboration as the best way to align relationships for buyers and sellers. The analysis here shows that this argument is at best misguided and at worst guilty of a simplistic logic. The grounds for this criticism fall into two areas: first, on whether collaboration is always superior to arm's length relationship management; second, on whether or not win–win outcomes are commercially feasible.

The analysis here shows that whether or not buyers and sellers should collaborate operationally is an open question. There is no necessary benefit to any party in creating close operational linkages unless the commercial and operational value that is appropriated as a result outweighs the benefits of being arm's length. It is worth stating that, given the buying organisation's focus on its own core competencies, there are likely to be only a few buying organisations that have the capability to provide anything that suppliers need to improve their own operational efficiency and effectiveness. This implies that arm's length rather than collaborative operational ways of working are likely to predominant in the future just as they have in the past. This means that, while one cannot deny the value for some buyers and sellers of collaborative ways of working, claiming that this is always the preferred way of working is simply nonsensical.

But perhaps the most damning criticism of those who espouse the value of win–win collaboration arises from the realisation that win–win outcomes are not commercially feasible in vertical exchange transactions between buyers and suppliers. As discussed earlier, if win–win outcomes are not feasible for buyers and sellers (although they may be in horizontal forms of exchange), then encouraging the search for this outcome is likely to be a recipe for disappointment to both parties. The analysis presented here demonstrates that, while one party in vertical exchange relationships can achieve the maximisation of their ideal goals or interests (a win), this cannot be achieved simultaneously by the other party due to their non-commensurable interests.

Given this, the best that can be achieved for collaborative ways of operational working is not a positive-sum outcome based on win–win, but that value is appropriated along a continuum in which either the buyer or the supplier wins, with the other party partially winning (cells B and F in Figure 6.1), or neither party wins and both parties only partially win (cell E in Figure 6.1). If these non zero-sum outcomes occur, then it is likely that, while both parties will not be simultaneously content, the relationship has the potential to be sustained – despite one or both parties being unhappy with the commercial outcome relative to their ideal.

Aligning non zero-sum outcomes that result in buyer, reciprocal or supplier dominant collaboration is the best that can be said for sustaining collaborative relationships because win–win collaboration is a chimera. Having said that, the pursuit of zero-sum (win–lose or partial win–lose) outcomes is also likely to be a recipe for disaster if collaborative ways of working are operationally necessary for both parties to an exchange relationship. It can be argued, therefore, that those seeking to sustain collaborative operational ways of working must ensure that non zero-sum outcomes occur. If the commercial outcome slips into zero-sum or negative-sum, then it is likely that one or both parties will terminate the relationship. Saying that non zero-sum outcomes are essential to sustain collaborative relationships is not, however, saying that win–win collaboration is feasible.

It is not sensible to argue that *reciprocal collaboration* resulting in partial win–partial win, non zero-sum outcomes (cell E in Figure 6.1) is always preferable to *buyer* or *supplier dominant collaboration*. The problem with partial win–partial win outcomes is that, while the other party in the exchange fails to maximise their interests, neither party is able to achieve their own deal. Given that it is logical for the owners of the buying and selling organisation to seek to maximise their commercial interests, it can be argued that both the supplier and buyer have superior win–partial win, non zero-sum outcomes to pursue under either *buyer* or *supplier dominant collaboration*.

Unfortunately, this means that seeking to find relationship management outcomes that eradicate the essential tension and conflict that exists in buyer and supplier exchange will prove illusive. This is because the interests of buyers and sellers are not fully commensurable and never will be. This is not just because, for some buyers and suppliers in one-off games, zero-sum outcomes can be desirable (Cox 2004a, 2004b). On the contrary, it is because even in repeat games – where collaboration is essential for both parties operationally – there is a never-ending struggle over who appropriates the most value.

Conclusions: practical steps to create and avoid the destruction of value

Hopefully this discussion has demonstrated that current social science thinking about the concepts of value, interests and mutuality in transactional exchange is under-developed. This is because current thinking tends to over-emphasise the value of collaboration operationally and win–win outcomes commercially for sustaining relationships, without fully specifying what are the trade-offs for both parties to an exchange, and without fully recognising that mutuality is an elusive and variable rather than an absolute concept.

Furthermore, it has been argued that the current largely uncritical reliance on mutuality as the most appropriate way for buyers and suppliers to manage exchange relationships may be misguided. This is because, paradoxically, there are circumstances when buyers and supplies may willingly accept win–lose (zero-sum) outcomes in pursuit of broader operational and commercial goals. A fully rigorous and robust disciplinary approach to transactional exchange must be able to accommodate this possibility.

Despite this, collaboration is a very useful way for buyers and suppliers to work together operationally to create value – even though win–win outcomes are not feasible commercially. This means that when buyers and suppliers collaborate they must develop a tradecraft about effective and ineffective ways of working. To this end, a number of practical steps can be taken by buyers and suppliers to ensure that they create rather than destroy value when they engage in collaboration. The first step is to understand that all forms of relationship management are investment decisions and should be managed accordingly (Cox *et al.* 2004). This means that a rigorous and robust methodology that focuses on the internal and the external benefits to the buyer and the supplier of the collaboration must be in place to guide the investment decision (Cox *et al.* 2003).

The second step is for both parties to recognise that business involves the creation and destruction of power resources that enable one party to an exchange to create a situation of dominance from which commercial advantage can be leveraged. To this end, buyers have to understand that, while collaboration can provide tremendous opportunities for value creation, if they are not aware of the risks of post-contractual moral hazard through supplier lock-in and opportunism, then over time collaboration may destroy rather than create value (Cox 2004c). Similarly, suppliers have to recognise that, while collaboration can create opportunities for buyer lock-in and market closure against competitors, it also brings risks of hold-up post-contractually. If practitioners do not understand these issues, then it is likely that they will be taken advantage of by those who have a better understanding of the rules of the game of commercial exchange.

References

Cannon J. and W.D. Perreault (1999), Buyer–supplier relationships in business markets *Journal of Marketing Research*, 36: 439–460.

Christopher, Martin and Dennis Towill (2002), Developing market specific supply chain strategies, *International Journal of Logistics Management*, 13(1): 1–14.

Contractor, Farok J. and Peter Lorange (eds) (1988), *Co-operative Strategies in International Business*, Lexington Books, New York.

Cousins, Paul, (2002), Defining value and managing the value gap: a supply chain management perspective, *Proceedings of the 11th IPSERA Conference*, University of Twente, pp. 162–173.

Cox, Andrew (2004a), Business relationship alignment: on the commensurability of value capture and mutuality in buyer and supplier exchange, *Supply Chain Management: An International Journal*, 9(5): 410–420.

Cox, Andrew (2004b), *Win–Win?*, Earlsgate Press, Stratford-upon-Avon.

Cox, Andrew (2004c), Strategic outsourcing: avoiding the loss of critical assets and the problems of adverse selection and moral hazard, in *Business Briefing: Global Purchasing and Supply Chain Strategies*, World Markets Research Centre, London, pp. 67–70.

Cox, Andrew, Joe Sanderson and Glyn Watson (2000), *Power Regimes*, Earlsgate Press, Stratford-upon-Avon.

Cox, Andrew, Paul Ireland, Chris Lonsdale, Joe Sanderson and Glyn Watson (2002), *Supply Chains, Markets and Power*, Routledge, London.

Cox, Andrew, Paul Ireland, Chris Lonsdale, Joe Sanderson and Glyn Watson (2003), *Supply Chain Management: A Guide to Best Practice*, Financial Times/Prentice Hall, London.

Cox, Andrew, Chris Lonsdale, Joe Sanderson and Glyn Watson (2004), *Business Relationships for Competitive Advantage*, Palgrave Macmillan, Basingstoke.

Cox, Andrew, Chris Lonsdale, Glyn Watson and Yi Wu, (2005), Supplier relationship management as an investment: evidence from a UK study, *Journal of General Management*, 30(4): 27–42.

Hines, Peter, Richard Lamming, Dan Jones, Paul Cousins and Nick Rich (2000), *Value Stream Management: Strategy and Excellence in the Supply Chain*, Financial Times/ Prentice Hall, London.

Lamming, Richard (2001), Transparency in supplier relationships: concept and practice, *Journal of Supply Chain Management*, 37(4): 4–10.

Lee, H. L. (2004), The triple-A supply chain, *Harvard Business Review*, October: 102–112.

MacNeil, Ian R. (1983), Values in contract: internal and external, *Northwestern University Law Review*, 78(2): 168–180.

Narayanan, V. G. and Ananth Raman (2004), Aligning incentives in supply chains, *Harvard Business Review*, November: 94–102.

Ramsay, John (2005), The real meaning of value in trading relationships, *International Journal of Operations and Production Management*, 25(6): 549–565.

Rumelt, Richard, P. (1987), Theory, strategy and entrepreneurship, in David Teece (ed.), *The Competitive Challenge: Strategies for Industrial Innovation and Renewal*, Ballinger, Cambridge, MA., pp. 137–158.

Wilkinson, Ian F. and Louise C. Young (2002), Business dancing – the nature and role of inter-firm relations in business strategy, in David Ford (ed.), *Understanding Business Markets and Purchasing*, 3rd edition, Thomson Learning, London, pp. 107–120.

Williamson, Oliver. E. (1996), *The Mechanisms of Governance*, Free Press, New York.

Zajac, Edward J. and Charles P. Olsen, (1993), From transaction cost to transactional value analysis: implications for the study of inter-organizational strategies, *Journal of Management Studies*, 30(1): 130–142.

7

The style/involvement model of consumer innovation

Gordon Foxall and Victoria James

Introduction

Consumer researchers have shown an interest in the first adopters of new products and brands that exceeds their concern for almost any other aspect of purchase and consumption. Both theoretical and practical studies have sought to locate these 'consumer innovators' and to establish the role they play in the creation of markets and the communication of innovations (Foxall and Goldsmith 1994). This chapter argues that, for all its popularity among investigators, 'consumer innovativeness' remains a field of enquiry beset by confusion over basic terminology and an inability to come to terms with the weak evidence on which its generalizations about the personality profiles of 'consumer innovators' are based.

The problem of terminology presents a major critical issue, one which hinges around the use of the word 'innovative' and its derivatives. It is not just a matter of too casual use of this word, but a more deeply held misconception, common among students of creativity, including marketing, that 'innovative' equals 'new', 'novel', 'exciting', 'modern', and even 'good', 'appropriate' and 'superior'. If only it could be measured well, then how convenient this would be for those who believe that 'innovators', the risk-taking trend-setters, are the very people who can be expected to buy *any* new product! It is this hypothesis that this chapter examines critically on the basis of empirical evidence as well as *a priori* argument.

The chapter begins by summarizing why consumer innovativeness has become a central topic in both new product marketing and the explanation of early adoption. In doing so, it comments on the elusive nature of the personality traits assumed to be associated with consumer innovativeness. Although the conventional terminology is necessarily employed thus far, a solution can now be proposed to the confusion it has engendered. This chapter argues that the personality profiles of early adopters can be usefully investigated by the Kirton Adaption-Innovation Inventory or KAI (Kirton 2003), which measures both the cognitive/personality style generally associated with consumer innovativeness (that of the *innovator*) and that which is, by implication, diametrically opposite (the *adaptor*). The KAI correlates significantly with precisely those traits of personality that have been consistently identified as characterizing the earliest adopters of new products.

The findings of ten empirical studies of 'innovative' consumer behaviour which employ the

KAI are then summarized and discussed. Finally, the implications of these findings for marketing practice and the explanation of early adoption are discussed and directions for further research are suggested.

Consumer innovators in marketing practice and consumer theory

New product strategy

The marketing literature imputes one or other of two strategies to consumers according to the stage in the product life cycle. The first adopters of new products, who differ socially and economically from later adopters, are portrayed as more involved in the product field and are said to engage in extended problem solving prior to purchase. These so-called 'consumer innovators' are socially independent, requiring little or no personal communication before adopting (Midgely 1977). By contrast, later adopters need other people to 'legitimate' the purchase and use of new products; the product life cycle may have progressed well into its maturity stage before the last of them buy for the first time. Later purchasers are said to be less involved in the product field; by the time they adopt, pre-purchase decision making has become safe and routine (Rogers 1983).

The expected patterns of behavioural and psychographic difference between early and later adopters form the basis of a strategic prescription for product development, according to which marketing mixes should be tailored to the distinctive requirements of successive adopter categories. The resulting temporal market segmentation is described as leading to the profitable development of both new and established products (Baker 1983). If potential initial and later adopters of new products can be identified at appropriate stages of the new product development process, the tailoring can begin that much earlier and be incorporated into the market testing of alternative prototypes.

Non-product elements of the marketing mix, notably persuasive communications, can be directed specifically towards the needs and vulnerabilities of the homogeneously conceived primary market. Numerous attempts have been made to differentiate these adopter categories psychographically, on the basis of links between early adoption and such traits as risk-taking, impulsiveness, dominance, inner-directedness, flexibility and venturesomeness, and perception of new product characteristics (Foxall and Goldsmith 1988; Gatignon and Robertson 1991; Midgley 1977; Rogers 1983).

Personality traits of first adopters

Identification of the personality characteristics of these initial adopters has also excited intellectual curiosity. One of the more sophisticated theoretical quests for the nature of 'the innovative personality' is that of Midgley and Dowling (1978), who draw attention to the situational influences that facilitate or impede early adoption. However, the principal explanatory element in their model is a hypothetical construct, 'innate innovativeness', mediated by product field interest.

They argue that, in order to account for different levels of 'actualized innovation' – the single act defined by time elapsed from launch, the adoption of several new products in the same field measured by a cross-sectional method, and the adoption of new products across product fields measured by a generalized cross-sectional method – it is necessary to posit increasingly abstract concepts of 'innovativeness', an abstract personality trait assumed to be possessed in some degree by everybody, but actually existing only in the mind of the investigator. The extent of an individual's early adoption is ultimately explained by a reference to his or her degree of innate innovativeness, which is 'a function of (yet to be specified) dimensions of the human personality' (ibid.: 235). Another contingency theorist, Hirschman (1980), speaks similarly of 'inherent' innovativeness and 'inherent' novelty seeking without specifying the traits with which they might be associated.

Both managerial and theoretical views of the personality profiles of innovative consumers anticipate a relationship between the behaviours of interest and the psychographics of the people who perform them. But empirical confirmation of such expectations has been elusive; the quest for operationally measurable traits of personality related to innovative behaviour has a long history in marketing and consumer psychology but has produced nothing more than a mass of weak, if positive, correlations. Reviews of the empirical literature on innovativeness have long acknowledged the scant evidence that personality is linked at all to innovativeness and have derided the notion that a universal set of traits predicts or explains innovative behaviour (e.g. Rogers 1983). The strong assertion of the contingency theorists that innovative consumer behaviour is conceptually attributable to an abstract personality construct which is empirically available in the form of operationally measurable personality traits would seem, therefore, to fail. However, while a broad range of personality traits has been incorporated in the empirical research to which these reviews refer, the results are not unequivocally adverse.

A thorough consideration of the totality of empirical evidence indicates that innovative consumer behaviour is consistently related to five cognitive-behavioural traits supported by theoretical reasoning and empirical findings from investigations of both personality and cognitive style in relation to consumer choice. The five cognitive-behavioural traits are: category width, flexibility, tolerance of ambiguity, self-esteem, and sensation-seeking (for reviews of the theoretical and empirical evidence, see Goldsmith 1989; Midgley 1977; Mudd 1990; Pinson 1978; Pinson et al. 1988; Rogers 1983). The implication is that if the personality traits that explain actualized innovativeness (which, by implication, are the 'yet to be specified' dimensions of personality of which innate innovativeness is a function) are to be identified, then these cognitive-behavioural variables must define the area in which we should look. It would be especially desirable to employ a composite measure of all these cognitive-behavioural variables were there a theoretically grounded instrument available. The following section proposes that Kirton's (1976) Adaption-Innovation Inventory (KAI) constitutes such a measure.

Adaption-innovation theory

Adaption-innovation theory (Kirton 2003) suggests a means of understanding both the disappointing outcomes of previous research into the personality-based precursors of consumer innovativeness and the persistence of personality constructs as explicators of early adoption. The Kirton Adaption-Innovation Inventory (KAI), which provides an operational measure of the adaptive and innovative cognitive styles posited by Kirton (1976), appears also to be a suitable instrument for further empirical research, given its externally validated links with the personality traits known to determine, consistently albeit weakly, initial adoption: namely category-width, tolerance of ambiguity, flexibility, self-esteem and sensation-seeking. Cognitive style refers to an individual's way of processing information, his or her preferred approach to decision making and problem solving as distinct from his or her cognitive level, ability or complexity (Kirton 2003). A range of publications has developed and summarised the literature on the many types of intellectual and cognitive style, which may produce useful background information for the reader and allow a positioning of KAI theory (e.g. Kaufmann 2005; Zhang and Sternberg 2005). The adaption-innovation theory proposes a continuum of such styles and relates them to the individual's characteristic manner of approaching change. The extreme adaptor prefers order and precision, and is concerned with the accuracy of details, prudence, soundness, efficiency and a degree of conformity. The adaptor is happiest working within a well-established pattern of rule and operating procedures.

By contrast, the innovator prefers to think tangentially, challenges rules and procedures and is less inhibited about breaking with established methods and advocating novel perspectives and solutions. The innovator is easily bored by routine and seeks novelty and stimulation in discontinuous change; he or she tends towards risk-taking, exploration and trial (Kirton 2003). The behavioural characteristics of adaptors and innovators are explained in more detail in Kirton (ibid.).

As relatively narrow categorizers, adaptors are more likely than innovators to seek to avoid mistakes, even if this means missing some positive opportunities (Foxall 1988). Their preference for structure (Kirton 2003) leads them to take a more cautious and conservative view, confining their search for information within the frame of reference dictated by their direct personal experience. Since adaptors are more intolerant of change and disruption than are innovators, are unwilling to accept ambiguity and are more dogmatic and inflexible (Goldsmith 1989; Gryskiewicz 1982; Kirton 1976, 2003), they are predictably less amenable to the most discontinuous innovative product trial. Their consequent lack of experience of these products further reinforces their unwillingness to explore. Innovators, who by contrast are broad categorizers, risking errors and costs to take advantage of potential positive chances, are more likely to try new products, accepting the risk of buying an unsatisfactory item. They use more environmental stimuli, exploring more ideas outside of the consensually agreed and using them more actively to find a solution. Their more abstract thinking leads them to ask more questions, search widely for information, and investigate more relationships.

The KAI requires respondents to estimate on 32 five-point ratings how easy or difficult they would find it to sustain particular adaptive and innovative behaviours over long periods of time. The measure is scored in the direction of innovativeness from an adaptive extreme (32) to an innovative extreme (160), and with a theoretical mean suggested by the scale midpoint (96).

Terminological confusion and its resolution

Before showing how the KAI has been used in consumer research and how the results have elucidated the relationship between personality and innovative choice, it is necessary to address the terminological confusion that pervades this topic. The scope for confusion in the use of terms such as 'innovator' and 'innovativeness' will already be apparent to the reader. At its simplest, it takes the form of quite distinct conceptual levels being described in similar terms, from the hypothetical and abstract 'innate innovativeness' and 'inherent innovativeness', to the concrete and observable 'actualized innovativeness'. To use the same term in each case, whilst claiming that the former provides an explanatory basis for the latter, is to prejudge the issue of whether innovative behaviour is attributable to an underlying personality trait or system. At the intermediate level, there is a plethora of terms to refer to measurable intervening variables: sensory innovativeness, cognitive innovativeness, hedonic innovativeness, adaption-innovation, etc. (Hirschman 1984; Kirton 1976). Finally, at the level of consumption rather than purchasing, the term 'use-innovativeness' has been suggested to refer to the deployment of a product that has already been adopted to solve a new problem of consumption (Hirschmann 1980).

Foxall (1989) proposed the substitution of 'market initiators' for 'purchase innovators'. The term emphasizes that such adopters are initial purchasers but also that they have an initiating role in the communication and diffusion of new brands and products. This usage is in line with that found in both marketing studies of adoption and diffusion and the wider analysis of these phenomena in a broad range of other fields (Foxall and Bhate 1993a; Rogers 1983). A synonym is 'initial adopters'. Both designate an observable level of analysis, the relationship of which to a trait of personality, or to a group of associated traits that predispose a consumer towards innovative behaviour, is an empirical question rather than a matter of preordination.

Market-initiation also covers consumers' reactions to the range of newness available in new brands and products more successfully than the blanket term 'innovators'. The word 'innovation' describes an entire spectrum of new products from the discontinuous, which has highly disruptive consequences for consumer behaviour, to the continuous, which requires almost no accommodation on the part of the consumer (Robertson 1967). Similarly, the term 'use-initiation' might cover the phenomenon of so-called 'use-innovativeness'. Again, it describes the behavioural level on which the consumer initiates novel functions for an accepted product, without confusing this observable action with any underlying personality trait or system that might account for it. But it again has the advantage of covering uses of an already adopted product that range from radically inventive, qualitative changes to the more quantitative deployment of a product in a number of more basic alternative functions (Foxall and Bhate 1991). An example of the former is consumers using household bleach as a germicide (which involves a high degree of discontinuity and dissimilarity); the latter is exemplified by the use of a home computer for spreadsheet analysis in addition to word processing (a more continuous re-application that involves much greater similarity of behaviour). Once again, the continuity/discontinuity of the product function is conceptually separate from the consumption behaviour of the consumer.

These terms are used in the following description of a research programme, concerned with both market-initiation and use-initiation, which incorporated as explanatory cognitive/personality variables the adaptive-innovative cognitive styles defined by Kirton. In the following account, the first purchasers of a new brand/product are called *market-initiators* or *initial adopters*; consumers who turn a product they already own to novel uses are called *use-initiators*. The generic term to cover both types is consumer initiators. Only those who score appropriately on the KAI are called *innovators*, and this term is used to refer to consumers whose cognitive style is innovative as defined by Kirton.

Implications for new product adoption

The implication of adaption-innovation theory and the approximately normal distribution of the range of cognitive styles it represents is that both research and marketing management must henceforth take into account the existence of both adaptors and innovators among consumer initiators.

In particular, it is essential to consider the probable differences in decision-making styles for adaptors and innovators as they influence product perceptions and responses to persuasive marketing communications. The following discussion rests on substantial bodies of knowledge concerning the personality basis of adaptive-innovative cognitive style (Goldsmith 1989; Kirton 2003) and the relationship of cognitive style to consumer behaviour (Foxall 1988; Foxall and Bhate 1993a; Foxall and Goldsmith 1994; Pinson 1978; Pinson *et al.* 1988).

Category width, the extent to which the consumer perceives an innovation to differ from the norm established by existing products or practices, partly determines the degree of risk he or she perceives in buying and using an innovation. Broad categorizers are more willing than narrow categorizers to embrace innovations that diverge from the norm (Venkatesan 1973). Broad categorizers are also likely to adopt genuine innovations (radical or discontinuous) even at the risk of being dissatisfied, while narrow categorizers prefer artificially new items, i.e. those within their structure, minimizing the possibility of a mistake. Adaptors are more likely to be narrow categorizers, seeking to avoid mistakes even if this means their missing some positive opportunities (Foxall 1988).

Adaptors are also more intolerant of change and disruption, unwilling to accept ambiguity, more dogmatic and inflexible than innovators (Goldsmith 1989; Gryskiewicz 1982; Kirton 2003). Hence it is to be expected that adaptors will be less amenable to new product trial. Their resulting lack of experience of new products further reinforces their unwillingness to explore.

Innovators, by contrast, are likely to be broad categorizers, risking errors and costs to take advantage of potential positive chances. They are likely to try new products, accepting the risk of buying an unsatisfactory item. They may also use more environmental stimuli, taking in more of the data that impinge on them and using them more actively to find a solution. Their more abstract thinking is likely to lead them to ask more questions, search widely for information and investigate more relationships.

Method and results

Table 7.1 contains a summary of the results of ten studies that have explored KAI and related ideas in consumer research, with the intention of relating a pattern of personality traits to market- and use-initiation. Specific details and methodological discussion and considerations can be found in Foxall (1988), Foxall and Bhate (1991, 1993a, 1993b, 1993c), Szmigin and Foxall (1998, 1999), Pallister and Foxall (1998), Wang *et al.* (2006a, 2006b, 2006c) and Pallister *et al.* (2007).

Table 7.1 Summary of research findings

Study	Expectations/background	Results	Conclusions
Study 1: New food brands	This exploratory study tested the broad proposition that innovators would evince a greater volume of market-initiation than adaptors, i.e. buy more new brands of food products.	This hypothesis was not confirmed, but the results pointed to a more complicated pattern of initial adoption. A positive but extremely weak and non-significant correlation was found between the number of new brands purchased and KAI: r = 0.09, p = 0.22. Purchasers of the highest number of new brands (6–8) scored unexpectedly adaptively (r = 90.75, sd = 19.48, n = 12).	1. Contrary to expectations, there is no correlation between KAI and the number of new brands purchased. 2. Both adaptors and innovators are substantially represented among the initial purchasers of recently launched brands. 3. Buyers of the largest number of recently launched brands are adaptors.

Study 2: New 'healthy' food products 1	This study pursued the possibility of the heaviest purchasers of new brands to be adaptive rather than innovative by investigating initial purchase within a coherent product field, namely 'healthy' food products.	Purchasing innovativeness was not linearly related to KAI: $r = 0.04, p = 0.26$. Neither the KAI mean of purchasers of up to two new products, nor that of purchasers of 16–19 products, differs significantly from the female general population mean. Means of both of these groups are distinctly adaptive. However, means of the purchasers of intermediate quantities of new products are significantly higher than that of the female general population.	1. KAI is not correlated with volume of initial purchasing. 2. Adaptors as well as innovators are found among the primary segment that displays initial purchasing. 3. The purchasers of the highest number of products recently introduced into supermarkets are adaptors.
Study 3: New 'healthy' food products 2	Adaptors who had become committed to the cause of healthy eating and therefore to this product field would indeed be more likely than innovators or other, less involved adaptors to seek out assiduously not a few but as many as possible relevant food items. This was operationalized in terms of personal involvement with healthy eating, which was measured by the Zaichkowsky Personal Involvement Inventory (PII).	Purchase initiation was not linearly related to adaption–innovation: $r = 0.04$. Two-way ANOVA, with number of 'healthy' food brands purchased as the dependent variable and KAI and PII as the independent variables, showed no significant main effects for either adaption/innovation ($F_{1.47} < 1$) or for personal involvement ($F_{1.147} = 1.88, p > 0.17$). The mean of the less involved innovators (2.83, $sd = 1.83, n = 24$) and that of the more involved innovators (2.65, $sd = 1.54, n = 43$) fell between those of the adaptor groups but were not significantly different.	1. The pattern of findings found in Studies 1 and 2 has now been shown at the brand level of a coherent product group. 2. The importance of consumers' involvement with the product has been shown to relate to adaption in determining initial adoption. The interaction of involvement and (adaptive) cognitive style as determinants of the behaviour of the group purchasing the highest number of new brands (the more involved adaptors). High involvement was not associated with purchase level (number of brands bought in the case of innovators).

(Continued Overleaf)

77

Table 7.1 Continued

Study	Expectations/background	Results	Conclusions
Study 4: Use-initiation in home computing software applications	The research design was developed at this stage to include products that were intrinsically more involving than foods, namely, computing software applications. Respondents used between 1 and 7 software applications.	KAI is not linearly related to use-initiation: $r = -0.01$. The KAI and PII means of users of up to four applications were compared with those of users of 5–7 applications. The KAI mean of the latter group (111.00, $sd = 18.69$, $n = 7$) was significantly more innovative than that of the users of 1–4 (98.47, $sd = 17.72$, $n = 143$): $z = 1.82$, $p < 0.05$.	1. Both innovative cognitive style and a high level of personal involvement with computing are significantly related to the number of software packages used but only for a small segment of users who score very highly on both KAI and PII. 2. Situational variables, as well as cognitive factors, are closely related to computer use.
Study 5: Software applications in organisational contexts	This study involved 107 computer users on graduate programmes. The Business Information Technology Systems program (BITS) simulated situations of required use of computers; the Marketing program, situations of discretionary use; and the Legal Practice program, situations of minimal use.	KAI scores were skewed towards the innovative pole (range 70–138). The sample was divided into four 'style/involvement' groups, based on whether their KAI and PII scores exceeded or fell short of the sample means. One-way ANOVA was used to examine the relationship of each group's KAI and PII scores to each of the dependent variables. Significant F ratios were found for overall computer usage ($F_{3,103} = 8.38$, $p = 0.000$), programming experience ($F_{3,103} = 3.16$, $p = 3.027$), frequency of computer use ($F = 11.13$, $p = 0.000$) and number of packages used ($F = 5.03$, $p = 0.002$). In the case of duration of computing experience, $F_{3,103} = 0.53$, $p = 0.66$.	1. Regardless of cognitive style, a high level of involvement with computing is positively related to overall extent of computer use. Again, while this is not novel in itself, it is important to recognize that both adaptors and innovators are represented in both low and high involvement conditions. 2. While situational influences are determinative of overall computer use levels, adaptive-innovative cognitive style and personal involvement are differentially related to specific uses of the computer, such as number of packages used and frequency of computer use.
Study 6: Innovation resistance in users of debit and credit cards	Study 6 used a qualitative approach (in-depth interviews) to explore the resistance of consumers to using	In fact non-credit taking (those who pay off in full each month), credit card holders where almost entirely drawn from the	1. Full payer credit card consumers, characterized by more adaptive personalities, exhibit a form of

debit/credit cards in terms of their cognitive style. Resistance to innovation, in rejecting new methods of payment, can take the form of outright rejection (the most extreme response), postponement and opposition.

adapter categories. They suggested that debit cards had no differential advantage and so stuck to using credit cards.

use-initiation, which involves using the product in a way that was not designed, i.e. by not taking credit.
2. Laggards and later adopters of these financial services products may have a good reason for being so – their apparent resistance may belie a deeper understanding of how the product works and may actually be partaking in extensive innovative behaviour.

Study 7: Styles of cashless consumption

The study categorized consumers into four styles of cashless consumption. *Product enthusiasts* use cards primarily for emotional benefits, with functional benefits being secondary, and often have a variety of different cards but are committed to a particular payment method. *Controllers* are cautious about their money, keep a careful track on their spending and generally stick to what they know in terms of payment methods. *Finessers* choose a broad range of methods and try to get the best value in terms of interest-free periods, etc. Finally, *Money managers* accept the payment of interest to the provider as an acceptable fee for a useful service much more readily. They are characterized by active and positive use of a range of methods and feel comfortable with credit.

See background section.

1. Both *Controllers* and *Product enthusiasts* were more interested in the outcome of the payment method and tended towards adaption.
2. It is suggested that the *Product enthusiasts*, although at the adapter end, are similar to the profile of the involved adapter suggested by Foxall and Bhate.
3. *Finessers* and *Money managers* were most concerned that the methods worked smoothly and efficiently and tended towards innovation. *Finessers* where often in the middle of the KAI continuum but were principally innovators.

Study 8: Financial services consumer innovativeness

Study 8 involved a factor analysis of the Hurt–Joseph–Cook scales, which are an inventory

The factor analyses, taking into account the full and shortened versions of the scales (of

1. The *conforming* factor is reminiscent of the adapter category.

(Continued Overleaf)

Table 7.1 Continued

Study	Expectations/background	Results	Conclusions
	for the measurement of innovativeness. A questionnaire (n = 308) was distributed to British consumers of pensions, life assurance, mortgages and savings and investment products.	which all produce high and acceptable levels of reliability and discriminant validity), highlighted a number of factors. The first of these, *conformity*, suggested that consumers of financial services are frequently sceptical, confused, pressured, suspicious, dominated and poorly treated. A second, *eager innovativeness*, suggested a more influential, creative, original and inventive style.	2. The *eager innovativeness* factor is reminiscent of the innovator category. 3. 'The buyers of all four financial services can be described predominantly as conformists, as can the non-buyers of life assurance and mortgages. However, the non-buyers of savings and investments and pensions appear to be more eagerly innovative, apparently shifting at the point of purchase to a more conforming mode' (Pallister and Foxall 1998: 675).
Study 9: Website loyalty – innovativeness and involvement	This study looked at website loyalty in terms of innovation and involvement. Taiwanese internet buyers (n = 1044) on a B2C printer company website responded via an online questionnaire which measured their involvement, innovativeness (using the Domain Specific Innovativeness (DSI) scale), commitment, re-purchase intention, distrust, personal loss, website loyalty and actual website buying frequency. Innovativeness as a cognitive style was not measured by the KAI, unlike earlier studies.	The study broke down the respondents by their innovativeness and involvement scores into four significant ($p < 0.05$) segments: *less-involved adapters* (n = 296, 28.3%), *less-involved innovators* (n = 172, 16.5%), *more-involved adapters* (n = 285, 27.3%) and *more-involved innovators* (n = 291, 27.9%). More-involved groups (both adapters and innovators) have significantly ($p < 0.05$) higher brand commitment, re-purchase intention regarding the brand in the traditional market and website loyalty to the brand's website. In less-involved situations, adapters' commitment was found to be significantly ($p < 0.05$) higher than that of	1. Consumers, in terms of loyalty to a website, can be separated into four distinct and significant categories, *less-involved adapters*, *less-involved innovators*, *more-involved adapters* and *more-involved innovators*, extending the earlier segmentations. 2. The combinations of cognitive style and involvement aspects can be related to specific attitudes, such as commitment, re-purchase intention, distrust and website loyalty, and also to actual website buying frequency.

		innovators. It was suggested that less-involved adapters buy out of inertia and have the lowest brand commitment $(F_{34.74} = -0.42, p < 0.05)$.	
Study 10: Style/ involvement in financial services	UK consumers of pensions, life assurance, mortgages and savings and investments (n = 308) were questioned using KAI and the Hurt–Joseph– Cook scales.	Consumers were segmented into high, medium and low innovativeness groups. Findings suggest that mortgages and pensions are purchased by *highly-involved adapters*, life assurance is purchased by *less-involved adapters* and savings and investments are purchased by *highly involved innovators*. In products regarded as more innovative, i.e. savings and investments, buyers' innovativeness scores are found to be significantly (p < 0.05) higher than non-buyers.	1. Consumers could be segmented into the expected high/low involvement and high/low innovativeness groupings, as had been observed for a range of products which were both innovative and established. 2. For the same individual, their involvement level will differ between different products/ services according to the items' features, even when those products/services are in the same category.

Implications for theory and practice

Theoretical implications

The findings resolve the problem of low correlations between measures of personality and consumer behaviour that were repeatedly a feature of early research. Low correlations were presumably the outcome of researchers measuring the traits of personality embodied by innovators and overlooking those of the adaptors who are also substantially represented among consumer initiators. Low correlation of KAI and consumer initiation would be a problem for this measure only if it operationalized innovativeness alone; however, as a bipolar measure of adaptiveness as well as innovativeness, it has consistently produced results that are intelligible once the coexistence of adaptors and innovators among market initiators is recognized.

The view that the behaviour of consumer initiators is explained by a set of personality traits that define 'innate' or 'inherent' innovativeness is naïve (incomplete). The Midgley–Dowling thesis (1978) that actualized innovativeness is explicable by innate innovativeness, mediated by product field interest and situational factors, is upheld in the case of computing. However, the import of the food studies is that consumer initiators may manifest either adaptive or innovative personality characteristics rather than the profile suggested by research in marketing and cognitive/ personality psychology. Although psychometric techniques will continue to improve, it seems infeasible that traits other than those investigated in the five studies will emerge as related to 'innate innovativeness'.

Any notion that consumer initiators' behaviour can be unequivocally explained by reference to an underlying trait of innate or inherent innovativeness is, therefore, disconfirmed. Far from indicating that actualized innovativeness is inevitably a function of an underlying personality configuration, the results show that adaption-innovation, a dimension of cognitive style that correlates reliably with traits generally associated with initial adoption, is only weakly and usually nonlinearly related to market initiation (operationally measured as the number of new brands purchased or as use-innovativeness).

Moreover, in the case of new foods, the cognitive style profiles of market initiators were approximately evenly divided between the adaptive and the innovative, while a subset of the adaptors was responsible for the highest level of purchase. In the case of use-initiators for software products, both adaptors and innovators were again well represented; although, in the organizational context, personal involvement in computing played a dominant role in determining the extent of use-initiation, both adaptors and innovators were present in substantial proportions. The results also suggest that Midgley and Dowling were right in calling attention to the mediation of innovative behaviour by situational events, but do not unequivocally confirm those authors' preoccupation with an ultimately trait-based explanation of observed early adoption. For both financial services and website loyalty, innovators and adapters – both in terms of high and low involvement – were found and were statistically significant groupings.

The coexistence of adaptive and innovative buyers *at the initial stage of the brand–product life–cycle* indicates two separate and interdependent styles of mental processing among the market segment that has hitherto been labelled 'consumer innovators' and which we now propose to call 'consumer initiators'. It is not feasible, therefore, to identify the innovators and adaptors that we have found to be members of this primary or initial market with the innovators and initiators proposed in other frameworks (e.g. Bass 1969).

Why is the Midgley–Dowling thesis confirmed for one product type (computer software) and consumer behaviour (use-initiation) but not for another product (food) and behaviour (initial adoption)? A possible explanation is that the thesis applies principally to products and situations that are inherently highly involving (computer software under task orientations requiring externally enforced adoption versus food choice under discretionary control). This possibility is borne out by the finding reported by Foxall and Bhate (1994) that adaption-innovation was most closely associated with computer utilization in the case of the Business Information Technology program.

Further research should concentrate on the paradoxical finding that both systematic buyers and systematic non-buyers might be the same kind of people, *adaptors* who differ according to their personal involvement with the product field. This result, since replicated (Mudd 1990) for the adoption of new educational practices by college professors in the United States, flies in the face of conventional adoption theory. It emphasizes the need, which further research should recognize, to treat adaption-innovation as a continuum rather than as the dichotomy that work to date has assumed in order to simplify analysis. Since a unique configuration of personality traits can no longer be expected to characterize initial adopters, researchers should finally turn their attention to the situational influences on consumer initiation.

Implications for adoption modeling

Accounts of consumers' information processing must recognize differences in cognitive style and personal involvement that distinguish adaptors' and innovators' behaviour at each stage of the consumer decision-making sequence.

By confirming that market initiators may have one of two diametrically opposed personality profiles, only one of which is predicted by adoption theory, the results have profound implications for the understanding of consumers' cognitive processing. They disconfirm the widely held view that initial buyers are inevitably highly involved and engaged in extended problem solving, while low involvement, manifesting in routine decision making and purchasing, is characteristic of later adopters. Moreover, in the case of new foods, while involvement makes no difference to the purchase level of innovators, for adaptors it marks a crucial distinction.

The problem-solving behaviours of consumer initiators can be expected to differ at each stage of the adoption decision process, depending on their adaptive-innovative cognitive style and, in the case of adaptors, their level of involvement with the product field. It is proposed that the differences may be by reference to the decision styles of the three segments found in innovative food markets, and the four segments found within website loyalty ad financial services, etc. For example, stages in the decision process will be different for less-involved adapters, innovators, etc. Less-involved adapters' problem recognition will be reactive and for innovators will be active. Moving through the adoption process, less-involved adapters are likely to make more conservative decisions while innovators will make more radical decisions. More-involved adapters will differ from both, being proactive in their problem recognition and search and making prudent and goal-oriented decisions.

Further research should seek to elucidate the behavioural implications of the coexistence of adaptive and innovative segments within markets for new brands and products. Adaptors' narrow category width, relative inflexibility, intolerance of ambiguity, lower self-esteem and sensation seeking suggest they are more likely to be attracted to relatively continuous new products (continuous innovations) than more discontinuous ones. Foxall (1989) reported evidence that consumers' perceptions of the degree of continuity/discontinuity of new food brands were reflected in the predominance of adaptors and innovators, respectively, among their purchasers.

This result, if replicated by further work, would explain why more-involved adaptors bought the highest numbers of food brands/products, items, which at their most radically new, tend still to be fairly continuous. By comparison, the more discretely new software applications could be expected to be used in the largest volumes by more involved innovators. Research aimed at testing these propositions is not only relatively straightforward to carry out but capable of clarifying the place of adaptive-innovative cognitive style in models of adoption.

Implications for new product marketing

The post-launch marketing mix for new products should include both adaptors and innovators, whose reactions to marketing communications and other elements of the marketing mix are likely to be diametrically opposed.

The research has identified not only market segments whose coexistence at the beginning of the product life cycle may be inimical to the successful introduction of a unified launch marketing mix, but also the psychographic basis on which they differ. The consistent finding that both adaptive and innovative market segments must be addressed at the launch stage of the product life cycle raises obvious questions for marketing strategy. The work suggests that the market for new 'healthy' foods can be psychographically segmented in three ways, while that for computing applications software contains both adaptive and innovative sub-segments for both more- and less-involved consumer segments. It is essential, therefore, to consider the probable differences in decision-making styles for adaptors and innovators as they influence product perceptions and responses to persuasive marketing communications. Advertising, for instance, plays a crucial role in the persuasion of initial adopters since it is virtually the sole means by which new brands and products can be communicated to this primary market. Yet adaptors and innovators will likely respond quite differently to new product advertising.

Further research at the managerial level should seek solutions to the problem of accommodating marketing strategy for new products to the psychographic segments revealed in the research.

Both academic consumer research into the psychographic segmentation of initial markets for products and services and practical attempts to influence demand for these items have often assumed a homogeneous consumer profile. But the implication of adaption-innovation theory is that both research and marketing management must henceforth take into account the existence of both adaptors and innovators among consumer initiators. In particular, it is essential to consider the probable differences in decision-making styles for adaptors and innovators as they influence product perceptions and responses to persuasive marketing communications.

One possibility is that the product development process may produce novel items that are tailor-made for one segment – on the conventional wisdom, this would be the 'innovative' but is better expressed as the 'initial' segment – but which are simply ignored as inappropriate by the other. At worst, persuasive appeals aimed toward one segment may simply alienate the other. Authoritarian appeals, likely to appeal to extreme adaptors, might stimulate antipathetic feelings in innovators that preclude their trying the new item; and more freewheeling appeals aimed at innovators that stress the novelty and radical difference of a new product or brand could similarly alienate adaptors. However, the extent to which these considerations actually influence market take-up of specific new offerings remains to be empirically established product-market by product-market. If confirmed, they may suggest why most new products fail. But, more hopefully research may indicate how new product marketing appeals might be made simultaneously to the segments of new markets.

There are also implications for adaptors' and innovators' differential responses to new product promotions. Considerations of category width, boredom with the familiar and a capacity to work with several paradigms rather than within one framework imply that innovators would, for instance, respond more positively than adaptors to two-sided appeals. It is actually possible that innovators appreciate messages that embody pro and con arguments and that they become easily bored with repeated messages that are consistent with their current beliefs. Adaptors are more likely than innovators to respond favourably to one-sided messages, consistent with their current attitudes and habits. They are more likely than innovators to need credible sources of information to handle discrepant advertising messages and to change their attitudes and behaviour.

Innovators, being more flexible, can accommodate more discrepant information. They therefore can cope with cognitive dissonance and indeed may be motivated by it. They are more likely than adaptors, who have strong needs for clarity, to remember incomplete messages and therefore may be more susceptible to postmodern advertising. Since adaptors are more cautious and analytical in their judgements and more reflective and tentative in their decision making, they are open to rational, apparently objective appeals based on reasoned arguments. It appears likely that adaptors will be more amenable to reasoned argumentative advertising, even if it leads to allegedly incontrovertible conclusions that would appear dogmatic and authoritarian to innovators. All of these possibilities are strongly suggested by the research programme that has been described and by what is known of adaptive-innovative cognitive and behavioural styles. But there is clearly great scope for further research to examine them further.

Summary and conclusion

Theoretical and practical studies of 'consumer innovativeness' are currently beset by two problems. First, is the proliferation of terms referring to 'innovators', 'use-innovators', 'innovative personality traits' and so on, which are both confusing and conceptually inexact. Second, is the failure to account for the mass of weak evidence on which the notion of an innovation-prone personality is based.

This chapter has proposed a more coherent set of terms to designate the behavioural and psychological dimensions of innovative consumer behaviour. Ten empirical studies have been presented of the cognitive style/personality profiles related to new brand/product purchasing and the use of computers for novel purposes. Contrary to the literature on adoption and diffusion, while many of the consumers with a propensity for these behaviours showed the cognitive/personality styles widely attributed to 'consumer innovators', a substantial proportion, sometimes a majority, had the obverse profile. In terms of Kirton's adaption-innovation theory, so-called consumer innovators might exhibit either adaptive or innovative cognitive styles. Personal involvement with the product field also emerged as a powerful explicator of 'innovative' consumer behaviour.

Hence purchasers of the highest level of food innovations were adaptors who were also highly involved in the product field; and while the heaviest users of software applications were those who were highly involved, both adaptors and innovators figured strongly among them. In financial services, innovators tended towards saving and investment products while adapters favoured mortgages and pensions. Adapters were also found to exhibit a form of *use-initiation*, which involved using a product in a way it was not designed for. The findings suggest a more complicated psychographic composition of initial consumers than is generally appreciated in managerial prescriptions for new product development and marketing, and in theoretical explanations of consumer behaviour which rely on conceptual abstractions such as 'innate' or 'inherent' innovativeness. The overall conclusion is the need to reject emphatically the idea that the behaviour of consumer initiators can be explained by a set of personality traits that uniquely defines 'innate' or 'inherent' innovativeness.

The study of consumer initiation has been dogged for too long by loose terminology and simplistic reasoning. As a field that has prided itself on its scientific approach to the acquisition of knowledge, consumer research ought now to reject those hypothetical constructs and tenuous relationships among variables that are no longer relevant to a field in which knowledge rather than speculation is demonstrably possible. This chapter has not only suggested a resolution of the problem of inexact and misleading terminology; it has also shown a way forward through the incorporation of operational variables rather than abstract conjecture into our models of consumer initiation.

Acknowledgements

This chapter draws on and develops material that originally appeared in the *British Journal of Management*, 5(2) in 1994, *Technovation*, 15(5) in 1995 and in Michael Kirton's (1994) *Adaptors and Innovators: Styles of Creativity and Problem Solving*.

References

Baker, M.J. (1983) *Market Development*. Penguin, Harmondsworth.

Bass, F.M (1969) A new product growth model for consumer durables. *Management Science*, 15, 215–227.

Foxall, G.R. (1988) Consumer innovativeness: creativity, novelty-seeking, and cognitive style. In: E.C. Hirschman and J.N. Sheth (eds), *Research in Consumer Behavior*, Vol. 3. JAI Press, Greenwich, CT, pp. 79–113.

Foxall, G.R. (1989) Adaptive-innovative cognitive styles of market initiators. In: M.J. Kirton (ed.), *Adaptors and Innovators: Styles of Creativity and Problem Solving*. Routledge, London, pp. 125–157.

Foxall, G.R. and Bhate, S. (1991) Cognitive style, personal involvement and situation as determinants of computer use. *Technovation*, 11, 183–200.

Foxall, G.R. and Bhate, S. (1993a) Cognitive styles and personal involvement of market initiators for 'healthy' food brands: Implications for adoption theory. *Journal of Economic Psychology*, 14, 33–56.

Foxall, G.R. and Bhate, S. (1993b) Cognitive style and use-innovativeness for applications software in home computing: implications for new product strategy. *Technovation*, 13(5), 311–323.

Foxall, G.R. and Bhate, S. (1993c) Cognitive style and personal involvement as explicators of innovative purchasing of 'healthy' food brands. *European Journal of Marketing*, 27(2), 5–16.

Foxall, G.R. and Bhate, S. (1994) How task orientation and individual differences influence computer utilization: the effects of cognitive style and personal involvement in three situational contexts. Unpublished working paper, University of Birmingham.

Foxall, G.R. and Goldsmith, R.E. (1994) *Consumer Psychology for Marketing*. Routledge, London and New York.

Foxall, G.R. and Goldsmith, R.E. (1988) Personality and consumer choice: another look. *Journal of the Market Research Society*, 30, 111–129.

Gatignon, H. and Robertson, T.S. (1991) Innovative decision processes. In: T.S. Robertson and H.H. Kassarjian (eds), *Handbook of Consumer Behavior*. Prentice Hall, Englewood Cliffs, NJ, pp. 316–346.

Goldsmith, R.E. (1989) Creative style and personality theory. In: M.J. Kirton (ed.), *Adaptors and Innovators: Styles of Creativity and Problem Solving*. Routledge, London, pp. 37–55.

Gryskiewicz, S.S. (1982) The Kirton Adaption-Innovation Inventory in creative leadership development. *Proceedings of the British Psychological Society*, University of Sussex, Brighton.

Hirschman, E.C. (1980) Innovativeness, novelty seeking and consumer creativity. *Journal of Consumer Research*, 7, 28, 3–295.

Hirschman, E.C. (1984) Experience seeking: a subjectivist perspective of consumption. *Journal of Business Research*, 12, 115–136.

Kaufmann, G. (2005) Two faces of creativity. In: O. Fisscher and P. de Weerd-Nederhof (eds), *Proceedings of the 1st Creativity and Innovation Community Workshop*, Oxford, Blackwell, pp. 131–145.

Kirton, M.J. (1994) *Adaptors and Innovators: Styles of Creativity and Problem Solving*, second edition. Routledge, London.

Kirton, M.J. (2003) *Adaption-innovation: In the Context of Diversity and Change*, Routledge, London

Midgley, D.F. (1977) *Innovation and New Product Marketing*. Croom Helm, London.

Midgley, D.F. and Dowling, G.R. (1978) Innovativeness: the concept and its measurement. *Journal of Consumer Research*, 4, 229–240.

Mudd, S.A. (1990) The place of innovativeness in models of the adoption process: an integrative review. *Technovation*, 10, 119–136.

Pallister, J.G. and Foxall, G.R. (1998) Psychometric properties of the Hurt-Joseph-Cook scales for the measurement of innovativeness. *Technovation*, 18(11), 663–675.

Pallister, J.G., Wang, H.-C. and Foxall, G.R. (2007) An application of the style/involvement model to financial services, *Technovation*, 27, 78–88.

Pinson, C. (1978) Consumer cognitive styles: review and implications for marketers. In: E. Topritzhofer (ed.), *Marketing: Neue Ergenbnisse aus Forschung und Praxis*. Gabler, Wiesbaden, pp. 163–184.

Pinson, C., Malhotra, N.K. and Jain, A.K. (1988) Les styles cognitifs des consommateurs. *Recherche et Applications en Marketing*, III, 53–73.

Robertson, T.S. (1967). The process of innovation and the diffusion of innovation. *Journal of Marketing*, 31, 14–19.

Rogers, E.M. (1983) *The Diffusion of Innovations*. Free Press, New York.

Szmigin, I. and Foxall, G. (1998) Three forms of innovation resistance: the case of retail payment methods. *Technovation*, 18 (6/7), 459–468.

Szmigin, I. and Foxall, G. (1999) Styles of cashless consumption. *International Review of Retail, Distribution and Consumer Research*, 9(4), 349–365.

Venkatesan, M. (1973) Cognitive consistency and novelty-seeking. In: S. Ward and T.S. Robertson (eds), *Consumer Behavior: Theoretical Sources*. Prentice Hall, Englewood Cliffs, NJ, pp. 354–384.

Wang, H.-C., Pallister, J.G. and Foxall, G.R. (2006a) Innovativeness and involvement as determinants of website loyalty: I. A test of the style/involvement model in the context of internet buying. *Technovation*, 26, 1357–1365.

Wang, H.-C., Pallister, J.G. and Foxall, G.R. (2006b) Innovativeness and involvement as determinants of website loyalty: II. Determinants of consumer loyalty in B2C e-commerce. *Technovation*, 26, 1366–1373.

Wang, H.-C., Pallister, J.G. and Foxall, G.R. (2006c) Innovativeness and involvement as determinants of website loyalty: III. Theoretical and managerial contributions. *Technovation*, 26, 1366–1373.

Zhang, L.F. and Sternberg, R.J. (2005) A threefold model of intellectual styles. *Educational Psychology Review*, 17(1), 1–53.

8

Creativity and knowledge relationships in the creative industries

Paul Jeffcutt

Introduction

In recent years, creativity has become a very popular term with both the wider public and business communities. In one sense, this attention is obvious – which person, group, firm, city or region would aspire to be uncreative? However, the recent enthusiasm for creativity needs to be put in context and, in particular, related to ongoing government and corporate strategic responses to globalized challenges in the contemporary knowledge economy.

This chapter pursues this by examining creativity and the creative industries in a broad organizational field of knowledge relationships and transactions – as a cultural economy. In considering significant issues and debates across this complex territory, the chapter concentrates on the key generic problems of investigating, understanding and influencing this cultural economy. These generic problems are considered and assessed via discussion of a pioneering in-depth study of the creative industries in a region of the UK which came to understand this creative economy as an *ecosystem*. The chapter concludes by setting out key challenges for research and policy in the building of situated and strategic knowledge on cultural economies.

The creative industries

Over the past decade in particular, influential national (DCMS 1998, 2001, 2007; NESTA 2005) and transnational (EC 2001, 2006; NEF 2002) reports have recognized the value (measured by employment and turnover) and dynamism (measured by growth) of creative work to contemporary economies. In this light, a new arena of action, the creative industries, has become constructed for the development of cities, regions and nations. In terms of conventional indicators, the volume and value of activity in the creative industries is highly significant for Western economies. For example, in the UK the creative industries have been valued at 7.2 per cent of GDP and assessed as employing 1.8 million people and as growing at 5 per cent per annum – twice the rate of the rest of the economy (DCMS 2007). The creative industries have been defined as follows:

Those activities which have their origin in individual creativity, skill and talent and which have a potential for wealth and job creation through the generation and exploitation of intellectual property. These have been taken to include the following key sectors: advertising, architecture, the art and antiques market, crafts, design, designer fashion, film, interactive leisure software, music, the performing arts, publishing, software and television and radio.

(DCMS 1998: 1)

The creative industries have come to represent a key indicator of vitality in a knowledge economy – not only valuable and dynamic, but also cool and sophisticated. However, attention needs to be directed towards identifying the generic forces and factors that are shaping their development; three main themes of connectivity can be observed (see also Jeffcutt 2004):

- Creative industries are *trans-sectoral* because they are shaped by connectivity between the media/information industries and the cultural/arts sector (i.e. the cultural industries) – this is evident at all levels of activity, from the growth of new cultural entrepreneurs in diverse locales to dynamic change in the global economy.
- Creative industries are *trans-professional* because they are shaped by connectivity between diverse domains of creative endeavour (i.e. visual art, craft, print, video, music, etc.) brought together for the development of goods and services through new opportunities for the use of digital media technologies. For example, over the past fifteen years, the UK videogame sector has developed from the cult activity of teenagers in suburban bedrooms to an international export industry greater in value than that of television and radio (an already substantial, mature and internationally significant sub-sector of the UK economy).
- Finally, creative industries are *trans-governmental* in that this field of policy and practice (at whatever level) brings together a complex network of stakeholders – departments of culture and of industry, as well as trade, professional, educational and community bodies – to try to do effective 'joined up' policy-making and governance.

Knowledge relationships in the creative industries

The creative industries are thus defined and shaped by complex connectivities, but there is limited strategic knowledge about the relationships and networks that enable and sustain the creative process in this important part of the knowledge economy (often termed the cultural economy).

The creative industries span a range of activities (i.e. arts, genres, crafts, specialisms and domains of endeavour), all of which have creativity at their core; here, creativity is being understood as 'processes that produce new and valued ideas' (Rickards 1999). The terrain of the creative industries is thus characterized by a very mixed economy of forms, from freelancers and micro-businesses to transnational organizations (encompassing the range from sole artists to global media corporations). The creative process in these organizations is distinguished by a complex cycle of knowledge flows, from the generation of original ideas to their realization, whether as products or performances. At its core, the creative process is driven by inspiration and informed by talent, vitality and commitment (Bilton 2006; Leadbeater and Oakley 1999); this makes creative work volatile, dynamic and risk-taking, shaped by important tacit skills (or expertise) that are frequently submerged (even mystified) within domains of endeavour.

The recent public popularity of the creative industries has been a rather double-edged sword. Marking out the creative industries has provided, on the one hand, a welcome emphasis on the significance and value of creativity for knowledge economies; but, on the other hand, the currently dominant approach (i.e. derived from the DCMS 1998 definition, which has attained a global influence) provides a rather arbitrary bounding of this creativity that diverts emphasis from key generic issues, such as the core dynamics of the creative process in knowledge economies.

Accordingly, to concentrate attention on sectors where creativity is more visible in the knowledge economy does not imply that creativity is redundant in the remainder of industry. Indeed, in terms of the DCMS definition, science, technology and manufacturing are primarily 'non-creative' industries; however, this is not a depiction that would fit the many highly inventive enterprises active in these fields (e.g. Intel, Dyson, etc.). This is a separation that also extends into the conventional treatment of the relationship between creativity and innovation (which we shall return to anon) that is being revised by work on the democratizing of innovation (NESTA 2006).

Strategic knowledge about the creative industries

Detailed knowledge about the make-up and dynamics of particular knowledge economies is a crucial strategic resource for policy- and decision-makers. A comprehensive evidence base is needed for intelligence, the analysis of key development factors and the focusing of policy action towards strategic opportunities. However, such strategic knowledge is currently limited, in general, about knowledge economies and, in particular, about the creative industries. The major knowledge deficits can be outlined as follows.

National statistics

In the UK, as in other developed nations, data on the economy are regularly collected (by the Office of National Statistics), predominantly from established employers, in national surveys that are available in regional breakdowns. The data are robust and in time series, typically providing the key source for strategic decision-makers in both the public and private sectors. The main limitations are as follows:

- The statistical codes (e.g. Standard Industrial and Occupational Classification) under which data are collected and organized are agreed internationally; these focus on established occupations. However, they reflect an outmoded picture of the contemporary economy as they tend not to capture the developing knowledge economy (in general) and the creative industries (in particular) at all well (e.g. despite its significance, the UK has no category of videogames yet). Furthermore, there is an approximately ten-year time lag in the substantive revision of these national statistical codes.
- National surveys of established employers (VAT registered, in the UK) measure the established economy and tend not to capture either the self-employed or new businesses trading below the threshold of VAT registration (£55,000 turnover per annum, in the UK). Consequently, national statistics do not capture many freelancers and micro-businesses that make up a significant proportion of the total of creative enterprises (e.g. such enterprises accounted for 36 per cent of total creative enterprises in Northern Ireland; see Jeffcutt 2003). As a consequence, it has been necessary to develop methods of

manipulating national statistics to provide estimates of the size of areas of activity that the coding system does not capture (such as the creative industries; see Pratt 1997).

Public research on economic regions

As creative industries became recognized as significant to regional economies, regional governmental bodies (in the UK, Europe and Australia) have commissioned primary data-gathering on this sector. For example, in recent years three comprehensive regional studies have been completed in the UK (in Yorkshire, Northern Ireland and the East Midlands). With a local focus on a rapidly developing sector of the economy, such studies have been seeking to capture both the baseline data and key dynamics that national statistics have been unable to access. The main generic limitations of such work are as follows:

- Ready-made regional databases of the creative industries do not exist; they have to be compiled by the research team – this is an arduous task on a rapidly changing sector and its degree of thoroughness limits the accuracy and comparability of the results.
- A standard analytic frame for the investigation of creative industries in a region does not yet exist. Each regional study in the UK, although similar in its overall structure and approach, has made choices about sampling and analysis that reflect local priorities – this provides limits for comparability across studies.
- The detailed results of regional studies are confidential to the commissioning bodies and have only been made public in highly truncated forms – this limits the ability to make comprehensive comparisons across studies.

As a consequence, in the UK (a nation that has been recognized for its pioneering approach to this field) the public evidence base on the creative industries is patchy in its coverage and largely lacking in both comprehensiveness and depth. The major national studies that have been completed (DCMS 1998, 2001, 2007) have produced estimates of work activity and business performance derived from national statistics (on the old economy) and/or secondary sources, without making a serious attempt to examine the key dynamics that produced the results. The overall position is a surprising lack of detailed and in-depth strategic knowledge about the cultural economy in the UK; incongruous given the UK's global status as a policy leader in this field.

A key question that follows is how to maximize creativity in any individual, enterprise, region or economy. In order to respond effectively, one has to understand where creativity is located. Obviously, individuals are a primary source of creativity, but (like innovation) it is somewhat shortsighted (although very popular) simply to seek to increase the creativity quotient of each individual in the hope that this will make a significant difference. Just as with innovation, new ideas require a context in which they may be nurtured, developed and passed on, or made into something more generally useful. It is also clear that some contexts and organizational formations enable creativity to flourish (Bilton 2006), and others seem to induce the opposite. This is not to suggest that creativity is all context – for creativity requires both context and organization. Hence, the answer to the key question above must lie in a complex interaction of the two. In other words, creativity needs to be addressed as a process (requiring knowledge, networks and technologies) that enables the generation and translation of novel ideas into innovative goods and services. This key (but still poorly understood) process in the contemporary knowledge economy, which interconnects creativity and innovation, has been both underlined and obscured by the surge of interest in creative industries.

Creativity and innovation in the creative industries

The shortcomings in the conventional definition of creative industries (derived from DCMS 1998) are put into perspective by recent work on what has been called the 'cultural economy'. In Scott's view (see Power and Scott 2004; Scott 1999, 2000), the rising importance of the cultural economy signifies a phase of convergence in the global economy in which goods and services are becoming 'aestheticized' and culture and leisure are becoming 'commodified'.

The cultural economy comprises all those sectors in modern capitalism which cater to consumer demands for amusement, ornamentation, self-affirmation, social display and so on. These sectors comprise various craft, fashion, media, entertainment and service industries, with outputs like jewellery, perfume, clothing, films, recorded music or tourist services (Scott 1999: 807).

Better understanding the cultural economy is thus significant for the improved understanding of the contemporary knowledge economy. However, there is limited strategic knowledge about the relationships and networks that enable and sustain the creative process in knowledge economies. Recent work on these problems (see Jeffcutt and Pratt 2008, for an overview) emphasizes the significance of particular types of knowledge relationships in particular situations.

In the cultural economy, significant knowledge relationships occur between the diverse contributors to the creative process (whether more engaged with the 'inspiration' or the 'perspiration') and are focused towards the achievement of successful outcomes (whether realized in terms of performances or products). These knowledge relationships (Hesmondhalgh 2007) involve the bringing together of diverse expertise (both creative and non-creative) in complex value circuits of symbolic goods that connect the originators of novel ideas with the consumers of novel experiences (see Caves 2000; Scott 1999, 2000). These knowledge-intensive relationships are both situated and networked – sustained by diverse communities of activity, from project-based/hybrid/virtual organizations (Grabher 2003, 2004) to cultural quarters and digital media hubs (Pratt 2002, 2006). Clearly, these diverse relationships and networks are *organised*, even if they may not always be managed (in the conventional sense of the term).

The crucial organizational properties of these creative processes can be summarized as follows (see also Jeffcutt 2004). First, they are *situated* in communities and spaces, both local and global; second, they are *networked* through dense transactions and knowledge relationships which articulate both traded and untraded interdependencies; and third, they are *temporal*, in that an infinite variety of highly differentiated symbolic goods juxtapose for attention in an interplay between producer and consumer through originality, identity and market opportunity.

In knowledge economies, these creative processes need to be understood as both transactional and contextual (see Grabher 2003; Jeffcutt and Pratt 2002). An effective analogy that captures this dynamic, multi-layered complexity is that of an ecosystem (Grabher 2004; Jeffcutt 2003, 2004; NESTA 2005), which will be further explored in the following section of the chapter.

In considering the dimensions of the creative economy, it must be appreciated that creative processes are not uniquely found in a relatively small number of expressive activities. Whilst there are clearly some organizational fields in which creativity is configured at a premium, in others it tends to be either discouraged, or discounted. It is thus logically consistent to undertake situated analyses and examine how 'creativity' is constructed in particular settings and segments of the contemporary knowledge economy. In this respect, organizations operational in the cultural economy, because they explicitly produce 'creative' products, are an important and interesting particularity. However, it must be noted that creative industries are (in principle) no more or less creative than others.

Understanding the dynamics of the creative industries ecosystem

The work of Amin and Thrift (1994), Best (2001) and Scott (2000) on the nature of knowledge economies has made clear that attention needs to be focused on agglomerations of diverse firms that, through dense transactions and knowledge relationships, achieve distinctive capabilities in particular areas of the cultural economy. Furthermore, it is also clear that these dense networks of firms of different scale and purpose (sometimes termed clusters) are situated in distinctive communities and spaces (see Florida 2002, 2005) that are local as well as global (see Landry 2000).

In this light, the comprehensive and in-depth analysis of creative industries in a distinctive economic region provides just such a locus of study. However, few such studies have been completed in the UK and, as was recognized in an earlier section, comparative research between them is constrained. Accordingly, to provide a strategic context for the examination of key generic issues in the cultural economy, this chapter will refer to the work of one of these studies in particular – a study of the Creative Industries in NI (see also Jeffcutt 2003).

The core process for enterprises in the cultural economy is the building of intellectual property in a value circuit for products and services that extends from initial idea to end user. These value circuits are diverse, ranging from the relatively simple (e.g. craft) to the more complex (e.g. film), each of which typically goes through the major phases of content origination, production, reproduction and exhibition (Pratt 1997). Enterprises occupy different niches along these value circuits, ranging from the more robust to the more insecure. Four main generic features were found across value circuits (that were observed in the research on enterprises in the creative industries in Northern Ireland); these occurred in different mixes and strengths in different enterprises and shaped the distinctive niches that these enterprises occupied in the cultural economy. The interrelationship of these four main generic features of the CI ecosystem is displayed in Figure 8.1; further information about each feature is set out below:

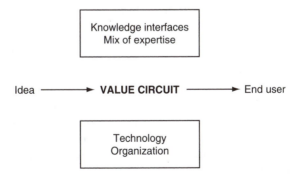

Figure 8.1 CI ecosystem: key features

■ *Knowledge interfaces* The mix of social, cultural and professional relationships and networks that the enterprise sustains and can access.

    – *Key issues*: the range, narrowness, breadth, overlap, barriers and gaps in these knowledge interfaces.

■ *Mix of expertise* The matrix of expertise that the enterprise possesses and can access.

    – *Key issues*: the mix of specialisms (creative and business), the balance of specialisms across individuals and teams, the richness and mobility of the existing pool of expertise in the region, the availability and supply of fresh expertise.

■ *Technology* The medium of creative activity of the enterprise.

    – *Key issues*: the mix of craft and digital processes, the uniqueness and sharedness of the technology, the rate of change.

■ *Organization* The structural and operational capabilities of the enterprise.

    – *Key issues*: the complexity of operations (scale and scope), the longevity and flexibility of operations (continuing/one-off), the density of transactions, the competitive position.

A cultural economy is thus made up of a rich mix of enterprises in an evolving configuration of value circuits for creative goods and services – an ecosystem of creative space. However, as Scott, Florida and Best argue, the development factors for the cultural economy of a region extend beyond the traded and untraded relationships in any value circuit – they are embedded in the material and social context within (and from) which these value circuits develop and are sustained. The research on the creative industries of Northern Ireland identified key development factors that enabled or limited the mix of generic features found in any enterprise (i.e. knowledge interfaces, mix of expertise, technology, organization). These key factors are briefly outlined below and were found to interrelate at three main levels (micro, meso and macro) of capability:

■ *Individual capabilities* Originality and potential, both creative and entrepreneurial.
■ *Organizational/sectoral capabilities* The availability/accessibility of expertise and resources.
■ *Environmental capabilities* The market/milieu for creativity; regional infrastructure and support.

Key challenges for enhancing creativity in the creative industries

The dual challenge for researchers and policy-makers is to better understand the crucial dynamics of cultural economies so that insightful and supportive action may be pursued in particular locales (e.g. cities and economic regions). This challenge is all the more important in a contemporary context where the outputs of the creative industries are trumpeted (as sexy and significant) and a whole plethora of policy initiatives are being undertaken (nationally and internationally, across the developed and developing worlds), searching to expand these outcomes in the short term. A major concern is that the motivation for this activity is often the hope of joining a bandwagon (for fear of being left behind), with insufficient regard for the complexity of these creative dynamics and with little attention to the evaluation of cause and effect. The crucial strategic logic of the research into the creative industries of NI was the finding that, to be effective, development action had to be focused on the CI ecosystem as a whole. As a consequence, any development strategy needed to be both generic and integrated rather than piecemeal – in other words, it needed to be ecological.

Importantly, the NI research reiterated that there was no 'magic bullet' for the development of a cultural economy (much to the disappointment of some local policy-makers). In this light, development needs would be specific to particular cultural economies, taking account of inherited capabilities and the development dynamics of the CI ecosystem. The necessary starting point for any development strategy was thus a detailed appraisal of these circumstances and a realistic evaluation of both capabilities and opportunities. The worst-case scenario would be a policy of late 'me too' – an economic region that, from a situation of unexplored disadvantage, desires to imitate the economy of elsewhere in the vain hope that their success will also arrive once a copy (of what is believed to be the secrets of their success) is established locally. This naïve imitative process is perhaps best described as a policy-makers' 'cargo cult', in which the totems of aspirational development are regularly constructed (usually with the help of 'witch doctors') but the spirits of success are rarely bestowed. As Scott has repeatedly argued, despite the many attempted imitations across the world, there is still only one Hollywood.

In contrast, the real development work for policy-makers in economic regions is the complex and longer-term strategy of capacity building across a portfolio of areas of development need (see also Florida 2002, 2005; Landry 2000). Considering the dynamics of the ecosystem of the creative industries in NI, a development framework for the sustainability of the cultural economy was proposed in which development action would be focused on key dynamics and leverage points. The strategic framework for sustainable development was made up of a series of interrelated action lines in five main thematic areas:

- *Creative learning*: improving the supply of new entrants to the sector.
- *Creative opportunity*: developing the existing workforce in the sector.
- *Creative business*: developing enterprises in the sector (new and existing).
- *Creative sector*: developing sectoral infrastructure (hard and soft).
- *Creative governance*: developing 'joined-up' policy between stakeholders.

The rationale for this approach was that, although Northern Ireland had recently developed a significant creative industries sector, this rapid growth had largely been driven by creative entrepreneurs, without effective support and resource systems that could sustain the medium- and longer-term development of the sector in NI. Hence the strategic framework sought to address the breadth and diversity of the needs that had been exposed (through the research) by building sustainable pathways for development (across the value chains of the CI ecosystem) that brought together key stakeholders in effective partnerships and programmes of coherent and coordinated action. In essence, the development strategy was ecological, being built around enabling initiatives (e.g. interfaces, brokerage and intermediaries) that could bridge gaps, enhance and extend relationships between creative enterprises and the existing patchwork of support and resource systems of NI. As a whole, the portfolio of actions was focused on sustaining the regional knowledge economy of NI in a crucial area of opportunity – the creative industries.

Conclusions

The chapter has considered key issues and debates across a complex field concerned with creativity in knowledge economies, examining the key generic problems of investigating, understanding and influencing the cultural economy. This process has necessarily considered a rich mix of problems and opportunities, situating these in a discussion of a pioneering in-depth study of the creative industries in an economic region of the UK.

The first main conclusion is that there is not one cultural economy but many. Each cultural economy will be situated in a particular locale, with distinctive layers, features, dimensions, knowledge relationships and capabilities. Hence any analysis of and action on the cultural economy needs to be both situated and strategic. Such work necessarily involves a number of key challenges, which can be outlined as follows.

The key research challenge is to insightfully analyse the ecosystem of creative space in particular knowledge economies. This involves examining multi-layered knowledge networks and transactions in particular locales that are local, temporal and mobile but organized. The organization of the creative process in particular locales is realized as an evolving order, articulated by an emerging dynamics of interconnection (i.e. clusters, interfaces, margins and hybrids). The key policy challenge is to insightfully work with this situated knowledge (and its stakeholders) to sustainably enhance the creative space of particular knowledge economies. This involves an ecological approach that is generic, integrated and which focuses on key dynamics (i.e. enabling connections at interfaces through brokerage and intermediaries).

The second main conclusion is that there is a need to build strategic knowledge on cultural economies (across locales) that is thematic, flexible and responsive. Such work necessarily involves a number of key challenges, which can be outlined as follows.

The key research challenge is to overcome existing problems in the availability and sharing of detailed research knowledge on particular cultural economies and establish a generic framework for knowledge building. This knowledge is necessarily interdisciplinary and interoperational (see Hesmondhalgh 2007; Jeffcutt and Pratt 2002, 2008).

The key policy challenge concerns the numerous and diverse policy actions that are being undertaken (across the developed and developing worlds) in particular cultural economies. These are largely local and fragmented and are rarely being coherently evaluated in ways that will enable the strategic development of cumulative applied knowledge (within and across locales).

The crucial socio-economic problems of the twenty-first century don't come conveniently sectioned up in terms of pre-existing structures of knowledge; hence, to address them effectively, we are required to work in ways that are more interactive, distributed and dynamic. Because of its dynamics of connectivity, the territory concerned with creativity in knowledge economies should be capable of rising to the above challenges and pursuing more boundary-crossing approaches to the development of strategic knowledge. It is clearly a field of distributed expertise (between researchers, policy-makers and practitioners) built around multiple networks that do not value convention. It is also a field of multiple stakeholders, where key questions need to be framed and reframed across contexts in an interactive process of analysis, response and action.

Arenas that practise such strongly contextualized co-development between distributed expertise and stakeholders have been characterized as fields of 'mode 2' knowledge (Gibbons et al. 1994; Nowotny et al. 2001) and are thought to be more effective at dealing with the challenges of complexity in knowledge societies. Within the territory concerned with creativity in knowledge economies, there is a growing recognition of the importance of 'mode 2' methods of knowledge development (see, for example, the We-Think project; Leadbeater 2008). In essence, such work is concerned with the building of an effective 'in-between', characterized by sustainable pathways and effective partnerships between research, policy and practice. This work is not only crucial for the development of creativity in knowledge economies, but also for the development of valuable 'mode 2' knowledge about the cultural economy.

References

Amin, Ash and Thrift, Nigel (1994). *Globalization, Institutions and Regional Development in Europe*. Oxford: Oxford University Press.

Best, Michael (2001). *The New Competitive Advantage*. Oxford: Oxford University Press.

Bilton, Chris (2006). *Management and Creativity*. Oxford: Blackwell.

Caves, Richard (2000). *The Creative Industries*. Cambridge, MA: Harvard University Press.

Department of Culture, Media and Sport (DCMS) (1998). *The Creative Industries Mapping Report*. London: HMSO.

DCMS (2001). *The Creative Industries Mapping Report*. London: HMSO.

DCMS (2007). *Staying Ahead: The Economic Performance of the UK's Creative Industries*. London: HMSO.

European Commission (Directorate-General for Employment and Social Affairs) (2001). *Exploitation and Development of the Job Potential in the Cultural Sector in the Age of Digitisation*. Munich: MKW.

European Commission (Directorate-General for Education and Culture) (2006). *The Economy of Culture in Europe*. Munich: KEA.

Florida, Richard (2002). *The Rise of the Creative Class*. New York: Basic Books.

Florida, Richard (2005). *Cities and the Creative Class*. Abingdon, Oxon: Routledge

Gibbons, Micheal *et al.* (1994). *The New Production of Knowledge*. London: Sage.

Grabher, Gernot (2003). Learning in projects, remembering in networks. *European Urban and Regional Studies* 11: 99–119.

Grabher, Gernot (2004). Knowledge governance in project ecologies. *Organization Studies* 25: 1491–1514.

Hesmondhalugh, David (2007). *The Cultural Industries* (second edition). London: Sage.

Jeffcutt, Paul (2003). *Creative Enterprise: Developing and Sustaining the Creative Industries in Northern Ireland*. Belfast: Centre for Creative Industry, Queen's University.

Jeffcutt, Paul (2004). Knowledge relationships and transactions in a cultural economy: analysing the creative industries ecosystem. *Media International Australia* 112: 67–82.

Jeffcutt, Paul and Pratt, Andy C. (2002). Managing creativity and the creative industries. *Creativity and Innovation Management* 11: 225–233.

Jeffcutt, Paul and Pratt, Andy C. (2008). *Creativity and Innovation in the Cultural Economy*. Abingdon, Oxon: Routledge.

Landry, Charles (2000). *The Creative City*. Leicester: Earthscan.

Leadbeater, Charles (2008). *We-Think*. London: Profile.

Leadbeater, Charles and Oakley, Kate (1999). *The Independents*. London: Demos.

National Endowment for Science, Technology and the Arts (NESTA) (2005). *Creating Growth: How the UK Can Develop World Class Creative Businesses*. London: NESTA.

NESTA (2006). *The Innovation Gap*. London: NESTA.

Network of European Foundations for Innovative Co-operation (NEF) (2002). *Creative Europe*. Bonn: ERICarts.

Nowotny, Helga, Scott, Peter and Gibbons, Michael (2001). *Rethinking Science, Knowledge and the Public in an Age of Uncertainty*. Cambridge: Polity.

Power, Dominic and Scott, Allen C. (2004). *The Cultural Industries and the Production of Culture*. London: Routledge.

Pratt, Andy, C. (1997). Employment in the cultural industries sector: a case study of Britain 1984–1991. *Environment and Planning A* 29: 1953–1976.

Pratt, Andy, C. (2002). Hot jobs in cool places: the material cultures of new media product spaces: the case of San Francisco. *Information, Communication and Society* 5: 27–50.

Pratt, Andy, C. (2006). Advertising and creativity: a governance approach. *Environment and Planning A* 38: 1883–1899.

Rickards, Tudor (1999) *Creativity and the Management of Change*. Oxford: Blackwell.

Scott, Allen (1999). The cultural economy: geography and the creative field. *Media, Culture and Society* 21: 807–817.

Scott, Allen (2000). *The Cultural Economy of Cities*. London: Sage.

9

Leading for renewal: the value of positive turbulence

Stanley S. Gryskiewicz

Leaders who develop the ability to read turbulence and who respond to it by bringing a controlled amount of it into the organization create a condition of organizational renewal called *positive turbulence* – the primary means of ensuring that organizations not only survive change but also prosper from it.

Probably the most important challenge a leader faces today is building an organization that continually renews itself – an organization in which creativity (the generation of new and useful ideas) and innovation (the successful implementation of these ideas) are ongoing. This challenge is heightened by the constant – many would say, accelerating – change that has been buffeting us all.

I have spent many years working with and studying organizations seeking renewal in the midst of such turbulence, and I have found that there are leaders who are able to connect the two. They have developed the ability to read turbulence and have responded to it, not by attempting to wall it out, but by bringing controlled amounts of it into the organization. In doing this, they have created a condition of renewal that I refer to as *positive turbulence*; in my view, creating positive turbulence can be the primary means of promoting renewal so that organizations not only survive change but also prosper from it.

Difference and speed

Reading turbulence is a continual activity – the leader must understand the multitude of forces that the organization is subject to, decide which forces to bring in and how to do it, then gauge the turbulence that is brought in so it may be kept positive.

Turbulence can be difficult to read because it occurs in so many interrelated forms: information, the competitive environment and organizational structure, to name only a few. In the discussion that follows I refer primarily to informational turbulence, which may be the most important form at present, but the same principles apply to any of the forms. In addition, the experience of turbulence is not just a matter of external events; how one reacts to these events also plays a part. Therefore, in order to read turbulence, you must understand both its objective and subjective aspects.

Turbulence possesses two basic objective aspects: degree of difference and speed. The former has to do with how different new information coming into the organization is from previous information, and the latter has to do with the rate at which the information arrives. Likewise, there are two basic subjective aspects: receptivity and the capacity to reframe. Individuals differ widely in their ability to accept different information and in their style of processing it. Information is only data until it is converted into something meaningful, which usually involves looking at it from a new frame of reference.

Objective aspects

When new, or different, information comes into the organization, turbulence occurs. The amount of turbulence depends largely on just how different the information is and how fast it is coming in.

If the difference is small, you can expect the turbulence to be slight; it may even go unnoticed. If, however, the difference is large, you can expect the turbulence to be great and probably experienced as threatening and disruptive. Very large differences, and therefore very great turbulence, will likely stimulate the organizational equivalent of antibodies, with white corpuscles surrounding the new information and isolating it. In some cases, an extremely large difference may paralyze the organization and send it into a downward slide. Trying to deal with new information that is coming in very fast is like trying to get a drink of water from a high-speed hose. It's messy and it hurts. Conversely, dealing with information that comes in too slowly is like trying to get a drink from a faucet that is shut off but leaking. It should be noted that speed is often closely related to volume; a fire hose is hard to drink from not only because of the speed of the water but also because of the amount of it.

It is also not uncommon for new information to present itself both at a high rate of speed *and* with a high degree of difference. You can get help in reading these objective aspects of turbulence from the news media (particularly the business press). The media are particularly on the lookout for information with a high degree of difference. They are, of course, less likely to report on an event that exhibits little difference. And even if the degree of difference is high, they may miss information when the speed is low. If the time between the first and the second reports of new information is great, they may not connect the two events and see the emerging pattern. Thus, it is important to bring experience and a good memory to bear when you are reading turbulence.

Subjective aspects

Not surprisingly, the subjective aspects of turbulence are more complex than the objective ones. Three things have an effect on how turbulence is received: creativity style (problem-defining behavior), tolerance of ambiguity, and the ability to make remote associations.

A person's creativity style is how he or she responds when presented with a problem to solve: is the problem accepted as defined or is it redefined? Some people become irritated or anxious when they find themselves in conditions of uncertainty when they cannot anticipate likely outcomes or understand exactly what is driving the situation. Others manage uncertainty by simply ignoring it. Research suggests that the best way to manage it is to develop a stance in which you entertain ambiguity.

Ambiguity is a state in which many possibilities exist. Complete ambiguity is, practically speaking, the same thing as chaos, and all of us are nervous in total chaos. So we all have an urge to impose order. Some of us move very quickly to close boundaries and contain ambiguity. Others prefer to entertain ambiguity or at least some element of it; they are in less of a rush to nail everything down, preferring to leave a little wiggle room in the product or process they are creating.

Many of us by temperament and training find it easier and very practical to think and speak in controlled, concise terms. We stay on the subject at hand; one idea follows closely after another in an orderly manner. This style of thinking has been called *linear*. Others see that there are advantages to occasionally departing from linear thinking. They have been known to unleash their thoughts to range about like hunting dogs in a wide-open field. The term *remote association* is often applied to this style of thinking.

In addition to how we take in turbulence, our capacity to make something out of what we receive is crucial. The capacity to reframe is probably the master key that unlocks everything else. It thus relates to all the responses to turbulence that are detailed below.

Reframing is the ability to look at something from a slightly different angle or several different angles in order to find new meaning. How we experience turbulence depends on how much sense we can make of new information that is, by its nature, not fully clear.

An example of reframing can be seen in the reaction to the incredible growth of new technology. No one is unaware of new technology: it is different enough and happening fast enough that we cannot help but notice. But some people actively wonder what it means for a company or an industry or an organization. What new perspective will explain it best?

The subjective aspect of turbulence is further complicated by the fact that it occurs at three interrelated but distinct organizational levels: the individual, the group or team, and the organization as a whole. In order to read turbulence effectively, you must pay attention to each of these levels.

Using turbulence

Responding to turbulence should also be a continual activity. Because turbulence can be so threatening, leaders have often responded to it by trying to build organizations that wall it out or eliminate it. I believe that many systematic management techniques, although they have worthwhile goals and incorporate potentially useful procedures, are actually often driven by the desire of leaders to eliminate turbulence. Leaders who succeed in eliminating turbulence make the organization comfortable for a time but cut off its sources of renewal – its ability to respond creatively to change.

In order for an organization to continually renew itself, it must incorporate, in a controlled and thoughtful way, some of the turbulence it is surrounded by, particularly changing information. There are various mechanisms (which I have seen tested over the years by various organizations) that can be used to create positive turbulence and then to pay disciplined attention to new information, both internally and at the periphery of the organization. These mechanisms can be grouped according to the subjective level that each focuses on.

Individual level

There are a number of mechanisms that work on the individual level. These, of course, add to an individual's knowledge, but they also serve to bring new information, and therefore some controlled turbulence, into the organization.

Publications

A good means of bringing in new information is to have professionals subscribe to publications from fields outside their areas of expertise and find one that is clearly ahead of current thinking. In addition, there are publications, which I call *credible fringe business periodicals*, that can be very helpful in bringing in new information. These are periodicals that, although currently at the periphery of a field, contain ideas of value. The list of such publications that I consult includes *Fast Company, Strategy and Leadership, Red Herring, GOOD* and *Nordicum*.

These are primarily business publications because that is the world in which I live and work and also because overall business and economic trends are significant for all industries. Leaders should develop their own lists of credible fringe periodicals that depict the signs of change within their own fields, those that challenge the established way.

Conferences

Sending individuals to one conference a year outside their professional fields will provide an unsettling source of new information. (This should not take the place of conferences that people attend for professional and personal growth.)

Networks

Encouraging individuals to take part in professional networks is another way to bring new information into the organization. Such networks function best when members actively participate and give to, not just take from, the experience of the network.

One very intriguing variation on this mechanism is the internal network – a collaboration of organizational members who get together either formally or informally to share ideas and brainstorm solutions. Organizations that employ internal networks include Motorola, Hallmark, Eastman Chemical, the US Air Force and S.C. Johnson.

Travel and foreign assignments

I don't think any single activity does more for bringing new information into an organization than travel. Consider the case of Hallmark. At this company, both artists and writers are sent outside the organization to attend major openings at museums around the world or to soak up atmosphere and information. Hallmark refers to this as *creative travel* and call such trips *mini sabbaticals*. Travelers are expected to come back and use their new stimulation to suggest new product lines.

Closely related to travel is the mechanism of assigning key people to positions in overseas offices, a practice that is increasing. For example, 75 per cent of 3M's top managers have lived abroad for at least three years. The company actively looks for opportunities to send managers abroad for experience, thus exposing them to new information.

Internal sabbaticals

In education and the military, sabbaticals are common and well established as a source of physical and psychological renewal. The idea is not as often used in business, but there is no reason it should not be. Again, Hallmark provides us with a model. This company gives employees a way to be exposed to some new thinking or to learn a new skill through what we might call *internal sabbaticals*.

Changing roles

Another way to generate new information (at least information that is new to a specific locale in the organization) is to move individuals outside their well-learned roles or functional positions.

Team level

The following mechanisms can be used on the team level to produce positive turbulence.

Diversity of membership

The single most important strategy for building positive turbulence into a team is diversity of membership. When members have a broad range of skills and backgrounds, then the information the team generates will not be uniform. One good way to accomplish this diversity is to draw on people from different functional areas (for instance, manufacturing, marketing, finance and human resources). If it is impossible to do this (for example, because the team's purpose requires a focused effort in a particular discipline), then diversity can be accomplished by putting people with different personalities on the team or by rotating in new members.

Outside experts

A team can also generate new information by bringing in experts, from either inside or outside the organization, in subjects related to but not exactly the same as the area the team is working on. Such experts are not team members and may have contact with the team only once or twice.

Creative thinking

In order for a team to generate new information and new ideas, it is necessary that both its individual members and the team as a whole learn to avoid stereotyped thinking and, as people say, to think outside the box. In my experience, this thinking needs to be done systematically, and there are various methods available.

Stirring

In order to keep the information churning within a team, the members should have ongoing contact, rather than just coming together at regular, sometimes lengthy, intervals. There are various ways to do this: for instance, teams can hold daily mini-meetings in which members provide information on where they are with respect to their projects or assignments. Even if it is common for people to be at the same place today that they were the day before, this will stimulate movement.

Another way to stir the pot is to locate members together as much as possible. This will increase their contact and promote serendipitous conversations in the halls.

Technology

It is, of course, often impossible to bring team members together physically. They may be in different buildings, states or countries. The advances in communications technology can help with this. E-mail and group decision-making software can help members exchange information regularly and quickly. In fact, this technology can more than offset distance – that's why it is used even by people who aren't geographically dispersed. It facilitates the circulation of information, which increases the frequency with which new information is generated.

Organizational level

There are many mechanisms that can be used on the organizational level to promote a condition of positive turbulence.

Guest experts

Bell Laboratories is a classic example of an organization that successfully renews itself, coming up with novel and useful ideas in the communications arena. Since its inception, Bell Laboratories has averaged more than two new patents a day. Besides hiring talented experts in particular fields and providing them with resources such as time, materials and other talented people just like them, it brings in people who can describe the thinking found in tangentially-related fields of knowledge.

One forum for this type of stimulation is a monthly event to which outsiders are invited; its sole purpose is to provide some provocative thinking and even outrageous ideas for the lab scientists who choose to attend.

Two criteria have been put in place that go a long way toward guaranteeing the high quality of each presentation: the person presenting must be a recognized world expert in his or her field, and the expertise of the invited presenter must not currently exist inside the laboratory itself.

Corporation-wide trade shows

It is a fact of human nature that we accord more weight to the words of outsiders than to those of our immediate colleagues (witness the phenomenon of outside consultants.) But we would be foolish indeed to ignore the talent at home. The bright, clever, maybe even off-the-wall thinkers in our own organizations have the potential to perform the same function as outside experts to generate information that is different. This can be accomplished through the mechanism of what I call *corporation-wide trade shows*. People can learn what their colleagues in other departments, divisions, and even subsidiary companies are doing in a show-and-tell format.

Corporation-wide trade shows can be especially valuable to very large organizations, those with separate operating divisions that traditionally have had very little to do with one another.

Workforce diversity

It takes only brief reflection to realize that the potential for different information is greatly enhanced in organizations that have a wide cross-section of employees. Diversity in the workplace is thus a helpful mechanism for generating positive turbulence. The best way to achieve this diversity is to hire it.

Alliances, mergers and joint ventures

Working closely with other organizations is a good way to bring in new information. Of course, this needs to be done carefully so that the turbulence it generates is kept positive. Its success also has much to do with the circumstances – remember the aspects of speed and degree of difference.

Mergers are much in the news these days. The worst case is when the two organizations are extremely similar; then there is great overlap and redundancy without a single bit of new information. The best case is when the two organizations are reasonably different; then there can be synergy, successful collaboration and new approaches to long-standing problems.

Crisis response

No sane person would suggest deliberately engineering a crisis as a way of stimulating renewal, but the unfortunate fact is that crises do occur, and they do have to be dealt with. When trouble strikes an organization that already has a creative climate, often that crisis is the catalyst for significant innovation.

Listening posts

Truly listening to customers in their own settings provides invaluable information as well as giving direction, uncovering opportunities, motivating the product development team, and stimulating creative thinking. The type of listening I am talking about here goes far beyond the findings of market research. This listening supplements and energizes the numeric conclusions and links the actions of a product developer directly with an end user.

In 1975, Theodore Levitt's groundbreaking article in the *Harvard Business Review* on marketing myopia suggested listening to clients to identify gaps in the services or products offered. Note that Levitt didn't suppose that the client would give detailed specifications for the service or product he or she wanted, though sometimes that happens. Rather, the client, if gently encouraged, can describe an outcome or a gizmo that would be beneficial. The organization can then ask R&D or product development, 'Can you design a process that will deliver outcome X to clients?' or, 'Can we make a gizmo that's like our product Y but has the following characteristics?'

Interaction

I must point out here that by identifying a mechanism with a particular level I do not mean to imply that it does not have an effect on other levels. The information-generated turbulence experienced by an individual will most likely have an effect on the teams he or she serves on and also an impact on the organization as a whole. The most intense effect, however, will in most cases be at the level the turbulence is introduced. (And all turbulence is experienced to some degree on the individual level.)

I have presented the mechanisms in levels, because to promote renewal it is necessary to have positive turbulence at all levels. The best way to ensure this is to apply mechanisms consciously at each one.

Process of renewal

The mechanisms described above, plus many others I don't have space to describe, are means of initiating and controlling turbulence, making it positive so it can contribute to the process of organizational renewal. To use these mechanisms effectively, you should have a sense of the basics of this process.

You must overcome a reliance on single-source information. The turbulence of having new and different information come into the organization will lead to new ideas as people try to make sense of the information and generate explanations for it. Some of these ideas, if the organization has ways to pay attention to them and consider their possible application, will be seen to be useful in helping the organization meet the needs of its customers more effectively. This is the creative part of the process of renewal.

The organization will then do the work of implementing these ideas, and the informational turbulence will generate ideas that will facilitate implementation. This is the innovative part of the process.

If the mechanisms of positive turbulence are applied systematically and over time, thus helping ensure that creativity and innovation are ongoing, then the organization will in fact be likely to renew itself. And if this process is made a central organizational activity, then it can truly be said that a climate of renewal has been created.

In practice, the parts of the renewal process can happen so rapidly, and interact in so many ways, that they can be difficult to distinguish. You may find yourself talking about using a particular mechanism to promote creativity, skipping positive turbulence and not mentioning renewal. Nevertheless, all the basic parts of the process are at work.

Reading and responding to turbulence are simultaneous and ongoing activities, requiring leaders to pay attention to such issues as how the subjective aspects of receptivity (creativity style, tolerance of ambiguity, and the ability to make remote associations) work at different levels and play out in different mechanisms. If a leader carried out this reading and responding systematically, the complexity can be turned into renewal.

Acknowledgement

This material is reprinted with permission from *Leadership in Action*, Volume 25, No. 1, March/ April 2005, © Jossey-Bass, a Wiley imprint.

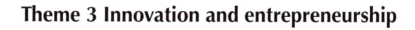

Theme 3 Innovation and entrepreneurship

Evolutionary models of innovation and creativity

Colin Martindale

When analyzed, a creative idea is almost always found to consist of a combination of old ideas previously thought to be unrelated to one another (Poincaré 1913). Poets seldom coin new words but usually put together old words in new ways. If we consider Einstein's equation, $E = mc^2$, it is clear that the idea is creative because it put together well-known ideas in a new and unexpected way. Though creative ideas arise in a variety of ways, self-reports (e.g. Ghiselin 1985) suggest that several stages are usually involved. Based on comments by Helmholtz (1895), Wallas (1926) described these as preparation (gathering information presumed to be relevant to a problem and trying to solve it in an intellectual fashion; an attempt that very often fails), incubation (setting the problem aside and working on another problem), inspiration (the sudden occurrence of the creative idea; something that suggests that the problem had been being worked on in the fringes of awareness or the unconscious mind during incubation), and verification or elaboration (making sure that the idea arising from inspiration in fact solves the problem).

This process may be accounted for by models that may be described as evolutionary in nature. Any system may be said to evolve if it involves variants, some of which are consistently selected over others and preserved in some manner. That a system can be described by an evolutionary model does not mean that it would be profitable to do so. The formation of a crystal or virtually all types of learning could be described in an evolutionary fashion. However, there are better ways of describing these processes.

Our thoughts are quite variable indeed. If we are confronted with a problem that we wish to solve, we shall certainly select and retain those ideas that give most promise of solving the problem. As we shall see, some mental environments are far more conducive to the production of creative ideas than are others, so an evolutionary theory of creativity must account for environment as well as for sources of variation, selection and preservation. Self-reports indicate that creative ideas tend to originate in states of reverie as opposed to conceptual or rational states. Furthermore, it has been estimated that it takes about ten years of very hard work to learn the ideas and skills one needs in order to think of creative ideas (Simonton 1999). This suggests that a certain matrix of interests, motives and traits are needed for the production of such ideas.

Evolutionary theories were first proposed in biology and sociology in order to account for the historical development and differentiation of species, languages and types of culture. It is not obvious on the face of it that such theories are the best manner of accounting for the origin of creative ideas. As Harding (1942) remarked, an idea is eventually applied to everything to which it is applicable. I might add that it is also applied to things to which it is not especially applicable.

As first formulated, evolutionary theory involved the iteration of variation, selection and retention across long periods of time that produced classes of species, languages or cultures. Before I confront the question of whether such theories are appropriate for accounting for the origin of creative ideas, let me look briefly at the origin of evolutionary theories.

Biological and sociocultural origins of evolutionary theory

Until the eighteenth century, theological explanations of the diversity of species were widely accepted with little question. All species had been independently created around six thousand years previously. Similarities between and differences in complexity of species were attributed to the fact that they had been organized into a hierarchy or great chain of being, with man occupying the highest rank.

Erasmus Darwin (1794) was one of the first to dispute this belief. He argued that all creatures may have evolved from a common ancestor. As to how this occurred, some of his ideas are close to those of Lamarck concerning use and disuse of organs as the main force behind evolution, but he also mentioned competition between males for mates and sexual selection. Although their theories were extremely similar, Erasmus Darwin and Lamarck were apparently unaware of each other's work.

Lamarck (1809) argued that changes in the environment cause some organs to be used more and others to be used less. This causes the organs to increase or decrease or even disappear. He called this his 'First Law'. His 'Second Law' was that such acquired traits are heritable. The laws bring about a continuous change in all organisms. Lamarck explicitly assumed that the course of evolution is from simple organisms toward greater complexity or 'perfection'. While the cause of Lamackian evolution is different than the cause later postulated by Darwin, the result is exactly the same: a huge number of species each adapted to its particular environmental niche. He even explicitly mentioned natural selection but felt that it was not an important factor in speciation. Until Mendel's (1866) laws of genetics were rediscovered in the twentieth century (de Vries 1900), Lamarck's ideas seemed perfectly reasonable and were very widely accepted by scientists as an alternative or adjunct to Darwin's ideas.

The theories of Lamarck and Erasmus Darwin were at first rejected, but had gained wide currency by the 1840s. Chambers' (1844) *Vestiges of the Natural History of Creation* was a popularization of Lamarckian theory. It was first published anonymously, and the name of the author was only revealed in 1884. Though it aroused both scientific and religious antipathy, the book enjoyed greater sales than the work of Darwin throughout the nineteen century. Hostility toward the book led Darwin to delay publication of his ideas, which he had worked out by 1844, for several decades.

Far from being a follower of Darwin, Herbert Spencer (1852) had first published his theory of biological evolution, based on Lamarck, seven years before Darwin published his theory. Though he later embraced Darwin's ideas concerning natural selection, throughout his career, Spencer thought Lamarckian evolution to be a far more important force. Spencer's (1864) central idea was that the evolution of everything from the cosmos through biology and psychology to society involves a movement from simplicity toward complexity. Where relevant, this involves increasing differentiation of parts along with increasing hierarchal integration. He does give reasons for this trend. One, for example, is simply size. An amoeba the size of a human would be impossible, so it must become multi-cellular. Without hierarchical integration, the cells would drift off on their own. Lamarckian evolution is not relevant to the history of the cosmos, so it did no harm to what Spencer said. It did lead him to some errors concerning biological evolution. His ideas about socio-cultural evolution were quite sophisticated but often misunderstood because they are quoted out of context (Carniero 2001). In this case, he saw that Lamarckian theory is in fact a better basis than is Darwinian evolution, as the latter operates far too slowly on random variations. The bane of Darwinian theory when applied beyond biology is its dependence upon random variations. Clearly, acquired traits are passed on in the case of sociocultural evolution. Given that sociocultural evolution involves innovations on the level of social structures and the presence of technology, Spencer's theory is a theory of innovation, though he did not make this explicit or deal in any detail with the mechanisms of innovation.

It is interesting that Malthus' (1798) book, *An Essay on the Principles of Population*, was the inspiration for both Darwin's (1859) and Alfred Russel Wallace's almost identical theories of natural selection. Malthus pointed out that, if unchecked, human population would grow geometrically, whereas agricultural production could at best grow arithmetically. The result would be mass starvation. Of course, the food available to animals does not increase at all, so there must be competition for it, leading to the survival of the fittest (the phrase was suggested by Spencer). Thus Darwin's and Wallace's theories of evolution are often used as an example of the combination of remote ideas leading to a creative idea.

Darwin and Wallace presented papers explaining their ideas to the Linnean Society in 1858. Darwin (1859) presented three main selection mechanisms: natural selection, sexual selection (elaborated in Darwin 1871), and use verses disuse. The last is of course the basic principle of Lamarckian evolution, which Darwin fully accepted. He saw that natural selection would take an extremely long time to have any effect, whereas sexual selection could act more quickly. Whenever called upon to give an evolutionary account of extremely fast changes, Darwin always invoked the principle of use verses disuse. Sexual selection subsumes at least three quite different things: aesthetic or hedonic selection (selection of mates on the basis of perceived beauty), selection on the perception of vigor of mates, and conquest of mates on the basis of overcoming members of the same sex (almost always male). It is clearly not a unitary concept.

Variation is now thought of as arising from mutations or errors as a result of gene recombination due to sexual reproduction. These are random events and virtually always deleterious. On the biological level, they will take millions of years to have any effect. Most traits are distributed in at least a quasi-Gaussian fashion, so some variation is virtually always present. Selection is due to adaptation to the environment, sexual selection, or use as opposed to disuse. Of course, preservation refers to the survival of offspring. That variation is due to random factors in Darwinian evolution raises doubts as to whether evolutionary models of creativity will work. In most cases, the problem space is far too large to be searched in a random fashion, and people do not think in a random manner.

Darwin meant his evolutionary theory to be applicable to more than biology. This is made clear by his approval by attempts to apply it to non-biological phenomena. For example, Schleicher (1863) looked upon languages as genuses and species that evolve according to Darwinian principles. Not only could linguistic speciation be viewed as being explained by evolutionary principles, but it could also be used to test them. Thus, the 1868 translation of his book was titled, *Darwinism Tested by the Science of Language*. The book was quoted approvingly by Darwin (1871).

After the rediscovery of Mendel's laws of inheritance by de Vries (1900), what is called the modern synthesis of evolutionary biology was possible. It is mainly the work of Dobzhansky, Haldane and Mayr. R. A. Fisher put sexual selection, which had never been popular with biologists, on a firm footing. Recently, Dawkins (1976) has introduced the term 'meme' to denote something mental that acts like a gene but is applied to social and cultural evolution. It is unclear why we need the term meme, as it seems to be merely a synonym for 'idea'. However, Dawkins (ibid.) and others have introduced some interesting and profitable (and unprofitable) analogies between memes and genes.

Evolutionary models of creativity

Bain

It is certainly possible to formulate an evolutionary theory of creativity with no mention at all of Darwinian evolution. We are far too ready to invoke Darwin not because his theories are relevant but because they are popular. In fact, Bain (1855) did precisely this, because he wrote before Darwin. Bain, if remembered at all, is remembered as the foremost British psychologist of the nineteenth century. It is less well known that he (Bain 1872) proposed the first neural-network theory of mind and very explicitly formulated the Hebb (1949) rule of learning long before Hebb was born. Bain espoused British associationistic psychology. In his opinion the association of ideas is due only to similarity and contiguity. More importantly, he disposed of implausible associationistic laws by arguing that a number of ideas are not learned but present at birth because of Lamarckian evolution.

Bain (1855) devoted considerable space to explaining creative ideas. He takes it for granted that one must have the right ideas to combine in order to arrive at a creative idea. He ascribes creativity to trial and error, but given what he has said in the previous several hundred pages, we are safe in assuming that one will think of closer associates before thinking of more remote associates, so trial and error is not random. Bain does not say anything about the mental environment most conducive to creative thought, but stresses that a 'fanatical' interest in a topic is necessary in order to arrive at a creative solution. Without such an interest, one would give up trying to solve a problem that was at all difficult. His ideas, including 'fitness or unfitness' are all present in the 1855 edition of his book but are more clearly expressed in the third edition (Bain 1874):

> Possessing thus the material of the construction and a clear sense of the fitness or unfit-
> ness of each new tentative, the operator proceeds to ply the third requisite of con-
> structiveness – trial and error – to attain the desired result. The number of trials necessary
> to arrive at a new construction is commonly so great that without something of an
> affection or fascination for the subject one grows weary of the task.

> This is the *emotional* condition of originality of mind in any department (p. 593). In the
> process of *deduction* the same constructive process has often to be introduced. The mind
> being prepared beforehand with the principles most likely for the purpose, incubates in
> patient thought over the problem, trying and rejecting, until at last the proper elements
> come together in the view, and fall into their places in a fitting combination.

> (p. 594)

> With reference to originality in all departments, whether science, practice, or fine art,
> there is a point of character that deserves notice – I mean an active turn, or a profuseness
> of energy, put forth in trials of all kinds on the chance of making lucky hits. Nothing less
> than a fanaticism of experimentation could have given birth to some of our grandest

practical combinations. The great discovery of Daguerre, for example, could not have been regularly worked out by any systematic and orderly research; there was no way but to stumble upon it. The discovery is unaccountable, until we learn that the author got deeply involved in trials and operations far removed from the beaten paths of inquiry.

(p. 595)

Bain seems only to describe the preparation stage of creativity. Helmholtz (1895) remarked that some trivial problems may be solved during this stage. A huge number of self-reports from creators of all sorts say nothing about trial and error. Poets very often say that their poetry is dictated. Great novels have been written in six weeks (e.g. Haggard 1926), with the author saying nothing about trial and error and saying that he himself was often not sure what was going to happen next.

Poincaré

Poincaré (1913) proposed a more satisfactory model of creativity. He is explicit that the mental environment for the production of creative ideas resembles a state of reverie and that such ideas arise effortlessly: 'One evening, contrary to my custom, I drank black coffee and could not sleep. Ideas rose in crowds; I felt them collide until pairs interlocked, so to speak, making a stable combination' (ibid.: 387).

He argues that some sort of trial and error may occur but at an unconscious level. He expresses his ideas so well that it is better to quote him than to attempt to paraphrase him:

It is certain that the combinations which present themselves to the mind in a sort of sudden illumination, after an unconscious working somewhat prolonged, are generally useful and fertile combinations, which seem the result of a first impression. Does it follow that the subliminal self, having divined by a delicate intuition that these combinations would be useful, has formed only these, or has it rather formed many others which were lacking in interest and have remained unconscious?

In this way . . . of looking at it, all the combinations would be formed in consequence of the automatism of the subliminal self, but only the interesting ones would break into the domain of consciousness. And this is still very mysterious. What is the cause that, among the thousand products of our unconscious activity, some are called to pass the threshold, while others remain below? Is it a simple chance which confers this privilege? Evidently not; among all the stimuli of our senses, for example, only the most intense fix our attention, unless it has been drawn to them by other causes. More generally the privileged unconscious phenomena, those susceptible of becoming conscious, are those which, directly or indirectly, affect most profoundly our emotional sensibility.

(p. 391)

Poincaré's idea that the quasi-random trial and error involved in creativity occurs unconsciously, accounts for the fact that creators do not generally mention trial and error in describing how creative ideas occur. However, it is difficult to see how his idea could be tested and made susceptible to falsification. It is interesting that he invokes aesthetic selection rather than fitness as the selection process; we reach the following conclusion:

The useful combinations are precisely the most beautiful, I mean those best able to charm this special sensibility that all mathematicians know, but of which the profane are so ignorant as often to be tempted to smile at it. What happens then? Among the great numbers of combinations blindly formed by the subliminal self, almost all are without interest and without utility; but just for that reason they are also without effect upon the aesthetic sensibility. Consciousness will never know them; only certain ones are harmonious, and, consequently, at once useful and beautiful. They will be capable of touching this special sensibility of the geometer of which I have just spoken, and which, once aroused, will call our attention to them, and thus give them occasion to become conscious.

This is only a hypothesis, and yet here is an observation which may confirm it: when a sudden illumination seizes upon the mind of the mathematician, it usually happens that it does not deceive him, but it also sometimes happens, as I have said, that it does not stand the test of verification; well, we almost always notice that this false idea, had it been true, would have gratified our natural feeling for mathematical elegance. Thus it is this special aesthetic sensibility which plays the role of the delicate sieve of which I spoke.

(pp. 391–392)

There is a perfectly mechanistic way of explaining why only beautiful solutions present themselves to the conscious mind. In neural-network terms, Martindale (2007) has shown that beauty corresponds to a state in which activation of nodes is maximized and inhibition amongst them is minimized. This will correspond to a state in which only a few nodes are very highly activated. On the cognitive level, we know that only highly activated nodes enter consciousness awareness. Martindale argues that the laws of aesthetics and of cognition are isomorphic. Combinations of ideas that are not beautiful or are not correct will involve too much inhibition or confusion or contradiction. They will not therefore enter consciousness. This line of reasoning would explain why innumerable combinations of ideas could occur outside conscious awareness but only combinations that are beautiful or very close to correct would enter consciousness.

Yet all the difficulties have not disappeared. The conscious self is narrowly limited, and as for the subliminal self we know not its limitations, and this is why we are not too reluctant in supposing that it has been able in a short time to make more different combinations than the whole life of a conscious being could encompass. Yet these limitations exist. Is it likely that it is able to form all the possible combinations, whose number would frighten the imagination? Nevertheless that would seem necessary, because if it produces only a small part of these combinations, and if it makes them at random, there would be small chance that the *good*, the one we should choose, would be found among them.

Perhaps we ought to seek the explanation in that preliminary period of conscious work which always precedes all fruitful unconscious labor. Permit me a rough comparison. Figure the future elements of our combinations as something like the hooked atoms of Epicurus. During the complete repose of the mind, these atoms are motionless, they are, so to speak, hooked to the wall: so this complete rest may be indefinitely prolonged without the atoms meeting, and consequently without any combination between them.

On the other hand, during a period of apparent rest and unconscious work, certain of them are detached from the wall and put in motion. They flash in every direction through the space where they are enclosed, as would, for example, a swarm of gnats or, if you prefer a more learned comparison, like the molecules of gas in the kinematic theory of gases. Then their mutual impacts may produce new combinations. What is the role of the preliminary conscious work? It is evidently to mobilize certain of these atoms, to unhook them from the wall and put them in swing. We think we have done no good, because we have moved these elements a thousand different ways in seeking to assemble them, and have found no satisfactory aggregate. . . . They freely continue their dance.

Now, our will did not choose them at random, it pursued a perfectly determined aim. The mobilized atoms are therefore not any atoms whatsoever; they are those from which we might reasonably expect the desired solution. Then the mobilized atoms undergo impacts that make them enter into combinations among themselves or with other atoms at rest which they struck against in their course. However it may be, the only combinations that have a chance of forming are those where at least one of the elements is one of those atoms freely chosen by our will. Now, it is evidently among these that is found what I call the *good combination*. Perhaps this is a way of lessening the paradoxical in the original hypothesis. Another observation is that it never happens that the unconscious work gives us the result of a somewhat long calculation *all made*, where we have only to apply fixed rules. We might think the wholly automatic subliminal self particularly apt for this sort of work, which is in a way exclusively mechanical. It seems that thinking in the evening upon the factors of a multiplication we might hope to find the product ready made upon our awakening, or again that an algebraic calculation, for example a verification, would be made unconsciously. Nothing of the sort, as observation proves. All one may hope from these inspirations, fruits of unconscious work, is a point of departure for such calculations. As for the calculations themselves, they must be made in the second period of conscious work, that which follows the inspiration, that in which one verifies the results of this inspiration and deduces their consequences. The rules of these calculations are strict and complicated.

They require discipline, attention, will, and therefore consciousness. In the subliminal self, on the contrary, reigns what I should call liberty, if we might give this name to the simple absence of discipline and to the disorder born of chance. Only, this disorder itself permits unexpected combinations.

(pp. 392–394)

Poincaré makes several important points. Specific equations are not solved unconsciously, as this requires conscious calculation. The implication is that the ideas combined in unconscious incubation are extremely abstract. Furthermore, the creator has a good idea as to which ideas will result in a creative idea, but does not know exactly how to combine them. This helps to solve the problem of the search space being too large to be searched in a quasi-random fashion.

Campbell

D. T. Campbell (1960) is often cited as proposing an evolutionary model of creativity. However, he does little more than quote at greater length than I have done what Bain and Poincaré wrote, assert that they are correct, and attempt to counter some obvious criticisms of their models. Campbell's main contribution was to make explicit that what Bain and Poincaré had said can be formulated as a Darwinian evolutionary process of blind variation and selective retention. The main problem with his formulation is that he does not very well explain how the search space of a problem could be reduced to a reasonable size if creative ideas arise from a blind or quasi-random process. He does make suggestions, but they are not very convincing. For example, he points out that a large number of people may be working on a problem so that the search space is in a sense divided amongst them.

Simonton

In a remarkable book, Dean Keith Simonton (1999) has used a social or cultural Darwinian framework to explain artistic and scientific creativity. His approach is similar to D. T. Campbell's (1960) explanation of creativity as variation and selective retention but goes far beyond Campbell's original formulation. The creative genius has a facility for generating variations (new combinations of ideas) and retaining those that are most 'fit' or useful. Simonton does not tie himself down to a specific way in which creative ideas arise. The process described by Poincaré will do or pure chance will do. He provides a useful taxonomy of how random or chance events may lead to creative ideas:

> One is working on a problem and cannot solve it. A purely random experience may provide the clue necessary to make the creative connection. Martindale (1995) argued that creative people are able to keep more ideas in the focus and fringe of awareness than are uncreative people. An uncreative person will forget about an insoluble problem, whereas the ideas to be combined remain in the back of the creative person's mind.

Along with Simonton, he argues that some stimulus encountered at random may provide the clue that connects the ideas that need to be connected in order to solve the problem. In this view, no unconscious mentation occurs during incubation. Rather, the problem merely remains in the fringe of awareness and an event seemingly random with respect to the problem provides the solution.

Solution of a problem occurs because of a purely chance event. Goodyear's quite accidentally dropping some material on a stove led him to discover how to vulcanize rubber. In solving one problem, the creator also unwittingly solves another. The classic example is Maxwell's explanation of electricity and magnetism, which unexpectedly turned out also to be an explanation of light. In seeking to solve one problem, a person makes another discovery quite by chance. In seeking a route to India, Columbus discovered America. The creator is not trying to solve any particular problem and accidentally makes a discovery. Leeuenhoek was looking at random things through the newly discovered microscope and discovered microscopic organisms.

Using rigorous quantitative methods applied to archival data, he has investigated how a huge range of factors (e.g. genetics, child rearing, age, birth order, intelligence, personality, mental illness, productivity and contemporary social and cultural conditions) relates to creative eminence. Simonton has provided us with a useful framework into which we can integrate what we know, or are likely to discover, about creativity. The reader is referred to the article by Simonton in this volume for details.

Miller

The models described above deal with how creative ideas are thought of. Geoffrey Miller (2001) discusses why they are thought of, at least in the case of the arts. Until quite recently, biologists have not liked Darwin's (1871) theory of sexual selection and have tried in various ways, without much success, to reduce it to his ideas about adaptation to the environment. It can be used as a possible explanation of several things that cannot easily be accounted for by adaptation. The human brain is far larger than it need be to adapt to any conceivable environment. Language is adaptive, but the vocabularies of all languages are far larger than they need to be. Of course music and the arts are nice, but it could be argued that they serve no real function. Perhaps these facts can be accounted for by sexual selection. The idea is speculative, but it may be that humans wanted mates who were especially intelligent or could make up pleasing poems or sing nice songs. Miller (ibid.) attempts to explain the origin and function of the arts in terms of sexual selection. In his view, they are displays created to attract potential mates. His theory may be more applicable to the popular performing arts than to the high arts. Some popular musicians do attract large numbers of seemingly sex crazed 'groupies', but eminently creative artists and writers working in the high arts are not so successful at getting the attention of anyone.

Conclusions

Evolutionary models of creativity suffer from several difficulties. On the practical level, creative ideas and works often seem to arise far more quickly than they should given the search space the models allow them. It must be that various yet unknown search algorithms exist to allow a vast search space to be searched in a very short time.

Given appropriate heuristics, it may be that the search space is not as vast as is commonly thought. If one stores ideas in a sufficiently abstract manner, one will see that millions of more concrete ideas need not be searched at all. The solution to a scientific problem is not going to come from ideas concerning recipes from the kitchen. Most ideas in a creator's mind are utterly irrelevant to the problem at hand, so need not be examined. Say that the goal is to think of a creative idea about the psychology of memory. Most ideas will not lead to such an idea. Probably, the ideas that most certainly must be avoided are those concerning memory itself. They are too similar to the idea that one seeks to yield remote associations but will only yield uncreative ideas of the sort found in normal science. Even less relevant are any ideas emanating from humanistic domains. Creative ideas are in general derived by appropriating ideas from a more rigorous discipline. Thus, one's ideas concerning biology or chemistry or physics are most likely to yield the creative combination.

Of these ideas, most are also irrelevant. One knows beforehand that theories of gravitation or of the theory of relativity are not likely to yield fruitful combinations. Our best bet would be to limit the search space to what we know about immunology, for example. Thus, most of what one knows is known beforehand to be extremely unlikely to yield a creative idea. It would merely waste one's time to ponder such domains. It must be that at least creative people have the ability to inhibit vast domains of knowledge that could not possibly produce a solution to a problem.

Like atoms, ideas have elective affinities for one anther. They attract and repel and combine in certain manners only. It is not beyond the bounds of comprehension that a theory or a poem or an entire novel may self-organize itself beyond the bounds of consciousness. It has been said that there are only about a dozen stories to be told. May we not think that the right ideas may self-organize themselves around a schema for one of these and present itself almost full blown to the creator? I certainly do not know, but let us remember that psychology is a young science, and we know very little about the manner in which the mind works.

On the theoretical level, there are no plausible genetic analogues of processes reported to accompany creative insight. The experiences that Poincaré (1913) reports seem to be more analogous to chemistry or statistical mechanics than to genetics. We can certainly think of models of creativity that are analogous to Darwinian evolution, but this may not in fact be the best analogy.

Creative ideas are often thought of as 'invaders' from another discipline. What is puzzling to scientists working in one discipline may be analogous to something that is totally obvious in another discipline. Thus, a mere glance at the problem immediately suggests a solution. Harding (1942) gives a large number of examples of such ideas. Hybrid vigor may be much stronger in the mental, than in the biological realm.

References

Bain, A. (1855). *The senses and the intellect* (1st edition). London: Longmans, Green.

Bain, A. (1872). *Mind and body: The theories of their relationship.* London: Henry S. King.

Bain, A. (1874). *The senses and the intellect* (3rd edition). New York: Appleton.

Campbell, D.T. (1960). Blind variation and selective retention in creative thought as in other knowledge processes. *Psychological Review, 67,* 380–400.

Carneiro, R.L. (2001). *Evolutionism in cultural anthropology: A critical history.* Boulder, CO: Westview.

Chambers, R. (1844) *Vestiges of the natural history of creation.* London: John Churchill.

Darwin, C. (1859). *On the origin of species.* London: Watts.

Darwin, C. (1871). *The descent of man, and selection in relation to sex.* New York: D. Appleton, 1896.

Darwin, E. (1794). *Zoonomia.* London: J. Johnson.

Dawkins, R. (1976). *The selfish gene.* New York: Oxford University Press.

Ghiselin, B. (ed.) (1985). *The creative process: Reflections on the invention in the arts and sciences.* Berkeley: University of California Press.

Haggard, H.R. (1926). *The days of my life: An autobiography.* London: Longmans, Green.

Harding, R. (1942). *An anatomy of inspiration.* Cambridge: Hoffer and Sons.

Hebb, D.O. (1949). *The organization of behavior.* New York: Wiley.

Helmholtz, H. von (1895). *Popular lectures on scientific subjects.* London: Longmans, Green.

Lamarck, J.B. de (1809). *Zoological philosophy: An exposition with regard to the natural history of animals.* Chicago: University of Chicago Press 1984.

Malthus, T. (1798). *An essay on the principles of population.* London: T. Johnson, 1806.

Martindale, C. (1995). Creativity and connectionism. In S. Smith, T. Ward and R. Finke (eds), *The creative cognition approach* (pp. 249–268). Cambridge: MIT Press.

Martindale, C. (2007). A neural-network theory of beauty. In C. Martindale, P. Locher and V. Petrov (eds), *Evolutionary and neurocognitive approaches to aesthetics, creativity, and the arts* (pp. 182–193). Amityville NY: Baywood.

Mendel, G. (1866). Versuche über Pflanzen-Hybriden. Verhandlungen des naturforschenden Vereines, Abhandlungen, *Brünn, 4,* 3–47.

Miller, G. (2001). *The mating mind: How sexual choice shaped the evolution of human nature.* New York: Anchor.

Poincaré, H. (1913). *The foundations of science.* New York: Science Press.

Schleicher, A. (1863). *Die Darwinsche Theorie und die Sprachwissenschaft – offenes Sendschreiben an Herrn Dr. Ernst Haeckel (Darwinism tested by the science of language).* Transl. H. Boehlau. London: John Camden Hotten, 1869.

Simonton, D.K. (1999). *Origins of genius: Darwinian perspectives on creativity.* NewYork: Oxford University Press.

Spencer, H. (1852). The Haythorne papers. In *Essays scientific, political and speculative* (Vol. 1, pp. 1–7). London: Williams and Norgate, 1891.

Spencer, H. (1864). *First principles of a new system of philosophy.* New York: D. Appleton.

Vries, H. de (1900). Das Spaltungsgesetz der Bastarde, *Berichte der deutschen botanischen Gesellschaft, 18,* 83–90.

Wallas, G. (1926). *The art of thought.* New York: Harcourt Brace.

11

Creativity and entrepreneurship

Mathew Manimala

Introduction

Creativity and innovation are often mentioned as integral ingredients of entrepreneurship ever since this thesis was proposed by Schumpeter (1934) in a book that changed the paradigms in which entrepreneurship research had been previously carried out. Prior to this the focus of research on the subject was primarily on the investment and risk-taking capabilities of the individual. While recognizing the importance of innovation for entrepreneurship, subsequent researchers (e.g. Gilad 1984; Whiting 1988) have attempted to identify the specific links between creativity and entrepreneurship. The need for entrepreneurs to be creative is almost intrinsically linked with the very nature of entrepreneurship itself. Entrepreneurs are creators of something new, though not *ex nihilo*, and have to come up with innovative re-combinations of resources (Hayek 1945; Kirzner 1973; Schumpeter 1934; Shane 2003) in order to make profits as well as gain and sustain a strong presence in the competitive arena, often by offering new products and services. Innovation, therefore, is not just a desirable add-on to entrepreneurship but an integral component of it.

Creativity of entrepreneurs is therefore a function of their special circumstances as well as the personality characteristics of venturesome individuals. It is obvious that start-up activities are unlikely to be performed in a resource-rich situation. Besides, first-generation entrepreneurs are known to be burdened by the 'liability of newness' (Stinchcombe 1965), as well as the 'liability of smallness' (Hannan and Freeman 1984). Unlike established organizations, new entrepreneurs do not have slack resources; neither do they have the track record and credibility to attract financial and/or human resources. Their products and services do not have any brand image, and their enterprises have not yet built any corporate image, nor any systems and procedures to handle the many routine activities involved in the management of their enterprises. The entrepreneurial situation is therefore characterized by a series of paradoxes.

In a physical sense, the most critical of these paradoxes, as apparent from the situation described above, is the mismatch between the requirements and availability of resources. Building a new enterprise and establishing it in the competitive field would need a lot of resources, which the newness and smallness of the enterprise/entrepreneur prevents them from attracting. In prioritizing the tasks to be performed while implementing their entrepreneurial vision, entrepreneurs have to focus on the critical tasks, but paradoxically have to take care of every routine, in the absence of robust organizational systems and procedures. Such paradoxes can also cloud the mental processes of the entrepreneur. For example, in introducing a new product in the market, entrepreneurs will have to combine novelty and familiarity, the former for catching attention and the latter to prevent outright rejection (Ward 2004). Moreover, in the broader process of entrepreneurial innovation, there is a paradoxical situation that the innovator should be capable of the apparently unrelated processes of divergent as well as convergent thinking (Guilford 1967), one for generating the new idea and the other for implementing it.

Thus entrepreneurs have to live with paradoxes both in terms of the internal processes as well as the external circumstances of their operations. No wonder they have to be innovative in almost everything that they do. Their innovativeness is not restricted to the product, process, market, supply and industry organization, as Schumpeter (1934) originally suggested, but covers other related areas such as the management of finance, people, enterprise organization and culture, research and development, external agencies, and the like (Manimala 1992a).

Nature of entrepreneurial innovation

Though there are several ways of characterizing and classifying entrepreneurial innovation, one of the most useful ways of appreciating its significance is to examine its impact on: (a) the enterprise itself, and (b) the society at large. With reference to the former, it was suggested above that the scope of entrepreneurial innovation is so wide-ranging as to cover any activity related to the creation and management of enterprises, however insignificant they may appear to be. The test of innovativeness is whether the change would enhance the competitive advantage of the enterprise, not whether it is in an area of operation that is generally perceived to be significant. Following this line of argument, one could redefine 'entrepreneurial innovation' as a change in any aspect of an enterprise's design, products, services and/or operations that would enhance its competitive advantage. It would imply that innovations in areas that are apparently unrelated to the products/services being offered (such as the shop-floor organization, enterprise structuring, human resource policies, marketing strategies, procurement of resources, dealing with external agencies, etc.) could also lead to significant competitive advantages for the enterprise. An oft-quoted example of this is how in the 1970s the Japanese automobile industry gained significant competitive advantage over their Western counterparts through simple innovations on the shopfloor, with hardly any changes in the product or technology (Cusumano 1988).

It may be noted that the impact of innovation on the enterprise is evaluated primarily through the competitive advantage gained by the enterprise, which is suggestive of the linkages between the internal and external impacts. Since competitive advantage is a function of stakeholder acceptance, it is imperative that entrepreneurial innovations emerge from a persistent concern of the entrepreneur about the developments in the environment. It is the fitment between the stakeholders' needs and the outcomes of entrepreneurial innovations that makes them acceptable to stakeholders and thereby gives an advantage to the innovator. Hence, the quality of innovations and their impact on the larger society would depend primarily on the degree of concern that the entrepreneur has about the developments in the environment.

While the sensitivity to the external environment is critical for the success of entrepreneurial innovations, there can be various degrees of such success. One way to understand these differences is to classify them into 'incremental' and 'radical' innovations, the former contributing to the reduction of costs and/or improvement of features of existing products/services, and the latter creating new products, services and/or industries. The basic processes underlying these two types of innovation could be described as 'exploitation' and 'exploration', respectively (March 1991). In view of the impact of these two types of innovation on the economy, they are sometimes called the 'competence-enhancing' and 'competence-destroying' innovations (Tushman and Anderson 1986), the former supporting and improving on the existing competencies and the latter destroying them. This distinction is obviously rooted in the concept of 'creative destruction' proposed by Schumpeter (1942), who made a distinction between 'natural growth' and 'development', where the latter happens as a consequence of the creative destruction brought about by entrepreneurial actions. The most important contribution of entrepreneurs to the economy, therefore, is that they take the economy to a new level of 'development', and the society to a new quality of life through the discontinuous changes brought about through 'competence-destroying' innovations.

It may be noted that the 'destruction' of competencies is characterized as 'creative' because it takes the economy and society to a new level of competencies, wealth and quality of life. Take, for example, the case of the invention and commercialization of the internal combustion engine. While it destroyed the competence of animal-drawn vehicles, it had a tremendous impact on the size, structure and quality of the transportation industry and led to significant increases in the wealth of certain economies and the quality of life in general. This example, and many others of similar nature, would also suggest that the 'competence-destroying' innovations are stimulated primarily by 'technology push' rather than 'market pull' (Mowery and Rosenberg 1979; Scherer 1982). The latter, on the other hand, would form the basis for incremental innovations, as customer feedback is likely to focus on the problems they experience with the existing products and the need to improve their performance.

It is against this need to 'destroy' the existing competencies in the interest of attaining new stages in economic development and higher levels in the general quality of life that the critical role of the innovative entrepreneur becomes apparent. Established organizations would obviously have a vested interest in preserving the current technologies because they have already heavily invested in them. This is why new ventures become the major vehicles for bringing in new and disruptive technologies, as is demonstrated by the related statistics from the United States (Hisrich and O'Cinneide 1996), where it is shown that almost 70 per cent of the new products and 90 per cent of new jobs are from new ventures. While the contributions of new ventures to the economy are often evaluated by the employment and wealth generated by them, their most important contribution is undoubtedly the raising of the economy and the society to new levels (Stel et al. 2005) through their disruptive innovations in the marketplace. This, however, cannot be done except through focused implementation of creative ideas that would serve the latent or perceived needs of the society. The need for creativity for entrepreneurs, therefore, cannot be overemphasized.

The entrepreneurial individual

In view of the fact that entrepreneurs have to be innovative in order to ensure the survival and growth of their ventures and contribute to economic development, it may be argued that the most critical trait of an entrepreneur is creativity. However, research on entrepreneurial traits has identified many more of them than just 'creativity'. Prominent among them are: risk-taking ability (Knight 1921), need for achievement (McClelland 1961), internal locus of control (Rotter 1966), desire for independence (Collins and Moore 1970), and so on.

While the role and importance of such traits have become redefined in subsequent studies, an aggregate view of the findings of trait research has been developed by Timmons (1994) through an analysis of more than fifty research studies, where he found consensus on six general characteristics of entrepreneurs: (i) commitment and determination, (ii) leadership, (iii) opportunity obsession, (iv) tolerance of risk, ambiguity and uncertainty, (v) creativity, self-reliance and ability to adapt, and (vi) motivation to excel. It may be noted that Timmons combines 'creativity' with 'self-reliance' and 'ability to adapt', suggesting that while creativity is a necessary condition for entrepreneurship, it may not be a sufficient one, and that most of the innovations by entrepreneurs are adaptations rather than break-through innovations (see Kirton 1976, for the distinction between adaptors and innovators). Extending this logic, one could say that, creativity being a general but rather ill-defined (Runco 2004) capability of the human individual, its use in an entrepreneurial pursuit would depend on several other characteristics of the individual as well as the situation. It may be the desire for independence (Collins and Moore 1970), the motivation to excel (McClelland 1961), or the intrinsic interest in the field or the issue (Amabile 1992) that stimulates the search for creative solutions and leads to entrepreneurial actions. In fact, the linkage between intrinsic interest and creative frustration was also highlighted in one of the studies done by the author, wherein it was found that entrepreneurial creativity flourishes when the exercise of a person's intrinsic interest becomes blocked by the work environment (Manimala 2005a).

Facilitating entrepreneurial activity among citizens is obviously a priority for national economies, for which the most logical course of action seems to be to improve the entrepreneurial environment, which is alternatively called the entrepreneurial framework conditions (EFCs). While this was the hypothesis with which the multi-country 'Global Entrepreneurship Monitor (GEM)' research project was started, their findings did not support it; there were greater levels of entrepreneurial activity in countries with relatively poor EFCs (Reynolds et al. 2002). When similar results persisted over the years, the GEM research team brought in an explanation that the impact of the EFCs would be more on the quality of entrepreneurship rather than on its level (Minniti 2005). In other words, improvements in EFCs could lead to improvements in the quality of entrepreneurship without necessarily increasing the number of enterprises. GEM's focus, incidentally, was on assessing the numbers, not the quality, of new ventures created annually. While this is a plausible explanation for the anomalous findings of GEM, there is still a need for explaining the nature of environmental influences on new venture creation.

Against this context it is useful to call to mind a distinction made by organization theorists between the *task* (Thompson 1967) and *general* (Khandwalla 1977) environments. The former consists of factors that have specific impact on business activities, such as the types of customers, suppliers, labour markets, financial institutions, training systems, regulatory groups, competitors, etc., whereas the latter consists of the economic, socio-cultural, legal-political and educational systems of a society. There is some research evidence to suggest that it is the general environment that influences the development of entrepreneurial individuals in a society, whereas the task environment would influence the fields and quality of their entrepreneurial action (Manimala 2005b).

The observation by McClelland (1961) that the development of entrepreneurial individuals in a society largely depends on the child-rearing and early socialization practices (including the choice of nursery rhymes and stories) followed in that society also highlights the importance of the general environment. An obvious implication of this is that unless a society has a general environment that promotes the development of creative (entrepreneurial) individuals, they will not be able to make use of the opportunities made available by the facilitation of the task environment. This is why the entrepreneurship development efforts (especially in developing countries) based on the facilitation of task environment without addressing the issues related to the general environment have become largely ineffective.

As noted above, the stimulation of entrepreneurial creativity may happen because of the presence of different characteristics in the individuals under different circumstances. For this reason, it is logical to assume that there will be different types of entrepreneurs. Hence there have been some attempts to identify the different sub-types among entrepreneurs. As McKelvey (1975) has pointed out, even a non-stable taxonomy has a role in delineating some of the fundamental characteristics of the phenomenon being studied. It is with this intention of highlighting a variety of personality characteristics that might stimulate entrepreneurial creativity that we mention a few attempts at classifying entrepreneurs. Starting with the dichotomous classification of entrepreneurs by Smith (1967) into 'craftsmen' and 'opportunistic' entrepreneurs, the number of categories gradually increased, wherein each category name is suggestive of a dominant trait or motive that stimulates entrepreneurial creativity in such individuals.

A few additional taxonomies/typologies are listed below: artisan, classical and managerial (Stanworth and Curran 1976), craft, promotion and administrative (Filley and Aldag 1978), Cantillon-entrepreneur, industry-maker, administrative, small business owner and independent (Webster 1977), small business owner and entrepreneur (Carland *et al.* 1984), craftsmen, family men, risk lovers and managers (Lafuente and Salas 1989), self-actualizers, negative entrepreneurs and family men (Dubini 1989), escapists, deal-makers, skills/contact-based purchasers, expertise-based service providers, pursuers of unique ideas and organizers (Gartner *et al.* 1989), inventor, adventurer, problem-solver, gap-filler, social visionary, opportunity grabber and specialist (Manimala 1996). The last of these taxonomies was based on an analysis of the more innovative entrepreneurs, and hence has special relevance for understanding the nature of entrepreneurial creativity.

Processes of entrepreneurial creativity

While it is recognized that the motivation for creativity could be different for different types of entrepreneurs, there is not much agreement about the process of entrepreneurial creativity. A very general statement on this is that there could be different stages to the process, such as problem finding, ideation and evaluation, which interact with one another and with the prior knowledge and motivation of the person to produce creative outcomes (Runco and Chand 1995). The role and importance of prior knowledge in the process (Shane 2000), especially the knowledge generated through prior work experience of the person (Ronstadt 1988) cannot be overemphasized. Developing first-hand experience of the phenomenon is like coming out of a building into a corridor that gives a broader view of what is happening outside (ibid.). Moreover, experience is the primary source of new knowledge that, according to Kolb (1984), is generated through a four-stage process of experiencing, reflecting, conceptualizing and experimenting. Work experience in the relevant field, therefore, is an important stimulant for the entrepreneurial individual to implement creative ideas, as it not only enables the person to identify the market gaps that fit with one's own capabilities and resources and provides insights into the ways in which the business is currently operating, but also enhances one's financial and social capital, which are essential for the successful implementation of such ideas. Thus, entrepreneurial creativity is to be seen as resulting from the interaction of experience-based knowledge, competencies, confidence and attitudes of the individual with the dynamic changes in the environment.

There is considerable debate on whether or not this process of generating entrepreneurial ideas and identifying business opportunities is a conscious process. Kirzner (1979), who attempted to capture the essence of this process, stated that 'entrepreneurial alertness consists, after all, in the ability to notice, without search, opportunities that have been hitherto over-looked' (p. 148), implying that it is essentially a subconscious process. Most other researchers, while generally agreeing with this view, try to explain the nature and extent of subconscious activity involved in the process. Hills *et al.* (1997) observed that opportunity identification by entrepreneurs is based on their gut feeling rather than formal research and analysis. Similarly, Long and McMullan (1984) argued that the entrepreneur exerts only a partial control over the process of opportunity identification. Herron and Sapienza (1992) further clarified the role of 'conscious' and 'subconscious' evaluation, specifying that the latter method is used for the identification of opportunities, whereas the former (conscious evaluation) is used to evaluate an identified opportunity. The general tenor of these arguments is consistent with the findings of Manimala (1999), that the more innovative entrepreneurs tend to make important decisions on the basis of their hunches and gut feelings rather than logical inferences based on scientific analyses. In other words, they rely more on their 'intuitions' supported by holistic perceptions than on inferences supported by analytic data, suggesting that entrepreneurial decision making relies more on the 'right brain', which is the source of creative ideas (Sperry 1969). This is why their decision making is characterized by the use of heuristics or decision rules emerging from a holistic perception of the total situation (Alvarez and Busenitz 2001; Manimala 1992b).

Even though much of entrepreneurial creativity happens without conscious effort on the part of the individual, there is some benefit in the use of formal techniques of creativity for generating business ideas and identifying opportunities. These are particularly useful for people who have developed certain mindsets that block new ideas, where creativity techniques would unblock them by providing a 'set to break set' (Rickards 1988: 69). It is against this background that researchers have tried to discover the techniques (conscious or subconscious) used by entrepreneurs to identify business opportunities. Ward *et al.* (2004) have identified three such commonly adopted techniques: namely, conceptual combination, analogy and problem defin-ition. Having studied the lives of about 100 entrepreneurs, Vesper (1993) came to some interest-ing conclusions about opportunity identification for new venture creation. While he found strong support for the view (as explained above) that entrepreneurial ideas are an outgrowth of the individual's background (including education, work experience, hobbies, attitudes and motivation), he did not find any evidence to support the popular perception that such ideas are rare and extraordinary and are born out of a mysterious combination of day-dreaming and inspiration. Entrepreneurial ideas can arise from one's day-to-day routines and can also be developed deliberately and systematically, as was also pointed out by Rickards (1988).

A basic prerequisite for this is that the individual should have a sense of control over their life and work, and have the freedom and capability to work on their own ideas (Rickards 1985). When such autonomous, empowered and motivated individuals live their lives the way they normally do, they create innovative ideas also. Faltin (2001) describes the characteristics of such a process from a practitioner's perspective. These include: discovering something already exist-ing, focusing on the functions rather than conventions, combining existing ideas, products and/ or services, finding additional uses for an existing product or technology, converting a com-monly felt problem into a business opportunity, converting hobbies into work/business, and vice versa, persisting with and pursuing one's vision and unique ideas, and thinking with society and sharing its concerns and value systems. The simplicity and effectiveness of these processes illustrate how entrepreneurs combine spontaneity with deliberateness for generating great ideas and opportunities from ordinary situations.

Idea sources and implementation strategies

The processes described above are also suggestive of the sources of entrepreneurial ideas. In one of the studies by the author (Manimala 1999), it was found that the principal sources of new venture ideas for potential entrepreneurs are contacts with other people, especially (potential) customers, and their own experience with available products and services. The more innovative entrepreneurs, in addition, get new ideas from their experience of changes in the general environment, technological developments, especially in other countries, research and investigations based on their own special interests, as well as those of their own colleagues and associates, and the failed and abandoned ideas of others. Similarly, studies in developed countries like the United States have also highlighted the importance of prior work experience for generating and implementing new venture ideas. For example, Singh *et al.* (1999) found that more than 73 per cent of entrepreneurs in their sample got their new venture ideas from their prior work experience, whereas only about 11 per cent got them from some sort of market research. These findings point to the importance for the individual of being open to a wide range of experiences so that any one or a combination of them, interacting with their own competencies and motivation, could stimulate the emergence of innovative new venture ideas.

As far as the implementation of entrepreneurial ideas is concerned, it is argued that the most important factor affecting implementation of entrepreneurial ideas is the individual's intention to act (Bird 1988). Based on the argument of William James (1890/1950) that the 'will' is a separate and independent faculty of the mind, Bird (1988) has gathered evidences from prior research to demonstrate the role and importance of intentionality in the process of implementing entrepreneurial ideas, bringing out, in the process, many other psychological variables that positively affect intentionality, such as: time-orientation focusing on the present and a wide range of future scenarios rather than on the past, greater vigilance and openness to the environment resulting from intuition and pattern-recognition capabilities, dynamic flexibility in actions resulting from the above-mentioned cognitive complexity even while retaining clear and specific organization-based goals, openness to one's own experiences and willingness to learn from them, networking skills and the ability to recognize and reward the contributions of others and thereby build several layers of teams, both within and outside one's enterprise, and above all, the ability to manage the conflicting needs, values and beliefs of oneself by developing a strong internal coherence and alignment among them.

It may be noted that many of these psychological traits and attitudes figure in our own discussion of the nature of the entrepreneurial individual and the process of entrepreneurial creativity. Besides, it was also found in the author's research on enterprise growth cited above (Manimala 2005), that it is the entrepreneur's personal willingness and inclinations that are the most important influence on enterprise growth. It is not surprising that the same factor is critical to the implementation of the original idea in the first place.

It should be noted that among the various factors that facilitate the individual's intention to implement an entrepreneurial idea, there is a special role for the networking skills of the entrepreneur. Personal and professional networks constituted of relatives and friends, religion and community members, hobby clubs, trade associations, business associates, etc. are used by entrepreneurs for a variety of tasks involved in idea implementation such as refining the original idea, developing expertise, identifying and attracting talents, raising funds, developing supply sources, organizing for the initial production at low or no investment, finding and influencing customers, managing business and financial risks, building corporate image, and so on (Manimala 1998). Several other studies have also reported similar findings. Singh *et al.* (1999) found that a dominant method used by entrepreneurial individuals to convert their initial ideas into business opportunities is to discuss it with business associates and potential customers (50 per cent) and family and friends (46 per cent), and as a result about 37 per cent made moderate to major changes to their initial ideas.

Entrepreneurs use their personal networks for securing scarce resources at low costs (Birley *et al.* 1991) and thereby reducing their overall costs (Jarillo 1986). They also use networks to mobilize support from investors and build credibility with customers, suppliers and employees (Johannison 1986; MacMillan 1983), as well as compensate for the absence of track record and public image (O'Farrell and Hitchins 1988). While the use of social networks for the generation of new ideas (Hills *et al.* 1997) could largely be a subconscious process, their use for idea implementation is conscious, deliberate and planned. In fact, it is observed that the thinking processes involved in the early and later stages of entrepreneurship are of different natures. In the early stages it is the divergent, holistic and intuitive thinking that helps the idea generation process, but in the later stages the entrepreneur has to shift to convergent, analytical and reductionist thinking to bring about the cognitive closure and refinement necessary for implementing the idea (Csikszentmihalyi 1996; Nystrom 1979).

Conclusion

Entrepreneurship, by the very fact that it results in something new, has to have intrinsic linkages with human creativity. Resource and acceptability constraints emanating from the liabilities of newness and smallness make it impossible for the new venture to survive without innovativeness. The entrepreneurial individual therefore has to have a different nature. The factors leading to the development of such individuals and those facilitating their entrepreneurial activities are presented in the model in Figure 11.1. It is clear that the entrepreneur has to be a divergent thinker (for idea generation), as well as a convergent thinker (for idea evaluation and implementation). The former is often a subconscious process and the latter conscious and deliberate, often in collaboration with one's social network.

While divergent thinking is a common capability of the human individual, the extent of its development varies from individual to individual depending on the nature of their formative environment. Furthermore, the use of divergent thinking capability for entrepreneurial opportunity identification depends on the presence of certain other characteristics in the individual, such as curiosity, adventurism, social concerns, intrinsic interest and specialization in a field, need for achievement, desire for independence, and so on. The development of such characteristics in an individual is also a function of the general (formative) environment constituted by the socio-cultural, legal–political, educational and economic conditions of the region. The general environment also has secondary influences in providing the individual with opportunities for holistic experience, competence development and/or creative frustration. This is a two-way process whereby some individuals actively create such opportunities while others make use of the available ones. Identification of entrepreneurial opportunities, therefore, is the result of the interaction among the special characteristics, motives, competencies, prior experience and knowledge of the individual, as well as the dynamic needs of the market.

Identification of an entrepreneurial opportunity does not necessarily ensure its implementation. Evaluation and implementation of the new idea is largely a conscious and deliberate process (even though subconscious processes are also at work, especially for the identification of further new ideas to overcome the constraints posed by the liabilities of newness and smallness in the way of implementation). The implementation process too is facilitated by individual as well as environmental factors. Three individual factors are significant: freedom to act, will to

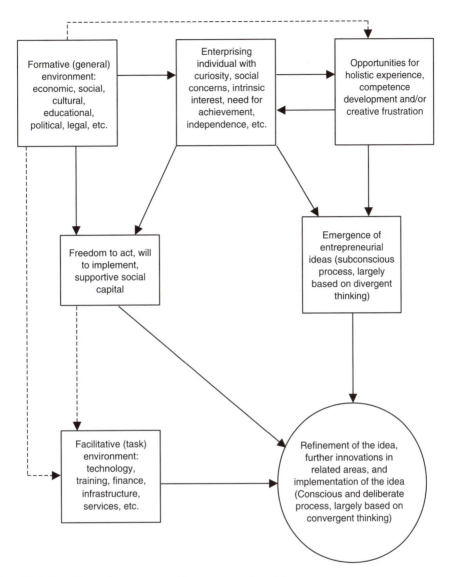

Figure 11.1 Creativity and entrepreneurship: a conceptual model

Note: Dotted lines indicate weak or long-term influences.

implement, and supportive social capital, all of which are influenced by the general (formative) environment. Such individual factors interact with the task (facilitative) environment to refine the idea and to innovate on the methods of implementation. Though the general tendency of the entrepreneurial individual is to make use of the facilities provided by the task environment, the individual's personality has a role in securing the right kind of services from the task environment and sometimes even in creating such facilities. Thus entrepreneurial creativity is an outcome of the interaction between the characteristics of the general and task environments with those of the individual, aided by the individual's ease of intermittently using divergent and convergent thinking skills as and when required.

In taking the readers on the trail of the literature linking entrepreneurship and creativity, it is hoped that they too benefit from the insights derived in the process. For the general reader, this chapter attempts to demystify entrepreneurial creativity and clarify its nature, stages and *modus operandi*. The more important among the issues highlighted are: (1) the natural linkage between entrepreneurship and creativity arising from the liabilities and paradoxes that are definitionally linked to it; (2) the need for entrepreneurs to relate their innovations to the larger needs of society so as to enhance their acceptability, sustainability and impact; (3) the special role of entrepreneurs in taking the economy and society through successive stages of development and progressively higher quality of life through their sponsorship of disruptive innovations (which is in sharp contrast with the general perception among policy-makers that the main contribution of entrepreneurs is the generation of employment and wealth); (4) the need for 'entrepreneur-ial' characteristics that can stimulate and provoke the creative abilities of individuals so that they are used in entrepreneurial pursuits; (5) the role of the general environment in developing 'entrepreneurial' traits and enterprising behaviour, and the role of the task environment in channelling the latter into business pursuits; (6) the importance of experiential knowledge, competencies and confidence for stimulating idea generation and the entrepreneurs' preference for a combination of heuristics and analysis for implementation, implying that subconscious processes dominate during the early stages and conscious ones during the later stages of new venture creation; (7) the role of different entrepreneurial and related traits and motives in creating different sub-types among innovative entrepreneurs; and (8) the importance of free-dom and will to act and the social capital of the individual, which have been identified as the essential prerequisites for idea implementation.

While the conceptual clarity being brought to bear on entrepreneurial creativity is surely of academic and research interest, there could also be benefits for other types of readers such as entrepreneurs and policy-makers. Aspiring entrepreneurs, for example, could recognize the importance of relevant work experience in stimulating entrepreneurial ideas as well as in developing financial and social capital and therefore be selective about their work experience and, while working, deliberately look for new venture ideas and opportunities. They should also eject the generally accepted stereotype that business ideas occur to entrepreneurs only by intuition, and try to aid this process by adopting creativity techniques and idea generation exercises identified by researchers and practitioners, especially those discussed in this chapter. It should also be noted that in the later stages of the entrepreneurial process, which consists predominantly of the implementation tasks, there have to be increasing inputs based on planning, information-gathering and professional knowledge.

One other issue that an entrepreneur has to keep in mind is that the need for innovativeness on the part of the entrepreneur does not cease with the generation of the initial idea, but continues through the implementation and growth phases, even though the areas of innovation might change. The entrepreneur should not leave out any aspect of the business from the purview of innovation because even the apparently small innovations in related areas can significantly enhance the competitive advantage of the enterprise. In fact, the impact of an innovation depends more on the ability of the entrepreneur to relate it to the larger concerns of society than the self-perceived relevance/importance of the technology involved or the area of business the innova-tion is related to. Hence, the two most critical assets of an innovative entrepreneur are apparently the social concerns (for idea generation) and the social capital (for idea implementation).

Since entrepreneurial innovation is primarily a function of the creative abilities, attitudes, competencies and confidence, as well as the freedom and will to act on the part of the indi-vidual, the focus of policy-makers' initiatives should be on the development of such individuals in society. This would imply that they should primarily focus on the general environment rather than the task environment specific to business creation. In their anxiety to facilitate new venture creation, governments and policy-makers, especially in developing countries, have been making sustained efforts at creating a benign task environment for business creation. Such efforts have been found to be largely ineffective, apparently because the people are not developed enough to have the right kinds of attitudes and competencies required for effectively making use of such task facilitation. On the other hand, if such attitudes and competencies are available among individuals, they can themselves find ways to get the tasks organized.

The suggestion here is not that task facilitation is unimportant, but that it is ineffective if not preceded by an appropriate formative environment. Hence the priority for policy-makers should be for facilitating the general/formative environment comprising the economic, social, cultural, legal, political, educational and infrastructural (energy, water, transport, communication, etc.) factors. Among these, the factor that is most amenable to changes in the short run is the learning and education system. Also, changes implemented in the learning and education system are known to have far-reaching impacts on the other constituents of the general as well as the task environments. It may be noted that the knowledge explosion and entrepreneurial creativity during the Industrial Revolution in Europe were a consequence of the Renaissance, which was essentially a movement for liberating the learning system. As far as the policy-makers are concerned, one of the major implications of the findings about the differential roles of the general and task environments in facilitating entrepreneurial creativity is that the governmental initiatives for providing enterprise support should start with the general environment, particularly the learning and education system, so as to increase the supply of entrepreneurial individuals in the society. The general policy of the governments should therefore be to develop and empower the entrepreneurial individuals and then leave it to these enterprising individuals to take care of the tasks associated with venture creation and management.

References

Alvarez, S. A. and Busenitz, L. W. (2001) The entrepreneurship of resource-based theory, *Journal of Management*, 27: 755–775.

Amabile, T. M. (1992) *Growing up creative: nurturing a lifetime of creativity*, second edition, New York: Creative Education Foundation.

Bird, B. (1988) Implementing entrepreneurial ideas: the case for intention, *Academy of Management Review*, 13 (3): 442–453.

Birley, S., Cromie, S. and Myers, A. (1991) Entrepreneurial networks: their emergence in Ireland and overseas, *International Small Business Journal*, 9 (4): 56–74.

Carland, J. W., Hoy, F., Boulton, W. R. and Carland, J. A. C. (1984) Differentiating entrepreneurs from small business owners: a conceptualization, *Academy of Management Review*, 9 (2): 353–359.

Collins, O. F. and Moore, D. G. (1970) *The organization makers: a behavioral study of independent entrepreneurs*, New York: Appleton-Century-Crofts Inc.

Csikszentmihalyi, M. (1996) *Creativity: flow and psychology of discovery and invention*, New York: Harper Collins.

Cusumano, M. A. (1988) Manufacturing innovation: lessons from the Japanese auto industry, *Sloan Management Review*, 30 (1): 29–39.

Dubini, P. (1989) The influence of motivation and environment on business start-ups: some hints for public policies, *Journal of Business Venturing*, 4 (1): 11–26.

Faltin, G. (2001) Creating a culture of innovative entrepreneurship, *Journal of International Business and Economy*, Fall: 123–140.

Filley, A. C. and Aldag, R. J. (1978) Characteristics and measurement of an organizational typology, *Academy of Management Journal*, 21: 578–591.

Gartner, W. B., Mitchell, T. R. and Vesper, K. H. (1989) A taxonomy of new business ventures, *Journal of Business Venturing*, 4 (3): 169–186.

Gilad, B. (1984) Entrepreneurship: the issue of creativity in the market place, *Journal of Creative Behaviour*, 18: 151–161.

Guilford, J. P. (1967) *The nature of human intelligence*, New York: McGraw-Hill.

Hannan, M. T. and Freeman, J. H. (1984) Structural inertia and organizational change, *American Sociological Review*, 49: 149–164.

Hayek, F. A. (1945) The use of knowledge in society, *American Economic Review*, 35: 519–530.

Herron, L. and Sapienza, H. J. (1992) The entrepreneur and the initiation of new venture launch activities, *Entrepreneurship Theory and Practice*, 17(1): 49–55.

Hills, G. E., Lumpkin, G. T. and Singh, R. (1997) Opportunity recognition by successful entrepreneurs: perceptions and behaviors of entrepreneurs. In Reynolds, P. D., Bygrave, W. D., Carter, N., Davidsson, P., Gartner, W. B., Mason, C. M. and McDougall, P. P. (eds), *Frontiers of entrepreneurship research*, Wellesley, MA: Babson College, 168–182.

Hisrich, R. D. and OCinneide, B. (1996) Entrepreneurial activities in Europe-oriented institutions, *Journal of Managerial Psychology*, 11(2): 45–64.

James, W. (1950) *The principles of psychology, Vol. 2*, New York: Dover (original work published in 1890).

Jarillo, J. C. (1986) Entrepreneurship and growth: the strategic use of external resources, *Journal of Business Venturing*, 4: 133–147.

Johannison, B. (1986) Network strategies: management, technology and change, *International Small Business Journal*, 5 (1): 19–30.

Khandwalla, P. N. (1977) *Design of organizations*, New York: Harcourt Brace Jovanovich.

Kirton, M. J. (1976) Adaptors and innovators: a description and measure, *Journal of Applied Psychology*, 61 (5): 622–635.

Kirzner, I. (1973) *Competition and entrepreneurship*, Chicago, IL: University of Chicago Press.

Kirzner, I. (1979) *Perception, opportunity, and profit*, Chicago, IL: University of Chicago Press.

Knight, F. (1921) *Risk, uncertainty, and profit*, Boston: Houghton-Mifflin.

Kolb, D. A. (1984) *Experiential learning: experience as the source of learning and development*, Englewood Cliffs, NJ: Prentice Hall.

Lafuente, A. and Salas, V. (1989) Types of entrepreneurs and firms: the case of new Spanish firms, *Strategic Management Journal*, 10 (1): 17–30.

Long, W. and McMullan, W. E. (1984) Mapping the new venture opportunity identification process. In Hornaday, J. A. *et al.* (eds), *Frontiers of entrepreneurship research*, Wellesley, MA: Babson College, 567–590.

MacMillan, I. C. (1983) The politics of new venture management, *Harvard Business Review*, November–December: 8–16.

Manimala, M. J. (1992a) Entrepreneurial innovation: beyond Schumpeter, *Creativity and Innovation Management*, 1 (1): 46–55.

Manimala, M. J. (1992b) Entrepreneurial heuristics: a comparison between high PI (pioneering-innovative) and low PI ventures, *Journal of Business Venturing*, 7: 477–504.

Manimala, M. J. (1996) Beyond innovators and imitators: a taxonomy of entrepreneurs, *Creativity and Innovation Management*, 5 (3): 179–189.

Manimala, M. J. (1998) Networking for innovation: anecdotal evidences from a large-sample study of innovative enterprises, *Journal of Entrepreneurship*, 7 (2): 153–169.

Manimala, M. J. (1999) *Entrepreneurial policies and strategies: the innovator's choice*, New Delhi: Sage.

Manimala, M. J. (2005a) Growth venture policies and founder characteristics: evidence from British high-growth and low-growth ventures, Chapter 11 of Manimala, M. J. (2005) *Entrepreneurship theory at the crossroads: paradigms and praxis*, second edition, New Delhi: Wiley-Dreamtech.

Manimala, M. J. (2005b) Innovative entrepreneurship: testing the theory of environmental determinism, Chapter 1 of Manimala, M. J. (2005) *Entrepreneurship theory at the crossroads: paradigms and praxis*, second edition, New Delhi: Wiley-Dreamtech.

March, J. G. (1991) Exploration and exploitation in organizational learning, *Organizational Science*, 2 (1): 71–87.

McClelland, D. C. (1961) *The achieving society*, Princeton, NJ: Van Nostrand.

McKelvey, B. (1975) Guidelines for the empirical classification of organizations, *Administrative Science Quarterly* 20: 509–525.

Minniti, M. (with Bygrave, W. D. and Autio, E.) (2005) Global Entrepreneurship Monitor 2005 Executive Report, Wellesley, MA: Babson College and London: London Business School.

Mowery, D. and Rosenberg, N. (1979) The influence of market demand upon innovation: a critical review of some recent empirical studies, *Research Policy*, 8: 102–153.

Nystrom, H. (1979) *Creativity and innovation*, New York: Wiley.

OFarrell, P. N. and Hitchins, D. W. N. (1988) Alternative theories of small firm growth: a critical review, *Environment and Planning* 20: 365–382.

Reynolds, P. D., Bygrave, W. D., Autio, E., Cox, L. W. and Hay, M. (2002) *Global Entrepreneurship Monitor 2002 Executive Report*, Wellesley, MA: Babson College, Ewing Marion Kauffman Foundation, and London: London Business School.

Rickards, T. (1985) *Stimulating innovation*, London: Frances Pinter.

Rickards, T. (1988) *Creativity at work*, Aldershot: Gower.

Ronstadt, R. (1988) The corridor principle, *Journal of Business Venturing*, 3 (11): 31–40.

Rotter, J. B. (1966) Generalized expectancies for internal versus external control of reinforcement, *Psychological Monographs*, 80 (609).

Runco, M. (2004) Creativity, *Annual Review of Psychology*, 55: 657–687.

Runco, M. and Chand, I. (1995) Cognition and creativity, *Educational Psychology Review*, 7: 243–267.

Scherer, F. M. (1982) Demand pull and technological invention: Schmookler revisited, *Journal of Industrial Economics*, 30 (3): 225–237.

Schumpeter, J. A. (1934) *The theory of economic development*, Cambridge, MA: Harvard University Press.

Schumpeter, J. A. (1942) *Capitalism, socialism, and democracy*, New York: Harper and Brothers.

Shane, S. (2000) Prior knowledge and the discovery of entrepreneurial opportunities, *Organizational Science*, 11: 448–469.

Shane, S. (2003) *A general theory of entrepreneurship: the individual–opportunity nexus*, Cheltenham: Edward Elgar.

Singh, R. P., Hills, G. E. and Lumpkin, G. T. (1999) New venture ideas and entrepreneurial opportunities: understanding the process of opportunity recognition, United States Association of Small Business and Entrepreneurship (USABE) 13th Annual National Conference, January 16.

Smith, N. R. (1967) *The entrepreneur and his firm: the relationship between type of man and type of company*, East Lansing: Michigan State University.

Sperry, R. W. (1969) A modified concept of consciousness, *Psychological Review*, 76: 532–536.

Stanworth, M. I. K. and Curran, J. (1976) Growth and the small firm: an alternative view, *Journal of Management Studies*, 13: 95–110.

Stel, A. van, Carree, M. and Thurik, A. R. (2005) The effect of entrepreneurial activity on national economic growth, *Small Business Economics*, 24: 311–321.

Stinchcombe, A. L. (1965) Organizations and social structure. In J. G. March (ed.), *Handbook of organizations*: 142–193, Chicago: Rand-McNally.

Thompson, J. D. (1967) *Organizations in action*, New York: McGraw-Hill.

Timmons, J. A. (1994) *New venture creation: entrepreneurship for the 21st century*, fourth edition, Homewood, IL: Irwin.

Tushman, M. L. and Anderson, P. (1986) Technological discontinuities and organizational environments, *Administrative Science Quarterly*, 31: 439–465.

Vesper, K. H. (1993) *New venture mechanics*, Englewood Cliffs, NJ: Prentice Hall.

Ward, T. B. (2004) Cognition, creativity, and entrepreneurship, *Journal of Business Venturing* 19: 173–188.

Webster, F. A. (1977) Entrepreneurs and ventures: an attempt at classification and clarification, *Academy of Management Review*, 2 (1): 54–61.

Whiting, B. G. (1988) Creativity and entrepreneurship: how do they relate?, *Journal of Creative Behaviour*, 22 (3): 178–183.

12

Social networks and creativity: combining expertise in complex innovations

Arent Greve

Introduction

Creativity depends on opportunities that arise from a conjunction of social networks and knowledge development that create opportunities to create technologies. Using a nested multi-level approach, looking at institutional characteristics at industry level, firm level networks, and interpersonal interactions, I argue that industry level beliefs influence technology innovation. Social networks open opportunities for creative minds to interact with others and combine resources to create new technologies. We illustrate this theory by looking at complex technologies. I present two case studies: (1) the development of two new technologies for floating off-loading and production of oil, and (2) how engineers in ten firms battle pollution problems from paper and pulp mills. Social network analysis reveals how nested networks of industries, organizations and individuals contribute opportunities and resources to complete the innovations.

Engineering and creativity in complex multi-disciplinary settings

Some entrepreneurs start firms in high technology industries based on a creative invention. However, most firms make only one break-through innovation during their lifetime. Thus, we need to understand why some engineers display creativity at one point in time, but not later, and why others may have the same abilities to be creative, but they may not be able to finalize their visions. This chapter focuses on creation of complex technologies, developing theory on creativity in multi-level social networks. This approach shows how opportunities are shaped and how social systems become essential in creating technological concepts and carrying out innovations. I present two exploratory case studies of engineers involved in radical technological innovations. The two case studies presented here show how creativity depends on scientific knowledge at the research frontier. The first study looks at the social networks of engineers participating in the development of two revolutionary off-shore oil technologies. The second study compares the knowledge environment of ten paper and pulp mills struggling with developing technologies to reduce pollution. The successful firms are in close contact with research institutes and universities, whereas other less successful firms do not reach into this domain.

The chapter follows up two shortcomings of creativity research highlighted by Mumford (2003): (1) the field has had an emphasis on individuals or small groups, and we need to know more about how social systems contribute to creativity; and (2) a majority of creativity research has addressed issues either in an experimental setting or have studied so called *creative occupations*. The definitions have been narrow, and mostly included artists, scientists and musicians. The field has ignored engineers, software programmers, and many more occupations. In recent years we have seen a refocusing of creativity research in this direction. This chapter contributes to the field by showing the importance of the evolution of social networks. It also shows that cross-disciplinary and cross-industry relations, and timing of problem awareness and breaking of new knowledge can create opportunities for connecting diverse knowledge into radical innovations. Engineers who are on the intersection of social networks where new knowledge is developed, and where this knowledge has a potential for solving problems they are struggling with, have an advantage in combining resources in novel ways. Moreover, to be able to solve complex technological problems they need to have social networks that include people from different disciplines. Such social networks may be a result of careers spanning across disciplines and firms, so that they know where to mobilize complementary knowledge and resources in a creative way in order to complete their inventions.

Guilford (1950) proposed that divergent thinking, the ability to generate several solutions to problems, is a main characteristic of creative thinking (Runco *et al.* 2001). Following this tradition, I define creativity as thinking outside of general frames of reference, leading to the generation of novel ideas, and solutions to problems. With this definition I see creativity as a starting point of all innovations. I define complex technologies as those that require cross-disciplinary combinations of knowledge. Radical innovations require changes in components as well as architecture[1] (Henderson and Clark 1990).

Previous research on creativity in social settings

Individual creativity and organizations

There is much research on individual creativity. Creative persons may be exceptionally talented and well trained (Amabile 1988). Such writers view creativity as an individual trait, with divergent thinking as the main driver of creativity (Mumford 2003). Others look into motivational factors behind creative innovations. They investigate how intrinsic and extrinsic factors may influence performance and attention to change (Collins and Amabile 1999).

Some look at the social processes that support or inhibit individual creativity (Amabile 1996; Kanter 1983). Looking for innovative cultures, Kanter (1983) shows that routines, existing activities and the 'Not Invented Here' syndrome curb creativity. In organizational research there has been a tendency to concentrate on factors inhibiting creativity more than those that enhance creativity. Kanter (1988) shows that interactions with diverse others support creativity. Exposure to alternatives enables people to use wider categories and come up with more divergent solutions. Other researchers look at organizational processes and leadership that further individual creativity (Redmond *et al.* 1993; Shalley *et al.* 2004).

Yeh (2004) shows that organizational factors as opportunities and needs, support, team work, and supervision can help organizations make room for creativity among their employees. Shalley *et al.* (2004) point out that job complexity that raises intrinsic motivation may increase creativity in organizations. They also review research that shows mixed findings for factors such

133

as relationship with supervisors and co-workers, evaluations, time deadlines and spatial configurations of work. They explain these inconsistent findings with how contextual characteristics may influence how individuals perceive cues as informational or controlling. The former is the foundation for intrinsic motivation, the latter focuses employees on organizational demands and expectations. However, questioning how contextual factors may interact to either increase or decrease creativity gave mixed results.

Another unresolved issue is the role of expertise in creativity (Mumford 2003). Weisberg (1999) argues that expertise and extensive practice are essential to all forms of creative thought. Experts provide rich conceptually-based knowledge needed for combination of different elements that go into the creative process. Csikszentmihalyi (1999) focuses on how situational factors, in particular domain and field, influence creative work. Providing knowledge, resources and technological capabilities, the field influences standards and how people judge work. Expertise also enters into the ability of people to engage in divergent thinking, problem recognition and ability to solve problems (Vincent *et al.* 2002). Creativity research is still striving to develop comprehensive models of problem recognition (Mumford 2003; Runco 1994).

Creativity depends on time off routine activities (Salter and Gann 2003). Some research probes whether available time, type of information or interaction spark creativity in organizations. Engineering designers problem solve better when they can both spend time on their own and face-to-face with co-workers (Perlow 1999). Tight deadlines and production goals may reduce intrinsic motivation and creativity (Amabile *et al.* 2002). A few studies find contradicting results on how deadlines affect creativity. Andrews and Farris (1972) found that scientists and engineers working under deadlines were often more creative. It looks as if deadlines inhibit some but not others; therefore, we need to look at under what conditions deadlines further or inhibit creativity.

Woodman and Schoenfeldt (1990) suggest an interactionist model of individual creativity with person–situation interaction as a main focus. This model is extended to individual interactions in groups, so that creativity leads to organizational outcomes (Woodman *et al.* 1993). Much research looks at formal groups or organizations. However, creative innovations may originate in informal groups or social networks that span inter-organizational networks (Perry-Smith and Shalley 2003). Thus, a social network perspective complements research at individual and group levels, by formalizing and mapping social relations that enter into the creative process that eventually produces innovations.

Organizations and innovations

Organizational researchers typically do not focus on creativity. They center on the outcome of creative processes, without taking issue with the extent of creativity that enters innovations. This literature offers insights into how higher-level structures and environments can influence innovations, and under what conditions such efforts fail. In the biotechnology industry, few firms can mobilize sufficient internal resources for R&D, patenting, clinical trials, governmental approval, production and commercialization on their own. Strategic alliances help smaller organizations access a wider array of resources to enable the completion of innovations (Powell *et al.* 1999). However, collaborations often fail because of mismatched complementarity, rivalries, social and cultural conflicts, and problems of communication and coordination (Omta and Rossum 1999). Many problems related to the R&D process are rooted in lack of clear knowledge of what partners can accomplish, and how to organize an alliance (Niosi 2003). Partner selection often misses the social and cultural aspects and the give-and-take aspects of collaboration (Erens *et al.* 1996). It is hard to prescribe how people should interact to innovate; if managers select partners based on prestige or market share, without pre-existing relations, the alliance may fail. Therefore, this chapter looks at how informal social structures emerge over time to evolve into formal relations. Favorable connections arise from career mobility and inter-organizational work experiences, and these connections may result in better partner selection.

Complementary resources are only useful if innovators know about them and understand how to take advantage of them. The knowledge behind technologies often resides in a network of firms, not in single firms alone (Afuah 2000). These firm-level networks have evolved over some time, and employees learn to use them. Working in a firm, individuals add contacts to their personal networks. Employees also bring their personal networks into firms, which enlarge the firm's network (Gabbay and Leenders 1999). Firms connected to other firms, or with employees that have experiences and connections across disciplines, have nested networks. Through these contacts employees learn about the resources colleagues in other disciplines command, and how they solve problems, and what capabilities different firms have to solve specific problems.

In contrast, core firms within an industry often develop practice and beliefs in specific technological systems. They may dominate markets, becoming carriers of the dominating knowledge and technological paradigms. These firms rarely produce new, radical technologies, because they are entrenched in the dominating technological paradigms (Tushman and Anderson 1986). This makes them less able to recognize problems with the current state of affairs. Firms that take their technology for granted during designing and running complex technologies may fall into the competency trap when searching for solutions to problems within their familiar paradigm (March 1991). They are good at raising questions and solving problems within their own knowledge domains by incremental changes and improvements of the technology. However, they are not able to find radical solutions and go beyond incremental improvements. Current knowledge and problem solving, frames of reference and habitual cognition blind actors from raising crucial questions. If problems cannot be solved within their paradigm, engineers in such closed firms do not know whom to ask. Nor would they know how to communicate with those from other fields (Pinkus *et al.* 1997). Expertise within certain institutional settings may not be beneficial to creative problem solving. Discovering how knowledge and assets can be redefined and connected in novel ways requires heterogeneous networks that can expose people to diversity that can inspire and enable creativity (Amabile *et al.* 1996).

Technology changes and institutional settings

Industries and technologies go through periods of creative exploration and innovation, and other periods of incremental changes or exploitation (March 1991). Some innovations succeed; others fail, not always for the right reasons. As industries go through these cycles, some innovations are never explored. Selection mechanisms may not favor the technologically best solutions. Selection in some organizational environments lands on bad solutions; institutional standardization may impede technology development; choice of the wrong technology may lead to a dead end. Breaking with an accepted path may be very difficult, even if that technology suffers from inherent problems (Garud and Rappa 1994). Creative solutions may break with established technological trajectories. Radical innovations break with existing knowledge by combining new components in a new architecture, which refers to how components are linked and work together. To make such breakthroughs requires a change in the perception of

135

causal relations (Henderson and Clark 1990). These changes are the most difficult to construct and adopt. Connecting pieces of new knowledge requires cross-disciplinary contacts and knowing who can do what.

Theory of creativity in social networks

Nested multi-level networks

An important concept for studying innovative settings is nested systems, or how systems at different levels are connected to each other. Researchers study innovations (and creativity) from at least four different levels; the industry level, inter-organizational level, firm level (including groups), and individual level. When conditions in each of these levels affect behavior across levels, we refer to this interdependence as nested systems or multi-level social networks. Since creativity and innovation activities may exist in firms in different positions in these networks, the interaction of parts of the system may spark innovation elsewhere, which alerts us to the structural properties of systems. People develop contacts with firms and individuals throughout their careers. Some engineers develop social networks in more than one industry, which give them the experience to understand cross-disciplinary knowledge. Through their network contacts they may discover how knowledge and technologies develop in other settings, and these developments open possibilities of combining new resources in novel ways to produce innovations.

Individual creativity in organizational settings

Tushman and Anderson (1986) observe that innovations emerge from embeddedness or the cross-cutting of diverse social networks at the fringes of industries. These innovators are not committed to existing technologies, they discern deficiencies, and are more willing than core firms to take the risk of exploring alternatives; they are not bound by institutional norms of appropriate practice, which often impede creativity. Firms on the fringe of an industry offer people a network position that crosses different domains, which makes it possible to follow developments in fields other than their own. Through career mobility, they are likely to know more people in other organizations. The rate of knowledge development in different fields varies, and conversations and problem solving with other engineers, customers and other professionals that are part of their connections often result in new ideas or creative solutions to problems by combining new resources (Afuah 2000). Thus I suggest Proposition 1.

Proposition 1: People and firms with cross-disciplinary networks on the fringe of an industry are in better positions to create new solution to problems

Some individuals have contacts to people in other organizations that may possess or develop knowledge that can have an impact on their current work. These individuals may have contacts to the academic system and knowledge-producing firms that may come up with new knowledge that can solve problems or question current practices. Their network position gives them insights into how knowledge develops in related or complementary fields. Depending on the timing of developments, a situation may occur when missing pieces of knowledge come together or when someone discovers a novel combination of knowledge components. Thus, I suggest Proposition 2.

Proposition 2: People who are embedded in social networks that span several firms and institutions are more likely to be creative innovators than those lacking such connections

Complex technologies depend on cross-disciplinary cooperation; the innovators have to be positioned in social networks that embed them into nested networks at several levels. However, social processes tend to divert people away from cross-disciplinary networks. The homophily principle influences choice of network partners (McPherson *et al.* 2001). Since people are attracted to those that are similar to them, this may limit people's networks and give them less information (Burt 1992). Likewise, when organizations choose partners, cultural similarity attracts organizations (Pinfield 1973). Since trust and mutual solidarity are the basis of establishing and maintaining both personal and inter-organizational relations, homophily in inter-organizational relations can limit exposure to diverse disciplines. Thus, the most common network structures make it harder to break through inherited paradigms.

In contrast, others whose careers span several organizations with different task domains will meet a diverse set of people. Cross-domain relevant knowledge is likely to be non-redundant information that can enhance creativity (Csikszentmihalyi 1996). Some connections between different firms will not only diversify people's networks, they can also create trust and access to new knowledge frontiers. Inter-organizational networks benefit knowledge transfers between organizations if there are personal relations between employees (Swan *et al.* 1995). Lack of personal networks between organizations impedes such knowledge transfer (Groenewegen 1992). Personal relationships are important not only within an organization but also between organizations. However, Perry-Smith *et al.* (2006) found that it was not optimal for internally central scientists to have many outside ties. Thus, there seems to be a division of roles, some people connect colleagues within an organization and others act as bridges between organizations. Therefore, I suggest Proposition 3.

Proposition 3: People who have career paths through several different firms in different industries are more likely to have interdisciplinary networks than people without such careers

This conjecture rests on an assumption that participating in diverse networks is a necessary but not sufficient condition to take advantage of interdisciplinary networks. To understand what other disciplines can offer to solve complex problems, people need to share frames of reference. In solving complex problems, each specialist provides part of the expertise necessary to the total knowledge required. Communications depend on developing a shared frame of reference to understand cross-disciplinary contributions. Engineers need to understand how components developed in another discipline can contribute to solving a problem. To have this overview of what is going on in different fields requires a network containing the necessary expertise.

Professionals communicate and tend to trust each other when they have common denominators (Bouty 2000). Their past interactions help develop similar cognitive representations (Garud and Rappa 1994). Shared frames of reference develop when participants perceive and interpret information in similar ways, are able to cooperate to solve interdisciplinary problems, and develop a common repertoire of communication practices (Orlikowski and Yates 1994). Thus, communications and cooperation in cross-disciplinary projects contribute to domain familiarity of other fields. Social relations produce and maintain intellectual resources. Having a career path that crosses many firms and many projects gives an opportunity for life-long learning and developing domain familiarity and shared frames of reference with other disciplines. Such networks enable technology developers to see implications of progress in knowledge in other fields, and thus creatively join new components into a new architecture to produce radically new technologies. Thus, I suggest Proposition 4.

137

Proposition 4: People participating in cross-disciplinary cooperations and communications are more likely to come up with creative ideas that combine knowledge domains than people without this experience

Two case studies

Interviews and data collection

To illustrate how people take advantage of multi-level nested networks to create radical innovations I present two case studies. The first study shows how networks contributed to the creation of two successful off-shore oil loading and production technologies, and the second shows how some firms succeeded while others failed to produce or adopt workable innovations to control pollution in the paper and pulp industry. The oil technology network consists of one hundred and thirteen individuals from thirty-two firms from nine countries, I use numbers to identify respondents. The paper and pulp network consists of ten focal firms that represent around 80 per cent of the Norwegian paper and pulp output. They participate in a network of 126 firms or institutions from eight countries. I use letter codes to name firms.

Case 1: Oil technologies

The development of the technologies

Two off-shore technologies are stellar examples of developing complex technologies. Submerged Turret Loading (STL) is a technology for uploading oil from a production platform to a tanker. Submerged Turret Production (STP) is a technology for producing oil in a ship directly from the well-head. The concepts for both of these technologies are new and radical, diverging from all conventional oil loading and production technologies available. The STL concept emerged among a group of people working at MCG (Marine Consultants Group). During the planning of oil pipelines from the fields in the North Sea, Statoil and other oil operators decided to start production using buoy loading to tankers at the field while waiting for the design and construction of pipe lines. This process, despite a lot of problems, was so successful that the oil field operators cancelled plans for oil pipelines. MCG works on improving buoy loading. The weather is the most serious problem; high waves and shifting wind directions cause constant stoppages, with dangers of oil spills. Thus, one condition for creative thinking is present: the engineers have a high awareness of a host of problems with current technologies.

Three independent breakthroughs in knowledge occurred prior to and during the development of these innovations. One was the development of computer simulation models for stable position anchoring in high waves in open seas. The research institute Marintek developed these models, building on recent knowledge of wave dynamics. The second breakthrough came when Framo Engineering constructed a rotating connector to seal oil flows at high temperature and pressure. Third, from the field of physics, new knowledge of multiphase flows and pumping solved the problem of pumping oil, gas, water and other fluids through the same risers (flexible pipes connecting the well-head with the pumping unit), and re-injecting gas and seawater to maintain well pressure.

STL is a submerged cone-shaped buoy that is connected to a tanker through a hole in the bottom of the bow of the ship to load oil from a production platform. STL depends on two of the breakthroughs in knowledge: the rotating connector and the anchoring models. The anchoring system is the technologically most advanced part, which must be designed and constructed separately for each location to fit local sea depths, wave patterns and ocean currents.

- The concept for STL comes from 1004.
- The idea is conceived and elaborated together with 1013, who is the more theoretically oriented of the two, 21001 (a Marintek employee), and other engineers working in MCG in 1990.
- 1004 follows the progress in knowledge of wave dynamics through close connections to 21001, keys in the development of anchoring models, and 1013 (the most central person of the group).
- 1004 is also connected to 3012, who from 1983 to 1991 was chief executive officer (CEO) of Framo Engineering that developed the rotating connector around 1990.
- The MCG engineers began working on an STL prototype, which was finished by 1992.
- 1004, MCG and Statoil establish the firm Applied Production Loading (APL)[2] in early 1993 to dedicate the firm to STL.
- Almost half of the employees from MCG followed 1004 and 1013 to join APL.

At the firm level of networks, the developers of STL draw on other firms and research institutions. Most of the APL employees are educated at the University of Science and Technology in Trondheim (NTNU) as marine engineers. 1013 was a faculty member at NTNU before joining MCG in 1990 and, later, APL. Several of his former students participate in the project. The developers also have work-related contacts made through their career paths working or collaborating with other firms on projects in the North Sea.

The second technology is STP, which in addition to the STL technologies depends on multiphase flows and pumping. By maintaining oil well pressure, the process more than doubles the yield of an oil field.[3] Late in 1993, 3012, a Statoil employee, while working with APL on the STL project, gets the idea of combining multiphase pumping with the STL buoy. This would eliminate the need for a production platform. He takes his idea to his colleague and long-time friend, 3005, and together with 1004 and 1013 they develop the concept of STP. It is a modified STL buoy that produces oil directly from the well-head, with risers and communication cables to monitor and govern multiphase pumping. 3012 has a good understanding of Framo Engineering's capabilities. He presents the possibility of developing multiphase pumping units small enough to be placed in a ship connected to a modified STL buoy. Framo Engineering accepts this project, and after working on it during 1994 comes up with a working prototype.

The evolution of the network structures

The oldest relations among this core group of engineers were established before 1970 (some in the early to mid-1960s). Their long careers within the marine-based oil industry endow them with social networks that span all functions across the value chain of offshore oil production. The 23 most central engineers have held a mean number of 5.4 jobs (range 2–12) in 44 firms and institutions. Altogether, 32 firms participate in the development of STL/STP, including 21 of the 44 firms that had employed one or more of these engineers. This demonstrates how the engineers draw on the social networks they have built during their careers. The innovators have direct contacts to organizations that do fundamental research and technology development. They also connect directly to potential users of the technologies. This position enables them to discover new knowledge while it is being developed, and they are close to areas with problems that need a solution. These cross-cutting ties, combined with creative abilities, made it possible to combine and apply new knowledge to radical innovations that solved a host of problems while increasing efficiency and safety.

The ideas that enabled these two radical innovations were conceived and developed in firms that are on the fringe of the oil industry; they belong to a set of firms that supply technology to off-shore oil platforms. This satisfies Proposition 1. During the idea and development phases these engineers interacted with a diverse set of people from several firms representing different disciplines and value chains in off-shore oil production. The originators[4] of the STL and STP buoys were closely linked to institutions and firms that developed the basic knowledge (Proposition 2). These engineers, all of them at that time around 45–52 years old, had developed the networks during their long careers that spanned several firms and institutions covering a variety of disciplines, thus they could connect several levels of networks (Proposition 3). These engineers saw that by combining newly developed knowledge in three areas, they created two totally new concepts for off-loading and producing oil off shore. The timing of knowledge development and the crossing of the networks of these developers, who were all working on improving buoy loading, made it possible for them to see this opportunity to radically change the current technologies. Through their networks they were able to mobilize and communicate across a wide array of disciplines to enable the construction of the buoys (Proposition 4).

Case 2: Pollution control

Technology innovations

By the time we did our network data collection, in 1997–98, the industry had been working on reducing pollution for about 25 years, starting in the early 1970s. By 1990 they had not seen much progress, primarily because of lack of knowledge and strategies for technology development. The mills had negotiated lax pollution standards with the regulatory agency (SFT) that regulates each mill individually. During this long spell of technology development some mills completely changed process technology, converting from chemical pulping to TMP (Thermo Mechanical Pulping) or CTP (Chemical Thermo Pulping) and two firms developed closed chemical processing systems burning waste for energy production. Some firms rely on end-of-pipe cleaning in addition to the other changes; this is a multi-step process involving sedimentation, biological and chemical cleaning. These changes required technological re-orientation, and some mills succeeded while others failed miserably to develop, adopt or run the new technologies.

The development of the networks

At the industry level, the networks are open for all kinds of technological discussions. A mill that runs an experiment constructs small-sized pilot plants to test new technology and compare solutions. Inviting other mills to share results gives all engineers contacts from other mills. Firm-level networks are created through contacts with suppliers, customers, consultants, other paper and pulp mills, research institutes and universities. Most of the contacts also involve personal contacts between specific persons. These open communications and plant visits substitute for cross-firm career mobility in developing social networks.

The differences in pollution levels between the firms range between 0.82 and 19.8 per cent of produced tons of paper or pulp. We divided the networks of the 126 firms into four groups (blocks) based on structural equivalence (Wasserman and Faust 1994). Firms in blocks 1 and 3 have low pollution levels; block 4 firms have very high pollution levels, and block 2 is mixed. Block 1 consists of firms centered around NS. All mills in this group are TMP mills. There are also three R&D organizations in this group. NS has its own R&D unit, NSR that in addition to its own research participates in projects with other mills in the NS system. UNI, in which NS has minority ownership, is also part of the R&D system of the three NS mills. Joint R&D is done at the mills, with people from NSR cooperating with local engineers. Apart from these mills, the block 1 firms are also connected to other small research institutes. The firms in this block have successfully developed new process technologies and sophisticated end-of-pipe cleaning systems.

Block 2, with HUN and HUR, have been less able to solve their pollution problems, and face several serious problems. These two firms are connected to consultants and some public administrative bodies that are used mainly for lobbying purposes. HUN[5] was particularly successful in gaining lax regulations and financial support. Their networks are not directly connected to organizations that develop fundamental knowledge.

Block 3 consists of two sulphate pulp mills (PET and TOF), which confront difficult techno-logical problems in reducing emissions. Their network consists of universities, R&D institutes and machine suppliers that are technology leaders in their fields. They have successfully dealt with the most complex problems of all the mills. Their technology solution, closed processing, is unusual and difficult to construct and run. PET's technology developer is the grand old man in the industry, just passed 70 years by the time we collected our data, and officially retired. He runs his own firm, using his old offices at PET. Holding a doctoral degree, his career spans faculty positions in the US and Norway. He has been the theses advisor for several people in the industry, including his colleague in TOF. They still cooperate on projects. I asked him why there were so few consulting firms in his network, and his reply reflected his close ties to the academic system: 'Why should we pay consultants for yesterday's knowledge when today's knowledge is free?'

Block 4 firms, two chemical processing mills, SAN and BOR, have quite different tech-nologies. Their connections reflect SAN's efforts to get expertise from BOR related to chemicals. Cross-block ties are dense to many firms in the industry, and to a large network of chemical suppliers and consultants. BOR is a world leader in vanillin production, a by-product made of pollutants from chemical pulping. Both firms in this block pollute more than any other of the firms. SAN tried to run an end-of-pipe system, but it failed miserably, and they were never able to stabilize the processes, despite their ties to block 1 firms that are very successfully running the same cleaning process. However, the block 4 firms, in contrast to block 1, have very few ties to block 3, where most of the fundamental research takes place, which may explain their failure to control pollution. The failure to control pollution led to SAN's demise.

The difference in success in reducing pollution between our ten focal actors shows that networks play a significant role. What counts is to whom the firms have ties. None of these firms are fringe firms in the paper and pulp industry (Proposition 1). The networks of the technology developers follow closely the technologies they are using. However, block 3 is an exception, with connections to most of the institutions that do basic research that are relevant for pollution control. Firms in block 1 participate in networks with R&D firms and institutes that mainly do applied research. Network ties to consultants are less effective. This study shows the importance of having close relations with institutions developing basic knowledge. Firms in blocks 1 and 3 have more of these ties, including cross-disciplinary ties, than the other two blocks, supporting Propositions 2 and 4. All the successful technology developers had long careers connecting them to several firms and institutions; the youngest was 48 years old, the oldest 70.

Conclusion: the role of networks and careers

Rigid institutional structures curb creativity. As one proceeds through the layers of nested networks, from the core to the periphery, structures become increasingly fragmented. Firms on the fringe of the oil industry created radical innovations. Their knowledge and traditions come from outfitting tankers loading oil from off-shore platforms. Their earliest customers are two newly-established oil companies. Statoil and Norsk Hydro have few traditions and set paradigms for uploading and processing crude oil. On the contrary, Statoil, observing that traditional technologies already had failed in the harsh conditions of the North Sea, participates in many innovations that have revolutionized oil technology. The paper and pulp industry had tried for almost 20 years to control pollution. It took a lot of experimenting before the knowledge base was sufficient to succeed. However, open networks made access to knowledge easy. People and firms participated in experiments looking for progress in knowledge to improve technology.

Firm level relations, the second layer of the nested networks, show that the innovators are well connected to firms and institutions that develop basic knowledge. The central firms in the oil technology development are placed within the nested structures that connect them directly to organizations that break fundamental knowledge barriers. Similarly, in the paper and pulp industry we found two different groups of firms that were also parts of social networks on the research frontier. The firms in block 1 around NS shared technology and helped each other backed by their connections to other research institutes. Block 3 firms were integrated into the university system in Scandinavia and the USA. We found that people who are embedded in social networks that span several firms and research institutions are more likely than people lacking such connections to be creative innovators. The crucial links are to institutions that do basic research. All successful firms had those links; the less successful did not.

At the individual level, we find that people who have a career path going through several different firms or who have participated in R&D in several firms, are more likely to have interdisciplinary networks than people without such careers. The STL/STP originators had central positions in the network, connecting them directly to several diverse firms providing the necessary knowledge and complementary resources. Without these contacts, the innovations may not have been realized. Building social networks over long careers gave the most successful innovators valuable contacts that were willing to participate in the development of radical new ideas.

One thing is having connections to a diverse set of specialized firms and research institutes; another thing is being able to communicate across disciplines and seeing what they can contribute to a project. Having long careers spanning several firms and projects increases the innovators' ability to communicate across disciplines. Despite the complexity of the technologies, the successful development indicates effective communications. Interactions in social networks are necessary for creative processes. Their long careers and diversified networks made them able to understand how other disciplines could contribute to problem solving. The less successful innovators lacked these relations and were not able to take advantage of all available knowledge.

These two case studies show how communications in social networks expose people to new knowledge that enables them to create radical concepts and transform them into workable technologies. The oil industry case highlights the role of timing, which can explain why several firms rarely come up with more than one radical innovation. The central innovators had a combination of long careers and multi-disciplinary networks that at the time of knowledge breakthroughs intersected all the relevant firms and institutions to combine new knowledge to create radical technologies. The paper and pulp firms had struggled over decades to invent technologies, and some firms failed in making workable technologies. Their networks differed from the successful firms in lacking the connections to universities and research institutes creating fundamental knowledge that enable radical changes in technology.

Most research takes for granted that young people are the most creative. These cases show that creativity was only feasible after a lifetime of building networks. These innovations needed complex, interdisciplinary knowledge. Only long careers can establish the interdisciplinary and inter-organizational networks that can produce complex technologies. This combinative ability is a kind of creativity that comes with age. By focusing mainly on individuals, our field over-looks the wider social milieu that infuse mature persons with the ability to create and take advantage of long careers building social networks and learning how other disciplines can contribute to complex problem solving. These opportunities depend on the intersection of networks and timing of knowledge breakthroughs.

Notes

1 Architecture refers to how components are connected to each other.
2 See http://www.apl.no/. Based on the STL/STP concepts, APL has now a wide range of similar technologies for more benevolent seas than the North Sea.
3 Conventional technologies extract 15–25 per cent of the resources, while multiphase pumping extracts 50–70 per cent. Engineers in the North Sea are now aiming at levels beyond 70 per cent.
4 1004 and 1013 later moved from APL and founded a new firm to create another family of radical technologies for the oil industry, http://www.sevanmarine.com.
5 This firm later declared bankruptcy.

References

Afuah, A. (2000). How much do your competitors' capabilities matter in the face of technological change? *Strategic Management Journal, 20*(3), 397–404.

Amabile, T. M. (1988). A model of creativity and innovation in organizations. *Research in Organizational Behavior, 10*, 123–167.

Amabile, T. M. (1996). *Creativity in context.* Boulder, CO: Westview.

Amabile, T. M., Conti, R., Coon, H., Lazenby, J. and Herron, M. (1996). Assessing the work environment for creativity. *Academy of Management Journal, 39*(5), 1154–1184.

Amabile, T. M., Hadley, C. N. and Kramer, S. J. (2002). Creativity under the gun. *Harvard Business Review, 80*, 52–61.

Andrews, F. M. and Farris, G. F. (1972). Time pressure and performance among scientists and engineers: a five-year panel study. *Organizational Behavior and Human Decision Processes, 8*, 185–200.

Bouty, I. (2000). Interpersonal and interaction influences on informal resource exchanges between R&D researchers across organizational boundaries. *Academy of Management Journal, 43*(1), 50–65.

Burt, R. S. (1992). *Structural holes: the social structure of competition.* Cambridge, MA: Harvard University Press.

Collins, M. A. and Amabile, T. M. (1999). Motivation and creativity. In R. J. Sternberg (ed.), *Handbook of creativity* (pp. 297–312). Cambridge: Cambridge University Press.

Csikszentmihalyi, M. (1996). *Creativity: flow and the psychology of discovery and invention.* New York: Harper Collins.

Csikszentmihalyi, M. (1999). Implications of a systems perspective for the study of creativity. In R. J. Sternberg (ed.), *Handbook of creativity* (pp. 313–338). Cambridge: Cambridge University Press.

Erens, F., Stoffelen, R., van de Ven, R. and Wildeman, L. (1996). Alliance and networks: the next generation. Paper presented at the Proceedings of the 6th International Forum on Technology Management.

Gabbay, S. M. and Leenders, R. T. A. J. (1999). CSC: the structure of advantage and disadvantage. In R. T. A. J. Leenders and S. M. Gabbay (eds), *Corporate social capital and liability* (pp. 1–14). Boston: Kluwer Academic Press.

Garud, R. and Rappa, M. A. (1994). A socio-cognitive model of technology evolution: the case of cochlear implants. *Organization Science, 5*(3), 344–362.

Groenewegen, P. (1992). Stimulating 'hot technologies:' interorganizational networks in Dutch ceramic research. *R&D Management, 22*, 293–305.

Guilford, J. P. (1950). Creativity. *American Psychologist, 5*, 444–454.

Henderson, R. M. and Clark, K. B. (1990). Architectural innovation: the reconfiguration of existing product technologies and the failure of existing firms. *Administrative Science Quarterly, 35*(1), 9–30.

Kanter, R. M. (1983). *The change masters: innovation for productivity in American corporations.* New York: Simon and Schuster.

Kanter, R. M. (1988). When a thousand flowers bloom: structural, collective, and social conditions for innovation in organization. *Research in Organizational Behavior, 10*, 169–211.

March, J. G. (1991). Exploration and exploitation in organizational learning. *Organization Science, 2*(1), 71–87.

McPherson, J. M., Smith-Lovin, L. and Cook, J. M. (2001). Birds of a feather: homophily in social networks. *Annual Review of Sociology, 27*, 107–120.

Mumford, M. D. (2003). Where have we been, where are we going? Taking stock in creativity research. *Creativity Research Journal, 15*(2 and 3), 107–120.

Niosi, J. (2003). Alliances are not enough: explaining rapid growth in biotechnology firms. *Research Policy, 32*, 737–750.

Omta, O. and Rossum, W. v. (1999). The management of social capital in R&D collaborations. In R. T. A. J. Leenders and S. M. Gabbay (eds), *Corporate social capital and liability* (pp. 356–376). Boston, MA: Kluwer Academic Publishers.

Orlikowski, W. J. and Yates, J. A. (1994). Genre repertoire: the structuring of communicative practices in organizations. *Administrative Science Quarterley, 39*, 541–574.

Perlow, L. A. (1999). The time frame: toward a sociology of work time. *Administrative Science Quarterley, 44*(1), 57–81.

Perry-Smith, J. E. (2006). Social yet creative: the role of social relationships in facilitating individual creativity. *Academy of Management Journal, 49*(1), 85–101.

Perry-Smith, J. E. and Shalley, C. E. (2003). The social side of creativity: a static and dynamic social network perspective. *Academy of Management Review, 28*(1), 89–106.

Pinfield, L. (1973). Socio-cultural factors and interorganizational relations. *Academy of Management Best Paper Proceedings, August*, 100–106.

Pinkus, R. L. B., Shuman, L. J., Hummon, N. P. and Wolfe, H. (1997). *Engineering ethics: balancing cost, schedule, risk – lessons learned from the Space Shuttle.* Cambridge: Cambridge University Press.

Powell, W. W., Koput, K. W., Smith-Doerr, L. and Owen-Smith, J. (1999). Network position and firm performance: organizational returns to collaboration. In S. Andrews and D. Knoke (eds), *Research in the sociology of organizations, Vol. 16* (pp. 129–159). Greenwich, CT: JAI Press.

Redmond, M. R., Mumford, M. D. and Teach, R. J. (1993). Putting creativity to work: leader influences on subordinate creativity. *Organizational Behavior and Human Decision Processes, 55*, 120–151.

Runco, M. A. (ed.) (1994). *Problem finding, problem solving, and creativity.* Norwood, NJ: Ablex Publishing Corporation.

Runco, M. A., Plucker, J. A. and Lim, W. (2001). Development and psychometric integrity of a measure of ideational behavior. *Creativity Research Journal, 13*(3 and 4), 385–391.

Salter, A. J. and Gann, D. M. (2003). Sources of ideas for innovation in engineering design. *Research Policy, 32*(8), 1309–1324.

Shalley, C. E., Zhou, J. and Oldham, G. R. (2004). The effects of personal and contextual characteristics on creativity: where should we go from here? *Journal of Management, 30*(6), 933–958.

Swan, J., Newell, S. and Robertson, M. (1995). The diffusion of knowledge and the role of cognitions in technology design. *Management Research News*, *18*(10 and 11), 30–41.

Tushman, M. L. and Anderson, P. C. (1986). Technological discontinuities and organizational environments. *Administrative Science Quarterly*, *31*(3), 439–465.

Vincent, A. S., Decker, B. P. and Mumford, M. D. (2002). Divergent thinking, intelligence, and expertise: a test of alternative models. *Creativity Research Journal*, *14*(2), 163–178.

Wasserman, S. and Faust, K. (1994). *Social network analysis: methods and applications*. Cambridge, MA: Cambridge University Press.

Weisberg, R. W. (1999). Creativity and knowledge: a challenge to theories. In R. J. Sternberg (ed.), *Handbook of creativity* (pp. 226–250). Cambridge: Cambridge University Press.

Woodman, R. W. and Schoenfeldt, L. F. (1990). An interactionist model of creative behavior. *Journal of Creative Behavior*, *24*, 279–290.

Woodman, R. W., Sawyer, J. E. and Griffin, R. W. (1993). Toward a theory of organizational creativity. *Academy of Management Review*, *18*(2), 293–321.

Yeh, Y.-C. (2004). The interactive influences of three ecological systems on R&D employees' technological creativity. *Creativity Research Journal*, *16*(1), 11–25.

Part 4

Creativity and knowledge

Theme 4 Knowledge management

13

Knowledge management and the management of creativity

Geir Kaufmann and Mark A. Runco

Knowledge management and the management of creativity: the new emperor?

During the two recent decades of management research we have seen an almost explosive development in interest in the concept of knowledge and the practical issues of how to manage the acquisition, storing, use and creation of knowledge. The concept of knowledge management has become the leading currency in the field of management theory and the new kid on the block in management practice. Such a development certainly is congenial to the notion of a knowledge society, which has supplanted the traditional manual labour-based industrial society in developed countries. The knowledge capital of a firm has replaced financial capital as its most important asset and has become the new feedstock of competitive advantage (e.g. Osterloh 2007). This development is often described in revolutionary terms. Nevertheless, some basic critical comments are in order.

An emperor without clothes?

Some critics worry that the new perspective on knowledge has no grounding in reality. After all, knowledge, broadly conceived as both procedural and declarative, has always been the core constituent of any job, and highly qualified professional skills and advanced forms of job knowledge certainly are not commodities that were invented during the last two decades. This reminder may serve as an effective inoculation against premature and even feverish overstatements of a development with a history perhaps as old as work itself.

Yet tempering the most wide-reaching claims of the revolutionary avant garde of the knowledge management crowd runs the risk of moving to the other extreme. More specifically, it may slide into a dangerous understatement of the tilting of balance that clearly is in progress in the modern economy and workplace. In neo-classical economics, workers are easily substitutable and replaceable. When workers are gone, given the minimal training required, replacements can easily be found. This is not the case in a knowledge-based economy. The knowledge it takes to do a job is now, more often than not, extensive, complex, abstract and creative. Often it requires substantial education and professional training, as well as considerable practical experience. There are frequent instances where employees have more advanced operational job knowledge than their managers. This leads directly to the question, 'how do you supervise employees that are more competent to do the job then you are yourself?'

Significantly, the relevant knowledge is often to a large degree subjective and contextually bound. It is based on *tacit knowledge*. Tacit knowledge may be very sophisticated, operational and effective, but resides in a knowledge repository that is difficult, or even impossible, to consciously access, and is therefore difficult or impossible to articulate and explain to another person. We may think of a stocktrader who is very successful but may not be capable of articulating much, either to him or herself, or to another less successful stocktrader, in regards to the kind of insightful knowledge on which the superior performance is grounded. Compounding this problem is the finding in cognitive psychology (Nisbett and Ross 1980), namely that when some introspection is described by the creative owner of the insightful knowledge, most of what is said often boils down to rationalization and does not reveal the true knowledge source of the superior performance. It turns out to be a fabricated story that the narrator truly believes, but that may be largely irrelevant to the true source of knowledge that mysteriously resides in a hidden layer of knowledge, deep down in the mind. There are several reasons to be leery of knowledge as a purely objective commodity.

Knowledge as a means and knowledge as a goal

To a certain degree, knowledge has always been at the root of the requisite skills for a job. But knowledge may take simple and complex forms. It can be concrete and manual or abstract and intellectual. The first category may be termed routine-procedural knowledge, whereas the latter may be classified as declarative-generative knowledge. There is a natural, evolutionary progression here.

The automatization of knowledge and skills by way of tools and technologies has a very long history. With the invention of information technology, the process of delegating routine procedural jobs to automatons in the widest sense has exponentially increased. Moreover, ever more sophisticated forms of artificial intelligence are invading the arena of natural intelligence and are replacing even fairly complex intellectual job operations. Faculty at universities may realistically dream of a future when large segments of the administrative bureaucracy that are now stifling creative activities with their invasive procedures are minimal. For example, the time may soon be ripe for replacing human agents in the study administration at colleges and universities with sophisticated, intelligent systems to do the highly complex logistics of assigning classroom and times to courses. It is very likely that we will see intelligent systems that can do a large part of the grading of essay exam papers on complex subject matters. This may have the positive effect of leaving more time for creative research activities among faculty.

Such considerations lead us naturally into the following general proposition: if a tilting point in the favour of generative-declarative knowledge as the most valuable asset has not been reached yet, it will eventually be reached. The apex of generative-declarative knowledge is creative knowledge, in the sense of knowledge creation. And now we can see the full force of the increasing relevance of creativity in the general enterprise of knowledge management.

The inevitable conclusion is as follows. The kind of problem solving, and the knowledge, declarative and procedural, that go with this form of problem solving and that forms the substance of the typical job in the knowledge-based economy is highly sophisticated, and evolving more and more towards the generative-creative end of the problem-solving continuum along the task novelty dimension. In principle, human job activities have to exceed the operative and declarative knowledge and performance capabilities of an intelligent automaton. According to the new credo, the more creative and intelligent juice there is in the required knowledge and skill it takes to do a good job, the more valuable the knowledge capital asset. This is the primary source of the competitive advantage of a firm in the knowledge economy.

Florida (2002) may indeed be vindicated on his core thesis that the knowledge economy may soon be more aptly described as creative economy, and that the emerging new labour class in modern societies is the creative class. This is the ever-increasing group of people who are primarily working on creating new content and new forms as their core job obligation. More and more work requires not only the intelligent use of knowledge, in the sense of rule-based application of existing knowledge to new situations, but also the capability to create new knowledge of an innovative kind (e.g. Kaufmann 2004). As pointed out by Florida (2002), to an increasing degree, society relies on individuality, originality and creativity in its products and services. In fact, the average household in a modern society now spends more of their budget on new products than on the ordinary survival goods and services that satisfy our basic material needs. We no longer go to the hairdresser, stylist or barber simply to cut our too long hair shorter. Rather, we are in for a treat that provides a novel expression of our individual self-image.

Knowledge as means and as goal

It is important to observe that the required knowledge in question may well be of the instrumental sort, and the goal may be to produce a material object, such as a Honda scooter or widget. When talking about knowledge asset as a competitive advantage in this context, we are talking about a tipping point when the knowledge involved in producing such an object is of a highly advanced form, not accessible to emulation by artificial intelligence systems (e.g. Nonaka and Ichijo 2007). Adding to the complexity of the required knowledge is the point that much important knowledge is not a pure individual entity, ultimately residing in a brain of an individual person. Some is synergetic knowledge generated by teams and organizational arrangements that may transcend the sum of the individual knowledge that enter into this dynamic environment.

Another significant knowledge asset exists when advanced knowledge is not only on the means side, but also is on the goal side of the production. Here, knowledge produces new knowledge, such as in the case of the development of new software, and new scientific theories.

Have all critics been silenced?

All of these arguments are logical, yet sceptics may not be convinced of such developments. Most are continuous and do not represent anything as grandiose as a Kuhnian paradigm shift in modern economics and management theory and practice. Scepticism certainly resides in both the consultant and academic community. This is how it should be. After all, it would not be the first time that a call to arms for a new revolution has turned out to be premature. Still, the conclusion is not that the new emperor (generative knowledge as salient commodity) has no clothes after all, and that false prophets fooled us into embracing what turned out to be a hype that contained no new academic or practical-professional calories.

To avoid plunging into a premature discussion of the role of creativity in knowledge management, then the major complaints of remaining critics should be carefully considered. These may be captured in four slogan-like complaints, as follows.

It is 'nothing else than'

The first criticism that pops up anytime something new is offered is the deafening shout of 'it is nothing else than'. This shout has indeed been loudly heard in the knowledge management community. The claim has been made, as pointed out recently by Grossman (2007), that knowledge management is nothing but repacked information technology in the form of information management systems. True, the first decade of KM leaned heavily on information technology, and the focus was to a large extent on stockpiling knowledge that had been gained in the firm. The objective was to avoid losing the precious and hard won knowledge if the knowledge owners disappeared. The importance of tacit knowledge was emphasized, and the precious nature of this knowledge was praised. The high market value of this kind of know-ledge is borne out of the difficulty of telling and explaining what you know in this particular currency of knowledge. One of the leading visions formulated was that of making implicit, or tacit, knowledge explicit, by way of codifying, systematizing and storing it in general, schematic or principled forms. In this form it was thought to be accessible for others to share and use. This emphasis on 'canned knowledge' is still present in a significant way. But it does not hold the same sway as in the early stage, and it has drawn criticism because of the limitations and even perplexities involved in this notion. Recently, Schulze and Stabell (2004) argued rather con-vincingly that the putative knowledge asset that existed in its 'hidden' and implicit form might be lost when it is translated into explicit form. Then it becomes information that could easily be copied by competitors. From a psychological vantage point, we may add to this argument by pointing to the very real possibility that when implicit knowledge is turned into explicit knowledge, it is no longer the same kind of flexible, and generative, creative knowledge. Thus, we see that people who are instructed to employ explicit knowledge (verbalizing) in solving creative insight problems do more poorly than those who are encouraged to trust their implicit knowledge, by using more intuitive sort of knowledge, such as imagery (Schooler *et al.* 1993). Thoughts beyond words: when language overshadows insight. *Journal of Experimental Psychology: General*, 12, 166–183.

In its more current version KM seems to be turning into 'softer' approaches, and the emphasis on the aspect of knowledge creation that has always been there (Nonaka 1994) has been strongly augmented (Grossman 2007; Nonaka and Ichijo 2007). Thus the link to creativity and innovation has indeed come more to the foreground in the later development of KM. When the creative aspect of knowledge is subsumed in KM, and when limitations of informa-tion technology with regard to both the study and practice of KM are underscored, it seems that the 'nothing else than' argument becomes a likely candidate for rejection.

It is 'everything and nothing'

Escaping from Scylla may throw you into the jaws of the beast of Charybdis. The opposite side of the coin of the previous argument is this: in accommodating the limitations imposed by a strict, information science (information technology definition of KM), and allowing its domain to stretch much wider into the logical geography, we may place the concept in the opposite corner, which is also open to criticism. Allowing for both 'hard' and 'soft' KM, and so on, raises the question of where the concept starts and ends. More specifically, one might ask what is *not* KM in the domain of information processing. This argument has recently been made by

Mårtensson (2003), who argued that, through the generous adaptation and softening up of the concept to meet the challenges of limitations that have been thrown at it, there is a real danger that the concept of KM may be turned into a sort of conceptual 'Jack of all trades'. This is a point well taken, and is probably closer to the truth than the argument under the first objection above. After all, has anyone ever been in doubt that it is important to create knowledge and to take good care of it, and pass it generously on to your colleagues, so that they can solve their problems without inventing the wheel on their own?

In defense of KM, we may argue that the power of the concept is to see learning, retention, thinking and creativity as being in the same loop, and not regard them as separate, distinct and encapsulated processes, that may at best interact. This argument is stated implicitly in the literature and deserves to be made more explicit and to be discussed and criticized in a more targeted way. It is also quite important to note that in his seminal article, Nonaka (1994) was quite specific in rejecting the standard information-processing paradigm of cognitive science. This is apparent in the humiliating conceptual inability of standard information processing theory to handle innovation as a complete process in the way that it actually occurs in the daily practice of the firm.

The Achilles heel is the more proactive dimension of finding new and interesting problems to solve, rather than being limited to a given 'input' and respond with some sort of 'output'. The argument to this effect has also been made in contemporary cognitive psychology, with specific reference to the importance of problem finding as an activity that goes beyond mere problem solving, and that is most intimately linked to creativity (e.g. Arlin 1975; Csiksentmyhalyi 1990; Kaufmann 2004; Runco 1994; Unsworth 2001). While we do not claim to have been able to make the 'everything and nothing' argument go away altogether, we do think that the concept of KM holds considerable promise to satisfy the delimitation and demarcation criteria that are necessary to for a legitimate scientific concept to abide by.

It is 'a fad'

Certainly, this is another common argument against aspiring candidates for novelty in the scientific and the management arena. 'This is a bug and nuisance right now, but it will go away.' In this particular case of criticism, we have to listen very carefully to the argument. If there is something that we know to be true, it is that business and management are full of examples of such irritating bugs that eventually go away after having sent people astray for all too long, and after having emptied decent but naive pockets for consultancy money that turned out to be as good as thrown out of the window. We all remember how disappointed we were when those wonderful firms praised for their excellence in Peters and Waters' (1982) *In Search of Excellence*, by the next brutal confrontation in time turned out to be the ones that did the worst. In light of this and many other fads, we may therefore be acutely alarmed when Nonaka and Ichijo (2007) admitted that the same happened to the Japanese firms that he praised so highly in his seminal writings, and that inspired his new theory of the knowledge-creating firm.

It is a 'contradiction in terms'

This objection is definitely not a standard objection against a novel concept striving for membership in the scientific family. Nevertheless, it can be made with considerable force. According to Alvesson and Korreman (2001), 'management' and 'knowledge' are 'odd couples'. We might, perhaps, have entertained the viability of such a concept under a notion of the existence of objective knowledge, defined as justified true belief. But according to Alvesson and Korreman, the concept of knowledge does not belong to the positivist, physical world as an object that can be assigned the status of an objective entity over and above our subjective constructions of the world. Recently, Nonaka (e.g. Nonaka and Ichijo 2007) has gone a long way down the same path. According to the post-modern, constructionist philosophy favoured by Alvesson and Korreman (2001: 997), knowledge is 'subjective', 'tacit situational', and 'dynamic'. Furthermore, knowledge is seen, not as a static, enduring object with constant properties, like physical objects, but is 'recreated in the present moment'. From this perspective it does not make much sense to claim that knowledge, in its prototypical sense, is something that can be managed, in the sense of being codified into explicit knowledge, stored and disseminated by way of information technology. At best, we may be able to control knowledge normatively, through prescribed interpretations for good practices. Thus, we may *enable*, rather than 'manage', knowledge creation.

The arguments made by Alvesson and Korreman (2001) are interesting, but they go too far and are also ill founded philosophically. Not even John Locke, the originator of the concept of the blank slate, thought that ideas of knowledge were literal copies of external objective entities. Some interpretative framework was thought to be necessary, even on this extreme empiricist theory of knowledge.

Alternatively, it seems much more reasonable to us to view knowledge on a continuum. Here, subjective and objective knowledge represent the poles of the continuum, where the extremes are boundary conditions and do not exist in pure form, i.e. there is no such thing as either pure subjective or pure objective knowledge, only marginal approximations at the extreme poles, and all kinds of combinations in between. Thus, there may be 'clocks' and 'clouds', and all sorts of combinations in between, so Popper claimed (2002) in his profound discussion on the possibility of objective knowledge. In this light, those emphasizing the subjective side of the continuum offer a one-sided view of the nature of knowledge, with little if any grounding in epistemological philosophy. The alarm bell comes on clearly and loudly when we hear from this camp such slogans as, 'there is no absolute truth'. Then we may legitimately side with Bandura (1976), and wonder how it is possible to entertain such a belief, which in itself is a claim for absolute truth! Coming down to earth, and practical matters of knowledge, we're certain it must be possible for a bakery to take care of a new, creative way of making American apple pie in a controlled, managed way in a distilled form of explicit, codified rule-specified prescriptions.

This is not to say that the argument made by Alvesson and Korreman (2001) is unimportant. Quite the contrary, we think they point to serious limitations in the current concept of knowledge management, particularly in the domain of economic administrative theory, where unrealistic ideals about objectivity and formalizations of knowledge are rampant. If the lesson of Alvesson and Korreman is taken in the right dosage, it may pave the way for new and more enriched understandings of what KM might entail under different conditions. Also, the argument is at its sharpest when it is applied to the knowledge creation side of KM. This is the point where it is appropriate to raise the issue of what role, if any, there is for concepts like 'management of creativity' in this enterprise, and how such a concept might figure in theories and practices of knowledge management.

Can creativity be managed?

The idea that creativity can be managed is firmly entrenched in the literature (Bilton 2007; Florida 2002; Isaksen and Todd 2006), and the practice of training and managing knowledge and skill in the domain of creativity has existed in a formalized way since Alex Osborne published his seminal book on 'applied imagination' (1957). Master degrees in creative studies started out in the 1960s under the visionary leadership of Sidney Parnes (Parnes *et al.* 1977). It may, however, be argued that the kind of creativity that is managed in these programmes represents the very low end of creativity, with its emphasis on superficial, and uncritical idea production. Thus, under the scrutiny of scientific conceptual analysis, the idea of managing creativity in its full flower sense may nevertheless not hold up. It may even turn out to be an oxymoron. Our position here is that there are uses of the concept of management of creativity that are squarely paradoxical and also untenable. There are, however, other uses of the concept of creativity of management that are defensible, and, most importantly, give rise to both scientific inquiry and professional practices that are fruitful and valuable. To explain this view, we turn to the link between creativity and knowledge management.

Where is psychology?

The major disciplinary hub of the scientific study of creativity is certainly psychology. With 'knowledge creation' as the title of their book, it may therefore come as more than a surprise when Nonaka and Ichijo (2007) do not even index the word 'psychology'. The surprise becomes even stronger when we discover that they do not index the concept of 'creativity' either. With few exceptions (e.g. Osterloh 2007), no link is made between the new focus on knowledge creation and research in the well-established scientific study of creativity. Basadur (1994) has also recently addressed this vacuum in the enterprise of knowledge management research. We fully agree with him that this is a serious limitation in the story told by KM researchers so far.

We may wonder if 'knowledge creation' is supposed to be something other than the development of new and valuable ideas, which is the standard definition of creativity. An argument of this kind has apparently yet to be made, either explicitly or implicitly. At the same time, we see that in standard definitions of KM, the field is categorized as multidisciplinary, yet the field of psychology is not included (Alvesson and Korreman 2001; Grossman 2007). The closest we come is the inclusion of cognitive science in the family of KM, but here the focus is on the information systems side of that discipline.

Given the central place of psychology in the study of creativity, we may here be faced with a major shortcoming in both the research programme designed for KM and the putative development of KM as a professional practice.

Nonaka (1994) pointed out that knowledge is something that ultimately dates back to ideas in the individual mind. The emphasis is, however, squarely on structural and functional organizational conditions that may facilitate knowledge creation. We may wonder if the field is in the grip of the traditional, Marxist social science view of creativity as something that is solely borne out of collectives, and that creative ideas in the individual mind are mere epiphenomena that are the real products of underlying collective forces at work. Or we may wonder if the field is so new that its development has not yet reached into psychology. Certainly psychology has much to offer in this endeavour, both at the individual, personal micro-level and at the macro-levels, such as groups and teams, not to speak of the psychology of leadership. We should also point out that psychology has for a considerable time now made significant contributions to our understanding of creativity at the organizational level, particularly with respect to leadership conditions that facilitate and inhibit creativity (Amabile 1996).

Knowledge and process in KM

In discussions most clearly related to creativity as an element in KM, the emphasis is on the problem of how to translate implicit knowledge into explicit knowledge (e.g. Nonaka 1994; Nonaka and Ichijo 2007). This is surely an important part of the enterprise. Few will doubt that having our intuitions come to the explicit foreground is important in creativity. In particular, this is important in the aspect of creativity that Boden (1993) termed 'explorative creativity', where the knowledge in question is immanent in an existing conceptual space, and where the discovery is the implication that has always been there, but had yet to be realized. We may think of wave energy as an example of explorative creativity, in the sense that it is an example of the forceful application of a lens principle to another domain. No new basic idea is created here, but a very imaginative and effective new implication of a known principle has been discovered.

Yet, creativity, or knowledge creation, is not only about making existing (tacit) knowledge explicit. It is also about the creation of entirely new knowledge, where we break the rules intrinsic to an existing conceptual matrix, and make a leap over to a new one. This happened, for instance, when Dick Fosbury invented his new high jumping style by moving in from the back and rolling over in a vertical way with the back of his head first. The rule of the game was changed from 'go in forward' to 'go in backwards'. Fosbury won the Olympic Gold Medal, with his Fosbury Flop, in 1968.

An important part of knowledge creation is not just about making implicit knowledge explicit. And this takes us to the next conceptual step. Rather than focusing on knowledge exclusively in the KM process, we should expand the perspective and focus on the processes at work in creativity. Processes involved in knowledge creation may also be divided into explicit and implicit. A major consensus in the creativity literature would emphasize the importance of implicit processes in this respect. It would view new knowledge as something that arises from implicit processes such as incubation and intuition. Such processes can now be understood in more sophisticated ways as examples of spreading activation in knowledge networks (Smith *et al.* 1995). Then the chances are that we may be able to use the remote associations that are often seen to lie at the heart of creative cognition (Mednick 1962; Milgram and Rabkin 1980).

Where is the individual?

According to Nonaka (1994: 15), 'ideas are formed in the minds of individuals'. However, he immediately adds the following caveat: 'interaction between individuals typically plays a critical role in developing these ideas'. It is not entirely clear what is involved in this claim. If the argument is made that ideas can only be 'half-baked' in the individual mind, and that the full, juicy bread of knowledge requires that other people assist in fully making clear and developing these ideas, then we would strongly disagree. Here we can point to empirical evidence to the effect that, very often, when great breakthrough ideas are made, the individual has an opportunity for isolation. This is sometimes interpreted as a sign that collective forces are, indeed, often detrimental to creativity, since creativity is essentially about 'going against the crowd' (Sternberg and Lubart 1995). It is true that Nonaka more or less explicitly delimits the kind of knowledge in question that is relevant here to *organizational* knowledge. Even then, we would argue that it is neither necessary, nor correct nor fruitful, to exclude the micro-level as such for independent scrutiny as a relevant determinant in the total equation of organizational knowledge (e.g. Elster 2007). Within organizational science, the argument is often made that the macro-level is an autonomous level, and not simply an additive aggregation of individuals.

Groups and collectives have their own properties and dynamics, due to the way they are organized (e.g. Alvesson and Korreman 2001; Grossman 2007). Hence, macro-levels have emergent properties that cannot be reduced to their constituent individual micro-elements. Even if we grant that this argument is fundamentally sound, it does not follow that hereby the micro-level is irrelevant! Logically, this is a totally non-sequitur argument. Obliterating the relevance of the micro-level is a fundamental mistake in the current conceptualizations of knowledge management. In particular, this move cuts out all the blood supply that is so vital in terms of the extensive knowledge of fifty years of research on the psychology of creativity. It also alienates the knowledge management enterprise from a large portion of the results of fifty years of highly sophisticated research in the field of cognitive psychology. Indeed, many of the core concepts in the knowledge management field, like tacit knowledge, have been far better developed in cognitive psychological research under concepts like implicit cognition.

We do, of course, agree that a broader scope is needed, and that we need to consider the dynamics in teams, the fertile dialogues that go on in organizations on a regular basis, as well as structural organizational arrangements that may facilitate the dynamic knowledge creation process. In these pursuits we must also take care not to forget the interactions among levels that sometimes may be of crucial importance. Much evidence in psychology points to the interesting and practically important conclusion that creative individuals are particularly context sensitive when it comes to bringing their talents to fruition. This means both that if creative individuals are nurtured in the right way through culture, climate and leadership, they respond generously by delivering handsome and creative ideational output in return. But this is a double-edged sword. If, on the contrary, creative individuals are met with such negative organizational climate factors such as lack of autonomy and held strictly under the sway of bureaucratic, administrative rules and regulations, and possibly also by worries of a shaky tenure situation, they respond adversely. They may even end up placing themselves in the very bottom of the creativity and productivity distribution among their organizational colleagues (Andrews 1975; Oldham and Cummings 1996; Runco 1994). The first shall become the last. Maybe we could call this 'the revenge of creativity'.

Implications and conclusions

The idea that knowledge is created and that innovation will be best served by enabling rather than managing leads directly to several practical implications. First is that micro-management is likely to be one of the worst things for innovative thinking. Innovative thinking is likely if individuals within a firm know that creative ideas are valued and if they know that they are encouraged in independent and original thinking. Basadur (1994) described various techniques used in Japanese firms for explicitly valuing original thinking, and in fact translated the concept of 'golden eggs', which is apparently often used to describe new ideas in Japanese firms. Employees know that ideas are golden.

The idea that knowledge is recreated in each moment parallels the Piagetian idea of understanding. For Piaget (1976), 'to understand is to create'. There again, the implication is to allow individuals to think for themselves in an original fashion. They possess the potential to do so and it is more a matter of getting out of their way than teaching them how. Runco (2003, 2004) applied this logic to creative work and suggested that the most important targets when encouraging creative thinking are actually extra-cognitive. They are *self-confidence* and *ego-strength*. These are important because too often social settings pressure individuals in the direction of conventional thinking. Even though each person has the potential for original and innovative thought, social pressures imply that it is better to conform. If individuals have ego-strength, however, they are willing to share their original ideas, even if they are unconventional and innovative. Note that this perspective describes implicit processes within a social setting.

Rubenson and Runco (1995) also recognized the implicit pressures of organizations and specifically cautioned against large work teams and brainstorming groups. These tend to maximize the stigma of being different (i.e. innovative) and maximize the risk involved with original thinking. Rubenson and Runco (ibid.) used psycho-economic logic to describe how innovation is most likely in firms and groups when (a) costs are minimal and (b) benefits are maximal (see also Rubenson and Runco 1992). The 'benefit' of innovative thinking is much like the idea of value, just described. If an organization clearly values innovative and independent ideation, the benefits will be clear to individuals within that firm. And here again, it is vital to allow and enable creative thinking. To that end, costs must be minimal. Large work teams are inappropriate because the individual producing an original idea has more at risk; more people may question the new idea.

This perspective also suggests that innovative thinking is most likely when various perspectives are found within the teams and organization. Rubenson and Runco (1995) looked specifically at teams and brainstorming groups, but the logic applies more generally to the entire organization. If heterogeneity of backgrounds, interests and experiences is maintained, it is easier to appreciate differences, including those inherent in new ideas. In fact, implicit in the organization which values diversity and heterogeneity is that different perspectives each have value. In a sense, this is the social analogue of the cognitive process that underlies ideational flexibility. Ideational flexibility is an important part of divergent thinking and is apparent when problems are approached from diverse perspectives. An individual is unlikely to be innovative if he or she sticks with the same approach or conceptual path; originality is more likely if different paths are tested. Individuals must avoid conceptual ruts (Adams 1986). The same holds true for groups and teams, which means that the process is more likely in diverse organizations, both because different perspectives will exist and because there will no doubt be an implicit message that diversity is valuable. If diversity is valuable, individuals are most likely to share their own original ideas, even if these ideas are unique and different. Conformity and conventionality are unlikely, and creative and innovative thinking are probable.

References

Adams, J. (1986). *Conceptual blockbusting*. New York: Norton.

Alvesson, M. and Korreman, D. (2001) Odd couple: Making sense of the curious concept of knowledge management. *Journal of Management Studies*, 38, 995–1018.

Amabile, T. (1996). *Context of creativity*. Boulder, CO: Westview Press.

Andrews, F.M. (1975). Social and psychological factors which influence the creative process, in I. K. Taylor and J. W. Getzels (eds), *Perspectives in creativity* (pp. 117–145). Chicago, IL: Aldine.

Arlin, P.K. (1975). Cognitive development in adulthood: A fifth stage? *Developmental Psychology*, 11, 602–606.

Bandura, A. (1976) *Social learning theory*. Englewood Cliffs, NJ: Prentice Hall.

Basadur, M. (1994). Managing the creative process, in M. A. Runco (ed.), *Problem finding, problem solving and creativity*. Norwood, NJ: Ablex.

Bilton, C. (2007). *Management and creativity*. Oxford: Blackwell.

Boden, M. (1993). *The creative mind: Myths and mechanisms*. New York: Routledge.

Csikszentmihályi, M. (1990). The domain of creativity, in M. A. Runco and R. S. Albert (eds), *Theories of creativity* (pp. 190–212). Newbury Park, CA: Sage.

Elster, J. (2007). *Explaining social behavior*. New York: Cambridge University Press.

Florida, R. (2002). *The rise of the creative class: And how it's transforming work, leisure, community an everyday life*. New York: Basic Books.

Grossman, M. (2007). The emerging academic discipline of knowledge management. *Journal of Information Systems Education*, 18, 1–9.

Isaksen, S.G. and Todd, J. (2006). *Meeting the innovation challenge*. Chichester: Wiley.

Kaufmann, G. (2004). Two kinds of creativity – but which ones? *Creativity and Innovation Management*, 13, 54–164.

Mårtensson, M. (2003). A critical review of knowledge management as a management tool. *Journal of Knowledge Management*, 4 204–216.

Mednick, S.A. (1962). The associative basis of the creative process. *Psychological Review*, 69, 220–232.

Milgram, R.M. and Rabkin, L. (1980). Developmental test of Mednick's associative hierarchies of original thinking. *Developmental Psychology*, 16, 157–158.

Nisbett, R. and Ross, L. (1980) *Human inference: Strategies and shortcomings of social judgment*. Englewood Cliffs, NJ: Prentice Hall.

Nonaka, I. (1994). A dynamic theory of knowledge creation. *Organization Science*, 5, 14–37.

Nonaka, I. and Ichijo, K. (2007). *Knowledge creation and management: New challenges for management*. Oxford: Oxford University Press.

Oldham, G.B. and Cummings, A. (1996). Employee creativity: Personal and contextual studies. *Academy of Management Journal*, 39, 607–634.

Osborne, A.A. (1957) *Applied imagination*. New York: Scribner.

Osterloh, M. (2007). Human resource management and knowledge creation. In I. Nonaka and K. Ichijo (eds), *Knowledge creation and management: New challenges for management* (pp.158–177). Oxford: Oxford University Press.

Parnes, S.J., Noller, R.B. and Biondi, A.M. (1977). *Guide to creative action*. New York: Scribner.

Peters, T.J. and Waters, R.H. (1982). *In search of excellence*. New York: Harper Business Essentials.

Piaget, J. (1976). *To understand is to invent*. New York: Penguin.

Popper, K. (2002) *The logic of scientific discovery*. New York: Routledge.

Rubenson, D.L. and Runco, M.A. (1992). The psychoeconomic approach to creativity. *New Ideas in Psychology*, 10, 131–147.

Rubenson, D.L. and Runco, M.A. (1995). The psychoeconomic view of creative work in groups and organisations. *Creativity and Innovation Management*, 4, 232–241.

Runco, M.A. (1994). *Problem finding, problem solving and creativity*. Norwood, NJ: Ablex.

Runco, M.A. (2003). Education for creative potential. *Scandinavian Journal of Education*, 47, 317–324.

Runco, M.A. (2004). Everyone is creative, in R. J. Sternberg, E. L. Grigorenko and J. L. Singer (eds), *Creativity: From potential to realization* (pp. 21–30). Washington, DC: American Psychological Association.

Smith, S.M., Ward, T.B. and Finke, R.A. (1995). *The creative cognition approach*. Cambridge: MIT Press.

Schooler, J.W., Ohlsson, S. and Brooks, K. (1993). Thoughts beyond words: When language overshadows insight. *Journal of Experimental Psychology: General*, 12, 166–183.

Schultze, U. and Stabell, C. (2004). Knowing what you don't know? Discourses and contradictions in knowledge management research. *Journal of Knowledge Management and Research*, 41, 350–373.

Sternberg, R. J. and Lubart, T. I. (1995). *Defying the crowd*. New York: Free Press.

Underwood, G. (1986). *Implicit cognition*. Oxford: Oxford University Press.

Unsworth, K. (2001). Unpacking creativity. *Academy of Management Review*, 26, 289–297.

14

Creating organizational knowledge dialogically: an outline of a theory

Haridimos Tsoukas

Introduction

Despite several insightful studies on how new knowledge is created in organizations, there is still no satisfactory answer to the question, 'what are the generative mechanisms through which new organizational knowledge is created?' The purpose of this chapter is to answer this question by drawing on the work of phenomenological philosophers such as Dreyfus and Taylor, literary theorists such as Bakhtin, and sociocultural psychologists such as Mead, Shotter and Hermans. Building on the concept of 'interaction', which previous studies of organizational knowledge have identified to be the bedrock for knowledge creation, the chapter argues that new knowledge comes from the exercise of judgment – the individual ability to draw new distinctions concerning a task at hand, typically in the context of a group. New distinctions may be developed through organizational members engaging in three kinds of dialogical (or quasi-dialogical) relationships: with real others, with imaginal others and with artifacts. Each dialogical relationship is conceptualized and illustrated. The overall dialogical approach adopted here is illustrated by drawing on the work of Donald Schön.

Despite the proliferation of empirical studies concerning the creation of new knowledge in organizations (Calhoun and Starbuck 2003; Leonard and Sensiper 1998; Obstfeld 2002; Robertson et al. 2003; von Krogh et al. 2000), we do not yet have a general theoretical account of how new organizational knowledge (NOK) is created. Scholars who have studied NOK have focused, quite rightly, on the social interaction through which new knowledge is generated, but have not specified what is in interaction that gives rise to NOK, nor what particular forms interaction takes (Cook and Brown 1999; Carlile 2002, 2004; Hargadon and Fanelli 2002; Orlikowski 2002; Tsoukas 2003). A more process-oriented account is required that will explicate, in general terms, how NOK is created through interaction.

The most detailed model of knowledge creation in organizations has been suggested by Nonaka and his associates, and deserves closer examination. In their seminal book *The Knowledge-creating Company*, Nonaka and Takeuchi (1995: 62) argued that 'knowledge is created through the interaction between tacit and explicit knowledge', which takes the form of four types of knowledge conversion (socialization, externalization, combination and internalization). In subsequent extensions to their model, Nonaka and his associates have retained the centrality of 'knowledge conversion' or, what they have later called, 'the dynamic interaction between subjectivity and objectivity' (Nonaka and Toyama 2005: 419), as the main driving force for knowledge creation (Nonaka *et al.* 2001).

Even leaving aside whether tacit knowledge should be seen as 'convertible' to explicit knowledge, a claim that has been disputed by several researchers (Brown and Duguid 2001: 203–4; Cook and Brown 1999: 394; Orlikowski 2002: 250–1; Tsoukas 1996: 14, 2003: 422–424), the nature of 'interaction' between tacit and explicit knowledge, or between subjectivity and objectivity, has not been sufficiently theorized in the work of Nonaka and his associates. How does such interaction take place and what is involved in it? How does human agency create new knowledge?

The importance of these questions is shown in an example Nonaka and Takeuchi use to illustrate their model, in which they describe the product-development process of Matsushita's Home Bakery, the first fully-automated machine for home use. According to the authors, the knowledge-creation process consisted of three cycles. First a prototype was created. Second, to improve the prototype, a software developer took an apprenticeship with a master baker at a major Japanese hotel in order to learn first-hand how to knead bread. A team of engineers was also brought to the hotel to experience the kneading and baking of bread. Following several discussions and a lot of experimentation, the prototype was significantly improved. Finally, the commercialization team further improved the prototype and made it a commercially viable product (Nonaka and Takeuchi 1995: 103–106).

The second cycle is the most important, since it is there where the breakthrough occurred. Nonaka and Takeuchi (ibid.: 104–5) note the tacit knowledge the software developer picked up through her apprenticeship, as well as the several discussions the members of the development team (the software developer and the engineers) had and their trial-and-error efforts to improve the prototype. What, however, the authors have left out is a theoretical account of what was involved in the interactions they described: the interactions members of the development team had among themselves and with the prototype. How, for example, did the software developer come up with the concept of 'twisting stretch' in order to describe her experience of kneading, a concept that turned out to be of pivotal importance to improving the prototype? How did conversations among the members of the development team enable them to make new distinctions leading to improving the prototype? Why the need for a prototype, in the first place?

To answer such questions a fine-grained theoretical account is needed that will specify the mechanisms through which the improved prototype – hence, new knowledge – emerged. Such an account will have to address some key theoretical issues, such as the link between human experience and its articulation, and the dynamic of creative action. In other words, while Nonaka and his associates have made a very important first step toward developing a general theoretical framework for explaining knowledge creation, we need to take it further by conceptualizing the mechanisms that underlie knowledge creation.

In this chapter I seek to build on the insights offered by the preceding researchers and suggest a general theoretical framework of knowledge creation in organizations. The approach adopted here is a *dialogical* one: this approach considers dialogicality an inherent feature of human thought and communication in general, and the most important characteristic of interaction in particular (Bakhtin 1981; Holquist 2002; Shotter 1997). The essence of dialogicality is sensitivity to otherness; the realization that the categories we think and communicate with are no mere individual creations but dialogically constituted through communication with others.

The core of my argument is as follows. New knowledge in organizations stems from the exercise of human judgment – from the individual ability to draw new distinctions concerning a task at hand, typically in the context of a team. The drawing of new distinctions is made possible through organizational members engaging in three kinds of dialogical (or quasi-dialogical) relationships: with real others, with imaginal others (especially the generalized other), and with artifacts. Dialogicality is at the heart of interaction and is the basis for making new distinctions and, hence, developing new knowledge.

The chapter is structured as follows. In the next section it is described how the making of new distinctions by actors is made possible through the dialogical structure of thinking. Following this, the concept of dialogue is explained and three forms of dialogical exchanges that are conducive to the emergence of new distinctions are described and illustrated. The creation of NOK, namely actors' ability to make new distinctions, is illustrated in a separate section by drawing on the work of Donald Schön. A summary of the argument, along with a broader discussion and suggestions for further research are included in the final section.

Dialogicality and the making of new distinctions

According to Bell (1999: lxi–lxiv), what differentiates 'knowledge' from 'information' and 'data' is the maximal exercise of human judgment. An individual is knowledgeable, notes Bell, by the extent to which she has the capacity to exercise judgment, which is either based on an appreciation of context or is derived from theory, or both (see also Tsoukas and Vladimirou 2001). What does the capacity to exercise judgment amount to? Drawing on Dewey (1934), Bell (1999: lxiv) argues that judgment involves the individual ability to draw new distinctions concerning a task. In his words: 'judgment arises from the self-conscious use of the prefix *re*: the desire to *re*-order, to *re*-arrange, to *re*-design what one knows and thus create new angles of vision or new knowledge for scientific or aesthetic purposes.'

This point is echoed by several studies of practitioners (be they nurses, doctors, fire fighters, managers, etc.) in natural work settings, which emphasize how reflective experience enables practitioners to make ever-finer distinctions (Benner *et al.* 1999: 33; Klein 1998). As several ethnographic studies have shown, when new distinctions are made, new knowledge emerges; and when the new distinctions are developed into new products, or are embodied in new actions, innovation and learning, respectively, occur (Hargadon and Sutton 1997; Edmondson 2002: 128; Reyes and Zarama 1998: 22–4). For example, often new ideas develop from seeing that old ideas can be applied in new contexts to solve new problems (Hargadon and Sutton 1997, 2000). When this happens, practitioners *re*-order what they know and by doing so they develop new distinctions.

What is it about self-consciousness that enables individuals to articulate new distinctions? For Mead (1934) the defining feature of self-consciousness is arousing in oneself the group of attitudes one is arousing in others; the taking of the attitude of another and acting towards oneself as others act. Or to put it more simply, seeing myself as others see me (Aboulafia 1986: 8–14; Joas 1996: 186–9; Mead 1934: 171; Strauss 1977: xxvi–xxviii). I am an object of my own perception through the categories of others. To see myself, I must appropriate the vision of others (Holquist 2002: 28).

For Mead (1934: 152–64), taking the role of the other occurs in a three-stage developmental process of the self. At the 'play stage', the individual imitates others' outer appearances without however, seeing the world from their point of view. At the 'game stage', the individual adopts the attitudes of all the others involved in the game and learns to see the world from their point of view. And, finally, at the stage of the 'generalized other', the individual, having learned to take the role of the other and having grasped the relationships between the roles of others in a game, further learns to adopt the attitude of the whole community or social group of which she is a part. Gradually, a 'generalized other' emerges epitomizing the attitude of the whole group, entering into the experience of any one of its individual members (Dodds *et al.* 1997: 497–8). As Mead remarks with reference to baseball, 'what [a player] does is controlled by his being everyone else on that team, at least in so far as those attitudes affect his own particular response. We get then an "other" which is an organization of the attitudes of those involved in the same process' (Mead 1934: 154). The individual adopts the group attitudes by 'further organizing, and then generalizing, the attitudes of particular other individuals in terms of their organized social bearings and implications' (ibid.: 158). In this way, the individual gradually learns not only to take the role of others in scripted interactions, but also to *imagine* the role of others in situations that have not yet arisen and, by so doing, the individual can try out new points of view and invent new approaches to the world (Scheff 2000: 10).

To illustrate the notion of the 'generalized other', consider Cook and Yanow's (1996) study of flute makers. The authors report that in deciding whether a particular flute is of sufficiently high quality, a flute maker 'would typically make only cryptic remarks, such as, "it doesn't feel right" or "this bit doesn't look quite right"' (ibid.: 442). Notice that in saying 'it doesn't feel right; it's cranky', a flute maker invokes an 'organized attitude' (Mead 1934: 161) with reference to flute making, which is common to all members of the organization, other-wise such an affirmation would not make sense. The flute maker is calling out the response of a generalized other so that when he says 'it's cranky', he arouses in himself the response of the generalized other. What makes an organization possible are such common responses and organized attitudes – 'a moral and notional consistency' (Kogut and Zander 1996: 502) in individuals' activities – with reference to the tasks at hand (Mead 1934: 161).

Mead's seminal contribution is to have made us see that the self, rather than being a self-contained, unitary entity, as common sense would have it, is actually *interactively* shaped. Similar insights are derived from the work of Vygotsky (1986), for whom individual conceptual development first occurs at the social level, through dialogues with others, which are then internalized to become part of the individual cognitive functioning (see Shotter 1993a, 1993b; Wertsch 1991: Chapter 2; Whetherell and Maybin 1996: 248–53). In developmental terms, the self is initially formed by external dialogues, which, at later stages of individual development, are transformed into internalized dialogues with the generalized other. Indeed, according to this view, intramental dialogue makes up the content of self-consciousness, and individual thinking consists of internalized social dialogues. As Mead (1934: 156) put it, 'only by taking the attitude of the generalized other toward himself, can [an individual] think at all; for only thus can thinking – or the internalized conversation of gestures which constitutes thinking – occur.'

Mead's and Vygotsky's emphasis on the interactive shaping of the self and the *dialogical* structure of thinking has intriguing parallels with the work of Bakhtin, the theorist of dialogi-cality *par excellence*. For Bakhtin, dialogicality is an ontological category of being, rather than a mere mode of communication (Taylor 1991a: 33, 1991b: 311). Dialogicality is an essential feature of discourse since the very capacity to think is grounded on *otherness* (Holquist 2002: 18; Taylor 1991a: 33). This is so because of the irreducibly social character of language. Language is not, and cannot be, private (Wittgenstein 1958: §243–307): it is developed and used in particu-lar forms of life, within which its terms gain meaning. Most of the time, language speakers use terms that are *already* defined and used by others. At the same time, speakers may renew the meaning of those terms and give them their own twist. The use of language presupposes the other and, in that sense, it is necessarily dialogical. As Bakhtin (1981: 293) remarks, 'The word in language is half someone else's. It becomes "one's own" only when the speaker populates it with his own intention, his own accent, when he appropriates the word, adapting it to his own semantic and expressive intention.'

Thus, although utterances are the unique products of language speakers, they are not *ex nihilo* constructions, since they inescapably draw on the utterances of others (Bakhtin 1986: 92–5). When I write or speak about a certain topic I am not the first one to do so. I am not, as Bakhtin (ibid.: 93) says, 'a biblical Adam, dealing only with virgin and still unnamed objects, giving them names for the first time'. Others have expressed views about it or in relation to it and, inevitably, my topic becomes the arena in which I meet the opinions, views and perspectives of others. It is not only others' previous utterances that I respond to in my speech or writing. I also anticipate others' possible responsive reactions (Bakhtin ibid.: 94). My utterances are constructed in anticipation of encountering their responses. In other words, the other is present in my speech both in the form of past utterances I address and in the form of future responses I anticipate.

For Bakhtin, the notion of 'utterance' is closely linked with the notions of 'voice' and 'addressivity'. An utterance, spoken or written, is always expressed through a voice – it expresses the perspective of someone. At the same time, a voice is never alone, since the utterance it expresses is directed at someone – it has an addressee – and it draws on others' preceding voices. In an intriguing parallel with Mead's 'generalized other', Bakhtin acknowledges that an addressee can be an immediate interlocutor and/or 'an indefinite, unconcretized other' (ibid.: 95; see also Barrett 1999: 143; Baxter and Montgomery 1996: 28–9). The dialogue with the 'generalized' or 'unconcretized other' usually takes the form of 'hidden dialogicality' (Bakhtin 1984: 97), which reflects earlier dialogues with real others. The generalized other's utterances are pre-supposed and responded to in intramental dialogue. Bakhtin describes hidden dialogicality as follows. 'Imagine a dialogue of two persons in which the statements of the second speaker are omitted, but in such a way that the general sense is not at all violated. The second speaker is present invisibly, his words are not there, but deep traces left by these words have a determining influence on all the present and visible words of the first speaker. We sense that this is a conversation, although only one person is speaking [. . .]' (ibid.: 197).

An instance of hidden dialogicality is seen in the case of Cook and Yanow's (1996: 442) flute maker who utters 'it doesn't feel right; it's cranky'. It is as if the flute maker responds to a question put to him by the generalized other. The reason why this claim can be made is that this intramental hidden dialogue is homologous to earlier exchanges that, in all probability, occurred at the intermental level, between the flute maker and his supervisor or trainer (Wertsch 1991: 89–90). The same can be said about the software developer and the intramental hidden dialogue she undoubtedly had with the master baker, as she was trying to perfect her bread-kneading skills after she had served her apprenticeship (Nonaka and Takeuchi 1995: 104).

Three dialogical mechanisms for creating new organizational knowledge

What is in dialogue that makes it possible for new distinctions to emerge? To take the paradigmatic case of a face-to-face dialogue between two individuals, dialogue involves the possibility of mutual influence, which leads to the gradual creation of common ground between interlocutors, without, however, them losing their individual distinctiveness. The common ground is created by interlocutors' efforts to actively assimilate mutually experienced strangeness (Markova 2003a: 104, 2003b: 257). In dialogue, participants' utterances 'are called forth by the state of the discussion, and they are inserted into a shared operation of which neither is the creator' (Merlau-Ponty 1962: 354). In other words, dialogue is enacted when interlocutors both fuse their perspectives *and* retain the uniqueness of their voices (Baxter and Montgomery 1996: 24).

There can be no dialogue unless participants differ from one another, which creates tension between them along with a desire to overcome it. Dialogue thrives insofar as participants refuse to become predictable and 'finalized' (Bakhtin 1984: 59), while actively striving to assimilate the strangeness of the other. In Plato's early dialogues there is a distinct feeling of perplexity and confusion created, a sensation of *aporia* (impasse), which acts as a stimulus to participants to overcome through assimilating the strange, thus moving to a fuller understanding (Mace 1999: 17). This happens because each interlocutor makes the other realize the limitations of his perspective and stimulates a search for a more universal perspective, thus each one potentially surprising themselves. Since dialogue involves the effort to assimilate experienced strangeness, interlocutors are stimulated to re-articulate their views and, thus, draw new distinctions. When they do so, interlocutors overcome the particularity of their perspectives and reach a higher universality in their understanding (Bohm 1996: Chapter 2; Gadamer 1989: 305; Kögler 1999: 43).

Although in its paradigmatic form dialogue is a language-based, face-to-face communication process that involves the synchronization of two streams of consciousness (Barrett 1999: 137; Bohm 1996: Chapter 2; Gergen *et al.* 2004: 7; Isaacs 1999: 19–20; Luckmann 1990: 52–3), nonetheless dialogue can be seen in broader terms if one wants to do justice to the *otherness* that human communication presupposes, namely that utterances are never wholly one's own (Shotter and Katz 1996: 228; Taylor 1991a: 33). Volosinov (1986: 95)[1] defines dialogue 'in a broader sense, meaning not only direct, face-to-face, vocalized verbal communication between persons, but also verbal communication of any type whatsoever'. A book, for example, is a verbal performance in print. While a book may become an object of discussion in a real-life dialogue, it is also 'calculated for active perception' (op.cit.): it invites the reader to search for the writer's intended meanings; it orients itself to previous performances in the particular field it contributes; and leads to other printed reactions in the form of book reviews, critical surveys, etc. In short, as an element of verbal communication, a book engages in a broader colloquy (see also Gadamer 1989: 368; Markova 1990: 4).

It is this broader view of dialogue that is adopted here. According to such a view, the dialogical partner is not necessarily a real other but may well be an imaginary other (e.g. an author) or an artifact (e.g. a drawing) (Holquist 2002: 30). In such cases, of course, we cannot speak of proper dialogue, since the other is not immediately available to reciprocate, but of quasi-dialogue. What is important to note, however, is that even quasi-dialogues preserve what is most distinctive in dialogicality, namely sensitivity to otherness (Holquist 2002: 41; Taylor 1991b: 310–14). Imaginary others or artifacts provide the opportunity for real actors to further develop themselves, since actors are seen as open-ended and relationally constituted. Quasi-dialogical exchanges generate strangeness, insofar as the actor tries to understand better his own earlier responses to imaginary others or artifacts, which the actor then needs to assimilate, and by so doing he is stimulated to make new distinctions. Dialogicality implies potentially endless semiosis – the constant recreation of meaning.

There are three forms of dialogical and quasi-dialogical exchanges individuals may engage in: dialogical exchanges with real others, quasi-dialogical exchanges with imaginal others, and quasi-dialogical exchanges with artifacts. Each one of them will be described and illustrated below. New knowledge may emerge when organizational members, in their attempts to tackle a problem, typically in the context of a team, engage in the preceding three dialogical and quasi-dialogical exchanges.

Dialogical exchanges with real others

How does dialogue with real others lead actors to obtain a clearer sense of their experiences and reach a higher level of universality in their understanding? Let us take the paradigmatic case of a face-to-face dialogue between two individuals, since it provides the template for the other two forms of quasi-dialogue. Suppose that individuals A and B are engaged in a conversation. A makes an utterance a, which is reciprocated by B's utterance b, to which A then responds through utterance a_1. Weick (1979: 89) calls such an exchange 'double interact'. Two things are worth noting about double interacts. First, they include three *logical* steps. Having made utterance a (first step), A has access to B through her receiving of b (second step), but B cannot know how b fits in with a, unless a third logical step is undertaken by A through utterance a_1 (Markova 1987: 294–5). And secondly, a_1 is a *reflexive* utterance; namely, it is made by A while bearing in mind both interactants' previous utterances (a and b) (Linell and Markova 1993: 182; Mead 1934: 135–52). In other words, a_1 partly signifies that A understands her own earlier utterance a in light of B's response to it (Gergen *et al.* 2004: 12–13).

The importance of dialogical exchanges for enabling practitioners to re-articulate their experiences and, thus, make new distinctions, has been illustrated in several ethnographic studies of innovation and knowledge creation (Carlile 2002, 2004; Dougherty 2004; Hargadon and Sutton 1997, 2000; Obstfeld 2005). Nonaka and Takeuchi's (1995) example of the bread-making machine is a good case in point. Without the conversations within the development team, the software developer would have been unable to articulate what was important in what she had learned through her apprenticeship. The dialogical exchange drew out from her thoughts she had no idea she possessed. Her attention was drawn by other team members to certain hitherto unnoticed aspects of her experience of bread kneading, which she subsequently formulated as 'twisting stretch' (Tsoukas 2003: 156).

Researchers from several disciplines have similarly illustrated the dialogical process through which new distinctions emerge in contexts as diverse as detective work (Hintikka 1983), nursing practice (Benner *et al.* 1999), medical diagnoses (Hunter 1991), educational practice (Hayes and Matusov 2005; Mercer 1995; Wertsch 1991), mentoring (Katz and Shotter 1996) and hospital administration (Middleton 1998).

Quasi-dialogical exchanges with imaginal others

A dialogue need not take place between real others only, but also with imaginal others, although, more accurately, in this case it is a quasi-dialogue, since the other is not immediately available to reciprocate one's utterances. Watkins (2000) describes how dialogues with imaginal others play an important role in human lives. She notes that individuals are never really alone. Even when they are silent, they find themselves talking, arguing and responding to others, such as critics, friends, gods, their own consciences, photographs, figures in their dreams or in the media (Hermans and Hermans-Jansen 2003; Hermans *et al.* 1993). The other is within us.

Examples of imaginal dialogues range from spontaneous ones, such as when an author is in a quasi-dialogue with reviewers while revising his manuscript (Hermans 1996a: 43), to designed ones as when, in executive seminars, participants are asked to write up an imaginal dialogue they might have with a colleague and reflect on how it might develop (Argyris 1993; Watkins 2000). For reasons explained earlier, in an organizational context, the most theoretically salient imaginal other is the generalized other. Individuals in organizations quasi-converse with the generalized other in the course of carrying out a task and their conversations take the form of hidden dialogicality.

To see how an imaginal quasi-dialogue works, consider the following example provided by Hermans and Kempen (1993: 158–61). Frank, a 48-year-old manager, is asked by the authors to enter into imaginal dialogue with a person depicted in a painting. The latter shows a middle-aged woman who is placed in a frontal position so that eye contact with the viewer is possible. Frank is first asked to describe a 'valuation' (namely, a unit of meaning deriving from important experiences in his life) and then to imagine how the woman would respond to his valuation, to which response he would then have to counter-respond. Thus, their quasi-dialogue consists of three steps: valuation, imaginal response, counter-response. Although space limitations prevent us from reproducing the entire quasi-dialogical exchange between Frank and the woman in the painting, it is interesting to note that, by counter-responding to her, Frank incorporates her imaginal response to his thinking, thus transforming his initial valuation. His counter-response in Step 3 involves a main element of his original valuation (in this case, his tendency for negative thinking) *and* a main element of the woman's response (in this case, her advice to have a more reserved trust in people). His counter-response (i.e. his new valuation) is novel because he allowed himself to be influenced by an imaginal other's point of view. Hermans and Kempen (ibid.: 160–1) recognize that this is not always the case and have given examples of subjects with whom imaginal dialogues failed to generate novelty. An imaginal quasi-dialogue is an open-ended process just like a dialogue with real others is.

Quasi-dialogical exchanges with artefacts

New distinctions may also be drawn when, in the process of carrying out their tasks, individuals interact with artifacts. Paradigmatic cases of quasi-dialogues between an actor and an artifact are the activities of painting, architectural design and prototyping (Boland and Colopy 2004; Gombrich 1977: 302; Hargadon and Sutton 2000: 163; Popper 1979: 253–4; Preda 1999; Schrage 2000). What these cases have in common is what Schön (1987: 31) calls 'the reflective conversation with the material of a situation'. The three logical steps of dialogical exchange with real others described earlier are at work here too. The individual acts, is attentive to surprises (namely, to the possibility his expectations may not be met), and acts again.

The artifacts actors create in the course of carrying out their tasks are called by Bamberger and Schön (1991: 192) 'reference entities' and by Knorr Cetina (2001: 181) 'epistemic objects'. What is characteristic of them is their ambivalent ontological status as knowledge carriers – they are both stable *and* mutable entities; they incorporate given knowledge and manifest knowledge-in-the-making (Bechky 2003a: 729; Preda 1999: 353). On the one hand, epistemic objects are repositories of what actors focally know so far (Bamberger and Schön 1991: 192), hence they are stable; on the other hand, however, they also incorporate knowledge of which actors are not focally aware of, hence they are open for further development. Such epistemic ambivalence enables epistemic objects to serve at once as 'a materialized "log" of the making process' (op. cit.), thus serving as useful memory-preservation aids, *and* as mutable objects that are inherently incomplete, thus being capable of further development (Ewenstein and Whyte 2005: 4–5; Knorr Cetina 2001: 181).

The importance of epistemic objects for knowledge creation has been highlighted by several management and organizational researchers (Bechky 2003a, 2003b; Carlile 2002, 2004; Hargadon and Sutton 2000; Leonard-Barton 1995; Nonaka and Takeuchi 1995; Schrage 2000; von Krogh *et al.* 2000). For the purpose of this chapter, Schrage's account is particularly revealing. He describes how leading companies create prototypes, models and simulations to help them innovate. Prototyping is important, suggests Schrage (2000: 13), because it facilitates the interplay between individuals and the expression of their ideas. An effective physical prototype of, say, an automobile dashboard or a bread-making machine, shows things that cannot be verbalized and, thus, leads to richer conversations (Dodgson *et al.* 2005: 100–101, 151; Nonaka and Takeuchi 1995: 105). It also enables practitioners to test ideas early enough in the process to learn from those tests (Hargadon and Sutton 2000: 163).

Organizational members often do not really know what they need, or are looking for, until they see it (Schrage 2000: 20, 126; Weick 1979: 133). They can articulate better what they want by interacting with prototypes and visual aids than by enumerating requirements or needs (Leonard-Barton 1995: 127–33; von Krogh *et al.* 2000: 89–90). Building prototypes and inter-acting with them helps individuals 'rearticulate' (Schrage 2000: 166) the problems they deal with, as was shown in Nonaka and Takeuchi's (1995) bread-making machine. A good proto-type can almost acquire life of its own and become a non-human quasi-agent (Ewnestein and Whyte 2005: 5; Law 1992; Preda 1999: 353). When it does, the prototype becomes the medium to generate surprise – it challenges its makers and elicits further responses from them (Schrage 2000: 118).

In light of the above, the process of organizational knowledge creation may now be described as follows (see Figure 14.1).

In organized settings new knowledge is created by individuals, typically, although not

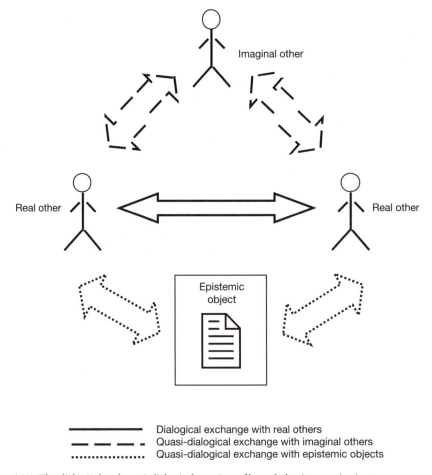

Figure 14.1 The dialogical and quasi-dialogical creation of knowledge in organizations

necessarily, within a project team, through the development of fresh distinctions concerning the task at hand. New distinctions may be developed through individuals engaging in dialogical relationships with real others, with imaginal others, and with artifacts. In dialogue with real others, interlocutors attempt to assimilate mutually experienced strangeness, and by doing so they are stimulated to make new distinctions. Quasi-dialogue with imaginal others mainly involves quasi-dialogue with the generalized other: those are internal (intramental) dialogues which are developed out of earlier external (intermental) dialogues with authority or senior figures in a discursive practice. The quasi-dialogue with the generalized other usually takes the form of hidden dialogicality, whereby earlier external dialogues with authority or senior figures are internalized so that, later, individual utterances in the course of carrying out a task may be seen as responses to questions raised by the generalized other.

Finally, actors engage in quasi-dialogical interactions with epistemic objects. The latter are invaluable in problem solving because they help make the individual handling of problems more cognitively efficient; draw together diverse specialists and provide a common language for problem solving; and, crucially, provide opportunities for actors to see aspects of their tacitly known backgrounds. Epistemic objects enhance perception, incorporate available knowledge, and enable individuals to bring forth aspects of their backgrounds of which they were not focally aware before. By doing so, actors can re-articulate the proto-interpretations that are already manifested in the epistemic objects and, thus, make new distinctions.

This theoretical account will be illustrated below by drawing on the work of Donald Schön.

An illustration

Throughout his work, Schön (1983, 1987) sought to elucidate the thought processes that are implicated in professional work. Unhappy with the image of technical rationality that was long assumed to underlie professional work, Schön argued that the latter is permeated by experimentation and uncertainty. In the illustration below the focus is on architectural designing, one of Schön's favorite themes.

Schön and Wiggins (1992) have described architectural designing as a 'reflective conversation' with the materials of a design situation. Their description is rich and a part of it is reproduced below, followed by an analysis employing the concepts developed in this chapter.

Schön and Wiggins (ibid.: 68) provide the following description of architectural design (see also Schön 1983: 82–4, 150–6):

Imagine a first-year design studio in a department of architecture. The studio project is the design of a school, for which the students have been given both a programme and a site. They have been working on this project for about a month when the studio master, Quist, sits down next to one of the students, Petra, to conduct a design review. Petra begins by describing how she has had 'trouble getting past the diagrammatic phase'. Then, in response to Quist's question, 'What other big problems?' she sets out the following account of her process to date:

'I had six of these classroom units but they were too small in scale to do much with. So I changed them to this more significant layout (the L-shapes). It relates grade one to two, three to four, and five to six grades, which is more what I wanted to do educationally anyway. What I have here is a space which is more of a home base. I'll have an outside/ inside which can be used and an outside/outside which can be used – then that opens into your resource/library thing.' (See Figure 14.2.)

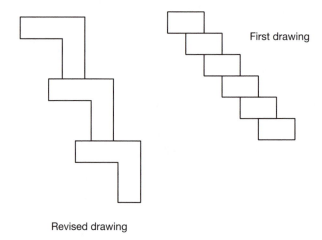

First drawing

Revised drawing

Figure 14.2 Petra's architectural drawings

Source: Adapted from Schön and Wiggins (1992: 69).

In terms of the concepts developed here, Schön and Wiggins' account may be analyzed as follows. Petra first produced a design, which, on reflection, was not to her satisfaction. She lets us get a glimpse of her thinking when she makes an evaluative judgment ('they were too small in scale to do much with') in response to Quist's question ('What other big problems?'). With her statement she articulates a distinction concerning the scale of what she had drawn: she recognizes an undesirable quality of the spatial configuration she had first designed and proceeds to name the quality ('too small in scale'). Petra was able to articulate her assessment of what she had done because her dissatisfaction with her initial design had already involved a certain level of articulation. One can easily imagine her thinking to herself, 'I am not happy with this', or 'this does not look right'. She was able to have such an experience precisely because, as a trainee, she had been learning certain qualitative distinctions that constituted the discursive practice she was involved in (namely, architecture) – what is and is not acceptable, adequate and desirable. It is because her initial dissatisfaction is not language-independent but already involves a characterization (a proto-interpretation), that she is able to wonder whether her design is adequate.

Having further articulated her experience, Petra could now have a better grasp of what she had done, making her able to further reflect and work on it. Indeed, her articulation led her to undertake new action, and she produced a revised design. In her response to Quist we can see traces of hidden dialogicality: her first two utterances may be plausibly reconstructed as responses to hypothetical questions: 'Why did you change the first design?' [Because the items in it] were too small in scale to do much with.' 'Why did you give the six classroom units this particular L-shape?' [Because] this [is a] more significant layout (the L-shapes); it relates grade one to two, etc.' Notice that Petra's response is part of a face-to-face dialogue with Quist, and the thinking that is revealed in her response is itself dialogically structured: it consists of utterances that can be seen as responses to questions that, most likely, would have earlier occurred on the intermental plane. Like in the example of the flute maker, this is a plausible assumption since, most likely, Petra's utterances are homologous to utterances in earlier training episodes that were replies to the studio master's overt questions (Wertsch 1991: 90). In Petra's response we have a hidden quasi-dialogue with Quist-as-the-generalized-other nested within a dialogue with Quist-as-the-real-other.

In other words, Petra's response expresses her voice and has an addressee (Quist) in two roles: as an immediate interlocutor and as a generalized other. Quist is clearly the immediate interlocutor (the real other) in this instance; but he is also the generalized other, the authority figure (the studio master) who has been teaching her for a year and whose utterances are pre-supposed and responded to by Petra's utterances. Her response is not totally idiosyncratic. By combining words to produce her utterance, she follows a generic form – a particular speech genre (Cook and Brown 1999: 392). The discursive practice into which she was being introduced made it necessary that she learned a specialized language and cast her utterances in certain generic forms that were characteristic of architectural practice. Thus to the Bakhtinian question 'who is doing the talking in Petra's response?', the answer is both Petra and Quist, and, through the particular genre used, the entire architectural practice.

Petra was led to produce the L-shapes in her second move – thus she was led to create new distinctions and, therefore, new knowledge – through her dialogical encounter with both Quist and her designs. When she produced the first design, she was able to evaluate it by some form of dialogical thinking: as seen above, it is as if Quist, the generalized other, was asking her certain questions to ascertain the adequacy of her design, to which she had to respond. And having literally seen what she had first drawn, she began to reflect on the epistemic object she had produced. She realized that scale was not 'significant' enough and she proceeded to correct it. Her initial design served as a display in which she could see what she was not focally aware of before (the importance of scale). She entered into a quasi-dialogue with that display until she obtained the result she wished.

In her second move, Petra pays focal attention to scale but, by doing so, she relies subsidiarily on broader notions of space and spatial use. While she produces something of more significant scale this time, she finds, on reflection, that she has unintentionally done other things as well. She has produced, for example, a space of three Ls that is more of a 'home base', and she has created two kinds of spaces ('outside/inside' and 'outside/outside') that she finds useable ('which can be used') (Schön and Wiggins 1992: 71). In other words, the epistemic object (the drawing) she has produced at each stage of the design process is epistemically important because it helps her discover the unintended consequences of her move (positive ones in this case), which she could not have articulated before (ibid.: 72). By creating an epistemic object she is enabled to bring forth aspects of her tacit background and thus enter into a quasi-dialogue with it. By doing so, she can articulate further what is already included in the background in an inchoate form.

To sum up, Petra's new design, judged satisfactory this time, came about through her engaging in dialogue with a real other (Quist), a quasi-dialogue with an imaginal other (Quist as the generalized other), and a quasi-dialogue with the epistemic objects she created along the way. Through those dialogical and quasi-dialogical interactions Petra's thinking was enabled to move forward, leading her to make new distinctions and thus create new knowledge.

Conclusions

This chapter has attempted to answer the question, 'what are the mechanisms through which new knowledge emerges in organizations?' and by so doing to offer a theoretical account that is compatible with what is currently known *and* takes it further. The approach adopted has been a dialogical one. It has been argued that, in organized settings, new knowledge comes from the exercise of human judgment – the individual ability to draw new distinctions concerning a task at hand, typically in the context of a team. New distinctions may be developed through organizational members engaging in three kinds of dialogical (or quasi-dialogical) encounters: with real others, with imaginal others and with artifacts.

Not all kinds of dialogue, however, may lead to 'productive differences' (Gergen *et al.* 2004: 13–14), namely, differences that can extend the potential of a preceding utterance. As the case studies by Beech *et al.* (2002) and Hodgkinson and Wright (2002) document, groups may be locked in patterns of conflict, or authority may be oppressively used, thus stifling generative dialogue and the creation of productive differences. In such cases, dialogue may be impoverished or is likely to generate 'destructive differences' – 'utterances that curtail or negate what has preceded' (Gergen *et al.* 2004: 14). Further research may explore the empirical conditions under which dialogical exchanges take place and what results they generate (Hermans 1996b; Markova and Foppa 1990). How, for example, does group diversity influence the dialogues its members may have when engaged in problem solving? How do politics and the exercise of power in a group impact on dialogue? Under what conditions are 'productive differences' more likely to be generated than 'destructive' ones? Moreover, what kinds of epistemic objects are more likely to help create new knowledge in organizations?

Finally, dialogue mobilizes thinking; it provides the fuel for the thinking process to unfold and thus for new distinctions to potentially emerge. To what extent do organizations dialogize the prevalent modes of cognition they employ? What thinking devices do they use (e.g. analogical thinking, dialectical thinking, etc.) in order to facilitate dialogue across the organization, with what results? How is reflection organized in the organization, with what results? A dialogical perspective opens up new areas for research in order to further advance our understanding of the processes through which new knowledge in organizations is created.

Acknowledgements

The author has benefited from presenting earlier versions of this chapter at conferences and seminars at the London Business School, University of New South Wales, University of Michigan (ICOS Seminar), University of Sussex, University of Cambridge, University of Brighton, University of Valencia, and the Universidade Nova de Lisboa. My thanks to Michael D. Cohen, Paul C. van Fenema, Robert Cooper, John Shotter and Karl Weick for their useful comments on earlier drafts.

Note

1 There is some dispute as to who actually wrote *Marxism and the Philosophy of Language*. For some Bakhtinian scholars like Holquist (2002: 8), Bakhtin is primarily responsible for writing this book, albeit under the name of his friend Volosinov, while for others this is not the case. For a summary of the dispute, see Wertsch (1991: 48–49).

References

Aboulafia, M. 1986. *The Mediating Self: Mead, Sartre, and Self-determination*. New Haven: Yale University Press.

Argyris, C. 1993. *Knowledge for Action*. San Francisco: Jossey-Bass.

Bakhtin, M.M. 1981. *The Dialogic Imagination*, edited by M. Holquist; translated by C. Emerson and M. Holquist. Austin: University of Texas Press.

Bakhtin, M. 1984. *Problems of Dostoevsky's Poetics*. Minneapolis: University of Minnesota Press.

Bakhtin, M. 1986. *Speech Genres and Other Essays*. Austin: University of Texas Press.

Bamberger, J. and Schön, D.A. 1991. Learning as reflective conversation with materials. In F. Steier (ed.), *Research and Reflexivity*, 186–209. London: Sage.

Barrett, F.J. 1999. Knowledge creating as dialogic accomplishment: a constructionist perspective. In A. Montuori and R.E. Purser (eds), *Social Creativity*, Volume, 1, 133–151. Cresskill, NJ: Hampton Press.

Baxter, L.A. and B.M. Montgomery. 1996. *Relating*. New York: Guilford Press.

Bechky, B.A. 2003a. Object lessons: workplace artefacts as representations of occupational jurisdiction. *American Journal of Sociology*, 109: 720–752.

Bechky, B.A. 2003b. Sharing meaning across occupational communities: the transformation of understanding on a production floor. *Organization Science*, 14: 312–330.

Beech, N., MacIntosh, R., MacLean, D., Shepherd, J. and Stokes, J. 2002. Exploring constraints on developing knowledge: on the need for conflict. *Management Learning*, 33: 459–476.

Bell, D. 1999. The axial age of technology foreword. In D. Bell, *The Coming of the Post-Industrial Society*, ix–lxxxv. New York: Basic Books, special anniversary edition.

Benner, P., Hooper-Kyriakidis, P. and Stannard, D. 1999. *Clinical Wisdom and Interventions in Critical Care*. Philadelphia, PA: Saunders.

Bohm, D. 1996. *On Dialogue*. London: Routledge.

Boland, R.J. and Collopy, F. 2004. Design matters for management. In R.J. Boland and F. Collopy (eds), *Managing as Designing*, 3–18. Stanford, CA: Stanford Business Books.

Brown, J.S. and Duguid, P. 2001. Knowledge and organization: A social-practice perspective. *Organization Science*, 12: 198–213.

Calhoun, M.A and Starbuck, W.H. 2003. Barriers to creating knowledge. In M. Easterby-Smith and M. A. Lyles (eds) 2003. *The Blackwell Handbook of Organizational Learning and Knowledge Management*, 473–492. Oxford: Blackwell.

Carlile, R. P. 2002. A pragmatic view of knowledge and boundaries: Boundary objects in new product development. *Organization Science*, 13: 442–455.

Carlile, R.P. 2004. Transferring, translating, and transforming: An integrative framework for managing knowledge across boundaries. *Organization Science*, 15: 555–568.

Cook, S. D. and Brown, J.S. 1999. Bridging epistemologies: The generative dance between organizational knowledge and organizational knowing. *Organization Science*, 10: 81–400.

Cook, S.D. and Yanow, D. 1996. Culture and organizational learning. In M.D. Cohen and L.S. Sproull (eds), *Organizational Learning*, 430–459. Thousand Oaks, CA: Sage.

Dewey, J. 1934. *Art as Experience*. New York: Perigee Books.

Dodds, A.E., Lawrence J.A. and Valsiner, J. 1997. The personal and the social: Mead's theory of the 'Generalizad Other'. *Theory and Psychology*, 7: 483–503.

Dodgson, M., Gann, D. and Salter, A. 2005. *Think, Play, Do*. Oxford: Oxford University Press.

Dougherty, D. 2004. Organizing practice in services: capturing practice-based knowledge for innovation. *Strategic Organization*, 2: 35–64.

Edmondson, E. 2002. The local and variegated nature of learning in organizations: A group-level perspective. *Organization Science*, 13: 128–146.

Ewenstein, B. and Whyte, J.K. 2005. Knowledge practices in design: The role of visual representations as 'epistemic objects'. Paper presented at the 21st EGOS Colloquium, Berlin, July.

Gadamer, H.-G. 1989. *Truth and method*, second edition. London: Sheed and Ward.

Gawande, A. 2002. *Complications*. New York: Metropolitan Books.

Gergen, M.M., Gergen, K.J. and Barrett, F. 2004. Appreciative inquiry as dialogue: Generative and transformative. *Advances in Appreciative Inquiry*, 1: 3–27.

Gombrich, E.H. 1977. *Art and Illusion* fifth edition. London: Phaidon Press.

Grant, R. 2002. The knowledge-based view of the firm. In C.W. Choo and N. Bontis (eds), *The Strategic*

Management of Intellectual Capital and Organizational Knowledge, 133–148. Oxford: Oxford University Press.

Hargadon, A. and Fanelli, A. 2002. Action and possibility: Reconciling dual perspectives of knowledge in organizations. *Organization Science*, 13: 290–302.

Hargadon, A. and Sutton, R.I. 1997. Technology brokering and innovation in a product development firm. *Administrative Science Quarterly*, 42: 716–749.

Hargadon, A. and Sutton, R.I. 2000. Building an innovation factory. *Harvard Business Review*, 78/5: 157–166.

Hayes, R. and Matusov, E. 2005. Designing for dialogue in place of teacher talk and student silence. *Culture and Psychology*, 11: 339–357.

Hermans, H.J.M. 1996a. Voicing the self: From information processing to dialogical interchange. *Psychological Bulletin*, 119: 31–50.

Hermans, H.J.M. 1996b. Opposites in a dialogical self: Constructs as characters. *Journal of Constructivist Psychology*, 9: 1–26.

Hermans, H.J., and Hermans-Jansen, E. 2003. Dialogical processes and development of the self. In J. Valsiner and K. Connolly (eds), *Handbook of Developmental Psychology*, 534–539. Thousand Oaks, CA: Sage.

Hermans, H.J.M. and Kempen, H.J.G. 1993. *The Dialogical Self*. San Diego, CA: Academic Press.

Hermans, H.J.M., Rijks, T.I. and Kempen, H.J.G. 1993. Imaginal dialogues in the self: Theory and method. *Journal of Personality*, 61: 207–236.

Hintikka, J. 1983. Sherlock Holmes formalized. In U. Eco and T.A. Sebeok (eds), *The Sign of Three*. Bloomington: Indiana University Press.

Hodgkinson, G.P. and Wright, G. 2002. Confronting strategic inertia in a top management team: Learning from failure. *Organization Studies*, 23: 949–977.

Holquist, M. 2002. *Dialogism*, second edition. London: Routledge.

Hunter, K.M. 1991. *Doctors' Stories*. Princeton, NJ: Princeton University Press

Isaacs, W. 1999. *Dialogue and the Art of Thinking Together*. New York: Currency.

Joas, H. 1996. *The Creativity of Action*. Cambridge: Polity Press.

Katz, A.M. and Shotter, J. 1996. Resonances from within the practice: Social poetics in a mentorship program. *Concepts and Transformation*, 1: 239–247.

Klein, G. 1998. *Sources of Power*. Cambridge, MA: MIT Press.

Knorr Cetina, K. 2001. Objectual practice. In T.R. Schatzki, K. Knorr Cetina and E. von Savigny (eds), *The Practice Turn in Contemporary Theory*, 175–188. London: Routledge.

Kögler, H.H. 1999. *The Power of Dialogue*. Cambridge, MA: MIT Press.

Kogut, B. and Zander, U. 1996. What firms do? Coordination, identity, and learning. *Organization Science*, 7: 502–518.

Larkin, J.H. and Simon, H.A. 1987. Why a diagram is (sometimes) worth ten thousand words. *Cognitive Science*, 11: 65–99.

Law, J. 1992. Notes on the theory of the Actor-Network: Ordering, strategy, and heterogeneity. *Systems Practice*, 5: 379–394.

Leonard, D. and Sensiper, S. 1998. The role of tacit knowledge in group innovation. *California Management Review*, 40: 112–132.

Leonard-Barton, D. 1995. *Wellsprings of Knowledge*. Boston, MA: Harvard Business School Press.

Linell, P. and Markova, I. 1993. Acts in discourse: From monological speech acts to dialogical inter-acts. *Journal for the Theory of Social Behaviour*, 23: 173–195.

Luckmann, T. 1990. Social communication, dialogue and conversation. In I. Markova and K. Foppa (eds) *The Dynamics of Dialogue*, 45–61. Hemel Hempstead: Harvester Wheatsheaf.

Markova, I. 1987. On the interaction of opposites in psychological processes. *Journal for the Theory of Social Behaviour*, 17: 279–299.

Markova, I. 1990. Introduction. In I. Markova and K. Foppa, *The Dynamics of Dialogue*, 1–22. New York: Harvester Wheatsheaf.

Markova, I. 2003a. *Dialogicality and Social Representations*. Cambridge: Cambridge University Press.

Markova, I. 2003b. Constitution of the self: Intersubjectivity and dialogicality. *Culture and Psychology*, 8: 249–259.

Markova, I. and Foppa, K. 1990. *The Dynamics of Dialogue*. New York: Harvester Wheatsheaf.

Mead, G.H. 1934. *Mind, Self, and Society*. Edited by C.W. Morris. Chicago: Chicago University Press.

Mercer, N. 1995. *The Guided Construction of Knowledge*. Clevedon: Multilingual Matters.

Merleau-Ponty, M. 1962. *Phenomenology of Perception*. Translated by C. Smith. London: Routledge.

Middleton, D. 1998. Talking work: Argument, common knowledge, and improvisation in teamwork. In Y. Engeström and D. Middleton (eds), *Cognition and Communication at Work*, 233–256. Cambridge: Cambridge University Press.

Nonaka, I. and Takeuchi H. 1995. *The Knowledge-creating Company*. New York: Oxford University Press.

Nonaka, I. and Toyama, R. 2005. The theory of the knowledge-creating firm: Subjectivity, objectivity and synthesis. *Industrial and Corporate Change*, 14: 419–436.

Nonaka, I., Toyama, R. and Byosiére, P. 2001. A theory of organizational knowledge creation: Understanding the dynamic process of creating knowledge. In M.D. Dierkes, A. Berthoin Antal, J. Child and I. Nonaka, *Handbook of Organizational Learning and Knowledge*, 491–517. Oxford: Oxford University Press.

Obstfeld, D. 2002. Knowledge creation, social networks and innovation: An integrative study. *Academy of Management Proceedings 2002*, H1–H6.

Obstfeld, D. 2005. Saying more and less of what we know: Knowledge articulation and the social process of knowledge creation and innovation. Working Paper, Graduate School of Management, University of California, Irvine.

Orlikowski, W.J. 2002. Knowing in practice: Enacting a collective capability in distributed organizing. *Organization Science*, 13: 249–273.

Preda, A. 1999. The turn to things: Arguments for a sociological theory of things. *Sociological Quarterly*, 40: 347–366.

Reyes, A. and Zarama, R. 1998. The process of embodying distinctions: A re-construction of the process of learning. *Cybernetics and Human Knowing*, 5: 19–33.

Robertson, M., Scarbrough, H. and Swan J. 2003. Knowledge creation in professional service firms: Institutional effects. *Organization Studies*, 24: 831–858.

Scheff, T.J. 2000. Multipersonal dialogue in consciousness: An incident in Virginia Woolf's *To the Lighthouse*. *Journal of Consciousness Studies*, 7: 3–19.

Schön, D. 1983. *The Reflective Practitioner*. New York: Basic Books.

Schön, D. 1987. *Educating the Reflective Practitioner*. San Francisco: Jossey-Bass.

Schön, D., and Wiggins, G. 1992. Kinds of seeing in designing. *Creativity and Innovation Management*, 1: 68–74.

Schrage, M. 2000. *Serious Play*. Boston, MA: Harvard Business School Press.

Shotter, J. 1993a. Vygotsky: The social negotiation of semiotic mediation. *New Ideas in Psycology*, 11: 61–75.

Shotter, J. 1993b. Bakhtin and Vygotsky: Internalization as a boundary phenomenon. *New Ideas in Psychology*, 11: 979–990.

Shotter, J. 1997. Dialogical realities: The ordinary, the everyday, and other strange new worlds. *Journal for the Theory of Social Behaviour*, 27: 345–357.

Shotter, J., and Katz, A.M. 1996. Articulating a practice from within the practice itself: Establishing formative dialogues by the use of a 'social poetics'. *Concepts and Transformation*, 1: 213–237.

Strauss, A. 1977. Introduction. In G.H. Mead, *On Social Psychology*, vii–xxi. Chicago: Chicago University Press.

Taylor, C. 1991a. *The Ethics of Authenticity*. Cambridge, MA: Harvard University Press.

Taylor, C. 1991b. The dialogical self. In D.R. Hiley, J.F. Bohman, and R. Shusterman (eds), *The Interpretive Turn*, 304–314. Ithaca, NY: Cornell University Press.

Tsoukas, H. 2003. Do we really understand tacit knowledge? In M. Easterby-Smith and M.A. Lyles (eds), *Handbook of Organizational Learning and Knowledge*, 410–427. Oxford: Blackwell.

Tsoukas, H., and Vladimirou, E. 2001. What is organizational knowledge? *Journal of Management Studies*, 38: 973–993.

Volosinov, V.N. 1986. *Marxism and the Philosophy of Language*. Translated by L. Matejka and I.R. Titunik. Cambridge, MA: Harvard University Press.

von Krogh, G., Ichijo, K., and Nonaka, I. 2000. *Enabling Knowledge Creation*. New York: Oxford University Press.

Vygotsky, L. 1986. *Thought and Language*. Cambridge, MA: MIT Press.

Watkins, M. 2000. *Invisible Guests*, third edition. Woodstock, CT: Spring Publications.

Weick, K.E. 1979. *The Social Psychology of Organizing*, second edition. Reading, MA: Addison-Wesley.

Wertsch, J.V. 1991. *Voices of the Mind*. Cambridge, MA: Harvard University Press.

Wertsch, J.V. 1998. *Mind as Action*. New York: Oxford University Press.

Wetherell, M. and Maybin J. 1996. The distributed self: A social constructionist perspective. In R. Stevens (ed.), *Understanding the Self*, 219–279. London: Sage.

Wittgenstein, L. 1958. *Philosophical Investigations*. Translated by G.E.M. Anscombe. Oxford: Blackwell.

Theme 5 Meta-theories of creativity

Computers and creativity: models and applications

Margaret Boden

Introduction: what is creativity?

Creativity is the ability to generate ideas (structures, artefacts . . .) that are novel, surprising and valuable. Each of those three terms is ambiguous – hence the countless disagreements that occur in everyday, and even professional, discussions about creativity. A theory of creativity should clarify the ambiguities, and explain why they arise.

The same applies to computational theories of creativity. These employ computational concepts of various sorts to explain creative thinking. Computational concepts are drawn from computer science and control theory, and in particular from artificial intelligence (AI) and artificial life (A-Life). These fields rely on several different approaches, including symbolic, connectionist and evolutionary programming – each of which has been used to model and/or explain the psychology of creativity. (And, as we'll see later, each has generated some practically useful applications.)

This scientific activity is not the same thing as trying to make computers 'truly' creative. Whether any computer can really be creative is a hotly contested philosophical question, as explained below. Whether a particular computer ever *appears* to be creative – because it generates ideas that we find novel, surprising and valuable – is an empirical question. It's that question which most concerns scientists using computational concepts to explain human creativity. For understanding how the computer does this can be helpful to psychologists interested in human thought, or information-processing, even if the answer to the philosophical question is 'No'.

Novelty, in this context, has a twofold ambiguity. If a new idea is novel *with respect to the person/system concerned*, we may speak of P-creativity (P for 'psychological'). If it is also, so far as is known, new *with respect to the whole of human history*, we may speak of H-creativity (H for 'history'). Clearly, H-creativity is a special case of P-creativity. To understand how creativity is possible, it is P-creativity that is crucial.

A new idea can be surprising in three different ways. First, it can be 'statistically' surprising. We always knew that it could happen, or anyway we'd have recognized that possibility instantly if we'd been asked, but we didn't expect it – much as we didn't expect an outsider to win the Derby. Second, a novel idea can surprise us by making us see that it had been possible all along, although we hadn't realized that; we may even be intrigued to find that the previous way of thinking had, in fact, allowed for it. And third, a new idea may cause 'impossibility' surprise, wherein we're amazed that it ever could have happened at all: it seems to be impossible, given the previous way of thinking. In such cases, our amazement may endure for a while even after the novel idea has been encountered.

Those three types of surprise correspond to three different types of psychological process by which novel ideas can be generated: combinational, exploratory and transformational creativity, respectively (Boden 2004). These distinctions are analytic, not temporal: the production of a single idea/artifact (a poem, or pot, or painting . . .) may have involved more than one of the three creative processes.

In combinational creativity, new ideas arise by making unfamiliar combinations of familiar ideas. (Think of collage in the visual arts, or of much poetic imagery.) Exploratory creativity explores the generative possibilities implicit in a previously accepted style of thinking, or conceptual space. (Think of styles of painting, or distinct areas of mathematics or theoretical chemistry.) And transformational creativity produces ideas that are indeed impossible, relative to the previous conceptual space, by altering/dropping one or more of the dimensions (constraints) that defined that space. (Think of Arnold Schoenberg's shift to atonality from tonal music, by dropping the previous insistence on having a home key; or remember Friedrich von Kekule's shift to ring-molecules from string-molecules.)

The third term in the definition of creativity, namely 'valuable', is the most slippery of all. For 'valuable' can mean many different things. What's valuable (interesting, fruitful, useful, economical, beautiful, arresting . . .) in music isn't what's valuable in chemistry or painting. Worse, what's valuable in any particular domain is something about which even domain-experts may disagree (especially in the case of transformational creativity, where – by definition – some stylistic rules have been broken/ignored). The final judgment, if any, is made as a result of often-lengthy disputes and negotiations, where the views of what's regarded as the most relevant social group have the strongest weight. Worse still, a 'final' judgment may change, due to historical factors varying from the declaration of war/peace to what a famous person chooses to wear to a birthday party. Judgments of value can even swing like a pendulum over the years (in the contemporary and historical appreciation of a poet or composer, for example).

Since science, in principle, can't adjudicate on matters of value (even though it can sometimes explain why it is that we accept certain values rather than others) (Boden 2006: Chapter 8, iv), there can never be a scientific theory/explanation that would enable us to settle all disputes about creativity. There can, however, be a science focused on *the psychological processes that generate the creative ideas*. For creativity doesn't happen by magic, nor by divine inspiration. (And as for 'intuition', this is the name of a question, not of an answer: we need to understand the psychological processes involved in intuition.)

This doesn't mean that creativity can be predicted. Contrary to what most people believe, a theory doesn't have to be predictive to be scientific: think of Darwin's theory of evolution, for instance. Rather, it explains why certain structures are found in the world around us, how they relate to others, and why some conceivable structures aren't found at all (Boden 2006: Chapter 7, iii.d). (Compare the way in which grammar explains the occurrence of certain word-strings rather than others.) Predictive science, such as most parts of physics, is a special case. Accordingly, a scientific theory needn't be able to predict the occurrence of specific creative ideas. (Given the richness and idiosyncracy of the ideas in individual human minds, it usually *won't* be able to do this.) It may not even be able to explain such ideas in detail *post hoc* (again, because we don't normally know what ideas are in the person's mind, still less which ones were involved in that particular episode of thought). Its task, rather, is to explain *how it's possible* for creative ideas to arise at all.

Creativity and artificial intelligence

Artificial intelligence (AI) is the study of how to make computers do the sorts of things that human (and animal) minds can do. It includes traditional, symbolic, AI (sometimes called GOFAI: Good Old-Fashioned AI), connectionist AI, evolutionary AI, and various types of robotics. It also includes artificial life (A-Life), although A-Life researchers usually make a point of distancing themselves from GOFAI.

AI is helpful in studying creativity for the same reasons that it's helpful in other areas of psychology. Computational concepts, drawn from AI/A-Life, sharpen psychological questions, because they can express ideas about mental processes more clearly than can verbal concepts.

That applies even when no computer modelling is involved. But when a psychological theory is implemented in functioning machines, the computer model that results can test the theory's coherence and implications much more rigorously than can be done by verbal reasoning and discussion. Often, it shows that a previously favoured theory has unsuspected gaps in it. Sometimes, it suggests how those gaps might be filled.

A computer model can show that a theory of creativity *could be* true, because (assuming that the model achieves the results expected) it undoubtedly specifies one way in which the phenomenon being studied can happen. (To know whether it *is* true, we need psychological and/or neuroscientific evidence as well.) In the case of creativity, even getting the AI model to perform as required is an interesting scientific achievement, for many people are utterly bemused about *how creativity is even possible.*

These remarks refer to the *scientific* usefulness of computer models that appear to be creative, insofar as they match the type of performance which in human beings we'd be happy to call creative. As remarked above, whether the computer model itself is 'really' creative is a separate, *philosophical*, question that's irrelevant here. It can't be answered without considering several fundamental, and highly controversial, philosophical topics – such as consciousness, the mind/brain relation, and intentionality, or meaning (Boden 2004: Chapter 11). But even if one decides that the answer is 'No', the relevance of computer models for expressing psychological theories of creativity remains.

Computer models of creativity

For reasons explained in the following section, combinational creativity is more difficult to model than one might expect. In other words, it's more difficult than most people think to make a computer come up with surprising-yet-valuable combinations. However, one area of AI has offered us some specific ideas about how mental combinations in general – alias associations – are possible. Connectionist AI, or the study of artificial neural networks, has focused on various aspects of associative memory – which is more often driven by subtle and fleeting comparisons than by exceptionless similarities (Boden 2006: Chapter 12).

The importance of mental associations in generating poetic imagery, for instance, was stressed by Samuel Taylor Coleridge. Coleridge's poetry has been insightfully analysed in this regard by the literary critic John Livingston Lowes (1930), who has identified the sources of many of the specific images in *The Ancient Mariner* (Boden 2004: Chapter 6). But Livingston Lowes, like Coleridge himself, had to take it for granted *that* associations are possible, without having any inkling of *how* they are possible. Today, connectionist AI can offer many hypotheses in answer to that question.

The most promising area for computer modelling is exploratory creativity. This requires, of course, that the programmer – or a cooperating colleague – has a good enough grasp of the domain concerned to specify the stylistic rules involved. This is rarely an easy matter. We're typically unaware of many of the stylistic aspects we respect when we create new structures/ ideas, and even if we do become aware of them, it's a challenging task to express them clearly in computational form. Indeed, a successful computer model can often teach the human experts something new about their specialist domain: musicology, for example, or architecture.

One impressive example of an exploratory AI model is Harold Cohen's AARON, a program for doing – and, more recently, for colouring – line drawings that's been under development for about 30 years (Cohen 1995, 2002). Cohen was already a highly acclaimed abstract painter before turning to computer art in the late 1960s. He did this not because he was seduced by the then-new gizmos, but because he believed that it would help him to understand his own creative processes.

The styles, or conceptual spaces, explored by AARON have varied over time, becoming richer in a number of ways. The line-drawing versions of the program developed increasingly subtle representations of 3D space over the years, and its images – each one unique, although clearly situated within a certain style – were exhibited in galleries around the world. The colouring version took longer to develop to a level that satisfied the human artist. But in 2006 it not only satisfied him, but actually surpassed him: 'I am a first-rate colourist,' Cohen said, 'but AARON is a world-class colourist' (p.c.). (This is analogous to the fact that, even by 1960, a draughts-playing program had beaten its own programmer – something that many people assume is impossible in principle.)

Two more exploratory AI systems within the visual arts concern architecture: one designs Palladian villas (Hersey and Freedman 1992), while the other sketches Frank Lloyd Wright 'Prairie Houses' (Koning and Eizenberg 1981). In both cases, the programmers learnt some-thing new about the styles concerned as a result of their work. (Notice the sub-title of the book on possible Palladian villas: *Plus a Few Instructively Impossible Ones*.) The Prairie House program is especially interesting. Not only has it generated designs for all the Prairie Houses actually created by Lloyd Wright, and others clearly in the same style – while *never* producing an unacceptable design; in addition, it has clarified various aspects of this genre – one which a specialist architectural historian, having tried unsuccessfully to define it, had declared to be 'occult' (Boden 2004: 309f.; Koning and Eizenberg 1981: 322).

An especially challenging example deals with the creation of new alphabetic fonts (Boden 2004: 306ff.; Hofstadter and McGraw 1995; Rehling 2002). Each letter must be written in the same style as its 25 fellows, and must also be recognizable as a particular letter – as an *a* or a *b*, for instance. However, the typical features of two letters may be very different, so that the style in question 'suits' a *w* better than an *a*; in that case, one may need to see the *w* in order to recognize the *a*. Further instances of artificial exploration concern the creation of story plots, taking into account not only the goals of the characters in the story but also the storyteller's own rhetorical goals in telling the tale (Boden 2004: 315–318; Turner 1994), and of music in many different styles – including both classical and modern composers and real-time jazz improvisation (Boden 2006: Chapter 13, iv.b; Cope 2001, 2006; Hodgson 2005).

Most of these research projects have been in development for some years, and are still being improved. For instance, the current version of the font-design program accepts five letter-seeds (*b, c, e, f* and *g*), classifies them with 93.5 per cent success (people achieve only 83.4 per cent), and designs a variety of coherent 26-letter fonts on the basis of the original (often modified) seeds. The programmers plan to enable it to do this on the basis of only one letter-seed. After that, they hope to extend it still further so that it can create letter-seeds for itself.

Science isn't excluded. A suite of discovery programs capable of inducing scientific laws from (sometimes noisy) input data has been developed by a team led by the AI pioneer, Herbert Simon (Langley *et al.* 1987). They might be better termed 'rediscovery' programs, since the laws generated by them were already known (although novel *formulations* of known laws sometimes arose). But AI programs have sometimes come up with new scientific knowledge (Langley 1998; Lindsay *et al.* 1980).

Yet more examples could be given: exploratory AI models are increasingly thick on the ground. And most of them generate *novel* ideas within the conceptual space concerned. Since that space, or style, is typically already valued (why bother to model a 'worthless' way of thinking?), the new structures generated within it will be regarded as valuable too. Or rather, they'll be regarded as valuable *prima facie*: we'll see in the next section that some people, after discovering the computer provenance of the novelties concerned, would firmly *refuse* to attribute value to them.

What of transformational creativity? It might seem that this is wholly denied to computers, which simply follow the program they're given. Although exploration is possible (as we've seen), surely transformation isn't?

That's not so. A program doesn't necessarily have to follow unchanging guidelines, for it can be given ways of changing its guidelines. Specifically, AI includes evolutionary methods, whereby programs are equipped with genetic algorithms (GAs) inspired by biological evolution (Boden 2006: Chapter 15, vi). A GA enables the program to make random changes in its own rules, so that new structures are generated which previously were *impossible*.

In effect, the GA reproduces (copies) the rules of the parent generation, making unpredictable 'errors' when doing so. As in biology, most of these random changes are either simple point-mutations or crossovers wherein brief *strings* of symbols switch position. Sometimes, however, an entire mini-program can be hierarchically nested within another, or two such mini-programs can be concatenated – one being added after the other. When that happens, the result (a coloured image, for example) may be very different from its 'parent/s', and radically different from its not-very-distant ancestors. So much so, indeed, that someone looking at the results wouldn't suspect the existence of any family relationship (Sims 1991).

The choice of parent/s to be reproduced at each generation is sometimes done automatically, by the program itself. In that case, the programmer has to provide a computational fitness function to make the selection at each stage. (The fitness function should implement the programmer's values with respect to the task concerned.) Alternatively, a human being may do the selection interactively. Research in evolutionary programming can be directed to non-biological problems. The very first GA program, for instance, was written – in the mid-1980s – to optimise a method for locating leaks in oil pipelines (Boden 2004: 229–232). But much is focused on biological problems, or analogues thereof. Work in A-Life ranges from the study of coevolution to the automatic evolution of the 'brains' and 'bodies' of robots. For instance, the distance between the robot's two eyes can evolve to be small in predators and large in prey – think of foxes and rabbits, respectively (Cliff and Miller 1995); and pressure-sensing whiskers that don't provide any information not provided also by vision may eventually lose their connection to the robot's brain (Cliff *et al.* 1993).

In addition, this computer-modelling approach is increasingly being used to produce what's termed evolutionary art (Whitelaw 2004). Evolutionary artists usually opt for interactive (not automatic) selection, because this gives them a chance to guide the evolutionary process along preferred paths. They typically say that the results (images, musical phrases . . .) include many that they simply *could not* have imagined themselves (Todd and Latham 1992). In other words, they normally see this as a more creative – certainly, more surprising – activity than using exploratory AI models to produce new artworks, which they might have imagined, but didn't.

Obstacles to computer creativity

The greatest obstacles to computer creativity are the computer's lack of knowledge, the difficulty of producing truly radical transformations, and the elusiveness of values. Those three factors limit the actual achievements of AI models of creativity. But we must also consider the general public's sceptical attitude with respect to computer creativity. Whether this is justified or not, it acts as a disincentive to people who might otherwise be drawn into computer modelling – especially of art. Let's consider these obstacles in turn.

It might appear that combinational creativity is child's play for computers. For a computer can easily be made to churn out novel combinations of familiar ideas. It could list indefinitely many sets of half-a-dozen normally unrelated objects to be assembled together in a collage, for instance.

In fact, however, combinational creativity is the most difficult (out of the three types of creativity) to model in computers. That's because it's relatively free: no immediately obvious stylistic rules, or guidance, are involved. Nevertheless, rules there are: it's not the case that 'anything goes'. These rules concern (many kinds of) relevance, rather than style. If they are ignored, then most of the novel combinations produced by the machine will be uninteresting, or valueless. For example, not every set of six objects would make a satisfying, or even intriguing, visual collage. Since a creative idea is *by definition* valuable, this is a major obstacle.

In general, the relevance-monitoring 'rules' and 'guidance' involved are grounded in a rich base of world-knowledge (sometimes including cultural familiarity with a certain area of art), and often a rich knowledge of various aspects of language, too. In principle, this knowledge could be simulated in a computer – although that might require major advances on the types of computer we have today. In practice, it can't. (Admittedly, some interesting work on the recognition of relevance is computationally informed, and suggests hypotheses about the information processing required (Sperber and Wilson 1986). But turning this into a functioning computer model, for anything other than tiny 'toy' examples, isn't a feasible project.) In short, there's no hope of the computer surpassing its programmer in combinational creativity, as AARON surpassed Cohen in colouring ability. Accordingly, the combinational creativity achieved by AI models is very crude in comparison with the human case.

This is clear, for example, in a joke-writing program called JAPE (Binsted and Ritchie 1997). The program originates punning riddles fitting nine familiar templates, such as *What do you get when you cross an X with a Y?, What kind of X has Y?, What kind of X can Y?* and *What's the difference between an X and a Y?* It uses a semantic network of over 30,000 words, with link-labels marked for syllables, spelling, sound and syntax, as well as for semantics and synonymy. The program consults the templates (no simple matter) to generate results, including these: *What do you call a depressed train? A low-comotive; What do you call a strange market? A bizarre bazaar;* and *What kind of murderer has fibre? A cereal killer.*

As those examples illustrate, JAPE's puns are pretty good. Indeed, it's the most successful of today's AI jokers (Ritchie 2003: Chapter 10). But its relevance here is in helping us to appreciate the complexity involved in coming up with *appropriate* combinations. On the one hand, there are many previously unsuspected psychological subtleties in play when someone finds (or understands) jokes to match these familiar templates. On the other hand, to generate or appreciate these apparently simple riddles demands both rich world-knowledge and significant linguistic knowledge (of syllables, spelling, sound, syntax, semantics and synonymy . . .). Even if computers don't/can't have 'real' knowledge (or understanding) of anything, an AI model of combinational creativity has to have some simulation of the human knowledge required. As JAPE shows, this is no small order.

The second major obstacle concerns the depth of the 'creative' transformations that can be effected by computer models. Evolutionary programs can give rise to apparently radical transformations, as we've seen. But critics sometimes argue that truly fundamental changes are impossible, because everything that happens must lie within the pre-ordained limits, or potential, of the program.

One way of avoiding this limitation is to enable the evolving system to be influenced by its physical environment – not just by its program. In that case, unplanned, and occasionally advantageous, types of causal interaction may occur. A wholly new sensor (for radio waves) was unexpectedly evolved in this way, where what the team were actually trying to evolve was an oscillator circuit (Bird and Layzell 2002).

With respect to arts and science, however, the relevant 'environment' is only rarely physical. More usually, it's cultural. For example, human creators can be led to fundamentally new ideas by reading the literature in the domain concerned, or even chatting with a friend over coffee. But, again, this is a tall order. Huge – and highly improbable – advances in AI (especially natural language processing) would be needed to enable a scientific-discovery program, or a computerised poet, to evolve new ideas in this way.

The greatest obstacle to the achievement of AI creativity is the issue of values. The problem is not that the computers themselves can't truly have values. The problem, rather, is that the human programmers can't reliably model their own values. It's often nigh impossible for us to identify our values – to say just why we appreciate a certain style of painting or music, for example. Even professional art critics and art historians may have difficulty in doing this. And supposing that they can, it may be extremely difficult to express a certain value clearly enough for it to be programmed.

Moreover, in many areas of life our values change and shift: a program that generated highly creative (valued) ideas last year, or even last month, might be dismissed as irrelevant today. Finally, human values aren't universally shared across cultures, or even within cultures. So if someone were able to model their individual preferences in a computer, other people might not appreciate the results. In short, both the computer simulation of values and the acceptability of value-simulations are problematic.

Two last obstacles must be mentioned – which concern the public's *refusal to accept* computer models of creativity, rather than the extent of those models' actual achievements/failures.

The first is a version of what AI scientists call the superhuman-human fallacy. Critics constantly complain, for instance, that a computer composer doesn't match up to Mozart or Beethoven, or that a computer painter is no Picasso. For sure, no computer poet is a Shakespeare or a Donne. (Remember JAPE, and you'll be reminded of why that is.) But such critics forget that most of the human species don't match up to those individuals either. We don't normally deny that Jo Bloggs is a creative musician, just because he's no Mozart. Creativity exists in people who aren't 'superhuman'. Indeed, it exists in all of us, since it's an aspect of normal intelligence (Perkins 1981). Think of the creativity involved in the political cartoons in your daily newspaper, and in the analogies mentioned in the newspaper's editorials; or give a thought to the jokes and sarcasm that pepper your own, and your next door neighbour's, conversation.

It's not clear whether highly exceptional individuals such as Mozart or Shakespeare, have much the same powers as us, only more so, or whether they have some mysterious 'extra'. My own bet would be on the former (Boden 2004: Chapter 10). But we'll never know until we understand the everyday cases. Jo Bloggs, here, plays much the same role as inclined planes do in physics: if Galileo had started out by rolling his balls on ploughed fields, he wouldn't have got very far. In other words, for the purpose of understanding creativity, Mozart can wait.

The second obstacle to public acceptance is the common (though by no means universal) conviction that computers and creativity simply don't mix. An especially telling example involved a music critic who wrote a damning 'review' of a concert of computer-composed music *two weeks before the concert took place*, and who refused to accept an invitation to the concert when contacted by the human composer-programmer himself (Cope 2006: 345). The very idea of such an occasion, in his view, was so inauthentic – not to say fraudulent – that he didn't need to judge the *degree* of creative 'success' of the program concerned. Success, he felt, was simply inconceivable. That is, even if the program had managed to compose new music in the style of Bach, or Mozart (which indeed it had), this critic wouldn't have been impressed. The program would be ingenious, no doubt: but valuable? *No!*

A comparable refusal to allow that any artwork could be generated by a computer has been argued by a philosopher of aesthetics for whom art, by definition, involves an act of communication between one human being and another (O'Hear 1995). On that view, even the most seemingly successful computer art can at best be only a pale shadow of the real thing.

Applications in the real world

Despite all the problems mentioned above, some areas of AI creativity are already bearing fruit. Indeed, a computer program won a real-world creativity competition, in which all the other contestants were human, as long ago as the early 1980s. The task in that case was to play a war game, in which one has to design and test a battlefleet within certain cost limits. Whether playing war games counts as a practical application, you may think, is a moot point (although presumably the military would say that it does). But since the early 1980s many other results have been generated which clearly do have uses in the real world.

In the visual arts, both exploratory computer artists (such as Cohen) and evolutionary artists (such as William Latham) (Todd and Latham 1992) exhibit – and sell – their work to the general public. Similarly, compositions by music programs are sometimes played and sold.

In the area of commercial/industrial design, all three programming approaches discussed here have been used to practical effect. Occasionally, innovations have been generated by an AI model that are sufficiently new, and (potentially) useful, to be patented: an early example was a three-dimensional computer chip (Boden 2004: 228).

Exploratory and evolutionary models are used in certain areas of science. In pharmacology, for example, new molecules (drugs) likely to have useful properties are routinely suggested by such means.

Practical applications to real-world problems of strategy, or leadership, are less apparent – not to say invisible. The reason is twofold. On the one hand, such problems, since they apply to human behaviour, are typically highly complex – and may also be affected by specific local conditions and/or personal idiosyncrasies. As explained in the discussion of combinatorial creativity (above), it's not feasible to include all such potentially relevant factors in the database of a computer program or neural network. On the other hand, even professional management consultants don't actually know just which features are important in enabling successful leadership. And insofar as they have plausible hunches about this, those hunches can't be expressed clearly enough for computational purposes. For the present, then (and, in my view, for the foreseeable future too), our best resource for addressing such problems is good old-fashioned human intuition.

Exploratory programs can also be used for purposes of training or education. A budding architect, or music student, may learn a lot from playing around with a suitably designed domain-specific computer program. For example, an early version of the jazz improviser mentioned above has been applied in this way (Hodgson 2005).

In addition, if theoretical psychology counts as an application in the real world, then AI models of creativity can claim credit here, too. Our understanding of the sorts of psychological process that underlie creative thinking is being advanced by this work. By the same token, we're learning more about the types of situation that can encourage or impede creativity, whether in children or adults. We're able, for instance, to resist the lazy suggestion that autodidacts are especially creative: some are and some aren't, depending both on the type of autodidact concerned and on the type of creativity in question (Boden 2003).

Conclusions

All research on creativity – whether historical, psychological, philosophical or computational – is bedevilled by the complexity of the concept, and by the fact that different people use the term in different ways. Accordingly, a host of conceptual issues need to be clarified before any satisfactory systematic study can be done.

In the AI modelling of creativity there's an added difficulty, namely, that anything we say has to be said clearly enough to be programmed. It's not enough for it to be intuitively intelligible. This clarity is needed at all stages of modelling: for defining conceptual spaces (styles) and the rules for exploring them, for identifying processes that can combine familiar ideas in new and interesting ways, and for the valuation of novel results.

That's the bad news. The good news is that when AI scientists do manage to achieve the necessary clarity, and write programs that generate creative – novel, surprising and valuable – results, they usually increase our understanding of the psychological processes involved. Creativity remains a marvel, to be sure. But it's no longer an unfathomable mystery.

References

Binsted, K., and Ritchie, G. D. (1997) Computational Rules for Punning Riddles, *Humor: International Journal of Humor Research*, 10: 25–76.

Bird, J., and Layzell, P. (2002) The Evolved Radio and its Implications for Modelling the Evolution of Novel Sensors, *Proceedings of Congress on Evolutionary Computation*, CEC-2002, 1836–1841.

Boden, M. A. (2003) Are Autodidacts Creative?, in J. Solomon (ed.), *The Passion to Learn: An Inquiry Into Autodidactism*, London: RoutledgeFalmer, 24–31.

Boden, M. A. (2004) *The Creative Mind: Myths and Mechanisms*, second edition, expanded/revised, London: Routledge.

Boden, M. A. (2006) *Mind as Machine: A History of Cognitive Science*, Oxford: Oxford University Press.

Cliff, D. and Miller, G. F. (1995) Tracking the Red Queen: Measurements of Adaptive Progress in Coevolutionary Simulations, in F. Moran, A. Moreno, J. J. Merelo and P. Chacon (eds), Advances in Artificial Life, *Proceedings of the Third European Conference on Artificial Life (ECAL95)*, Berlin: Springer-Verlag 200–218.

Cliff, D., Harvey, I. and Husbands, P. (1993) Explorations in Evolutionary Robotics, *Adaptive Behavior*, 2: 73–110.

Cohen, H. (1995) The Further Exploits of AARON Painter, in S. Franchi and G. Guzeldere (eds), *Constructions of the Mind: Artificial Intelligence and the Humanities*, special edition of *Stanford Humanities Review*, 4(2): 141–160.

Cohen, H. (2002) A Million Millennial Medicis, in L. Candy and E. Edmonds (eds), *Explorations in Art and Technology*, London: Springer, 91–104.

Cope, D. (2001) *Virtual Music: Computer Synthesis of Musical Style*, Cambridge, MA: MIT Press.

Cope, D. (2006) *Computer Models of Musical Creativity*, Cambridge, MA: MIT Press.

Hersey, G. and Freedman, R. (1992) *Possible Palladian Villas (Plus a Few Instructively Impossible Ones)*, Cambridge, MA: MIT Press.

Hodgson, P. W. (2005) Modeling Cognition in Creative Musical Improvisation, unpublished D.Phil. thesis, Department of Informatics, University of Sussex.

Hofstadter, D. R. and McGraw, G. (1995) Letter Spirit: Esthetic Perception and Creative Play in the Rich Microcosm of the Roman Alphabet, in D. R. Hofstadter and FARG (The Fluid Analogies Research Group), *Fluid Concepts and Creative Analogies: Computer Models of the Fundamental Mechanisms of Thought*, New York: Basic Books, 407–466.

Koning, H. and Eizenberg, J. (1981) The Language of the Prairie: Frank Lloyd Wright's Prairie Houses, *Environment and Planning, B: Planning and Design*, 8(3), 295–323.

Langley, P. W. (1998) The Computer-aided Discovery of Scientific Knowledge, in S. Arikawa and H. Motoda (eds), Discovery Science, *Proceedings of the First International Conference on Discovery Science, Fukuoka, Japan*, Berlin: Springer, 25–39.

Langley, P. W., Simon, H. A., Bradshaw, G. L. and Zytkow, J. M. (1987) *Scientific Discovery: Computational Explorations of the Creative Process*, Cambridge, MA: MIT Press.

Lindsay, R. K., Buchanan, B. G., Feigenbaum, E. A. and Lederburg, J. (1980) *Applications of Artificial Intelligence for Organic Chemistry: The Dendral Project*, New York: McGraw-Hill.

Livingston Lowes, J. (1930) *The Road to Xanadu: A Study in the Ways of the Imagination*, London: Houghton.

O'Hear, A. (1995) Art and Technology: An Old Tension, in R. Fellows (ed.), *Philosophy and Technology*, Cambridge: Cambridge University Press, 143–158.

Perkins, D. N. (1981) *The Mind's Best Work*, Cambridge, MA: Harvard University Press.

Rehling, J. A. (2002) Results in the Letter Spirit Project, in T. Dartnall (ed.), *Creativity, Cognition, and Knowledge: An Interaction*, London: Praeger, 273–282.

Ritchie, G. D. (2003) *The Linguistic Analysis of Jokes*, London: Routledge.

Sims, K. (1991) Artificial Evolution for Computer Graphics, *Computer Graphics*, 25(4): 319–328.

Sperber, D. and Wilson, D. (1986) *Relevance: Communication and Cognition*, Oxford: Blackwell.

Todd, S. C. and Latham, W. (1992) *Evolutionary Art and Computers*, London: Academic Press.

Turner, S. R. (1994) *The Creative Process: A Computer Model of Storytelling and Creativity*, Hillsdale, NJ: Lawrence Erlbaum.

Whitelaw, M. (2004) *Metacreation: Art and Artificial Life*, London: MIT Press.

16

Relationship creativity in collectives at multiple levels

Subrata Chakrabarty and Richard W. Woodman

Moving beyond the traditional focus on individual creativity, we argue that relationships are important for creative action, and that relationships can exist at multiple levels. A team is a collective of persons with inter-person relationships, an organization is a collective of teams with inter-team relationships, and a collective of organizations can exist in the market with inter-organization relationships. Relationships matter for creativity because relationships are often a preferred choice for creative action and provide access to useful knowledge. Relationships at multiple levels are structured according to the shared vision. Actors limit themselves to inspiring relationships when they prefer to undertake creative action in solitude, and build either integrating or synergizing relationships for undertaking creative action collectively.

Woodman *et al.* (1993) proposed one of the first models that discussed the pursuit of creativity at multiple levels of persons, groups/teams and organizations. However, a thorough understanding of why and how actors at these levels interact towards the realization of creativity has eluded us. For example, is a creative team just a collection of highly creative persons, or does there need to be creative synergy between team members? Can a unified creative idea be generated by a synergistic 'meeting of minds'? Will emphasis on just individual creativity lead to fragmented or disconnected creative outcomes from multiple people in a group? Why do some actors engage in creative action on their own (in solitude), while some others engage in collective creative action? How do these preferences play out in a social structure? We propose to address these questions, and hence better explain creative behavior at the inter-person, inter-team and inter-organization levels.

We define relationship creativity as a theoretical perspective for understanding the use of inter-actor relationships for creative action within a collective (at multiple levels of analysis) (for theory and details, kindly see Chakrabarty and Woodman 2008). In this chapter, we will argue that structuring different types of inter-actor relationships allow for different ways of engaging in creative action, which ultimately result in different creative outcomes (Chakrabarty and Woodman 2007, 2008). We discuss why and how the structuring of relationships among actors in collectives has a bearing on the nature of creative action.

First, for the actors at each of the chosen levels of analysis (namely persons, teams or organizations), the 'why?' will be explained by discussing two of the important motors that drive the usage of relationships for creative action. Specifically, we address why individuals with differing self-construals have different preferences for relationships, and why relationships provide access to useful knowledge.

Second, the major emphasis of this chapter is the 'how?' We will discuss the concept of shared vision (a shared motivation and common goal to come up with a unified creative outcome), the structuring of suitable inter-actor relationships (that provide a platform to work towards the realization of the creative goals), the creative action process (the act of making use of the structured relationships and working for creative outcomes), and the realization of the creative outcome.

Why do relationships matter for creativity?

Relationships are often a preferred choice and they allow access to knowledge that is useful for creative action.

Relationships are a preferred choice for some individuals

Self-construal is one's perception of self as either 'independent or interdependent', where a person with independent self-construal perceives that he or she 'is a separate entity with a unique repertoire of feelings and thoughts' and a person with interdependent self-construal feels 'connected to those around her or him' (Oetzel 2002: 127). Hence, a person's independent self-construal is a more direct and explicit measure of his or her individualistic tendencies, and a person's interdependent self-construal is a more direct and explicit measure of his or her collectivist tendencies at an individual level (Gudykunst et al. 1996; Oetzel 2002).

The independent self-construal places a greater emphasis on the self rather than the relationship (Gudykunst et al. 1996: 518; Oetzel 1998: 127). A person having a dominant independent self-construal views themself as a unique and independent actor, and the need for such 'independence requires construing oneself as an individual whose behavior is organized and made meaningful primarily by reference to one's own internal repertoire of thoughts, feelings, and action, rather than by reference to the thoughts, feelings, and actions of others' (Markus and Kitayama 1991). Hence, persons of independent self-construal with a creative urge would be driven towards creative action in isolation from others (in solitude), by largely relying only on their own internal cognition of thoughts, feelings and actions.

The interdependent self-construal places a greater emphasis on the relationship rather than the self (Gudykunst et al. 1996: 518; Oetzel 1998: 127). Unlike the independent self-construal, for the interdependent self-construal 'others will be assigned much more importance, will carry more weight' (Markus and Kitayama 1991: 229). To the interdependent self-construal 'the self becomes most meaningful and complete when it is cast in the appropriate social relationship' and great value is placed on the 'thoughts, feelings, and actions of others in the relationship' (ibid.: 227).

Oetzel's (2002: 127) studies found that groups dominated by independent self-construals were more likely to use competitive tactics (that would make the person stand apart from others and be perceived as unique) and less likely to use cooperative tactics. On the other hand, teams dominated by interdependent self-construals were likely to use cooperative tactics (that are essential for collective action) and less likely to use competitive tactics (that can be detrimental to collective action) (op. cit.). A person of independent self-construal would be most comfortable with either having no creative relationships with others or having relationships that are just inspirational enough for their own creative action in solitude. Within groups dominated by people with such independent self-construal, the members would be more oriented towards solitary creative action on their own (rather than collective creative action). In comparison, a person with greater interdependent self-construal is more likely to prefer engaging in collective creative action by using relationships with other persons. Within teams dominated by people with such interdependent self-construal, the members would be more oriented towards collective creative action towards a unified team outcome.

Very likely, when a collection of persons are dominated by people of independent self-construals, then one may find that each person is highly motivated to prove their own distinct creative self-worth; however, it might be difficult to get the collective to overcome their internal competition and start cooperating with each other. At the other extreme, when a collection of persons are dominated by people of interdependent self-construals, then all would follow the team's norms and work collectively with unity; however, members may shy away from highlighting their own individual creative contributions and may avoid fighting for their own individual rights (such as recognition or fair compensation) and avoid highlighting any unpleasant truths (such as deficiencies in the team's creative product) as it might displease the other team members and break the unity of their team.

Relationships provide access to useful knowledge

In a relationship between actors (persons, teams or organizations), if we consider a continuum ranging from low knowledge diversity (high commonality) to high knowledge diversity, then there is an optimum point on this continuum where the knowledge has high usefulness (Cohen and Levinthal 1990; Milliken and Martins 1996). Interactions with high knowledge usefulness would be beneficial to actors, as they would expose them to diverse knowledge that is also common enough for them to relate to. The benefits of access to useful knowledge are not limited to just inter-person and inter-team relationships within the boundaries of an organization. At an inter-organizational level, organizations in the market attempt to stay competitive by striving to access and benefit from the knowledge and expertise of the other organizations, and the management research literature has found strong evidence for such inter-organizational learning, formation of inter-organizational alliances for leveraging knowledge (Hitt *et al.* 2000), and inter-organizational mimicking (Haveman 1993; Mizruchi and Fein 1999). A person may be able to improve their own individual creativity by having inspiring interactions with others, and an organization can produce more creative products if it can study and derive inspirations from the products of other organizations in the market. When actors engage in creative action collectively (towards a unified creative outcome from the collective), then mutual knowledge usefulness can allow either (a) integration of their respective creative works (that were carried out by each actor alone) into a unified creative outcome, or (b) creative action in synergy, that is acting with high collective intensity, towards the realization of their unified creative outcome.

How do relationships allow creative action?

Shared vision and the structuring of creative relationships

An individual can become drawn into a creative endeavor in a number of ways. It may be that spark of imagination in solitude that intrinsically motivates the person to search, discover and delve deeper into the chosen domain. However, it may also be that moment of time when interacting with another person allows an individual to become exposed to a better way of looking at a problem that he or she has been trying to solve.

191

Not all social interactions are beneficial for creativity, and many such interactions are simply for routine or habitual purposes (Ford 1996). A creative relationship should allow beneficial interactions that are useful for creative action, and we suggest that they can be further classified into either an inspiring relationship, an integrating relationship or a synergizing relationship. An actor can have multiple dyadic relationships, and hence, it is very likely that creative inspirations emanate from one's relationships rather than just from within the actor. For a relationship to lead to collective creative action, it is important for the actors in the relationship to have a shared vision, which is a bonding mechanism that allows 'goal congruence' (Tsai and Ghoshal 1998: 467). When actors in a relationship have a shared vision, they then: (a) have the 'same perceptions about how to interact with one another'; (b) have 'collective goals and aspirations'; and (c) 'can avoid possible misunderstandings in their communications and have more opportunities to exchange their ideas or resources freely' (op. cit.). The nature of interactions between actors in a relationship and each of the actor's own preferences define the nature of the relationship (see Figure 16.1):

- *No creative relationship.* Interactions among the actors do not spark any additional creative ideas, and a shared vision is also absent in the relationship. However, in spite of not having any creatively beneficial relationships with other actors, the actor can undertake creative action in isolation (in solitude).
- *Inspiring relationship.* Interactions with another actor provide information that is beneficial for creative action, and the actor feels inspired by the talk; however there is absence of a shared vision where the actors fail to work out an arrangement whereby they can work collectively towards a unified creative outcome. In this scenario, the actor can retreat into solitude to delve deeper into the issue alone (without involving the other person) with the fresh creative insight gained from the inspiring relationship.
- *Integrating relationship.* The actors agree on a shared vision, but since each actor prefers to work alone, they decide to mutually divide their roles (based on their abilities) to engage in creative action in solitude, and to integrate (aggregate or sum together) their creative work into a unified creative outcome that represents the realization of their shared vision later on.
- *Synergizing relationship.* The actors agree on a shared vision, and they decide to work in a fashion whereby they can gradually move towards a unified creative outcome drawn from a mutual 'meeting of minds' and intense collaboration. This relationship allows creative action in synergy, which is a form of intense collaborative action, which results in a unified novel outcome that is above and beyond what each actor could have produced individually in solitude or by the mere summation or integration of their work. The interactions in this type of relationship have the potential to fructify into a unified creative outcome that is novel and unique to such an extent that only the synergy in the relationship could have produced it.

These interactions need not be limited to relationships among persons, and can be extended to higher levels of relationship among different team units (Alderfer and Smith 1982; Joshi 2006; Pettigrew 1998), and relationships among organizations (Ireland *et al.* 2002).

Table 16.1 briefly sums up the overarching concepts used in this chapter, that is, of shared vision and the structuring of creative relationships (either inspiring, integrating or synergizing relationships) that allow the process of creative action (either through solitude, solitude-plus-integration or synergy) that ultimately result in creative outcomes at multiple levels.

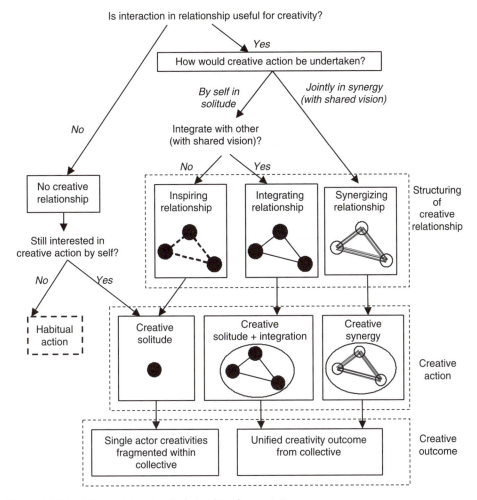

Figure 16.1 The 'How' of the role of relationships for creativity

Creative action: solitude, solitude-plus-integration and synergy at multiple levels of analysis

Ford (1996) suggested that creative action and habitual action represent competing behavioral option choices. While habitual actions imply routine or mundane behavior that does not display any potential for a creative outcome, creative actions lead to novel and valuable creative outcomes (ibid.). Ford (ibid.: 1117) explained that creative actions 'result from the joint influence of sensemaking, motivation, and knowledge and ability'. In this chapter, we term sensemaking, motivation and knowledge/ability as creative action inputs whose joint influence result in creative action (see Table 16.2). Furthermore, Ford (ibid.) suggested that individuals continually engage in sensemaking 'that reflects the reciprocal interaction of information seeking, meaning ascription, and action' (p. 1119) and that sensemaking 'typically elicits intentions and expectations regarding the appropriateness and likely effectiveness of future actions' (p. 1120). Additionally, motivation to take up a creative action is a function of the 'goals,

Table 16.1 Overall process leading to creativity in collectives

Concept	Description
Shared vision	The presence or absence of a shared vision that motivates persons, teams and organizations to forge (or not forge) relationships for creative purposes.
Structuring of suitable inter-actor relationships	The type of relationship formed, in terms of the nature and intensity of creative interactions. It can be either an inspirational relationship (for creative inspirations only, and does not allow any scope for collective action), an integrating relationship (allows each of the actors to work separately using their own expertise, but can eventually integrate their creative works into a unified one), or a synergizing relationship (allows the actors to work together with intense collaboration to take advantage of mutual expertise at all times).
The creative action	The actual process of creative action, which leads to the creative outcomes. It can be either creative action in solitude only (where the actor works relies primarily alone to achieve a creative outcome), creative action in solitude-plus-integration (where the actors work on their own, but also work towards integrating their creative works into a unified outcome), or creative action in synergy (where actors work together towards a unified creative outcome).
The realization of creative outcome	The outcome of creative action, which can be either fragmented creativities by actors within the collective (creative parts cannot be summed), or a unified creative outcome from the collective (equal to or greater than the sum of its parts).

Table 16.2 Creative action process

Action =	Predominant status of dimension		
	Sensemaking x	*Motivation x*	*Knowledge/ability*
Habitual action	*(Non-creative)*	*(Non-creative)*	*(Non-creative)*
Creative action in solitude	*Self*	*Self*	Primarily from *Self*, Maybe some inspiration from others
Creative action in solitude plus integration	*Self* while in solitude, and *Mutual* during integration stage	*Self*	Largely from *Self* while in solitude, but some mutual knowledge and abilities come into play during integration stage
Creative action in synergy	*Joint/mutual/iterative/ reciprocal*	*Mutual*	*Mutual knowledge/abilities*, that is optimum in diversity and commonality

expectations related to those intentions, and emotions' and knowledge and ability includes domain-related knowledge, behavioral abilities and creative thinking abilities (op. cit.) (for more details, see Amabile *et al.* 1996; Ford 1996; Woodman *et al.* 1993).

Though often applied at the individual level, the creative action inputs of sensemaking, motivation and knowledge/ability exist at higher levels (teams and organizations) too. This chapter assumes that an actor can be a person, team or organization, that a relationship can exist at multiple levels of inter-person, inter-team and inter-organization, and that the creative action inputs of sensemaking, motivation and knowledge/ability can exist at these multiple levels. The creative action inputs at each of the higher levels (teams and firms) are a function of both the aggregates of creative action inputs at levels below it and also the unique creative action inputs at the level itself. For example, individuals within a team can have their own individual sensemaking, motivation and knowledge/abilities that can be aggregated to the team level. At the same time, a team as a whole can behave as a distinct actor that has its own sensemaking, motivation and knowledge/abilities that are derived from collective constructs at the team/group level, such as the team's collective cognition, shared mental models, transactive memory, motivation, personality, efficacy, learning, tacit knowledge, mutual knowledge and abilities (Gibson 1999; Kirkman *et al.* 2004; Morgeson and Hofmann 1999; Walsh and Ungson 1991). Similarly, while creative action inputs at individual and team levels can be aggregated to organizational levels, the organization itself may behave as a distinct actor with its own sensemaking, motivation, and knowledge/abilities that are derived from organization-level constructs such as organizational memory, strategic intent, strategic leadership and organizational learning (Anand and Manz 1998; Hitt *et al.* 2000; Ireland and Hitt 2005; Morgeson and Hofmann 1999; Walsh and Ungson 1991).

Hence, our view is that the three dimensions of sensemaking, motivation and knowledge/ability can apply at multiple levels (person, team and organization). Additionally, we argue that the predominant status of the dimensions of creative action inputs varies across the creative action processes (see Table 16.2), namely (a) habitual action, (b) creative action in solitude, (c) creative action in solitude-plus-integration, and (d) creative action in synergy. For habitual action, these dimensions (or at least one of these) would be non-existent from a creative perspective. For creative action in solitude, these dimensions would be driven primarily from within the actor (see Table 16.2). Ford (1996: 1116–1125) has commendably elaborated on these aspects for habitual action and individual creative action (solitude).

Going beyond Ford's (1996) individual level cognition perspective, we explore the use of relationships for collective creative action. Inspiring creative relationships allow beneficial interactions with other actors, which inspire an actor's thoughts and feelings for the creative action being pursued. For creative action purely in solitude, inspiring relationships are especially useful. In the process of creative action in solitude, an actor is engaged in solitary creative action, and there is a preference towards detachment or isolation to varying extents. Creative solitude can involve either an extreme state of social isolation where there is no creativity-related interaction with the outside world, or it can also involve a less extreme state of isolation, where interactions are primarily geared towards gaining inspiring inputs from other actors for one's own creative action. For creative action in solitude, the inputs of sensemaking, motivation and knowledge/ability would be primarily derived by each actor from within (see Table 16.2). During creative action in solitude, an actor's creativity largely emanates from the 'self' or from 'within', and therefore each actor can be creative in a very unique way. When an actor is engaging in a particular creative endeavor in solitude, the actor's creative relationships with others are limited to just 'inspiring' relationships, or none at all. Such an actor draws creative inspirations while interacting with others, without any obligation to involve the other actor in the creative endeavor. Creative action in solitude by an actor is seen across society and organizations, where the actor is accountable and responsible for only their own creative actions, and interactions with others (if any) are often for sharing information that might be inspirational.

On the other hand, integrating and synergizing relationships allow much more than inspirations, and provide a social platform for multiple actors that are bound by a shared vision to work towards a unified creative outcome. In both synergizing relationships and integrating relationships, the individuals in the relationship need to together produce a unified creative outcome. In support of our perspective, Cohen and Levinthal (1990: 133) had earlier argued that 'assuming a sufficient level of knowledge overlap to ensure effective communication, interactions across individuals who each possess diverse and different knowledge structures will augment the organization's capacity for making novel linkages and associations – innovating – beyond what any one individual can achieve.' In an integrating relationship, a person's creative outcome in solitude would be considered 'incomplete' until it is integrated (aggregated) with that of the other person in the relationship. In comparison, synergy is the process of intense collective creative action by actors that results in novel and unique creative outcomes above and beyond what the actors could have achieved either on their own (as in solitude) or by simply summing or aggregating their work (as in integration).

Creativity is the novel and valuable outcome of creative action (Ford 1996: 115). The forms of creativity outcomes are: (1) an outcome of creativity of a single actor (individual creativity from a person, team creativity from a team, organizational creativity from an organization), and (2) the unified creative outcome from a collective of multiple actors that emanates from either (a) the integration of each actor's creativity (in solitude) within the collective into a larger unified whole, or from (b) the synergy in the relationships among the actors. Note that only integrating relationships or synergizing relationships allow collective creative action that lead to a unified creative outcome, and not inspiring relationships (which allow creative action in solitude only). Figure 16.2 provides a 3 × 3 framework whereby relationships can be structured in three ways (inspiring, integrating or synergizing), and can exist at three levels (inter-person within a team, inter-team within an organization or inter-organization within the market).

Inspiring relationships for creative action in solitude

Inspiring inter-person relationships for creative action in solitude: individual creativities fragmented within group

In fragmented groups, each individual's creative relationships with other group members and the external world are limited to just 'inspiring' relationships, or none at all. That is, an individual might be creatively inspired while interacting with others, but these relevant others do not involve themselves in the individual's creative endeavor in any manner whatsoever. Such fragmented groups are widespread and useful in organizations where people come together to 'share information, perspectives, and insights'; however, the focus is always on 'individual goals and accountabilities', 'members don't take responsibility for results other than their own' and there is no effort towards 'contributions requiring the combined work of two or more members' (Katzenbach and Smith 1993: 112).

During a person's creative action in solitude, the person would derive the inputs of sense-making, motivation and knowledge/ability from within (Ford 1996). Inspirational relationships (if any) with others are merely to source information or to discuss information that can spark off creative thoughts in the person's mind and help the person during his or her creative action in solitude (see Table 16.2). In solitude, the person can reflect back on the information received and discussions had with others, and use them to further refine and develop their own ideas. Within a group, where each person is working in solitude, there can be inspiring relationships among the persons with interactions that stimulate each other. However, since each person would have their own vision that is distinct from those of others, each person would engage in creative action that is in a distinct domain and does not need to depend on the creative outcomes of others to be eventually considered as 'complete'. The creative work of a person in solitude should be 'able to stand on its own feet' and have an 'identity of its own' when

			Level of analysis		
			Inter-person (within team/group)	**Inter-team** (within organization)	**Inter-organization** (in market)
Creativity	**Fragmented outcome**		**Relationships = Inspiring or none**	Inspiring relationships among persons (within *group*)	Inspiring relationships among teams (within organization)	Inspiring relationships with other organizations (in market)
			Creative action = solitude	by person in solitude	by team in solitude	by organization in solitude
			Outcome = fragmented within collective	Individual creativities (fragmented within group)	Team creativities (fragmented within organization) *(either 'T1' or 'T2')*	Organizational creativities (fragmented in market) *(either 'O1' or 'O2')*
	Unified outcome	**Integrated**	**Relationships = integrating**	Integrating relationships among persons (within *team*)	Integrating relationships among teams (within organization)	Integrating relationships among organizations (in market)
			Creative action = solitude + integration	by persons in solitude, with efforts for integration	by teams in solitude, with efforts for integration	by organizations in solitude, with efforts for integration
			Outcome = unified	Team creativity (T1)	Organizational creativity (O1)	Inter-organization creativity in market
		Synergized	**Relationships = synergizing**	Synergizing relationships among individuals (within *team*)	Synergizing relationships among teams (within organization)	Synergizing relationships among organizations (in market)
			Creative action = synergy	by individuals in synergy	by teams in synergy	by organizations in synergy
			Outcome = unified	Team creativity (T2)	Organizational Creativity (O2)	Inter-organization creativity in market

Figure 16.2 Framework: three creativity outcomes at three levels of analysis

completed; that is, it would be a creative outcome that is both independent and complete. In such a scenario, the group would potentially produce multiple distinct creative outcomes. This fragmentation can be beneficial, since the potential quantity of creative outcomes from the group can be very high, and at the same time members of the group can take advantage of their inspiring relationships, despite each member primarily engaging in creative action in solitude.

In fragmented groups, the individual creative abilities lead to different creative outcomes altogether that will not be unified. A fragmented group's creativity is the dispersed creative outcomes of its individual members in solitude, where each individual can produce a creative outcome that is very distinct from another's. In other words, fragmented group creativity emanates from creative action in solitude by individual members on very different creative endeavors. Hence, limiting inter-person relationships to either habitual or inspiring inter-person relationships allows for creative action in solitude by persons (within a group), which in turn is likely to result in multiple individual creativity outcomes that are fragmented within the group. Such fragmented individual creativities cannot be summed into a unified creative outcome for the group.

Inspiring inter-team relationships for creative action in solitude: team creativities fragmented within organization

When team creativity outcomes are fragmented within an organization, it is because teams in the organization work independently (each team in solitude), deliver independent creative products, and their creative interactions (if any) with other teams are only for 'inspiring' purposes that can aid their own team's creative outcome. For example, in a software firm, a marketing team may be engaged in devising a new ad campaign, and the sole purpose of their interaction with a software development team is to discover some basic information about the new software being developed that can be highlighted in the ad campaign. Both the marketing team and software team deliver very different creative products that cannot be unified, and their interaction is purely inspirational in nature.

A team unit's creativity in solitude (within the organization) is a function of the team's internal composition, internal characteristics, internal procedures, and also the external contextual/situational influences (Woodman et al. 1993). Though each team unit (within the organization) would act in solitude (that is, limit relationships with other teams to just inspirational ones), the members within the team can engage in creative action through either synergizing or integrating inter-person relationships, so that the team as a whole provides a unified creative outcome. Even though the members within the team work in a synergizing or integrating fashion, the team itself may be in 'solitude' because it is delivering an independent team outcome. Such teams contribute to fragmented organizational creativity, and any inter-team interactions are at best 'inspiring' relationships. This fragmentation within the organization can be beneficial, since each of the teams within the organization work towards independent creative outcomes, and hence the organization can potentially benefit from the sheer quantity of distinct creative outcomes that can be eventually produced. Hence, limiting inter-team relationships to either habitual or inspiring inter-team relationships allows for creative action in solitude by teams (within an organization), which in turn is likely to result in multiple team creativity outcomes that are fragmented within the organization. Such fragmented team creativities cannot be summed into a unified creative outcome for the organization.

Inspiring inter-organization relationships for creative action in solitude: organizational creativities fragmented in the market

In the market, an organization might be inspired by the procedures used by its competitors, or by the way one of its suppliers is marketing its products. These inspirations can come from direct interactions with other organizations (such as supplier or customer organizations), through observation of competitor organizations, or from consultants. Here, the organization is under no obligation to involve the source of inspiration in the creative endeavor that the organization is pursuing in solitude.

In a state of solitude, a single organization's creativity largely emanates from within, and therefore each organization can be creative in a very unique way based on the core capability of the organization. When an organization is engaging in a particular creative endeavor in solitude, the organization's creative relationships with other organizations are limited to just 'inspiring' tangible or intangible relationships, or none at all. Such single organization creativity is highly prevalent, where the organization is accountable and responsible only for its own creative actions, and the interactions with other organizations (if any) are often for obtaining inspirational information only. For example, the literature discusses 'mimicking', whereby one organization tries to study (or even copy) the work of its competitors or other successful organizations (Haveman 1993; Mizruchi and Fein 1999), and once an organization learns more from other organizations, then it would implement its 'learning' in solitude.

Fragmentation in a competitive market, where multiple organizations are working towards competing and diverse creative products, is a bonus for customers. When multiple organizations are competing to satisfy their customers with creative products, then the customers would benefit from the choice and also the lowering in costs paid for the creative product. However, it can be a problematic scenario for the organizations because of the intense competition, where there is intense pressure to continually produce creative outcomes (such as in the automobile industry where there is pressure to update the look and design of cars every year to suit the 'latest trends' and keep the new customers interested). Therefore the weak organizations, which are less creative, would fail to survive and be weeded out from the market.

Such competition does not however exist when there is a 'monopoly', that is, there is no fragmentation in the market and just one major organization dominates the market with its one creative product (for example, the monopoly of the Microsoft Windows operating system in the personal computer market). Organizations can move towards becoming monopolies by merging or acquiring competitor organizations, and therefore becoming a more dominant player in the market. Organizations can also form inter-organizational alliances to collectively develop a creative product, and this again can limit the choices for customers in the market. When there is monopoly in the market, governments often intervene and introduce laws to break the monopoly, to create a level playing for field for potential competitor organizations and to encourage greater competition. When the inter-organization relationships can be limited to just inspiring ones, then the multiple organizations can compete with each other and work towards creating diverse creative products in the market. These numerous organizational products are distinct from one another. In summary, limiting inter-organization relationships to either habitual or inspiring inter-organization relationships, allows for creative action in solitude by organizations (in the market), which in turn is likely to result in multiple organizational creativity outcomes that are fragmented in the market. Such fragmented organizational creativities cannot be summed into a unified creative outcome.

Integrating relationships for creative action in solitude-plus-integration

An integrating relationship allows the participants to work in solitude while collectively being driven by a shared vision to ultimately integrate their work in a unified creative outcome. In the process of creative solitude-plus-integration, each actor is engaged in creative action on its own (in solitude), with the well-entrenched belief that the creative work has to eventually be integrated with that of others to form a unified creative outcome. Integration is the mechanism of unifying existing creative outcomes into a larger whole. It is the mechanism of summing or fitting together the already available creative outcomes for a larger creative purpose. Though most creative action is produced by each actor in solitude, occasional interactions might be needed throughout the creative action process. This is to mutually ensure that each creator adheres to his or her shared vision even while working in solitude, so that later the integration happens smoothly.

Integrating relationships allow each actor to engage in creative action in solitude, and then allow the actors to integrate their creative outputs into a unified creative outcome that represents the aggregated and unified efforts of the entire collective. Integration is the mechanism of unifying existing creative outcomes into a larger whole. It is the mechanism of summing or fitting together the already available creative outcomes for a larger creative purpose.

Inter-person relationships for creative action in solitude-plus-integration: team creativity

When members start with a shared vision, which calls for commitment to a common purpose, then 'they hold themselves mutually accountable' (Katzenbach and Smith 1993: 112). As suggested by Katzenbach and Smith (ibid.: 112–113), such teams 'develop direction, momentum, and commitment by working to shape a meaningful purpose', and 'invest a tremendous amount of time and effort exploring, shaping, and agreeing on a purpose that belongs to them both collectively and individually.' Such a presence of shared vision is crucial, since it helps the members to forge integrating inter-person relationships, which allows individual creative action in solitude accompanied by the need for eventual integration, with the goal of attaining a unified team creativity outcome. Once a shared vision is developed, members of teams with integrated inter-person relationships work on their respective tasks in solitude and integrate them later into a unified whole to fulfil the vision. Specifically, in integrated inter-person relationships, individuals engage in creative behavior in solitude, and the purpose of the relationships is that of integrating the smaller creative outcomes of each member into a larger unified team outcome. In a team with integrated inter-person relationships, each individual's smaller creative outcome would be considered 'incomplete' until it is integrated to the larger unified whole. In teams where there are integrated inter-person relationships, the individuals need to work largely in solitude and at the same time produce a unified creative outcome.

Integrating relationships involves individual and mutual accountability towards their goal of eventually integrating the creative work performed by each member in solitude, and there is discussion, debate and decision that allows their creative work in solitude to be integrated smoothly into a unified creative outcome for the whole team (Katzenbach and Smith 1993). For example, imagine two girls who are participating as a team in a 'flower vase' contest. The potter-girl uses clay to create a beautiful handcrafted vase in solitude, and the florist-girl creates a beautiful bouquet of cut flowers in solitude, and then the mechanism of integration requires appropriate placement of the flowers in the vase, without which both the flowers and vase would otherwise have appeared somewhat 'incomplete'. For the integration to be most effective, ideally both the potter-girl and florist-girl should have had a shared vision to begin with. That is the size and shape of the vase should be such that the flowers can be well arranged; and similarly the size and shape of the flowers should be so chosen that they fit well in the vase. The integration involves combining the smaller individual creative outcomes (by members in solitude) into a larger unified one. In team creativity emanating from a structure of integrated inter-person relationships, the unified creative outcome is equivalent to the sum of the individual creative abilities (or smaller creative outcomes). Hence, the structuring of integrating inter-person relationships that are held together by a shared vision for the team allows for creative action in solitude-plus-integration among persons (within the team), which in turn is likely to result in the unified creative outcome. This unified outcome is a form of team creativity that represents the summation of creativities by persons within the team.

Inter-team relationships for creative action in solitude-plus-integration: organizational creativity

Once a shared vision is developed among teams, the teams can develop a structure of integrating relationships that would allow each of the multiple teams to work in solitude and at the same time provide a framework for eventual integration of their creative work towards realization of their shared vision. The relevant multiple teams in the organization have a shared vision; however, each team works on its own in solitude, and they later integrate their creative results into a unified one. For example, while designing a new concept car, the exterior-body team, the interior-décor team and the engineering team first agree on a shared vision, then work separately (in solitude) on their respective team creative goals, and eventually integrate their creative work into a unified one through interactions.

The relevant multiple teams need to collectively produce a unified creative outcome, and this unified creative outcome produces the integration of smaller creative team outcomes (by teams in solitude) into a larger unified organizational outcome. For an organizational example, one might consider the development of a concept car, where one team is responsible for exterior-body design and another team is responsible for interior-décor design. The creative exterior-body design should 'fit' well with the creative interior-décor design, so that both can be integrated easily. Though integration is primarily a post-creative mechanism, occasional interactions might be needed throughout the creative process to mutually ensure that each creator adheres to the mutual shared vision even while working in solitude, so that the integration happens smoothly later. Hence, the structuring of integrating inter-team relationships that are held together by a shared vision for the organization allows for creative action of solitude-plus-integration among teams (within an organization), which in turn is likely to result in the unified creative outcome This unified outcome is a form of organizational creativity that represents the summation of creativities by teams within the organization.

Inter-organization relationships for creative action in solitude-plus-integration: inter-organization creativity in market

Though decades ago some organizations had a monopolistic hold over certain market segments, the situation is rapidly changing and the market is becoming more fragmented, with numerous organizations and numerous competing creative products. To beat the increasing competition and to capture a dominant market share, organizations try to develop more novel and valuable creative products through various forms of inter-organization relationships. Two or more organizations start with a shared vision that requires a commitment from each organization to work in solitude towards their common purpose, keeping in mind that their creative work needs eventually to be integrated to realize the shared vision, and for which the involved organizations hold themselves mutually accountable. Once a shared vision is developed among organizations, they can develop a structure of integrating relationships that allows each of the multiple organizations to work in solitude and at the same time provide a framework for eventual integration of their creative work towards realization of their shared vision.

In an integrating inter-organization relationship, each organization can be expected to work in their respective core capabilities in solitude, and eventually integrate them to produce a unified creative outcome. For example, the outsourcing of work to specialized supplier organizations has received significant attention, both in the popular press and journals (Chakrabarty 2006; Dibbern *et al.* 2004). An organization in the oil and natural gas industry can focus on its own core capabilities, such as the designing of their own technology hardware, but the task of writing the software code for the technology system can be outsourced to a software service organization. The software code written by the software organization would ultimately be integrated with the technology hardware designed by the oil and natural gas organization for the entire technology system (combined hardware and software) to function properly. For integrated inter-organization creativity, the organizations in the relationship need to collectively produce a unified creative outcome, and this happens through the integration of smaller creative organization outcomes (by organizations in solitude) into a larger unified inter-organization outcome. Hence, the structuring of integrating inter-organization relationships that are held together by a shared vision allows for creative action of solitude-plus-integration among organizations (in the market), which in turn is likely to result in the unified inter-organization creativity outcome. This unified outcome represents the summation of creativities by the respective organizations.

Synergizing relationships for creative action in synergy

A synergizing creative relationship allows a creative action process of creative synergy towards a unified creative outcome. In the process of 'creative action in synergy' or simply 'creative synergy', two actors share a strong creative relationship and there is a mutual creative action with a shared vision. Creative synergy implies a disposition by two (or more) actors towards jointly undertaking a creative action that has the potential to generate a creative outcome that only their relationship(s) could have generated. During creative action in synergy, sensemaking would be done in a mutual and iterative fashion, where each actor in the relationship has the ability to perceive situations from multiple angles, find problems, and ask questions that challenge and inspire each other towards their shared vision (see Table 16.2). Apart from the intrinsic creative motivation that each actor has, they can also motivate each other in terms of their mutual goals, receptivity, capability and emotions (Ford 1996: 1118). For example, they would set goals for each other to enhance creative thinking, be receptive to each other's thoughts, encourage each other's progress, affirm confidence in each other's capability and arouse mutual interest. Similarly, they can be of mutual benefit to each other when their diverse knowledge/ability is channeled through their shared vision. The knowledge/ability dimension includes aspects such as domain-related knowledge, behavioral abilities and creative-thinking ability (op. cit.). Hence, there is a preference towards continual mutual engagement, and there is a strong relationship that drives the creative synergy towards a unified creative outcome.

Inter-person relationships for creative action in synergy: team creativity

As discussed earlier, when members have a shared vision, there is a commitment to shape a meaningful common purpose, they invest a tremendous amount of time and effort exploring, shaping and agreeing on a purpose, hold themselves mutually accountable and develop a strong sense of collective belongingness with the purpose (Katzenbach and Smith 1993). Such a presence of shared vision is crucial, since it helps the members to forge synergizing inter-person relationships, which allow collective creative action in synergy, with the goal of attaining a unified creative outcome. Once a shared vision is developed, members of teams with synergized inter-person relationships act on the vision in synergy towards a unified outcome. Specifically, in synergized inter-person relationships the members engage in creative behavior together, have enlightening interactions; there is a 'meeting of minds', and therefore the relationships lead to a common synergized outcome at a team level (see Figure 16.2). In teams where there are synergized relationships, the individuals are driven to work largely together to collectively produce a unified creative outcome.

The mutual accountability in synergizing relationships drives the collective creative action in synergy, and this involves intense discussion, debate and decision throughout the creative action process to realize a unified creative outcome for the whole team (ibid.). In team creativity from synergized inter-person relationships, the unified creative outcome is greater that the sum of the individual creative abilities. Hence, the structuring of synergizing inter-person relationships that are held together by a shared vision for the team allows for creative action in synergy among persons (within a team), which in turn is likely to result in the unified team creativity outcome. This is a form of team creativity that represents a very novel and unique outcome of joint action (from synergy), which cannot be achieved by each person alone or by the mere summation of the creativities of each individual.

Inter-team relationships for creative action in synergy: organizational creativity

Once a shared vision is developed among teams, the teams develop a structure of synergizing relationships that allows the multiple teams within the organization to collectively contribute to the vision and engage with each other. For example, HR and marketing teams may join forces to create a novel recruiting campaign, or a US army team and a US air force team may come together to devise and carry out a joint creative battle strategy. The relevant multiple teams need to collectively produce a unified creative outcome, and this unified creative outcome emanates from the synergy in relationships among teams. Hence, the structuring of synergizing inter-team relationships that are held together by a shared vision for the organization allows for creative action in synergy among teams (within an organization), which in turn is likely to result in the unified organization creativity outcome. This is a form of organizational creativity that represents a very novel and unique outcome of joint action (from synergy), which cannot be achieved by each team alone or by the mere summation of the creativities of each of the teams.

Inter-organization relationships for creative action in synergy: inter-organization creativity in market

The management literature suggests that 'through voluntary arrangements', such as strategic alliances and joint ventures, the organizations 'pool their resources to create goods and services with economic value', and using such inter-organization relationships they 'create knowledge that, in turn, facilitates the development of competitively valuable goods or services' (Ireland and Hitt 2005: 73). Organizations start with a shared vision, which requires a commitment of working jointly towards their common purpose, and for which the involved organizations hold themselves mutually accountable. Once a shared vision is developed among organizations, the organizations develop a structure of synergizing relationships that allows them to collectively contribute to the vision and engage with each other.

Many such relationships are formed on the basis of willingness to share expertise, and to leverage mutual organization-level capabilities, such as local market knowledge, technical abilities and various resources (Hitt *et al.* 2000: 449). For synergized inter-organization creativity, the organizations in the relationship need to collectively produce a unified creative outcome by using the synergy in relationships between organizations. Hence, the structuring of synergizing inter-organization relationships that are held together by a shared vision allows creative action in synergy among organizations (in the market), which in turn is likely to result in a unified inter-organizational creative outcome. This is a form of inter-organization creativity that represents a very novel and unique outcome of joint action (from synergy), which cannot be achieved by each organization alone or by the mere summation of the creativities of each of the organizations.

Conclusion

This chapter argued that the structuring of relationships among actors could influence creative outcomes. We provided a 3 × 3 framework whereby relationships can be structured in three ways, and can exist at three levels (see Figure 16.2). We encourage future researchers to address relationship creativity at the multiple levels of inter-person, inter-team and inter-organization.

References

Alderfer, C. P. and Smith, K. K. (1982) Studying Intergroup Relations Embedded in Organizations. *Administrative Science Quarterly*, 27, 35.

Amabile, T. M., Conti, R., Coon, H., Lazenby, J. and Herron, M. (1996) Assessing the Work Environment for Creativity. *Academy of Management Journal*, 39, 1154–1184.

Anand, V. and Manz, C. C. (1998) An Organizational Memory Approach to Information Management. *Academy of Management Review*, 23, 796–809.

Chakrabarty, S. (2006) Making Sense of the Sourcing and Shoring Maze: The Various Outsourcing and Offshoring Alternatives. In Kehal, H. S. and Singh, V. P. (eds), *Outsourcing and Offshoring in the 21st Century: A socio-economic perspective*, first edition. Hershey, PA: IGI Publishing.

Chakrabarty, S. and Woodman, R. W. (2007) A Theory of Relationship Creativity. *Academy of Management Annual Meeting*. Philadelphia, PA.

Chakrabarty, S. and Woodman, R. W. (2008) Toward a Theory of Relationship Creativity. Working Paper.

Cohen, W. M. and Levinthal, D. A. (1990) Absorptive Capacity: A New Perspective on Learning and Innovation. *Administrative Science Quarterly*, 35, 128–152.

Dibbern, J., Goles, T., Hirschheim, R. and Jayatilaka, B. (2004) Information systems outsourcing: a survey and analysis of the literature. *ACM SIGMIS Database*, 35, 6–102.

Ford, C. M. (1996) A Theory of Individual Creative Action in Multiple Social Domains. *Academy of Management Review*, 21, 1112–1142.

Gibson, C. B. (1999) Do They Do What They Believe They Can? Group Efficacy and Group Effectiveness Across Tasks and Cultures. *Academy of Management Journal*, 42, 138–152.

Gudykunst, W. B., Matsumoto, Y., Ting-Toomey, S., Nishida, T., Kim, K. and Heyman, S. A. M. (1996) The Influence of Cultural Individualism-Collectivism, Self-construals, and Individual Values on Communication Styles Across Cultures. *Human Communication Research*, 22, 510–543.

Haveman, H. A. (1993) Follow the Leader: Mimetic Isomorphism and Entry into New Markets. *Administrative Science Quarterly*, 38, 593–627.

Hitt, M. A., Dacin, M. T., Levitas, E., Arregle, J.-L. and Borza, A. (2000) Partner Selection in Emerging and Developed Market Contexts: Resource-Based and Organizational Learning Perspectives. *Academy of Management Journal*, 43, 449–467.

Ireland, R. D. and Hitt, M. A. (2005) Achieving and maintaining strategic competitiveness in the 21st century: The role of strategic leadership. *Academy of Management Executive* 19, 63–77.

Ireland, R. D., Hitt, M. A. and Vaidyanath, D. (2002) Alliance Management as a Source of Competitive Advantage. *Journal of Management*, 28, 413–446.

Joshi, A. (2006) The Influence of Organizational Demography on the External Networking Behavior of Teams. *Academy of Management Review*, 31, 583–595.

Katzenbach, J. R. and Smith, D. K. (1993) The Discipline of Teams. *Harvard Business Review*, 71, 111–120.

Kirkman, B. L., Rosen, B., Tesluk, P. E. and Gibson, C. B. (2004) The Impact of Team Empowerment on Virtual Team Performance: The Moderating Role of Face-to-face Interaction. *Academy of Management Journal*, 47, 175–192.

Markus, H. R. and Kitayama, S. (1991) Culture and the Self: Implications for Cognition, Emotion, and Motivation. *Psychological Review*, 98, 224–253.

Milliken, F. J. and Martins, L. L. (1996) Searching for Common Threads: Understanding the Multiple Effects of Diversity in Organizational Groups. *Academy of Management Review*, 21, 402–433.

Mizruchi, M. S. and Fein, L. C. (1999) The Social Construction of Organizational Knowledge: A Study of the Uses of Coercive, Mimetic, and Normative Isomorphism. *Administrative Science Quarterly*, 44, 653–683.

Morgeson, F. P. and Hofmann, D. A. (1999) The Structure and Function of Collective Constructs: Implications for Multilevel Research and Theory Development. *Academy of Management Review*, 24, 249–265.

Oetzel, J. G. (1998) Explaining Individual Communication Processes in Homogeneous and Heterogeneous Groups Through Individualism-Collectivism and Self-Construal. *Human Communication Research*, 25 202–224.

Oetzel, J. G. (2002) The effects of culture and cultural diversity on communication in work groups: Synthesizing vertical and cultural differences with a face-negotiation perspective. In Frey, L. R. (ed.), *New Directions in Group Communication*. Thousand Oaks, CA: Sage.

Pettigrew, T. F. (1998) Intergroup contact theory. *Annual Review of Psychology*, 49, 65.

Tsai, W. and Ghoshal, S. (1998) Social Capital and Value Creation: The Role of Intrafirm Networks. *Academy of Management Journal*, 41, 464–476.

Walsh, J. P. and Ungson, G. R. (1991) Organizational Memory. *Academy of Management Review*, 16, 57–91.

Woodman, R. W., Sawyer, J. E. and Griffin, R. W. (1993) Toward a Theory of Organizational Creativity. *Academy of Management Review*, 18, 293–321.

17

Creativity and economics: current perspectives

Isaac Getz and Todd Lubart

This chapter examines various ways in which creativity and economics relate to each other. In the first part, work on creativity that draws upon concepts in economics to highlight facets of the phenomenon of creativity is reviewed. In particular, economic concepts drawn from the investment domain have been applied to creativity, as have other economic terms such as human capital, and supply and demand. In the second part, work in the field of economics that concerns creativity, by integrating the creative process directly in economic models, or by highlighting considerations of institutional and organizational levels of economic analysis, is examined.

The economic perspective on creativity

Creativity theorists have used economic phenomena to develop and convey ideas about the nature of creativity. This cross-disciplinary work is based on the notion that bringing concepts from one domain (e.g. economics) to bear on another domain (e.g. psychology) will offer new insights into the topic under investigation (e.g. creativity). Thus, certain aspects of creativity, unnoticed or under-investigated within a purely psychological perspective, may be revealed or brought into focus by taking an economic perspective.

The principle of buying low and selling high

Sternberg and Lubart (1991, 1995), in their 'investment' theory of creativity, proposed that creative people are like successful investors in the financial marketplace: they buy low and sell high. Buying low in the realm of creativity means pursuing new or undervalued ideas that have growth potential – that may be successful for solving one's problem. Selling high means releasing a novel idea on the market when it has gained value and not holding an idea so long that others eventually have the same idea. Rather than jump on the bandwagon, producing work that may be good but similar to what others are doing, people who seek to be creative must deviate from the crowd, generating and advancing ideas that may eventually be recognized as new and valuable. Kuhn (1970) observed that for scientific activity, most researchers work within established theoretical or methodological paradigms rather than pursuing ideas outside such paradigms, ideas that have initially a low value but could lead to a paradigm revolution.

The buy low–sell high principle is partly descriptive of what creative people do (naturally) and partly prescriptive of a strategy that people may try consciously to implement to improve their creativity. In other words, people can develop a 'buy low–sell high' attitude, similar to the 'contrarian' attitude that Dreman (1977, 1982), the stock market analyst, advocates for stock investors. Engaging in 'buy low–sell high' behavior may involve an analysis of potential of ideas and of the marketplace for launching these ideas. Thus creators may use strategies similar to market analysts for choosing among several possible ideas. One strategy is fundamental analysis, in which key elements of a new idea may be evaluated for their intrinsic quality, originality, appropriateness to the problem-solving goal, as well as other qualities such as the aesthetic appeal of the idea or its coherence. This strategy can be seen in some accounts by inventors, in which they debate the strengths and weaknesses of their ideas before fully engaging work on a project. An alternative strategy is technical analysis in which trends in the problem domain may be examined in order to predict where a field is moving and what will be considered by the target audience as novel, appropriate or aesthetic. This strategy can be observed in some accounts of artistic creativity, including work in fashion design and advertising. According to the buy low–sell high principle, people fail to be creative because they: (a) buy high, pursuing ideas that are already valued or known (perhaps to avoid risk) (b) buy low, pursuing ideas that do not have growth potential, or (c) sell low, exposing an idea before the audience is ready, before the idea has gained in value, or, inversely, hold the idea too long so that it becomes commonplace.

The resources for creativity

Capital refers to assets that enter into the productive process and lead to income. Although we think often of physical capital (e.g. land, machines) or financial capital (money), there is also human capital. Human capital can be defined broadly as the knowledge, abilities and skills of workers as well as their time and energy. For creativity, the necessary human capital consists of a set of cognitive, emotional and conative resources. These resources are specific intellectual abilities, cognitive styles, knowledge, emotion, personality traits (e.g. risk taking) and motivations. Individuals vary in the extent to which they possess each resource. For example, one person may be a risk taker whereas another person is rather risk avoidant. The resources are hypothesized to develop and change over the lifespan.

A large body of research in psychology has examined the precise nature of the intellectual abilities, cognitive styles, knowledge, emotion, personality traits, motivations and environmental circumstances favorable to creativity. This work can be synthesized within the economic perspective on creativity: each person possesses a portfolio of resources (skills and traits) relevant to creativity. As Walberg (1988) noted, this portfolio of psychological resources for creativity is part of a person's 'human capital', which may be actively invested in creative projects. From this perspective, the level of creative performance observed depends on: (a) a person's level on each of the resources necessary for creativity, (b) the person's active engagement of their resources, and (c) the match between the portfolio of resources that a person has and the profile of resources required for creative work in a domain (or a task) (i.e. the market demands).

With regard to the specific resources for creativity, such as knowledge, Rubenson and Runco (1992) suggested that some fundamental economic principles may account for observed non-linear relationships between the resources and creative performance as well as lifespan changes in the resources. For example, some studies suggest that a greater and greater amount of certain resources is not always best for creativity. Based on Simonton's (1997) work, knowledge and specifically formal education seem to show an inverted-U relationship to creativity, with an intermediate level of education being preferable to a very advanced level. There may be a trade-off between two desirable but conflicting attributes. For example, knowledge is beneficial because it permits an individual to avoid re-inventing existing ideas (which already have a high value) and to avoid errors that others have already made in trying to work on a problem. However, increases in knowledge towards an expert level tend to have a negative effect on another desirable attribute, namely flexibility of thought. Experts often get stuck into using certain techniques for attacking a problem. Indeed, they have spent so much time and energy in acquiring these advanced techniques that it only makes sense to capitalize on their initial investment. In terms of intelligence and creativity, it has often been hypothesized that increases in intelligence contribute greatly to creativity initially, and then less and less. This is the economic phenomenon of diminishing returns.

With regard to lifespan changes in the resources for creativity, the well-known economic phenomenon of depreciation may be one of the processes at work. For example, knowledge acquired at a certain moment may become outdated. There is depreciation of the value of the initially acquired knowledge as a field advances. To the extent that a person acquires a substantial knowledge base in their field at their entry to the field, we may expect that their capital in terms of knowledge will gradually become devalued with age. The desire to avoid depreciation of one's existing knowledge may explain results showing that older scientists resist in some cases new theories more than do younger scientists, as Diamond (2001) showed in a study of the acceptance of Darwin's evolutionary theory by scientists of Darwin's era.

In addition to these explanatory insights offered by the investment perspective, this perspective brings into focus some aspects of creativity more than others (as is the case with any particular point of view). For example, special attention is devoted to risk taking, part of the personality resources for creativity. Risk taking is generally accepted as a key to investment decisions. Risk taking involves decision making in the face of potential gains or losses when the outcome is uncertain. Greater risks tend to be associated with greater potential gains. Concerning the pursuit of creative ideas, McClelland (1956) emphasized the importance of taking calculated risks; he contrasted people who do 'the safe thing' with 'wild-eyed people, the ones who like penny uranium stock' and suggested that creative people are those in-between these two extremes (p. 105). Generally, people tend to be risk averse, following the proverb 'a bird in the hand is worth two in the bush'. Studies of schoolchildren suggest that a low tolerance for failure develops starting in elementary school, perhaps because of the importance of obtaining good grades (Clifford 1988). People may underinvest because the potential rewards of a new idea are somewhat ambiguous as compared to pursuing technically sound but mundane ideas for which the limited rewards are clear (Rubenson 2003; Rubenson and Runco 1992). However, work by Kahneman and Tversky (1982) on risk taking in situations framed in terms of losses shows that people would take risks to minimize potential losses. Thus creative ideas may be pursued actively when they represent a possible but risky solution to a bad situation, whereas creative ideas may be avoided when a person faces a choice among options involving potential gains. Some techniques for stimulating creativity help people to frame problems in ways that reduce risk aversion (Adams 1986).

Creativity training builds human capital

The resources for creativity can be enhanced, at least partially, through training. For example, a person may study creative thinking techniques through a self-help book or by participating in a training program. Most creativity training focuses on enhancing the cognitive resources for creativity. Training is possible with regard to the personality and motivational resources for creativity but this type of training is less common.

An investment in creativity training leads to an accumulation of human capital that can later be put to use. The investment in training depends on the marginal utility (value added) to the individual (see Rubenson and Runco 1992). Age and occupation are two variables that may influence decisions to pursue creativity training. Younger workers may derive benefits of train- ing for a longer time than would older workers, thus increasing the utility of training for younger workers. Some occupations may demand creativity more than others, thus modulating the marginal benefits of training.

The benefits of creativity training, which may vary from person to person, include intrinsic rewards (e.g. personal enjoyment) and extrinsic rewards (e.g. increased job performance, earn- ings and opportunities for job advancement). The costs of creativity training include book expenses, tuition for courses, and opportunity costs of work not accomplished during the time spent on creativity training. For some individuals, the costs are reduced because their company sponsors the training program.

The decision to pursue creativity training is based on the marginal utility of each unit of training. A person with little human capital for creativity will benefit more than a person who already possesses many resources for creativity. Each of these individuals, however, can be expected to benefit less and less from each additional unit of creativity training, which is the phenomenon of diminishing returns. At some point, the marginal cost of additional creativity training will exceed the marginal benefit and the individual will not seek further training. With regard to the choice of creativity training versus traditional education, Rubenson and Runco (1992; Rubenson 2003) pointed out that people are more likely to invest in traditional educa- tion than in creativity-related education. The former has more predictable, less risky returns than the latter. Thus, even if people think that the effect of creativity training may be potentially more positive than traditional expertise training, the effects of creativity training are less certain than those expected with traditional education.

Similar to traditional economic capital, which enables potential economic productions, creative capital accumulation or enhancement enables potential creative productions. This potential is exploited maximally when productions satisfy some existing or latent needs – in other words, when they find a market.

The market for creativity

At the societal (aggregate) level, there is a supply and a demand for creative activity. The supply of creativity refers to the number of novel, useful productions (ideas, inventions, artistic works, etc.) that the members of a social unit (such as an organization or a society) provide. The demand for creativity is the need or desire in a society for creative productions. This demand may vary across domains (art, science, business, etc.) and across time. For example, during periods of political instability or war there may be greater demands for technological creativity than for artistic creativity. In financially tight periods, there may be a greater market for innovations that propose less expensive alternatives than for bold, but costly new products (Sternberg and Lubart 1995). The demand for creativity also varies from one place to another (Lubart 1999). Some societies value conformity and maintenance of the status quo more than others. Sternberg and Lubart (1991, 1995) characterize environments – markets – for creativity as ranging from those that are bullish, overtly supporting creative activity, to those that are bearish, hindering creativity. A bullish environment can spark creativity by providing financial and social resources for creativity. During the renaissance, for example, there were patrons who financially supported creative activity. Social interactions between artists of the time and competitions for prizes or commissioned works further contributed to a bullish environment for creativity. We can take the example of bullish markets enhancing the fulfillment of potential for creativity at the end of 1990s with the strong demand for dot.com creative start-ups. The emergence of the internet contributed to the flourishment of many creative entrepreneurs whose potential would have never been realized in other times. However, some case studies of eminent creators suggest that a bearish environment is not always bad for creativity. A bearish environment provides obstacles that provoke creative solutions, following the motto that necessity is the mother of invention.

Societies may influence the supply of creativity by increasing or decreasing incentives to produce new ideas. These adjustments can be accomplished, for example, through grants to stimulate activity in certain domains, through educational initiatives, or through changes to the patent system. Sometimes, however, the supply and demand get out of balance. First, a society may misallocate its resources for stimulating creativity, as with misguided educational programs. Second, a society may underestimate its need for creativity because it does not adequately take into account the long-term benefits of creative ideas, instead focusing on short-term, immediate needs (Rubenson and Runco 1992). This underestimation of the demand for creativity can result in occasional shortages of creativity, as was perceived in the United States in the 1950s upon the Soviet launch of Sputnik (see Atkinson 1990). Of course, societies must balance their need for creativity with other non-creativity related needs such as building roads or maintaining healthcare benefits.

Another dimension of the societal investment in creative human capital is the policy decision of who will receive this investment. Walberg (1988) has discussed this societal choice in terms of investing in the education of average children to increase the general level of creativity in the population versus investing in a smaller number of gifted children who could eventually achieve the highest levels in their fields of endeavor. To the extent that a society invests in those who have already succeeded in the past, there is a 'Matthew effect' (from Matthew 25:29 'unto every one that hath shall be given, and he shall have abundance'). Hence, the creatively 'rich' get richer, and the creatively 'poor' stay poor; for example, a grant may be more likely to be awarded to a researcher who already had a grant than to one who is just starting and never had funding. This pattern of investment in human capital increases the probability that investments in creative human capital will yield some returns. However, some authors have argued that a society may derive a greater benefit from enhancing the creativity of the 'average' person (through educational programs) rather than investing the same amount in a restricted group of highly creative people who may show a relatively small increment in their creativity.

Finally with regard to the market for creativity, Sternberg and Lubart's (1991, 1995) investment approach highlights additionally the social consensual nature of creativity. John Maynard Keynes noted that the value of stocks on the stock exchange or other financial instruments depends on the extent to which those actively involved in the market value and collectively desire a stock. In a parallel way, the value of an idea depends on the audience and the extent to which the audience collectively values the idea. Thus ideas (or productions) can appreciate or depreciate in value with time or with a change of audience. We are able therefore to understand better why some creative geniuses are 'discovered' posthumously and other 'greats' in their day disappear into oblivion.

Costs and benefits of creative activity

Sternberg and Lubart's (1991, 1995) investment perspective as well as Rubenson and Runco's (1992) psychoeconomic approach note that there are costs and benefits of creative work. Often, because creativity is a socially valued behavior, we tend to focus on the benefits of creative work. For an individual, there are both extrinsic benefits such as recognition and financial gains, and intrinsic benefits, such as satisfaction with one's work and a feeling of accomplishment. Also, creative accomplishments can open the door to further opportunities, creating a positive 'snowball' effect. However, there are also costs to creative work. First, there are pecuniary costs such as time and resources expended during the work. Though often considered under the term of constraints (to the creative process; cf. Gruber 1988; Rubenson 2003), time is surely the most precious of human resources. A lack of time usually blocks the creative process, although some research points out that time pressure may be beneficial through the enhanced focus on the problem-finding and problem-definition (Rubenson 2003). Costs can also play a role in switching creative energies from a costly domain to a less costly one. For example, Rubenson (ibid.) explains how Chinese written language – based on ideograms – made literary creativity highly costly. This led many artists to switch their creative expression into calligraphy – a lower-cost activity when using ideograms instead of full painting images. Second, there are psychic costs such as emotional wear and tear of overcoming the obstacles often encountered in creative work. The initial negative reaction that often accompanies creative work may affect one's self-confidence or task motivation. Psychic costs may furthermore include social isolation for one's 'deviant ideas'. Peers, whose own work is devalued by the appearance of the new, creative ideas, may seek to punish or ostracize the person who 'upsets the apple cart' (Sternberg and Lubart 1995).

There are opportunity costs as well: the individual could have been pursuing other projects that may have provided some positive results themselves. Finally, as Fuller (1992) has noted, there are transaction costs – costs that the creative person pays to a third party to facilitate the exchange with the audience. These transaction costs may be tangible, such as a commission paid to art gallery owners for displaying an artist's work, or intangible, such as limitations that one places on one's thinking to express ideas within the implicit rules of a discipline. In addition to the costs already mentioned, there are 'taxes' that are collected after a creative success (Sternberg and Lubart 1995). For example, following a creative success a scholar may be asked to review grant proposals or articles, serve on administrative committees, or give presentations summarizing previous work, which all take time from future creative work.

Parallel to the level of individual creators, there are also costs and benefits to creative work at the societal or macroeconomic level. The benefits of creativity include an enhanced quality of life for the society in general, as well as possible stimulation in the economic sphere. Each creative idea may have a trickle-down effect in which new supplementary products and services result from an initial idea. For example, the invention of the micro-computer fostered the emergence of many new computer-related services that have enhanced economic growth in recent times. The costs include direct financial costs and the use of physical and human resources. The opportunity costs refer to foregone advancements on other activities of the society (e.g. maintenance of roads). Opportunity costs also include the foregone advances on alternative creative domains. For example, given limited societal resources, if scientific creativity is promoted then artistic creativity may suffer a lack of advancement.

Conclusions

To summarize, we have examined how economic concepts have been applied to creativity in an effort to expand our understanding of this complex psychological phenomenon. The economic perspective highlights aspects of creativity at the microeconomic and macro-economic levels of analysis. Microeconomic phenomena include the investment in ideas that are unknown and/or undervalued, human capital as an input in the creative process, the notion of actively increasing human capital through creativity training, and the costs and benefits of creative work for the individual. Macroeconomic phenomena include the market for creativity, the supply and demand for creativity, societal policies toward investing in creativity, and the costs and benefits of creativity at the aggregate level. It should be noted, that for some authors taking the economic perspective, creativity is metaphorically similar to economic behavior, as in Sternberg and Lubart's proposal of creative people as successful investors, whereas for other authors, such as Rubenson and Runco in their work on active investment in creativity training, creative activity is directly influenced by economic concerns.

Economics of innovation and creativity research

In contrast to the previous section of this chapter in which economic phenomena were used to develop and convey ideas about the nature of creativity, we turn now to fields of economics and examine work in which creativity and innovation play an important role.

Endogenous growth theory and the economics of ideas

In the 1950s, a theory of economic growth was proposed in which technological change and innovation was the main factor – growth residual – explaining the permanent per capita growth since the industrial revolution (Abramovitz 1956; Solow 1957). Specifically, it explained the paradox that from the 1870s to the 1950s the growth rate of capital and labor accounted for only about 10 per cent of the growth rate in per capita output. Essentially due to the difficulties of mathematical formalization, this growth theory did not consider the nature of the innovation factor, postulating instead that it is determined by inputs external to the economic system (e.g. research in universities); it became known as *exogenous* growth theory (Solow 1994; Weitzman 1996).

In the late 1980s, a new, *endogenous* growth theory was advanced (Romer 1990). Similar to the exogenous one, this theory emphasized the critical role of technological change and innovation but viewed them as determined by inputs internal to the economic system and not external to it. Endogenous growth theory seeks to explain how economic systems' or countries' internal choices relevant to technological change and innovation (e.g. regarding investment in R&D) account for the variation among these systems on the rate of the growth residual.

Consider the 'economics of ideas' (Romer 1993) – one influential version of endogenous growth theory. It proposes that new ideas embedded in technological change and innovation are the main factor of economic growth and that the unbounded amount of potential new ideas is a main reason why growth after the industrial revolution has been constant and may continue to be so in the future. To illustrate this proposal, Romer (1995) replaces the 'factory' metaphor used traditionally in neoclassical growth theory by a 'computer' metaphor. Take for example, growth in agricultural output. Viewed through the 'factory' metaphor, this growth could come from an increase in 'raw materials' (arable land) and in 'equipment' (agricultural equipment, fertilizers). However, viewed through the 'computer' metaphor, this growth could come from new 'software' (methods of farming and farm management and methods to produce better equipment and fertilizers) rather than from an increase in amount of 'hardware' (arable land, agricultural equipment and fertilizers). This metaphorical shift allows Romer to change the common view of the main growth factor and of growth itself. In the 'factory' metaphor, instructions are provided and fixed by the external state of technological knowledge and non-production workers are considered as overhead; growth may come only from increases in 'raw materials', 'equipment' and 'production workers'. In this metaphor, because of the scarcity of the latter inputs, growth is viewed as limited. In contrast, in the 'computer' metaphor growth comes from inventing and accessing new and better 'software' – new ways to combine raw elements to create valuable things; because of the unbounded amount of potential new 'software' and because of the minimal costs for producing an extra 'software' copy, growth is seen as unlimited.

What are the endogenous economics' views of the process of creating 'software' which is so critical to this theory, and how do they relate to the psychological views of the creative process?

Endogenous economics' views of the creative process

As mentioned earlier, exogenous growth theory postulates the growth-relevant technological change and innovation factor to be a black box external to the economic system. In contrast, endogenous growth theory postulates that this factor is determined by the activity within an economic system. There seem to be two endogenous growth economics' views of this activity (Weitzman 1996). One view holds that this factor is a function of 'research effort'. For example, Grossman and Helpman (1994) postulate that 'firms devoting resources to R&D buy themselves a *chance* at developing the next generation of some targeted product' (p. 33). The nature of this functional relationship remains an open issue. For example, Solow (1994) wonders whether this function is continuous, or 'jump-like' – greater research effort leading to a one-time jump in technological change and innovation.

Alternatively, there is another view. Innovation results from a combinatorial creative discovery process; new ideas are combinations, hybrids of existing ideas or elements (Romer 1993, 1995; Weitzman 1996). This view is appealing to endogenous growth theorists because the combinatorial dynamics of possible new ideas evolve faster than the exponential dynamics of potential diminishing returns of the two other production factors – capital and labor. However, only a fraction of potential new ideas is transformed into useful, actually implemented ideas, and resources are required for this transformation. As Weitzman puts it, the growth residual 'is determined by the amount and productivity of the resources devoted to developing some finite subset of the unboundedly large number of *potentially* useful new hybrid ideas into *actually* useful new ideas' (p. 211).

Thus the growth residual depends on resources devoted to generating possible ideas combinations, selecting among them, and then developing them. For example, Weitzman (1996: 211) writes:

> The number of previously untried combinations of existing ideas eventually grows much faster than anything else in the economy. So too, for reasonable success fractions, does the number of viable seed ideas, which represent potentially sensible combinations that could be turned into workable new ideas if only the resources were available to develop them.

The same basic assumptions are held by Romer (1995, 1996), who, furthermore, suggests that both theory-guided and random experimentation research are required to discover new and useful ideas. He stresses the need for random experimentation consisting of random combinations of existing ideas because the restricted, 'deterministic' search guided by theory is not sufficient.

However critical it is for their theory, the endogenous growth economists do not elucidate what is meant by 'cleverly combining existing ideas to fashion useful new ideas' (Weitzman 1996: 211). Weitzman notes that current economic research has no realistic estimation of the resources needed for the creative process leading to technological change and innovation and he appeals for future economic-historical study of invention and creativity. Similarly, in his analysis of the endogenous economy of growth, Solow (1994: 53) suggests that:

> the best candidate for a research agenda . . . would be an attempt to extract a few workable hypotheses from the variegated mass of case studies, business histories, interviews, expert testimonies, anything that might throw light on good ways to model the flow of productivity-increasing innovations and improvements.

The elucidation however needs neither to wait nor to come from the empirical analysis carried out within the discipline of economics. Indeed, an important body of empirical evidence and modeling of the creative process accumulated during the last several decades in creativity research offers some insights into how ideas are produced and developed (see Magee 2005). Additional explanation of the latter is offered by organizational research on ideas and creativity.

Psychological views of the creative process

At least two lines of psychological research on creativity can contribute to a better understanding of the creative process by endogenous growth economists: idea combination/association and restricted search in the idea space. Regarding idea combination, a large number of researchers proposed that creative ideas are born from the association of remote concepts (Getz and Lubart 1998; Koestler 1964; Lubart and Getz 1997; Martindale 1993, see also this volume; Mednick 1962; Simonton 1988). Indeed, a whole body of research on the role of metaphor and analogy in the creative process is an illustration of the power of remote associations in the creative act. Combining remote concepts is not enough, however. Given the unlimited number of possible combinations, the issue is how a creative person restricts the search to those with more creative potential, rather than to those with less. Regarding this restricted search issue, Cambell (1960) proposed the 'blind variation and selective retention' view of the creative process, and Simonton's (1988) chance-configuration theory holds that the creator 'employs some criteria or heuristics to restrict the initial range of the search; [only when] the point is reached where the creator has minimal guidance from logic or past experience [he/she] must rely on an effectively non-directed search for new ideational variations among the population of relevant concepts' (Simonton 1997: 67). In fact, a non-directed search for idea combinations seems to be a last-resort strategy due to its inherent inefficiency.

A key issue for creativity research, therefore, is to account for factors that help a creator to restrict her or his search for creative ideas to the 'population of relevant concepts'. This issue is the focus of a diverse array of psychological mechanisms proposed to underlie the creative process, including cognitive and emotion-based, pattern-recognition and associationistic, psychodynamic and other ones (e.g. Boden 1992; Getz and Lubart 1998; Lubart and Getz 1997; Suler 1980; Weisberg 1986).

In addition to the importance of selectively combining ideas and retaining the most promising ones, there are the resources needed to actualize these fledgling ideas. Drawing again on the psychological literature on creativity, we can postulate certain resources that will help in both the selection of potentially useful ideas and in the development or implementation of these ideas.

One such resource is knowledge, involving stored information on the task, knowledge of the task domain, and knowledge of domains remote from the task. Relevant knowledge may be acquired through both formal education, as well as through informal exposure. It may take the form of explicit information, which can be recalled from memory, as well as implicit information captured in the heuristics that a person uses to guide work. With regard to the specific information about a task, research suggests that a person needs to acquire enough information to make the problem tractable for its preliminary analysis and definition. With regard to task domain knowledge, a person needs to acquire a critical but not too extensive amount of it (without the critical amount of task domain knowledge, every idea will seem 'new'; however, with too much knowledge a person will likely adopt the dominant perspective, thus impeding new ideas; see Simonton 1984). With regard to the knowledge of domains remote from the task and often helpful to find creative solutions, this is often obtained outside of formal education, for example from reading science magazines or visiting museum exhibits. In general, task-specific, domain-relevant and more general knowledge will help a person to recognize and use chance combinations and events as sources of ideas. As Louis Pasteur said, 'chance favors the prepared mind.' This knowledge also helps to develop ideas that are retained as potentially valuable.

Another important resource is emotion – stored emotional information and emotional abilities. We have shown (Getz and Lubart 1998, 2000; Lubart and Getz 1997) that rather than cognitive information, emotional information is a key resource in the preconscious process of concept combination. Furthermore, certain emotional abilities are a key for recognizing these combinations in working memory. Emotional information is acquired through experience with objects, people and situations, whereas emotional abilities are developed through formal and informal education.

Other psychological resources involved in idea selection and idea development include intellectual skills such as selectively comparing ideas through analogical thinking, or planning abilities. Overall, the availability of such cognitive and emotional resources as well as physical and financial ones means that people *can* engage in the creative process of developing new ideas, not necessarily that they *will* select and pursue potentially creative ideas. Personality traits (such as perseverance to overcome obstacles during idea development), and the motivation – intrinsic and extrinsic – to pursue new ideas, to engage in the efforts needed to develop new ideas (such as achievement motivation) are equally important. Thus, the level of these conative character-istics may be viewed as special, 'will' resources. If this level is very low, then its multiplication by other resources will also be low.

Taken together, this psychological work on the creative process has important implications for endogenous growth economics and by extension to economics in which the nature of creativity and invention is still a 'terra incognita' (Magee 2005). First, creative ideas are the outcome of a complex psychosocial creative process that cannot be approximated by mathematical combinatorial dynamics. Second, this process does not yield creative ideas as a constant fraction of the total number of essentially unbounded combinations of existing ideas into new ideas. Third, cognitive and emotional resources make the production of creative ideas possible, but they have to be accompanied by people's 'will' for creativity to make the production of creative ideas effective.

Organizational views of the creative process

Similarly to psychological views, organizational ones also offer a complex picture of idea generation and development. Acknowledging that many organizations have tremendous cognitive and emotional resources for ideas, and thus a high creative potential, this research shows that very few put in place a set of managerial practices to make people willing to express and implement their ideas. This set – called an idea management system – allows every employee to express, implement and be recognized for his or her ideas (Getz and Robinson 2003, 2007; Robinson and Stern 1998). Thus, instead of the average 0.46 ideas generated annually per employee, with 61 per cent being implemented in Germany and 0.13 and 49 per cent, respectively, in the US in companies mostly with traditional – idea blocking – command and control managerial practices, in companies having excellent idea management systems, employees generate over 20 ideas annually, with over 80 per cent being implemented. This actualization of employees' creative potential also has a direct impact on the combination of ideas.

First, employees are encouraged to express their ideas, thus increasing the likelihood that one employee's ideas will be known by others. Second, because employees are encouraged to implement their ideas by themselves, the likelihood of cooperation around the ideas of several employees – and thus of their combination – is increased. Finally, because employees are encouraged to consider that 'good is never good enough', the likelihood that one employee's implemented idea will be further improved with an idea of another employee is increased. This increased likelihood of combining employees' ideas has important implications for endogenous growth economics.

First, the best practices in idea management shed light – as Solow (1994) suggested – on the mechanisms facilitating the flow of ideas and innovation. Second, it shows that the assumption of a steady flow of ideas, in general, and of their combination, in particular, can be made only for some – excellent – companies, but not for entire industries or economies. Finally, it shows that the assumption of a small fraction of generated ideas being actually implemented is paradoxically true for companies who do little to facilitate their employees' creative ideas; it is wrong, however for the companies with excellent idea management systems in which most ideas are, on the contrary, implemented – up to 99 per cent in Toyota's Georgetown, KY plant.

In the previous section, the links between creativity research and economics was explored with regard to endogenous growth theories. The following sections focus on theories of institutional and organizational economics.

Institutional economics

Regarding creativity and innovation, institutional economics seems to pick up where growth economics leaves off. Broadly, this field of economics examines how institutions shape the capabilities and behavior of economic actors, and thus influence economic productivity, including through heightened innovation. Historically, the scale of institutions studied has varied (see Nelson 2006). Thus, with the strengthening of the USSR, Schumpeter (1942) and Hayek (1945) explored whether a market economy or a planned economy is the most favorable for innovation and productivity. After the Second World War, economists explored specific institutional aspects that influence productivity; they found stocks of physical and human capital, and investment available in the developed countries but not elsewhere. Further, when Japanese companies stormed US and Western Europe with better cars and electronics (and while communist countries lagged behind all three regions despite high investment in both physical and human capital), economists' interest switched to how businesses are structured and run, and the financial and labor market systems supporting them. Total Quality, continuous improvement and MITI became examples of institutional elements that explained Japanese superior productivity and innovation.

Then, when in the 1990s Japan's economy declined and the US information- and bio-technology sectors boomed, economists switched to start-ups, venture capital (VC) and fluid labor markets. Silicon Valley for IT and Southern California for biotech became examples of intertwined institutional systems that influence innovation and productivity. Consider 'innovation systems' (Nelson 1993) – one recent institutional economics theory particularly focused on innovation. It explores how companies are embedded in and supported by a variety of non-market institutions, leading to corporate innovation. A typical example is universities funded by the government to undertake research and training in fields relevant to an industry thus supporting the latter's companies' innovation. Another example is consumers' willingness to try new things that support corporate innovation. Thus Bhidé (2006) explains the US' superior corporate innovation not by large US government funding of public research but by the world's most 'venturesome' US consumers.

The multitude of actors and their environments uncovered by institutional economics is potentially relevant to the study of creativity. We turn now to organizational economics, and then discuss the implications of both fields of economics.

Organizational economics

Though this field is traced to Adam Smith who explained the advantages of the division of work for economic productivity, its modern history begins with Coase (1937). Coase explained why the company is a more economically efficient mechanism of coordination between productive actors than the market mechanism of individual actors (e.g. suppliers, producers, sellers, etc.) transacting with each other. Since then, organizational economists explored what organizational forms are best for economic productivity and innovation. Regarding productivity, the GM-pioneered multidivisional form (M-form), the matrix form, the network form and others have been studied. Regarding innovation, the field explored the so-called 'new organizational forms': internal hybrid – a mix of a typical organizational hierarchy with market mechanisms (e.g. Zenger 2002), and complementary practices – several work processes reinforcing each other (Ichniowski and Shaw 2003; also see Milgrom and Roberts 1990; note: many of the forms studied by organizational economics are also studied by organizational and management scholars.)

For the case of hybrid forms, economists study market mechanisms that companies introduce to compensate for their inadequate-for-innovation hierarchical control structure. These market mechanisms involve a diverse array of work practices termed as people-based, participative, team-based, empowerment, employee-involvement, idea management, TQM, etc. The common thread of all these practices is that problems, ideas, solutions and initiatives are not coming from the bosses but from the employees themselves. This creates an internal 'market for ideas' in which the most useful, and in many cases innovative, ideas are put in place, instead of remaining untold or unimplemented in a typical hierarchical structure. The hybrid character remains because the 'buyers' of ideas, those who listen to, evaluate and authorize the implementation of ideas, are still in the hierarchy. Enron – famous for its financial scandal – is a known case of such an internal market for ideas, claiming that it brought the 'Silicon Valley inside'.

In the case of complementary practices, economists describe how the groupings of mostly human resource practices in specific companies/industries are related to their productivity and innovation. A key finding is that in order to be effective, a critical grouping of complementary work practices has to be implemented (any single practice being insufficient which runs against a key trend in the management literature). Interestingly, Zenger (2002) uses the complementarity principle to explain why hybrid forms prove to be unstable. Indeed, hierarchical control practices and market mechanisms are not complementary but rather push hybrid forms either to return to a pure hierarchy or, inversely, to disaggregate into the market and to become a network of individual actors instead of a company.

Finally, some organizational economists go beyond description and look at organizations not merely as a structured mode of coordination favorable to innovation, but as an innovation itself. Indeed, new forms do not simply emerge but are invented and implemented, often under the guidance of a visionary leader in specific companies.

Implications for creativity

Overall, institutional and organizational economics have interesting implications for creativity spanning its person, process, product and 'press' aspects (Rhodes 1961). Concerning the creative person, creativity research relevant to organizations often examines individuals or small, eventually cross-functional project teams acting essentially at the 'upstream' of innovation as inventors and entrepreneurs (Amabile 1988; Rickards and Moger 1999; Rubenson and Runco 1995). Institutional economics show that individual/small team creators were preponderant in the nineteenth century but not after. Instead, at the beginning of the twentieth century, large firms and their labs assumed this role, university labs with marketable innovations rising after the Second World War and, more recently, the venture capital-backed start-ups; all these types of creators remaining co-present (Bhidé 2006). For creativity research, this implies that in order to be ecologically valid today, we need to focus not only on individuals/teams but also on all types of creators, most of which are *organizational* in nature. Furthermore, as implied by organizational economics, organizations should not be viewed as groupings of individuals but rather as groupings of *work practices* with a diverse degree of complementarity, which offer the possibility to create and to innovate. Ultimately, it may mean that in order to understand 'the creator', psychological approaches focusing on traits and abilities have to be complemented by organizational ones focusing on work practices.

Concerning the creative process, creativity research tends to focus on the preparation–incubation–illumination–validation model (see Lubart 2001–2002). The last – validation – phase is viewed as demanding time and effort but once the market recognizes an invention's usefulness, not much happens (this view has also been proposed by Schumpeter). Institutional economics paint a more complex picture. For example, Rosenberg (1976) showed that most innovations acquire their full market usefulness through a – an often decades' long – string of complementary useful inventions, whereas Bhidé (2006) affirms that this concerns not most but all commercial innovations. There are two implications of this view of the creative process. First, the study of the validation phase should not assume a single invention but rather a string of new useful inventions, each increasing the usefulness of the initial one until it is fully recognized by the market. Second, the study of validity criteria should view the initial invention's usefulness not as something given but evolving, based on further inventions that enhance it. For example, the first PDA – Apple's Newton – invented in the early 1980s, has been seen as a market failure. However, the spread of the PC, and a possibility to synchronize the PDA with it, increased the PDA's usefulness and the internet has increased even further the possibility for the PDA to access and download a variety of data and software. All those posterior inventions increased the PDA's usefulness to the level at which it became fully recognized by the market. Finally, the organizational view of the creative process sheds an interesting light on the validation phase. In fact, in organizational processes validation occurs in two steps: idea evaluation and idea implementation. Evaluation occurs typically 'on paper'. For example, in the already-mentioned idea management systems, a manager evaluates idea usefulness based on the discussion with the author and the estimations and numbers that the latter proposes. Similarly, in the entrepreneurial processes, venture capitalists and investors evaluate the idea based on the business plan and assessment of the team's qualities. However, not all ideas judged useful succeed in implementation (see Getz and Robinson 2003). Also, concrete implementation begins much before the new product hits the market: products are tested in pilot markets, produced first in small numbers, shipped to limited locations. Implementation may fail at each of these steps thus invalidating the idea; a creative idea's final proof is in its successful market implementation.

Concerning the creative product, creativity research tends to focus essentially on new and successful products, technologies, services, business processes, and eventually companies – start-ups. Organizational economics add a new type of innovation – the organizational form – resulting from a grouping of complementary work practices. For creativity research, it implies that for some products, such as new organizational forms, usefulness is time sensitive: a form judged useless can become useful with an addition of a key complementary practice, and, inversely, a form judged useful can cease being so once its work practices lose their complementarity thus damaging the overall organizational performance.

Finally, concerning the creative 'press' environment, creativity research often examined such individual/small team relevant aspects as family, educational background and professional fields/cultural movements (Csikszentmihalyi 1996; Lubart 1999; Simonton 1984). Institutional economics show that environments relevant to creative organizations involve an array of larger aspects such as funding bodies, public research and even consumers open to trying new things. Another implication for creativity studies is that, in addition to past and present environmental aspects, future ones may be critically important, as in the above illustration of the PDA innovation.

To summarize, economics and creativity cross-fertilize each other in several important ways. Economic phenomena allow research on creativity to develop and convey ideas about the nature of creativity. Inversely, creativity studies make explicit for economic theories the nature of the idea combination creative process, which is critical to these theories (e.g. endogenous growth economics). Finally, some economic fields that have focused on the nature of innovation, such as institutional and organizational economics, offer the field of creativity research ideas that extend and deepen the understanding of the person, process, product and press components of the phenomenon of creativity.

References

Abramovitz, M. (1956). Resource and output trends in the United States since 1870. *American Economic Review*, 46, 5–23.

Adams, J. L. (1986). *The care and feeding of ideas: A guide to encouraging creativity*. Reading, MA: Addison-Wesley.

Amabile, T. M. (1988). A model of creativity and innovation in organizations. *Research in Organizational Behavior*, 10, 123–167.

Atkinson, R. C. (1990). Supply and demand for scientists and engineers: A national crisis in the making. *Science*, 248, 425–432.

Bhidé, A. (2006). Venturesome consumption, innovation and globalization. Paper for a Joint Conference of CESIFO and Center on Capitalism and Society 'Perspectives on the Performance of the Continent's Economies'. Venice.

Boden, M. (1992). *The creative mind: Myths and mechanisms*. New York: Basic Books.

Campbell, D. T. (1960). Blind variation and selective retention in creative thought as in other knowledge processes. *Psychological Review*, 67, 380–400.

Clifford, M. M. (1988). Failure tolerance and academic risk taking in ten- to twelve-year-old children. *British Journal of Educational Psychology*, 58(1), 15–27.

Coase, R. H. (1937). The nature of the firm. *Economica*, 4(November), 386–405.

Csikszentmihalyi, M. (1996). *Creativity*. New York: HarperCollins.

Diamond, J.M. (2001). Foreword. In E. Mayr, *What evolution is* (pp. vii–xii). New York: Basic Books.

Dreman, D. (1977). *Psychology and the stock market*. New York: Amacom.

Dreman, D. (1982). *The new contrarian investment strategy*. New York: Random House.

Fuller, S. (1992). What price creativity? *New Ideas in Psychology*, 10(2), 161–165.

Getz, I. and Lubart, T. I. (1998). The emotional resonance model of creativity: Theoretical and practical extensions. In S. W. Russ (ed.), *Affect, creative experience, and psychological adjustment* (pp. 41–56). Philadelphia, PA: Brunner/Mazel.

Getz, I. and Lubart, T.I. (2000). An emotional-experiential perspective on creative symbolic-metaphorical processes. *Consciousness and Emotion*, 1, 89–118.

Getz, I. and Robinson, A. G. (2003). Innovate or die: Is that a fact? *Creativity and Innovation Management*, 12, 130–136.

Getz, I. and Robinson, A. G. (2007). *Vos idées changent tout!*, Paris: Éditions d'Organisation.

Grossman, G. M. and Helpman, E. (1994). Endogenous innovation in the theory of growth. *Journal of Economic Perspectives*, 8(1), 23–44.

Gruber, H. (1988). The evolving systems approach to creative work. *Creativity Research Journal*, 1, 27–51

Hayek, F. von (1945). The use of knowledge in society. *American Economic Review*, 35(4), 519–530.

Ichniowski, C. and Shaw, K. (2003). Beyond incentive pay: Insiders' estimates of the value of complementary Human Resource management practices. *Journal of Economic Perspectives*, 17, 155–180.

Khaneman, D. and Tversky, A. (1982). The psychology of preferences. *Scientific American*, 246(1), 160–173.

Koestler, A. (1964). *The act of creation*. New York: Macmillan.

Kuhn, T. S. (1970). *The structure of scientific revolutions*. Chicago: University of Chicago Press.

Lubart, T. I. (1999). Creativity across cultures. In R. J. Sternberg (ed.), *Handbook of human creativity* (pp. 339–350). Cambridge: Cambridge University Press.

Lubart, T. I. (2001–2002). Models of the creative process: Past, present and future. *Creativity Research Journal*, 13, 295–308

Lubart, T. I., and Getz, I. (1997). Emotion, metaphor, and creative process. *Creativity Research Journal*, 10, 285–301.

Magee, G. B. (2005). Rethinking invention: Cognition and the economics of technological creativity. *Journal of Economic Behavior and Organization*, 57, 29–48.

Martindale, C. (1993). *Cognitive psychology: A neural network approach*. Belmont, CA: Wadsworth, Inc.

McClelland, D. C. (1956). The calculated risk: An aspect of scientific performance. In C. W. Taylor (ed.), *The 1955 University of Utah research conference on the identification of creative scientific talent* (pp. 96–110). Salt Lake City: University of Utah Press.

Mednick, S. A. (1962). The associative basis of the creative process. *Psychological Review*, 69, 220–232.

Milgrom, P. and Roberts, J. (1990). The economics of modern manufacturing: Technology, strategy, and organization. *American Economic Review*, 80, 511–528.

Nelson, R. R. (1993). *National Innovation Systems: A Comparative Analysis*. Oxford: Oxford University Press.

Nelson, R. R. (2006). What makes an economy productive and progressive? What are the needed institutions? Working Paper 24. Laboratory of Economics and Management, Sant'Anna School of Advanced Studies, Pisa, Italy.

Rhodes, M. (1961). An analysis of creativity. *Phi Delta Kappan*, 42, 305–311.

Rickards, T. and Moger, S. (1999). The development of benign structures: Towards a framework for understanding exceptional performance in project teams. *Journal of New Product Development and Innovation Management*, 1(2), 115–128.

Robinson, A.G. and Stern, S. (1998). *Corporate creativity: How innovation and improvement actually happen.* San Francisco, CA: Berrett-Koehler.

Romer, P. M. (1990). Endogenous technological change. *Journal of Political Economy*, 985(2), S71–S102.

Romer, P. M. (1993). Idea gaps and object gaps in economic development. *Journal of Monetary Economics*, 32, 543–573.

Romer, P. M. (1995). La croissance économique et l'investissement dans les enfants. L'Actualité Economique. *Revue d'Analyse Economique*, 71(4), 384–396.

Romer, P. M. (1996). Why, indeed, in America? Theory, history, and the origins of modern economic growth. *American Economic Review*, 86(2) 202–206.

Rosenberg, N. (1976). *Perspectives on technology.* Cambridge: Cambridge University Press.

Rubenson, D. L. (2003). Art and science, ancient and modern: A psychoeconomic perspective on domain differences in creativity. In D. Ambrose, L. M. Cohen and A. J. Tannenbaum (eds), *Creative intelligence: Toward theoretic integration* (pp. 131–146). Cresskill, NJ: Hampton Press.

Rubenson, D. L. and Runco, M. A. (1992). The psychoeconomic approach to creativity. *New Ideas In Psychology*, 10(2), 131–147.

Rubenson, D.L. and Runco, M.A. (1995). The psychoeconomic view of creative work in groups and organizations. *Creativity and Innovation Management*, 4(2), 232–241.

Schumpeter, J. (1942). *Capitalism, socialism, and democracy.* New York: Harper and Rowe.

Simonton, D. K. (1984). *Genius, creativity, and leadership.* Cambridge, MA: Harvard University Press.

Simonton, D. K. (1988). *Scientific genius.* New York: Cambridge University Press.

Simonton, D. K. (1997). Creative productivity: A predictive and explanatory model of career trajectories and landmarks. *Psychological Review*, 104, 66–89.

Solow, R. M. (1957). Technical change and the aggregate production function. *Review of Economics and Statistics*, 39, 312–320.

Solow, R. M. (1994). Perspectives on growth theory. *Journal of Economic Perspectives*, 8(1), 45–54.

Sternberg, R. J. and Lubart, T. I. (1991). An investment theory of creativity and its development. *Human Development*, 34, 1–31.

Sternberg, R. J. and Lubart, T. I. (1995). *Defying the crowd: Cultivating creativity in a culture of conformity.* New York: Free Press.

Suler, J. R. (1980). Primary process thinking and creativity. *Psychological Bulletin*, 88(1), 144–165.

Walberg, H. (1988). Creativity and talent as learning. In R. J. Sternberg (ed.), *The nature of creativity* (pp. 340–361). New York: Cambridge University Press.

Weisberg, R. W. (1986). *Creativity, genius and other myths.* New York: Freeman.

Weitzman, M. L. (1996). Hybridizing growth theory. *American Economic Review*, 86(2) 207–212.

Zenger, T.R. (2002). Crafting internal hybrids: Complementarities, common change initiatives, and the team-based organization. *International Journal of the Economics of Business*, 9(1), 79–95.

18

Deconstructing creativity

Alf Rehn and Christian De Cock

It is also conceivable, at least hypothetically, that human thought (in so far as it is itself praxis and a moment of praxis) is fundamentally the understanding of novelty (as a perpetual re-organisation of the given in accordance with acts explicable by their end).

(Sartre 1976: 61)

In this chapter we will introduce a theorization of creativity which may well feel counter-intuitive to many at first. We contend that traditional discourses and theorizations of creativity have unconsciously limited its very nature to a set of preconceived ideas, thus distancing 'creativity' as a theoretical concept from the *praxis* of creativity. If creativity is a matter of 'going beyond', of exploring that which might be not so obvious and clear-cut and of challenging the taken-for-granted, then this puts the researcher of creativity in something of a bind. In order to be a 'creativity researcher' one needs to align oneself with a set of assumptions, but in order to stay 'creative' (as a moment of *praxis*), one has to continuously challenge these same assumptions. In fact, in order for creativity to remain 'creative' it, by its very nature and definition, needs to go 'beyond creativity'. We will discuss here this ontological problem of creativity, the fact that at the very core of creativity lies an *aporia*,[1] a difference to itself lodged in its very being. We aim to show that a critical and philosophical analysis might be needed to get a grip on this *aporia*. The kind of critical analysis we want to introduce here goes by the name of deconstruction.

Deconstructing creativity? What might this mean? Well, we aim to do something to the concept of 'creativity', and that 'something' is to subject it to a process of 'deconstruction' as developed by Jacques Derrida. Deconstruction is a practice rather than a theory, particularly as the latter has one fundamental requirement: that of closure. As such, it sidesteps what Rickards and De Cock (1999: 239) called the ontological paradox in creativity research: 'How might the generative process of creativity be expressed within a model or theory seeking some generalizability if an essential part of the process is its uniqueness from that which existed before?' Deconstruction resists theory precisely because it demonstrates the impossibility of closure. Deconstruction fastens on the symptomatic points, the *aporia* or impasses of meaning, where texts and concepts get into trouble, come unstuck, offer to contradict themselves (Eagleton 1996). It can be best described as a way of reading or perceiving that destabilizes a hierarchical order by stating what the hierarchy has suppressed. As Derrida (1981: 41) puts it:

> In a traditional philosophical opposition we have not a peaceful coexistence of facing terms but a violent hierarchy. One of the terms dominates the other (axiologically, logically, etc.), occupies the commanding position. To deconstruct the opposition is above all, at a particular moment, to reverse the hierarchy.

For Derrida, dominant positions have no foundation in themselves but are sustained by what they differ from. Deconstruction is for Derrida ultimately a political practice, an attempt to dismantle the logic by which a particular system of thought maintains its force.

What deconstruction does is the careful teasing out of warring forces of signification within a particular situation, text or concept. Whatever is present is not self-sustaining but lives on what it excludes, and by marking this difference deconstruction makes the excluded bounce back on the excluder (Iser 2006). Deconstruction spotlights what the dominant features have relegated to absence, the articulation of which makes the hierarchy fall apart. The conflicts within a concept like creativity, which the hierarchical order is supposed to pacify, thus come to the fore again.

Whilst there does not exist a commonly accepted definition of creativity, most commentators would agree that creativity involves the ability to come up with something 'new', which is of 'value' or 'useful' (Bills and Genasi 2003; Cox 2005; Ford 1996; Rickards and De Cock 1999).[2] Furthermore, it is often seen as critical for organizational success (Elsbach and Kramer 2003; de Brabandere 2005; Gogatz and Mondejar 2005; Proctor 2005). In a deconstructive move we want to explore what this focus on 'the new', on 'value' and 'organizational success' actually suppresses. Put somewhat differently, it is important, in order to develop the theoretical basis of creativity, to shake up this 'hierarchy' and see where this might take us. Indeed, isn't it so that in our reliance on creativity theories and models, on ever-more 'productive' creativity techniques, we are actually in danger of losing 'a general alertness which makes us aware, from moment to moment, of how the process of thought is getting caught in fixed sets of categories' (Bohm 2004: 75)? Doesn't the obsession with 'novelty', with 'frame-breaking' and 'thinking outside the box' – 'ideas' for the sake of 'ideas' – suppress that what is actually happening under so much active and activistic energy reflects rather conservative norms: 'compulsory individualism, compulsory "innovation", compulsory performativity and productiveness, the compulsory valorization of the putatively new' (Osborne 2003: 507)? Does the recent interest in creativity from policy makers (e.g. the 2005 *Cox Review of Creativity in Business*, commissioned by Gordon Brown, then UK Chancellor of the Exchequer[3] and now Prime Minister) not contain a strong ideological dimension: a need to respond to and fit in with the perceived needs of contemporary capitalism in a globalized risk society?

In the remainder of the chapter we want to explore the suppressed dimensions inherent in the notion of 'the new' and open up possibilities for creativity beyond the dominant neo-liberal, market-focused ideology of 'creativity' as a well-behaved category and phenomenon. In other words, we want to reclaim creativity and take it seriously, without remaining fixed in a strict hierarchy of pre-suppositions and preconceived notions. To put it more succinctly: we want to think creatively about creativity.

First deconstructive move: novelty and progress

> The palpable contradiction between the absolute claim for novelty and the inevitable repetition, the eternal return, of the same gesture of innovation over and over again, does not disqualify the characterization but rather lends it a mesmerizing, forever perplexing and fascinating, spell . . .
>
> (Jameson 2002: 125)

Asserting that creativity is about creating novelty may seem little more than a tautology. Yet, whilst it is undoubtedly true that creativity can be about creating the new, one could inquire whether this assertion holds always-already. One could also question whether the underlying assumption of creativity as essentially linked to such beneficial novelty and progress is justified, or whether both these aspects are parts of an ideological construction geared at normalizing and accentuating one set of notions over others. The process of deconstruction aims at this kind of 'picking apart', arguing that the creation of unspoken hierarchies and implied necessities are in fact limitations to thought, driven by a particular Western desire to purify and control. In this case the object being purified and controlled is creativity, the one thing one claims is beyond pure control – an inherent contradiction in thought.

Creativity, as a concept put to the use of contemporary capitalism, emphasizes the value of novelty, and positions this as a primary process in the economy. If we follow the argument developed by Schumpeter in *Capitalism, Socialism and Democracy* (1942), creativity is that which entrepreneurs showcase when they introduce new things into a market, and it is the 'creative destruction' they wield that makes them such potent agents of change. Furthermore, it is this process of innovation that enables progress in the world, as witnessed in advanced technologies and economies.[4] In current versions of this argument (see e.g. Bills and Genasi 2003; Cox 2005; de Brabandere 2005), creativity is presented as existing in juxtaposition with an old world/ economy (that which was) and as forming a signaling device for the birth of something better. Put slightly differently, it is often stated that creativity is important because it helps deliver the new into the world. The assumption that the new is clearly superior to what went before has an important corollary: failure to move from one to the other is to be explained by 'conservatism', not to mention stupidity or straightforward ignorance (Edgerton 2006). In other words, the concept of creativity serves as a way of creating a binary along the lines of old/bad – new/good. Creativity, seen as a morally upstanding phenomenon, emphasizes novelty and through this positions the new as necessarily better than the old, thus creating one of the hierarchies that deconstruction aims to topple. Where such a statement might be understandable and quite sensible in local cases, we must question whether we are prepared to accept it as a general statement. We must further ask whether it is, in fact, a neutral statement, but will leave this consideration to our third deconstructive movement.

To create a brand new product or start a new company is obviously a creative act. At the same time, virtually all such acts contain at least some traces of old ideas, and this 'old' content might in fact be quite substantial. If we look to the world of art, we see that creators such as Marcel Duchamp and Claes Oldenburg used already existing things – the ready-mades – to create high art (cf. Guillet de Monthoux 2004), thus problematizing the notion of novelty.[5] For them, there was no original, only an endless chain of derivatives. The world of the commodity had become a degraded one, in which things had been drained of their intrinsic value; but precisely because of this, they were now free to be put to all kinds of ingenious, innovative uses. What someone like Marcel Duchamp produced out of this non-innovation is ultimately one of the most original forms of art of modern times (Eagleton 2005). Žižek (2006) points out how Luther accomplished the greatest revolution in the history of Christianity, thinking he was merely unearthing the truth obfuscated by centuries of Catholic degeneration. In cultural theory, Walter Benjamin emphasized the notion of ruin and remembrance as central aspects of any creative act (cf. Rehn and Vachhani 2006), and in innovation studies one has long recognized that the most common form of innovation is incremental, i.e. one where the creative component is in fact the smallest part of the final product. All these facts are in themselves not 'new' and indeed some have been discussed at some length in creativity theory. Yet, this discussion has in almost all cases taken the form of emphasizing that it is still the new aspect, however minor this might be, that defines a particular act as creative.

Our first deconstructive move, then, is to claim that creativity need not be about novelty. Even though novelty may be present in creative acts, this can in fact be a fairly minor part thereof. The emphasis on novelty is needed to ideologically position creativity as part of an economic movement and to connect it to the modernist ideology of progress. But why would it be essential for creativity? Creativity can also be a question of returning, going to the roots, getting back to basics. Creativity can be about taking away things, simplifying, or creating by ignoring novelties. A neo-liberal ideological understanding may see the new as that which creates value, but a skeptical reading of this would ask whether this not merely involves recasting some old ideological chestnuts and enlisting the concept of creativity to drive these forward. If, for instance, we look at how MIT's John Maeda (2006) champions simplicity and thereby design and innovation principles that have been taken on board by companies such as Philips, we see that he encourages scaling back and reducing, rather than enhancing and adding on. Cook and Brown (1999) discovered that for a group of design teams at Xerox interacting with old artifacts is often a source of insights that are valuable in designing new technologies. The design team have a 'hands on' interaction with those artifacts that afford the recapture of those particular bits of knowledge associated with a particular competency, thus demonstrating the generative power of the practices associated with recapturing old knowledge. Here, creativity is about seeing what is truly valuable and permanent in something, rather than adding the newfangled onto it.

Thus the *praxis* of creativity does not necessarily underwrite the valuing of novelty over the already existing, as it deals mainly in achieving a goal. The reading of this process, however, has opted to promote novelty as the central aspect in order to achieve ideological goals. Our first deconstructive move thus suggests that we cannot allow the concept of creativity to be always-already defined by novelty, nor to fall under the ideological framework of progress and modernism, but instead to allow for a concept of creativity which says that it might at times be better to be old-fashioned. The notion of novelty as defining creativity is in such a reading not only analytically problematic, it is also uncreative as it discounts other possibilities.

Second deconstructive move: originality and uniqueness

> The staggering popularity of Reality TV programmes which consist simply in someone pottering mindlessly around his kitchen for hours on end suggests one interesting truth: that many of us find the pleasures of the routine and repetitive even more seductive than we do the stimulus of adventure.
>
> (Eagleton 2005: 8)

The painter Paul Cézanne, generally considered as one of the most important innovators in the history of painting[6] (cf. Berger 2001; Foster *et al.* 2004), demonstrated a very peculiar kind of 'creativity', one that eschewed novelty and instead focused on work and repetition. As he put it himself 'The quest for novelty and originality is an artificial need which can never disguise banality and the absence of artistic temperament' (quoted in Doran 2001: 17). What to make, for example, of Cézanne's stubbornness in wanting to paint the same view of Mont Sainte-Victoire over and over again? For Cézanne, the *work* of painting involved repetition, 'repetition in the name not just of seeking an answer to something but of locating, deepening, embellishing a problem . . .' (Osborne 2003: 520). Through the Mont Sainte-Victoire landscape – because Cézanne used it over and over again as his raw material – one comes to see what creativity can mean (in his particular context). It is what Paul Ricoeur (1998: 179) referred to as the 'enigma of creation':

> The modesty or the pride of the artist – in this case, it amounts to the same thing – is probably to know at this very moment how to make the gesture that every person should make. In apprehending the singularity of the question there is the sentiment of an incredible obligation; in the case of Cézanne or Van Gogh we know that it was over-whelming. It is as if the artist experienced the urgency of an unpaid debt with respect to something singular that had to be said in a singular manner.

The explanation of creativity thus has to be sought in the *process* of production itself; the power of the paintings lies in their *painting*. Nothing appeared more sacred to Cézanne than work: 'My method is to love working' (Doran 2001: 127). He thus subscribes to the very Marxist notion that reality can best be approached through work, precisely because reality itself is a form of production. Here, we find another ideological problem. Many commentators on creativity insist that the reason that creativity is important is because it generates unique and original things, and that this in turn produces value. But in accepting this we have taken in a theory of value as already unchallenged and objectively true when this theory is in fact a hotbed of dissenting opinions (see e.g. Gibson-Graham 1996). Furthermore, in the twentieth and twenty-first centuries, historians have become increasingly preoccupied with the phenomenon of repetition; not as Hegel described it by saying that everything in world history happens twice, but rather as Marx expanded this in his *18th Brumaire of Louis Napoleon* when he corrected what Hegel forgot to add: the first time as tragedy, the second as farce (Foster *et al.* 2004).

Our second deconstructive move, then, is to challenge the notion that creativity by necessity must contain original properties. Instead, we suggest that copying, imitation and mimicry, not to mention just hard (re)productive work, can be just as important. For instance, the new realist movement in the pictorial arts (as represented, for example, by the Florence Academy) attempts to achieve almost photo-realism in their art, which positions hard work and reproduction as more critical aspects of creative work than originality. Similarly, one can find cases in archi-tecture where the creator has tried to copy a style almost religiously, maybe adding a small twist, and presenting this as both a creative work and as homage. Another example would be indus-trial design which tries to mimic natural forms (e.g. the Anglepoise task light) or bands that try to capture the style and image of a bygone era (blues revivals, neo-crooners). In all these examples the hallmark of success in a creative endeavour is that one has succeeded in copying that which one references: 'It's just like the old times!', 'I can't believe this is not an Eames!' Exactness in mimicry can also create exquisite ironic effects, such as when Oscar Wilde created a new form of comedy simply by perfectly duplicating English high society mannerisms in print and on the stage.

Such a deconstructive move points to the fact that originality lies in the relational dynamics, not in the thing itself, and thus not in creativity itself either. Originality is a process, not an essential characteristic. We are always constrained by both the matter we are forced to work with and an audience we are trying to communicate with. Edgerton (2006: 84–85), for example, illustrates how car repairers in Ghana develop an intimate knowledge of cars and engines and how to keep them going using local materials, in the process transforming the cars: 'Replacement gaskets were made from old tyres, fuses were replaced by copper wire, nails were used as lock-pins . . . what might seem like dangerous and costly indifference to the rules set out in maintenance manuals was a remarkable example of extreme technical artifice brought within human understanding.' Creativity emerges here when one produces something that paradoxically adheres to the rules of the game and at the same time establishes new rules. The compulsion to emphasize uniqueness simply reduces creativity to one of its aspects, in the interest of better fitting it into a preconceived structure. As the modernist notion of progress, which in neoliberal discourse is ascribed to the workings of the market economy, *ipso facto* necessitates the existence of essential and replenishable originality, it is obvious why this aspect of creativity has been emphasized, even though this points to an ideological positioning rather than an analytical one.

Our second deconstructive turn thus involves a position where creativity might very well be about doing the same thing over and over again, and that things do not necessarily have to be original to be creative – or at least that one should not overemphasize this part of the binary. It might be that it is the very process of working that shows us creativity, rather than it being revealed in the originality of the final product. Therefore we shouldn't exaggerate the role of originality or uniqueness in the definition of creativity either, as this reduces what creativity can be or mean. This turn, however, should be seen as much more radical than merely a definitional *volte-face*, as it points to how the productive nature of creativity can be (alternatively) understood.

Third deconstructive move: neutrality, or, recasting the ideology of creativity

It is generally accepted that both innovation and entrepreneurship depend upon and utilize the creative impulse. As both have been politically and ideologically cast as necessary for economic growth and development in post-industrial economies, creativity has thus become something of a poster-child for the potential inherent in the market economy (viz. the *Cox Review of Creativity in Business*). Such a positioning, however pleasing it might be for creativity researchers, is not uncontroversial. It assumes that creativity is an external, outside thing, which can be harnessed by market agents such as the 'innovator' or the 'entrepreneur', and thus casts creativity as both neutral and necessarily beneficial. There is scant if any discussion about how this casting of creativity has made it into a moral category, and by extension a political one.

Little attention has been paid to how creativity can be a negative thing, or even an immoral or illicit affair. Similarly, the assumption that creativity is always a joyous thing, the mark of a free society, and the handmaiden of contemporary capitalism has been seldom put into question. This assumption is remarkably strong and affects much of theoretical work on creativity. While it is obvious that creativity can exist in fields such as accounting, crime, torture or paedophilia, such negative aspects are rarely if ever brought up in the discussion thereon, as this would make the concept seem less bright and decidedly positive than in its current dominant representations. Following the same logic, we can ask why it would necessarily be the case that creativity is furthered and utilized best in market economies?

In their study of *blat* networks in the Soviet Union, Rehn and Taalas (2004) argue that contrary to popular assumption the USSR may have been the most entrepreneurial country ever, and by extension, the most creative economy of all. In a system where even the simple act of buying meat was hindered by a Byzantine system of laws, regulations, five-year plans and a stifling bureaucracy, creativity and entrepreneurial action were not simply things a few special individuals engaged in, but became a necessary part of survival. Focusing on a system of favours and gift-exchanges known as *blat*, Rehn and Taalas discuss how the Soviet citizens would set up intricate and often highly creative networks of exchanges and mutual assistance in order to keep the everyday economy running in the undergrowth of the state-run system. For instance, a person with access to medicine could help a friend who in turn knew a butcher who might need a new coat, which might be had from a person who had earlier got a discounted Aeroflot-ticket from somebody's brother, and so on in a complex and ever-changing network of assistance. This obviously demanded quite a lot of creative finagling, interesting exchanges and out-of-the-box approaches to exchanges. At the same time, such *blat* networks obviously worked against the system and were basically illegal. They might have been beneficial for the people taking part in them, yet siphoned off resources from the greater system and could be understood both as a way to make the economy more efficient and as a system of exploitation. Such a system can of course not be seen as neutral – our view of it is inevitably tied to our views on what constitutes a 'good' society. Creativity, considered from this perspective, is not neutral at all but part of how we ideologically construct the world (cf. Žižek 2006). We can state that *blat* was creative or showed creativity, but whether this statement is seen as meaningful ultimately depends on our view of the world.

Peculiarly enough, this reaction to the oppression of the Soviet bureaucracy can be seen as a fundamentally Marxist move. The hallmark of Marxism is precisely the idea that human beings create both the world and themselves. Bernard Williams (1977: 206) put it thus:

> At the very centre of Marxism is an extraordinary emphasis on human creativity and self-creation. Extraordinary because most of the systems with which it contends stress the derivation of most human activity from an external cause: from God, from an abstracted Nature or human nature, from permanent instinctual systems, or from an animal inheritance. The notion of self-creation, extended to civil society and to language by pre-Marxist thinkers, was radically extended by Marxism to the basic work processes and thence to a deeply (creatively) altered physical world and a self-created humanity.

Our third deconstructive move, then, is to say that creativity is not a neutral thing, nor a self-evidently good thing, but instead necessarily tied to a moral and ideological context. Maybe, instead of 'creativity', we have things like 'neo-liberal creativity', 'late-modernist creativity', 'Marxist creativity' and so on. We might even have something like a neutral concept of creativity, but this would possibly have to accept things such as torture and systematic abuse as part of its expression. In other words, it is not enough to focus on *praxis*, we must also (echoing Sartre) think about the fundamentals of human thought (including the notion of ethics and how we construct the framework of our thinking). What deconstruction can do is to show how we (through the mechanisms of ideological thinking) neutralize and valorize a concept like creativity, and how we need to be aware of the possibilities for imbuing the concept with different values. The deconstructive method, which is mindful of how valorizations are turned into ontological claims, can help us disentangle the sometimes muddled moral discourse of creativity in contemporary society. As to the question of how we then would define creativity, we must turn one last time to Derrida (2001: 188):

The answer must each time be invented, singular, signed, and each time only one time like the gift of a work, a giving of art and life, unique and, right up until the end of the world, played back. Given back. To the impossible, I mean right up to the impossible.

Discussing deconstructed creativity

Why these deconstructive moves? What do we want to show? A critical reader could now challenge us and say we are merely playing a semantic game, and even suggest that we are draining the concept of creativity of meaning by suggesting that any-and-everything can be fitted into it. In one sense this latter accusation might be true. We do want to empty the word of its dogmatic and ideological meanings, as these in fact never can capture the concept of creativity in its entirety, and instead work as a form of straitjacket for enabling only particular types of analyses. We do not want to present a novel definition of creativity, but rather point to the problems with defining that which may lie beyond the graspable.

On one level, deconstruction should be a natural and normal process to all and sundry working in the creativity field, for it is reminiscent of many of the practical methods we use to develop ideas. Rule reversal, lateral thinking and all techniques working with interruptions or discontinuities are connected to the notion of deconstruction, even if the latter works on a more philosophical level. In this sense, deconstructing creativity is just a question of being creative about creativity, testing its borders by way of techniques used and prescribed by the field itself. On this level, deconstruction could even be seen as a sort of necessary ethics for the field of creativity studies; one that would assume that the field would practise what it preaches and not be afraid of 'walking the talk'.

Yet, there is obviously something much more radical at stake here. When one starts to subject the concept of creativity to such deconstructive moves, something happens. The familiar creativity territory becomes alien and strange and we seem to lose our bearings. The taken-for-granted grounding of the concept of creativity starts to look like just so many assumptions, created to fit nicely in with other assumptions. Creativity, from being a sign of humanity's potential, becomes just another word in the arsenal of politicians and CEOs. Rather than the nice, productive concept of good productive cheer we are left with a neo-liberal slogan or perhaps a Marxist rallying-cry.

Our aim is not simply to suggest that creativity is always-already ideologically tainted. It is not more so than any other concept one cares to analyse. Instead, our interest lies in bringing to the fore that which is normally hidden. By valorising novelty over the pre-existing, one turns creativity into part of a modernist narrative of unending progress and the necessity of continuous capitalistic development. By valorising originality, one hides away notions of production and work, not to mention history. By valorising creativity as a neutral concept, one hides away the many assumptions about ethics and the nature of social life that form the possibility of normalizing concepts. We cannot fully escape the framework within which we think, nor the context from where we think, but we must work on our awareness of the foundations of our thinking.

In an age where creativity has been corralled into the service of both big business and the nation state, we must be able to display a degree of intellectual honesty and show that we can subject even the concept of creativity to critique. Deconstruction is a technique for opening up concepts, subjecting them to difficult questions, and escaping the totalizing tendency inherent in all attempts at definition. By applying it to creativity, we have tried to suggest possibilities for a creativity theory of tomorrow; one that would generate more interesting insights from, and surprising twists to, the old tales.

Notes

1 Aporia is a term borrowed from literary theory which indicates the impasse of an undecidable oscillation, as when the chicken depends upon the egg but the egg depends on the chicken (Culler 1997: 100).

2 Ford's (1996: 1116) definition is succinct and typical: 'I define creativity as a domain-specific, subjective judgement of the novelty and value of an outcome of a particular action.'

3 The report offered the following recommendations (p. 16):

■ A nationwide programme should be introduced and supported to engage SMEs and demonstrate the practical benefits of applying creativity.

■ Steps should be taken to get greater understanding of creativity and innovation into the boardroom by recruiting people with creative experience onto company boards.

■ 'Managing creativity' should be a topic in the Institute of Directors (IoD) Chartered Director syllabus.

■ Broadcasters should take the same approach to encouraging creativity that they have recently shown towards enterprise.

4 Schumpeter attributed his insight that capitalism is an evolutionary process to Marx, whose vision already comprehended the raw power of capitalism. For Schumpeter, capitalism is never stationary but driven by a process of innovation, which is itself driven by the pursuit of profit, with profit-hungry entrepreneurs in the driving seat.

5 Duchamp's quintessential device in this respect was the readymade (e.g. bicycle wheel 1913; bottle rack 1914; Fountain 1917), an appropriated product positioned as art. This device allowed him to leap past old aesthetic questions of craft, medium and taste to new questions that were potentially ontological ('what is art?'), epistemological ('how do we know it?'), and institutional ('who determines it?'). His famous urinal (or 'Fountain') was the only one out of 2,125 works from 1,235 artists that was rejected for exhibition in April 1917 by the American Society of Independent Artists. As Foster *et al.* (2004: 129) put it: 'Never shown in its initial guise, *Fountain* was suspended in time, its questions deferred to later moments. In this way it became one of the most influential objects in twentieth-century art well after the fact.' Duchamp's main lesson was that no artist determines his work finally. Not only does the viewer have a share, but subsequent artists also interpret a body of work, reposition it retroactively, and so carry it forward as well.

6 John Berger (2001: 225–227) paid Cézanne the following homage: 'Everyone is agreed that Cézanne's paintings appear to be different from those of any painter who preceded him; whilst the works of those who came after seem scarcely comparable, for they were produced out of the profound crisis which Cézanne half foresaw and helped to provoke. . . . Cézanne, who consciously strove towards a new synthesis between art and nature, who wanted to renew the European tradition, in fact destroyed forever the foundation of that tradition by insisting, more radically as his work developed, that visibility is as much an extension of ourselves as it is a quality-in-itself of things.'

References

Berger, J. (2001). *Selected Essays*. New York: Vintage.

Bills, T. and Genasi, C. (2003). *Creative Business: Achieving Your Goals Through Creative Thinking and Action*. London: Palgrave.

Bohm, D. (2004). *On Creativity*. London: Routledge.

de Brabandere, L. (2005). *The Forgotten Half of Change: Achieving Greater Creativity through Changes in Perception*. Chicago: Dearborn.

Cook, S. D. N. and Brown, J. S. (1999). Bridging Epistemologies: The Generative Dance Between Organizational Knowledge and Organizational Knowing. *Organization Science*, 10(4), 381–400.

Cox, G. (2005). *The Cox Review of Creativity in Business*. London: HM Treasury, at: http://www.hm-treasury.gov.uk/cox.

Culler, J. (1997). *A Very Short Introduction to Literary Theory*. Oxford: Oxford University Press.

Derrida, J. (1981). *Positions* (A. Bass, Trans.). Chicago: Chicago University Press.

Derrida, J. (2001). *The Work of Mourning*. Chicago: Chicago University Press.

Doran, M. (Ed.). (2001). *Conversations with Cézanne*. Berkeley: University of California Press.

Eagleton, T. (1996). *Literary Theory: An Introduction*, second edition. Oxford: Blackwell.

Eagleton, T. (2005). *The English Novel: An Introduction*. Oxford: Blackwell.

Edgerton, D. (2006). *The Shock of the Old: Technology and global history since 1900*. London: Profile.

Elsbach, K. D. and Kramer, R. M. (2003). Assessing Creativity in Hollywood Pitch Meetings: Evidence for a Dual-Process Model of Creativity Judgements. *Academy of Management Journal*, 46(3), 283–301.

Ford, C. M. (1996). A Theory of Individual Creative Action in Multiple Social Domains. *Academy of Management Review*, 21(4), 1112–1142.

Foster, H., Krauss, R., Bois, Y.-A. and Buchloh, B. (2004). *Art since 1900: Modernism, antimodernism, postmodernism*. London: Thames and Hudson.

Gibson-Graham, J. K. (1996), *The End of Capitalism (As We Knew It): A Feminist Critique of Political Economy*. Oxford: Blackwell.

Gogatz, A. and Mondejar, R. (2005). *Business Creativity: Breaking the Invisible Barriers*. Basingstoke: Palgrave Macmillan.

Guillet de Monthoux, P. (2004). *The Art Firm: Aesthetic Management and Metaphysical Marketing*. Stanford: Stanford Business Books.

Iser, W. (2006). *How to Do Theory*. Oxford: Blackwell.

Jameson, F. (2002). *A Singular Modernity: Essay on the Ontology of the Present*. London: Verso.

Maeda, J. (2006). *The Laws of Simplicity*. Cambridge, MA: MIT Press.

Osborne, T. (2003). Against 'Creativity': A Philistine Rant. *Economy and Society*, 32(4), 507–525.

Proctor, T. (2005). *Creative Problem Solving for Managers: Developing skills for decision making and innovation*. Abingdon, Oxon: Routledge.

Rehn, A. and Taalas, S. (2004). 'Znakomstva I Svyazi' (Acquaintances and connections) – Blat, the Soviet Union, and mundane entrepreneurship. *Entrepreneurship and Regional Development*, 16(3), 235–250.

Rehn, A. and Vachhani, S. (2006). Innovation and the Post-original: On Moral Stances and Reproduction. *Creativity and Innovation Management*, 15(3), 310–322.

Rickards, T. and De Cock, C. (1999). Sociological Paradigms and Organizational Creativity. In R. E. Purser and A. Montuori (eds.), *Social Creativity* (Vol. 2, pp. 235–256). Cresskill: Hampton Press.

Ricoeur, P. (1998). *Critique and Conviction: Conversations with François Azouvi and Marc de Launay* (K. Blamey, Trans.). Cambridge: Polity Press.

Sartre, J.-P. (1976/2004). *Critique of Dialectical Reason* (A. Sheridan-Smith, Trans.). London: Verso.

Schumpeter, J. (1942). *Capitalism, Socialism and Democracy*. Cambridge, MA: Harvard University Press.

Williams, B. (1977). *Marxism and Literature*. Oxford: Oxford University Press.

Žižek, S. (2006). *The Parallax View*. Cambridge, MA: MIT Press.

19

Idea activity in our nations and workplaces

Glenn Rothberg

Introduction

Ideas might be considered as thoughts, concepts, beliefs or suggestions, involving *possible* courses of action. In this way, ideas are seen as the precursors of change. What *actually* happens to ideas is also an important part of creativity, innovation and economic advance.

Ideas are one of the great intangibles of our organizations, nations and workplaces. Even when restricted to commerce, a topic about ideas is wide. That is because ideas generate improved products, services, work teams and even leadership styles. As markets and environments change, the assumptions upon which the organization has been built, and is being run, become outdated. The organizational mission, core competencies, structure, and operations, cease to fit. Sometimes our uniqueness, our skills and our originality, embodied in our ideas, remain too long: ideas that brought us capabilities begin to provide us with disabilities. Innovation gaps arise. In these instances, there is a need to change ideas which, in their day, were possibly the best.

Typically, a change process will involve identifiable activity associated with the origin, acceptance and implementation of contributing ideas. This 'idea activity' indicates what is happening to ideas in the workplace. So, to understand whether and how ideas are contributing to improved performance in our nations and workplaces, we also need to discuss idea activity.

Florida (2003, 2005, 2007) discussed the scope and importance of the creative class, their association with cities, and talent retention. Clearly, trade and activity in ideas has a major role in the creative class demographic, estimated to be about 30 per cent of employees (Florida 2003: 330). However, largely unanswered are questions about the importance of ideas, and what is happening to them, both within the creative class and across the broader population.

In contrast with tools that measure activity in science, finance, accounting and economics, I suggest that there is inadequate attention to tools that measure activity in ideas. More generally, I suggest that there is a shortfall in monitoring and evaluating what is happening to ideas. To address ideas in a dynamic, action-based way, and monitor idea activity in our organizations will, I suggest, require managers and researchers to move beyond what I call a static mindset.

Therefore, the approach I take is fourfold. First, to emphasize how activity in ideas contributes to the creation of value, we need to distinguish between what I call the dynamic and static aspects of ideas. Second, discussed, is a tendency for the management literature to emphasize static aspects of ideas, which, as valuable as they are, do not focus on what is actually happening to ideas. So, third, I provide local workplace and national economic perspectives on measuring and harnessing what happens to ideas. Across these two perspectives, the presence of innovation gaps is indicated: firstly, when idea activity is measured in local workplaces; and secondly, when the contribution of innovation capacity to economic growth is compared across nations. Finally, to support decision makers in addressing ideas and improving innovation across workplaces and nations, the approach suggests invoking an ideas framework, through an idea activity metric.

Ideas contribute to value creation

To understand their contribution to the creation of value, we need to distinguish between the dynamic and static aspects of ideas. In a dynamic view, we measure idea flow and activity; in a static view, we measure idea capability and outcomes. I suggest that, relying on conventional theory and practice, managers tend to derive value from a static (and limited) approach to ideas.

Dynamic aspect of ideas

There is usually very little to be gained by not doing anything. Ultimately, it is the *activity* in ideas that is fundamental to future innovative outcomes. In short, for something to happen with ideas, they need to be active. A dynamic approach to ideas is to enquire about what is happening to them; this includes idea interaction, progression and responsiveness. The dynamic view provides a picture of idea flows. Contributing to the creation of value will depend on activity in ideas or what I call 'idea activity' (http:www.ideaactivity.com).

Activity in ideas includes their origin, acceptance and implementation. Turning, converting and translating ideas into high value added products and services is an activity in ideas. Ideation is also activity in ideas. This occurs, for example, when we are creating strategy, as well as when we are implementing it. Similarly, our management skills, processes, key result areas and outcomes depend on *activity* in diverse areas such as: design, production, finance, accounting, leadership, marketing, management, people, business, trade, community and environment. All involve an active role for past, current or future ideas. I suggest that, in the management literature, there is inadequate emphasis on the flow of ideas.

Static aspect of ideas

In a static approach to ideas, the emphasis is on the description, classification and warehousing of ideas. The static view provides a picture reflecting potentiality, possibility, capability, competence, and what might be delivered in the organization.

When managers address diverse workplace issues (such as: mission, vision and leadership; tasks, processes, techniques and technology; people, personalities and stakeholders; context and environment) they are addressing an existing profile of embedded ideas. These are accumulated ideas, currently retained and which, in their time, were possibly the best. In the static view, ideas are treated as objects, rather than as works-in-progress. However, if they are to bring change, managers will need to change the existing static profile of ideas.

As valuable as the static profile is in our understanding of mainstream management functions and disciplines, it does not reflect the level of idea activity that is actually occurring. It is suggested that there is an undue emphasis on the static view of ideas in the management literature.

Idea activity in mainstream management

Importance of activity in ideas

Learning and knowledge depend on activity in ideas. For example 'learning' includes the *transfer* of ideas, their dispensing, and take up, while 'knowledge management' includes the *flow* of ideas, their accumulation, warehousing, accessing and dispensing. The active flow of ideas (dynamic) contributes to knowledge, which, once attained, provides a capability (static). The *adaptation* of ideas occurs in 'organizational improvement' through leadership, tasks, processes and the way people interact. The 'diffusion of innovation' is essentially about the *take up* of ideas, including their acceptance and implementation.

For example, Boden (1994) queries the possible creative process and asks whether creativity can be measured (ibid.: 1). This is essentially a static analytical perspective about the nature of creativity. In contrast, when colleagues test the actual interactive flow and progression of ideas, and the creative projects occurring in the workplace, they are engaged in a dynamic activity.

The static view is typically present when the flow of ideas stops; such as when ideas are uninvited, unprocessed or ignored. Disdain for ideas is an effective way of reducing their effective flow. For example, dismissive claims that generating ideas is easy, or that there is no shortage of ideas can hide a barrier to their further progression. Often, to be stuck in a static view about ideas, there is a failure to see that the existing ideas will require additional idea *activity* for their progression through some combination of idea origination, acceptance and implementation.

It is not sufficient to advocate that ideas should somehow influence the way business gets done. We need a framework for ideas and their activity; we also need to be able to measure idea activity. Mainstream management functions become dynamic when ideas interact with them and progress (Rothberg 2005b).

To understand the role of ideas in our nations and workplaces, we need to recognize that 'idea activity' is not a topic that is readily identified in the management literature. However, as noted below, while measurement of transactions is common, mainstream management concepts, including leadership and competitive advantage, tend to focus on the static role of ideas, rather than on idea activity.

Idea activity metric and framework needed

Accountants measure financial and cash activity. Engineers measure time, distance and weight ratios. Manufacturers measure production throughput, and attributes of quality and errors. Economists use metrics in macroeconomics, including consumption expenditure and aggregate demand; and in microeconomics, including cost, production and sales transactions. In short, many aspects of activity are already measured in the typical enterprise. What about activity in ideas?

Is there an equivalent workplace idea metric? If ideas, creativity and innovation are important for business success, decision makers need to know what they are and what is happening to ideas in the workplace and throughout the economy. Are managers accountable for innovation and idea activity? If they are, how are they assessed? We need to capture the creative (and uncreative) interface between colleagues, their organization and the environment.

Indicators of activity in price, building, economic growth, consumption, sales and production are found through market surveys. Similarly, we can survey what participants say is happening to ideas in their workplaces. And we can aggregate these results across workplaces to the enterprise level, and beyond. Although we cannot observe ideas, we can record the presence or absence of idea activity, based on what participants tell us is happening among them (Rothberg 2004, 2007). This will include idea interaction and idea progression.

Filtered views

We need to detect whether and when ideas are being inappropriately screened out, as well as activity about their inclusion.

Mindsets and paradigms of whatever persuasion construct and apply ideas in selective ways. This is discussed by many writers, including: Burrell and Morgan (1979), Choi (1993), Clark and Clegg (1998), Geertz (1973) and Kuhn (1962, 1977). These idea filters are evident in the attention given by writers to errors, crises, disruptions, mind traps, uncertainty and ambiguity in management theory (Argyris 1985, 1990; Argyris and Schön 1978; D'Aveni 1998, 1999; D'Aveni and Gunther 1994; Hamel 2000). Images (Morgan 1997) are also used to provide partial views including: enterprise life cycle from birth to maturity (Schein 1985); strategy creation from animal-like behaviours found on safari (Mintzberg *et al.* 1998); and participants who fail to conform in a visionary company being removed like a virus (Collins and Porras 1998).

Leadership and longevity

In considering companies that have lasted for several hundred years, deGeus (1997) observes that a key characteristic of enterprise longevity includes tolerance of new ideas and valuing people, rather than assets. We are informed about the characteristics and benefits of transactional, transformational and servant leadership (Bass 1990, 1997, 1999; Spears 1998). Similarly, there is discussion about how differences in the enterprise's performance are attributed to their leaders (Collins 2001). In contrast, Drucker (2002: 289) observes that chief executives are expected to take on jobs that have become undoable.

In all these cases, we know that value is being created and destroyed. What we do not know is what is actually happening to ideas under the influence of the different leadership regimes. To detect these differences in the workplace, an idea activity metric is suggested (Rothberg 2005a). Such information may also provide leadership with practical options for intervention.

Resource activity

Organizations gain competitive advantage through their people questioning the norms and doing something useful with ideas. However, mainstream views about competitive advantage have been substantially based on a resource allocation model (Porter 1980, 1985), which highlights new competitors, substitutes, bargaining power and competitor rivalry (Porter 1985).

I suggest that it is now time to extend the resource view and acknowledge that an organization's competitive advantage is a profile of accumulated ideas. That is, ideas and their progressions are invisibly embedded when resources are assembled to form workplaces, industries and nations. This implies that changes in competitive advantage will be based on improved understanding and assessment of ideas. The traditional emphasis has been on the resource allocation outcome, rather than on the idea activity required to achieve it.

235

If we want evidence about how we have marginalized, fragmented, disintegrated and isolated ideas from regular workplace activity, we need look no further than the institutions of the 'suggestion box', 'the brainstorm session', the 'think tank' and the planning 'retreat'.

An activity-based focus for ideas encourages design that is ongoing and constantly offers new perceptions, and that is not restricted to efficiency, technology, task, leadership and people, but embraces them all: an ongoing dynamic approach.

These processes and events tell us more about how mainstream management has tended to contain rather than liberate ideas in routine activities. Idea filters are often initiated by customers and decision-makers who cannot see beyond their current way of doing things (Christensen 2000; Christensen and Raynor 2003). Better idea activity metrics can be used to detect and correct the extent to which ideas are filtered and biased in favour of existing beliefs, customers, products and markets.

Measurement of idea activity

What can we say about the measurement of idea activity in our workplaces and in our national economies? Firstly, in our workplaces we can measure the interaction and progression of ideas from views provided by workplace participants. Secondly, in our national economies, we can review the apparent impact of innovative capacity on overall economic performance.

Workplace perspective

An exploratory study of what happens to ideas in the workplace provided guidance on idea activity in organizations (Rothberg 2004). The results suggest opportunity for improved acknowledgement of ideas, scope for more consistent responsiveness, and opportunity to more reliably consider a range of constructive in-house skills among colleagues. The workplace idea activity results can be used to understand the contribution of ideas to other aspects of the organization, such as leadership and management (Rothberg 2005a) and to integrate the role of ideas into a reconstructed view of management theory and practice (Rothberg 2005b). An extension (Rothberg 2006) indicated the application of the idea metric internationally, and provided further evidence of how to measure and access ideas.

Illustrated in Figure 19.1 is the type of idea interaction and idea progression information that is available in the workplace (Rothberg 2004, 2006). The results from these studies provide doubt as to whether ideas have been adequately acknowledged or rewarded in the sample organizations. Using this type of approach, it is possible to reveal issues such as: whether respondents know better ways of performing their tasks; the nature and profile of support for ideas in the workplace; and the extent to which workplaces are reportedly to be friendly or unfriendly to ideas. In addition to idea interaction, idea progression can also be assessed, such as by finding out whether colleagues consider that it is possible to have ideas accepted and implemented in their workplace.

Through the components of idea activity (idea interaction and idea progression) we can measure what is happening to ideas in the workplace. By extending the approach across many workplace (and community) participants, we estimate aggregate idea activity for workplaces, businesses, cities, regions and national economies.

(a) Idea interaction: illustration

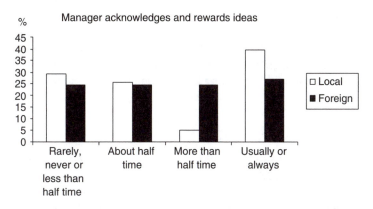

(b) Idea progression: illustration

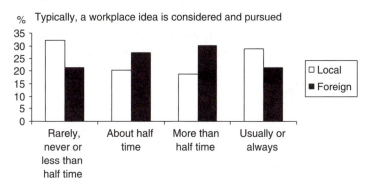

Figure 19.1 Workplace perspective on idea activity

Source: Rothberg (2006).

International economic perspective

Innovative capacity

What might we say about the impact of innovative capacity on economic outcomes among countries of the Organisation for Economic Cooperation and Development (OECD)?

The concept of national innovative *capacity* is the ability of a country to produce and commercialize a flow of new-to-the-world technologies over the long term (Furman *et al.* 2002). The innovation index uses patents and patent growth from each country to reflect ideas generated and the growth of idea production. The innovation concept and index is sourced to: a strong common innovation infrastructure; the country's industrial clusters; and innovation linkages, including universities and new venture funding sources (ibid.). The innovation index estimates are progressively updated (Gans and Hayes 2004, 2005, 2006; Gans and Stern 2003; Porter and Stern 1999).

The authors claim that the index is generally applicable as an explanator of national innovation, providing: 'an indication of the relative capability of the economy to produce innovative outputs' (Gans and Stern 2003: 23); and 'our clearest picture yet of the innovative state of the world' (Gans and Hayes 2004: 2), capturing 'R&D personnel and funding even in those sectors which do not rely heavily on patenting' (Gans and Stern 2003: 21).

That is, the Innovation Index is claimed to have generally applicable qualities for national economies. In short, these authors argue that we can use their innovation index as a proxy for economy-wide innovation in those nations for which they have developed it. The question is: does the additional innovative capacity translate to additional national economic growth? How do we know?

Creativity themes and innovative activity

In their retrospective, Rickards and Moger (2006) set out to review emerging creativity and innovation journal themes in the decade 1991 to 2000. Their discussion of emerging themes in innovation raises the question of innovation's impact on economic performance. This discussion of innovation journal themes overlaps the period during which there is also discussion and measurement of the innovation capacity index.

How would we know if discussions of innovation or changes in innovation capacity actually have an impact on economic performance in this period? The answer is to include an innovation index with other national economic data, to see if any statistical association exists. That is, we can review data among OECD nations to estimate the apparent contribution of innovation as a factor input that is associated with changes in national economic growth. Here, we are talking about measuring the responsiveness of real gross domestic product (GDP) against an existing measure of innovation.

This is addressed in two steps. Firstly, we can compare annual national percentage changes in the innovation index with annual national percentage rates of real GDP growth within the OECD (see Table 19.1). Secondly, we can derive an equation that updates the functional form (1) of the Solow (1957) aggregate production function. That is, we can estimate the apparent factor input contributions of annual percentage growth in labour, capital and innovation to the annual percentage growth of national economic output among countries within the OECD (see Table 19.2):

$$Y = f \text{ (Capital, Labour, Time, Innovation)} \tag{1}$$

Here, Y represents real gross domestic product, while capital and labour are represented in 'physical' units. Allowance for any kind of shift in the production function, slowdowns, speedups, improvements in the education of the labour force, and other sources of technical change (Solow 1957: 312) can be accommodated by the traditional variable Time, which is now

Table 19.1 Average growth in real GDP and innovation among OECD countries, 1985–2004

Period	Real GDP	Innovation Capacity Index	Innovation 'gap'	Observations
	A (%)	B (%)	C = B − A (%)	No.
1985–2004	2.71	6.38	3.67	328
1995–2004	2.93	8.17	5.24	160
1985–1994	2.51	4.68	2.17	168

Source: See Table 19.2.

Table 19.2 Average of annual growth rates estimated factor contributions to OECD economic growth, selected countries 1985–2004

Period	Equation estimated by stepwise regression		Data considered	
	Variables considered	Variables included (regression coefficients)	Mean	Annual data points
1985–2004	Real GDP		2.71	328
	Constant	1.56		
	Time		19.27	
	Hours worked	0.66	0.71	
	Capital services	0.19	3.68	
	Innovation (T)		6.38	
	Innovation (T-1)		7.15	
	Innovation (T-2)		7.20	
	Innovation (T-3)		6.50	
	R^2	0.52		
1995–2004	Real GDP		2.93	160
	Constant	3.36		
	Time	−0.09	24.23	
	Hours worked	0.62	1.07	
	Capital services	0.32	3.83	
	Innovation (T)		8.17	
	Innovation (T-1)	−0.03	8.51	
	Innovation (T-2)		8.57	
	Innovation (T-3)	0.02	8.55	
	R^2	0.58		
1985–1994	Real GDP		2.51	168
	Constant	2.26		
	Time		14.55	
	Hours worked	0.68	0.37	
	Capital services		3.53	
	Innovation (T)		4.68	
	Innovation (T-1)		4.93	
	Innovation (T-2)		4.94	
	Innovation (T-3)		4.68	
	R^2	0.53		

Notes: RGDP – Real Gross Domestic Product, annual % change (*OECD Factbook* 2006a); evolution of GDP (OECD 2006b); Constant – regression constant; Time – survey year number 1 = 1985; Hours worked – total hours worked, annual % change (*OECD Productivity Database*, selected countries, September 2006, 2006b); Capital services – capital input into production for the total economy, annual % change (OECD capital services, by type of asset based on harmonised price indices for ICT capital goods, October 2006, 2006b); Innovation (T), (T-1), (T-2), (T-3) – innovation index, annual % change, in year T (derived from Gans and Hayes 2005).

Sources: OECD nations – OECD countries selected for data series completeness: Australia, Belgium, Canada, Denmark, Finland, France, Germany, Ireland, Italy, Japan, Netherlands, New Zealand, Portugal, Spain, Sweden, UK and USA.

enhanced by the inclusion of an innovation index. The availability of data for capital services limited the research survey period to be within 1985 to 2004, and seventeen OECD countries. Using forward stepwise regression, only statistically significant factor input variables are included in the least squares equation fitted to the GDP data.

Results

Innovation gap

When the full period (1985 to 2004) is split into two sub-periods, there is a noticeable difference in reported economic performance and innovation (see Table 19.1).

Combining the performances of the GDP and the innovation series over these periods indicates that an apparently significant lift in innovation (capacity) is associated with a considerably smaller increase in real economic growth across these OECD economies. That is, the apparent innovation capacity increase is failing to translate into an equivalent increase in GDP real growth performance. This is equivalent to some combination of: a national economy performance shortfall, an 'innovation gap' or an innovation backlog. In these cases, the reported increase in innovation is not fully reflected in changed economic outcomes. There is a decline in the rate of utilization of the innovation capacity.

If the innovation is not producing improved outcomes in GDP performance, this is consistent with performance impediments in national workplaces throughout the OECD countries. It is also consistent with the reported difficulties for ideas in the workplace, along the lines indicated in the workplace pilot studies about idea activity.

Estimated innovation contribution

Consider the equation (1) that estimates the statistical contribution of innovation to the growth of real GDP among the OECD nations (see Table 19.2). For the estimated equation, more than half of the variation in annual growth in real GDP in the period 1985 to 2004 across the seventeen OECD countries is associated with changes in labour hours worked and the supply of capital services. The innovation index is not a statistically significant explanator of real GDP growth in the full period 1985 to 2004 across the seventeen OECD countries tested.

Overall, in the above regression equation (Table 19.2), when we have included an innovation (capacity) variable, as an additional factor input to see whether it is statistically associated with national economic performance, we find that it provides negligible additional explanatory power.

Implications

When an innovation index variable arising from national innovative capacity research is put to the test against overall economic activity, internationally, over two decades, it reflects potentiality and possibilities, rather than what actually happens in the economy. It appears that national innovation capacity does not materially contribute to explaining movement in the performance of economic growth, across seventeen countries of the OECD (Table 19.2: 1985–2004).

While the supply of innovation capacity is increasing, its relative take up, or implementation, is not (Table 19.1). This suggests that using the approach indicated, ideas embodied in the national innovation infrastructure are not being effectively transformed into economic activity. I have argued that, for these nations, and others, idea activity is a key to understanding economic performance.

Why might this result arise? Perhaps, contrary to the claims of its advocates, an innovation index based on patents activity does *not* adequately reflect economy-wide innovation activity. In this case, we need a revised measure of innovation. However, if the innovation index is a fair reflection of innovative capacity, this means that innovation activity is either not materially contributing to, or is not resulting in, a commensurate improvement in economic activity. This implies that it is an international (OECD) phenomenon that the creation of value is falling short of its innovative potential. This is also consistent with adverse findings about what happens to ideas in the workplace, as evidenced through the explicit measurement of idea activity reported by professional managers.

Conclusions

What happens to ideas is an important aspect of creativity. Both pilot workplace feedback and aggregate OECD data provide evidence that the conversion of ideas to beneficial outcomes and economic growth is operating below potential.

Developing knowledge about the nature of ideas, in their static and dynamic forms, remains a worthwhile challenge. The measurement and evaluation of idea activity is likely to provide organizational indicators about how ideas are addressed, encouraged, discouraged, espoused, suppressed, supported or resisted. Such idea metrics place us in a better position to intervene in the workplace to convert creativity, capacity, potential and possibilities into worthwhile outcomes. Also, what happens to ideas has application that builds upon the creative class discussed by Florida (2003, 2005, 2007) and others.

This perspective about ideas has profound managerial implications. Firstly, there is a need to employ a new framework that emphasizes the role of idea activity. This will go some way to overcoming the way ideas are unwittingly filtered in the organization, such as through static approaches to ideas in management, leadership and comparative advantage. Secondly, when we treat ideas as dynamic rather than static, we enhance opportunities for stakeholders in organizational, political and social domains. Thirdly, as a change agent of creativity, idea activity can be measured in the workplace. This includes an idea framework that identifies idea interaction and idea progression. Finally, this type of framework and ideas metric enables decision-makers to be better informed in relation to more productive interventions across workplaces, enterprises, regions, cities and nations.

References

Argyris, C. (1985) *Strategy, Change and Defensive Routines*, Marshfield, MA: Pitman.

Argyris, C. (1990) *Overcoming Organizational Defences: Facilitating Organizational Learning*, Needham Heights, MA: Allyn and Bacon.

Argyris, C. and Schön, D. (1978) *Organizational Learning: A Theory of Action Perspective*, Reading, MA: Addison-Wesley.

Bass, B.M. (1990) From Transactional to Transformational Leadership: Learning to Share the Vision, *Organizational Dynamics*, 18(3): 19–31.

Bass, B.M. (1997) Does the Transactional-transformational Leadership Paradigm Transcend Organizational and National Boundaries?, *American Psychologist*, 52(2): 130–139.

Bass, B.M. (1999) Two Decades of Research and Development in Transformational Leadership, *European Journal of Work and Organizational Psychology*, 8(1): 9–32.

Boden, M.A. (1994) *Dimensions of Creativity*, Cambridge, MA: MIT Press.

Burrell, G. and Morgan, G. (1979) *Sociological Paradigms and Organizational Analysis: Elements of the Sociology of Corporate Life*, Aldershot: Gower.

Choi, Y.B. (1993) *Paradigms and Conventions: Uncertainty, Decision Making, and Entrepreneurship*, Ann Arbor: University of Michigan Press.

Christensen, C. (2000) *The Innovator's Dilemma*, New York: HarperCollins.

Christensen, C. and Raynor, M.E. (2003) *The Innovator's Solution*, Boston, MA: Harvard Business School Press.

Clarke, T. and Clegg, S. (1998) *Changing Paradigms: The Transformation of Management Knowledge for the 21st Century*, London: HarperCollins Business.

Collins, J. (2001) Level 5 Leadership: The Triumph of Humility and Fierce Resolve, *Harvard Business Review*, January: 67–76.

Collins, J.C. and Porras, J.I. (1998) *Built To Last: Successful Habits of Visionary Companies*, London: Century Ltd.

D'Aveni, R.A. (1998) Waking Up to the New Era of Hypercompetition, *Washington Quarterly*, Winter, 21(1): 183–196.

D'Aveni, R.A. (1999) Strategic Supremacy through Disruption and Dominance, *Sloan Management Review*, 40(3): 127–136.

D'Aveni, R.A. and Gunther, R. (1994) *Hypercompetition: Managing the Dynamics of Strategic Maneuvring*, New York: Free Press.

deGeus, A. (1997) The Living Company, *Harvard Business Review*, 75(2): 51–60.

Drucker, P.F. (2002) *Managing in the Next Society*, Oxford: Butterworth Heinemann.

Florida, R. (2003) *The Rise of the Creative Class: And How it's Transforming Work, Leisure, Community and Everyday Life*, Australia: Pluto Press.

Florida, R. (2005) *Cities and the Creative Class*, Abingdon, Oxon: Routledge.

Florida, R. (2007) *The Flight of the Creative Class: The New Global Competition for Talent*, New York: HarperCollins.

Furman, J. L., Porter, Michael, E. and Stern, S. (2002) The Determinants of National Innovative Capacity, *Research Policy*, 31: 899–933.

Gans, J. and Hayes, R. (2004) Assessing Australia's Innovative Capacity: 2004 Update, Report 03/04, Melbourne Business School and Intellectual Property Research Institute of Australia, University of Melbourne, December, pp.1–25, at: www.ipria.org/publications.

Gans, J. and Hayes, R. (2005) Assessing Australia's Innovative Capacity: 2005 Update, Report 03/04, Melbourne Business School and Intellectual Property Research Institute of Australia, University of Melbourne, December, pp.1–29.

Gans, J. and Hayes, R. (2006) Assessing Australia's Innovative Capacity: 2006 Update, Report 03/04, Melbourne Business School and Intellectual Property Research Institute of Australia, University of Melbourne, December, pp.1–30, at: http://www.mbs.edu/igans.

Gans, J. and Stern, S. (2003) Assessing Australia's Innovative Capacity in the 21st Century, Intellectual Property Research Institute of Australia, University of Melbourne, pp.1–64.

Geertz, C. (1973) *The Interpretation of Cultures: Selected Essays*, New York: Basic Books.

Hamel, G. (2000) *Leading the Revolution*, Boston, MA: Harvard Business School Press.

Kuhn, T.S. (1962) *The Structure of Scientific Revolutions*, Chicago: University of Chicago Press.

Kuhn, T.S. (1977) *The Essential Tension: Selected Studies in Scientific Tradition and Change*, Chicago, IL: University of Chicago Press.

Mintzberg, H., Ahlstrand, B. and Lampel, J. (1998) *Strategy Safari: A Guided Tour through the Wilds of Strategic Management*, London: Prentice Hall.

Morgan, G. (1997) *Images of Organization*, Thousand Oaks, CA: Sage.

OECD (2006a) *OECD Factbook 2005*, Organisation for Economic Cooperation and Development, Paris, at: http://www.oecd.org.

OECD (2006b) *OECD Productivity Database*, Organisation for Economic Cooperation and Development, Paris.

Porter, M.E. (1980) *Competitive Strategy: Techniques for Analyzing Industries and Competitors*, New York: Free Press.

Porter, M.E. (1985) *Competitive Advantage: Creating and Sustaining Superior Performance*, New York: Free Press.

Porter, M.E. and Stern, S. (1999) *The New Challenge to America's Prosperity: Findings from the Innovation Index*, Washington, DC: Council on Competitiveness.

Rickards, T. and Moger, S. (2006) Creative Leaders: A Decade of Contributions from the *Creativity and Innovation Management* journal, *Creativity and Innovation Management*, 15(1): 4–18.

Rothberg, G. (2004) The Role of Ideas in the Manager's Workplace: Theory and Practice, *Management Decision*, 42(9): 1060–1081.

Rothberg, G. (2005a) Accessing Ideas to Develop Leadership and Organization, *Leadership and Organization Development Journal*, 26(6): 476–491.

Rothberg, G. (2005b) Beyond Mainstream Management: A Breakthrough Passage Construct, *Journal of Management Development*, 24(10): 896–912.

Rothberg, G. (2006) Idea Activity: Comparison of Australian and Malaysian Managers, unpublished survey.

Rothberg, G. (2007) Idea Activity: An Innovation Intervention, *Executive Matters*, American Management Association, New York, January: 3.

Schein, E.H. (1985) *Organizational Culture and Leadership*, San Francisco, CA: Jossey-Bass.

Solow, R. (1957) Technological Change and the Aggregate Production Function, *Review of Economics and Statistics*, 39(3): 312–320.

Spears, L.C. (1998) *The Power of Servant-Leadership: Essays by Robert K. Greenleaf*, San Francisco, CA: Berrett-Koehler.

Part 5

The creative individual

Theme 6 Personal creativity

20

Genius, creativity and leadership

Dean Keith Simonton

In 1804, Ludwig van Beethoven completed the composition of the famous Third Symphony, now known as the *Eroica* ('Heroic'). Initially dedicated to Napoleon Bonaparte, who the composer greatly admired as the champion of freedom, Beethoven had a sudden change of heart upon learning that Napoleon had just crowned himself Emperor of the French. Beethoven immediately obliterated his hero's name from the title page – so violently that it left a hole in the paper of the original score. A couple of years later, when Beethoven just heard that Napoleon had won the great battle at Jena, the composer exclaimed 'It's a pity that I do not understand the art of war as well as I do the art of music, I would conquer him!' (Forbes 1967: 403). Of course, Napoleon could no more have composed Beethoven's Third Symphony than Beethoven could have defeated Napoleon at Jena. Their respective domains of achievement are too far apart. Beethoven was a creator, Napoleon a leader. Creativity and leadership appear too different to be considered comparable phenomena.

Yet in another sense, Beethoven and Napoleon do represent two aspects of the same phenomenon. They are both called 'geniuses'. Beethoven may be a musical genius and Napoleon a military one, but the genius attribution applies equally to both personalities. This joint application is explicit in Galton's (1869) classic *Hereditary Genius*, the first empirical study of creativity and leadership. Just as Beethoven is discussed in the chapter on musicians, so is Napoleon treated in the chapter on commanders. Indeed, Galton also includes great scientists, poets and painters along with politicians and religious leaders. All seem to pass muster as geniuses in their respective domains. But what do such luminaries have in common that allows them to pass under the same rubric? Do creators and leaders of the highest order really deserve assignment to the same inclusive category?

It is my purpose in this chapter to outline an answer to this question. I begin by looking at the definitions of creativity and leadership, showing how they overlap in a meaningful manner. I then compare the empirical findings regarding the psychology of genius, creativity and leadership – making comparisons that indicate considerable convergence.

Defining creativity and leadership

Most creativity researchers have agreed on a basic definition of the phenomenon (Simonton 2000b). An idea is said to be creative when it fulfills two requirements. First, the idea must be original, novel or surprising, not routine or commonplace. Second, the idea must be adaptive, functional or effective. That is, it must work. For example, problem solving is deemed creative when the solution is not only new but it also actually solves the problem. Given this definition, psychologists have tended to focus on three distinct aspects of the phenomenon (ibid.). Some concentrate on the *process* that generates creative ideas, others focus on the *person* who produces creative ideas, and yet others scrutinize the *product* in which creative ideas are communicated or expressed. Naturally, these three perspectives should be closely related. Presumably, creative persons who have engaged in the creative process produce creative products.

Although leadership can be defined in multiple ways, one definition has the advantage that it bears a connection with the foregoing (Simonton 1995): a leader is a group member whose influence over group cohesion, decision making or productivity exceeds the average member of that group. According to this conception, a group can have more than one leader, and those leaders may differ in the amount of leadership they exert according to the specified criteria. Furthermore, the group itself may consist of anything between a small group and an entire nation. In the latter case, we can speak of an economic leader as one who exerts an inordinate impact on the nation's economy and a political leader as one who has a tremendous influence on the nation's politics.

When we turn to supreme exemplars of these two definitions, it is possible to see common ground. The highest-grade creators are like extraordinary leaders in that they exert an exceptional influence on their chosen domains of achievement – and perhaps on the world at large. Moreover, that impact usually takes place through discrete products, whether patents, journal articles, poems, paintings, drawings or compositions. Likewise, the highest-grade leaders are like extraordinary creators in that they also display influence through specific products. In their case, however, those products will be policies, programs, reforms, initiatives, strategies, tactics and laws. Just as Beethoven influenced the music world through his compositions, so did Napoleon influence the military and political world through his decisions as general and statesman. Both made a name for themselves, or left a mark on history, by exerting impact through products. The particular products may vary from one domain to the next – indeed, the products define the domain – but the impact still comes from products.

This integrated conception of high-level creativity and leadership then converges nicely with Galton's (1869) definition of genius. This he defined in terms of reputation, which he defined as 'the opinion of contemporaries, revised by posterity' that identifies a person as 'a leader of opinion, of an originator, of a man to whom the world deliberately acknowledges itself largely indebted' (Galton 1982/1972, p. 77). In short, genius is defined by excellence in achievements, achievements that may range from breakthrough symphonies to battlefield victories – and any other manner of exerting impact through products.

Comparing creativity and leadership

I have just argued that the highest forms of both creativity and leadership become just manifestations of genius. However different the nature of their achievements, Beethoven and Napoleon can be called geniuses on the basis of their domain-specific achievements. To be sure, that does not mean that the two had the same impact. On the contrary, leaders generally tend to attain higher levels of eminence than do creators (Simonton 1976, 1998). The average person on the street is more likely to name the current president of the United States than to identify the most recent Nobel Laureate in Literature. In fact, when Hart (1987) ranked the 100 most influential persons in history, Napoleon was ranked 34th to Beethoven's 42nd. Similarly, when Cattell (1903) scored 1000 creators and leaders on eminence, Napoleon came in first while Beethoven came in 121st (Cox 1926). Even so, Beethoven was ranked higher than any other composer except Mozart, and both of them ranked far higher than the lesser composers on Cattell's list.

But do outstanding creators and leaders converge on anything else besides being geniuses? The answer is affirmative. Psychologists who study genius-level creativity and leadership have discovered several convergences between the two types of exceptional achievement. This research emerged from two subdisciplines: differential psychology and developmental psychology.

Differential psychology

Differential psychologists are intrigued by how people vary. Clearly, geniuses are different from non-geniuses, just as notable creators and leaders differ from their less distinguished colleagues. Researchers have investigated three crucial facets to this variation, namely, behavior, cognition and personality.

Behavioral variation

In a sense, our definition of genius is intrinsically behavioral (Albert 1975). Genius is defined in terms of high-impact products. It is these achievements on which the genius must base his or her reputation. Even more significantly, individuals can vary in the number of products and this variation can be used to gauge the magnitude of genius. This assessment is best illustrated with respect to creative genius. Beethoven's reputation is not predicated on solely a single symphony. He has over a 100 major compositions. These include the opera *Fidelio*, the *Missa Solemnis*, nine symphonies, five piano concertos, a violin concerto, 16 string quartets, 32 piano sonatas, the song cycle *An die ferne Geliebte*, and dozens of other works, such as overtures, piano trios, violin sonatas and miscellaneous piano pieces. Many of these are considered masterpieces of their respective genre. As a consequence, Beethoven would still be one of the greatest composers who ever lived even if he had never written the *Eroica*.

The empirical literature shows that Beethoven is typical. The best single predictor of the eminence of any creator is the total amount of creative products he or she contributes to a chosen domain of achievement (Simonton 1997). This relationship holds not just for the arts, such as music (Simonton 1977, 1991b), but also for the sciences (Simonton 1991a). Yet there is another feature of this variation in lifetime output that deserves special emphasis: The cross-sectional distribution is highly skewed (Simonton 1997). A small proportion of the creators in any domain accounts for a disproportionate number of contributions to that domain. On average, the top 10 per cent in output can be credited with about half of the contributions while the bottom 50 per cent in output can claim only about 15 per cent of the contributions.

A very similar set of findings applies to the other guise of genius, namely, leadership (Simonton 1994). Napoleon's reputation as a great military genius does not rest solely on the Battle at Jena. Quite the contrary: He fought more battles than any other commander in recent history. Take away that one battle and there are still plenty of others on which he can rest his acclaim, such as the decisive Battle of Friedland one year later. Additionally, there is reason to believe the distribution of leadership contributions is also highly skewed. This is most evident in the area of economic leadership, where a very small percentage of the entrepreneurs will control a disproportionate amount of material wealth. Typically, the top 20 per cent can claim 80 per cent of the economic power. Bill Gates of Microsoft is to the economy what Beethoven is to music and Napoleon is to war.

Cognitive variation

One concept that is closely related to that of genius is general intelligence, especially as measured by the so-called IQ test. Indeed, genius is often defined in terms of having an IQ of 140 or higher. By this criterion, Beethoven and Napoleon barely qualify, if at all, because their IQs have been estimated to lie between 135 and 140 (Cox 1926). Nonetheless, the association between intelligence and either creativity or leadership is much more ambivalent (Simonton 1994). The correlation is only around 0.25, and sometimes even smaller. In fact, for some types of leadership one can be too intelligent to be effective, the peak appearing around an IQ of 120 (Simonton 1985). Interestingly, some creativity researchers have suggested that a 120 IQ marks a threshold beyond which additional increases in intelligence may not translate into enhanced creativity (Baron and Harrington 1981). Thus, although the consequence diverges, an IQ of this magnitude – which represents about the top 10 per cent in intelligence – appears to provide a benchmark of significance for creativity and leadership.

One explanation for the modest impact of IQ is that other cognitive variables are also involved, variables that may not be strongly linked to intelligence. In particular, it is conceivable that it is not just the *power* of thought that is important but also the *style* of thought. Certain cognitive styles may be conductive to creativity and leadership independent of a person's general intelligence. Let me give two examples.

The first possibility is integrative complexity. This is a measure of a person's ability to view some person or idea from more than one point of view and to integrate those alternative viewpoints. Someone low in integrative complexity can only see the world from a single perspective, whereas someone high in integrative complexity perceives a much more complex, finely differentiated reality. Empirical evidence suggests that the capacity for high integrative complexity is conducive to both creativity and leadership (Feist 1994; Suedfeld 1985; Suedfeld *et al.* 2003). It is easy to see why this would be the case for a military genius like Napoleon. A successful military commander has to approach the battlefield from various points of view, including that of the opposing general. Victory often depends on knowing how the opponent would respond to an attack here or a fake retreat there. In any event, variation on this characteristic may explain why some highly intelligent individuals do not always display genius.

The second potential factor is imagination. The importance of this variable is most obvious in creative genius, especially in the arts, such as music. Beethoven had to create whole symphonies from scratch, and to do so without obviously repeating himself, producing a portfolio of symphonic output that is as varied as Shakespeare's plays or Rembrandt's paintings. The importance of this factor is apparent in investigations using Martindale's (1990) Regressive Imagery Dictionary (RID) in computerized content analyses. The RID contains an inventory of words that indicate primary process imagery, or what was later termed primordial cognition. The words concern aspects of concrete human experience, like drink, kiss, smell, lick, touch, taste, hear, see, dream, smell, fly, fall and wake. Content analyses of literary masterworks have indicated that primordial cognition plays a critical role in creativity in general and literary creativity in particular (Martindale 1990). Among demonstrated effects is one very germane to the current issue: more creative poems appear to score higher on this variable than do less creative poems. At least this has been shown for the 154 sonnets penned by William

Shakespeare (Simonton 1989). Curiously, this result has an echo in research on presidential leadership: those presidents whose speeches score higher in primordial cognition according to a RID-based content analysis tend to be those presidents who score higher on independent measures of charisma (Emrich *et al.* 2001). Put differently, charismatic presidents deliver addresses that use the same basic words as found in great poetry. Carrying the argument full circle, charismatic presidents also score higher on measures of creativity (Simonton 1988b). Significantly, the latter is measured by such traits as the chief executive's inclination to initiate new programs and legislation – the creative products of executive leadership. Needless to say, even extremely bright individuals may be disinclined to engage in primordial cognition, providing another factor that may take off where intelligence leaves off.

Personality variation

Many investigators have pointed out that personality traits may be every bit as important as cognitive traits in the determination of genius, creativity and leadership (e.g. Baron and Harrington 1981; Simonton 1995). One candidate trait is one of the Big Five Personality Factors, namely, Openness to Experience. This factor assesses a person's ability to be venturesome with respect to travel, food and recreation, to question traditional values and to be receptive to new ideas and emotional experiences, to be highly curious, to possess a life rich in imagination and fantasy, and to be appreciative of poetry, art and music. Individual variation on this factor correlates positively with both creativity and leadership (Harris 2004; McCrae 1987; Rubenzer *et al.* 2000). Perhaps this finding would be anticipated from what was learned in the previous section. Openness to Experience would seem to have some connection with both complex and imaginative thought. Indeed, one could argue that what this factor represents is as much a cognitive style as it is a personality disposition.

The last statement would not apply to individual differences in motivation. Energy, drive, determination and persistence – these qualities have been consistently associated with genius-grade creativity and leadership since the very onset of empirical research (e.g. Cox 1926; Galton 1869). Nevertheless, it bears emphasis that motivation is not a homogeneous entity. Instead, there are different types of motives, each having distinct consequences for creativity and leadership. This heterogeneity is evidenced in research on political leadership (Winter 2003). This research uses a content analysis method that yields scores on three motives: (a) the need for power (the desire to control and influence others and to occupy positions of high prestige), (b) the need for achievement (the desire to reach excellence, to win in competition or to attain an unprecedented or unique accomplishment), and (c) the need for affiliation (the desire for companionship, friendship, nurturance or love). Although the content analytical scheme has been applied to a wide range of leaders, it has been most extensively applied to political leaders, and especially to US presidents (ibid.). These studies have revealed a distinctive motive pattern: The greatest presidents are highest in power motivation and, to a somewhat lesser extent, achievement motivation, but are much lower in affiliation motivation (ibid.).

Unfortunately, this same technique has not been applied to outstanding creativity. Even so, indirect evidence suggests a somewhat similar pattern for that alternative form of genius. Certainly, creative genius is not associated with an intense affiliation motive. If anything, exceptional creativity is correlated with a high degree of introversion and even antisocial behavior (Eysenck 1995). However, it is also likely that the achievement motive is more critical than the power motive as the primary impetus behind creative genius (e.g. Helmreich *et al.* 1980, 1988). Creators are driven to achieve excellence, whereas leaders are driven to attain power. Even so, it would seem that this contrast is inherent in the nature of the two forms of genius. A genius like Beethoven can achieve success in a far more solitary fashion than a genius like Napoleon. The former could create an achievement such as the Third Symphony in the privacy of his study, whereas the latter could not win the battle at Jena without ordering thousands of soldiers to their deaths.

Developmental psychology

Developmental psychologists are interested in how people develop and grow over the life span. Developmental research on genius, creativity and leadership has indicated several areas of potential convergence. In particular, genius-grade creators and leaders can be compared with respect to family background and career development.

Family background

Galton (1874) was the first psychologist to show that creative genius tends to appear in specific family environments. Among the environmental factors he investigated was birth order. Specifically, he observed that eminent scientists were most likely to be firstborns. Considerable research has been conducted on this factor since then, and a much more complex picture emerges. Sometimes firstborns have the advantage, and other times laterborns appear to enjoy the edge (Simonton 1994). For instance, whereas classical composers and mainstream scientists are most likely to be firstborns, artists, writers and revolutionary scientists are more likely to be laterborns. Likewise, whereas status quo politicians are most prone to be firstborns, revolutionary politicians are more prone to be laterborns. The pattern cutting across both creators and leaders is that firstborns are more inclined to succeed in domains that are high in tradition, status or prestige, whereas laterborns are more inclined to succeed in domains that are less conventional or lower in status or prestige. It goes without saying that birth-order effects are not so large as to preclude exceptions to the statistical pattern (Sulloway 1996). Even so, it is interesting that Beethoven was a firstborn, while Napoleon was a laterborn, as would be expected.

It is also interesting that Beethoven and Napoleon both lost a parent at a relatively young age. Beethoven was 17 when his mother died, and Napoleon was 16 when his father died – Beethoven's mother at age 43 and Napoleon's father at age 39. These specific biographical facts illustrate a general tendency for geniuses to have endured traumatic experiences during childhood and adolescence (e.g. Eisenstadt 1978). These adverse events can include the loss of one or both parents, parental alcoholism, downturns in family finances and even personal disabilities. These occurrences are especially prominent for creators and leaders who pursue more unconventional, even revolutionary careers (Sulloway 1996). For instance, parental loss is extremely high among eminent poets (Martindale 1972).

Career development

Galton (1869) had argued that genius was born, not made. Later he backed away from this extreme position, arguing that genius was the upshot of both nature and nurture (Galton 1874). Subsequent research concurs. Although it is clear that genetic endowment plays some role in determining a person's basic talents, it is also manifest that genius-level creativity and leadership must be nurtured. One particular manifestation of this necessity is the so-called ten-year rule (Simonton 2000a). According to empirical research, it takes about a decade of intense study and practice within a particular domain of expertise before an individual can make world-class contributions to that domain. This rule appears to apply to both creativity and leadership, albeit empirical data also suggest that the most eminent geniuses require somewhat less time to attain domain mastery (ibid.). Napoleon, for example, began his military training at age nine and received his military commission at age 16, having completed the two-year course of study at the École Royale Militaire in only a single year.

Another aspect of domain-specific expertise acquisition is the involvement of role models and mentors. The development of the future genius is usually enhanced by exposure to predecessors who have attained distinction in the same or a similar domain of achievement (e.g. Simonton 1984, 1992b). These predecessors can include direct relationships with teachers and mentors, but can also entail more distant relationships with persons who the developing talent looks up to and admires. Indeed, it is partly for this reason that geniuses, whether creators or leaders, tend to cluster into particular historical periods often labeled 'golden ages' (Simonton 1988a, 1992a). Beethoven, for instance, greatly admired both Mozart and Haydn, and had studied composition under the latter.

Once launching their careers, exceptional creators and leaders follow a distinctive career trajectory (Simonton 1994). They begin with relatively minor accomplishments, rise to a peak in which they achieve the work for which they are best known, and then often exhibit a gradual decline. It is typical for the peak to occur somewhere in the late thirties or early forties. To illustrate, Beethoven wrote his most famous composition, the Fifth Symphony, when he was 37 years old. The symphony was composed in 1807, the same year that the 38-year-old Napoleon attained the height of his power by defeating the Fourth Coalition at the Battle of Friedland. Nonetheless, it is also critical to recognize that the expected career trajectories differ for various domains of achievement (Lehman 1953; Simonton 1997). In some fields the peaks appear relatively early in life and the declines can be a bit more precipitous. This trajectory holds for abstract mathematics and lyric poetry, and for political revolutionaries and the founders of new religious faiths. In other fields the peaks come somewhat later, and the declines are much more gradual. This longitudinal pattern appears in the earth sciences and history, and in status quo politicians and leaders of established religious faiths.

Conclusion

In this chapter I have shown that genius-level creativity and leadership have a lot in common. In the first place, it is possible to find common ground in how the two terms are defined. Furthermore, outstanding creators and leaders are comparable on numerous individual-difference variables, including cognitive and personality factors. They also share a lot with respect to developmental variables, as witnessed in family background and career development. What has been presented should suffice to make the case for a fundamental unity in the seeming diversity. While Beethoven was writing on music paper, Napoleon was riding over the map – but they remain kindred spirits in their respective products of genius.

References

Albert, R. S. (1975). Toward a behavioral definition of genius. *American Psychologist, 30,* 140–151.
Barron, F. X. and Harrington, D. M. (1981). Creativity, intelligence, and personality. *Annual Review of Psychology, 32,* 439–476.
Cattell, J. M. (1903). A statistical study of eminent men. *Popular Science Monthly, 62,* 359–377.
Cox, C. (1926). *The early mental traits of three hundred geniuses.* Stanford, CA: Stanford University Press.

Eisenstadt, J. M. (1978). Parental loss and genius. *American Psychologist, 33,* 211–223.

Emrich, C. G., Brower, H. H., Feldman, J. M. and Garland, H. (2001). Images in words: Presidential rhetoric, charisma, and greatness. *Administrative Science Quarterly, 46,* 527–557.

Eysenck, H. J. (1995). *Genius: The natural history of creativity.* Cambridge: Cambridge University Press.

Feist, G. J. (1994). Personality and working style predictors of integrative complexity: A study of scientists' thinking about research and teaching. *Journal of Personality and Social Psychology, 67,* 474–484.

Forbes, E. (ed.) (1967). *Thayer's life of Beethoven* (revised edition). Princeton, NJ: Princeton University Press.

Galton, F. (1869). *Hereditary genius: An inquiry into its laws and consequences.* London: Macmillan.

Galton, F. (1874). *English men of science: Their nature and nurture.* London: Macmillan.

Galton, F. (1972). *Hereditary genius: An inquiry into its laws and consequences* (2nd edition). Gloucester, MA: Smith. (Original work published 1892.)

Harris, J. A. (2004). Measured intelligence, achievement, openness to experience, and creativity. *Personality and Individual Differences, 36,* 913–929.

Hart, M. H. (1987). *The 100: A ranking of the most influential persons in history.* Secaucus, NJ: Citadel Press.

Helmreich, R. L., Spence, J. T., Beane, W. E., Lucker, G. W. and Matthews, K. A. (1980). Making it in academic psychology: Demographic and personality correlates of attainment. *Journal of Personality and Social Psychology, 39,* 896–908.

Helmreich, R. L., Spence, J. T. and Pred, R. S. (1988). Making it without losing it: Type A, achievement motivation, and scientific attainment revisited. *Personality and Social Psychology Bulletin, 14,* 495–504.

Lehman, H. C. (1953). *Age and achievement.* Princeton, NJ: Princeton University Press.

Martindale, C. (1972). Father absence, psychopathology, and poetic eminence. *Psychological Reports, 31,* 843–847.

Martindale, C. (1990). *The clockwork muse: The predictability of artistic styles.* New York: Basic Books.

McCrae, R. R. (1987). Creativity, divergent thinking, and openness to experience. *Journal of Personality and Social Psychology, 52,* 1258–1265.

Rubenzer, S. J., Faschingbauer, T. R. and Ones, D. S. (2000). Assessing the U.S. presidents using the revised NEO Personality Inventory. *Assessment, 7,* 403–420.

Simonton, D. K. (1976). Biographical determinants of achieved eminence: A multivariate approach to the Cox data. *Journal of Personality and Social Psychology, 33,* 218–226.

Simonton, D. K. (1977). Eminence, creativity, and geographic marginality: A recursive structural equation model. *Journal of Personality and Social Psychology, 35,* 805–816.

Simonton, D. K. (1984). Artistic creativity and interpersonal relationships across and within generations. *Journal of Personality and Social Psychology, 46,* 1273–1286.

Simonton, D. K. (1985). Intelligence and personal influence in groups: Four nonlinear models. *Psychological Review, 92,* 532–547.

Simonton, D. K. (1988a). Galtonian genius, Kroeberian configurations, and emulation: A generational time-series analysis of Chinese civilization. *Journal of Personality and Social Psychology, 55,* 230–238.

Simonton, D. K. (1988b). Presidential style: Personality, biography, and performance. *Journal of Personality and Social Psychology, 55,* 928–936.

Simonton, D. K. (1989). Shakespeare's sonnets: A case of and for single-case historiometry. *Journal of Personality, 57,* 695–721.

Simonton, D. K. (1991a). Career landmarks in science: Individual differences and interdisciplinary contrasts. *Developmental Psychology, 27,* 119–130.

Simonton, D. K. (1991b). Emergence and realization of genius: The lives and works of 120 classical composers. *Journal of Personality and Social Psychology, 61,* 829–840.

Simonton, D. K. (1992a). Gender and genius in Japan: Feminine eminence in masculine culture. *Sex Roles, 27,* 101–119.

Simonton, D. K. (1992b). The social context of career success and course for 2,026 scientists and inventors. *Personality and Social Psychology Bulletin, 18,* 452–463.

Simonton, D. K. (1994). *Greatness: Who makes history and why.* New York: Guilford Press.

Simonton, D. K. (1995). Personality and intellectual predictors of leadership. In D. H. Saklofske and

M. Zeidner (eds), *International handbook of personality and intelligence* (pp. 739–757). New York: Plenum Press.

Simonton, D. K. (1997). Creative productivity: A predictive and explanatory model of career trajectories and landmarks. *Psychological Review, 104*, 66–89.

Simonton, D. K. (1998). Achieved eminence in minority and majority cultures: Convergence versus divergence in the assessments of 294 African Americans. *Journal of Personality and Social Psychology, 74*, 804–817.

Simonton, D. K. (2000a). Creative development as acquired expertise: Theoretical issues and an empirical test. *Developmental Review 20*, 283–318.

Simonton, D. K. (2000b). Creativity: Cognitive, developmental, personal, and social aspects. *American Psychologist, 55*, 151–158.

Stewart, L. H. (1977). Birth order and political leadership. In M. G. Hermann (ed.), *The psychological examination of political leaders* (pp. 205–236). New York: Free Press.

Suedfeld, P. (1985). APA presidential addresses: The relation of integrative complexity to historical, professional, and personal factors. *Journal of Personality and Social Psychology, 47*, 848–852.

Suedfeld, P., Guttieri, K. and Tetlock, P. E. (2003). Assessing integrative complexity at a distance: Archival analyses of thinking and decision making. In J. M. Post (ed.), *The psychological assessment of political leaders: With profiles of Saddam Hussein and Bill Clinton* (pp. 246–270). Ann Arbor, MI: University of Michigan Press.

Sulloway, F. J. (1996). *Born to rebel: Birth order, family dynamics, and creative lives.* New York: Pantheon.

Winter, D. G. (2003). Measuring the motives of political actors at a distance. In J. M. Post (ed.), *The psychological assessment of political leaders: With profiles of Saddam Hussein and Bill Clinton* (pp. 153–177). Ann Arbor, MI: University of Michigan Press.

21

Intellectual styles and creativity

Li-fang Zhang and Robert J. Sternberg

Introduction

In studying the nature of creativity, many scholars have elaborated on the characteristics of creative individuals (e.g. Barron 1955; Jalil and Boujettif 2005). Among these scholars, many have cogently argued for the importance of intellectual styles in creativity (e.g. Bloomberg 1967; Noppe 1996; Selby *et al.* 2005). Although empirical studies on the relationship between styles and creativity have been somewhat few and far between, the available research evidence indicates that work that seeks to understand creativity must take intellectual styles into account. What kinds of intellectual styles are conducive for the development of creativity? How can one foster creativity through addressing intellectual styles?

This chapter offers Zhang and Sternberg's (2005) Threefold Model of Intellectual Styles as a way of integrating the diverse work on intellectual styles and creativity. It is composed of four parts. The first part defines intellectual styles and creativity and explicates the conceptual links between the two constructs. The second provides research evidence on the relationship between them. The third proposes ways of fostering creativity through attending to intellectual styles. Finally, we draw some conclusions.

Intellectual styles and creativity: definitions and conceptual link

Intellectual styles and creativity defined

Intellectual style

Over the past seven decades, various labels with or without the root word 'style' have been proposed and diverse definitions of styles have been put forward. In an attempt to integrate the existing works in the field of styles, we (Zhang and Sternberg 2005) recently proposed the Threefold Model of Intellectual Styles, in which an intellectual style is defined as one's pre-ferred way of processing information and dealing with tasks. 'Intellectual style' is used as a general term to encompass the meanings of all major 'style' constructs postulated in the past several decades, including cognitive style, learning style, mind style and thinking style.

To varying degrees, an intellectual style is cognitive, affective, physiological, psychological and sociological. It is cognitive because whatever styles one uses to process information, one must be engaged in some kind of cognitive process. It is affective because one's way of processing information and of dealing with a task is partially determined by how one feels about the task. It is partially physiological because the use of a style is partially influenced by the way our senses (e.g. vision, hearing and touch) take in the information provided to us. It is psychological because the use of a particular style is partially contingent upon how one's personality interacts with one's environment. Finally, it is sociological because the use of a style is affected by the preferences of the society in which one lives for various ways of thinking.

Creativity

Creativity is the ability to produce work that is (a) relatively novel, (b) high in quality, and (c) appropriate to the task at hand (Amabile 1996; Stein 1953; Sternberg and Lubart 1995). To Sternberg and Lubart (1995), creativity is a confluence of six factors: intellectual abilities, knowledge, thinking styles, personality, motivation and environmental context. People who are more creative are more likely to think divergently, exhibit higher levels of cognitive complexity and flexibility (cognitive), and are better at coping with unstructured and ambiguous situations (see Kaufman 2002; Sternberg 2006, for comprehensive reviews).

Conceptual link

Numerous scholars have addressed the conceptual links between styles and creativity (Sternberg and Lubart 1995; Witkin *et al.* 1954). Noppe (1996) postulated five reasons why styles remain to be attractive variables to creativity researchers, with the most relevant to this chapter being: '. . . there is a range of individual variation in cognitive styles wide enough to encompass different domains of creativity and multiple levels of creative accomplishment . . .' (p. 370).

In the Threefold Model of Intellectual Styles, styles are grouped into three broad types (Zhang and Sternberg 2005): Type I, Type II and Type III styles. Type I intellectual styles denote preferences for tasks that have low degrees of structure, that require the individuals to process information in a more complex way, and that allow originality and high levels of freedom to do things in one's own way. These preferences correspond to those often expressed by highly creative individuals. Type II intellectual styles suggest preferences for tasks that are structured, that allow individuals to process information in a more simplistic way, and that require conformity to traditional ways of doing things and high levels of respect for authority. These preferences are consistent with those frequently observed in people with lower creative potential. Type III styles may manifest the characteristics of either Type I or Type II styles, depending on the stylistic demands of a specific situation.

Largely based on two criteria (popularity and empirical evidence), we organized ten existing style models/constructs into the Threefold Model of Intellectual Styles: (a) field-dependence/independence, (b) mode of thinking/brain dominance, (c) reflectivity-impulsivity, (d) adaptation–innovation, (e) thinking style, (f) personality type, (g) career interest type, (h) divergent–convergent thinking, (i) mind style, and (j) learning approach. Within each of these models, some individual styles satisfy the description of Type I styles, some fit in the description of Type II styles, while others meet with the definition of Type III styles (See Table 21.1).

Table 21.1 Intellectual styles

	Style type	Type I	Type II	Type III
Style Construct	Perceptual style Mode of thinking Conceptual tempo Decision-making style	Field independent Holistic Reflective Innovative	Field dependent Analytic Impulsive Adaptive	Integrative
	Thinking style	Legislative, Judicial, Global, Hierarchical, Judicial	Executive, Local, Monarchic, Conservative	Oligarchic, anarchic, internal, external
	Personality type	Intuitive, Perceiving	Sensing, Judging	Thinking, feeling, introverted, extraverted
	Career interest type	Artistic	Conventional	Realistic, investigative, social, enterprising
	Structure of intellect	Divergent thinking	Convergent thinking	
	Mind style	Concrete random	Concrete sequential	Abstract random, Abstract sequential
	Learning approach	Deep	Surface	Achieving

Note: The style constructs in bold type (Mind style and Learning approach) are yet to be directly tested with creativity.

Intellectual styles and creativity: empirical evidence

How can styles be understood within the framework of the Threefold Model of Intellectual Styles?

Field-dependence/independence

Alternatively known as psychological differentiation and perceptual style (Witkin *et al.* 1962), field-dependence/independence (FDI) refers to the extent to which people are dependent versus independent of the organization of the surrounding perceptual field. Field independent individuals are thought to be better at cognitive restructuring because of their propensity for being free from external referents. Field-dependent individuals are considered as being more socially oriented due to their higher levels of sensitivity to external referents.

The relationship between field independence and creativity is not straightforward. Several studies have yielded strong evidence indicating that the impact of field independence on creativity is through mediating factors such as dogmatism and fixity-mobility. For example, some researchers found that when examined individually, neither field independence nor dogmatism was useful in explaining variations in tasks that presumably reflect creative potential. However, when considered jointly, the explanatory power of the two variables for creative potential became significant.

In general, field independent people tend to be more creative than field dependent ones. What makes field independent people more creative is the greater range of modes of functioning that is at their disposal.

Mode of thinking (brain dominance)

Mode of thinking has been traditionally known as brain dominance or hemispheric specificity. Research from nearly the past three decades suggests that the two hemispheres are more dynamic than static and that they are more interactive than they were once believed to be. Thus, the terms 'brain dominance' and 'hemispheric specificity' have been gradually replaced by the terms 'hemispheric style' and 'hemispheric thinking style'. More recently, Zhang and Sternberg (2006) cast the term 'brain dominance' in yet another different light – that of mode of thinking. The three modes of thinking are analytic (originally left-brain dominance), holistic (originally right-brained dominance) and integrative (originally whole-brained).

Almost all studies have suggested that individuals with a holistic mode of thinking outperform those with an analytic mode of thinking on various measures of creativity (see Kaufman 2002). The relationship between modes of thinking and creativity may be stronger than that between modes of thinking and intelligence.

Several experimental studies attempted to examine creativity training methods and their effects on modes of thinking. Although all such studies suggested the malleability of modes of thinking, some concluded that the greatest increase was in the integrative mode of thinking, whereas others revealed that the greatest increase was in the holistic mode of thinking, regardless of treatment conditions.

Early in the 1980s, several scholars (e.g. Sinatra 1984) began to challenge the popular view that the holistic mode of thinking is the key to creativity and contended that both sides of the brain are needed for creativity. Indeed, it appears that different parts of the brain contribute to different stages of a creativity process (Torrance 1982).

Reflectivity–impulsivity

Reflectivity–impulsivity, also referred to as conceptual tempo, was originally introduced by Kagan and his colleagues (Kagan 1965; Kagan *et al.* 1964). Reflectivity is the tendency to consider and reflect on alternative solution possibilities. Impulsivity is the tendency to respond impulsively without sufficient forethought.

On average, reflectives consistently outperform impulsives on a variety of conceptual, perceptual and perceptumotor problem-solving tasks that involve response uncertainty. In researching and theorizing the relationship between conceptual tempo and creativity, scholars took opposing views in predicting the relationship between the two. Some (e.g. Fuqua *et al.* 1975) predicted that because of their nonconformity and uninhibited response style, impulsive children would perform better on creativity measures. Others (e.g. Mednick 1962) suggested that because of their slow and steady rate of responding, reflective children should outperform impulsive children on measures of creativity. Research suggests that, on average, reflective children tend to do better on various creativity measures than do impulsive ones. However, Kuziemski (1977) observed a significant interaction effect for gender and conceptual tempo, with reflective boys and impulsive girls scoring higher on creative thinking, which lent partial support to the prediction that impulsive children would outperform reflective ones.

Adaption-innovation

Kirton's (1976) adaption-innovation theory provides a basis for thinking about creativity. Adaptors have a tendency to deal with changes by working within the existing paradigm, whereas innovators have a propensity for challenging the existing system. Furthermore, when solving problems, innovators tend to access a wider repertoire of cognitive functioning than do adaptors. Kirton maintained that both adaptors and innovators are creative, although they differ in the ways in which they manifest their creativity.

Although results are mixed, the general tendency is that, compared with adaptors, innovators show higher levels of creativity (e.g. Puccio *et al.* 1995; Torrance and Horng 1980). Gelade (1995), however, found evidence that innovators are higher on some dimensions of creativity but not on others.

Thinking styles

Thinking styles refer to people's preferred ways of using the abilities that they have. According to Sternberg's (1988) theory of mental self-government, 13 thinking styles fall along five dimensions: functions, forms, levels, scopes and leanings. Based on empirical data, Zhang and Sternberg (2005, 2006) reconceptualized the 13 styles into three types.

Type I thinking styles tend to be more creativity-generating. They denote higher levels of cognitive complexity, including the legislative (being creative), judicial (evaluative of other people or products), hierarchical (prioritizing one's tasks), global (focusing on the holistic picture) and liberal (taking a new approach to tasks) styles. Type II thinking styles suggest a norm-favoring tendency. They denote lower levels of cognitive complexity, including the executive (implementing tasks with given orders), local (focusing on details), monarchic (working on one task at a time) and conservative (using traditional approaches to tasks) styles. Type III styles, including the anarchic (working on whatever tasks that come along), oligarchic (working on multiple tasks with no priority), internal (working on one's own) and external (working with others), may manifest the characteristics of the styles from both Type I and Type II groups, depending on the stylistic demands of a specific task.

Research findings are fairly consistent. In a Korean high school context (Park *et al.* 2005), students who performed better on a Scientific Giftedness Inventory (SGI – a measure of creativity as well as leadership, morality, motivation and scientific accomplishment) also scored higher on the legislative, judicial, global and liberal (all being Type I) styles. Meanwhile, those students whose performance on the SGI was inferior scored significantly higher on the executive and conservative (both being Type II) styles. Similarly, Kaufman (2001) discovered that creative writers scored higher on the legislative (Type I) style, but lower on the executive (Type II) style.

Zhang (in press) found that teachers (both school and university) in mainland China who taught in Type I teaching styles (i.e. teaching creatively) reported the use of both Type I and Type II thinking styles, whereas teachers with Type II teaching styles only reported the use of Type II thinking styles.

Personality types

Jung (1923) proposed that people attend selectively to elements in their environments, seeking out the ones compatible with their alleged personality type, and avoiding or leaving incompatible ones. These tendencies, according to Jung, lie along three dimensions: extroversion–introversion, sensing–intuitive, and thinking–feeling. Myers and McCaulley (1985) extended Jung's work by adding a fourth dimension – judging–perceiving. An extraverted person leans toward the outer world of objects, people and actions, whereas an introverted person prefers the inner world of concepts and ideas. A sensing person has a predilection for seeking the fullest possible experience of what is immediate and real. An intuitive person, in contrast, seeks the broadest view of what is possible and insightful. A thinking person likes to make decisions based on rational and logical planning, whereas a feeling person likes to make decisions based on harmony among subjective values. A judging person tends to be concerned with seeking closure without sufficient exploratory activities, whereas a perceiving person tends to be attuned to incoming information and open to new events and changes.

Some studies have revealed positive relationships of the intuitive and perceiving dimensions to divergent thinking tasks as well as to Kirton's innovators. While intuition is important for creativity, other things matter as well (Dollinger *et al.* 2004). Thus, high levels of creativity require a wide range of personality styles.

Career interest type

Holland (1973) proposed that people can be classified into six types corresponding to six occupational environments: realistic, investigative, artistic, social, enterprising and conventional. People of the realistic type like to work with things and enjoy outdoor activities. People with an investigative type of career interest like to be engaged in scientific kinds of work. People of the artistic type like to deal with tasks that provide them with the opportunities to use their imagination. Socially interested people like to work in situations in which they can interact and cooperate with other people. People of the enterprising type like to take on leadership roles when working with others. Finally, people of the conventional type like to work with data under well-structured situations.

Very few explicit efforts have been made to investigate the relationship of Holland's career interest types to creativity. Existing studies, all conducted in the early 1960s, found consistently that compared with people with low creativity, highly creative people express broader career interests; in particular, they are more artistic, unconventional and asocial (e.g. Holland 1961).

Divergent–convergent thinking

Divergent thinkers deal with problems in a flexible way and tend to generate multiple solutions to a single problem, whereas convergent thinkers deal with problems in a mechanical way and tend to see a problem and a solution as having a one-to-one relationship (Guilford 1950).

Creativity has come to mean divergent thinking in much research on creativity (Scrathley and Hakstian 2000–2001), despite the fact that there is more to creativity than just divergent thinking. Divergent thinking is a good predictor of creative achievement in both academic and non-academic settings, although divergent thinking generally has higher predictive value for older research participants than it does for younger ones.

However, note that, although divergent thinking is essential for being creative, to successfully channel one's divergent thinking into creative products, in particular when the process of creativity is relatively long, one invariably needs to incorporate convergent thinking. Precisely for this reason, teaching convergent thinking in such topics as logic, mathematics and physics is commonly seen.

Mind style

Gregorc (1982) suggested that individuals' tendency to use mediation channels or mind styles (also known as 'learning styles') could be understood in terms of two basic dimensions: use of space and use of time. Being either concrete (or physical) or abstract (or metaphorical), space refers to perceptual categories for acquiring and expressing information. Time is divided into two different ways of ordering facts and events: sequential (i.e. in a step-by-step or branchlike

261

manner) and random ordering (i.e. in a web-like or spiral manner). These two poles of the two dimensions form four styles that are referred to by Gregorc as mind styles: abstract random (approach learning holistically and prefer to learn in an unstructured way); concrete sequential (extract information through hands-on experiences and prefer well-structured work environments); abstract sequential (adopt a logical approach to learning and strong in decoding written, verbal and image symbols); and concrete random (take trial-and-error, intuitive and independent approaches to learning).

We have not located any empirical research on the relationship between the Gregorc styles and creativity. However, this relationship can be inferred indirectly via the association between the Gregorc styles and other intellectual styles. The two style constructs against which the Gregorc styles have been examined are the MBTI personality styles and the Kirton adaptive-innovative styles. Individuals who prefer the concrete-sequential learning style tend to be sensing and judging types of people, whereas individuals who prefer the concrete-random learning style tend to be intuitive and perceiving types of people. Thus, Gregorc's sequential types tend to be adaptors and the random types tend to be innovators. Given that the intuitive and perceiving types and the innovators tend to be more creative than their counterparts, as reviewed earlier, the random types should also be more creative than the sequential types.

Learning approach

Biggs (1978) proposed three common approaches to learning: surface, which involves a reproduction of what is taught to meet the minimum requirements; deep, which involves a real understanding of what is learned; and achieving, which involves using such a strategy that would maximize one's grades.

As in the case of the Gregorc styles, the relationship of learning approaches to creativity can be understood only indirectly through the literature on the relationship between learning approaches and other constructs that are presumably reflective of creative potential and that have been empirically proved to be correlates of creativity. For example, the deep learning approach has been identified to be highly correlated with Sternberg's Type I thinking styles, while the surface learning approach is highly related to Type II thinking styles. It has been found that openness, one of the Big Five personality traits, significantly predicts the deep learning approach and that conscientiousness is a good predictor for both the deep and the achieving approaches. Both Type I thinking styles and the openness personality trait have been proved to have a strong association with creativity.

Summary

Research on the relationship between intellectual styles and creativity is far from sufficient. Findings are mixed. What little we know suggests that intellectual styles matter for creativity. Across the findings from studies based on the style models reviewed in this chapter, Type I intellectual styles prove themselves to be a necessary, but not sufficient condition for creativity. To be successfully creative, one needs to possess a wide repertoire of intellectual styles, with Type I styles playing a critical role.

Fostering creativity through addressing intellectual styles

Can creativity be fostered through the encouragement of certain intellectual styles? Consider some possibilities.

Cultivating Type I intellectual styles

As we have seen, Type I intellectual styles are essential for creativity. This signifies that nurturing Type I intellectual styles may be conducive to the development of creativity. We propose several strategies for cultivating Type I intellectual styles that should apply to both the academic and business settings.

Serve as a role model for creative thinking

Role-modeling could be one of the major channels for promoting creativity-generating intellectual styles. We believe that if one has the opportunity to watch and emulate a role model who demonstrates the use of Type I intellectual styles, one can develop his or her own creativity-generating styles, at least in theory. In academic settings, the way teachers teach has a direct impact on how students learn. For example, if a teacher mostly lectures about the content of the textbooks, students are more likely to confine themselves to learning the contents of the textbooks as well. However, if a teacher draws from different resources, uses a wide variety of teaching methods and provokes creative thoughts, students may be inspired to go beyond the textbooks and initiate other means of learning.

Allow mistakes

No one wants to risk demonstrating creative thinking after having been penalized for a 'mistake' as a result of experimenting on a new idea. In schools and business organizations alike, people must be given chances to make mistakes. Creative ideas that lead to successful products are typically the result of trials and errors over a relatively long period of time. One cannot nurture Type I intellectual styles without tolerating mistakes and encouraging sensible risk-taking.

Reward creative ideas and products

It is not enough to tell others that we value Type I intellectual styles. We need to demonstrate that we really do so by rewarding creative thinking. For example, when a teacher grades assignments, not only should knowledge and analytical skills count, but also creative ideas. In a business setting, employees' performance should not only be evaluated on how well they can implement tasks, but also on how often they come up with innovative ideas or products that advance the organization.

Enriching experience

Much research suggests that Type I intellectual styles can be fostered by enriching people's experiences beyond their professional life. Underlying these experiences are the opportunities to receive the challenges that people are seldom presented with in their immediate work environments. There is strong evidence showing that creative thinking can be achieved through problem solving and that inadequate experience may interfere with creative thinking. Such evidence suggests that teachers, business leaders or any individuals in power could foster creative thinking by building environments that allow people to take on new challenges without being in fear of failure.

Allowing for diverse intellectual styles

Because creativity calls for a wide repertoire of intellectual styles, encouraging the use of a wide variety of intellectual styles becomes a promising strategy for fostering creativity. There are many possible ways to do so and diverse styles can be encouraged in many settings. We propose several strategies respectively in each of the following two broad settings: academic and business.

Academic settings

Teachers' consideration

There are at least two steps that teachers could take in facilitating the expansion of their students' style repertoire. The first concerns a change in teachers' attitudes. Very often, teachers without knowledge of intellectual styles tend to attribute students' poor academic performance to their low abilities. With some knowledge about intellectual styles, teachers may start considering other factors such as intellectual styles that affect student learning and performance, which may lead them to modify their attitudes towards students.

A logical step that follows is for teachers to take concrete actions in encouraging the use of diverse intellectual styles. Teachers should allow students to use different intellectual styles by diversifying their instructional methods and assessment schemes.

Administrators' considerations

There are many ways in which university/school administrators can facilitate the expansion of the style repertoire in their employees. We discuss the main one. Administrators must realize that teachers and staff vary in their intellectual styles and thereby they should create a work environment that allows teachers and staff sufficient autonomy to work at their own pace and in their own preferred ways. Being surrounded by colleagues who use a variety of intellectual styles increases the opportunities for teachers and staff to learn how to expand their own style repertoire.

Business settings

Human resource management

There are at least two critical points at which human resource management personnel should take diverse intellectual styles into account: recruiting and development. As Agor (1991: 13) stated: 'In the final analysis, what most helps an organization avoid errors and gain advantages from two perspectives, is the systematic integration of intuitive and traditional management skills and styles.'

Training and development programs

Providers of management training and development programs may help to expand business personnel's style repertoire by designing and implementing programs that can accommodate a broad range of intellectual styles. When training and development programs take into account people's diverse ways of processing information, they can not only allow people to find their 'comfort zone', but also challenge people to test themselves on new territories.

Conclusions

This chapter shows that intellectual styles and creativity are intricately entwined. While Type I intellectual styles are central for creativity, a wide repertoire of intellectual styles maximizes individuals' possibilities for successfully leading their creativity potential into creative productivity. Within the broad paradigm of creativity research, the encouragement of a great variety of styles, in particular Type I styles, offers promising opportunities in a range of academic and business settings.

References

Agor, W. H. (1991). How intuition can be used to enhance creativity in organizations. *Journal of Creative Behavior, 25* (1), 11–19.

Amabile T. M. (1996). *Creativity in context.* Boulder, CO: Westview-Harper Collins.

Barron, F. (1955). The disposition towards originality. *Journal of Abnormal and Social Psychology, 51,* 478–485.

Biggs, J. B. (1978). Individual and group differences in study processes. *British Journal of Educational Psychology, 48,* 266–279.

Bloomberg, M. (1967). An inquiry into the relationship between field independence-dependence and creativity. *Journal of Psychology, 67,* 127–140.

Dollinger, S. J., Palaskonis, D. G. and Pearson, J. L. (2004). Creativity and intuition revisited. *Journal of Creative Behavior, 38* (4), 244–259.

Fuqua, R. W., Bartsch, T. W. and Phye, G. D. (1975). An investigation of the relationship between cognitive tempo and creativity in preschool-age children. *Child Development, 46,* 779–782.

Gelade, G. (1995). Creative style and divergent production. *Journal of Creative Behavior, 29* (1), 36–53.

Gregorc, A. F. (1982). *Gregorc Style Delineator.* Maynard, MA: Gabriel Systems.

Guilford, J. P. (1950). Creativity research: Past, present and future. *American Psychologist, 5,* 444–454.

Holland, J. L. (1961). Creative and academic performance among talented adolescents. *Journal of Educational Psychology, 52,* 136–147.

Holland, J. L. (1973). *Making vocational choices: A theory of careers.* Englewood Cliffs, NJ: Prentice Hall.

Jalil, P. A. and and Boujettif, M. (2005). Some characteristics of Nobel laureates. *Creativity Research Journal, 17* (2 and 3), 265–272.

Jung, C. (1923). *Psychological types.* New York: Harcourt Brace.

Kagan, J. (1965). *Matching familiar figures test.* Cambridge, MA: Harvard University Press.

Kagan, J., Rosman, B. L., Day, D., Albert, J. and Philips, W. (1964). Information processing in the child: Significance of analytic and reflective attitudes. *Psychological Monographs, 78* (1), 578.

Kaufman, J. C. (2001). Thinking styles in creative writers and journalists. *Dissertation Abstracts International (Section B): The Sciences and Engineering, 62* (3B), 1069.

Kaufman, J. C. (2002). Dissecting the golden goose: Components of studying creative writers. *Creativity Research Journal, 14* (1), 27–40.

Kirton, M. J. (1976). Adaptors and innovators: A description and measure. *Journal of Applied Psychology, 61,* 622–629.

Kuziemski, N. E. (1977). Relationships among imaginative play predisposition, creative thinking, and reflection-impulsivity in second graders (Doctoral dissertation, Boston University). *Dissertation Abstracts International, 38,* 1861B.

Mednick, S. A. (1962). The associative basis of the creative process. *Psychological Review, 69,* 220–232.

Myers, I. B. and McCaulley, M. H. (1985). *Manual: A guide to the development and use of the Myers-Briggs Type Indicator.* Palo Alto, CA: Consulting Psychologists Press.

Noppe, L. D. (1996). Progression in the service of the ego, cognitive styles, and creative thinking. *Creativity Research Journal, 9* (4), 369–383.

Park, S. K., Park, K. H., and Choe, H. S. (2005). Relationship between thinking styles and scientific giftedness in Korea. *Journal of Secondary Gifted Education, 16* (2–3), 87–97.

Puccio, G. J., Treffinger, D. J. and Talbot, R. J. (1995). Exploratory examination of relationships between creativity styles and creative products. *Creativity Research Journal, 8* (2), 157–172.

Selby, E. C., Shaw, E. J. and Houtz, J. C. (2005). The creative personality. *Gifted Child Quarterly, 49* (4), 300–357.

Sinatra, R. (1984). Brain functioning and creative behavior. *Roeper Review, 7* (1), 48–54.

Stein, M. I. (1953). Creativity and culture. *Journal of Psychology, 36,* 311–322.

Sternberg, R. J. (1988). Mental self-government: A theory of intellectual styles and their development. *Human Development, 31* 197–224.

Sternberg, R. J. (2006). The nature of creativity. *Creativity Research Journal, 18* (1), 87–98.

Sternberg, R. J. and Lubart, T. I. (1995). *Defying the crowd: Cultivating creativity in a culture of conformity.* New York: Free Press.

Torrance, E. P. (1982). Hemisphericity and creative functioning. *Journal of Research and Development in Education, 15* (3), 29–37.

Torrance, E. P., and Horng, R. Y. (1980). Creativity and style of learning and thinking characteristics of adaptors and innovators. *Creative Child and Adult Quarterly, V* (2), 80–85.

Witkin, H. A., Dyk, R. B., Faterson, H. F., Goodenough, D. R. and Karp, S. A. (1962). *Psychological differentiation.* New York: Wiley.

Witkin, H. A., Lewis, H. B., Hertzman, M., Machover, K., Meissner, P. B., and Wapner, S. (1954). *Personality through perception.* New York: Harper.

Zhang, L. F. and Sternberg, R. J. (2005). A threefold model of intellectual styles. *Educational Psychology Review, 17* (1), 1–53.

Zhang, L. F., and Sternberg, R. J. (2006). *The nature of intellectual styles.* Mahwah, NJ: Lawrence Erlbaum.

Zhang, L. F. (in press). Teachers' styles of thinking: An exploratory study. *Journal of Psychology.*

22

Creativity and personality

Stephen J. Guastello

Introduction

This chapter summarizes the relationship between personality traits with creative behavior and incumbency in creative occupations. The review encompasses surface, source traits (Big Five), and cardinal traits of the normal range personality, and abnormal personality issues. The participants in the studies that are reported here were all adults, including college undergraduates and professionals in their early, middle and later career stages. At the surface trait level, about half of the spectrum of traits contributes to creative personalities. Although the relationships with external criteria are not as strong for the source traits, there is a consistent positive relationship between Openness with creative behavior, and a consistent negative relationship between Conscientiousness and creative behavior; the latter is truer among artists than among scientists. The cardinal trait Psychoticism forms a bridge between normal and abnormal personality ranges. The relationship between creativity and mood disorders is frequently reported but inconsistent empirically, however. The inconsistency appears to be explained by the presence of another variable, emotional intelligence.

Personality traits

This chapter is confined to trait-based theories of personality, which lend themselves to correlational analysis of data, and are thus the dominant form of research on personality and occupational selection. Allport's (1937) hierarchical theory of traits serves as the conceptual starting point for organizing this line of work. Allport's work culminated in a three-tiered taxonomy consisting of surface traits, source traits and cardinal traits.

The surface traits are the most specific, and are thus thought to be most proximally related to external behaviors. Cattell (1947) refined the concept of surface traits into a taxonomy of 16 bipolar traits. One of the 16 traits was a quick measure of general intelligence, which Cattell regarded as necessary for the proper interpretation of a person's profile on the other 15 traits (Cattell *et al.* 1970). The taxonomy of bipolar traits that make up the current versions of the Sixteen Personality Factor Questionnaire (16PF) can be divided into two groups for present purposes: those that are more relevant to creativity and those that are less so. The creative person was characterized as (16PF codes in parentheses): aloof or reserved (A−), intelligent or capable of abstract thought (B+; initially conceived as a culture factor), dominant (E+), serious (F−), expedient or inattentive to rules (G−), socially bold (H+), sensitive (I+), imaginative (M+), liberal or open to experience (Q1+) and self-sufficient (Q2+). The other traits are: emotional stability (C), trusting versus suspicious (L), unpretentious and self-disclosing versus politically savvy and private (N), self-doubting versus self-assured (O), impulsive versus self-controlled (Q3) and relaxed versus tense (Q4).

The source traits were the result of analyzing the factor structure of numerous personality tests that were thought to contain surface-level traits. The mainstay of the work on the Big Five source traits is attributed to McCrae and Costa (1985) and their subsequent work. According to Goldberg (1993), however, 'the honor of first discovery must be accorded to Donald Fiske (1949), who analyzed a set of 22 variables developed by Cattell and found five factors that replicated across samples of self-ratings, observer ratings and peer ratings' (p. 27). Cattell *et al.* (1970) reported their own five-factor re-analysis of the 16PF, but argued against placing too much weight on it precisely because the second-order traits were less specific than the primary 16; also, because the five factor solution resulted from a previous factor analysis, scales that result from the second factor analysis contain another source of error that lies between the final factors and the primary factors, and the primary factors and the original data. Both points strongly suggested that source traits would be less proximally correlated with external criteria.

The Big Five traits are neuroticism, extroversion, openness, agreeableness and conscientiousness. 16PF second-order counterparts (Cattell 1994) are, respectively, anxiety, extroversion, independence, tough-mindedness and self-control.

The cardinal traits were the focus of Eysenck's perspective and long-term research strategy in personality measurement. Eysenck's taxonomy consists of three broad traits − extroversion, neuroticism and psychoticism (Eysenck 1970). The former two resemble two from the Big Five. Psychoticism is the trait with the strongest implications for creative behavior (Eysenck 1993).

Two other taxonomies of personality traits surface in the literature on personality and creativity, the California Psychological Inventory (CPI; Gough and Bradley 1996), and the Myers-Briggs Type Indicator (MBTI; Briggs *et al.* 1998). The CPI was developed as a set of 20 'folk scales' that were meant to measure psychological constructs that appeared meaningful in a relatively conventional understanding of personality; unlike the 16PF they were not predicated on a factor-analytic theory. CPI also contains a dozen 'special purpose' scales. CPI scales are approximately as narrowly defined as surface traits, and they can be sorted into the Big Five taxonomy of source traits with factor analysis fairly well (Conn and Rieke 1994).

The MBTI was based on Jung's theory of personality types (Jung 1971). According to Jung, there were four dichotomies, and the combination of four dichotomies yields 16 possible types. Although Jung's taxonomy did not have a counterpart for neuroticism, the four MBTI scales that lead to the dichotomies align with the other four Big Five source traits reasonably well: introversion−extroversion with extroversion, sensing−intuition with agreeableness, thinking−feeling with openness and judgment−perception with conscientiousness (Conn and Rieke 1994). It is noteworthy that Jung used introversion−extroversion as the organizing construct for interpreting the nature of the other possible combinations. The intuition construct has surfaced in the recent literature on personality and creativity.

Types of creativity

For most purposes herein, there are two types of indicators of creativity that surface most often, which are in turn used as criteria in studies where personality variables are the predictors of success. The first type of indicator is incumbency in an occupation (e.g. science or art) that requires a strong component of creative output. Studies that used occupational group membership as a criterion were often part of a broader research agenda that was designed to identify profiles of personality traits that were associated with different occupations (e.g. Cattell *et al.* 1970). This type of information eventually led to the use of personality tests for career counseling.

The second type of criterion is the self-report measures of creative work products. The Artistic and Scientific Activities Survey (ASAS; Guastello and Shissler 1994; Guastello *et al.* 1992) is a self-report measure of creative behavior. It also reflects the principle that creative production occurs at a rate over time and that individual differences in rates of production could be substantial (Simonton 1989). The ASAS captures respondents' rates of production in visual arts, music, literature, theater, science and engineering, business ventures, apparel design, and video and photography. Some of the questions ask the respondents to indicate how often they engage in these activities over a period of three years. Other questions ask the respondents to indicate how often they have produced particular types of permanent works in each of these areas of endeavor.

The ASAS contains two oblique factors, one for science and business, and one for all the other arts combined. The correlation between the two factors was 0.32 (Guastello and Shissler 1994), indicating that creative behavior was only partially domain-specific. Within each factor there is a substantial overlap in activity between one sub-domain and another. Scratchley and Hakstian (2001) reported a similar two-factor result using a different self-report measure of creative accomplishments.

The literature also offers a few studies that used inventories of creative behavior that were based on principles of the ASAS, but with little or no emphasis on production rates (Carson *et al.* 2005; Dollinger *et al.* 2004; Griffin and McDermott 1998; Scratchley and Hakstian 2001). There were also others that utilized ratings of creative products as criteria, which are discussed in subsequent sections of the chapter.

Creativity and suface traits

Occupational profiles

The 16 primary traits are often used in weighted combination to form other useful measures such as the Creativity Index. The Creativity Index ia a combination of traits that distinguished creative people from a control sample of participants who were employed in the same profession but who did not have a history of original contributions (Cattell and Drevdahl 1955; Cattell *et al.* 1970; Cross *et al.* 1967; Drevdahl and Cattell 1958). A broad cross-section of content domains was represented in the original research that produced the list of traits associated with creativity that was mentioned earlier.

Like the other 16PF scales, the Creativity Index has a mean of 5.5, a range from 1 to 10 and a standard deviation of 2.0. One can then compare the mean for an occupational sample against the population mean, obtain a *t*-value or a *z*-value, and then convert the *t* or *z* to a point-biserial correlation, r_{pb}. Table 22.1 lists 15 different samples of creative people, their estimated *r* between the Creativity Index and occupational group membership. The average validity coefficient for the profile for occupational group membership is 0.72.

There appear to be only small domain-specific variations in the personality profiles of

Table 22.1 Validity coefficients for 16PF and CPS creativity indices based on profiles of incumbents in creative occupations and creative behavior

Sample	N	Description	Est. r
Occupational profiles, 16PF Creativity Index (fourth edition)			
1	142	Artists, USA and UK	0.87
2	94	Artists, USA, male	0.62
3	111	Artists, USA, female	0.73
4	107	Art instructors	0.79
5	54	Musicians	0.69
6	187	Research scientists	0.88
7	306	Scientists and engineers, not research	0.78
8	433	Engineers, not research, Australia	0.62
9	37	Research and development engineers, Australia	0.74
10	89	Creative writers	0.92
11	81	University professors	0.88
	1641	Fourth edition samples 1–11	0.75
Occupational profiles, 16PF Creativity Index (fifth edition)			
12	56	Artists	0.53
13	76	Musicians	0.53
14	117	Engineers, all levels and types	0.42
15	48	Research scientists	0.74
	297	Fifth edition samples 12–15	0.52
	1938	All 15 16PF samples	0.72
Creative Behavior, 16PF Individual Scales (fifth edition)			
16	440	Science–Business: H+ I– M+ Q2+ Q1+ A–	0.42
		All Arts: Q2+ I+ Q3+ Q1+ N– M+ F+	0.43
		ASAS Total: F+ M+ N– Q2+ Q1+ Q3+	0.42
Creative behavior, CPI CPS Scale			
17	204	Ratings of creative stories	0.25
18	94	Creative behavior inventory	0.43
19	94	Ratings of drawings	0.24
20	86	Creative Achievement Questionnaire	0.34
21	150	Experience in a variety of musical activities	0.34
	628	Weighted average samples 17–21	0.31

Notes:

Sources of samples: 1, 5–7, 10–11 from Cattell *et al.* (1970); 2–3 from Csikszentmihalyi and Getzels (1973); 4 from Kessler (1988); 8–9 from Dowling and Cieri (1992); 12–16 from Rieke *et al.* (1994) and Guastello and Shissler (1994); 17 from Wolfradt and Pretz (2001); 18–19 from Dollinger *et al.* (2004); 20 from Carson *et al.* (2005); 21 from Goney and Waehler (2006).

Sources of *r*: samples 1–15, conversions of *t*-tests for sample versus population means to point-biserial *r*; sample 16, multiple regression; samples 17–21, *r* as originally reported. Correlations are not corrected for reliability or restriction of range.

incumbents of creative occupations. Csikszentmihalyi and Getzels (1973) found that their artist sample scored lower on 16PF G and higher on M than scientists. Traits G and M were further connected to economic and aesthetic values when compared to other types of artists. Fine art students scored higher on a separate measure of aesthetic value, lower on economic values, lower on G, higher on M, and lower on N than other artists. Guastello and Shissler (1994) found that industrial scientists scored higher on N than their sample of artists.

In a meta-analytic study, Feist (1998) assessed the relationship between the CPI variables with membership in occupational groups of creative versus less creative scientists (total $N =$ 3918): 'Eight . . . scales yielded median effect sizes greater than or equal to 0.50 [. . .]: Tolerance . . . Self-acceptance . . . Sociability . . . Flexibility . . . Dominance . . . Intellectual Efficiency . . . Achievement via Independence . . . and Psychological Mindedness. . . . This pattern of scores on the CPI suggests a personality structure that is tolerant and open-minded, self-accepting, outgoing, confident, ambitious, persistent, and is a good judge of character' (p. 298).

For artists versus non-artists (total $N = 4397$), there were eight CPI variables that were negatively associated with artists: Responsibility, Socialization, Achievement via Conformance, Good Impression, Self-control, Well-being, Tolerance and Communality. Flexibility was positively associated with membership in the artist category. 'Such a strong pattern of results suggests personalities that are conflicted, impulsive, nonconformist, rule-doubting, skeptical, fiercely independent, and not concerned with obligations or duties. . . . [A]lthough they are conflicted and rebellious, artists seek change, are easily bored, and yet see themselves as talented and worthy people' (p. 298).

Creative behavior

The 16PF traits have been associated with creative output from the ASAS (Rieke et al. 1994). The sample was composed of 214 people who were employed in creative occupations (engineers, research scientists, beauticians, artists and musicians) and 226 undergraduates; many of the participants in the study indicated that they were involved in two or more types of creative behavior. Multiple regression coefficients were obtained for the science–business ($R = 0.42$) and art ($R = 0.43$) composites.

There were some notable trends. B+ was more relevant to creative production in the sciences than in the arts, although all profiles of creative persons were B+ relative to the general population. Scientific creativity and artistic creativity fell on opposite poles of I. H+ was more relevant to creative production in the sciences than the arts, although music was an exception. Finally, although Q3 was not relevant to creative production in any one discipline, it did emerge as a characteristic of multi-talented people, particularly in the arts factor.

Other contributions to the study of personality and creative behavior were made using the Creative Personality Scale (CPS) from the CPI. Gough (1979) initially developed the CPS from CPI items that distinguished incumbents in creative occupations from other people. Four studies have now been reported showing correlations between the CPS with creative behavior. Participants in those studies were all undergraduates. The weighted average for the six r coefficients is 0.31 (Table 22.1).

Source traits and creativity

The focus of research on personality and creativity shifted to source traits after McCrae's (1987) article showed a relationship between the trait Openness and divergent thinking. The

271

relationship between source traits with incumbency in creative occupations and creative behavior is considered next.

Occupational groups

In his meta-analysis of findings connecting source traits with membership in creative occupations, Feist (1998) examined numerous studies that reported relationships between surface traits from the 16PF, CPI and EPQ with membership in three occupational categories – scientists versus non-scientists, creative versus less creative scientists and artists versus non-artists. The surface traits were sorted into one of the Big Five themes based on the similarities of their constructs. Some of the source traits were coded as 'positive' and others as 'negative'; a trait was coded as 'positive' if it indicated neuroticism, for instance when neuroticism was intended, and 'negative' if they indicated a sign of positive mental health or lack of neuroticism. Effect sizes were reported in the form of standard deviation units between the target occupational group and the comparison group (Cohen's d).

Feist's results (1998: 295) are reorganized into simplified form in Table 22.2. The average of the two median effect sizes was taken for the positive and negative groupings, noting whether both signs of d were headed in consistent versus inconsistent directions. The values of d were then converted to point-biserial correlations.

The results shown in Table 22.2 indicate different profiles of source traits for the three occupational groups. Most of the correlations are low; in light of the large sample sizes involved, statistical significance is not an issue. The artists' profile indicated greater neuroticism and openness and less conscientiousness than the creative scientists. The two scientists' profiles indicate that strategies for selecting personnel should differ depending on whether creative or routine work is involved. It is noteworthy that if one were to use the mean d for positive openness, rather than a d based on the average of two medians, the estimated r_{pb} for Openness for creative scientists would be 0.20.

In one later study involving occupational group profiles, Burch et al. (2006) compared 53 visual artists (undergraduates) with 54 non-artists using the NEO-FFI (Costa and McCrae 1989) as the measurement of the Big Five traits. Their values of d were converted to r_{pb} in Table 22.2.

Creative behavior

Several studies have now reported links between the five source traits and creative behavior. The 16PF global traits are reported in Table 22.2 for the ASAS total score, followed by the separate scores for creative behavior in the arts and in science and business. The two sub-group profiles are relatively similar; the main results were that creative behavior is associated with Independence or Openness and Agreeableness, and negative scores on Self-control. The multiple regression coefficients for source traits predicting ASAS total, Arts, and Science-business were 0.32, 0.34 and 0.30, respectively. The 16PF scale that corresponds to Agreeableness is Tough-mindedness, which is the opposite of Agreeableness; thus the actual coefficients reported by Rieke et al. (1994) were changed from negative to positive. It is noteworthy that the 16PF results for Agreeableness fell in the opposite direction of trends reported and discussed by other recent commentators on the Big Five theory and creativity (Burch et al. 2006; Feist 1998; Wolfradt and Pretz 2001).

The intuition construct in the MBTI is described as thinking with a sixth sense or hunches rather than the five senses, thinking about what could be rather than what is, emphasizing

Table 22.2 Correlations between source traits and creative behavior

Sample	N	Test	Behavior	r				
				N	E	O	A	C
Occupational group membership								
1	4852	various	Scientists vs. nonscientists	−0.06	0.03	−0.05	0.06	0.25
2	3981	various	Creative scientists vs. less creative scientists	0.01	0.07	0.12	−0.06	−0.08
3	4397	various	Artists vs. non-artists	0.09	0.09	0.23	−0.09	−0.31
4	107	NEO	Visual artists, non-artists	0.25	−0.06	0.24	−0.21	−0.08
Creative behavior								
5	440	16PF	ASAS arts	0.05	0.13	0.21	0.32	−0.22
5	440	16PF	ASAS science-business	−0.09	−0.14	0.15	0.02	−0.06
6	132	NEO	Ratings, life-span creativity	−0.03	−0.10	0.40	−0.27	−0.12
7	204	NEO	Creative stories	0.05	−0.07	0.19	−0.22	−0.24
8	94	MBTI	Creative behavior inventory		0.27	0.19	0.54	0.29
8	94	MBTI	Drawings		−0.20	0.09	0.29	−0.20
9	211	OS	Suggestions, manufacturing			0.17		
10	86	OS	Creative Achievement Q.			0.33		
11	212	OS	Business, global change			0.43		
11	212	OS	Business, incremental change			0.20		
11	212	OS	General managerial creativity			0.42		
12	67	NEO	Undergraduate creative activities			0.58		
13	131	NEO	ASAS arts			0.53		
13	131	NEO	ASAS science-business			0.30		
			Weighted average	−0.01	−0.02	0.28	0.09	−0.14

Notes: N = Neuroticism, E = Extroversion, O = Openness, A = Agreeableness, C = conscientiousness, OS = open source. Total sample sizes for creative behavior: N, 1216; E, A, and C, 1404; O, 2669. Sources of samples: 1–3, Feist (1998); 4, Burch *et al.* (2006); 5, Rieke *et al.* (1994); 6, Soldz & Vaillant (1999); 7, Wolfradt and Pretz (2001); 8, Dollinger *et al.* (2004); 9, Baer and Oldham (2006); 10, Carson *et al.* (2005); 11, Scratchley and Hakstian (2001); 12, Griffin and McDermott (1998); 13, Perrine and Brodersen (2005). Source of r: samples 1–3, conversions of effect sizes to r; samples 4–13 as originally reported. Correlations are not corrected for reliability or restriction of range.

theoretical possibilities and novelty rather than practicalities or utility, learning new skills rather than using established skills (Hirsh and Kummerow 1990: 5). As such it bears a close resemblance to 16PF factors Q1+ and M+, or Openness in the Big Five theory, although the factor analysis (Conn and Rieke 1994) turned out differently. Only one study was found that linked the MBTI thinking–intuition scale (Dollinger *et al.* 2004) with creative behaviors.

Some conclusions can be drawn concerning the source traits and creativity. The most consistent effect was a positive correlation (*r* = 0.28) between Openness and creative behavior, which is consistent with McCrae's (1987) initial proposition. There was also a net negative correlation between Conscientiousness and creative behavior ($r = -0.14$).

There was no net relationship between Neuroticism and creativity ($r = 0.01$), or between extroversion and creative behavior ($r = -0.02$); there were no decipherable patterns of positive and negative coefficients that contributed to this average. Agreeableness showed the least consistent results of the source traits ($r = 0.09$), and it appears that negative correlations were obtained from the NEO, and positive correlations were obtained from the 16PF and the MBTI.

Cardinal traits and pathological conditions

The results on record for two of the three cardinal traits, extroversion and neuroticism, have been incorporated into the analysis of source traits report earlier. By one form of reckoning, the third cardinal trait, Psychoticism, is a combination of Agreeableness (negative), Openness to experience (positive) and Conscientiousness (negative). By another form of reckoning, there is something special occurring with the psychoticism trait, and that is the focus of attention in this section of the chapter. Psychoticism is perhaps best characterized as 'thinking differently'. Extremely low scores characterize highly altruistic and empathetic people; in other words, it characterizes people who put some concerted effort into thinking like most of the sane world. Conformists occupy the middle ranges of this scale (Eysenck 1993). As one moves toward the progressively higher scores, however, one starts to encounter criminal behavior, followed by progressively severe diagnoses of mood disorders, followed by schizotypal personality disorders and schizophrenia. Divergent thinking, which characterizes creative thinking, is not especially different from the over-inclusive thinking that characterizes some pathological thought processes; the differences between the two may just be matters of degree and controllability (ibid.).

Mood disorders

Andreasen (1987) compared 30 creative writers with 30 matched control cases and their first-degree relatives (parents and siblings) for incidence rates of depression-related diagnoses. She found that the creative writers were 2.7 times more likely to have any of several affective disorders. Specifically, they were 3.0 times more likely to have bipolar II disorder, 2.2 times more likely to have major depression, and 4.3 times more likely to report alcoholism than their matched controls. For the comparison of relatives, the 116 relatives of the creative writers were 9.0 times as likely to have had any affective disorder, 7.5 times more likely to have had major depression specifically, and 1.2 times more likely to report alcoholism than the 121 relatives of control subjects. Additionally, the relatives of the creative writers were 2.5 times more likely to display a 'well-recognized level of creative achievement' (p. 1290) compared to the relatives of control subjects.

Richards *et al.* (1988) addressed this connection from the opposite perspective. They composed three samples: (a) a clinical sample of 17 bipolar patients and 16 cyclothymes, (b) a sample of 11 normal first-degree relatives, and (c) a sample of 33 control subjects, of whom 15 were normal and 11 carried a different diagnosis. A comparison of subjects' scores on their Lifetime Creativity scales indicated greater creativity among the mood disorder subjects compared to other groups, but no incremental creativity for the first-degree relatives compared to controls. Thus when the perspective was reversed, mood disorders predicted greater creative achievement, but the previously reported association among first-degree relatives disappeared.

According to Jamison (1995), who studied eminently famous creative people, the creative persons' productivity varied with their mood cycle. As an example, Schubert's musical productivity was highest in years that were characterized by a manic cycle, and lowest in years characterized by deep depression. That connection between productivity and the mood cycle appeared to generalize to other creative bipolar individuals (Jamison 1993).

Other studies produced different conclusions, however. Waddell (1998) reviewed 29 studies and 34 review articles on the possible association between creativity and psychopathology. Of the 29 studies, '15 found no evidence to link creativity with mental illness, 9 found positive evidence, and 5 had unclear findings' (p. 166). The results within the 34 reviews were mixed, but the authors tended to conclude in favor of the linkage more often than was warranted, according to Waddell. Possible reasons for the negative or mixed evidence might be traced to definitions of creativity versus eminence, and the diagnostic classifications utilized. The occasional use of biographical sources can produce a bias, according to Eysenck (1993), because the more sensational lives are more likely to be captured in biographies compared to lives that were tamer.

Emotional intelligence

Although there are many studies that connect creativity with psychopathology, particularly mood disorders, humanistic psychologists have associated creativity with mental health and positive emotions. Furthermore eminently creative persons suffering from a mental illness sometimes find their affliction facilitates their work, while others are debilitated. The conflict of viewpoints appears to be rectified, at least partially so, by introducing emotional intelligence as a covariate in the connection between mood disorders and creative behavior (Guastello et al. 2004).

Emotional intelligence (EI) was initially defined as, 'a type of emotional information processing that includes accurate appraisal of emotions in oneself and others, appropriate expression of emotion, and adaptive regulation in such a way as to enhance living' (Mayer 2001: 9); the definition was later refined to reflect more strongly that EI is an ability. The available measurements of EI variables emphasize the personality and cognitive aspects of EI. Of relevance here, Schutte et al. (1998) developed a scale for measuring EI that correlated with the constructs of alexithymia, attention to feelings, clarity of feelings, mood repair, optimism and impulse control.

Guastello et al. (2004) examined the role of EI, as measured by the Schutte et al. (1998) scale as a covariate that moderates the relationship between mood disorders and creativity. A sample of 412 undergraduates completed five measures of divergent thinking, the ASAS, the EI scale by Schutte et al., a measure of cognitive style flexibility that is part of the ASAS (cognitive style is discussed later in this chapter) and a brief questionnaire about seeking clinical treatment. Clinical treatment actions were coded into four categories that comprised the independent variable in a MANCOVA analysis: did not think about treatment for bipolar or other mood disorders, thought about it but did not enter treatment, was in treatment, and completed treatment. EI was used as the covariate. The results showed that, after controlling for EI, clinical action category had a significant impact on one of the five measures of divergent thinking – ideational fluency ($\eta^2 = 0.02$, $r = 0.15$). In principle, ideational fluency is the type of divergent thinking that is most proximal to the contents of the uncontrolled thought trajectories of manic individuals. Ideational fluency was greatest for the group that completed therapy, and least for the group that was currently in therapy. The within-cells correlation between EI and ideational fluency was by itself not significant ($r = 0.07$).

Treatment categories were also related to the ASAS total score, after correcting for EI ($\eta^2 = 0.02$, $r = 0.15$). For this variable, the highest mean score was observed for those who were in therapy, and the lowest mean was observed for those who considered therapy but did not undertake it. The within-cells correlation between EI and ASAS total score was 0.22. Thus there were distinct relationships found between mood disorders and creative production among the undergraduates, and also between EI and creative production. EI played the expected mediating role between mood disorders and creative behavior, wherein people with higher EI were able to channel their angst into something productive.

References

Allport, G. W. (1937). *Personality: A psychological perspective*. New York: Holt.

Andreasen, N. C. (1987). Creativity and mental illness: Prevalence rates in writers and their first-degree relatives. *American Journal of Psychiatry*, 144, 1288–1292.

Baer, M. and Oldham, G. R. (2006). The curvilinear relation between experienced creative time pressures and creativity: Moderating effects of openness to experience and support for creativity. *Journal of Applied Psychology*, 91, 963–970.

Briggs, K. C., Myers, I. B., McCaulley, M. H., Quenck, N. L. and Hammer, A. L. (1998). *The Myers-Briggs Type Indicator*. Palo Alto, CA: Consulting Psychologists Press.

Burch, G. St. J., Pavelis, C., Hemsley, D. R. and Corr, P. J. (2006). Schizotypy and creativity in visual artists. *British Journal of Psychology*, 97, 177–190.

Carson, S. H., Peterson, J. B. and Higgins, D. M. (2005). Reliability, validity, and factor structure of the Creative Achievement Questionnaire. *Creativity Research Journal*, 17, 37–50.

Cattell, H. E. P. (1994). Development of the 16PF fifth edition. In S. Conn and M. L. Rieke (eds), *16PF fifth edition technical manual* (pp. 1–20). Champaign, IL: Institute for Personality and Ability Testing.

Cattell, R. B. (1947). Confirmation and clarification of primary personality factors. *Psychomrika*, 12 197–220.

Cattell, R. B. and Drevdahl, J. E. (1955). A comparison of the personality profile (16PF) of eminent researchers with that of eminent teachers and administrators and the general population. *British Journal of Psychology*, 46, 248–261.

Cattell, R. B., Eber, H. W. and Tatsuoka, M. M. (1970). *Handbook for the Sixteen Personality Factor Questionnaire*. Champaign, IL: Institute for Personality and Ability Testing.

Conn, S. and Rieke, M. L. (1994). Construct validation of the 16PF fifth edition. In S. Conn and M. L. Rieke (eds), *The 16PF fifth edition, technical manual* (pp. 101–142). Champaign, IL: Institute for Personality and Ability Testing.

Costa, P. T. and McCrae, R. R. (1989). *NEO-PI/FFI manual supplement*. Odessa, FL: Psychological Assessment Resources.

Cross, P. G., Cattell, R. B. and Butcher, H. J. (1967). The personality pattern of creative artists. *British Journal of Educational Psychology*, 37, 292–299.

Csikszentmihalyi, M. and Getzels, J. W. (1973). The personality of young artists: An empirical and theoretical exploration. *British Journal of Psychology*, 64, 94–104.

Dollinger, S. J., Palaskonis, D. G. and Pearson, J. L. (2004). Creativity and intuition revised. *Journal of Creative Behavior*, 38, 244–259.

Dowling, A. J. and DeCieri, H. (1992). Human resource management for engineers. In D. Samson (ed.). *Management for engineers* (pp. 179–207). Melbourne, Australia: Longman Chechire.

Drevdahl, J. E. and Cattell, R. B. (1958). Personality and creativity in artists and writers. *Journal of Clinical Psychology*, 14, 107–111.

Eysenck, H. J. (1970). *The structure of human personality* (third edition). London: Methuen.

Eysenck, H. J. (1993). Creativity and personality: Suggestions for a theory. *Psychological Inquiry*, 4, 147–178.

Feist, G. J. (1998). A meta-analysis of personality in scientific and artistic creativity. *Personality and Social Psychology Review*, 2, 290–309.

Fiske, D. W. (1949). Consistency of the factorial structures of personality ratings from different sources. *Journal of Abnormal and Social Psychology*, 44, 329–344.

Goldberg, L. R. (1993). The structure of phenotypic personality traits. *American Psychologist*, 48, 26–34.

Goncy, E. A., Waehler, C. A. (2006). An empirical investigation of creativity and musical experience. *Psychology of Music*, 34, 307–321.

Gough, H. G. (1979). A creative personality scale for the Adjective Check List. *Journal of Personality and Social Psychology*, 37, 1398–1405.

Gough, H. G. and Bradley, P. (1996). *The California Psychological Inventory* (third edition). Palo Alto, CA: Consulting Psychologists Press.

Griffin, M. and McDermott, M. H. (1998). Exploring a tripartite relationship between rebelliousness, openness to experience, and creativity. *Social Behavior and Personality*, 26, 347–356.

Guastello, S. J. and Shissler, J. (1994). A two-factor taxonomy of creative behavior. *Journal of Creative Behavior*, 28, 211–221.

Guastello, S. J., Bzdawka, A., Guastello, D. D. and Rieke, M. L. (1992). Cognitive measures of creative behavior: CAB-5 and consequences. *Journal of Creative Behavior*, 26, 260–267.

Guastello, S. J., Guastello, D. D. and Hanson, C. (2004). Creativity, mood disorders, and emotional intelligence. *Journal of Creative Behavior*, 38, 260–281.

Hirsh, S. K. and Kummerow, J. M. (1990). *Introduction to type in organizations* (second edition). Palo Alto, CA: Consulting Psychologists Press.

Jamison, K. (1993). *Touched with fire*. Toronto: Maxwell Macmillan Canada.

Jamison, K. (1995). Manic-depressive illness and creativity. *Scientific American*, February, 62–67.

Jung, C. G. (1971). *Psychological types* (collected works, Volume 6). Princeton NJ: Princeton University Press/Bollinger.

Kessler, E. (1988). Personality characteristics of college art instructors in seven Midwestern states. Unpublished doctoral dissertation, Illinois State University.

Mayer, J. D. (2001). A field guide to emotional intelligence. In J. Ciarrochi, J. P. Forgas and J. D. Mayer (eds), *Emotional development and emotional intelligence: Educational implications* (pp. 3–34). New York: Basic Books.

McCrae, R. R. (1987). Creativity, divergent thinking, and openness to experience. *Journal of Personality and Social Psychology*, 52, 1258–1265.

McCrae, R. R. and Costa, P. T., Jr. (1985). Updating Norman's 'adequate taxonomy': Intelligence and personality dimensions in natural language questionnaires. *Journal of Personality and Social Psychology*, 49, 710–721.

Perrine, N. E. and Brodersen, R. M. (2005). Artistic and scientific creative behavior: Openness and the mediating role of interests. *Journal of Creative Behavior*, 39, 217–236.

Richards, R., Kinney, D. K., Lunde, I., Benet, M. and Merzel, A. P. C. (1988). Creativity in manic-depressives, cyclothymes, their normal relatives and control subjects. *Journal of Abnormal Psychology*, 97, 281–288.

Rieke, M. L., Guastello, S. J. and Conn, S. (1994). Leadership and creativity. In S. Conn and M. L. Rieke (eds), *16PF fifth edition technical manual* (pp. 183–212). Champaign, IL: Institute for Personality and Ability Testing.

Schutte, N.S., Malouff, J.M., Hall, L.E., Haggerty, D.J., Cooper, J.T., Golden, C.J. and Dornheirn, L. (1998). Development and validation of a measure of emotional intelligence. *Personality and Individual Differences*, 25, 167–177.

Scratchley, L. S. and Hakstian, A. R. (2001). The measurement and prediction of managerial creativity. *Creativity Research Journal*, 13, 367–384.

Simonton, D. K. (1989). Age and creative productivity: Nonlinear estimation of an information processing model. *International Journal of Aging and Human Development*, 29, 23–37.

Soldz, S. and Vaillant, G. E. (1999). The Big Five personality traits and the life course: A 45-year longitudinal study. *Journal of Research in Personality*, 33 208–232.

Waddell, C. (1998). Creativity and mental illness: Is there a link? *Canadian Journal of Psychiatry*, 43, 166–172.

Wolfradt, U. and Pretz, J. E. (2001). Individual differences in creativity: Personality, story writing and hobbies. *European Journal of Personality*, 15, 297–310.

23

The thinking of creative leaders: outward focus, inward focus and integration

Michael D. Mumford, Cristina L. Byrne and Amanda S. Shipman

Introduction

Leadership is critical to the success of creative efforts. Although leaders serve many roles in directing creative efforts, the direction of these efforts requires creative thinking on the part of leaders. In this chapter, we argue that leaders' creative thinking involves an external focus with respect to the organization and its operational environment, and an internal focus with respect to the ideas being produced by the group. The integration of these two foci is held to be critical for the success of those who lead creative enterprises. Directions for future research with respect to the internal and external foci, and their integration, are discussed.

When one mentions the word creativity, images are called to mind of the lonely struggle of the great artist or the eminent scholar who works against all odds to produce a truly novel and useful product. As attractive as this image may be, it is not consistent with what we know about the nature of creative work. Creative work, more often than not, occurs in teams or as part of a collaborative effort. The ideas produced by this effort must be developed, implemented and marketed – activities that may involve a cast of hundreds if not thousands. And, the products resulting from this effort will be used, and adapted, by thousands more. The distinctly social nature of creative work (Csikszentmihalyi 1999) has an important, albeit often overlooked, implication. Like other forms of social work, leadership will make a difference, a big difference, to the nature and success of creative efforts.

One illustration of this point may be found in a study by West *et al.* (2003). They examined innovation in health care teams. It was found that clarity with regard to who was the leader of the group was related to innovation ($r = 0.40$), with leadership proving particularly important to innovation in larger groups. In another study along these lines, Tierney *et al.* (1999) examined creativity among 191 research and development employees of a large chemical company. Effective leadership was found to yield correlations in the 0.30s, not only with creativity ratings and patent applications but also with indices of intrinsic motivation and use of requisite creative problem-solving strategies. In still another study along these lines, Barnowe (1975) examined creative productivity among 81 research and development groups containing 963 chemists. He found that measures of leadership skills, particularly leader technical skills, produced correlations in the 0.40s with indices of creativity and innovation of group members.

These studies, of course, serve to make our basic point. Leadership does, in fact, make a difference, a big difference, to the success of creative work in organizations. This finding, however, broaches a broader substantive question. Exactly why does leadership make such a difference? Broadly speaking, two answers have been provided to this question. One answer holds that the effects of leadership on creative work are a function of the social outcomes of leader behavior (e.g. Amabile *et al.* 2004). The other answer holds that the effects of leadership on creative efforts are attributable to how leaders think about creative work (e.g. Mumford *et al.* 2003).

In fact, a variety of social behaviors initiated by leaders do seem to contribute to creativity (Mumford *et al.* 2002b). Leaders must sell creative products to the organization. They must create a climate where creative collaborations are likely to occur. And, they must provide people with socio-emotional support as they encounter the day-to-day frustrations that accompany any creative effort.

As important as the social influences of leader behavior are to creative efforts, one must not underestimate the importance of leader cognition (Mumford *et al.* 2003). How leaders define problems and structure the work of the group appears to be as important, if not more so, than social behavior. In fact, leader cognition may be a particularly complex phenomenon. It involves 'external' cognition, where leaders must think about the broader systems – both social and technological systems. It also calls for 'internal' cognition, where leaders think about the creativity of the work being done. And, the integration of this externally focused and internally focused cognition to bring a creative product into existence. In this chapter we will examine the nature of leaders' creative thought, examining this outward focus, inward focus and their integration.

Outward focus

Scanning

Leaders serve a unique and critical role in any creative venture. They define the mission, the technical production effort, to be pursued by the group (Mumford *et al.* 2002b). At one level, the importance of the mission defined by a leader is straightforward. It defines the focus and scope of people's creative efforts. At another level, however, effects of mission definition are more subtle. Creative people invest themselves and their identity in the mission being pursued. As a result, missions both direct and motivate creative efforts. This rather straightforward set of observations, however, has an important, albeit often overlooked, implication: viable missions, as defined by leaders, must be embedded in the environment – both the organizational and the technological environment. Thus leaders in formulating missions must gather information—a process referred to as scanning.

In fact, a variety of studies have shown that environmental scanning is critical to leader performance (Walsh 1988). It also appears that scanning is critical to the effective leadership of creative efforts. Thus, Koberg *et al.* (1996), in a study of innovation among mature high technology firms, found that environmental scanning and analysis by senior managers was critical to firm innovation. Similar findings have been obtained in studies by Souitaris (2001) and Rodan (2002). The question raised by these findings, however, is exactly what information those who lead creative efforts are seeking.

The available evidence indicates that leaders' information gathering through scanning is a selective activity. Typically, leaders' scanning focuses on competitors – competitors whose actions might represent a threat to current products. Leaders, moreover, also seek to acquire information from suppliers and customers. Although direct evidence bearing on the leaders of creative efforts is lacking, it seems likely that leaders of these efforts, like leaders in general, seek information bearing on competitors, suppliers and customers and use this information as a basis for defining missions.

However, the scanning activities of the leaders of creative efforts may be more complex. To begin, creative leaders must not only scan the organization's operating environment, they must also scan the technological environment (Weber and Perkins 1992). Scanning of the technological environment typically will focus on emerging themes that have implications for current organizational operations. This scanning of emerging themes in the technological environment, however, will require a deep search, with leaders examining not only the potential of emerging themes but also problems encountered in work pursuing these themes, key people conducting work on this theme, and those aspects of the theme that have, and have not, been explored. In other words, the leaders of creative efforts scan the technological environment, vis-à-vis the organizational environment, to identify themes and issues that might be worth pursuing.

The second way in which the scanning activities of creative leaders differ from 'standard' leader scanning involves absorptive capacity (Cohen and Levinthal 1990). Absorptive capacity concerns the organization's capacity to understand and respond to emerging new technological themes. Typically, organizations that lack absorptive capacity with respect to expertise, process and structure will fail to effectively exploit emergent opportunities. Accordingly, the leaders of creative efforts can be expected to actively seek out information bearing on strengths and weaknesses of the organizations' absorptive capacity often appraising these indicators of absorptive capacity to those of competitors.

Forecasting

Scanning provides leaders with information about emerging themes that might serve the organization and the organization's capabilities for exploiting these themes. However valuable this information may be, it is not, unto itself, useful as a basis for defining a creative mission. The information gathered in scanning, at least as it pertains to creative efforts, only provides signals about a potential future or set of futures. Thus creative leaders must be able to forecast the implications of various efforts.

Some evidence bearing on this point has been provided by O'Connor (1998). She conducted a qualitative study of eight radical technological innovations developed by various organizations. Her findings indicated that innovation was strongly influenced by the ability of senior leaders to 'see' the implications of a new technology, if it was developed, for the operations of the organization and the technological field. In keeping with these observations, Kickul and Gundry (2001) have provided evidence indicating that leaders' creative thinking abilities moderated the impact of scanning on firm innovation – presumably because divergent thinking allows people to formulate multiple forecasts of the future. In other words, the leaders of creative efforts must be able to forecast the downstream implications of technology vis-à-vis organizational operations.

What is important to recognize with regard to forecasting is that, ultimately, forecasting of the future, particularly in the case of creative efforts, is an inherently ambiguous activity. More specifically, leaders can not be assured what issues will arise in the pursuit of creative efforts nor can they be assured that these issues will be successfully resolved. These observations led Mumford et al. (in press) to argue that leaders address this inherent ambiguity in forecasting with regard to creative efforts by working at a higher level of abstraction. In other words, leaders

281

forecast the effects of themes rather than the success of a particular creative effort. In fact, Hughes (1989) has argued that the identification and exploration of high potential themes is critical to innovation in technology.

With regard to themes, and forecasting of their potential effects, however, three key considerations should be taken into account. First, forecasting depends on expertise, with experts showing far greater ability to predict future implications of actions than novices. This enhanced predictive ability appears to be based on experts' formulation of more sophisticated mental models, where these mental models permit forecasting based on a limited number of key, critical, variables. What is important to recognize here, however, is that while the nature of leaders' mental models makes effective forecasting possible, they simultaneously constrain the nature of the forecasts made. One way in which leaders cope with these constraints is by soliciting input from other people employing different mental models. Another way leaders cope with these constraints is by considering incongruities in the information gathered vis-à-vis applicable mental models. Thus, effective forecasting may require an extended analytical appraisal of multiple sources of information from multiple perspectives.

Second, the forecasting of creative leaders, while based on abstractions, or themes, must take a concrete tangible form (O'Connor 1998). Thus the leaders of creative efforts will envision products flowing from relevant technological themes. This concrete instantiation of forecasts provides leaders with a hypothetical case. These hypothetical cases are necessary because they provide a framework around which actions can be envisioned, along with relevant resources, restrictions and contingencies. In fact, in the case of highly creative leaders, it seems likely that they often envision multiple potential products emerging from a theme, along with potential 'spin-offs' of these products. Thus creative leaders, in forecasting, appear to be able to work with abstract themes to envision concrete products and their implications.

Third, forecasts of products are of interest for the leaders of creative efforts not with respect to the product, or set of products, being envisioned. Rather, the product, or set of products, being envisioned, allows leaders to analyze the key requirements likely to be imposed on product development with respect to technology, customers, competitors and suppliers. In anticipation of these requirements, leaders can begin to formulate missions for creative teams and recruit the talent needed to ensure successful completion of the mission.

Mission

A mission may be viewed as a specific form of a broader leader vision (Shamir *et al.* 1993). In contrast to a vision where leaders anticipate an idealized model of future organizational operations, a mission reflects an area of technological exploration pursuant to a certain set of products (Mumford *et al.* 2002b). Although missions and visions should not be arbitrarily equated, the cognitive processes underlying the formation of a mission and vision appear quite similar.

Recently, Strange and Mumford (2005) proposed a cognitive model of the processes underlying the formation of missions and visions on the part of leaders. Within this theory, it is assumed that people begin with a descriptive mental model of current operations. Either cases reflecting real-world events, or cases reflecting envisioned products, are then analyzed to identify critical causes influencing the attainment of select goals. These causes and goals are then reorganized and recombined in a conceptual combination process to give rise to a prescriptive mental model, which, with reflection on the implications of this model in terms of its implications for resources, contingencies and restrictions, allows leaders to formulate a mission. In fact, Strange and Mumford, in an experimental study, showed that this kind of creative analysis gave rise to the production of stronger vision statements, especially when 'leaders' evaluated critical causes of successful case models and the goals implied by failed case models.

One implication of these findings is that they point to a critical processing skill underlying leader creative thought on the part of leaders. More specifically, leader creative thought, at least with respect to the formulation of missions, will depend on conceptual combination skills (Scott *et al.* 2005). However, leaders' conceptual combinations will be inherently real-world based. Thus, the implications of the prescriptive mental model being formulated will be evaluated with respect to tangible consequences of this model on the lives of others and the development of new technologies. Indeed, Scott *et al.* have shown that strategies, such as (1) prediction of the implications of a concept, and (2) revision of concepts based on anticipated outcomes, may give rise to creative thought in conceptual combination efforts on the part of people in leadership roles.

The other implication of these observations involves identification of issues to be addressed as part of a leader's mission. With definition of a mission, a leader can anticipate potential outcomes of this mission if certain assumptions are satisfied. The definition of these assumptions, however, is noteworthy for two reasons. First, some assumptions will indicate requisite actions to be taken by the leader or the organization. Second, other assumptions will indicate areas of ambiguity – or unknowns. These unknowns, however, become particularly significant because they indicate the areas in which leaders must explore the implications of the unknowns vis-à-vis the prescriptive mental model they have constructed. Thus, the definition of these unknowns, and the initiation of exploratory efforts to resolve these unknowns, provides a basis for leaders' initiation of creative efforts.

In this regard, however, it is important to bear in mind another consideration. Not all unknowns are equally important. Thus, effective leaders of creative work will often prove unusually skilled at identifying critical unknowns. Moreover, they will organize these unknowns by resolving macro-issues first. The knowledge gained in resolving macro-issues will be used to specify later refinements of the idea being developed in relation to the demands imposed by the field, the organization and the organization's operating environment. Thus, integral to a leader's definition of a mission is ongoing learning and progressive refinement and extension of prescriptive mental models with exploration and feedback. Put more directly, creative leaders create experiences to learn and adjust their prescriptive mental models based on this experience – a point nicely illustrated in Edison's development of electric lighting systems (Hughes 1989).

Inward focus

Evaluation

Missions are significant in the leadership of creative groups in part because they define the kind of creative activities to be pursued. In fact, one can argue that with definitions of a challenging, high value mission, leaders have taken a key step to creating a climate likely to foster creativity (Mumford *et al.* in press). From the perspective of creative thought on the part of leaders, however, definition of a mission provides leaders with a framework, or a set of standards, for executing a key demand made in all leadership roles – the evaluation of others' work.

Traditionally, evaluation has not been seen as a critical aspect of creative thought. However, more recent work has indicated not only that evaluation skills and creative thinking skills are closely related (Basadur *et al.* 2000) but also that evaluation may provide the key locus around which leaders generate new ideas (Mumford *et al.* 2003). A recent study by Lonergan *et al.*

(2004) suggests how this creative evaluation might occur. They asked undergraduates to assume the role of a marketing director for an advertising firm developing campaigns for a new product – the 3D Holograph Television. These 'leaders' were asked to evaluate campaign proposals. More specifically, they were first asked to appraise ideas, then asked to suggest revisions to ideas, and then provide a plan for the advertising campaign. It was found that when 'leaders' suggested revisions for good, or original, ideas, application of operating efficiency standards contributed to the production of stronger advertising campaigns. On the other hand, when 'leaders' suggested revisions for weaker ideas, application of innovation standards contributed to the production of stronger advertising campaigns. Thus leaders' creative thought appears to occur in a compensatory manner intended to clarify implementation issues surrounding good ideas and to strengthen the creativity of weak ideas.

What is important to recognize here is that leaders' creative thought, with regard to ideas generated in working on the issues entailed in a mission, is not inherently productive in the sense that leaders do not necessarily generate the ideas. However, the evaluation and revision of these ideas does call for creative thought on the part of leaders; with leaders in some cases helping followers generate more original ideas and in other cases envisioning the requirements for implementation of these ideas – both activities that call for substantial creative thought on the part of leaders.

With regard to leaders' evaluation of ideas, however, it is important to bear in mind several other points. First, idea evaluation will often be based on case-based or experiential knowledge (Hammond 1990). The application of these case models in idea evaluation, of course, suggests that leaders will need (1) substantial real-world experience to permit effective revision of ideas, and (2) creative thought concerning the requirements for developing these ideas. Second, as Mumford *et al.* (2003) point out, the effectiveness of idea evaluation will depend, to a large extent, on the viable delivery of feedback. Thus leaders can be expected to think, and think in-depth, about how feedback should be delivered vis-à-vis both the individuals proposing an idea and the mission at hand. Third, in the case of creative leaders this feedback will be framed in terms of contribution to the mission, now and in the future, rather than immediate perform-ance. Thus creative leaders, in thinking about ideas, will examine implications, including down-stream implications, with respect to a broader mission not just short-term performance con-sideration. Fourth, and finally, however, evaluation will be based, in part, on the impact of ideas on system functioning. These system demands may, at times, result, even in the case of highly creative leaders, in the rejection of otherwise viable ideas.

These observations about the idea evaluation process on the part of creative leaders point to a broader implication. The creative thought of leaders is an inherently integrative activity, where the implications of ideas are thought about in the context of both the mission and the operating environment of the organization or field. This point is of some importance because it suggests that wisdom may be a particularly important influence on the creative thinking of leaders. And, in keeping with this observation, Connelly *et al.* (2000) have provided evidence indicating that wisdom has a particularly strong influence on the creative thinking of senior leaders.

Planning

It is not, of course, sufficient simply for leaders to evaluate and provide feedback with respect to ideas. Leaders must plan for the generation, development and fielding of these ideas (Yukl 2002). Traditionally, planning, including planning for creative efforts, has been viewed as lock-step execution of a set of predefined action scripts. More recently, however, models of planning have begun to emphasize the need for planners to construct a mental simulation of future activities (Mumford *et al.* 2002a). These mental simulations of future actions, of course, represent a form of complex cognition.

More centrally, however, the formulation of mental simulations involving the actions needed for idea implementation have been shown to call for creative thought. In one recent study along these lines, Osburn and Mumford (2006) developed strategies for training two key skills held to be involved in planning: (1) penetration and (2) forecasting. After receiving training, undergraduates were asked to assume the role of principal, the leader, of a new experimental school and formulate curriculum plans. It was found that stronger plans, especially for creative people, were obtained in the trained as opposed to the not-trained condition. These findings, moreover, point to the importance of 'leaders' being able to identify critical issues raised by new ideas and to forecast, or predict, the likely implications of pursuing these ideas within the social system at hand. Thus leaders must be able to identify critical issues and envision how these issues will shape development of an idea.

The envisioning of the social and technical issues involved in development of ideas, however, is a complex process, especially when creative ideas are under consideration. To begin, in pursuing creative ideas, all relevant facts will not be available to the leader. Thus creative leaders must arrange for conditions that will allow this information to be acquired. Accordingly, creative leaders, in formulating plans, will engage in ongoing, iterative, learning – revising plans for ideas and idea implementation as new information becomes available. This iterative learning will prove most effective, however, when tests, or experiments, focus on the exploration of critical causes, key contingencies and requisite resources (Mumford *et al.* 2002a). Thus creative leaders will take an experimental approach in constructing plans for pursuing new ideas (Eisenhardt and Tabrizi 1995).

What should be recognized here, however, is that the development and implementation of ideas is an inherently social process, both with regard to idea development and idea implementation. One implication of this observation is that leaders' planning will involve the careful arrangement of people and expertise to bring forth the development of new ideas. Thus leaders must consider the need for cross-functional teams or expertise-based teams, taking into account both the stage of idea development and the kinds of expertise bearing on idea development at this point in a cycle of activity. Another implication of this observation is that leaders must plan the conditions of interaction, creating a climate appropriate for creative work at that point in the idea development cycle (Mumford *et al.* in press). Still another implication of this observation is that leaders must create conditions vis-à-vis the social system as a whole that permit an idea to be pursued. Thus they must formulate strategies for acquiring resources and removing undue restrictions. In fact, one can argue that planning for the circumvention of these restrictions and contingencies, and the acquisition of requisite resources and support, represents one of the most powerful, and pervasive, forms of creative thought on the part of leaders.

Implicit in these observations about the social nature of plan development and generation is an important aspect of planning from a cognitive perspective. In the real world, plans, at least any given plan, often do not work out. Thus Xiao *et al.* (1997) found that skilled planners typically develop multiple backup plans, along with diagnostic markers for monitoring progress in plan execution. The generation of multiple backup plans, of course, calls for the divergent thinking commonly held to be critical for creativity. Not only must leaders be creative in developing these backup plans, they must also focus attention on the diagnostics being used to monitor plan implementation and mark the need for implementation of these backup plans. Hence the leaders of creative efforts can be expected to evidence both flexibility with regard to plans and intense information processing with regard to progress and problems encountered in the development and fielding of new ideas.

Crises

As noted above, in the development of new ideas and new products, things do not always go as planned. And, even the most extensive set of backup plans may not prove sufficient to address the problem. In other words, crises arise in the development and fielding of new ideas. Drazin *et al.* (1999) conducted a qualitative study of leaders' roles in developing one technological innovation – a new aircraft. They found not only that crises emerged throughout this project but also that a key role played by leaders was the effective resolution of these crises. Although the role of leaders in crisis resolution was not surprising (Yukl 2002), more surprising was the way leaders went about resolving these crises. More specifically, leaders, in crises, engaged in sense-making activities. In sense-making, the origin of the crisis is articulated, the significance of its potential impacts, and frameworks, or mental models, that might be used to understand and respond to the crisis are articulated and conveyed to group members.

Leader sense-making with respect to crises arising in the development of new ideas is noteworthy, with respect to leader cognition, for two reasons. First, leaders must develop and articulate mental models of the creative effort. Not only must leaders develop and articulate mental models, they must be able to tie these mental models to events arising in the course of developing a creative idea, revising their mental model to take into account emergent negative events. Thus leaders, particularly the leaders of creative efforts, must be capable of on-line adjustment of mental models – and of conveying this reconfiguration of their mental model to followers. In fact, the ability of creative leaders to 'act', a skill traditionally related to creativity, may represent one outcome of the need to articulate the significance of a crisis vis-à-vis the mission being pursued by a project team.

Second, in sense-making, leaders must be able to tie the significance of an event to the mission being pursued by a project team. One implication of this observation is that crises are framed and understood by leaders in terms of the mission being pursued. Thus leaders must appraise the implications of crisis events with respect to being capable of adapting missions to the demands imposed by crisis resolution. The other implication of this observation is that leaders must not simply respond to crises but must think about the implications of crises both for the mission being pursued and followers' actions with regard to this mission. Thus the thinking of creative leaders relates not only to the crisis but also to others' responses to the demands imposed by the crisis. This point is of some importance because it indicates that creative leaders must not only think about the crisis but they must also be able to anticipate the responses of the people doing the work. Given this demand, it is hardly surprising that creative leaders 'know their people' and establish conditions that allow 'their people' to work creatively.

Integration

Information

Perhaps the most striking conclusion that can be drawn from our foregoing observations concerns the need for leaders to be able to integrate multiple sources of information, external information and internal information, in generating creative problems and creative solutions. Moreover, within each of these two broad domains, leaders will be presented with multiple different pieces of information – information ranging from market conditions to followers' reactions to the crises emerging in the course of their work. This rather straightforward observation has an important implication with regard to creative thought on the part of leaders. More specifically, leaders' creative thought will require unusually high levels of synthesis.

In the thinking of creative leaders, however, the wide range of information that must be considered will necessarily place on leaders a requirement for balance. More specifically, creative leaders cannot overemphasize the promise of an idea. By the same token, they cannot accept the demands of the field or organization as it stands. This observation has three important implications.

First, creative leaders' thinking will focus on what is 'doable' with the social system at hand. Thus the leaders of creative efforts in their thinking, and their style of leadership, will evidence substantial pragmatism (Mumford and Van Doorn 2001). This pragmatic orientation will stress the active analysis and manipulation of key operations within the limits of what can be accomplished vis-à-vis the bounds set by current technological capabilities and the extant social system. Although this pragmatic orientation may at times cause the creative leader to reject sound ideas that require extensive development, it will also lead to skill in identifying those ideas that can be efficiently exploited within the extant social system. In fact, when one considers the creative thinking of leaders, such as Benjamin Franklin in establishing subscription libraries and volunteer fire departments, one clearly sees this trend towards the pragmatic analysis of ideas and their implications.

Second, the pragmatism of creative leaders suggests that these individuals will employ a rather complex set of standards in appraising information and acting on ideas. The cost, likely success and timeframe for exploring and developing ideas can all be expected to loom large in the thoughts of creative leaders. Not only will creative leaders take these pragmatic considerations into account, they will ask another, crucial, question. What is the readiness of an idea for exploitation both technically and by the social system? This focus on the analysis of readiness, of course, implies that timing will represent a significant consideration in the thoughts of creative leaders.

Third, these observations about pragmatism and timing are noteworthy, in part, because they point to an important conclusion with regard to expertise. The leaders of creative efforts will need two forms of expertise: (1) expertise with regard to the technology, and (2) expertise with regard to the social system. When considered in light of the fact that leaders must vis-à-vis missions be capable of integrating these two forms of expertise, these demands suggest that creative leadership will emerge relatively slowly. And, it can be expected to emerge rather late in a person's career as a result of the focus of early development of technical expertise.

Analysis versus action

The demands made by the need for creative leaders to synthesize two distinct forms of information are complicated by another factor unique to the thinking of creative leaders. Creative leaders will typically lack all of the information needed to both generate an idea, a mission, and develop viable products flowing from this mission. This point is of some importance because it suggests that the thinking of creative leaders will evidence a distinct action-oriented bias in their thinking. This action-oriented bias arises from the need to gather information both about the social system and the technology under consideration. In fact, often one can expect creative leaders to pursue experiments with regard to both the social system and the technology simply as a way of acquiring this information (Mumford *et al.* in press). In other words, creative leaders' thinking will be based on trial experiments intended to clarify missions and the social implications of new ideas. In fact, these experiments, or trials, provide creative leaders with the case-based knowledge needed to guide much of their thinking.

This bias towards real-world acquisition of experience, however, cannot override the need for analysis of the information gathered through experiments or trials. Leaders must not only understand the social system and the idea, they must also be capable of envisioning the consequences, both for the social system and the field, of pursuing an idea. More centrally, they must be able to see how an idea might contribute to, support or extend the mission being pursued. This observation, of course, points to the need for analysis, ongoing analysis, on the part of creative leaders. In fact, one might expect that among creative leaders the planning of 'experiments' and the analysis of the 'results' of these experiments vis-à-vis the social system and mission being pursued is a key strategy used to guide creative thought.

The synthesis of action and analysis on the part of creative leaders will prove critical in allowing them to address another key role demand. Ultimately, effective leaders, including creative leaders, must be able to respond to crises. In the case of leaders of creative efforts, this response requires sense-making with respect to the sources of this crisis – either technical or social sources. Leaders' sense-making activities, however, ultimately depend on the analysis, a thoughtful analysis, of the causes of a crisis. Thus the thinking of creative leaders, like leaders in general, must integrate both action and analysis vis-à-vis the social system and the technical issues at hand. Creative leaders, however, will pursue and learn from these crises with respect to the mission and technology at hand.

Balance

The need for creative leaders to work with both action and analysis and to work with two streams of expertise, system and technical expertise, has a final noteworthy implication. The leaders of creative efforts must be able to balance multiple demands and multiple sources of information. One aspect of this balance pertains to decision making on the part of creative leaders. Creative leaders must be able to weigh both systems and technical considerations. Thus they cannot pursue technical ideas with the single mindedness characteristic of creative people in general. Moreover, in formulating their missions, and selecting ideas worth pursuing, they must consider the capabilities and limitations of the social system in which they are operating.

The ability of creative leaders to balance these concerns has a final implication that should be noted. Creative leaders are passionate about their mission, ideas relevant to this mission, and the contribution of this mission to the social system. By the same token, they must be willing to forego the pursuit of even viable ideas that are unworkable within the social system. Contrawise, they must, at times, be willing to initiate efforts that, although illegitimate within the extant social system, will push this system in a new direction needed to adapt to technological advances (Eisenhardt and Tabrizi 1995). The need for balancing these competing concerns implies that the leaders of creative efforts will display a peculiarly controlled form of passion about ideas involving a pragmatic assessment of these ideas with regard to the mission they have decided to pursue. In fact, it is this balance that allows creative leaders to provide the kind of compensatory feedback integral to their creative thought and the success of the creative enterprise.

Conclusions

In this effort we have examined the cognition of those individuals who lead creative efforts. Perhaps the most clear-cut conclusion that can be drawn in this regard is that leaders are not simply a passive entity providing support for the creative activities of others. Instead, what appears to be the case is that creative leaders must think, and think creatively, about both the creative work being done and the system in which this work is occurring. Thus, the thinking of leaders is both system focused and technically focused. More specifically, leaders' thoughts about creative work involve three key externally focused processing activities: (1) scanning, (2) forecasting, and (3) mission definition. With definition of a mission, leaders' thinking can turn to the creative work being done. Three key processing activities relevant to the creative work being pursued were identified: (4) evaluation of ideas, (5) planning, and (6) crisis management. Figure 23.1 illustrates how these processes operate together in leaders' creative thought.

Although it seems possible to identify the cognitive processes underlying leaders' creative thought, it should be recognized that each of these processes, in its own right, is a complex phenomenon. Moreover, leaders must be capable of integrating external, social system knowledge, with internal, technical knowledge. This integration, moreover, must occur in a balanced pragmatic fashion that seeks to resolve ambiguities in available information. This relatively straightforward observation has an important, although often overlooked, implication. The thought of those who lead creative efforts may be as complicated, and perhaps more complicated, as those who are pursuing the creative work.

This observation is of some importance because it suggests that more attention, far more attention, needs to be given to how the leaders of creative efforts think. Not only do we need more research on the thinking of creative leaders, given the complexity of leaders' creative thought, we need studies examining interventions that will serve to develop this form of complex multi-faceted cognition. Hopefully, the present effort by delineating the key processes involved in creative thought on the part of leaders will lay a groundwork for future work along these lines.

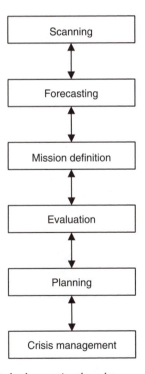

Figure 23.1 Key processes involved in leader creative thought

Acknowledgments

We would like to thank Sam Hunter, Katrina Bedell-Avers, Tamara Friedrich, Alison Antes and Jay Caughron for their contributions to the present effort. Correspondence concerning this chapter should be addressed to Dr Michael D. Mumford, Department of Psychology, the University of Oklahoma, Norman, Oklahoma 73019 or mmumford@ou.edu.

References

Amabile, T. M., Schatzel, E. A., Moneta, G. B., and Kramer, S. J. (2004). Leader behaviors and the work environment for creativity: Perceived leader support. *Leadership Quarterly, 15*, 5–32.

Barnowe, J. T. (1975). Leadership and performance outcomes in research organizations: The supervisor of scientists as a source of assistance. *Organizational Behavior and Human Performance, 14*, 264–280.

Basadur, M., Runco, M. A. and Vega, L. A. (2000). Understanding how creative thinking skills, attitudes and behaviors work together: A causal process model. *Journal of Creative Behavior, 34*, 77–100.

Cohen, W. M. and Levinthal, D. A. (1990). Absorptive capacity: A new perspective on learning and innovation. *Administrative Science Quarterly, 35*, 128–152.

Connelly, M. S., Gilbert, J. A., Zaccaro, S. J., Threlfall, K. V., Marks, M. A. and Mumford, M. D. (2000). Exploring the relationship of leadership skills and knowledge to leader performance. *Leadership Quarterly, 11*, 65–86.

Csikszentmihalyi, M. (1999). Where are you, Virgil, when we need you? *Psychoanalysis and Contemporary Thought, 22*, 649–663.

Drazin, R., Glynn, M. A. and Kazanjian, R. K. (1999). Multilevel theorizing about creativity in organizations: A sensemaking perspective. *Academy of Management Review, 24*, 286–307.

Eisenhardt, K. M. and Tabrizi, B. N. (1995). Accelerating adaptive processes: product innovation in the global computer industry. *Administrative Science Quarterly, 40*, 84–110.

Hammond, K. J. (1990). Case-based planning: A framework for planning from experience. *Cognitive Science, 14*, 385–443.

Hughes, T.P. (1989). *American genesis: A history of the American genius for invention*. New York: Penguin.

Kickul, J. and Gundry, L. K. (2001). Breaking through boundaries for organizational innovation: New managerial roles and practices in e-commerce firms. *Journal of Management, 27*, 347–361.

Koberg, C.S., Uhlenbruck, N. and Sarason, Y. (1996). Facilitators of organizational innovation: The role of life-cycle stage. *Journal of Business Venturing, 11*, 133–149.

Lonergan, D. C., Scott, G. M. and Mumford, M. D. (2004). Evaluative aspects of creative thought: Effects of appraisal and revision standards. *Creativity Research Journal, 16*, 231–246.

Mumford, M. D. and Van Doorn, J. R. (2001). The leadership of pragmatism: Reconsidering Franklin in the age of charisma. *Leadership Quarterly, 12*, 279–309.

Mumford, M. D., Bedell, K. E. and Hunter, S. T. (in press). Planning for innovation: A multi-level perspective. In M. D. Mumford, S. T. Hunter and K. E. Bedell (eds), *Research in Multi-level Issues: Vol. VII*. Oxford: Elsevier.

Mumford, M. D., Connelly, S. and Gaddis, B. (2003). How creative leaders think: Experimental findings and cases. *Leadership Quarterly, 14*, 411–432.

Mumford, M. D., Schultz, R. A. and Osburn, H. K., (2002a). Planning in organizations: Performance as a multi-level phenomenon. In F. J. Yammarino and F. Dansereau (eds), *The many faces of multi-level issues* (pp. 3–65). Oxford: Elsevier.

Mumford, M. D., Scott, G. M., Gaddis, B., and Strange, J. M. (2002b). Leading creative people: Orchestrating expertise and relationships. *Leadership Quarterly, 13*, 705–750.

O'Connor, G. C. (1998). Market learning and radical innovation: A cross case comparison of eight radical innovation projects. *Journal of Product Innovation Management, 15*, 151–166.

Osburn, H. K. and Mumford, M. D. (2006). Creativity and planning: Training interventions to develop creative problem-solving skills. *Creativity Research Journal, 18,* 173–190.

Rodan, S. (2002). Innovation and heterogeneous knowledge in managerial contact networks. *Journal of Knowledge Management, 6,* 152–163.

Scott, G. M., Lonergan, D. C. and Mumford, M. D. (2005). Conceptual combination: Alternative knowledge structures, alternative heuristics. *Creativity Research Journal, 17,* 79–98.

Shamir, B., House, R. J. and Arthur, M. B. (1993). The motivational effects of charismatic leadership: A self-concept based theory. *Organization Science, 4,* 577–594.

Souitaris, V. (2001). External communication determinants of innovation in the context of a newly industrialised country: a comparison of objective and perceptual results from Greece. *Technovation,* 21, 25–34.

Strange, J. M. and Mumford, M. D. (2005). The origins of vision: Effects of reflection, models, and analysis. *Leadership Quarterly, 16,* 121–148.

Tierney, P., Farmer, S. M. and Graen, G. B. (1999). An examination of leadership and employee creativity: The relevance of traits and relationships. *Personnel Psychology, 52,* 591–620.

Walsh, J. P. (1988). Selectivity and selective perception: An investigation of managers' belief structures and information processing. *Academy of Management Journal, 31,* 873–896.

Weber, R. J. and Perkins, D. N. (1992). *Inventive minds: Creativity in technology.* New York: Oxford University Press.

West, M. A., Borrill, C. S., Dawson, J. F., Brodbeck, F., Shapiro, D. A. and Haward, B. (2003). Leadership clarity and team innovation in health care. *Leadership Quarterly, 14,* 393–410.

Xiao, Y., Milgram, P. and Doyle, D. J. (1997). Capturing and modeling planning expertise in anesthesiology: Results of a field study. In C. E. Zsambok and G. Klein (eds), *Naturalistic decision making* (pp. 197–205). Mahwah, NJ: Lawrence Erlbaum.

Yukl, G. (2002). *Leadership in organizations.* Upper Saddle River, NJ: Prentice Hall.

24

Creativity: a systems perspective

Seana Moran

Synopsis: looking at the '4 Ps' interactively

Recent literature reviews (e.g. Runco 2004; Simonton 2000) suggest the creativity research community has settled on studying creativity based on four components, often referred to as the '4 Ps': person, process, press and product. Each component seems to have been favored during different decades of the twentieth century and to have settled into a different subdiscipline within psychology. Mid-century, creativity was considered a personal trait as part of psychometric and personality psychology. The focus was the individual. Concurrently, creativity was considered a problem-solving process by cognitive psychologists. The focus was how a person mentally engaged in the task. Since the 1980s, social or sociocultural psychologists have studied creativity as an aspect of context (press or persuasion), as a function of social interaction and social support. Underpinning all these approaches was creativity as a product: there was some outcome – an idea, artwork, scientific discovery, musical performance – that was assessed to be novel yet appropriate to the social or task situation. In this chapter, I present a systems approach based on role theory for examining the 4 Ps interactively, use literature as an exemplary case, and suggest benefits and challenges that result from such an approach.

The framework: a systems view of creativity

Vygotsky proposed a systems model nearly 100 years ago, examining what he called the 'zone of proximal development' (ZPD). Vygotsky's ideas about learning were embraced by the educational community, but his ideas about creativity – which were less cohesive and more scattered across his many writings – were less well received (see Moran and John-Steiner 2003). Thus, the ZPD concept was understood primarily as the setting where one individual learns from a more expert individual how to accomplish a well-defined cultural task – the individual learns from the culture. The ZPD concept did not catch on as a setting for the culture to learn from the individual, where one individual creates a response or meaning to a task that enlarges the repertoire for what future experts can teach.

Although several more creativity-oriented systems models have been proposed since then, Csikszentmihalyi's (1988) model seems to have become the most widely used. This model comprises an *individual* who fashions a contribution and makes it public to others who compose the *field*, a socially connected group – often organized into institutions – that practices, controls and standardizes tasks related to a particular *domain*, or organized body of knowledge and symbol systems. Csikszentmihalyi's model aggregates Vygotsky's model, positing not a dyad but a field of many people, and not a single symbolic task but a domain of many symbols and tasks. For example, the literary field encompasses the network of social connections among writers, editors, publishers, critics and awards grantors. Individuals assume these various jobs. This network collects, distributes and recognizes works from the literature domain, which is the library of works that have been accepted for publication.

Within this systems view, most individual contributions for a particular job task are fairly similar. Clients count on accountants to behave like other accountants; the same goes for realtors, receptionists and garbage collectors. Some individuals exhibit personal style or other variation – one realtor may have more 'flair' – and the extent of this variation depends on how important the work is to society, how strongly the field can control access to and use of the domain, and how wilful the individual is.

Sometimes an individual's contribution varies significantly from the standard or norm for the outcomes expected in a particular job and field. When the individual's contribution is novel, field members aggregately decide whether the contribution is an error or is creative (see Stacey 1996). If it is decided an error, the contribution is forgotten or marginalized. If it is creative, the contribution becomes part of the domain and eventually is taught to the next generation of practitioners.

When a contribution is accepted by the field, its impact or influence can vary. Importantly, creativity evaluations form a continuum. At one end is exact reproduction of a product or idea to preconceived specification (e.g. assembly line manufacturing). This end is usually considered uncreative, even if it is valuable expert performance. At the other end is originality, conceived of as a breaking from tradition to spawn new possibilities leading to cultural progress (e.g. Picasso's cubism or Einstein's relativity). In the middle are various forms, including proficiency, which is the extreme of useful but not novel, and eccentricity, which is the extreme of novel but not useful.

Creativity, then, is a novel yet appropriate outcome of the interaction of individual, field and domain that influences the way others in the field use domain resources. This system corresponds to the 4 Ps: the individual is the person, the field is the press with its social focus, the domain is the process with its cognitive focus, and the outcome is the product. The systems model, however, emphasizes not the Ps as independent elements, but rather their interactions. Creativity cannot be just personal style, variation or potential because it must have some impact on how others think or behave; that is, there is an influence of the individual on the domain (i.e. the influence of the domain on the individual would better be termed 'learning'). Creativity is not just a rebalancing of power within the field because, again, it must change how people think; that is, there is a field–domain interaction. Creativity is not just an individual accomplishment because it requires the considered judgment of knowledgeable others; that is, there is an individual–field interaction.

At least, in theory, that is how the systems model should work. Unfortunately, as with person, process, press and place, the three elements of the systems model – individual, field, and domain – have tended to be studied separately. The individual is the province of psychology, the field of sociology, and the domain of philosophy or criticism. Even in studies that use Csikszentmihalyi's model specifically (e.g. Gardner *et al.* 2001; Seitz 2003), each element is described separately.

How can these dimensions be studied interactively? That is, what lens might support scholars to focus not on the elements themselves but on the dynamics among elements?

The arena: the system functions within a role

One way may be to focus on the concept of the role. A role comprises how a person behaves in predictable ways depending on what she or he knows or believes and where she or he is situated socially in terms of identity and power relative to others (Biddle 1986). A role might be thought of as 'getting dressed': the individual's repertoire of personality traits and skills slips on the intellectual and political demands of a particular position within a social network.

The role is a microcosm of the individual–domain–field system. A role contains two dimensions – the social and the symbolic (e.g. Passy and Giugni 2000). The social dimension involves the relationship of the person-in-position to other persons-in-positions, groups and organizations through power, status and network contacts. The field governs the social dimension. The symbolic dimension involves the knowledge and beliefs the person must learn and utilize to complete the role's task demands. The domain governs the symbolic dimension.

The role also contributes to the creation and perpetuation of fields and domains. People make sense of their own and others' role performances and products, and make decisions about good and bad, acceptable and unacceptable, boring and interesting. These individual decisions can create conflicts or tension among roles but also can lead to aggregate norms as the many people in or related to a role stabilize their relationships, skill sets and preferences. This stabilization can lead to the institutionalization of social relations (i.e. a field) and of task constraints (i.e. a domain).

Many psychological studies use role theory. Some researchers assume person and demands are stable and try to match them (Holland 1996), whereas others study the adjustment dynamic between person and demands (Dawis and Lofquist 1984). Most prior studies tend to assume and to promote the notion of 'fit': the ideal is when persons and demands are in alignment (e.g. Gardner et al. 2001; Roberts and Robins 2004). This combined belief/goal has tended to limit the use of role theory to studying relatively standardized job positions within institutionalized networks that stabilize social interaction. That is, the value of cultural and social stability precedes the value of cultural progress.

As a result, creativity tends to be conceptualized as an aberration from standard performance in a well-specified role or as an aberrant type of role. For example, creativity is a special type of performance as a businessperson – usually in terms of entrepreneurial behaviour. Or creativity is standard performance for special roles that are 'set aside' by society to be particularly creative – such as an artist or musician. Note, however, that creativity – especially the 'big-C' genius type – also can result when a person in a 'creative' role engages in aberrant performance, even for the special role, which is accepted by the field. For example, Picasso was an artist, but he also created art that was far from the standard for his time. This aberration made him one of the most celebrated 'creative' artists of the twentieth century.

The role – where a person comes into contact with field and domain demands – is where creativity has the possibility or impossibility of occuring. Different ways in which an individual takes on a role can result in different effects or work products. Each individual who takes on a role – say, the writer role – brings to it a different set of skills, interests and styles. The individual also interprets the role a little differently than another writer may – perceiving or understanding the demands more or less specifically, prioritizing them along different criteria, or aiming them toward different outcome possibilities. As these writers engage in the role's tasks and interact with others in the field, such as editors and readers, they continue to perceive, understand, interpret and prioritize. Particular configurations of these interactions lead either to conventionalized work or creative work.

Conventionalized work in a domain at a given historical time includes the knowledge, ideas or know-how validated by current field members' decisions regarding relevance and usefulness. It is socially shared, habitual thought and action – 'common knowledge'. Such an alignment of the field/social and domain/symbolic equates with standardized, 'acceptable' work. The field, over time, has worked out the 'right way' to accomplish the tasks associated with a role so that people who assume that role are likely to produce nearly identical performances. This aligned state correlates with cultural stability. In literature, writers and editors know what they are expected to do, and readers know what they will receive upon purchase of most books. This aligned state is concurrently approached through socialization by the field and learning of the domain, based on how the role is currently agreed upon by field members.

There also is work produced in a domain that does not hold the field's approval at a particular historical time. In these instances, the field's and the domain's influences on the role do not coincide strongly. Confusion can arise as to the value of a particular writer's work or a person's performance in the role. It is not immediately apparent whether a particular novel or poem is 'good', or appropriate to be sanctioned by the field as worthy literature.

If the work is really original, field members may not have criteria for evaluating it. It takes time for field members to determine value. Bourdieu (1993) argues that people who produce cultural products, such as written works in the literary field, must not only create the product but also the value of that product. As field members grapple with this confusion, they come to judge a new work as either 'error' and dismiss it, and the current field–domain alignment remains intact; or they judge it as 'creative' and allow it to become a leading aspect of the domain transformed. This judgment can transform the field-domain into a new alignment by not only expanding the canon of literature but also by changing the power dynamics of the literary field. It can make some practitioners who adopt the change more influential and those who had invested in past ways less influential. This misaligned–then–realigned state – a dynamic concept in opposition to the static 'fit' concept – is where creativity is found. (See Rubenson and Runco 1992; Sternberg and Lubart 1995, for related 'psychoeconomic' models.)

The 'shadow': lower visibility of the symbolic dimension

Perhaps part of the difficulty in both studying and fostering creative work is that the social and the symbolic dimensions of a role are often not clearly distinguished. Foucault's (1980) power/knowledge arguments, as well as Sawyer's (1995) studies of improvisation, show how the social and the symbolic interweave so closely as to be seen as singular. For Foucault, power involves disciplining individuals' behaviour to conform to norms or standards; by using this force, those in power establish what knowledge is true. Power (of the field) and knowledge (from the domain) are so closely intertwined they are indistinguishable; might makes right. Sawyer's careful analysis of an improv theatre troupe exposes how each actor's utterance both defines the scene and controls what other actors can say or do. The social interaction of the actors defines and controls what the words mean, and what the words mean defines and controls how the actors interact. Again, the social and the symbolic become indistinguishable.

This failure to distinguish the social and the symbolic, or power and knowledge, dimensions of a role may stem from several sources. First, many leaders and researchers stop short of recognizing the symbolic dimension – the domain elements – as entities that exist in and of themselves. Scholars recognize that a person can set a goal or do a task. But they tend not to recognize that aspects of that task can serve as supports for the person's development (Bruner 1962), or objects in which the person can invest resources (e.g. Moran 2006), or entities that continue to develop after the creator has finished with them as others adopt or appropriate the idea and it becomes less idiosyncratic and more universal (Feldman 1994).

It is not common parlance to say that a writer commits to the sonnet form or that the sonnet form sometimes drives the writing. Bruner (1962) describes this support as 'freedom to be dominated by the object – you begin to write a poem. . . . Before long it, the poem, begins to develop metrical, stanzaic, symbolical requirements. You, as the writer of the poem, are serving it – it seems . . .' (p. 214). However, some writers *do* talk about their poetic forms as entities that are just as real and living as their siblings or friends (e.g. Taylor *et al.* 2002–2003). Furthermore, there is some developmental evidence that eminent adult creators established this 'personal' connection with the symbolic domain at an early age (Root-Bernstein 2006).

Second, the domain-controlled symbolic dimension is contained within individuals' minds, so it is less visible than the field-controlled social dimension. As a result, the individual–domain relationship is not conceived of as a relationship; it is conceived of as a behaviour and folded into individual traits. For example, intrinsic motivation, which could be seen as a strong relationship between an individual and the symbolic dimension, is recognized as different from extrinsic motivation, but is usually described as a trait of the person rather than an interaction (e.g. Amabile 1996). A few researchers who study 'distributed cognition' have addressed the individual's relationship with the symbolic dimension of the role while also recognizing the social dimension (e.g. Salomon 1993).

Third, it is difficult to 'see' or 'hear' the symbolic except through social interaction. Vygotsky (1962) and many others focused on language; it is a symbol system that is accessible to study via conversations. Anthropologists addressed symbols through social events like rituals and ceremonies (see discussion in Turner 1983). The symbolic dimension is especially difficult to see once the role has been conventionalized, automated and habitualized, so that it is no longer thought about by performers – as if the individual can no longer feel the clothes on his or her shoulders. Still, Lakoff (1986) put the symbolic dimension center stage in his discussion of how metaphor is not a special type of language but underpins thought in general – including conventionalized thought and clichés.

Despite these difficulties, this notion of the symbolic dimension may turn out to be key in understanding creativity. As Vygotsky explained, it is the fuzzy 'sense' – not the socially agreed-upon 'meaning' – that brings to cultural light new possibilities (see Moran and John-Steiner 2003). Lakoff (1986) further suggests it is this fuzzy area – what he talks about as metaphor – that underpins all understanding, not just the idiosyncratic or the poetic. Stacey (1996) focuses on the richer symbolic 'shadow' system behind the institutionalized, standardized ways of an organization as the crux of organizational creativity.

An example: commitment and creativity

I recently completed a study in which this social/symbolic distinction came to the fore. I examined how different patterns of commitment among writers related to how creative the literary field assessed their novels or poetry to be (Moran 2006). Commitment is a binding of person and role based on what the individual invests in a role and toward what aspects of a role she or he invests in. Work commitment researchers primarily have addressed social or field-focused commitment targets, such as the organization, occupation, work team or union. Recently, Meyer and Herscovitch (2001) put forth two categories of commitment: social foci and goals. These categories parallel the social and symbolic dimensions of the role and show a growing awareness of the symbolic 'shadow', but still conceive the symbolic dimension as an individual property of a goal.

I analyzed interviews with 36 writers whom various literary field members (e.g. awards committees, critics, professors) categorized as 'genre conforming' writers who stayed within conventional prescriptions for acceptable literature, 'experimental' writers who attempted novelty but whose contributions have not been fully accepted, and 'domain transforming' writers who altered the literary canon. My analysis revealed that commitment functioned in qualitatively different ways for these three statuses. The emphasis and relative importance of the two role dimensions in relation to the individual vary: for genre conformers, the social role dimension dominates the commitment; for experimentalists, the individual self dominates and the role is minimized; and for domain transformers, the symbolic role dimension dominates.

Genre conformers tend to invest in what powerful others in the literary field think they should invest in. They attend schools and workshops to learn the proper techniques, hone their craft, gain confidence through feedback from others, entice others to help them as much as possible so they can live up to the expectations set by teachers, editors, critics and others in power. Often they know these expectations and standards in advance. The payoff for their investment is higher standing within the literary community.

Experimentalists tend to invest in themselves by expressing that self through words. They barely engage with the environmental demands aspect of the role at all. They chafe at how authorities reinforce 'one right way', which experimentalists feel preempts exploration of other options. They resist or defy consolidation of power in the field or 'common knowledge' in the domain by providing alternative interpretations. Because others central to the literary community often are antagonistic to their deviant perspectives, experimentalists may receive little support from the literary field. Commitment – their own investments – must sustain their efforts to gain reader allies, courage and control. The payoff for their investment is self-perceived authenticity.

Domain transformers tend to invest in language itself, the symbolic medium in which they work. They fall in love with rhythm, grammar, form, meaning, characters or imagery. They develop a passion for language. Rather than subscribing to or fighting against members and mores of the literary field, they cultivate support from language itself. The payoff for their investment is making their ideas, stories and symbols understandable and moving to readers. This passion to share the possibilities of language can take on tones of a moral crusade.

Thus, I found that commitment is important when there is fit *and* misfit between the individual and the social and symbolic dimensions of the role. When there is a strong resonance between the person and the social dimension of the role, commitment functions to maintain that resonance through consistency of the person's performance and considerable reinforcing support from the field. Such is the state of the genre conformers in my writer sample.

When there is a misfit between the person and the social dimension of the role but only a moderate connection between the person and the symbolic dimension of the role, commitment functions as a protective device from the field's perceived obstacles and as a 'backup battery' to provide resources that are not forthcoming as field supports. Such is the state of the experimentalists in my writer sample.

When there is a strong resonance between the person and the symbolic dimension of the role regardless of the fit with the social dimension of the role, commitment functions to develop that resonance through persistence of the person's effort until the domain's possibilities provide some cognitive scaffolding for the work and buy time to reach readers. Such is the state of the domain transformers in my writer sample.

Other empirical findings corroborate these ideas. For example, Oldham and Cummings (1996) found that the combination of individual character plus high job complexity plus low supervisory control – that is, strong individual–symbolic/domain relationship and weak individual–social/field relationship – resulted in the most creative outcomes. Similarly, Perry-Smith (2006) found that weak social ties and, in certain cases, marginality (i.e. weak individual–field relationships) facilitate creativity. As with my study, these other studies show that the person must interact with or be part of the field, but not overpowered or confined by the field's expectations, to be able to bring forth latent aspects of the domain to share with others.

The benefits: creativity is part of the natural rhythm of fields and domains evolving

I have advocated a shift from thinking about creativity as a particular 'thing' to thinking about it as a particular configuration of relationships among the individual and the social and symbolic dimensions of the role, as governed by the field and domain. I think practitioners (e.g. educators, leaders and workers) already incorporate both dimensions – even if not consciously or intentionally. Teachers seem intuitively to balance or integrate building a relationship with a student as a person as well as midwifing a relationship between the student's mind and the content matter. Teachers who seem particularly adept at fostering creativity (e.g. Moran and Ritchhart 2003) have a knack for keeping the social support from interfering with symbolic exploration. Creative collaborators also seem to accomplish this same goal (e.g. Moran and John-Steiner 2004).

Ideological implications that this role-based systems approach brings to light include: (1) why much of the time people do not consider the domain because they limit themselves to field-approved knowledge and do not entertain areas of the domain outside field control; (2) why morality and creativity are often in contention when morality is equated with socially agreed-upon norms rather than the interplay of social and symbolic culture (see discussion in Runco and Nemiro 2003); (3) why creativity stirs up anxiety at both the individual and field levels because it encompasses change that alters intellectual conceptions as well as social power dynamics (Jaques 1990).

This role view makes creativity more of an evolutionary rather than a revolutionary phenomenon. It is a natural part of cultural progress, a certain configuration of the person and the two dimensions of the role that changes the landscape of the domain, and often of the field as well. Anyone in any job is interacting daily with the field and domain through the social and symbolic dimensions of the role. This approach suggests that a strong relationship between individual and symbolic/domain is more likely to lead to more creative outcomes, whereas a strong relationship between individual and social/field leads to more conventional outcomes.

Several empirical implications also emerge from this role-based systems approach. It opens research opportunities to move beyond categorizing persons, processes, contexts or products as more or less creative. For example, how does the way a person learns a task (individual–domain interaction) support or restrict what positions she or he can take on (individual–field interaction)? Or, vice versa, how does the position a person assumes (individual–field interaction) support or constrain the way she or he makes use of or structures domain symbols and knowledge (individual–domain interaction)? Or how aligned or misaligned are the expectations of the field with the standards of the domain at a particular historical point in time (field–domain interaction) to allow or inhibit a person from even putting forth a novel contribution (individual–domain interaction)? Many further questions can be developed.

Additional ideological and empirical work could impact future practice by providing tools that help people less intuitively attuned to the symbolic dimension to see it as a separate entity – to move beyond what the field authorities have told them is the 'right way'. Practical implications of this approach address career development, leadership and educational issues. Any job or work role could be decomposed along its social and symbolic dimensions. The social side would comprise the job's connections to other jobs or positions, its status within an institution, the power it wields and its centrality to the institution and field. The symbolic side would comprise the knowledge and skill requirements to do the job, the symbol systems or notations job tasks use, and the thinking or problem-solving demands.

To some degree, Holland's (1996) RIASEC model does this job decomposition. However, the model ends up categorizing the whole job or whole person as more or less creative instead of recognizing the fluidity of creative possibility in nearly any job. Instead of categorizing only some jobs (e.g. artist, scientist) as creative, such decomposition analyses could be used to assess ways a person could be creative within any job. Even bookkeepers or car assembly line workers have some leeway because the domains of accountancy and automobile manufacturing are open ended and flexible.

By better understanding how a role could result in standardized or creative outcomes, leaders and educators could help foster or control (depending on their goals and purposes) the likelihood of such creativity. Although, in this volume, the assumption is that creativity is valuable (an attitude I share), creativity is not necessarily appropriate at all times in all situations. For example, I would prefer my pilot not be creative while I'm 30,000 feet up except under extraordinary circumstances, and even then only as a last resort.

The challenge: methodology

Creativity scholars need to tackle methodological issues. A role-based systems approach demands more of the data than correlational approaches. Measurements must be taken of the *interactions* of the three system components – the individual, the field and the domain – and statistical interactions are not the same as system interactions. This requirement creates the need for an interactional model in which the measurements are not of the individual but of the interaction of the individual with the social role dimension and the individual with the symbolic role dimension. Furthermore, individual, field and domain are not independent; they compose each other. Individuals hold positions within the social network of the field. Domain knowledge is parsed among individuals' minds. This lack of independence puts additional demands on mathematical methods and multilevel modelling techniques. Furthermore, these interactions are not necessarily stable. As discussed, creativity is a form of temporary destabilization then restabilization of the system.

Existing methodologies might be useful, including dynamic modelling. This approach is growing, but is limited by the need for precise measurement, which is difficult to come by with creative phenomena. Game theory shows promise, but the 'creativity game' would be complex with many players, uncertainty, asymmetric information and unknown outcomes. Simonton's sophisticated statistical work (e.g. 1999) seems highly promising as a basis for further methodological development. He shows how newer time-series, structural-equation, nonlinear and latent-variable analytic tools better meet the challenges of studying 'significant samples', or people whose work would be outliers in comparison to the norm for a field (such as creators). For example, he produced a parsimonious growth model of differences in creative productivity across career trajectories with only six variables: two individual starting conditions of creative potential and age at career onset, two process rates of ideation and elaboration, and an 'equal-odds rule' that captures how quantity and quality of output are related (Simonton 1997).

Conclusion: there's more to a role than meets the eye

The Vygotskian microcosm view and the Csikszentmihalyian aggregate view support an examination of how creativity's 4 Ps interact with the social and symbolic dimensions of a role. To achieve a novel yet appropriate outcome (product), an individual (person) must interact with both the social dimension (press) and the symbolic dimension (process) of a work role. This social–symbolic distinction often is missed – one is reduced to the other – and confusion results. The terms 'field' and 'domain' are occasionally used interchangeably even though field addresses the social or power-oriented aspects of an interaction, and domain encompasses the task, symbolic or knowledge-oriented aspects of an interaction.

Still, the distinction is approached in several lines of research. Career development scholars draw on it when they make distinctions between jobs and individuals who are task oriented (domain/symbolic focused) versus people oriented (field/social focused). Similarly, motivational scholars draw on the distinction when they separate intrinsic motivation (from interacting with the domain through a task) from extrinsic motivation (which comes from the field and social interaction).

The distinction is important because it helps scholars and educators better pinpoint whether creativity is better served by influencing a person's learning and interaction with the domain or a person's socialization, interpersonal support and interaction with the field.

References

Amabile, T. *Creativity in context*, Boulder, CO: Westview Press 1996.

Biddle, B. J. Recent developments in role theory, *Annual Review of Sociology*, 12 1986, 67–92.

Bourdieu, P. *The field of cultural production*, New York: Columbia University Press 1993.

Bruner, J. S. *On knowing: Essays for the left hand*, New York: Cambridge University Press 1962.

Csikszentmihalyi, M. *The nature of creativity*, New York: Cambridge University Press 1988, pp. 325–339.

Dawis, R. V. and Lofquist, L. H. *The psychological theory of work adjustment*, Minneapolis: University of Minnesota Press 1984.

Feldman, D. H. *Beyond the universals of cognitive development*, 2nd edition, Norwood, NJ: Ablex 1994.

Foucault, M. *Power/knowledge: Selected interviews and other writings 1972–1977*, New York: Pantheon Books 1980.

Gardner, H. Csikszentmihalyi, M. and Damon, W. *Good work: When excellence and ethics meet*, New York: Basic Books 2001.

Holland, J. E. Exploring careers with a typology: What we have learned and some new directions, *American Psychologist*, 51 1996, 397–406.

Jaques, E. *Creativity and work*, Madison, WI: International Universities Press 1990.

Lakoff, G. A figure of thought, *Metaphor and Symbolic Activity*, 1 1986, 215–225.

Meyer, J. P. and Herscovitch, L. Commitment in the workplace: Toward a general model, *Human Resource Management Review*, 11 2001, 299–326.

Moran, S. Commitment and creativity, unpublished doctoral dissertation, Harvard Graduate School of Education 2006.

Moran, S. and John-Steiner, V. *Creativity and development*, New York: Oxford University Press 2003, pp. 61–90.

Moran, S. and John-Steiner, V. *Collaborative creativity: Contemporary perspectives*, London: Free Association Books 2004, pp. 11–25.

Moran, S. and Ritchhart, R. (eds) *Creative classrooms, vol. 4*, Burbank, CA: Disney Learning Partnership 2003.

Oldham, G. R. and Cummings, A. Employee creativity: Personal and contextual factors at work, *Academy of Management Journal*, 39 1996, 607–634.

Passy, F. and Giugni, M. Life-spheres, networks, and sustained participation in social movements: A phenomenological approach to political commitment, *Sociological Forum*, 15 2000, 117–144.

Perry-Smith, J. E. Social yet creative: The role of social relationships in facilitating individual creativity, *Academy of Management Journal*, 49 2006, 85–101.

Roberts, B. W. and Robins, R. W. Person-environment fit and its implications for personality development: A longitudinal study, *Journal of Personality*, 72 2004, 89–110.

Root-Bernstein, M. Imaginary worldplay in childhood and maturity and its impact on adult creativity, *Creativity Research Journal*, 18 2006, 405–425.

Rubenson, D. L. and Runco, M. A. The psychoeconomic approach to creativity, *New Ideas in Psychology*, 10 1992, 131–147.

Runco, M. A. Creativity, *Annual Review of Psychology*, 55 2004, 657–687.

Runco, M. A. and Nemiro, J. Creativity in the moral domain: Integration and implications, *Creativity Research Journal*, 15 2003, 91–105.

Salomon G. (ed.), *Distributed cognitions: Psychological and educational considerations*, New York: Cambridge University Press 1993.

Sawyer, R. K. Creativity as mediated action: A comparison of improvisational performance and product creativity, *Mind, Culture, and Activity*, 2 1995, 172–191.

Seitz, J. A. The political economy of creativity, *Creativity Research Journal*, 15 2003, 385–392.

Simonton, D. K. Creative productivity: A predictive and explanatory model of career trajectories and landmarks, *Psychological Review*, 104 1997, 66–89.

Simonton, D. K. Significant samples: The psychological study of eminent individuals, *Psychological Methods*, 4 1999, 425–451.

Simonton, D. K. Creativity: Cognitive, personal, developmental, and social aspects, *American Psychologist*, 55 2000, 151–158.

Stacey, R. D. *Complexity and creativity in organizations*, San Francisco, CA: Berrett-Koehler 1996.

Sternberg, R. J. and Lubart, T. I. *Defying the crowd: Cultivating creativity in a culture of conformity*, New York: Free Press 1995.

Taylor, M., Hodges, S. D. and Kohanyi, A. The illusion of independent agency: Do adult fiction writers experience their characters as having minds of their own?, *Imagination, Cognition and Personality*, 22 2002–2003, 361–380.

Turner, V. Body, brain, and culture, *Zygon*, 18 1983, 221–245.

Vygotsky, L. S. *Thought and language*, Cambridge, MA: MIT Press 1962.

25

Change-oriented leadership behaviour: a consequence of post-bureauratic organisations?

Jouko Arvonen

The purpose of this chapter is to describe a model of leadership that includes a change dimension as leadership behaviour. The new three-factor model adds the change-oriented leadership style to the earlier two (production- and employee-oriented) leadership styles. The emergence of a change-oriented style is suggested as being a consequence of greater turbulence and uncertainties in organisations and their environments in the late twentieth century, giving rise to post-bureaucratic structures.

The model was explored and verified in a range of studies within which 6434 subordinates in 13 countries rated the leadership styles of their immediate managers' behaviour. There were both broad samples and single-company samples. Exploratory and confirmatory factor analyses consistently demonstrated the three dimensions of change-, production- and employee-oriented leadership behaviours. We have labelled this the Cpe model. The predicted three-factor pattern has been found in Nordic countries and in the USA, across different company samples and professional domains.

The model suggests that change-oriented behaviour will be important in a wide range of contemporary situations. To be a successful change-oriented manager, however, a leader is likely to combine all three behaviour patterns in practice.

Change oriented leadership – a dimension?

The primary research issue addressed by this work is the extent to which it is justified to include a dimension of change orientation (including creativity) in a theory of leadership behaviour. The formal research questions are stated as follows:

1 Is there a leadership behaviour that can be defined and measured as change- and development-oriented observable behaviour?
2 Is change-oriented behaviour an additional dimension to the prevailing and traditional two-factor model?
3 To what extent has such a model validity across different populations comprising different kinds of culture, organisation, divisions, and so on?

By leadership in this chapter we refer to persons in leadership roles in formal organisations. Leadership is not studied in natural or spontaneous groups, nor in project teams. Furthermore, the focus of the study is leader (manager) behaviour, not the influence process between leader and others.

Leadership is examined in terms of how it is rated (observed) by subordinates. According to this perspective, the chosen metric deals with perceptions reported regarding the immediate or direct manager.

This methodological decision can be challenged, although it has been widely accepted in leadership studies (Bass 1985; Hersey and Blanchard 1982). The most important argument for the choice of the subordinate perspective is that the subjective interpretations of subordinates are psychological determinants of their potential and actual behaviour and thus relevant for organisational outcomes. We consider subordinates as important actors in order to promote effectiveness in organisations. The approach has shortcomings from a methodological point of view, which will be addressed below.

The emergence of the change dimension

Organisations have become more post-bureaucratic, i.e. more decentralised and often in the flat matrix form, with project teams working across organisational functions (Hackman and Wageman 1995; Shamir 1999). In this context of a changing and uncertain world, leadership issues have received more attention and assumed greater importance.

Leadership has demonstrated an important role in: influencing and transforming employees' needs and attitudes (Bass 1985; Burns 1978; Zaleznik 1977 1989); increasing a company's competitive advantage (Nyström 1990; Pascale 1990; Peters and Waterman 1982); implementing organisational change at the strategical level (Tichy 1983); creating high performance working groups (Lawler 1992); focusing on leaders as persons and increasing their informal power (Bennis and Nanus 1985; Conger and Kanungo 1988, 1998; House and Shamir 1993); communicating goals as visions (Bennis 1989, 1992; Kotter 1985, 1990; Tichy and Devanna 1990); creating informal organisational and corporate values (Selznick 1957); restructuring and vitalising companies (Iacocca and Novak 1985); and even in explaining national success (Pascale and Athos 1982).

Definitions of leadership

In formal organisations, leadership is connected with formal positions, roles and authority in order to reach the goal of the group and organisation in an effective way. Hemphill and Coons (cited in Yukl 1994: 2) define leadership as, 'the behaviour of an individual when [he or she] is directing the activities of a group toward a shared goal'. A similar definition is proposed by Hersey and Blanchard (1982: 3), who argue that leadership involves: 'working with and through individuals and groups to accomplish organisational goals'. Roethlisberger and Dickson (1939: 569), based on the experiences from the famous study at the Hawthorne plant, suggest that: 'the function of the management can be described as that of maintaining the social system in a state of equilibrium such that the purpose of the enterprise is realised'.

These definitions include the assumption that the formal authority does not merely contribute to the influence process in order to make others behave according to the leader's will or to accomplish the goal of the group. Hersey and Blanchard (1982) define power as *the potential for influence*. They write: 'Thus power is a resource, which may or may not be used. Therefore, leadership is simply any attempt to influence, while power is well described as leaders' influence potential' (p. 177).

In the leadership literature, the distinction is often made between managers (i.e. persons in formal positions to run the business according to routines), and leaders (i.e. those persons who possess an informal power): '[Leadership] is the persuasion of individuals and innovativeness in ideas and decision making that differentiates leadership from sheer possession of power' (Hall 1977: 240). Management and leadership may in this sense be seen as different organisational processes, more or less suitable in different situations in the organisation. As Yukl (1994: 4) maintained, '. . . managers are oriented toward stability and leaders are oriented toward innovation'.

From a systems theory point of view, Katz and Kahn (1978: 536) define leadership as the following:

> Three basic types of leadership occur in organisational settings: (1) the introduction of structural change, or policy formulation, (2) the interpolation of structure, that is, piecing out the incompleteness of existing formal structure, or improvisation, and (3) the use of structure formally provided to keep the organisation in motion and effective operation, or administration.

They recognise the importance of change and even the need for improvisation.

It is the conceptualization implied in this theoretical analysis that anticipates the possibility of a three-factor leadership model, and provides a rationale for the extra factor.

From such a perspective, twenty-first-century leadership is seen as involved in managing an environment of turbulence, uncertainty and change. Emphasis is often placed on the need to identify some kind of dissatisfaction with the status quo, formulation of a vision for the group to adjustment better to the environment, and the creation of trust and emotional appeal in the leader as a person, who will also be engaged in creation of informal organisations (networks) with a high degree of empowerment and shared values (Conger and Kanungo 1998; Kouzes and Posner 1995).

Theoretical background: the dominant two-factor model of leadership behaviour

These two dimensions of leadership behaviour are labelled differently by different researchers, for instance, as democratic or authoritarian leader behaviour (Lewin 1950); employee- and job-centred supervision (Likert 1961); consideration and initiation of structure (Bass 1960; Fleishman and Harris 1962); concern for people and concern for production (Blake and Mouton 1964, 1985); task-oriented and relationship-oriented behaviour (Hersey and Blanchard 1982); directive and participative leadership (Bass 1990); instrumental, supportive, participative and achievement-oriented leadership (Filley *et al.* 1976); boss- and subordinate-centred leadership (Tannenbaum and Schmidt 1958); control-oriented and involvement-oriented approach (Lawler 1992); and maintenance and performance (Misumi 1989).

It should be noted that items of 'change-orientation' were also included, for instance in different versions of the Ohio questionnaire (SBDQ, LDBQ). These items described management behaviours such as: '[H]e offers new approaches to problems; tries out his new ideas with the group; waits for people under him [or her] to push new ideas before he does.' However, analysis of results did not reveal a factor that could be labelled as 'change-orientation'. Neither have results from other studies concerning related aspects of management activities and practices included the change-oriented daily activities or practices in their scales (House and Rizzo 1972; Mintzberg 1973).

We conclude that the studies occurred in decades in which leaders encountered more stable industrial conditions. The environment of the companies examined, and the organisations themselves, were perceived as stable and organised to maximise the production capacity following prevailing beliefs of attending to organisational structures and showing consideration for human relations. The change dimension or pattern of management behaviour has not emerged nor has it been relevant in stable organisational conditions. According to Burns (1978), management and leadership behaviour under these conditions were characterised by the pattern of 'transactional' behaviour.

More recent research, however, has suggested that change orientation might well be included in a model of leadership (Ekvall et al. 1987). The underlying logic of this change-oriented leadership behaviour dimension is that corporate life shifted dramatically during the 1970s and 1980s. Companies and organisations are now facing an environment involving global competition, more differentiated customer needs, restructuring necessities, and utilising human resources. These demands will require new management abilities concerning development and creativity.

Studies and data

The basis of this chapter derives from results of five empirical studies. In total, 6434 respondents rated their managers, in 13 different countries but mainly from Sweden, Finland and the US. The single-company samples are Swedish. In the first study, the population consisted of 711 respondents in Sweden, Finland and the US. In the second study, the Swedish sample consisted of more than 1000 respondents, mainly in a supermarket chain, but also in other private industrial companies. The US sample was smaller and comprised respondents' ratings of managers from different companies. The third study involved 3857 respondents from 13 different countries. The respondents in this broad sample were managers taking part in general training programmes, and they were asked to rate their immediate manager to whom they report. These respondents came from different organisations; their work backgrounds were very heterogeneous by professional division, organisational level, function, age, sex, education, etc. In the fourth study, the sample consisted of two similar plants in a single company, i.e. a more specific and well-defined sample. The fifth study is also a single-company sample including different functions and levels.

Findings

All five studies included in this chapter support the proposition that change-oriented leadership behaviour may be seen as an additional dimension in a leadership model. The strongest evidence for the model is revealed by factor analyses.

All analyses provide three dimensions of leadership behaviour. The model is labelled as the Cpe model. The five studies consistently demonstrated the relevance of the *change and development* factor in management behaviour. Items based on the factor analyses and used in the measurement of the change dimension in management behaviour in the five studies are summarised in Table 25.1. The results show that the factor loadings are strong and stable across populations.

When the content of the total change factor is analysed according to the included items, it

Table 25.1 Factor analyses of the CPE measures from the five studies

	Study 1	Study 3	Study 2a★	Study 2b★★	Study 5
Change/Development Scale Items					
Offers ideas about new and different ways of doing things	0.74	0.71	0.81	0.78	0.89
Pushes for development / growth	0.74	0.69	0.81	0.67	0.90
Initiates new projects	0.73	0.67	0.81	0.76	0.84
Experiments with new ways of doing things	0.67	0.65	0.73	0.77	0.80
Shares thoughts and plans about the future	0.55	0.56	0.65	0.63	0.47
Mean loadings	0.67	0.66	0.76	0.72	0.78
Reliabilities (Chronbach alpha)	–	0.85	0.87	0.84	0.90
Employee behaviour scale items					
Shows regard for his/her colleagues as individuals	0.75	0.74	0.82	0.83	0.92
Is considerate	0.69	0.62	0.71	0.78	0.85
Is friendly	0.55	0.52	0.54	0.59	0.67
Trusts his/her subordinates	0.53	0.64	0.55	0.36	0.84
Allows his/her subordinates to decide	0.50	0.55	0.54	0.57	0.80
Mean loadings	0.60	0.61	0.63	0.63	0.82
Reliabilities (Chronbach alpha)	–	0.75	0.77	0.84	0.90
Production orientation scale items					
Is very exacting about plans being followed	0.62	0.63	0.73	0.76	0.90
Makes a point of following rules and principles	0.57	0.56	0.47	0.60	0.83
Plans carefully	0.69	0.69	0.72	0.80	0.82
Controls work closely	0.55	0.57	0.61	0.66	0.76
Gives clear instructions	0.62	0.61	0.66	0.76	0.72
Mean loadings	0.61	0.61	64	0.72	0.81
Reliabilities (Chronbach alpha)	–	0.76	0.77	0.76	0.88

★ Study 2a: Swedish sample; ★★Study 2b: US sample.

reveals that the question is broadly defined. Change and development are defined in terms of visionary qualities, creativity, action for implementation and risk-taking:

Visionary qualities

■ shares thoughts and plans about the future★

Creativity

■ offers ideas about new and different ways of doing things★
■ likes to discuss new ideas
■ sees possibilities rather than problems
■ encourages thinking along new lines

Action for implementation

■ pushes for development/growth★
■ initiates new projects★
■ experiments with new ways of doing things★

Risk-taking

- is willing to take risks in making decisions
- makes quick decisions

There are relatively more items indicating creativity than there are items for other factors. In the 'action for implementation', three items are included. 'Risk-taking' is measured by two items emphasising decision making. However, these items were not present in the five-item scale. Finally, there is one item about 'visionary qualities' of leader behaviour. The five-item scale was used to measure the change dimension, and the included items are marked with an asterisk in the list above. The content of the change dimension in the Cpe model has similarities with Bernard Bass' (1985) definition of transformative leadership regarding the 'intellectual stimulation' (provides new ideas, which challenge followers). There are also similarities with the model of Conger and Kanungo (1998) regarding charismatic leadership. Items of creativity (unconventional behaviour), visionary qualities and (personal) risk-taking are included. However, their scales include fewer items on implementing change than does the CPE scale.

The *employee dimension* is also stable across the five populations. This dimension can be compared with the well-known 'consideration' scale used in leadership studies. It is also comparable with the scale of 'individual consideration' in the transformational leadership model of Bass (1985) and the scale of 'sensitivity to members' needs' in the charismatic scale of Conger and Kanungo (1998).

Items in this factor (and on the scale represented by the five items) are quite homogenous, characterising behaviour such as: respect, trust, consideration, delegation, and so on. In Bass' (1985) model of transformational leadership, the behaviour of the manager is defined as more action-oriented in order to activate empowerment and high performance in individuals. Behaviours such as self-sacrificing, role modelling, showing self-confidence, using symbols, and promoting high performance (Bass 1985; Conger and Kanungo 1998; House 1995; Kouzes and Posner 1995) are not included as such in the relation dimension of the CPE model.

The *production dimension* also shows a clear factor pattern across populations. Theoretically this dimension has caused major problems when measured with different scales (SBDQ and LBDQ, for instance; see Schriesheim *et al.* 1976). The first one is more oriented toward autocratic, controlling and punitive behaviour of the leader. The second one includes more items on communication, role clarity and organising. In the Cpe model the production orientation does not include punitive or autocratic management behaviour. However, factor analyses attributed ten items to this dimension and the items with strongest loadings were included in the index measuring production orientation.

A scrutiny of the ten items in the production factor reveals that there are two groups of items in the factor. The items with strongest loadings are attributed to management of details, controlling, planning, giving instructions and making a point of rules. This is not punitive and autocratic behaviour, but formal and controlling. The other group of items describes a manager who provides clarity in relation to goals, roles, performance standards and job requirements. These could perhaps be a separate factor. However, splitting into two sub-factors could not be justified from the results obtained.

The structure dimension is in some way comparable to the transactional behaviour scale in the Bass model and the dimension of maintaining status quo in the scale of charismatic leadership of Conger and Kanungo. Both may be seen as in contrast to transformational and charismatic behaviour.

The dimension of structure in leadership and in organisation theory is problematic, especially when there is a simultaneous need for structure (efficiency) and change. Katz and Kahn made a difference between applying and creating structure by stating that these two aspects need different abilities of management behaviour. They also recognised that the failure to distinguish between the use and creation of structure limits the usefulness of the Ohio scales (Katz and Kahn 1978: 561). The CPE model provides a dimension of change-orientation, and thus the possibility to manage the issue of changing the organisational structure.

A major conclusion from this analysis seems to be that the CPE model includes three independent leadership behaviours (change, production and employee orientation). These dimensions are included also in other theories of leadership. For instance, the change dimension is accounted for also in other models, e.g. outstanding leadership, charismatic leadership and transformational leadership (Bass 1985; Conger and Kanungo 1998; House 1995). Actually, these dimensions describe the change-oriented manager as in the CPE model, i.e. visions, creativity, implementation of change, and so on. However, in these scales there are also items about relation-oriented behaviour, e.g. individual consideration, motivation, trust, and so on. This means that relation and change orientation are blended and considered as one dimension. In the CPE model these behaviours are kept separate theoretically and in measurement, which provides the possibility of considering scales independently of each other.

CPE dimensions and organisational effectiveness

Bivariate and multivariate analyses were conducted to assess the three dimensions within the CPE model on correlations with organisational effectiveness. The bivariate studies were carried out for Studies 1 and 5. A further refinement (for perceived effectiveness of the manager) was introduced in a multivariate analysis of data from Study 3.

The assessment ratings were as follows. Assessments of the proficiency of the manager/leader were obtained from responses to the question 'How good or bad is your manager from the point of view of the organisation and the enterprise?' The two other criteria, also addressed to individual subordinates, were based on ratings of cost and change effectiveness at the level of departments.

Table 25.2 shows significant correlations between all three dimensions in the CPE model and the effectiveness criteria. The competence assessment of the manager seems to be most strongly associated with the behavioural (employee) component. The partial correlation analyses also reveal this pattern. The employee-oriented manager seems to be less associated with proficiency when the respondent's attitude to the manager is held constant. However, the change-oriented manager is most strongly associated with ratings of high proficiency even when attitude is held constant.

The more specific criteria of effectiveness applied in Study 5 also indicate strong and significant correlations between the leadership components of the model and the organisational outcome in terms of change- and cost effectiveness. Only one of the correlations is not significant: the production-oriented manager is not related to change effectiveness. This can be seen as in accord with interpretations of transactional managers as defined by Bass (1985) and status quo managers defined by Conger and Kanungo (1998). However, it is interesting to note that both relations and change behaviour are also regarded as important (accounting for approximately 30 per cent of variance in change effectiveness).

It is of interest to note that cost-effectiveness seems to be related to all three of these behaviours. However, the regression analyses indicate that only relations- and production-oriented

Table 25.2 CPE dimensions and effectiveness assessments

		CPE dimension organisational criteria for effectiveness (employee ratings)		
		Organisational effectiveness: manager	Work group effectiveness: cost	Work group effectiveness: change
Study 1	Change	0.69★★★		
	Production	0.55★★★		
	Employee	0.62★★★		
Study 3	Change	0.59★★★		
	Production	0.43★★★		
	Employee	0.50★★★		
Study 5	Change		0.31★	0.49★★
	Production		0.42★★	0.14 ns
	Employee		0.41★★	0.47★★
R^2 (for CPE)			0.29★★★	0.31★★★

Notes:
★ = p < 0.05, ★★ = p < 0.01, ★★★ = p < 0.001.
Bi-variate analysis on results from Study 1 and Study 5. When adjusted for perceived effectiveness of the manager (multi-variate analysis), the correlations of Study 3 reduced to 0.48, 0.37 and 0.25, but were still all p < 0.001

behaviours contribute significantly and change-oriented behaviour does not have the same relevance for this perceived organisational outcome.

These results are in accordance with theories emphasising the concept of leadership (instead of management, which was the context of the earliest studies). In theories of transformational leadership and of charismatic leadership there are competencies of both change (creativity, risk-taking and trust), and relations (considering, inspiring and empowering). In this sense, the findings reported here are in line with what has been predicted in such work.

However, there are some differences. First, in the CPE model all three behavioural dimensions are defined as independent and can be combined as a set of profiles. Second, all three behavioural dimensions are reported as needed in most organisations. This means that behavioural components associated with both 'leadership' and 'management' have to be included in the model.

However, in situations characterised by a strong need for change, the profile of 'leadership' rather than 'management' is more successful (cf. Bass 1985; Kotter 1990; Yukl 1994).

Conclusions

Leadership research over the last decades has to a large extent been based on the two-factor model of leadership behaviour (Bass 1990; Yukl 1998). However, the context of leadership changed during the 1980s and 1990s. Global competition, changing environment, increasing importance of human resources development, flat organisational structures and flexible production systems put new demands on leadership (Howard 1995). These contextual factors have contributed to a need for adjustment in management roles and behaviour. Management is more frequently labelled as 'leadership', 'charismatic leadership', 'neo-charismatic leadership', 'transformational leadership', 'visionary leadership', 'outstanding leadership' and 'inspirational leadership' (Burns 1978; Conger and Kanungo 1998).

These both external and internal factors in organisations focus on the need for explicit change-oriented management behaviour. The main purpose of this chapter is to develop and empirically test a behaviour-oriented leadership model, including the change dimension. Considering the research problem and the empirical results, the following conclusions seem to be reasonable:

1 There was substantial evidence that the change dimension (including creativity) is relevant in leadership. It adds to the traditional dimensions of employee- and production-orientation. The model was labelled the CPE model. Factor analysis of the items in the change dimension suggested rather broad constructs of change. Behaviours associated with visionary qualities, creativity, action implementation and risk-taking are loaded in the dimension. Thus, measurement of these assumed theoretical dimensions displays high construct validity.

2 The dimensions of the model have a high degree of stability across different kinds of populations. This indicates that the model is of rather general relevance for management behaviour in different countries, in different kinds of companies and branches. Thus the model has substantial generality (external validity) in the Western countries in which it has been tested.

Future research and management development

There are some issues which should be of great concern for future research. As mentioned above, quantitative methods are not adequate alone for studying the quality of leadership. The leadership processes of influence, communication and symbolic behaviour are issues favouring investigation by means of qualitative case studies, for instance by observation (cf. Mintzberg 1973) or intensive interviewing (Bryman et al. 1988).

Yet, there is considerable agreement that situational interactions and adaptations are of relevance. However, quantitative methods and data have limited capacity to identify, and more importantly to interpret, higher-order interactions (cf. Cronbach 1975). Quantitative data can suggest general constructs and models, but cannot tell how variables are interacting in a specific management situation. A significant correlation between behaviour and effect variables in a large sample does not mean that this is valid in an individual case. To understand the individual manager's situation we have to apply other methods, qualitative inquiries, observations and reflexive methods (Alvesson 1996).

Self-report inventories have been accepted as valuable in management training and in providing feedback to managers in order to facilitate self-reflection. Such deductive and inductive methods may also be combined (Van Maanen 1983).

As said above, behavioural science and leadership research has often applied a variance approach in which phenomena are studied by means of isolated dimensions. These analyses say very little about the person, and how the person combines such dimensions in practice. The person approach could also 'decrease' the amount of interaction we dervive from variable research, and allow for more sense of how persons and situations are interacting, and how leadership of a person is developing across time (see Magnusson 1985; Nystedt 1983). The study of interaction between types of situations and leadership profiles should say more about managers' capability to handle different situations (Ropo 1989). This can also be done in quantitative analyses when different levels of analyses are included (cf. den Hartog 1997; Hall and Lord 1995).

There is, one could say, confusion about the different leadership measurement scales. The construct validity of these scales could be empirically tested (see Yukl 1999). There should be approaches where all these scales are included and empirically analysed in order to observe the correspondence between constructs.

Common method and common source problem in measuring behaviour and effects are dominant in leadership research. There should be more research on the effects of these possible biases and measurement using other sources of information (triangulation). Subordinates are in many cases a valid source of data on leadership, but data on effectiveness should be measured from other sources. The picture that subordinates and others have about their managers comprises accumulated perceptions over time. This condition provides a number of problems to locate behaviour in time and to relate it to other variables. This has been insufficiently noticed in the research. Studying critical incident or crisis situations may provide interesting knowledge about leadership in more specic situations when demands might be extraordinary.

The CPE model and scales can be further developed. It seems important to make a distinction between 'positive structure' (goal and role clarity, and expectations of performance) as one sub-dimension, and 'negative structure' (close control) as another sub-dimension (cf. SBDQ and LBDQ scales; Bass 1990; Schriesheim *et al.* 1976). The change dimension can be more distinctly divided into sub-scales (cf. Lindell and Rosenqvist 1992). The employee dimension may be completed in favour of more activity-facilitating relational behaviour: image building, feedback, stimulation of team spirit, role modelling, conflict resolving, and so on. However, it seems to be a strength that all three dimensions are measured independently of each other, especially when there can be different combinations of these dimensions in managerial behaviour. For instance, change may be combined with production- or employee-orientation, thus providing rather different types of management style.

Dimensions in CPE scales should be defined also in more organisational terms. Now they might be defined in 'psychological' terms and in 'factor analytical' terms. Dimensions can be seen as functions of business demands and should be defined as functional roles, management role behaviour or critical situational factors, which put demands on the person in the role. Thus a better distinction between organisational context, role description and qualifications of the person is needed. The number and variety of dimensions itself can be extended and be more specific. For instance, 'performance- and result-orientation' could be more distinct or considered as a dimension. This is obvious in companies where project organisation and project leadership are applied.

The CPE model has currently been well validated in Western cultures. There is no guarantee that the model is valid in cultures with differing values systems. Furthermore, if the culture attempts to deal with uncertainty and adaptation differently, 'change-oriented' leadership may not be found. This, we argued, is the explanation of its appearance in the studies reported here, while it did not appear in earlier Western studies. The model is offered as a pragmatic and bounded or contextualized one, rather than one that is ideological or universal across all contexts.

Change-oriented leadership will emerge when a society or organisation needs it. If organisational leaders fail to engage with change-oriented leadership they are less likely to be successful. Further work will increasingly indicate the contingencies that will have to be taken into account in effective change-oriented leadership.

References

Alvesson, M. (1996). Leadership studies: From procedure and abstraction to reflexivity and situation. *Leadership Quarterly*, 7 (4), 455–485.

Bass, B. M. (1960). *Leadership, psychology, and organisational behavior*. New York: Harper and Brothers.

Bass, B. M. (1985). *Leadership and performance beyond expectations*. New York: Free Press.

Bass, B. M. (1990). *Bass and Stogdill's handbook of leadership* (third edition). New York: Free Press.

Bennis, W. (1989). *Why leaders can't lead*. London: Jossey-Bass.

Bennis, W. (1992). The artform of leadership. In S. Srivastva (ed.), *The executive mind*. London: Jossey-Bass.

Bennis, W. and Nanus, B. (1985). *The strategies of taking charge*. New York: Harper and Row.

Blake, R. and Mouton, J. (1964). *The managerial grid*. Houston, TX: Gulf Publishing.

Blake, R. and Mouton, J. (1985). *The managerial grid III: The key to leadership excellence*. Houston, TX: Gulf Publishing.

Bryman, A., Bresnen, M., Beradsworth, A. and Keil, T. (1988). Qualitative research and the study of leadership. *Human Relations*, *41* (1), 13–30.

Burns, J. M. (1978). *Leadership*. New York: Harper and Row.

Conger, J. A. and Kanungo, R. B. (1998). *Charismatic leadership in organisations*. London: Sage.

Cronbach, L. J. (1975). Beyond the two disciplines of scientific psychology. *American Psychologist*, February, 116–127.

den Hartog, D. N. (1997). Inspirational leadership. Amsterdam University, Department of Work and Organizational Psychology (doctoral dissertation).

Ekvall, G., Arvonen, J. and Nyström H. (1987). *Organisation och innovation*. Lund: Studentlitteratur.

Filley, A., House, R. J. and Kerr, S. (1976). *Managerial process and organisational behavior* (second edition). Glenview, IL: Scott, Foresman.

Fleishman, E. A. and Harris, E. F. (1962). Patterns of leadership behavior related to employee grievances and turnover. *Personnel Psychology*, *15*, 43–56.

Hackman, J. R. and Wageman, R. (1995). Total quality management: Empirical, conceptual, and practical issues. *Administrative Science Quarterly*, *40*, 309–342.

Hall. R. J. (1977). *Organizations, Structure and Process* (second edition). Englewood Cliffs, NJ: Prentice Hall.

Hall, R. J. and Lord, R. G. (1995). Multi-level information-processing explanations of followers' leadership perceptions. *Leadership Quarterly*, *6* (3), 265–287.

Hersey, B. and Blanchard, K. (1982). *Management of organisational behavior* (fourth edition). Englewood Cliffs, NJ: Prentice Hall.

House, R. J. (1995). Leadership in the twenty-first century. In A. Howard (ed.), *The changing nature of wor.* (pp. 411–450). San Francisco, CA: Jossey-Bass.

House, J. R. and Rizzo, J. R. (1972). Toward the measurement of organisational practices: Scale development and validation. *Journal of Applied Psychology*, *56* (5), 388–396.

House, R. J. and Shamir, B. (1993). Toward the integration of transformational, charismatic, and visionary theories. In M. M. Chemers and R. Ayman (eds), *Leadership theory and research: Perspectives and directions* (pp. 81–107). San Diego, CA: Academic Press.

Howard, A. (ed.) (1995). *The changing nature of work*. San Francisco, CA: Jossey-Bass.

Iacocca, L. and Novak, W. (1985). *Iacocca. En självbiografi*. Stockholm: Svenska Dagbladets Förlag AB.

Katz, D. and Kahn, R. (1978). *The social psychology of organisations* (second edition). New York: Wiley.

Kotter, J. P. (1985). *Power and influence: Beyond formal authority*. New York: Free Press.

Kotter, J. P. (1990). *A force for change: How leadership differs from management*. New York: Free Press.

Kouzes, J. M. and Posner, B. Z. (1995). *The leadership challenge: How to keep getting extraordinary things done in organisations* (second edition). San Francisco, CA: Jossey-Bass.

Lawler, E. E., III (1992). *The ultimate advantage: Creating the high involvment organisation*. San Fransico, CA: Jossey-Bass.

Lewin, K. (1950). The consequences of an authoritarian and democratic leadership. In A. W. Gouldner (ed.), *Studies in leadership* (pp. 409–417). New York: Harper and Brothers.

Likert, R. (1961). *New patterns of management*. New York: McGraw-Hill.

Lindell, M. and Rosenqvist, G. (1992). Management behavior dimensions and development orientation. *Ledarship Quarterly, 3*, 355–377.

Magnusson, D. (1985). Implications of an interactional paradigm for research on human development. *International Journal of Behavioral Development, 8*, 115–137.

Mintzberg, H. (1973). *The nature of managerial work*. New York: Harper and Row.

Misumi, J. (1989). Research on leadership and group decisions in Japanese organisations. *Applied Psychology: An International Review, 38*, 321–336.

Nystedt, L. (1983). The situation: A constructivist approach. In J. Adams-Webber and J. C. Mancuso (eds), *Applications of personal construct theory* (pp. 93–114). Ontario: Academic Press.

Nyström, H. (1990). *Technological and marketing innovation*. New York: Wiley.

Pascale, R. (1990). *Managing on the edge*. New York: Simon and Schuster.

Pascale, R. and Athos, A. (1982). *The art of Japanese management*. Harmondsworth: Penguin.

Peters, T. and Waterman, R., Jr. (1982). *In search of excellence*. New York: Harper and Row.

Roethlisberger, F. J. and Dickson, W. D. (1939). *Management and the worker: An account of a research program conducted by the Western Electricity Company, Hawthorne Works, Chicago*. Cambridge MA: Harvard University Press.

Ropo, A. (1989). *Leadership and organisational change*. Acta Universitatis Tamperensis, ser A, 280. Tampere: University of Tampere, Finland (doctoral dissertation).

Schriesheim, C., House, R. and Kerr, S. (1976). Leader initiating structure: A reconciliation of discrepant research results and some empirical tests. *Organizational Behavior and Human Performance, 15*, 279–321.

Selznick, P. (1957). *Leadership in administration*. New York: Harper and Row.

Shamir, B. (1999). Leadership in boundaryless organisations: Disposable or indispensable? *European Journal of Work and Organizational Psychology, 8*, (1), 49–71.

Tannenbaum, R. and Schmidt, W. H. (1958). How to choose a leadership pattern. *Harvard Business Review, 36*, 95–101.

Tichy, N. M. (1983). *Managing strategic change: Technical, political, and cultural dynamics*. New York: Wiley Interscience.

Tichy, N. M. and Devanna, M. A. (1986). *The transformational leader*. New York: Wiley.

Van Maanen, J. (ed.) (1983). *Qualitative methodology*. Beverly Hills, CA: Sage.

Yukl, G. (1994). *Leadership in organisations* (third edition). London: Prentice Hall.

Yukl, G. (1998). *Leadership in organisations* (fourth edition). London: Prentice Hall.

Yukl, G. (1999). An evaluative essay on current conceptions of effective leadership. *European Journal of Work and Organizational Psychology, 8* (1), 33–48.

Zaleznik, A. (1977). Managers and leaders: Are they different? *Harvard Business Review*, May–June, 67–78.

Zaleznik, A. (1989). *The managerial mystique: Restoring leadership in business*. New York: Harper and Row.

Theme 7 Structured interventions

Prototyping processes that affect organizational creativity

Cameron Ford

Introduction

This chapter explores the role that prototyping processes play in the development of creative work proposals. I begin by presenting a process approach to understanding creativity that emphasizes the importance of individual and collective thought experiments as a means of generating novel proposals and assessing their potential value. I then describe how prototypes serve as a visualization media capable of promoting the quality and quantity of thought experiment trials. Specifically, designing and sharing prototypes is a visualization strategy that can promote analogical reasoning and effectuation, and serve as a repository where knowledge from diverse contributors can be integrated into creative solutions. I conclude by speculating how differences in prototyping media characteristics may affect organizational creativity.

This chapter will explore one potentially fruitful avenue for future organizational creativity process research. Specifically, I will describe ways in which prototyping strategies employed by individuals and collectives may help or hinder creative productivity. I define prototyping as *a process involving explicit efforts to create visualizations of novel proposals in an effort to facilitate the assessment of their potential usefulness or value*. This process may be undertaken by individuals as one considers various analogies, images or models that bring coherence and clarity to a proposal. Articulating a novel proposal in this manner is akin to addressing the sensemaking question posed by Weick (1979): 'How do *I* know what I think until I see what *I* say?' Prototyping may also occur at the nexus between individuals and collectives during occasions when an individual uses visualization strategies to seek help from others (Hargadon and Bechky 2006). Weick (1979) cleverly suggests alternating pronouns to create interesting new sensemaking research questions – in this case leading one to ask: 'How do I know what *they* think until I see what *they* say?' Furthermore, this process could engage interactions among a collective whose members use visualizations to provoke novel associations and consolidate valuable insights (Hargadon and Bechky 2006; Hargadon and Sutton 1997). This leads to another interesting sensemaking question that asks: 'How do *we* know what we think until we see what *we* say?' I believe that questions such as these offer promising justifications for future creativity research that examines relationships between creating and organizing processes within and across levels of analysis.

The role of visualization in the development of creative proposals and the advancement of academic disciplines has been richly described in the context of physics by Arthur Miller (1996). After conducting a far-ranging historical analysis that spans the contributions of Galileo, Newton, Einstein, Feynman and many others, Miller concludes that imagery and visualization processes play a central role in creativity and the advancement of scientific fields. Thought experiments, wherein one visualizes a particular theoretical conundrum and imagines the results of various experimental trials, were a key process revealed through his analysis. Einstein, for example, wrote extensively about the role of thought experiments in the development of his theories of special relativity and general relativity. Galileo was also noteworthy for proposing thought experiments (e.g. Galileo identified inconsistencies with Aristotle's proposals by pub-lishing thought experiments related to the acceleration of falling stones of varied weights), and used these proposals to engage others in scientific discourse that changed what came to stand for 'common sense' in the study of physics. Miller's analysis also points out how visualizations can retard the advancement of new ideas by describing how difficult it was for theorists to overturn the invalid visualization comparing atoms to solar systems.

I make note of Miller's analysis in an effort to provide readers with an analogy that may help to visualize the main points I intend to offer in this chapter. In particular, I follow the same reasoning by arguing that thought experiment trials are a productive way to consider sensemak-ing and organizing processes that facilitate and constrain creative action. This approach to theorizing is well aligned with the robust tenets of Campbellian evolutionary theorizing that has been widely and successfully employed in the administrative sciences. Adopting a theoretical language used by evolutionary theorists addressing an array of processes related to organizational and strategic change may provide a common meta-theoretical language capable of bringing greater clarity and coherence to the organizational creativity research literature.

The remainder of this chapter will progress as follows. I begin by offering a brief description of the benefits of process theorizing in the context of organizational behavior research. I then extend this reasoning by describing how variation and selective-retention processes may mani-fest themselves in thought experiments related to creative actions in organizational settings. Prototypes are then introduced as cognitive and material manifestations resulting from thought trials that may subsequently induce additional analogical reasoning or effectuation that elabor-ates and clarifies a specific proposition. I conclude by speculating about how differences in prototyping media, ranging from verbal analogies to crude models to computer animated scenarios, may affect the novelty and expected value of individual and collective action.

A process view of creativity

Creativity research in the context of organizational and professional settings has advanced significantly in the past decade. Recent reviews of this literature (Shalley *et al.* 2004) describe several characteristics of individuals and their work settings that have been associated with creative outcomes. Although these findings are clearly useful, most prior empirical research has been motivated by a variance approach to theorizing that is limited in its ability to explain dynamic interactions among individuals and their work settings that affect the development and utilization of creative solutions (Van de Ven and Engelman 2004). Recognition of these limitations has led to several recent efforts that attempt to portray dynamic processes that may foster creative professional productivity (see Drazen *et al.* 1999; Elsbach and Kramer 2003; Ford 1996; Hargadon and Bechky 2006; Perry-Smith and Shalley 2003). These contributions to process theorizing in the organizational creativity literature suggest many exciting new research opportunities associated with individual and collective creativity (cf. Ford 1996; Hargadon and Bechky 2006), and offer a path toward integrating the contributions offered by organizational creativity studies with broader, timeless challenges addressed by the administrative sciences (Ford and Kuenzi 2008).

Organizational behavior research in general has been criticized recently for failing to offer dynamic theoretical descriptions that explain how specific organizing practices affect economic and behavioral outcomes. Heath and Sitkin (2001) criticized organizational behavior research generally for its failure to sufficiently address processes that are central to the task of organizing. More specifically, they argue that organizational behavior research would have greater impact if it focused on how people solve the dynamic problems of aligning goals and coordinating action. This focus, they believe, would make researchers less likely to emphasize simple patterns of co-variation among 'a laundry list of behavioral variables' in their studies (p. 56) that do little to explain processes that produce these patterns. I believe this critique is important to this essay because visualization strategies such as prototyping are critical primarily because they impact the dynamic problems of aligning goals and coordinating action in organizational settings.

MacKenzie (2004) and Van de Ven and Engleman (2004) also argued that organizations are process-driven by nature, and that process theorizing is necessary for understanding how change occurs within organizational settings. If one views organizational creativity as instigating organizational change, then their arguments should lead one to conclude that process theorizing is necessary to adequately describe organizational creativity. MacKenzie (2004) also notes that process theorizing tends to be less sensitive to variations across contexts that produce unstable empirical findings that often characterize research traditions based on variance theorizing. Consequently, process theorizing may serve as a promising scheme for aligning organizational creativity research findings, and integrating them into other related domains of organizational and strategic change research.

The theory I favor, as a broad framework for understanding organizing processes related to creativity, is Campbell's (1960, 1965) widely employed variation and selective-retention (VSR) model of creativity and social change. Campbell's work has been employed broadly throughout the administrative sciences (see Baum and McKelvey 1999, for an appreciative review), and has also been suggested as a meta-theory for organizing the contributions of prior creativity research (Simonton 1999). Weick *et al.* (2005) also argue that Campbellian logic, as incorporated in Weick's enactment theory (1979), may serve as a process theoretical framework that links thinking, acting and organizing. I have used this perspective previously to explain the evolution of creative endeavors in general terms (Ford 1996, 2005; Ford and Sullivan 2005), and have found Campbellian theorizing to be especially impressive with respect to its broad application across research traditions and levels of analysis (Ford and Sullivan 2008). Weick *et al.* (2005: 414) reinforce this conclusion by advocating making VSR theorizing '. . . the microfoundation of organizing and sensemaking [because] it makes it easier to work with other meso- and macro-level formulations that are grounded in Campbell's work (e.g. Aldrich 1999; Baum and Singh 1994; Ocasio 2001).'

Thus, I adopt enactment theory's (Weick *et al.* 2005) depiction of VSR processes related to individual and collective sensemaking, acting and organizing to explore how prototyping processes affect organizational creativity. To anticipate the discussion that follows, I will describe prototyping as a process involving the visualization of analogies and alternative combinations of available resources (effectuation – Sarasvathy 2001). Variations are subjected to evaluation based on selection criteria and previously retained knowledge to derive an assessment of a proposal's value. Individuals may choose cognitive or verbal prototyping strategies such as utilizing analogies, or may choose to create tangible manifestations of proposals such as diagrams, sketches, written proposals, models, simulations or fully functioning designs. Once articulated, prototypes may be shared with others. This may instigate further sensemaking cycles wherein a proposal becomes infused with selection considerations and retained knowledge offered by a collective (Hargadon and Bechky 2006).

Thought experiments and creativity

As I mentioned previously, thought experiments are a central process associated with descriptions of sensemaking (Weick 1979) and creative insight (Miller 1996). Thought experiments involve developing an abstract proposition (i.e. variation) and subjecting that proposition to selective-retention considerations regarding what is known about contextual factors that might affect the success or value of the proposition (Weick 1989). Thus, individuals are proposed to think much like researchers who search previously retained knowledge (e.g. ideas and analogies) for novel solutions to bothersome problems. Once an individual formulates an initial novel proposal, that proposal is subjected to 'value screens' relevant to a particular problem (e.g. technology, market, organization, financial considerations) that can be used to assess the solution's usefulness. Positive assessments of a novel alternative may result in a proposal being retained as a workable solution, or partially selected as a promising draft requiring further revision. Thought experiments related to a particular problem may continue indefinitely as novel proposals are discarded, modified or retained.

These sensemaking and organizing cycles describe how VSR processes manifest themselves in individuals' ongoing efforts to address uncertainty in their work environments (Weick *et al.* 2005). Uncertainty fuels sensemaking efforts when individuals find current circumstances to be, in some fashion, problematic (cf. problemistic search – Cyert and March 1963). Therefore, one should expect significant variation in the frequency that individuals engage in thought trials based on the degree to which they face uncertainty in their respective organizational roles. Individuals who work in jobs where goals and processes are coordinated by organizational routines will have fewer opportunities to consider uncertainties and formulate novel propositions relative to those who work in roles that afford greater discretion regarding appropriate ends and means. Returning to the subject of prototyping as a means of conducting productive thought trials and spurring sensemaking, it is not surprising to see prototyping being used extensively to address complex and novel problems such as those associated with new product development, architecture and entertainment production. However, the benefits of prototyping thought trials may also be extended to less classically 'creative' pursuits, especially in settings where it is important to integrate knowledge resources from diverse stakeholders and to accommodate eclectic interests necessary to support the implementation of a creative solution.

Indeed, one of the benefits of considering thought trials related to creative proposals is that doing so provides a theoretical basis for understanding how repeated thought trials lead to enhanced learning and solution feasibility as knowledge resources are infused into a proposal (Ford 2005). Specifically, repeated thought trials may enrich the retained pool of knowledge available to build solutions, the fidelity of selection criteria employed to assess value, and the expected value of a proposed variation. As an analogy, this is similar to the processes through which academic research, and an academic researcher, improves as a result of peer reviews and author revisions. Successful thought trials result in a particular proposal being judged as increasingly plausible as key sources of uncertainty are addressed from one trial to the next. As thought trials result in higher plausibility and lower uncertainty, associated proposals become increasingly attractive alternatives with respect to a particular problem or objective (Weick *et al.* 2005).

Consequently, it becomes increasingly likely that a novel solution can gain support from key stakeholders and resource providers.

It is also important to note a few additional characteristics and limitations associated with thought trials. Although I've described sensemaking cycles characterized by thought experiment trials as leading towards progressively refined, plausible and valuable solutions, it is perhaps more likely for trials to reveal inherent weaknesses leading to a proposal's rejection. Furthermore, differences in previously retained knowledge, biases related to relevant selection processes, and relationships with helpful colleagues (Perry-Smith and Shalley 2003) make it likely that thought trials will result in different outcomes for different experimenters. Finally, as has been reported in many tales of scientific discovery (e.g. the discovery of penicillin), serendipity may intervene to affect the outcome of specific experimental trials. Such unexpected events could be fortuitous or disastrous, but considering creativity as a consequence of dynamic experimental processes wherein ideas are churned across increasingly refined thought trials provides a means of considering the role that luck plays in the discovery and realization of creative proposals.

Prototyping as a means of promoting analogical reasoning and effectuation

The previous discussion suggests that creativity research can benefit from an increased emphasis on process theorizing, that thought experiment trials are a fruitful way of describing VSR processes associated with creativity and social change (Campbell 1960), and that visualization strategies such as prototyping promote experimenting. With these theoretical premises in place, the remainder of this chapter will focus on describing how prototyping affects organizational creativity, and how variations in prototyping media differentially address the development of novel proposals and the assessment of a proposal's value.

Weick *et al.* (2005) describe sensemaking as *an activity that talks organizations into existence*. Previously I defined prototyping as *a process involving explicit efforts to create visualizations of novel proposals in an effort to facilitate the assessment of their potential value*. Considering these two notions together leads me to propose that prototyping affects creativity by providing increasingly sophisticated *conversation pieces* that instigate and sustain VSR thought trials. These conversation pieces help creators and their collaborators visualize key characteristics of a proposal, thus facilitating knowledge sharing, creative associations and proposal valuation. Prototypes also serve as a retention mechanism where ideas incorporated in a proposal design are preserved for future sensemaking conversations. Prototypes may range in quality from rough and inexpensive (e.g. verbal analogies, paper sketches, foam and wire models) to realistic and expensive (e.g. websites, miniaturizations, working models, computer animations).

There are two specific processes associated with organizational creativity that are especially likely to be affected by prototyping. Recent research related to innovation, creativity and strategic change have argued that analogical reasoning is especially important in organizational settings (Giovanni *et al.* 2005; Hargadon 2003). This research argues that creative business proposals typically result from generalizations from previously retained knowledge, often in the form of previously developed solutions or prior experiences, to a novel problem. Hargadon and Sutton (1997) describe this process of recognizing relevant analogies and generalizing prior solutions to new settings as 'knowledge brokering'. They even offer their own analogy by describing Thomas Edison's quote that, 'To invent, you need a good imagination and a pile of junk' (Hargadon and Sutton 2000). Edison is another well-known experimenter and prototyper, having tested approximately 2000 alternative solutions before finding an effective filament to use in his electric light bulb. These findings, and the analogy to Edison's famous Menlo Park 'Invention Factory' (ibid.), demonstrate how previously retained knowledge fuels individual and collective creativity as increasingly plausible visualizations (analogies) are used to develop and validate novel proposals.

Another relevant and closely related process associated with creativity is effectuation (Sarasvathy 2001). Effectuation is a process that has been employed in the entrepreneurship literature to describe how individuals 'take a set of [previously retained] means as given, and focus on selecting between possible effects that can be created with that set of means' (p. 245). Sarasvathy also employs an analogy to help readers visualize and better understand her proposals. She compares effectuation with the process of making dinner by examining the contents of one's pantry and determining what can be made with the ingredients on hand. She presents this as an alternative to more normatively rational approaches to planning such as picking a recipe and going to the store to acquire the necessary ingredients. Effectuation theory is consistent with long-standing associationistic perspectives in creativity that describe how individual differences in finding connections among previously unrelated ideas promote creativity (Mednick 1962). This perspective reinforces research on analogical reasoning by illustrating the importance of broad experience and large social networks. These factors provide access to retained knowledge that offers access to analogies and ideas from which to support effectuation (Simonton 1999).

Analogical reasoning and effectuation are likely to benefit from prototyping. Ideas and enlightening comparisons can be made more vivid and engaging through visualizations offered by prototyping efforts. Each VSR thought trial might result in the rejection of a proposition because it is not personally appealing relative to current circumstances, or because it suffers from a 'fatal flaw' that makes it implausible for the time being. Alternatively, propositions may be partially selected so that some attributes are deemed potentially useful or valuable while others are found to be lacking. In this case, an individual may go 'back to the drawing board' and consider alternative or enhanced analogies, models or diagrams. Individuals may also engage in help-seeking (Hargadon and Bechky 2006) conversations that use a prototype as a conversation piece to engage attention and elicit useful expertise capable of enhancing the proposal. Help seeking is an active effort to gain assistance from others, and tends to evoke help giving from others who offer their attention, time and assistance (ibid.). Prototype driven thought trials are likely to proceed through many iterations of this type of 'revise and resubmit' process before a proposal seems plausible enough to implement.

As I mentioned, the initiator of a novel proposal may seek additional knowledge, resources and relationships by presenting a prototype (e.g. analogy, story, model, scenario, etc.) to others. This helps to create a shared understanding of a proposal's attributes, and allows others to assess its expected value and contribute ideas that may mitigate potential shortcomings. In this manner, collective sensemaking and learning is promoted by presenting and experimenting with prototypes. The result of collective sensemaking may be to improve a proposal's plausibility by removing doubt associated with a particular dimension. Hargadon and Bechky (2006) described how an individual working on a novel proposition may provoke conversations that lead to the coalescence of a creative collective. They present evidence from field studies that show how social interactions trigger alternative framings and novel elaborations that no individual involved in the conversations could have generated alone.

Collective creativity occurs during moments characterized by help seeking and help giving that result in reframing and elaborations. Prototypes as conversation pieces may increase the frequency of these collective behaviors, and are likely to promote the efficiency of collective thought trails (i.e. meetings) for eliciting and integrating relevant, useful knowledge from diverse participants. This notion is analogous to Kogut and Zander's (1992) description of combinative capability. They define this as a dynamic ability of actors to synthesize current and acquired knowledge. As such, they include both the existing knowledge of a proposal's originator as well as knowledge that might be obtained from others. Prototypes may facilitate combinative capability through enhanced learning and shared understandings.

Finally, prototypes that evoke positive value assessments from help givers may promote the formation of a creative collective. Novel proposals presented in the form of vivid, provocative prototypes are likely to attract new contributors, and new contributors are likely to add insights and resources that improve the proposal. In this way, prototypes as conversation pieces may instigate the kinds of processes wherein creative proposals and social networks co-evolve over time in a spiraling manner that leads proposals and relationships to become more organized over time (Perry-Smith and Shalley 2003).

Prototype media characteristics that affect individual and collective creativity

Ford and Sullivan (2004) described how novel contributions benefit project teams early in their development when their primary goals are to learn more about a problem, search for useful information and articulate tentative solutions. However, after teams experience a midpoint transition (Gersick 1988), and attention shifts toward executing a proposal and satisfying external stakeholders, additional attempts to introduce novel ideas may be disruptive. I extend this logic to prototyping processes by suggesting that low quality, inexpensive media such as verbal analogies, written proposals, paper sketches, foam and wire models, etc. that are easy to discard, replace and modify are most useful early in a proposal's development. This is because low quality, inexpensive media can be rapidly 'churned' through a large number of thought trails and quickly refined through individual and collective effort. Proposals can evolve rapidly when facilitated by crude prototypes that invite questioning, learning and revision. Low quality, inexpensive media are egalitarian in the sense that they invite interaction, improvisation and play by raising questions regarding basic attributes and assumptions.

Alternatively, high quality, expensive prototyping media such as interactive websites, miniaturizations (i.e. table-top replicas), working models and computer animations provide highly specific, vivid and difficult-to-change representations of novel proposals. Consequently, these prototypes are not effective for evolving a proposal through multiple individual or collective thought trails. These types of prototype do not invite questioning regarding basic attributes or assumptions, and are less appropriate for incorporating novel insights or constructive feedback. Those who control the prototype in this case control the premises of a proposal. However, high quality, expensive prototyping media are very effective at answering questions that might affect assessments of the value of a novel proposal. Thus, these prototypes help to reduce uncertainty and enhance plausibility, often in an effort to attract support necessary to implement a proposal. Because high quality prototypes are so vivid, they are likely to reduce consideration of alternative designs and propositions, and therefore limit further novel developments.

Overall, as the primary source of uncertainty related to a novel proposal shifts from creating something plausible to organizing resources capable of executing the proposal, the character of prototyping processes should change. Specifically, low quality, inexpensive prototyping media should be used early in an effort to promote novel associations and quickly enhance the plausibility of the proposition through repeated thought trails. High quality, expensive prototyping media should be employed when one seeks to demonstrate value and attract resources from those with limited understanding (e.g. those outside the immediate work setting or professional domain). It is interesting to consider the role that advanced information technologies may play in mitigating the trade-offs between quality, expense and interactivity. Technologies including computer-aided design, stereolithography (rapid prototyping) and augmented reality are already widely used in product development environments. It will be interesting to investigate whether increasingly vivid prototyping media help or hinder the development of novel propositions (controlling for media interactivity).

Conclusion

The purpose of this chapter has been to explore how prototypes may affect creativity resulting from individual and collective thought trials or experiments. My interest in this topic has been spurred by my own interactions with entrepreneurs who face the challenges of articulating their proposals, communicating them to others and evolving the offering to become increasingly plausible. I've helped entrepreneurs develop analogies, 'money machine' diagrams, interactive websites, table-top models, animated shorts, role plays and 'promo-types' (looks-like, not works-like prototypes). What I have found interesting about these kind of conversation pieces is that they benefit from non-verbal information that allows individuals who figuratively or literally speak different languages to understand, assess and contribute to a proposal. By facilitating analogical reasoning, effectuation and learning in this manner, I believe prototyping processes can be utilized more extensively and effectively in organizational settings as a means of promoting novel and valuable proposals.

Consideration of prototyping may also enrich our understanding of pitching processes as described by Elsbach and Kramer's (2003) pioneering research examining Hollywood pitch meetings. They describe pitching as an interactive communication process characterized by creativity, learning and negotiating. Elsbach and Kramer's research is an excellent contribution to process theorizing in that pitching is clearly a process that is central to organizing. It is also interesting to consider the extent to which prototypes affect value assessments, controlling for other features of a proposal. Although I have argued that proposal assessments will improve as prototypes incorporate knowledge and become less uncertain, it could also be that proposals become judged as more certainly awful as data accumulates regarding key assumptions and characteristics. Ultimately, like most processes, prototyping is likely to be only as effective as those who prototype. Retained knowledge, analogical reasoning, effectuation and selection criteria are likely to be limited and biased in some fashion from one individual to the next. Thus, I see the greatest hope in using prototyping as a means of facilitating help seeking and help giving that enriches the novelty, value and shared understanding of creative solutions to organizational problems.

References

Aldrich, H. (1999). *Organizations Evolving*. London: Sage.

Baum, J.A.C. and McKelvey, B. (eds) (1999). *Variations in Organization Science: In Honor of Donald T. Campbell*. Thousand Oaks, CA: Sage Publications.

Baum, J. and Singh, J. (1994). Organizational hierarchies and evolutionary processes: Some reflections on a theory of organizational evolution. *Evolutionary Dynamics of Organizations* (pp. 3–22). New York: Oxford University Press.

Campbell, D.T. (1960). Blind variation and selective retention in creative thought as in other knowledge processes. *Psychological Review*, 95, 380–400.

Campbell, D.T. (1965). Variation and selective retention in socio-cultural evolution. In H. R. Barringer, G. I. Blanksten and R. W. Mack (eds), *Social change in developing areas: A reinterpretation of evolutionary theory* (pp. 19–48). Cambridge, MA: Schenkman.

Cyert, R.M. and March, J.G. (1963). *A Behavioral Theory of the Firm*. Englewood Cliffs, NJ: Prentice Hall.

Drazin, R., Glynn, M.A. and Kazanjian, R.K. (1999). Multilevel theorizing about creativity in organizations: A sensemaking perspective. *Academy of Management Review*, 24 (2), 286.

Elsbach, K.D. and Kramer, R.M. (2003). Assessing creativity in Hollywood pitch meetings: Evidence for a dual-process model of creativity judgments. *Academy of Management Journal*, 46 (3), 283–301.

Ford, C.M. (1996). A theory of individual creative action in multiple social domains. *Academy of Management Review*, 21 (4), 1112–1142.

Ford, C.M. (2005). Creative associations and entrepreneurial opportunities. In L. Thompson and H. S. Choi (eds), *Creativity and innovation in organizations* (pp. 217–234). Hillsdale, NJ: Lawrence Erlbaum.

Ford, C.M. and Kuenzi, M. (2008). 'Organizing' creativity research through historical analysis of foundational administrative science texts. In J. Zhou and C. Shalley (eds), *Handbook of Organizational Creativity* (pp. 65–94). Hillsdale, NJ: Lawrence Erlbaum.

Ford, C.M. and Sullivan, D.M. (2004). A time for everything: How the timing of novel contributions influences project team outcomes. *Journal of Organizational Behavior*, 25 (2), 279–292.

Ford, C.M. and Sullivan, D.M. (2005). Creating and organizing processes in the business domain. In J. Kaufman and J. Baer (eds), *Creativity across Domains: Faces of the Muse* (pp. 245–260). Hillsdale, NJ: Lawrence Erlbaum.

Ford, C.M. and Sullivan, D.M. (2008). A multi-level process view of new venture emergence. In M. Mumford, S. Hunter and K. Bedell-Avers (eds), *Multi-level Issues in Creativity and Innovation*. Greenwich, CT: JAI Press.

Giovanni, G., Levinthal, D. and Rivkin, J. (2005). Strategy making in novel and complex worlds: The power of analogy. *Strategic Management Journal*, 26 (8), 691–712.

Gersick, C.J.G. (1988). Time and transition in work teams: Toward a new model of group development. *Academy of Management Journal*, 31 (1), 9–41.

Hargadon, A.B. (2003). *How Breakthroughs Happen*. Boston, MA: Harvard Business School Press.

Hargadon, A.B. and Bechky, B.A. 2006. When collection of creatives become creative collectives: A field study of problem solving at work. *Organization Science*, 17 (4), 484–500.

Hargadon, A.B. and Sutton, R.I. (1997). Technology brokering and innovation in a product development firm. *Administrative Science Quarterly*, 42, 716–749.

Hargadon, A.B. and Sutton, R.I. (2000). Building an innovation factory. *Harvard Business Review*, 78 (3), 157–166.

Heath, C. and Sitkin, S.B. (2001). Big-B versus Big-O: What is *organizational* about organizational behavior? *Journal of Organizational Behavior*, 22, 43–58.

Kogut, B. and Zander, U. (1992). Knowledge of the firm, combinative capabilities, and the replication of technology. *Organization Science*, 3 (3), 383–397.

Mackenzie, K.D. (2004). The process approach to multi-level organizational behavior. In F. Dansereau and F. J. Yammarino (eds), *Multi-level Issues in Organizational Behavior and Processes*. Greenwich, CT: JAI Press.

Mednick, S.A. (1962). The associative basis of the creative process. *Psychological Review*, 69, 220–232.

Miller, A. (1996). *Insights of Genius*. Cambridge, MA: MIT Press.

Ocasio, W. (2001). How do organizations think? In T. K. Lant and Z. Shapira (eds), *Organizational Cognition: Computation and Interpretation* (pp. 39–60). Mahwah, NJ: Lawrence Erlbaum.

Perry-Smith, J.E. and Shalley, C.E. (2003). The social side of creativity: A static and dynamic social network perspective. *Academy of Management Review*, 28 (1), 89–106.

Sarasvathy, S.D. (2001). Causation and effectuation: Toward a theoretical shift from economic inevitability to entrepreneurial contingency. *Academy of Management Review*, 26 (2), 243–263.

Shalley, C., Zhou, J. and Oldham, G. (2004). The effects of personal and contextual characteristics on creativity: Where should we go from here? *Journal of Management*, 30 (6), 933–958.

Simonton, D.K. (1999). Creativity as blind variation and selective retention: Is the creative process Darwinian? *Psychological Inquiry*, 10 (4), 309–328.

Van de Ven, A. and Engleman, R. (2004). Event-and outcome-driven explanations of entrepreneurship. *Journal of Business Venturing* 19, 343–358.

Weick, K. (1979). *The Social Psychology of Organizing* (second edition). New York: McGraw-Hill.

Weick, K.E. (1989). Theory construction as discipline's imagination. *Academy of Management Review*, 14, 516–531.

Weick, K.E., Sutcliffe, K.M. and Obstfeld, D. (2005). Organizing and the process of sensemaking. *Organization Science*, 16 (4), 409–421.

27

Creative problem solving: past, present and future

Gerard Puccio and John Cabra

The need for creativity in the new economy

Economic pressures associated with increased levels of global competition have companies scrambling to find ways to remain competitive. More and more organizations recognize that survival in large measure rests upon their ability to get new products and services to the market place. It has been argued that companies can no longer compete on cost and quality alone because others can produce the same product just as well and at a competitive cost; as a consequence imagination and innovation have taken on much greater import in sustaining a competitive edge. As Janszen (2000) observed, 'After the age of efficiency in the 1950s and 1960s, quality in the 1970s and 1980s, we now live in the age of innovation' (p. 3).

In response to these competitive forces, companies and governments alike are beginning to compel educational systems, both secondary and post-secondary, to consider ways in which they might better prepare young people to be productive employees in this age of innovation. Recent books, such as Friedman's (2006) *The World is Flat*, and popular periodicals, such as *Time* magazine, all tout the need for schools to develop creative thinking skills among students. In their *Time* magazine cover story, titled 'How to bring our schools out of the 20th century', Wallis and Steptoe (2006) delineated what are considered to be the skills required for success in the twentieth century. Second on this list was 'Thinking outside the box'. In describing this skill, Wallis and Steptoe observed, 'Jobs in the new economy – the ones that won't get outsourced or automated – put an enormous premium on creative and innovative skills, seeing patterns where other people see only chaos' (p. 52).

Organizations recognize the need to be innovative and that employees' creative imaginations are the wellspring for innovation; as noted by Amabile *et al.* (1999), 'Creativity is the crucial "front-end" of the innovation process; before innovation can happen, the creative ideas must be generated by individuals and teams so that they can be successfully implemented' (p. 1). This important link between innovation and creativity has compelled scholars, educators and those in business to search for proven strategies that might be used to enhance creative thinking skills. In the business sector there has been an active search for methods that might improve the creativity level of employees. Those in schools and universities have developed and studied specific programs, tools and strategies that can be offered to students to better equip them to apply their imaginations in the pursuit of solutions to complex problems. In reality, this quest is not new; Osborn explored these exact same issues more than 50 years ago. This business man's interest in developing methods to help individuals deliberately call on their creativity skills resulted in his seminal book *Applied Imagination: Principles and Procedures for Creative Problem-solving* (Osborn 1953). This was perhaps the first major work to delineate creativity methods that could be taught. Since the release of this book, the methodology he described, called 'Creative Problem Solving' (CPS for short), has been adopted in both schools and industry, and has been examined in numerous research studies. The purpose of this chapter is to review this widely used and researched creative process model, beginning with a brief exploration of the history of CPS and ending with a description of future trends. In-between we examine the current CPS model.

Creative problem solving: definiton and structure

What is CPS? Puccio *et al.* (2007) recently defined CPS as a 'comprehensive cognitive and affective system built on our natural creative processes that deliberately ignites creative thinking and, as a result, generates creative solutions and change' (p. 29). CPS is a model of the creative process; as such it delineates the operations that facilitate the kind of thinking required to successfully resolve complex problems.

The terms that comprise the acronym CPS can each be defined to provide a more complete picture as to the purpose of this creative process model (ibid.). First, and foremost, CPS is a creative process. CPS is designed to bring about deliberate creativity – the production of ideas that are both new and useful. As a creative process, CPS is specifically designed for situations where there is a need for a change, new thinking or a different approach. In CPS, creative thinking is called on to resolve a complex problem; a situation that is ill defined (i.e. there is no single solution path), novel (i.e. the situation is either changing or new) and ambiguous (i.e. information is missing or it is difficult to determine what is relevant). The final term in the CPS acronym, solving, refers to taking action – pursuing a course that effectively deals with a problem. The intended outcome of the application of CPS is the implementation of a novel solution to a complex problem designed ultimately to resolve that situation.

CPS is not designed to replace individuals' natural creative thinking processes, but to explicate this process in a way that allows them to be more systematic in how they approach challenges. Thinking is not always neat and orderly, thus the CPS model attempts to introduce structured thinking into our more intuitive creative attempts in a way that enhances effectiveness and increases the likelihood of producing novel solutions to perplexing problems. Research into the stages of thought individuals move through when resolving an ill-structured problem has yielded consistent findings (Kaufmann 1988). Kaufmann concluded that such research highlights three specific stages of thought. He observed, 'The three phases seem to be related logically to form a strict sequence with "identification" first, followed by "development", ending in "selection" ' (p. 99). The structure of the CPS model reflects these natural process steps.

Table 27.1 provides a summary of the various versions of CPS that have emerged over a more than 50-year period. Each version begins with the author(s), the year of publication and the name ascribed to that particular CPS model. The specific steps found in each of the respective models follow this information. To show how CPS reflects natural creative thinking, the steps have been aligned with the three phases referred to by Kaufmann (ibid.). The steps associated with the Identification phase of natural problem solving are aimed at forming an understanding

Table 27.1 Creative problem-solving models: developments and spin-offs

Natural creative process stages	Osborn (1953) The Original Model	Osborn (1963) CPS Stream Lined	Parnes (1967) Osborn–Parnes	Isaksen and Treffinger (1985) Basic Course	Parnes (1988, 1992) Visionizing	Isaksen, Dorval and Treffinger (1994) Components Model	Basadur (1994) Simplex®	Vehar, Firestien, and Miller (1997) Plain Language	Isaksen, Dorval, and Treffinger (2000) CPS Version 6.1	Puccio, Murdock, and Mance (2007) Thinking Skills Model
						Task appraisal and process planning			Planning Your Approach: Appraising Tasks and Designing Process	Assessing the Situation
Identification	Orientation			Mess-Finding	Desires (1988) Objective-Finding (1992)	Understanding the problem: mess-finding	Problem finding: Problem-Finding	Explore the Challenge: Identify the Goal Wish, Challenge	Understanding the Challenge: Constructing Opportunities	Clarifying: Exploring the Vision
	Preparation	Fact-Finding (problem definition and preparation)	Fact-Finding	Data-Finding	Fact-Finding	Understanding the problem: data-finding	Problem finding: fact-finding	Explore the Challenge: Gather Data	Understanding the Challenge: Exploring Data	(Occurs in Assessing the Situation)
	Analysis		Problem-Finding	Problem-Finding	Problem-Finding	Understanding the problem: problem-finding	Problem finding: problem-definition	Explore the Challenge: Clarify the Problem	Understanding the Challenge: Framing Problems	Clarifying: Formulating Challenges
Development	Hypothesis	Idea-Finding (idea production and development)	Idea-Finding	Idea-Finding	Idea-Finding	Generating ideas: Idea-Finding	Problem solving: idea-finding	Generate Ideas: Generate Ideas	Generating Ideas: Generating Ideas	Transforming: Exploring Ideas
	Incubation									
Selection	Synthesis									
	Verification	Solution-Finding (evaluation and adoption)	Solution-Finding	Solution-Finding	Solution-Finding	Planning for action: solution-finding	Problem solving: evaluate and select	Prepare for Action: Select and Strengthen Solutions	Preparing for Action: Developing Solutions	Transforming: Formulating Solutions
							Solution implementation: plan			
			Acceptance-Finding	Acceptance-Finding	Acceptance-Finding	Planning for action: acceptance-finding	Solution implementation: acceptance 'sell' idea	Prepare for Action: Plan for Action	Preparing for Action: Building Acceptance	Implementing: Exploring Acceptance
							Solution implementation: action			Implementing: Formulating a Plan

of the problem to be addressed. Those CPS steps designed to generate possible responses to the problem, which in natural process is called Development, are next. Finally, a decision must be reached about which course of action is most promising. In natural process this has been referred to as the Selection phase. By reviewing the versions of CPS found in Table 27.1, it is easy to see how the structure of these models closely aligns with the phases of natural thinking. For a thorough description of the evolution of the structure of the CPS process, see Puccio *et al.* (2005) and Isaksen and Treffinger (2004). We will now turn our attention to a more in-depth review of the most recent version of CPS.

Creative problem solving: the Thinking Skills Model

Figure 27.1 shows a graphic depiction of a recently published version of CPS, referred to as the *Thinking Skills Model* (Puccio *et al.* 2007). While this model retains many of the historical features of the CPS framework, it does introduce new developments that depart from past models. This description of the Thinking Skills Model progresses from what might be considered the standard features of CPS, which will also serve to underscore and illuminate the historical roots of this creative process model, to current developments.

As with previous models, the steps in the Thinking Skills Model align with the phases associated with individuals' natural creative processes, which in this model are found on the

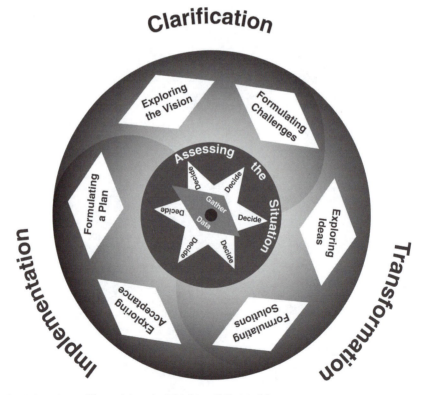

Figure 27.1 Creative problem solving: the Thinking Skills Model

© Puccio, Murdock and Mance (2007). Reprinted with permission.

outside and are labelled Clarification, Transformation and Implementation. Each of these phases contains two specific CPS steps. In the Clarification stage, a vision of the desired outcome is developed; this occurs in the Exploring the Vision step; and then the gaps that must be closed to achieve this vision are identified during Formulating the Challenges. The two steps within the Transformation stage are Exploring Ideas and Formulating Solutions. The focus of Exploring Ideas is to generate novel ideas that address the challenges that impede progress towards the desired outcome. These ideas are then transformed into workable solutions in Formulating Solutions. The Implementation stage begins with Exploring Acceptance. Having a great solution is not sufficient for success, particularly if this solution means that others must embrace change – a new way of performing, thinking or carrying out work. Before rushing to implement a new solution, the goal of Exploring Acceptance is to cause individuals, teams or organizations to pause and examine factors in their context that must be taken into consideration in order for the solution to be adopted. The insights gained through this step are directly applied in the last step, Formulating a Plan. At this point, a specific implementation plan is devised that will move the solution into action.

The structure of the Thinking Skills Model, and the specific steps themselves, are consistent with past models. Although the names for the CPS steps have changed over time, there is a predictable progression from steps that focus on developing a better understanding of the problem at hand, to the generation and development of ideas that respond to the identified problem, with the final steps focused on the formulation of an action plan. Over time, new steps have been added and existing steps have been refined within these three basic areas of operation. For instance, Isaksen and Treffinger (2004) added the Mess-Finding step in 1985 to bring focus to the extent to which the individual or group had 'ownership' of the problem to be addressed (see Table 27.1). The *Basic Course* model also provided an example of a step that was modified to improve the effectiveness of the process. Specifically, the step previously known as Fact-Finding was changed to Data-Finding to encompass the contribution that feelings, observations, impressions and questions make to the understanding of a problem.

This continued refinement of existing steps can be found in the present model, most notably the Implementation stage in which the examination of acceptance issues (Exploring Acceptance) is separated from the creation of an action plan (Formulating a Plan). With the exception of Basadur's (1994) Simplex® model, these two activities were traditionally combined into one step, called either Acceptance-Finding or Plan for Action. Since CPS is aimed at the introduction of something new, and given the fact that change is not always readily accepted, it was deemed important to allow for a concentrated period of time to examine a broad array of factors, such as key stakeholders, resources, timing issues, cultural norms, work climate issues, etc., that might impact the successful introduction of the solution or change.

Although research has demonstrated, with some consistency, the existence of a sequence of discrete steps in the creative process, it has also been observed that individuals rarely move through the cognitive phases of the creative process in an orderly fashion. Again Kaufmann (1988) observed that, 'the cycle of phases is a lot more complex, and a high degree of overlapping occurs with lots of commuting between the different phases' (p. 99). The CPS model has accounted for this natural inclination for the mind to fast-forward through steps of the process or to rewind and revisit previous steps, as well as the need for the problem solver to adjust the application of the CPS process according to circumstances associated with the situation. This departure from a lock-step sequential application of the CPS process, in which the individual or group always begins with an identified first step and moves through the process model in a linear manner, was initially challenged by the componential model published by Isaksen *et al.* in

1994. With this process framework came the introduction of two initial process activities, called Task Appraisal and Process Planning, that enabled an individual or group to determine whether CPS was appropriate for the problem and, if so, where to begin in the process.

The Thinking Skills Model extends the view that CPS is a non-linear process. Specifically, the Thinking Skills Model always begins with a step called Assessing the Situation. The purpose of Assessing the Situation is twofold: first to identify and describe the data relevant to the problem under examination; and second, to determine the next process step. Since the thinking involved in Assessing the Situation occurs at a metacognitive level, that is, an ability to actively monitor and regulate thinking processes in accordance to one's cognitive objectives, this step is referred to as the executive step as it stands above the others and thus enables an individual or group to determine the most effective progression through the CPS framework. To encourage ongoing monitoring, Assessing the Situation occurs throughout the process, thereby allowing individuals and groups to jump forward or revisit steps as necessary.

A hallmark of the CPS process, which is retained in the Thinking Skills Model, is the dynamic balance between divergent and convergent thinking that occurs in every step of the process. In fact, the current illustration of the process (see Figure 27.1) maintains the longstanding tradition of graphically representing each step of the CPS process in a diamond shape (e.g. Osborn-Parnes, Basic Course, Simplex®). The expanding upper portion of the diamond shape represents the application of divergent thinking, which is the broad search for many diverse and novel alternatives. The bottom portion of the diamond, where it closes in on a particular point, represents convergent thinking – a focused and affirmative evaluation of alternatives.

This balance between the search for options and then selection among these alternatives is crucial to effective thinking. It allows individuals and groups to be more successful in finding creative solutions by encouraging them to first set aside premature evaluation and to think up all the possible alternatives, followed by the application of good decision-making skills to find those alternatives that are most promising in that particular step of the process. The dynamic balance of divergent and convergent thinking optimizes the thinking as it ensures that sufficient ground is covered before taking a decision. As Ruggiero (1998: 5) concluded:

> For decades psychologists of thinking stressed that the mind has two distinctive phases – the production phase and the judgment phase – that complement each other during thinking. They stressed further that proficiency in thinking requires the mastery of all approaches appropriate to each phase and skill in moving back and forth between them.

CPS has been referred to as a cognitive process model; however, the identification of the kinds of thinking skills necessary to successfully engage in CPS has been limited to divergent and convergent thought. Perhaps the most significant evolution with respect to the current CPS model is not found in any modification to the structure or steps of the model, but rather in the articulation of the thinking skills associated with this process. In the Thinking Skills Model, Puccio et al. (2005, 2007) have set out to identify a main thinking skill involved in each step of the process. Based on extensive experience in teaching and researching the CPS model, seven main thinking skills were delineated. An extensive review of the literature was undertaken to confirm whether scholars in the fields of creativity, education, business and psychology had isolated and described the same or similar cognitive skills (Barbero-Switalski 2003). Information garnered through this literature review led to a revised list of thinking skills and definitions that were then evaluated by a panel of content experts (ibid.). A summary of these thinking skills, and their respective step, is found below:

- *Diagnostic thinking* (assessing the situation): making a careful examination of the situation, describing the nature of the problem, and making decisions about appropriate process steps to be taken (curiosity).
- *Visionary thinking* (exploring the vision): articulating a vivid image of what you desire to create (dreaming).
- *Strategic thinking* (formulating challenges): identifying the critical issues that must be addressed and pathways needed to move toward the desired future (sensing gaps).
- *Ideational thinking* (exploring ideas): producing original mental images and thoughts that respond to important challenges (playfulness).
- *Evaluative thinking* (formulating solutions): assessing the reasonableness and quality of ideas in order to develop workable solutions (avoiding premature closure).
- *Contextual thinking* (exploring acceptance): understanding the interrelated conditions and circumstances that will support or hinder success (sensitivity to environment).
- *Tactical thinking* (formulating a plan): devising a plan that includes specific and measurable steps for attaining a desired end and methods for monitoring its effectiveness (tolerance for risks).

A further development embodied by the Thinking Skills Model is the first attempt to articulate the specific affective skills that support effective use of CPS. Goleman (1998) suggested that, 'the act of innovation is both cognitive and emotional. Coming up with a creative insight is a cognitive act – but realizing its value, nurturing it and following through calls on emotional competencies, such as self-confidence, initiative, persistence, and the ability to persuade' (p. 100). Commensurate with Goleman's position on the interplay of cognition and emotion in the innovation process, Puccio et al. (2007) set out to describe the affective skills that complement the cognitive skills found in CPS. Three affective skills are deemed important for successful adoption of the CPS process in general: openness to novelty, tolerance for ambiguity and tolerance for complexity. Additionally, there are seven specific affective skills that align and support the thinking skills found in each step (see the parentheses found at the end of the thinking skills definitions). These ten affective skills are not presented as a comprehensive set. Rather, they are offered as a starting list intended to acknowledge some of the important ways in which emotional abilities support a cognitive creative process.

Puccio et al. (2005) provided an initial attempt to highlight some of the anticipated benefits of the development of the Thinking Skills Model. Now that we have had the opportunity to work with the Thinking Skills Model, we offer the following as a revised list of the theoretical and practical benefits associated with the current CPS framework; it:

1. Allows greater articulation of the qualitative distinctions found among steps of the CPS process.
2. Broadens the instructional methods used to teach and train CPS by incorporating additional approaches designed to promote thinking and affective skills.
3. Improves understanding of the potential impact and value of CPS training.
4. Adds specificity to the learning objectives associated with CPS teaching or training.
5. Enhances levels of internalization and transfer by linking effectively to a variety of areas of human endeavor.
6. Shifts the CPS model from a mechanical process framework more towards a meta-model capable of assisting individuals and groups in identifying the kind of thinking necessary to be successful in a wide variety of situations.
7. Serves as an organizing framework for problem-solving tools, thus allowing the CPS

model to draw in a greater variety of methods and strategies from other fields (i.e. strategic planning, continuous improvement, decision making, design thinking, etc.).

8 Specifies the kinds of leadership skills necessary in today's complex workplace (see Puccio *et al.* 2007).

In conclusion, the CPS model has enjoyed more than 50 years of development and application. A unique aspect of the history of CPS is that this model has not been relegated strictly to application, but such practice has been balanced by research into the efficacy of CPS. Puccio *et al.* (2006) provided a summary of the research that has explored the value of CPS training. After conducting a meta-analysis of creativity training, Scott *et al.* (2004) concluded that CPS is among the most effective models shown to positively impact divergent thinking, problem solving, performance, attitudes and behaviors. This combination of both research and practice renders CPS a unique model in the field of creativity.

Future trends

As CPS has been transformed over a five-decade period, there is little doubt that it will continue to evolve. Therefore, we close this chapter by examining three future trends that might continue to shape the use of CPS, as well as the model itself. The first trend is the integration of more Eastern philosophical approaches to creativity such as meditation and spiritual intelligence. The second trend is the integration of technology such as software programs that parallel the stages of CPS or the use of avatars to facilitate CPS in a multi-virtual environment. The third trend is the integration of CPS and methods applied in design thinking, such as ethnography.

Integration of Eastern philosophy

The development of CPS has been almost exclusively driven by a Western mindset. As globalization has forced businesses to embrace more Eastern ways of thinking and behaving, so too CPS must consider how to expand beyond its cognitive, rational and semantic orientation to problem solving. That is, problem-solving approaches in the future may evoke emotional, spiritual and intuitional intelligences that work in concert with cognitive intelligence to produce innovation. Emotional intelligence here is defined as the ability to understand one's innermost feelings and one's relationship with others (Goleman 1998). Spiritual intelligence is the willingness to observe, to notice without affixation, to observe with presence and alertness, the awareness of awareness (Aburdene 2005). Intuitional intelligence is defined as the preliminary instinctive knowing that does not occur at the conscious level, but not withstanding directs thinking (Bowers *et al.* 1990).

BusinessWeek magazine reported that companies are beginning to integrate Indian philosophy and business strategy (Engardio and McGregor 2006). *BusinessWeek* also reported that General Electric's CEO, Jeffrey Immelt, consults an Indian-born strategist to receive insight on mastering certain impulses and emotions that could get in the way of sound judgments. Elite business schools such as Harvard, Kellogg, Wharton, Michigan and Dartmouth now tout that 10 per cent of their faculty are of Indian descent (ibid.). Major companies such as AT&T, PepsiCo and Aetna are providing employees with training in reflection and meditation. *The Journal of Management Education* dedicated an entire issue to spirituality in contemporary work (Dehler and Neal 2000). So (1995) found that regular practice of transcendental meditation produced significant and positive increases in six areas of intelligence that included creativity.

With the *Thinking Skills Model* we have begun to explore how affective skills contribute to effective creative problem solving, but with the trend toward practices typically associated with Eastern thought, there is much more that can be done. For instance, methods might be incorporated to assist those who use CPS to explore their intuitive sense of the problem. Ideation in CPS may include processes that are based on heightened spiritual states of consciousness. When creating a plan of action, individuals may start to examine how their ideas might influence the organizational ecosystem comprising of vendors, clients, the community, employees, financial structure, resources and society at large.

Integration of technology

The processing speeds of computer microchips are increasing at dizzying rates. This phenomenon will open up endless possibilities for new technologies. For example, the head of Sony's electronic games business, Ken Kutaragi, with the help of engineers from IBM, Toshiba and Sony, was able to create a supercomputer chip that is 60 times faster and 1000 times more realistic than the PlayStation2 (Kirkpatrick 2005). Such an improvement in speed and in realism will inevitably transform computers, broadband, wireless phones, networks, and just about anything that involves digitization.

Increasingly, creative process methods are finding their way into computer programs. There are programs for mind-mapping and for visually tagging themes within a data set. There exists intelligent computing that learns in the same way humans do by applying algorithms to organize data into patterns and sequences and then calculates the probability of what will follow; memory nodes then transmit this information among themselves so that computing can in effect learn.

These prospects appear to have important implications for how and where innovation is facilitated individually or in groups. Companies such as American Airlines, Federal Express and Dell are using networks built on collaborative simulation systems (Schrage 2006). Software programs now permit digitized prototypes, models and simulations to go through endless iterations, which *Strategy + Business* is coining iterative capital (ibid.). Chrysler, for example, uses a software program called the Data Visualizer in concert with another program called Catai to perform 8646 iterative checks in 17 seconds to examine the interface possibilities among sheet metal components (ibid.). There are software programs that aid novices in creating storyboard illustrations or that process data to produce a variety of mission statements from which to choose.

Multi-user virtual environment interfaces such as Second Life (a virtual community) provide opportunities for avatars to facilitate CPS with the help of other avatars. Given advancements in technology, it is highly likely that users of Second Life will one day be able to don virtual reality eyewear coupled with full body force feedback systems to activate the five senses. In the future, the development of touch-screen technology may permit clients and resource group members to move digital flipchart paper or Post-Its™. Because the exchange of information will grow exponentially and in velocity, the role of a CPS facilitator is likely to shift to one of hyperediting in which he or she filters information much like portfolio managers do using methodologies such as the modern portfolio theory, which incorporates quantitative tools to assess risk and reward (ibid.). Because software programs will parallel CPS stages and tools, a facilitator will rely less and less on flipcharts and Post-Its™. Thus when working with virtual groups, facilitators in the future may find themselves in the role of an observer who monitors group process and intervenes based on feedback generated by software programs that interprets speech inflection and detects emotions.

335

Integration of ethnography

According to Nussbaum (2006), ethnography is fast becoming the new core leadership competence. Ethnography is a social science discipline that is now being applied in business to generate an empathic understanding of consumer needs (ibid.), needs that perhaps the consumers themselves may not realize. It is an inquiry into consumer activities from which information emerges that is then used to create innovations for market solutions. The core method for empathic understanding is observation. Observers immerse themselves in targeted settings. They use tools such as cameras, video recorders and sketchpads. Once observations have been completed, software programs then aid in analysis of a large volume of visual data. It would be wise for future versions of CPS to use data gathered through ethnography as a springboard to problem identification.

Summary

In a field replete with 'How to' books and applied approaches, CPS stands out as one of the few creative process models that has effectively integrated theory, research and practice. This unique combination provides CPS with a rich history and firm foundation from which to evolve. The trends briefly outlined in this chapter provide exciting future opportunities for the continued development of CPS. One enduring thread that has traversed the CPS processes of the past and the present, and in all probability will continue into the future, is the underlying principle long held by Osborn (1963) – to separate divergent and convergent thinking.

References

Aburdene, P. (2005). *Megatrends 2010: The rise of conscious capitalism*. Charlottesville, VA: Hampton Roads Publishing Company, Inc.

Amabile, T. M., Burnside, R. M. and Gryskiewicz, S. S. (1999). *User's manual for KEYS: Assessing the climate for creativity*. Greensboro, NC: Center for Creative Leadership.

Barbero-Switalski, L. (2003). Evaluating and organizing thinking tools in relationship to the CPS framework. Unpublished master's project, Buffalo State, State University of New York.

Basadur, M. (1994). *Simplex®: A flight to creativity*. Buffalo, NY: Creative Education Foundation.

Bowers, K. S., Regher, G., Balthazard, C. and Parker, K. (1990). Intuition in the context of discovery. *Cognitive Psychology*, 22, 72–110.

Dehler, G. and Neal, J. (2000). The guest editor's corner. *Journal of Management Education*, 24, 536–539.

Engardio, P. and McGregor, J. (2006). Karma capitalism. *BusinessWeek*, at: http://www.businessweek.com/globalbiz/content/oct2006/gb20061019_650475.ht?chan=search.

Friedman, T. L. (2006). *The world is flat: A brief history of the twenty-first century*. New York: Farrar, Straus and Giroux.

Goleman, D. (1998). *Working with emotional intelligence*. New York: Bantam.

Isaksen, S. G. and Treffinger, D. J. (2004). Celebrating 50 years of reflective practice: Versions of creative problem solving. *Journal of Creative Behavior*, 38, 75–101.

Isaksen, S. G., Dorval, K. B. and Treffinger, D. J. (1994). *Creative approaches to problem solving*. Dubuque, IA: Kendall/Hunt.

Isaksen, S. G., Dorval, K. B. and Treffinger, D. J. (2000). *Creative approaches to problem solving* (second edition). Dubuque, IA: Kendall/Hunt.

Janszen, F. (2000). *The age of innovation: Making business creativity a competence, not a coincidence*. London: Financial Times/Prentice Hall.

Kaufmann, G. (1988). Problem solving and creativity. In K. Gronhaug and G. Kaufmann (eds), *Innovation: A cross-disciplinary perspective* (pp. 87–137). Oslo: Norwegian University Press.

Kirkpatrick, D. (2005). The 9-in-1 wonder chip. *Fortune*, 5 September, 139–149.

Nussbaum, B. (2006). Ethnography is the new core competence. *IN*, 22 February, 10.

Osborn, A. F. (1953). *Applied imagination: Principles and procedures of creative problem-solving*. New York: Scribner's Sons.

Osborn, A. F. (1963). *Applied imagination: Principles and procedures of creative problem-solving* (third edition). New York: Scribner's Sons.

Parnes, S. J. (1967). *Creative behavior workbook*. New York: Scribner's Sons.

Parnes, S. J. (1988). *Visionizing*. East Aurora, NY: DOK Publishers.

Parnes, S. J. (1992). Creative problem solving and visionizing. In S. J. Parnes (ed.), *Sourcebook for creative problem solving* (pp. 133–154). Buffalo, NY: Creative Education Press.

Puccio, G. J., Firestien, R. L., Coyle, C. and Masucci, C. (2006). A review of the effectiveness of Creative Problem Solving training: A focus on workplace issues. *Creativity and Innovation Management*, 15 19–33.

Puccio, G. J., Murdock, M. C. and Mance, M. (2005). Current developments in creative problem solving for organizations: A focus on thinking skills and styles. *Korean Journal of Thinking and Problem Solving*, 15, 43–76.

Puccio, G. J., Murdock, M. C. and Mance, M. (2007). *Creative leadership: Skills that drive change*. Thousand Oaks, CA: Sage.

Ruggiero, V. R. (1998). *The art of thinking: A guide to critical and creative thought* (fifth edition). New York: Longman.

Schrage, M. (2006). Here comes hyperinnovation. *Strategy + Business*, at: http://www.strategy-business.com/press/article/10900?pg=0.

Scott, G. M., Leritz, L. E. and Mumford, M. D. (2004). The effectiveness of creativity training: A meta-analysis. *Creativity Research Journal*, 16, 361–388.

So, Kam-Tim (1995). Testing and improving intelligence and creativity in the Chinese culture with Maharishi's vedic psychology: Toward a holistic and universal assessment. Unpublished doctoral thesis, Maharishi International University.

Vehar, J. R., Firestien, R. L. and Miller, B. (1997). *Creativity unbound*. Williamsville, NY: Innovation Systems Group.

Wallis, C. and Steptoe, S. (2006). How to bring our schools out of the 20th century. *TIME*, 18 December, 50–56.

28

Thinking outside the box: Edward de Bono's lateral thinking

Sandra Dingli

What is lateral thinking?

Edward de Bono invented the concept of lateral thinking in 1967. While the term may have been used informally before, it has become almost universally associated with the body of work written by de Bono over the following decades.

Lateral thinking involves deliberate mental efforts to change more automatic or habitual responses that have been shaped through perceptual frameworks. The result is that unexpected and valuable ideas are unleashed. Such outcomes are primarily unexpected and valuable to the individual at the moment of insight, but may at times be of high impact to far wider groups of individuals, organizations, or even cultures.

As opposed to other methods for idea generation, lateral thinking may be used not only for problem solving but also for design purposes and for constructive thinking. Opportunities may be created or exploited in various areas, including science, technology, management, education, economics and policy making.

Belief in the application of lateral thinking goes against the assumption that some people are born creative while others are not. It furthermore implies the possibility of utilizing simple methods for a wide range of individuals to generate ideas on demand within a short timeframe.

The rationale behind lateral thinking

Edward de Bono was educated as a medical doctor at the University of Malta and he later continued his studies at the University of Cambridge. His early research led him to explore the nature of self-organizing biological systems and to relate it to what he called *The Mechanism of Mind* (de Bono 1969).

Lateral thinking is based on the hypothesis that the human brain is a self-organizing information-processor with output that depends on both internal and external environments and on previous experience. Through the use of lateral thinking, established cognitive patterns are deliberately disrupted and information is processed differently, increasing the chances of arriving at novel perspectives for the individual.

de Bono's hypothesis offers a cognitive explanation of the process of insight, which is often considered critical to the act of creativity and of humor (Koestler 1964; Sternberg and Davidson 1995). The process of insight, which is generated within a self-organizing patterning system, such as the human brain, is generally organized to generate a deterministic outcome rather than an unexpected one. When one listens to a joke being related, the brain receives successive cues (sequential over time), which reinforce anticipatory responses. The sequential delivery of information directs the listener's attention in a particular direction. Expectations are then suddenly disrupted, with the result that a moment of insight is instigated when the listener 'gets the joke'.

Similar disruptions in anticipated patterns of cognitive processing occur through the use of lateral thinking methods. Once again, the outcome is a moment of insight or what is often referred to as an 'aha' moment, when novel perspectives are generated. Insight may be regarded as a process simulated through what may initially appear to be illogical (or 'apparently illogical') methods. The lateral thinking tools seek to simulate in a purposive manner those haphazard processes (such as a chance event or a piece of information that acts as a catalyst) that occur in the human brain when insight occurs.

Serious creativity

The upshot is 'serious creativity', which de Bono views as distinct from 'whacky' or crazy creativity. The latter is considered to be analogous to a situation such as that of a person constrained from playing the violin because of her hands being securely tied with a rope. 'Cutting the rope,' de Bono maintains, 'does not make that person a violinist' (*The Guardian* 2005). This involves a distinction between processes that allow people to feel relaxed and comfortable and which remove inhibitions, and the skills which permit the generation of useful novelty which de Bono calls 'serious' creativity. Lateral thinking, therefore, involves the application of systematic methods as opposed to the view of creativity as a mysterious gift or talent that some people possess while others do not.

Although he admits that removing inhibitions may result in 'a mild level of creativity but not much' (de Bono 1993a: x), his distinction between serious and crazy or whacky creativity addresses:

> one of the most serious dilemmas of our whole thinking culture . . . [the assumption] that every valuable creative idea must always be logical in hindsight. If it were not logical in hindsight, we should never be able to appreciate its value. It would just be a crazy idea suspended without any support. We might catch up with it later or not at all. So we are able to appreciate only those creative ideas which are logical in hindsight.
>
> (de Bono 1990a: 89)

In this and other works, de Bono acknowledges the difficulty which the word 'creativity' presents, through lack of a widely accepted encompassing definition:

> The very word 'creativity' is a huge concept trap in the English language. It covers everything from just making something happen (like creating a mess) to artistic creativity, to mathematical insights, to finger painting by children. That is one of the reasons, among many, why we have done so little about the matter. It was precisely to escape this concept

339

trap that I invented the term 'lateral thinking' to apply very specifically to the changing of concepts and perceptions in a self-organizing patterning system.

(1990a: 105)

These accounts indicate an attempt to demystify the creative process, which other authors have also identified as a development beyond earlier views (Isaksen 1987; Parnes 1992). Lateral thinking is an innovative attempt to cut across the habitual processes through which perception occurs. This process can be deliberately instigated through the use of strategies that mimic what happens in the brain when new ideas are generated.

De Bono explicitly states that, 'in any self-organizing system, creativity is absolutely essential' (1993b: 63). This is evident as, '[t]here can be no doubt that creativity is the most important human resource of all. Without creativity there would be no progress, and we would be forever repeating the same patterns' (ibid.: 169). This does not however reject the benefits of routinization. Rather, he follows Simon's (1997) well-known description of such information process as self-limiting through satisficing:

If the brain were not a pattern-making system we would not be able to read, write or talk. Every activity, like getting dressed in the morning, would be a major time-consuming task. Sport would be impossible. . . . Consider the millions of people who drive along the roads every day using patterns of perception and reaction and only occasionally having to work things out.

(de Bono 1990a: 82)

Defining lateral thinking

The definition of lateral thinking found in a number of dictionaries is 'seeking to solve problems by unorthodox or apparently illogical methods'. It is important to note that the illogicality of the methods used is merely apparent and that the subsequent, after-the-event shift in perception reveals previously taken-for-granted assumptions as false or debatable:

The best way to describe lateral thinking is to say: 'You cannot dig a hole in a different place by digging the same hole deeper.' This emphasizes the searching for different approaches and different ways of looking at things. Lateral thinking contrasts with vertical thinking where 'you take a position and then you seek to build on that basis. . . . The next step has to be related and logically derived from where you are at this moment. This suggests building up from a base or digging deeper the same hole. . . .'

(de Bono 1993a: 52–53)

Lateral thinking augments the habitual and more routine processes that make up vertical thinking:

I regard creative thinking (lateral thinking) as a special type of information handling. It should take its place alongside our other methods of handling information: mathematics, logical analysis, computer simulation, and so on. There need be no mystique about it. A person sitting down with the deliberate intention of generating an idea in a certain area and then proceeding to use a lateral thinking technique systematically should represent a normal state of affairs.

(p. xii)

In the same text, lateral thinking is summarized as:

> the type of creative thinking that can be learned, practiced, and used by everyone. Some people will be better at it than others, as with any skill. Learning lateral thinking will not make everyone a genius, but it will supplement existing thinking skills with a valuable ability to generate new ideas.
>
> (p. 310)

The concept of skill is a key issue which de Bono does not take lightly – he considers thinking to be a skill which can be improved through practice, this being a claim which is reiterated in most of his publications and something that many of his methods aim to achieve.

Lateral thinking and other methodologies

The wider body of work sometimes known as lateral thinking includes other methodologies that are proposed as simple and effective ways through which one can generate new ideas and challenge existing concepts and perceptions. The list below (de Bono 1993a) provides a comprehensive list of tools and a description of their practical application and effects:

- *CoRT (Cognitive Research Programme)*: six programmes (CoRT 1 to CoRT 6), designed for educational contexts with the aim of broadening perceptual skills.
- *DATT™ (Direct Attention Thinking Tools)*: ten 'thinking tools' (seven of which are identical to the thinking tools in CoRT 1), primarily for management and staff training contexts.
- *Six Thinking Hats® (parallel thinking)*: this method involves six different modes of thinking, each being represented by a different colored hat, supporting conflict resolution, problem solving, decision making or generating new insights.
- *Six Action Shoes*: this method (which, to date, has not been commercialized) uses a similar technique to that of the Six Thinking Hats; however the focus is on *action*. Each 'shoe' has a different color and function, which represents a different mode of action applied to problem solving and decision making.
- *Simplicity*: based on a book with the same name (de Bono 1990b), the aim is to create a shift in perception from complexity to simplicity in an attempt to reduce unnecessary procedures, avoid duplication and increase efficiency.
- *Six Value Medals™*: this distinguishes six different value categories and the aim is to scan for values and to prioritize them, after which top values are addressed and maximized.
- *Focus on Facilitation™*: this involves the use of a combination of de Bono's tools for use in facilitating meetings successfully.

Most of these methods are propriatory, although descriptions of most of the methods are to be found in numerous publications. Some authors (González 2001, for example) tend to assume that all de Bono's methods fall under the general rubric of lateral thinking. This may be reinforced in some of de Bono's publications, such as *Serious Creativity* (1993a), where the Six Thinking Hats are described in the first chapter of Part 2 under the heading 'Lateral Thinking Tools and Techniques'. For the purposes of this chapter, these methods have been differentiated from lateral thinking (see Table 28.1).

Table 28.1 Summary of lateral thinking and related methodologies

CoRT 1 (Broadens perception)	DATT™ (Broadens perception)	Six Thinking Hats (Parallel thinking)	Lateral Thinking (Out-of-the-box thinking)
PMI Plus, Minus, Interesting	PMI Plus, Minus, Interesting	White Hat Information, Facts and Data	Alternatives
CAF Consider All Factors	CAF Consider All Factors	Red Hat Emotions, Hunches, Intuitions	Concept Triangle
Rules	RAD Recognize, Analyze, Divide	Yellow Hat Benefits, Optimism, Value	Concept Fan
C & S Consequence and Sequel	C & S Consequence and Sequel	Black Hat Difficulties, Problems, Risks	Provocation (PO)
AGO Aims, Goals, Objectives	AGO Aims, Goals, Objectives	Green Hat Creativity, New Ideas, Alternatives	Challenge
Planning	KVI Key Values Involved	Blue Hat Facilitation, Summarizing, Decision making	Movement
FIP First Important Priorities	FIP First Important Priorities		Random Input
APC Alternatives, Possibilities, Choices	APC Alternatives, Possibilities, Choices		The Creative Pause
Decisions	DOCA Design/Decision, Outcomes, Channel, Action		
OPV Other People's Views	OPV Other People's Views		

Two other lateral thinking 'tools', Focus and Harvesting, may be noted, besides the ones listed in Table 28.1. Focus is used for orientation at the start of a creative thinking session. Harvesting, on the other hand, is used subsequently to prioritize, select and manage ideas that have been generated.

Some clarifications need to be made concerning de Bono's methods. First of all, de Bono's CoRT programme consists of six programmes where CoRT 4, which consists of ten work cards for use in educational contexts, comprises a simple version of some of the lateral thinking methods. Secondly, de Bono's Green Hat, one of the 'Six Thinking Hats' which represents the generation of new ideas and alternatives, and within which the lateral thinking techniques may be used, represents out-of-the-box (or creative) thinking.

Theoretical considerations and applications

Three widely cited and applied lateral thinking tools are Challenge, Random Input and Provocation (see, for example, Tanner 1997, for applications of these tools and some others in a large organization).

Challenge (de Bono 1993a) involves reflecting upon and questioning deeply held assumptions or convictions. The practical applications are vast, covering many fields of endeavor and range from accepted procedures, products and services to concepts, actions or designs. Practically anything can be challenged in an attempt to search for improvement. A successful outcome would involve the generation of alternative possibilities, even when there is no apparent need to do so, through raising questions about matters such as established procedures and whether the reasons for following them are still valid. This comes about through challenging dominant assumptions in a manner that does away with conventional analysis, argument or criticism.

Successful use of this lateral thinking tool interestingly demonstrates de Bono's emphasis on creativity methods being used not solely for problem solving but also to add value or to achieve improvement in any existing product, process or service, or intangible concept or idea. The deliberate application of this tool can result in the elimination of excessive bureaucracy or the improvement of, for example, products or services which are deemed to be acceptable under present circumstances but which can be drastically improved or made to be more efficient or desirable. The result is cost cutting, added value and an increase in profitability and competitivity – these being factors generally cited as being the main motivation for allocating resources for the generation of ideas in organizations.

Random Input (de Bono 1993a) simulates what happens when the information received from an external source triggers awareness and attention. This method involves introducing a word, picture, object or any other stimulus unconnected with the topic to encourage discovery of new ideas. As de Bono states, 'The background principle is that if you start from a different point, then you increase the likelihood of opening up patterns different from those you would have used when starting from the "center" ' (de Bono 1993a: 318).

Various print, mechanical and electronic aids are known which assist in the delivery of randomly generated words or images. They include sets of printed cards with random words, a 'random word ball', and more recently stimuli accessed from electronic databases. The practical result appears to be similar to what happens when attempts are made to associate disparate elements or when connections are forced as a result of linking two separate concepts (Rickards and Moger 1999). New ideas can emerge when this method is used; however, it involves divergent thinking where not all the resultant ideas are necessarily feasible or appropriate. Use of the method demonstrates that it is efficient as it does not take up more than a few minutes when used skilfully and, as opposed to similar techniques such as Parnes' (1992) visualization, it does not require either relaxation or incubation, nor does it require additional visible stimuli as some Creative Problem Solving (CPS) techniques may do (such as music, pictures, smells, etc.).

Provocation (also known as 'PO', a new word coined by de Bono, which means 'Provocative Operation') involves a two-stage process. A provocation is first set up, following which 'movement' is used to explore the provocation and to 'move' towards a useful new idea:

> With deliberate provocation we have a systematic method that can produce the same effects [as chance, accident, mistake, or 'madness']. We do not have to wait for change, accident or mistake. We can be temporarily 'mad' for just thirty seconds at a time in a

343

controllable fashion. We can switch the madness on and off as we wish. That is why provocation is such a fundamental aspect of lateral thinking.

(de Bono 1993a: 145)

De Bono distinguishes provocation from brainstorming as:

At first it might seem that provocation is simply a scattergun approach in which you say anything that comes to mind in the hope that something just might prove useful. To some extent this is the way brainstorming is used by some people. Such an approach would be weak and very wasteful.

(p. 146)

The Escape method of provocation

De Bono proposes a number of ways in which a provocation can be set up. The Escape method involves two steps – that which is taken for granted is first stated, followed by its negation, which provides the provocation. This is then used to lead towards unexpected directions, with the result that novel ideas are generated.

The Stepping Stone method of provocation

The Stepping Stone method involves four formal and deliberate ways that can be used to set up provocations.

Reversal involves changing the regular direction of thought. De Bono provides this example of reversal:

'I have orange juice for breakfast' is reversed to 'PO, the orange juice has me for breakfast.' Using movement, this could lead to an image of a person falling into a huge glass of orange juice, emerging smelling of orange juice. The novel idea that emerges could be to create shower attachments with perfume which could scent the water that emerges from the shower.

(p. 170)

A provocation may be set up by means of *Exaggeration*. Examples provided by de Bono include: 'PO, telephones are too heavy to lift' and 'PO, each cinema ticket costs $100' (p. 172) New ideas are generated from these exaggerations through movement.

Distortion sets up a provocation by changing regular sequences of actions. One well-known example which de Bono provides is: 'PO, you die before you die.' 'This was,' he states, 'the sort of provocation that led Ron Barbaro of the Prudential Insurance company to develop the very successful idea of "living benefits" ' (p. 173).

Finally, *Wishful Thinking* sets up provocations by proposing fantasy situations, which, under normal circumstances, would be impossible to achieve. Some examples provided by de Bono are: 'PO, the pencil should write by itself' and 'PO, shoplifters identify themselves' (pp. 174–175). The use of movement and reflection on such fantasies leads to feasible and innovative ideas, which may add value, resolve problems and increase profitability and competitivity.

Research evidence

Research has been conducted on the effects of the Six Thinking Hats and the CoRT (Cognitive Research Trust) thinking skills (Azzopardi *et al.* 2001; Dingli and Sciortino 1998; Edwards 1988, 1994, 1996; Hill 1994; Leone Ganado 1997; O'Brien *et al.* 1994; Perkins and Prime 1996; Tidona 2001).

A group of schoolteachers in Malta regularly conducts action research on the effects of teaching de Bono's methods, including the Six Thinking Hats and the CoRT programme (Cognitive Research Trust) to children (http://schoolnet.gov.mt/thinkingskills). The introduction of the CoRT programme in educational settings has been criticized for insufficient research evidence of its effectiveness:

> We find the lack of adequate evaluation studies on the CoRT program to be both surprising and disturbing. The program has been in existence for over 10 years and is claimed to be in wide use both in the British Isles and in Venezuela. Furthermore, de Bono makes strong claims concerning the effectiveness of the CoRT program. Yet after 10 years of widespread use, we have no adequate evidence concerning those claims and thus no support for the effectiveness of the program or the theoretical assumptions from which it was derived.
>
> (Polson and Jeffries 1985: 445)

McPeck (1981: 96) comments: 'It is surprising that de Bono's work has not received the scrutiny that one would expect from professional philosophers of education and others concerned with the development of critical thinking.' He draws attention to de Bono's overt opposition to the traditional academic approach to knowledge and to the absence of footnotes, references or indices in his publications (p. 97), as he states: 'This is especially serious when his claims are clearly of an empirical nature, and his argument rests on them. This fact alone may explain why traditional academics have never taken his work very seriously.'

De Bono's[1] response to this accusation is that the only references he would need to make in his work would be to his own publications, and that this is not necessary for their further understanding.

The author of this chapter had collected and examined a list of publications to combat such criticism (Dingli 2001). These tend to report practical experiences, rather than attempt the considerable task of evaluating the corpus of work in a rigorous and empirical fashion and, moreover, do not include research on the effects of using lateral thinking.

Most of the examples, anecdotes and case studies found in his numerous publications originate either from his own experience conducting workshops with audiences of different ages and backgrounds in educational or organizational contexts or from feedback received from his vast international network of certified trainers.

De Bono holds consistently to the position that it is the *practical and effective application of his methods* that should be taken into consideration rather than sophistic arguments or empirical research, where fine details such as that concerning the transfer of learnt skills from educational or organizational settings to other contexts cannot always be adequately captured.

The extensive reach of de Bono's work is evident when one considers the millions of books sold, and the number of languages into which many have been translated. Further evidence of the application of his methods in both educational and organizational contexts is visible both from the number of papers presented at conferences worldwide and from the continual demand for his services as he regularly travels the globe, delivering keynote presentations and workshops and attempting to satisfy a constant demand for consultations.

Most of the available research on the effects of using de Bono's lateral thinking tools is anecdotal and a great deal of such 'evidence' is cited in de Bono's numerous publications. A typical example is found in the 'Note on the Author' in *Serious Creativity*, which states:

> In an interview with the *Washington Post* on September 30 1984, Peter Ueberroth, the organizer of the very successful 1984 Los Angeles Olympic Games, told how he had used lateral thinking to change the Games from an event that no city in the world wanted to an event for which cities competed. At an opera reception in Melbourne, Australia, John Betrand, the skipper of the successful 1983 Australian bid for the America's Cup, told Dr. de Bono how he and his crew had used lateral thinking at every point.
>
> (de Bono 1993a: v)

De Bono's presentations at the numerous workshops he conducts, together with his official websites, are peppered with these and other similar testimonies. This includes lists of renowned organisations, including IBM, Du Pont, Prudential, AT&T, British Airways, British Coal, NTT (Japan), Ericsson (Sweden) and Siemens, who are often quoted on de Bono's websites as saying that numerous ideas were generated using lateral thinking, as a result of which profits and competitivity increased.

A theoretical comparison of lateral thinking with synectics and creative problem solving conducted as research at Masters level draws out a number of similarities and differences and claims that it is not possible to rank these methods against each other in the hope of selecting a 'winner' (González 2001). This study confirms the lack of academic research on de Bono's work, as González states: 'In academic settings, very little exists in the way of his research. Most of his studies show business results and are anecdotal in nature' (p. 69). González quotes from an interview he conducted with de Bono, which reveals the manner in which de Bono views academic research:

> It's really not an interest of mine to publish work and case studies that demonstrate measurability and results, although it certainly exists, or have to justify my work among academia. Research tends to be so artificial . . . nobody has been able to prove that literature, history or mathematic classes have prepared people for society. The skills of action are every bit as important as the skills of knowledge. We neglect them completely and turn out students who have little to contribute to society.
>
> (de Bono, cited in González 2001: 69)

González does not appear to have pressed de Bono further on his claim that research has been conducted, although it is likely that de Bono was referring to work published on the effects of using his CoRT programme. However, it is important to return to de Bono's emphasis on the 'skills of action' in the above quotation, as he has always claimed that his methods, which are content neutral, counteract the natural tendency of the human brain to categorise and pigeon-hole information. Moreover, his definition of the term 'operacy', a term which he himself coined, is 'the skill of thinking leading to action' – a clear demonstration of the importance he places on the practical application of the methods he advocates.

Divergent thinking methodologies

How do de Bono's methods compare with other idea-generating methods? In a discussion on Creative Problem Solving (CPS), McFazdean (1999:111) distinguishes three types of technique:

- *Paradigm-preserving techniques*, such as brainstorming, force field analysis and brainwriting, retain existing boundaries surrounding a problem and allow participants to remain within their comfort zone with a minimal amount of risk-taking.
- *Paradigm-stretching techniques* involve the creation of new ideas through the forced association of unrelated concepts or stimuli.
- *Paradigm-breaking techniques*, including lateral thinking, draw new elements into the problem situation and develop new relationships, with the result that powerful novel ideas may be generated.

In a paper where the stated aim is to 'build bridges', Sutcliffe (1997) summarises the benefits and limitations of lateral thinking, as he states:

> The potential is clearly to create many, if not wholly, new ways of thinking about all sorts of things (not only practical or material problems); the limitation is quite simply that not every new idea is a good idea. There always remains, as de Bono often admits, a need to subject creative ideas to critical analysis as part of a continual drive towards real improvement.

Sutcliffe maintains that analysis and judgement should not be undervalued because it is as a result of good judgement that 'we recognise the need for better designs in the first place, apply appropriate strategies and procedures for coming up with them in the second place, and eventually appreciate the better designs when they are put forward' (ibid.). It is particularly important to analyse concepts since 'without clear analysis our thinking, and therefore our designs, cannot move forward' (ibid.).

Sutcliffe (ibid.) challenges de Bono for his claim that, ' "We need to be able to design ways forward – leaving the cause in place", which reflects "pessimism" and a particularly curious remark from one who earlier placed such great emphasis on "what may be" and "what can be" in a changing world, rather than on "what is" in a world misconceived as "stable".' There is, therefore, no reason to accept 'the notion that the causes of so many problems have to be "left in place".'

As a proponent of philosophical thinking, particularly in the form that is known as *Philosophy for Children*, Sutcliffe (ibid.) admits it is necessary to 'design ways forward'. However, in order to do so, 'we need to concentrate on the very tools of our thinking – especially the words or concepts that we use, more or less creatively, to resolve our problems.'

Sutcliffe draws a parallel between de Bono's methods and philosophy for children, both of which, he admits, 'are inspired by the same vision of "building" a better world'. This can be executed through 'cooperative thinking', which is similar to de Bono's 'parallel thinking' in a manner which overcomes the rejection of different values.

The work of influential philosopher George Pólya has been related to the lateral thinking approach (Hughes and Hughes 2007). Examining Provocation, Challenge and Alternatives methods, they conclude that:

> Pólya's heuristic techniques fall into de Bono's creative thinking framework. Specifically,

they [Specialisation and Generalisation] fall into the frameworks of Challenge and Alternatives. Notably, none of Pólya's heuristics fall into de Bono's framework of Provocation.

(p. 163)

Hughes and Hughes differentiate between the mechanisms implied by the various techniques. In their view,

A hypothesis is related to judgement[al] thinking because it tries to be reasonable, whereas provocation makes a deliberate attempt to be unreasonable. A hypothesis exists to be verified, whereas a provocation does not exist to be verified, but to be used as a bridge to a valuable and meaningful idea or concept.

(p. 160)

This analysis has much in common with ideas of neuro-linguistic programming and the internal dialogue (Hermans *et al.* 1992).

Lateral marketing and lateral puzzles

There have been a number of applications of lateral thinking to work and leisure occupations, the most well known being lateral thinking puzzles and lateral marketing.

Lateral thinking puzzles are popular and widely available. Sloane and MacHale (2005a) have published a number of such puzzles with unlikely and unexpected solutions, which, they claim, help to unleash the brain's potential for lateral thinking. They support the viewpoint that effective thinking in real life is rarely straightforward but is 'much more likely to be an unpredictable mixture of guesswork, hunches, funny feelings, insight, intuition, experience, sixth sense, serendipity, low cunning, street wisdom . . .' (p. 9). They illustrate the popular enthusiasm for the potency of lateral thinking as, 'one of the most powerful weapons the human mind can employ' (op. cit.).

Sloane and MacHale (2005b: 7) conceive of lateral thinking puzzles as presenting 'strange situations which require an explanation'. The puzzles present the reader with insufficient information on a topic and they instigate reflection and the questioning of assumptions.

Solving such puzzles may involve an internal dialogue (Hermans *et al.* 1992). There are interesting parallels to be found in writings on neurolinguistic programming. Anecdotal evidence and training experience demonstrate that lateral thinking puzzles are an effective way of motivating learners from underprivileged social groups such as prison inmates, residents at a drug rehabilitation centre and children in socially deprived areas.

Trías de Bes and Kotler (2003) contrast vertical marketing with lateral marketing, following de Bono's distinction between vertical and lateral thinking. The former follows a number of sequential and logical thinking processes, while the latter 'restructures the existing information and goes from the concrete to the global through less selective thinking, but rather more exploratory, probabilistic, provocative and creative thinking' (p. 75). Trías de Bes and Kotler claim that both types of thinking are 'necessary and complementary', without one being considered as superior to the other. Their ideas consist of a reaction to the claim that current marketing theories 'are not very effective in creating alternative or substitute products' (p. 20).

Lateral marketing involves the creation of a new category or market where a product is transformed in order to make it appropriate for satisfying new needs or new situations. This concept takes marketing beyond its regular sequential process where new products and services are variations of what was previously available. Lateral marketing goes one step further and an interesting example which the authors use to demonstrate this concerns breakfast cereals, which, when converted into cereal bars, are considered as snacks to be consumed at any time of the day, thus broadening the concept of cereal and creating new markets.

Conclusion

Lateral thinking is today as much a part of everyday English language as terms such as Kuhn's 'paradigm shifts' and Dawkins' 'memes'. There is an enormous body of practical work pointing to the efficient and effective use of lateral thinking tools, with claims for the generation of valuable ideas within a very short time span.

There is little doubt that the work which Edward de Bono himself has published has influenced individuals all over the world. His numerous publications, together with his frequent public and media appearances, have raised awareness of the benefits to be derived from deliberate efforts for instigating creative thinking.

However, there remain major challenges to establishing the theoretical grounding of the work. The very broad reach of the work contributes to the difficulties. de Bono's refusal to follow academic convention and to connect his work to earlier literature leaves it open to criticism as at best under-researched. Similar criticism has been levelled at other systems aimed at structuring and accelerating the creative process (Parnes 1992). Such criticism does not, however, detract in any way from the practical positive effects that are regularly reported as a result of the efficient use of de Bono's lateral thinking tools.

Note

1 Private communication to the author, but one that is consistent with his public response on the matter. His response to criticism is that anyone in doubt as to whether the tools are effective or not should carefully observe the powerful results that emerge from their use.

References

Azzopardi, A., Borg Savona, L., Busuttil, E., Mifsud, J., Pace, M. and Zammit, J. (2001) Teaching thinking in a secondary school in Malta. In S. Dingli (ed.), *Creative Thinking: An Indispensable Asset for a Successful Future, Selected Proceedings of the Fourth International Conference on Creative Thinking*. Msida: Malta University Press.

de Bono, E. (1967) *The Use of Lateral Thinking*. London: Jonathan Cape.

de Bono, E. (1969) *The Mechanism of Mind*. London: Penguin.

de Bono, E. (1990a) *I am Right You are Wrong: From this to the New Renaissance, from Rock Logic to Water Logic*. London: Penguin.

de Bono, E. (1990b) *Simplicity*. London: Penguin.

de Bono, E. (1993a) *Serious Creativity: Using the Power of Lateral Thinking to Create New Ideas*. London: HarperCollins Business.

de Bono, E. (1993b) *Sur/petition: Going Beyond Competition*. London: HarperCollins.

Dingli, S. (2001) Brief literature review, July, at: http://home.um.edu.mt/create.

Dingli, L. and Sciortino, L. (1998) Developing democratic values through a summer school curriculum. Unpublished B.Ed. (Hons.) dissertation, University of Malta.

Edwards, J. (1988) The direct teaching of thinking skills. CoRT 1: An evaluative case study. Unpublished Ph.D. thesis, James Cook University of North Queensland, Australia.

Edwards, J. (1994) Thinking and Change. In S. Dingli (ed.), *Creative Thinking: A Multifaceted Approach, Proceedings of the First International Conference on Creative Thinking*, pp. 16–29, Msida: Malta University Press.

Edwards, J. (1996) The direct teaching of thinking in education and business. In S. Dingli (ed.), *Creative Thinking: New Perspectives, Proceedings of the Second International Conference on Creative Thinking*, pp. 82–95, Msida: Malta University Press.

González, D. (2001) The art of solving problems: Comparing the similarities and differences between Creative Problem Solving (CPS), lateral thinking and synectics. Unpublished Master of Science dissertation, State University of New York, Buffalo State College, International Center for Studies in Creativity.

Guardian, The (2005) Where do you wear your thinking cap?, at: http://technology.guardian.co.uk/online/businesssolutions/story/0,,1399009,00.html downloaded 8 February 2007

Hermans, H.J.M., Kempen, H.J.G. and van Loon R.J.P. (1992). The dialogical self: Beyond individualism and rationalism. *American Psychologist*, 47, 23–33.

Hill, B. (1994) Growing people, growing crystals. In S. Dingli (ed.), *Creative Thinking: A Multifaceted Approach*, pp. 215–223. Msida: Malta University Press.

Hughes, A. and Hughes, P. (2007) Pólya and de Bono: A comparative study in problem solving heuristics. In S. Dingli (ed.), *Creative Thinking: Towards New Possibilities*. Msida: Malta University Press.

Isaksen, S.G. (1987) Introduction: An orientation to the frontiers of creativity research. In S. G. Isaksen (ed.), *Frontiers of Creativity Research: Beyond the Basics*, pp. 1–26. Buffalo, NY: Bearly.

Koestler, A. (1964) *The Act of Creation*. London: Macmillan.

Leone Ganado, J. (1997) Teaching children to think. Unpublished PGCE dissertation, University of Malta.

McFadzean, E. (1999) Creativity in MS/OR: Choosing the appropriate technique. *Interfaces*, 29 (5), 110–122, at: http://www.cs.wright.edu/~rhill/HFE_742/Choosing%20Creativity.pdf.

McPeck, J.E. (1981) *Critical Thinking and Education*. Oxford: Martin Robertson.

O'Brien, J., Stapledon, A., Edwards, J. and Diamond, P. (1994) An implementation of Cort-1, -IV and –VI in a large secondary school. In S. Dingli (ed.), *Creative Thinking: A Multifaceted Approach, Proceedings of the First International Conference on Creative Thinking*, pp. 93–110. Msida: Malta University Press.

Parnes, S.J. (ed.) (1992) *Sourcebook for Creative Problem-Solving*. Buffalo, NY: Creative Education Foundation Press.

Perkins, K. and Prime, T. (1996) They keep telling us we have to think differently, but no one shows us how to do it! In S. Dingli (ed.), *Creative Thinking: New Perspectives, Proceedings of the Second International Conference on Creative Thinking*, pp. 103–122. Msida: Malta University Press.

Polson, P.G. and Jeffries, R. (1985) Analysis-instruction in general problem solving skills: An analysis of four approaches. In J. W. Segal, S. F. Chipman and R. Glaser (eds), *Thinking and Learning Skills*, Volume 1, pp. 417–455. Hillsdale, NJ: Lawrence Erlbaum.

Rickards, T. and Moger, S.T. (1999) *Handbook for Creative Team Leaders*. Aldershot: Gower.

Simon, H.A. (1997) *Models of Bounded Rationality: Empirically Grounded Economic Reason*, Volume 3. Cambridge, MA: MIT Press.

Sloane, P. and MacHale, D. (2005a) *Outstanding Lateral Thinking Puzzles*. New York: Sterling.

Sloane, P. and MacHale, D. (2005b) *Classical Lateral Thinking Challenges* New York: Sterling.

Sternberg, R. and Davidson, J.E. (eds) (1995) *The Nature of Insight*. Cambridge, MA: MIT Press.

Sutcliffe, R. (1997) Constructive thinking and reconstructive thinking: Some thoughts about de Bono's thoughts. *Dialogue Works*, at: http://www.dialogueworks.co.uk/dw/wr/dbono.html.

Tanner, D. (1997) *Total Creativity in Business and Industry: A Road Map to Building a More Innovative Organization*. Advanced Practical Thinking Training, Inc.

Tidona, G. (2001) È possibile migliorare la creattivita e la riflessività dei ragazzi? (Can we improve thinking and creativity in school children?). *DIALOGO – mensile regionale di cultura, politica e attualità*, 7, XXVI.

Trías de Bes, F. and Kotler, P. (2003) *Lateral Marketing*. New York: Wiley.

350

29

Computer-supported idea generation

Rene Ziegler and Michael Diehl

Can computer-mediated communication facilitate idea generation?

Idea generation is a creativity task that involves productive thinking. Often, the generation of ideas is one of the early steps in problem solving. To foster idea generation, brainstorming (Osborn 1957) remains one of the most widely used techniques by individuals as well as groups (cf. Rickards 1999). It consists of a set of instructions designed to free the individual from the inhibiting effects of self-criticism and – in the case of group brainstorming – the criticism by others during a problem-solving session. In particular, brainstormers are instructed to keep the following in mind: the more ideas the better; the wilder the ideas the better; improve or combine ideas already suggested; and do not be critical. Probably the most important claim by Osborn was the statement that brainstorming would allow the average person to come up with 'twice as many ideas when working with a group than when working alone' (1957: 229). This claim is based on the assumption that members of a group will be mutually stimulated by the ideas of others and thus come up with ideas they would not have otherwise thought about. However, numerous studies have failed to support this optimistic prediction. Quite the contrary – perhaps one of the most consistent findings in social psychological research is the inferiority of brainstorming groups consisting of more than two members when compared to so-called 'nominal' groups (e.g. Diehl and Stroebe 1987). The productivity of such nominal groups is assessed as the quantity or quality of the non-redundant ideas from an equal number of individuals working alone.

Notwithstanding this consistent pattern of findings regarding idea production, there is an illusion of group effectivity (Stroebe *et al.* 1992). That is, group members feel facilitated in their idea production by the presence of other group members, find their work more enjoyable, and are more satisfied with their own performance.

Four major accounts have been suggested for the productivity loss in brainstorming groups (*downward social comparison, evaluation apprehension, free riding* and *production blocking*). With respect to downward comparison, groups are presumed to start performing at a relatively low level, which may cause high performers to feel deviant. As a result, high performers may lower their performance in the direction of the lower group standard, partly because of a desire to not look foolish or 'play the sucker' (Paulus and Dzindolet 1993). As Diehl and Stroebe (1987) were able to show, evaluation apprehension does have a small detrimental impact on idea generation. Thus, fear of negative evaluations from other group members may prevent individuals from presenting certain (e.g. controversial) ideas. In comparison, free riding was not found to be responsible for the production loss observed in real brainstorming groups. More importantly, however, production blocking has been identified as the major cause of the production loss in real groups (ibid.). Production blocking refers to the fact that only one member of a group can speak at a time during verbal brainstorming. In further experiments, Diehl and Stroebe (1991) found evidence that production blocking is not due to time constraints or motivational losses but is probably due to an impairment of the cognitive processes underlying idea production.

With the advent of modern computer technology, the problem of production blocking may be circumvented by the use of a computer network (e.g. Rickards 1987). Such a network allows all group members to express their ideas at any time and even so nevertheless might enable them to be stimulated by reading other group members' ideas. Further, the possibility of presenting the ideas expressed by a group member to other group members anonymously might help prevent evaluation apprehension on behalf of brainstormers. Given that stimulation is, first of all, a cognitive process, in the following we will turn to empirical evidence regarding interpersonal stimulation effects in free recall. This research area has explicitly referred to production blocking with respect to the effects of 'cuing' on memory performance.

Cognitive stimulation in idea generation: exploring the cognitive processes in free recall

The central assumption underlying (computer-supported) group brainstorming is that group members may be stimulated by the ideas of other group members by providing access to knowledge available in an individual's long-term memory. In this respect, work on the reproduction of learned items from memory is of interest. In particular, it has been studied whether the retrieval of a list of learned items is facilitated when part of the items are provided as a cue. On the one hand, and contrary to prediction, part-list cuing has been found to impair the retrieval of items rather than to facilitate it. On the other hand, retrieval cues may facilitate retrieval of items in the case of items from different categories (cf. Roediger 1974). Thus, at the individual level, cues may increase the flexibility of item reproduction, but decrease the number of items per category. Further, at the group level, it has been investigated whether items recalled by one group member may facilitate recall by other group members. However, no evidence of such cross-cuing has been found (e.g. Meudell et al. 1992), neither in the case of uncategorized material nor in the case of categorized lists. With respect to the latter, there also has been no evidence found for an increase in the number of categories from which items are recalled due to cross-cuing.

Moreover, other work on collective memory shows a similar effect of interactivity as work on group brainstorming. That is, real group memory is worse than nominal group memory (i.e. collaborative inhibition). As suggested by Basden et al. (1997), collaboration during retrieval of categorized lists may disrupt individual retrieval strategies (e.g. recall of items by position, alphabetically, by category, etc.). Especially, collaborative inhibition is attributed to a switching of categories during recall. In fact, on the one hand providing category names led to an increased number of recalled categories, but on the other hand it led also to collaborative inhibition, since more category switching occurred (ibid., Experiment 2).

With respect to idea generation, then, work on individual and collective memory suggests that ideas from other group members may have mixed effects. On the one hand, ideas of another group member may serve as cues that impair idea generation from the same categories. On the other hand, such ideas may make available categories more accessible. However, an important difference between reproduction of learned items versus production of ideas may be that the number of items that can be recalled is by definition limited to the learned list. In comparison, regarding the amount of ideas that may potentially be generated a limitation is set, in principle, only by an individual's knowledge base in long-term memory.

In the next section, we will review the literature on computer-supported idea generation. In this respect, as suggested by the above discussion of the effects of cuing (i.e. part-list cuing, accessibility of categories), it is necessary to take a look at different measures of productivity. In fact, to compare the productivity of different brainstorming groups, a number of different measures have been used. Basically, these measures can be grouped into measures of quantity and measures of quality. The first measure, fluidity, is defined as the sheer number of ideas generated. The second criterion is flexibility. This is defined as the number of different categories to which a set of ideas belongs (e.g. ideas pertaining to how to protect endangered animal species can be classified into categories such as 'changing consumer behavior' or 'policy changes', etc.). The higher the amount of different categories to which ideas belong, the more creative idea-production is considered to be. The third criterion, originality, is determined by the frequency with which any single idea is brought up in a given population – the less frequent, the more creative. Finally, the fourth criterion, elaboration, focuses on how concrete and thorough any single idea is. The more elaborated, the more creative.

Whereas the first criterion, fluidity, is a quantitative measure, the latter three are qualitative measures of creative thought. With regard to brainstorming, a basic finding in most of the research is the high correlation between both kinds of measures, i.e. quantity and quality (e.g. Diehl and Stroebe (1987) reported a correlation of $r = 0.87$ between the number of non-redundant ideas and the number of good ideas). Nevertheless, in order to gain insight into processes underlying idea generation in (computer-aided) brainstorming groups, it is instructive to consider both quantitative and qualitative outcome measures.

Computer-supported idea generation in groups and individuals: factors, processes and effects

In the following, we will review the empirical evidence regarding the role of production blocking, evaluation apprehension, free-riding, social comparison processes and – most importantly – cognitive stimulation in computer-supported idea generation. Although it may appear obvious, it seems necessary to point out that the question of whether computer-supported idea generation may help groups not only to overcome the process losses found in face-to-face (ftf) idea generation but to actually outperform their nominal counterparts can be answered only when computer-supported (cs) real groups are compared to nominal groups which also have to type their ideas using a keyboard. In comparison, any firm conclusions are difficult in the case of a comparison of computer-aided idea generation with idea generation by means of other kinds of idea expression (hand-writing, verbalizing) because of unknown individual differences with respect to speed of typing, hand-writing and speaking.

With respect to blocking, research shows that in computer-supported brainstorming the possibility for all group members to enter their ideas parallel with and independently of each other reduces the detrimental effect of blocking idea generation identified in ftf groups. Gallupe *et al.* (1994, Experiment 1) showed that idea production of real cs groups was reduced (and as low as in ftf groups) when there was a delay of 5 seconds during which an individual's keyboard was locked after he or she had entered an idea as compared to when there was no delay in cs groups. Secondly, turn taking in real cs groups (i.e. each group member can express one idea and then has to wait until all other group members have expressed one idea each) has been found to reduce productivity below the level of real cs groups without turn-taking (Experiment 3), and even below turn-taking ftf groups (Experiments 2 and 3). Third, a first-in procedure (i.e. an individual can only express an idea when the previous group member has finished expressing his or her idea) has been shown to reduce productivity of real cs groups as compared to nominal cs groups to the level of productivity of first-in ftf groups (Experiment 3). Thus, empirical evidence shows that the opportunity in real cs groups to enter ideas in parallel eliminates or at least reduces production blocking.

The effect of anonymity regarding evaluation apprehension and free-riding in idea generation has been tested in a number of studies. In most of these studies, no difference in the productivity between anonymous and non-anonymous idea generation was found (e.g. Pinsonneault *et al.* 1999). The only study to reveal higher productivity of anonymous cs groups as compared to non-anonymous cs groups (by entering their terminal number) was the one conducted by Cooper *et al.* (1998). Anonymous real cs groups were similar to nominal groups who had to hand-write their ideas. Thus, conclusions regarding this comparison are difficult because of a confound regarding anonymity and way of idea expression (typing versus writing). Further, this advantage came at the cost of increased numbers of unacceptable ideas.

The role of social comparison processes in computer-aided idea generation was investigated in two studies (Dugosh and Paulus 2005; Munkes and Diehl 2003). Dugosh and Paulus (2005) found an interaction trend such that many (versus few) stimulus ideas (from a pre-arranged database) led to somewhat more (fewer) ideas when the stimulus ideas were said to come from a previous participant with a similar creativity level (supposed to induce a high level of social comparison likelihood) rather than randomly drawn from an idea database (low likelihood). With respect to the number of original ideas generated, an interaction of number of stimulus ideas and social comparison likelihood revealed that whereas many stimulus ideas from a similar other (versus randomly drawn) led to more original ideas, few stimulus ideas led to more original ideas when they were allegedly drawn randomly (versus from a similar other).

Munkes and Diehl (2003) studied the role of the mere productivity of a similar other (i.e. information about another idea having been produced by a similar other via an idea counter without the idea itself being presented to participants). They found evidence for heightened productivity as a result of performance competition regardless of the level of performance of a similar comparison other (superior, equal or inferior). In contrast, no evidence for performance matching was found (Paulus and Dzindolet 1993). These findings were in line with predictions derived from Festinger's social comparison theory (1954), according to which social comparison should lead to competition due to a unidirectional upward pressure in the case of abilities.

With respect to the question of whether cognitive stimulation may lead real cs groups to outperform nominal cs groups, it has been argued that group size plays a crucial role such that large real cs groups outperform large nominal cs groups, whereas small real and nominal cs groups may not differ. In particular, computer-aided brainstorming is presumed to require a critical mass before process gains due to synergy have a significant effect on performance (Dennis and Valacich 1993). In their study, six-member and twelve-member real cs groups and nominal groups were compared. Whereas for six-member groups no difference was found depending on which technique was used, for twelve-member groups real cs groups outperformed nominal groups. However, one problem concerns the fact that nominal groups had to write down their ideas on paper rather than typing them. Further, it is of importance to distinguish effects of cognitive stimulation from redundancy reduction. Whereas redundancy can be avoided in real groups because group members are informed about the ideas of others, this is not possible in nominal groups. Since redundancy increases as an accelerated function of group size, larger groups are more disadvantaged than smaller groups. Thus, rather than providing evidence of heightened productivity with an increase in the number of group members in real cs groups, increasing levels of redundancy may lower the productivity with an increase in the number of group members in nominal groups. In fact, an analysis of the number of redundant ideas revealed that twelve-person real cs groups produced fewer redundant ideas than twelve-person nominal groups. The productivity difference between the two conditions ($d = 30$) was about equal to the difference in redundant ideas between the two conditions ($d = 34$; no difference regarding redundancy was found in six-person groups).

Other research involving smaller-sized groups has found mixed effects. For example, Ziegler et al. (2000) compared four-person real cs groups and nominal cs groups (as well as two-person real and nominal cs groups). In two studies, no difference regarding the number of non-redundant ideas was found between real and nominal cs groups (of either size). With respect to flexibility of idea generation, in one study it was found that four-person real cs groups (as compared to nominal cs groups) narrowed down their idea production to categories also searched by other group members. Further, ideas in nominal cs groups were found to be more elaborated than ideas of real cs groups. Dugosh et al. (2000, Experiment 3), in comparison, found increased idea generation of real cs groups as compared to nominal cs groups when four-person groups were instructed to pay attention to the group's ideas because they would have to recall them after the brainstorming session. As outlined above, the rationale behind the memory instruction was that other group members' ideas can only stimulate further ideas when they are not ignored.

For further studies comparing real cs groups and nominal cs groups, as well as a critique of some of the studies purported to show an advantage of real cs groups over nominal cs groups, see Ziegler et al. (2000) and Pinsonneault et al. (1999). Overall, the empirical evidence regarding cognitive stimulation suggests advantages for brainstorming in real cs groups. However, except for the experiment conducted by Dugosh et al. (2000), most studies do not allow firm conclusions to be drawn. Nonetheless, it seems fair to conclude that it is not the sheer number of group members that is crucial with respect to whether real cs groups outperform their nominal counterparts (see also, Pinsonneault et al. 1999). Rather, it may prove useful to test in more detail the processes that may help real cs groups to profit from a group's synergetic potential. In this respect, a number of studies have been conducted to research the effects of various factors regarding cognitive stimulation in computer-supported individual brainstorming.

Dugosh and Paulus (2005), for example, argued that common stimulus ideas should stimulate more new ideas than unique stimulus ideas because the former may overlap more with individuals' semantic networks. In line with expectations, the results showed that individuals generated more ideas when presented with 40 common stimulus ideas rather than 40 unique ideas (when only eight ideas were presented, idea type did not make a difference).

Nijstad et al. (2002) were interested in the effects of two factors on individual brainstorming. First, whether stimulus ideas were diverse or homogeneous (i.e. from many versus few categories); second, whether the presentation of the stimulus ideas was ordered or unordered (i.e. all stimulus ideas from the same path-goal category were presented in sequence versus randomized). Participants in all experimental conditions were given a recall instruction (cf. Dugosh et al. 2000). In a control condition, individuals brainstormed without any stimulus ideas. It was found that individuals in all four experimental conditions produced more ideas than individuals in the control condition. Diversity of idea production (i.e. flexibility) was higher in the case of diverse stimuli as compared to homogeneous or no stimuli. Within-category fluency was higher in the case of homogeneous stimuli as compared to diverse and no stimuli. Finally, Nijstad *et al.* (2002) found that clustering (i.e. the extent to which an idea is followed by an idea from the same category) was higher in the control condition than in the unordered presentation conditions.

While Nijstad *et al.* (ibid.) showed that compared to a control condition without any stimulation productivity was higher in individual brainstorming conditions in which ideas of others were presented, other studies (e.g. Ziegler *et al.* 2000) provide evidence that cognitive stimulation may actually reduce brainstorming performance at the group level. As research on collaborative remembering suggests, these mixed results may be explained by the fact that cognitive stimulation should only work if it does not interfere with memory processes underlying individual idea production. Therefore, first of all, ideas should be presented on demand (i.e. at will) of the brainstorming individual rather than contingent on factors not under the control of the individual. Moreover, presenting one's own ideas (i.e. self-cuing) should result in less interference than presenting ideas of other individuals (cross-cuing). Ideas, similar to learned items in free recall, are produced in semantically related clusters. Therefore, interference should be lowest when the last idea of a cluster is used for self-cuing.

Based on this reasoning, Müller *et al.* (2006) developed a software program that selects (in a first brainstorming phase) stimulation ideas according to their position within the temporal structure of the idea generation process. Results of an experiment comparing different kinds of stimulation with one's own ideas (self-cuing) showed, as expected, that (in a second brainstorming phase) a condition in which people were stimulated by the last idea of a cluster produced significantly more and better ideas compared to further experimental conditions with stimulus ideas not taken from the end of a cluster as well as a control condition without self-cuing. These results were replicated in a second study and contrasted with cross-cuing. Participants in the self-cuing condition outperformed the cross-cuing condition and the control group without cuing. Participants in the cross-cuing condition did not produce significantly more ideas than those in the condition without cuing. This demonstrates that self-cues from the cluster ends can increase individual performance much better than ideas from the cluster ends of another person.

Cognitive and motivational processes enhancing productivity in idea generation

The research reviewed in the previous section can be summarized as follows. Computer-supported group brainstorming can eliminate mutual production blocking as the major cause for the inferiority of real groups compared to nominal groups. However, even in the absence of production blocking, exchanging ideas in computer-supported brainstorming does not lead to more or more creative ideas at the group level. There is only one study, by Nijstad *et al.* (2002), providing evidence that the presentation of pre-selected ideas to individual brainstormers may affect idea production. Stimulating individuals with ideas from many versus few categories resulted in ideas from many or few categories, respectively. Stimulating individuals with ordered ideas or unordered ideas with respect to category affiliation led to more or less clustered idea production, respectively. The quantity or quality of the total amount of ideas produced by an individual, however, did not differ between the four experimental conditions. The only significant performance difference occurred when the four conditions with stimulation were compared to the control condition without stimulation.

Since higher performance may be due to enhanced motivation as well as to enhanced ability, it remains unclear what are the causes of the effects of stimulus ideas on individual productivity. As research by Munkes and Diehl (2003), as well as by Dugosh and Paulus (2005), shows, presenting ideas of others can lead to social comparison processes triggering the motivation to perform well. According to Festinger's (1954) social comparison theory, people have a need to evaluate their opinions and abilities. Whenever possible, they will use physical standards for these evaluations. If such physical standards are not available, they can be expected to use social standards (i.e. other persons). The tendency to make comparisons is highest when the comparison other is similar and it decreases as the comparison other becomes more discrepant. Festinger postulated that a pressure toward uniformity is present when an individual compares his or her opinions or abilities with those of other people. An additional unidirectional upward pressure is present when performances are compared in order to evaluate one's ability. This upward pressure motivates people to gain superiority over other people, which consequently leads to performance competition.

Whereas performance competition due to the presentation of stimulus ideas is restricted to interpersonal settings (cf. Munkes and Diehl 2003), performance comparison may occur whenever stimulus ideas are presented. Stimulus ideas in individual settings may not only provide information of which ideas (diverse versus homogeneous) or how the ideas (ordered versus unordered) should be generated (cf. Nijstad *et al.* 2002) but also may serve as a comparison standard regarding how many ideas are expected (cf. Dugosh and Paulus 2005). Therefore, empirical evidence showing that conditions in which stimulus ideas are presented result in higher productivity does not allow for the conclusion that this is due to a process of cognitive stimulation.

Cognitive stimulation refers to the process of making memory items more accessible. Memory items that are available may be temporarily inaccessible due to various reasons (e.g. priming of other topics or cognitive overload). In addition, items vary in their accessibility due the strength of their associative relations with other items in memory. There is an associative hierarchy from the most accessible to the least accessible items. When people are generating ideas, they will start with those categories that are most accessible and thus come to mind more easily. Generally, people will stick to a certain category until they get the impression that no further ideas will come to mind. In such a situation, people usually change the search domain and start generating ideas from another category. In order to come up with those remote items that are available but not easily accessible, two different approaches are possible: enhancing either the motivation or the ability to continue the search process. First, one could try harder, that is, not give up too early but search until the next item comes to mind. Second, one could come back to the category later by starting with a search cue that is most closely associated with the remote items, i.e. the last mentioned and thus least accessible item from the respective category. Stimulating idea generation by using the last item of a cluster instead of the first one does indeed result in more additional ideas from the given cluster (cf. Müller *et al.* 2006).

Implications for theory and practice of idea generation

Idea generation, like any other performance, is a product of ability and motivation. The ability to generate many ideas, and especially creative ideas, depends on the amount of domain-relevant knowledge stored in long-term memory. This knowledge is acquired by communicating directly with other people (e.g. face-to-face) or indirectly (e.g. via reading literature). The higher someone is intrinsically motivated, the more he or she will seek to advance his or her knowledge. The more domain-relevant knowledge is available, the better the potential to generate many creative ideas in a specific situation. However, in order to generate many creative ideas in regard to a certain problem, the available knowledge has to become accessible. This process also depends on ability and motivation. The situational ability of gaining access to remote ideas can be enhanced by stimulating diverse semantic categories (cf. Nijstad *et al.* 2002) or stimulating less accessible items within a semantic category (cf. Müller *et al.* 2006). The motivation to search for relevant knowledge items may be enhanced by social competition (cf. Munkes and Diehl 2003) or high comparison standards (Dugosh and Paulus 2005). This implies that a model of idea generation has to consider both cognitive and motivational processes. Whereas recent cognitive models of idea generation (e.g. Nijstad and Stroebe 2006) can account for possible facilitating effects of cognitive stimulation, they have problems in explaining inhibiting effects of cognitive stimulation. In addition, they ignore the effects of increases or decreases in the motivation to search for new ideas.

Computer-supported enhancement of idea generation

Computer-supported brainstorming in groups circumvents mutual production blocking and thus has proven to lead to higher productivity than brainstorming in face-to-face-groups, increasingly so with larger groups. However, real (i.e. interactive) computer-supported brainstorming groups are not necessarily more productive than nominal computer-supported brainstorming groups. At the very least, it seems unlikely that the sheer number of group members may ultimately prove to be the crucial factor necessary in order to reach the critical mass of cognitive stimulation making real cs groups outperform nominal cs groups. In fact, there is no clear-cut evidence that mutual cognitive stimulation will facilitate idea generation in a group brainstorming session. Therefore, instead of enhancing ability, computer support in group settings is, rather, a means to maintain participants' ability by avoiding production blocking and cognitive interference. In addition, it may enhance motivation through social competition. This may be achieved by using idea counters that disclose to the group members whenever someone has generated an additional idea (cf. Munkes and Diehl 2003).

In individual settings, the ability for idea generation can be enhanced by stimulating persons in a second phase using the last ideas of their idea-clusters generated in the first phase of a brainstorming session (cf. Müller *et al.* 2006). Since social competition is not possible in individual settings, an additional increase in motivation could be achieved by setting individually specified high performance standards (e.g. to produce 25 per cent more ideas than in the first phase of idea generation) and by providing information on the computer screen regarding how far someone is still away from this standard after each additional idea articulated. Computer-supported individual idea generation that facilitates access to remote problem-relevant knowledge and enhances motivation by high personal performance standards should therefore lead to superior creative performance compared to all other ways of generating creative ideas, whether individually or in groups.

Beyond such computer-supported idea generation of individuals or groups in small local or distributed networks, the internet offers various possibilities to exchange knowledge and ideas in extended virtual communities. The options and facilities of Web 2, especially, are generating new and challenging research questions regarding social influences on creativity and idea generation. What motivates people to share their knowledge and ideas with others? Does participating in web activities enhance knowledge and provide cognitive stimulation for generating creative ideas or products? Are specific applications or tools of Web 2 suitable for stimulating idea generation? Extending the research on computer-supported idea generation to the 'virtual world' may enhance our understanding of the social and motivational determinants of creativity in individuals and groups in the 'real world'.

References

Basden, B. H., Basden, D. R., Bryner, S. and Thomas, R. L., III. (1997). A comparison of group and individual remembering: Does collaboration disrupt retrieval strategies? *Journal of Experimental Psychology: Learning, Memory, and Cognition, 23*, 1176–1189.

Cooper, W. H., Gallupe, R. B., Pollard, S. and Cadsby, J. (1998). Some liberating effects of anonymous electronic brainstorming. *Small Group Research, 29*, 147–178.

Dennis, A. R. and Valacich, J. S. (1993). Computer brainstorms: More heads are better than one. *Journal of Applied Psychology, 78*, 531–537.

Diehl, M. and Stroebe, W. (1987). Productivity loss in brainstorming groups: Toward the solution of a riddle. *Journal of Personality and Social Psychology, 53*, 497–509.

Diehl, M. and Stroebe, W. (1991). Productivity loss in idea generating groups: Tracking down the blocking effect. *Journal of Personality and Social Psychology, 61*, 392–403.

Dugosh, K. L. and Paulus, P. B. (2005). Cognitive and social comparison processes in brainstorming. *Journal of Experimental Social Psychology, 41*, 313–320.

Dugosh, K. L., Paulus, P. B., Roland, E. J. and Yang, H. (2000). Cognitive stimulation in brainstorming. *Journal of Personality and Social Psychology, 79*, 722–735.

Festinger, L. (1954). A theory of social comparison processes. *Human Relations, 7*, 117–140.

Gallupe, R. B., Cooper, W. H., Grisé, M.-L. and Bastianutti, L. M. (1994). Blocking electronic brainstorms. *Journal of Applied Psychology, 79*, 77–86.

Meudell, P. R., Hitch, G. J. and Kirby, P. (1992). Are two heads better than one? Experimental investigations of the social facilitation of memory. *Applied Cognitive Psychology, 6*, 525–543.

Müller, S. C., Diehl, M. and Ziegler, R. (2006). Cross-cuing versus self-cuing: What enhances performance in a brainstorming task? *Proceedings of the 28th Annual Conference of the Cognitive Science Society* (pp. 1844–1849), Vancouver, Canada.

Munkes, J. and Diehl, M. (2003). Matching or competition? Performance comparison processes in an idea generation task. *Group Processes and Intergroup Relations, 6*(3), 305–320.

Nijstad, B. A. and Stroebe, W. (2006). How the group affects the mind: A cognitive model of idea generation in groups. *Personality and Social Psychology Review, 10*, 186–213.

Nijstad, B. A., Stroebe, W. and Lodewijkx, H. F. M. (2002). Cognitive stimulation and interference in groups: Exposure effects in an idea generation task. *Journal of Experimental Social Psychology, 38*, 535–544.

Osborn, A. F. (1957). *Applied imagination* (revised edition). New York: Scribner.

Paulus, P. B. and Dzindolet, M. T. (1993). Social influence processes in group brainstorming. *Journal of Personality and Social Psychology, 64*, 575–586.

Pinsonneault, A., Barki, H., Gallupe, R. B. and Hoppen, N. (1999). Electronic brainstorming: The illusion of productivity. *Information Systems Research, 10*, 110–133.

Rickards, T. (1987). Can computers help stimulate creativity? Training implications from a postgraduate MBA experience. *Management Education and Development Journal, 18*, 129–139.

Rickards, T. (1999). Brainstorming revisited: A question of context. *International Journal of Management Reviews, 1*, 91–110.

Roediger, H. L. (1974). Inhibiting effects of recall. *Memory and Cognition, 6*, 54–63.

Stroebe, W., Diehl, M. and Abakoumkin, G. (1992). The illusion of group effectivity. *Personality and Social Psychology Bulletin, 18*, 643–650.

Ziegler, R., Diehl, M. and Zijlstra, G. (2000). Idea production in nominal and virtual groups: Does computer-mediated communication improve group brainstorming? *Group Processes and Intergroup Relations, 3*, 141–158.

Part 6

Integration

30

Integration: prospects for future journeys

Mark A. Runco, Tudor Rickards and Susan Moger

Overview and future explorations of creativity and innovation

The introduction to this volume promised an intellectual journey through the various themes and chapters. The present chapter extends that journey by exploring intersections and convergences among the themes and paths and by identifying a few paths less travelled. The intention is to help place the ideas presented in this volume within the wider contexts of creativity research and practice.

Creative mechanisms and innovation processes

Many authors in this volume said something about the mechanisms underlying the creative process. Coyne (Chapter 3), for instance, described the relationship between sensory processes and creative thinking. Fisher and Amabile (Chapter 2) questioned the assumption of stages in creative work and suggested that it is most accurate to view innovation as improvisational. Stage theories have been used for years and years (Runco 1994; Wallas 1926) and can be quite useful, but Fisher and Amabile are correct that the underlying assumptions should be recognized. The general assumption that the creative process can be accurately understood by dividing up the work into discrete phases is obviously a kind of reductionism and unrealistic. Surely there is more fluidity and variation in the creative process than is captured by stage theories.

Such variation and fluidity is suggested by improvisation. Still, as is clear in the empirical research (Sawyer 1992), improvisation is not disorderly, nor even free of rules. There is, however, a great deal of latitude, and the objective is a creative performance. The 'rules' of improvisation are often implicit, but when everyone follows them, the result is creative. The result is, for that reason, sometimes described as *emergent* and surprising (De Cock and Rickards 2008; Estes and Ward 2002; Richards 1996).

Note that improvisation is often a matter of collaboration and teamwork. This is as much the case in organisational projects as it is in musical groups. The examples in Bruce's chapter (4) support the idea of organisations as improvisational systems.

Cox (Chapter 6) introduces the interesting idea of destruction within the creative process. This may not come as a surprise given Picasso's oft-quoted quip that 'all creativity is an act of destruction', and Schumpeter's influential concept of *creative destruction* from the economic literature. Nevertheless, it offers a provocative oxymoron. Thinking about oxymorons and apparent contradictions has been suggested as supporting reflective and creative thinking (Rothenberg 1999).

Turbulence is not far from the idea of destruction, and it too may play a role in creative work, as noted by Gryskiewicz in Chapter 9. Turbulence may function on an organisational level as anxiety does on an individual level: as an indication that some change is needed. The parallel between organisations and individuals can be taken further. Gryskiewicz encourages us to reinterpret turbulence as an opportunity for renewal and reinvention rather than a potential disaster!

Similar logic was applied some time ago by Wittgenstein (1961, quoted by Schuldburg 1994), though he was referring to personal problems which can disappear, in a manner of speaking, if reinterpreted as challenges to be valued, rather than undesirable. Such 'disappearance of problems' was explored in some depth by Runco (1999a) and Schuldberg (1994). There is, then, an intriguing theoretical intersection where individual and organisational thinking come together, and another concerning opportunities and turbulence, destruction and values.

Cox emphasised values as a necessary part of creative work. Several others have also explored the role played by values in the creative process (Dollinger *et al.* 2008; Kasof *et al.* in press). In the present volume, Cox (Chapter 6) ties values to collaboration and suggests that it is possible to construct win–win arrangements. Interestingly, Cox describes how values themselves are the result of creative thinking. He uses a transactional perspective, which fits nicely with several lines of current research on creativity within organisations (e.g. Sosik *et al.* 1998).

Runco (2004) took the extreme view and proposed that values may represent the most important part of the creativity complex. The rationale for this suggestion was that values determine how we direct our actions (e.g. towards things which we value), and as such determine the degree to which our creative potentials will be fulfilled. This holds true on the level of organisations (Amabile and Gryskiewicz 1989) and even cultures (Campbell 1960), as well. Paraphrasing Aristotle, 'What is honored in a culture will be cultivated there' (attributed to Aristotle by Torrance 2003: 277).

Context and creativity

Another intersection among paths (and thus a sort of consensus) is that creativity occurs within particular contexts. Two of the more important contexts described in the chapters of this volume are cultural and organisational. These do not merely act as influences and determinants, however, but instead are also influenced by creativity. In a word it is best to assume *bidirectionality*. It is simplistic to think that contexts are always the influence and creative thinking the result. Instead, an interplay implies that environments act on and are influenced by creative people and their efforts.

Chakrabarty and Woodman (in Chapter 16) show how considerations of multiple levels of creativity can point to this kind of interplay and interaction, as do the *person–environment interactions* (PEI), which are frequently cited in the organisational and psychological literatures (Drazin *et al.* 1999; Huber 1991; Runco 2007a).

Context may be domain- and field-specific. In the present volume, the field of design was several times given as an example. Bruce (Chapter 4), for instance, suggested that creative work is vital for a competitive advantage in the field of design, and much of what Tsoukas (Chapter 14) proposed applies very directly to the field of design.

Moran (Chapter 24) reminds us that the influences on creative and innovative work are not simple. Personal capacities play a role, as do domains, fields and contexts. It is not just a matter of one person and one environment, as might be implied by a simple PEI model, because various individuals are likely to be involved, as are teams, groups and other levels of an organisational hierarchy. Interactions among individuals and within an organisation then occur within a given culture, or even several of them, given the multinational basis of many contemporary organisations. Moran suggests that the full range of interactions can be captured with systems theory. Systems theory recognizes the various levels and the various directions of influence. Albert (1996), Csikszentmihalyi (1990) and Gruber (1988) have also offered parallel but slightly varied systems theories of creativity.

The chapters of Greve and Manimala about entrepreneurs reflect a specific kind of systems theory. Like Csikszentmihalyi's (1990) systems theory, with individuals influencing a field and perhaps eventually a domain, Manimala describes *acceptance* as an important part of the entrepreneurial process. An entrepreneur does not simply produce a good idea. Rather, the entrepreneurial process requires acceptance and commitment by a business and an audience, and for that reason efforts by entrepreneurs should include acceptance in their plans. This will contribute dramatically to their competitive advantage.

Greve's discussion of social networks links nicely the multilevel (and systems) perspective to the entrepreneurial process. His work applies very directly to complex technological innovations. The idea of targeting acceptance was discussed in depth by Kasof (1995), Runco (1995) and Amabile (1995).

Coyne (Chapter 3) and Price (Chapter 5) acknowledge context in their ideas about *situated creativity*. The former explores the significance of language and symbol systems for creativity, including sound and voice, which seems to be a unique contribution to the innovation and creativity literatures. The sensory basis of creativity indicates that creative work is not simply a metacognitive process but is also sometimes very basic and quite sensory. Price takes a more evolutionary perspective. Through such an approach, variations of ideas, insights or innovations are produced and then selected, based on their value or usefulness. Again, there is an assumption of 'fit,' though here it is between ideas and other products with an environment and earlier it was a person–environment (PEI) fit.

The evolutionary approach to creativity is an attractive one (Albert 2008; Gabora 2007; Simonton 1995, 2007; Weisberg and Hass 2007). It is, as you might expect, no longer considered to be an exclusively Darwinian process, as Martindale re-emphasises (Chapter 10).

Knowledge, personality and style

Although creativity may be supplanting knowledge as the most important commodity in industry and society as a whole (see Kaufmann and Runco, Chapter 13), knowledge is still enormously important for innovation. Fisher and Amabile (Chapter 2) emphasise the role of expertise, for example, and of course expertise is largely a reflection of an extensive and intricate knowledge base. Jeffcutt (Chapter 8) suggests that one of the more pressing issues is that of sharing knowledge and making it more widely available. It is not just a matter of generating new knowledge and ideas. Here, again, collaboration is significant.

Kaufmann and Runco (Chapter 13) question the boundaries of knowledge and creativity management. They raise the possibility that the two are inextricable, at least for truly meaningful knowledge. In this light, the shift from knowledge to creativity management is less a paradigm shift than a recognition of the role of knowledge in creativity, and vice versa. At the heart of this line of thought is the premise that 'to understand is to create' (Runco 2007b).

For Tsoukas, knowledge is developed via careful judgment and dialogue with both imagined and real collaborators. Such dialogue is consistent with the well-known tactic for creative thinking usually labeled 'shift perspectives', the idea being that real or imagined collaborators can provide or facilitate such a shift (Runco 1999b). The dialogues described by Tsoukas are also consistent with the imagined worlds and *paracosms* that are apparently frequently employed by highly creative scientists (Root-Bernstein and Root-Bernstein 2006).

Even on the level of the individual there is more to creative and innovative thinking than just knowledge and expertise. In the present volume, Guastello (Chapter 22) describes how personality influences creative work. Particular attention is given to mood, emotional intelligence and psychoticism. Earlier work even described how expertise can sometimes inhibit creative and innovative thinking! Apparently, the assumptions and routines that are used when there is a high level of expertise sometimes blind the expert to original ideas. Such is the occasional *price of expertise*.

Given the individual differences implied by the role of knowledge and personality, it is no surprise that Simonton suggests that some individuals are much more likely than others to influence fields and domains. These are the geniuses and leaders among us. In a sense, Simonton tells us how the *psychological creativity* defined by Boden (Chapter 15) can lead to *historical creativity*. (Much the same distinction is less elegantly but more commonly described as Little C Creativity and Big C Creativity.) Simonton's ideas also suggest that the concept of leadership is broader than it first may appear. Leaders may be business managers, supervisors and owners, but they may also be leaders in other domains. In fact, a leader is anyone whose thinking is influential and persuasive (Rickards and Clark 2005; Simonton 1990).

Arvonen (Chapter 25) and Mumford, Byrne and Shipman (Chapter 23) focus on leaders, the former emphasising the role of transformation and the latter the capacity to use both external and internal data. Zhang and Sternberg (Chapter 21) take a psychological approach to creative work, but they emphasise styles rather than cognitive capacity or ability. Once again, an intersection of research and theory should be acknowledged, for there is a substantial interest in styles and creativity (Basadur 1994; Martinsen 1995).

Methods and theories of creativity

Several chapters suggest methods for stimulating creative thinking. Ford (Chapter 26), for example, describes how visualisation can be used for prototyping and how thought experiments might be used with work proposals. Puccio and Cabra (Chapter 27) provide a thorough review of the *Creative Problem Solving* system of creative thinking, which has developed from the earlier efforts of Parnes and Osborn. They remind us how it can be useful to extricate critical processes from creative processes. This is an interesting and important idea for anyone interested in organisational creativity. New ideas are not only facilitated by tactical thinking but also by getting out of the way, or 'letting creativity happen'. This does of course not imply that critical and convergent processes are never useful for creative thinking (Runco 1994).

Dingli (Chapter 28) provides a much-needed critical review of the evidence for effectiveness of *lateral thinking* and its conceptual grounding. She also helps distinguish lateral thinking from Edward de Bono's other interesting contributions to cognitive studies.

As mentioned briefly just above, Boden (Chapter 15) distinguishes between *historical* and *psychological creativity*, and then describes how the latter can be simulated and assessed with computers and computer models. Ziegler and Diehl (Chapter 29) also identify a role for the computer, namely, as a tool for brainstorming and creative problem solving instead of for simulation and modeling. Of great practical importance is their idea that the problems that sometimes occur when brainstorming, such as production blocking, can be mitigated with computer-supported idea generation techniques.

Ideas are also at the heart of Rothberg's chapter. He suggests that existing measures, which look to inventions, patents and similar products, should be replaced with methods assessing idea activity. In addition to adding support to the role of ideas in creative work and innovation, Rothberg's logic complements Boden's argument about the distinction between historical creativity (which is objective and usually reflected in some result or product) with psychological creativity (which often involves ideation).

In a sense these views suggest yet another intersection of paths. In particular, they fit nicely with the systems theories mentioned above in that psychological and personal creative processes, including ideation and the invention of knowledge, are involved but could eventually become social, objective and consensual. This might involve the influence on fields and domains which are a part of systems theories.

Standing back, theories of artificial creativity suggest that we question the nature of creativity and innovation. Are they things that computers can do (Rickards 2002)? Similar grand questions are posed by Rehn and De Cock (Chapter 18), in their stimulating deconstruction of creativity and theories of innovation. Of special importance here is the question they ask about the novelty requirement for creativity. Even more significantly they draw attention to currently less travelled approaches to the study of creativity, as in Rickards and De Cock (1999).

Concluding remarks

The issues, possibilities and questions just mentioned indicate that our journey within this volume is finished, but other journeys await us. At this point, it should be clear that the chapters of this volume: (a) offer a fairly comprehensive overview of the current thinking about creativity and innovation, (b) are interconnected in numerous interesting ways, and connected to the larger innovation and creativity literatures, and (c) encourage our intellectual journeying along a variety of paths and directions. The field of creativity continues to fascinate with its variety and unanswered questions (George 2007). The journey promised in our introduction has not been a direct one, but the diverging paths have been worth exploration. Further explorations of creativity and innovation will no doubt prove to be enriched by the experience.

References

Albert, R. S. (1996). What the study of eminence can teach us. *Creativity Research Journal, 9*, 307–315.

Albert, R. S. (2008). The achievement of eminence as an evolutionary strategy. In M. A. Runco (ed.), *Creativity Research Handbook* (Vol. 3). Cresskill, NJ: Hampton Press.

Amabile, T. M. (1995). Attributions of creativity: What are the consequences? *Creativity Research Journal, 8*, 423–426.

Amabile, T.M. and Gryskiewicz, N.D. (1989). The creative environment scales: Work environment inventory. *Creativity Research Journal, 2*, 231–253.

Basadur, M. (1994). Managing creativity in organisations. In M. A. Runco (ed.), *Problem Finding, Problem Solving, and Creativity* (pp. 237–268). Norwood, NJ: Ablex.

Campbell, D. (1960). Blind variation and selective retention in creative thought as in other knowledge processes. *Psychological Review, 67*, 380–400.

Csikszentmihályi, M. (1990). The domain of creativity. In M. A. Runco and R. S. Albert (Eds.), *Theories of Creativity* (pp. 190–212). Newbury Park, CA: Sage.

De Cock, C. and Rickards, T. (2008). Understanding organisational creativity: Toward a multi-paradigmatic approach. In M. A. Runco (ed.), *Creativity Research Handbook* (Vol. 3). Cresskill, NJ: Hampton Press.

Dollinger, S., J., Burke, P. A. and Gump, N. W. (2008). Creativity and values. *Creativity Research Journal*, 19, 91–103.

Drazin, R., Glynn, M.A. and Kazanjian, R.K. (1999) Multilevel theorizing about creativity in organisations: A sense-making perspective. *Academy of Management Review, 24* (2), 286–307.

Estes, Z. and Ward, T. B. (2002). The emergence of novel attributes in concept modification. *Creativity Research Journal, 14,* 149–156.

Gabora, L. (2007). Why the creative process is not Darwinian. Comment on 'The creative process in Picasso's Guernica sketches: Monotonic improvements versus nonmonotonic variants'. *Creativity Research Journal, 19,* 361–365.

George, J.M. (2007) Creativity in organisations. *Academy of Management Annals,* 1, 439–477.

Gruber, H. E. (1988). The evolving systems approach to creative work. *Creativity Research Journal, 1,* 27–51.

Huber, J. (1991) *Macro–micro Linkages in Sociology.* Newbury Park, CA: Sage.

Kasof, J. (1995). Explaining creativity: The attributional perspective. *Creativity Research Journal, 8,* 311–366.

Kasof, J., Chen, C., Himsel, A. and Greenberger, E. (in press). Values and creativity. *Creativity Research Journal, 19,* 105–122.

Martinsen, O. (1995). Cognitive styles and experience in solving insight problems: Replication and extension. *Creativity Research Journal, 8,* 291–298.

Richards, R. (1996). Does the lone genius ride again? Chaos, creativity and community. *Journal of Humanistic Psychology, 36,* 44–60.

Rickards, T. (2002) Creativity in humans, computers and the rest of God's creatures: A meditation from within the economic world. In P. McKevitt, S. O'Nullain and C. Mulvihill (eds), *Language, Vision, and Music: Selected Papers from the 8th International Workshop on the Cognitive Science of Natural Language Processing,* pp. 373–384. Amsterdam: John Benjamins.

Rickards, T. and Clark, M.C. (2005) *Dilemmas of Leadership.* Abingdon, Oxon: Routledge.

Rickards, T. and De Cock, C. (1999). Sociological paradigms and organisational creativity. In A. Montuori and R. Purser (eds), *Social Creativity* (Vol. 2, pp. 235–256). Cresskill, NJ: Hampton Press.

Root-Bernstein, M. and Root-Bernstein, R. (2006). Imaginary worldplay in childhood and maturity and its impact on adult creativity. *Creativity Research Journal, 18,* 4, 405–425.

Rothenberg, A. (1999). Janusian process. In M. A. Runco and S. Pritzker (eds), *Encyclopedia of Creativity* (pp. 103–108). San Diego, CA: Academic Press.

Runco, M. A. (ed.) (1994). *Critical Creative Processes.* Cresskill, NJ: Hampton Press.

Runco, M. A. (1995). Insight for creativity, expression for impact. *Creativity Research Journal, 8,* 377–390.

Runco, M. A. (1999a). Tactics and strategies for creativity. In M. A. Runco and S. Pritzker (eds), *Encyclopedia of Creativity* (pp. 611–615). San Diego, CA: Academic Press.

Runco, M. A. (1999b). Tension, adaptability, and creativity. In S. W. Russ (ed.), *Affect, Creative Experience, and Psychological Adjustment* (pp. 165–194). Philadelphia, PA: Taylor and Francis.

Runco, M. A. (2004). Personal creativity and culture. In L. Sing, A. N. N. Hui and G. C. Ng. (eds), *Creativity: When East meets West* (pp. 9–21). Singapore: World Scientific Publishing.

Runco, M. A. (2007a). *Creativity: Theories and Themes: Research, Development, and Practice.* San Diego, CA: Academic Press.

Runco, M. A. (2007b). To understand is to create: An epistemological perspective on human nature and personal creativity. In R. Richards (ed.), *Everyday Creativity and New Views of human nature: Psychological, Social, and Spiritual Perspectives* (pp. 91–108). Washington, DC: American Psychological Association.

Sawyer, K. (1992). Improvisational creativity: An analysis of jazz performance. *Creativity Research Journal, 5,* 253–263.

Schuldberg, D. (1994). Giddiness and horror in the creative process. In M. P. Shaw and M. A. Runco (eds), *Creativity and Affect* (pp. 87–101). Norwood, NJ: Ablex.

Simonton, D. K. (1990). History, chemistry, psychology, and genius: An intellectual autobiography of historimetry. In M. A. Runco and R. S. Albert (eds), *Theories of Creativity* (pp. 190–212). Newbury Park, CA: Sage.

Simonton, D. K. (1995). Exceptional personal influence: An integrative paradigm. *Creativity Research Journal*, *8*, 371–376.

Simonton, D. K. (2007). The creative process in Picasso's Guernica sketches: Monotonic improvements versus nonmonotonic variants. *Creativity Research Journal*, *19*, 329–344.

Sosik, J. J., Kahai, S. S. and Avolio, B. J. (1998). Transformational leadership and dimensions of creativity: Motivating idea generation in computer-mediated groups. *Creativity Research Journal*, *11*, 111–121.

Torrance, E. P. (2003). Reflection on emerging insights on the educational psychology of creativity. In J. Houtz (ed.), *The Educational Psychology of Creativity* (pp. 273–286). Cresskill, NJ: Hampton Press.

Wallas, G. (1926). *The Art of Thought*. New York: Harcourt Brace and World.

Weisberg, R. A. and Hass, R. (2007). We are all partly right: Comment on Simonton. *Creativity Research Journal*, *19*, 345–360.

Index

4Ps, systems perspective 292–300

AARON program, exploratory AI 182, 184
absorptive capacity 281
abstract creativity 33
abstraction in forecasting 281–2
Acceptance-Finding step in CPS 331
action-oriented bias 287
actualized innovativeness 74, 81–2
adaption-innovation 73–4, 75, 257–8, 259–60
adaptors 74, 75–6, 82, 83–5, 122
addressivity in dialogue 164
administrators, intellectual styles 263
adoption-innovation theory 84
adoption modelling in marketing 82–3
adversarial management 65
advertising, initial adopters 83–4
affiliation need 251
agon 33
agreeableness, personality trait 268, 272, 274
algorithmic execution in organizational action
        17–18
algorithmic planning in organizational action
        17–18
Allport, G.W. 267
Alvesson, M. 153–4
Amabile, Teresa 13–24, 327, 363, 365
ambiguity tolerance
    consumer innovation 73
    positive turbulence 100–1
Amin, A. 93
analogical reasoning 321–3
analogy, entrepreneurship 124
Anderson, P.C. 136

Andreasen, N.C. 274
Andrews, F.M. 134
anonymity, idea generation 354
anxiety, personality trait 268
aporia, deconstructing creativity 29, 222
Applied Production Loading (APL) 139
architectural designing 169–71
Ardrey, R. 30
Aristotle 364
arm's length relationship, relationship
        management 65, 66–7
arms race 52
artifacts
    interaction 225
    quasi-dialogues 165, 167–71, 172
artificial intelligence (AI) 179, 181, 184
    applications 186–7
    connectionist 181
    public acceptance 185–6
artificial life (A-Life) 179, 181, 183
artistic person, career interest type 261
Artistic and Scientific Activities Survey (ASAS)
        269, 271, 275–6
Arvonen, J. 302–13, 366
Assessing the Situation step in CPS 332
associative memory, AI 181
autopoetic communities 47, 48

backup plans, creative leaders 285–6
Bain, A. 112–13
Bakhtin, M. 163–4
balance, leadership 288
Bamberger, J. 167
Bandura, A. 154

Barnowe, J.T. 279
Basadur, M. 157, 331
Basden, B.H. 352
Basic Course model in CPS 331
Bass, B. 307
bearish markets for creativity 210
beauty 114
Bechky, B.A. 322
Becker, F. 50
Beethoven, L. van 247, 248–9, 250, 252–3
behaviour, leadership 249–50
Bell, D. 162
Bell Laboratories 104
Benjamin, W. 225
Bessant, J. 38, 40, 42, 43
Best, M. 93, 94
Bhidé, A. 218
Biggs, J.B. 262
Binsted, K. 184
bipolar personality traits 267–8
Blanchard, K. 303–4
blat networks 228
blind variation and selective retention, ideas search 214
Boden, M. 156, 179–88, 234
Bourdieu, P. 295
brain dominance mode, intellectual style 257–8, 259
brainstorming 158, 344, 351–3
    computer-supported 353–9, 366–7
Brown, J.S. 225
Bruce, M. 37–45, 363
Bruner, J.S. 296
bullish markets for creativity 209–10
Burke, J. 14
Burns, J.M. 305
business value, creation or destruction 61–70
buyer dominance, relationship management 66–7
buy low, sell high principle, economic principle 206–7
Byrne, C. 279–91, 366

Cabra, J. 327–37, 366
California Psychological Inventory (CPI) 268, 270–1, 272
Campbell, D.T. 115, 214, 319
canned knowledge, knowledge management 152
capital, creativity resources 207, 208–9
cardinal personality traits 267, 268, 274–6
career development, geniuses 252–3
career interest type, intellectual style 257–8, 261
cargo cult of policy makers 95
category width, consumer innovation 73, 76, 84
Cattell, J.M. 249

Cattell, R.B. 267, 268
C,zanne, P. 225–6
Chakrabarty, S. 189–205, 364
Challenge, lateral thinking 343
Chambers, R. 110
chance-configuration theory, ideas search 214
change-oriented leadership behaviour 7, 302–13
chaos 101
charismatic scale 307
Chemical Thermo Pulping (CTP) 140
Clarification step in CPS 331
Coase, R.H. 217
cognitive-behavioural traits, consumer innovation 73
cognitive dissonance, innovators 84
Cognitive Research Programme (CoRT), lateral thinking 341–2, 345, 346
cognitive style 71–87, 256–7
    leadership 250–1
cognitive variation, leadership 250–1
Cohen, H. 182, 184
Cohen, W.M. 196
coherence, sound 26
Coleridge, S.T. 181
collaboration 363
    inhibition 352
    relationship 65, 66–7
    win–win 4–5, 61–70
collective creativity 322–4
collectives at multiple levels, relationship creativity 189–205
combination
    entrepreneurial techniques 124
    knowledge creation 160
combinational creativity 180, 181, 184, 186
combinative capability, prototypes 323
commitment, systems perspective 296–8
communities, evolutionary perspective 50–1
competence-destroying innovation 121
competence-enhancing innovation 121
competitive advantage
    entrepreneurial innovation 120
    resource activity 235
complementary practices, organizational economics 217–18
complex evolving systems 51–2
complexity 110–11, 133
componential model, CPS 331–2
componential theory of organizational creativity 15–16, 18
compositional creativity 14–21, 22
computers
    see also artificial intelligence; technology
    design use 41

idea generation 351–9, 366–7
models and application 179–88
public acceptance 185–6
conceptual entrepreneurial techniques 124
conceptualization, entrepreneurship 123
conferences, positive turbulence 102
Conger, J.A. 307, 308
conscientiousness, personality trait 268, 274
conscious evaluation, entrepreneurship 124
consideration scale, leadership 307
consumer innovation 5, 71–87
content analysis, RID 250–1
context 33, 364–5
creative industries 91, 92
individual creativity 134
situated creativity 365
contextual thinking 333
contrarian attitude, economic perspective 207
conventional person, career interest type 261
convergent thinking 120, 126, 257–8, 261, 332, 336
Cook, S.D. 162, 164, 225
Coons 303
copying, deconstructing creativity 226
Costa, P.T. Jr 268
counter-response, dialogue 167
Cox, A. 61–70, 363–4
Coyne, R. 25–36, 363, 365
CPE see change-oriented leadership behaviour
craftsmen, entrepreneurship 123
creative action
relationship creativity 191–204
in solitude 194, 195, 196–9
in solitude plus integration 194, 195, 199–202
in synergy 194, 195, 202–4
creative class 151, 232
creative destruction 121, 364
creative industries 5, 88–98
Creative Personality Scale 271
creative problem solving (CPS) 328–36, 343, 347, 366
Creativity Index, occupational profiles 269–70
creativity-relevant processes 15, 16, 21–2
crises
improvisation 20–1
improvisational creativity 14
leadership 286, 289
response, positive turbulence 105
cross-cuing, item recall 352
cross-disciplinary cooperation 137–8
cross-domain knowledge 137
Csikszentmihalyi, M. 49, 50, 52, 134, 271, 293–4, 300, 365
Csikszentmihalyi's fields 46, 48, 51

cultural economy, creative industries 92, 93, 94–7
culture
computers and creativity 185
context 364
Cummings, A. 298
customer active paradigm 41

Darwin, C. 46, 110
Darwin, E. 110
Data-Finding step 331
Dawkins, R. 49, 51, 53, 112
de Bono, E. 8, 338–50, 366
declarative-generative knowledge 150–1
declarative memory 21
de Cock, Christian 222–31, 367
deconstructing creativity 6, 29, 222–31
deGeus, A. 235
Deleuze, G. 31, 32
dependence, relationship creativity 190–1
depreciation, economic perspective 208
Derrida, J. 29, 222–3, 228–9
design 4, 11–57, 364–5
business 37–45
destruction 61–70, 121, 363–4
development
creative industries 94–5
entrepreneurship 121
problem solving 328–30
developmental psychology, genius and leadership 252–3
diagnostic thinking 333
dialogical relationships, organizational knowledge 6, 160–76
Diamond, J. 47, 208
Dickson, W.D. 303
Diehl, M. 351–9, 366–7
differential psychology 249–52
differentiated products 61
Dingli, S. 338–50, 366
Direct Attention Thinking Tools (DATT), lateral thinking 341–2
discovery programs 182–3
Distin, K. 53
Distortion, lateral thinking 344
divergent thinking 133, 134, 271–2, 274, 275–6
CPS 332, 336
entrepreneurs 120, 126
forecasting 281
intellectual style 257–8, 261
lateral thinking 347–8
domain 50–1, 298–9
systems approach 293–5, 296, 299, 300
domain-relevant skills 15, 16
domain-specific expertise 252–3

double interacts 166
downward social comparison 351, 353, 354
Drazin, R. 286
Dreman, D. 207
Duchamp, M. 224
Dugosh, K.L. 354, 355, 357

Eagleton, T. 225
early adopters 71–87
Eastern philosophy in CPS 334–5
Echo 27–8
ecology 50
economic leadership 248, 250
economic regions, creative industries 91, 93, 94,
    95, 96
economics
    costs and benefits 211
    current perspectives 6, 206–21
    idea activity 237–41
economy
    creative problem solving 327–8
    knowledge-based 149–51
ecosystems 50
    creative industries 88, 92, 93–4, 95–6
edge-of-chaos 52
Edgerton, D. 227
Edison, T. 321–2
effectuation, prototypes 322
ego-strength 157–8
Einstein, A. 318
elaboration, idea generation 109
Elsbach, K.D. 324
embodied creativity 32–3
emotion, CPS 333
emotional information 215
emotional intelligence 275–6, 334
employee orientation 308
enactment theory 319
endogenous growth theory 212–14
Engleman, R. 319
enigma of creation 226
enterprising person, career interest type 261
entrepreneurial framework conditions (EFCs) 122
entrepreneurs 5, 107–45, 365
    creativity 119–31
    effectuation 322
    social networks 132–45
    USSR blat networks 228
environment 4–5, 59–106
    business value 61–70
    compositional creativity 15
    computers and creativity 185
    creative industries 94
    creativity market 209–10

entrepreneurship 120, 122–3, 128–9
    knowledge relationships 88–98
    positive turbulence 99–106
    scanning 280–1
    style/involvement model 5, 71–87
epistemic objects, dialogue 167, 169, 172
Escape method of provocation 344
ethnography, integration 336
evaluation
    apprehension 351–2, 353, 354
    leadership 283–4, 289
evaluative thinking 333
everyday creativity 31–2
evolution 5, 48–51, 180, 365
    AI 183
    innovation and creativity 109–18
evolutionary art 183, 186
evolutionary programs 185
exchange relationships, business value 61–70
exogenous growth theory, economics 212, 213
experience, entrepreneurship 123
experimental culture 21
experimentation 287–8
    entrepreneurship 123
expertise 365
    complex innovations 132–45
    creative industries 94
    guest experts 104
    individual creativity 134
    outside experts 103
explicit knowledge 152, 156, 160–1
exploitation 121
exploration 121
exploratory art 186
exploratory creativity 156, 180, 181–3
exploratory programs 186–7
extrinsic benefits, economics 209, 211
extrinsic motivation 300
extroversion, personality trait 260, 268, 274
Eysenck, H.J. 268, 275

facilitation 341
Facilities Management 50
Faltin, G. 124
familiarity, entrepreneurship 120
family background, geniuses 252
Farris, G.F. 134
feeling person, personality 260–1, 268
Feist, G.J. 272
Festinger, L. 357
field 298–9
    systems approach 293–5, 298, 299, 300
field-dependence/independence, intellectual style
    257–8

filtered views, idea screening 235
Fisher, C. M. 13–24, 363, 365
Fisher, R. A. 111–12
Fiske, D. 268
fit, role theory 294
fitness function 183
fitness landscapes 52
flexibility, consumer innovation 73
Florida, R. 94, 151, 232
Focus, lateral thinking 342
Focus on Facilitation, lateral thinking 341
font-design program, computer models 182
Ford, C. 193, 195, 317–26, 366
forecasting, leadership 281–2, 285, 289
Foucault, M. 295
Foxall, G. 71–87
fragmented groups, inspiring relationships 196–9
frames of reference, social networks 137
Framo Engineering 138–9
free riding 351, 352, 353, 354
Freud, S. 27
Friedman, T.L. 327
frustration, entrepreneurship 122
Fuller, S. 211

Gallupe, R.B. 353–4
Galton, F. 25, 247, 248, 252
game theory 299
gaps, sound 30–1
Gates, W. 250
Gell-Mann, M. 52
general environment, entrepreneurship 122–3,
        128–9
generalized other, dialogue 162–3, 164, 169,
        170–1
genetic algorithms 183
genius, leadership 247–55
Getzels, J.W. 271
Getz, I. 206–21
Global Entrepreneurship Monitor (GEM) 122
goal congruence, relationships 192
Goldberg, L.R. 268
Goleman, D. 333
Gonz lez, D. 346
Good Old-Fashioned AI (GOFAI) 181
Gregorc, A.F. 261–2
Greve, Arent 132–45, 365
gross domestic product (GDP) 238–40
Grossman, G.M. 213
Grossman, M. 152
groups 44
    see also relationship creativity
    collaboration 363
    dialogue 172

effectivity 351–2
    innovative thinking 158
    memory 352–3
    positive turbulence 103–4
    self-construal 190–1
growth residual, economics 212, 213
Gryskiewicz, S.G. 99–106, 364
Guastello, S.J. 267–78, 366
Guattari, F. 31, 32
Guilford, J.P. 133
Gundry, L.K. 281

habitual action, relationships 193, 194, 195
habitual responses, improvisation 18, 22
Hallmark 102
Harding, R. 110, 117
Hargadon, A.B. 321, 322
Hart, M.H. 249
Harvesting, lateral thinking 342
Hatsopoulos, G. 14, 19, 20
Hayek, F. 216
Heath, C. 319
Hebb, D.O. 112
Hegel 226
Helmholtz, H. von 109, 113
Helpman, E. 213
hemispheric style, intellectual style 259
Hemphill 303
Hermans, H.J.M. 167
Hermes 29
Herron, L. 124
Herscovitch, L. 297
Hersey, B. 303–4
hidden innovation, design 37, 41
hidden knowledge 152
Hills, G.E. 124
historical creativity 179, 187, 366, 367
Holland, J.E. 299
Holland, J.L. 261
horizontal information transmission 51
horizontal relationships 63–4
Hughes, A. 348
Hughes, P. 348
Hughes, T.P. 282
human capital 207, 208–9
human resource management 263
hybrids, economics 217, 218

Ichijo, K. 153, 154, 155, 156
ideas
    activity 7, 232–43
    combination 214
    development 215–16
    dynamic approach 232–3, 234

economics 212–13
evaluation 283–4, 289
generation 14, 15, 109
    computer-supported 351–9, 366–7
    entrepreneurship 128
    lateral thinking 338
    unconsciousness 113–14
interaction 236–7
management system 216, 219
progression 236–7
selection 215
sources, entrepreneurship 125–6
static approach 232–4
ideational fluency 275–6
ideational thinking 333
identification, problem solving 328–9
IDEO 15
illumination, creative process step 14, 218
imagination
    design 38
    geniuses 250–1
imagined others, quasi-dialogues 165, 166–7, 169,
    172
imitation, deconstructing creativity 226
Immelt, J. 334
implementation 219
    entrepreneurship 125–8
    step in CPS 331
implicit knowledge 152, 156
improvisation 4, 13–24, 38, 39, 295, 363
incremental innovation 120–1
incubation, creative process step 13–14, 109, 218
independence
    entrepreneurship 121, 122
    exchange relationships 66–7
    personality trait 268
    relationship creativity 190–1
    voice 29
Indian philosophy 334
individuals 136–8
    capabilities, creative industries 94
    creativity 133–4
    knowledge management 156–7, 158
    personal creativity 245–313
    positive turbulence 101–3
    structured interventions 315–59
    systems approach 299
    systems model 293–4, 296, 298
information, integration 286–7
informational turbulence 99–106
information management systems 152
information processing 153
information technology see artificial intelligence;
    computers; technology

initial adopters in marketing 75
innate innovativeness 72–3, 74, 81–2, 85
innovation 5, 107–45, 363–4
    see also entrepreneurship
    capacity 237–8, 240
    complex, networks 132–45
    creative industries 92–3
    creative problem solving 327
    design 37–8, 40–4
    diffusion 234
    economics 212–19
    evolutionary models 109–18
    hidden 37, 41
    incremental 225
    index 237–40
    inherent 73, 74, 82, 85
    leadership 279
    style/involvement model 71–87
innovative cultures 133
innovative thinking 157–8
innovators 74, 75, 76, 82, 83–5, 122
    cross-disciplinary cooperation 137
    fringes of industry 136
insight 339
inspiration, idea generation 109
inspiring relationships 192–3, 195, 196–9
institutional economics 216–17, 218
integrating relationships 192–3, 195–6, 199–202
integration 8, 363–9
    leadership 279–91
integrative complexity, leadership 250
intellectual property, creative industries 93
intellectual styles 7, 256–66
intelligence, genius 250
intentionality, entrepreneurship 125
interactionist model, networks 134
interdependence, exchange relationships 66–7
interdisciplinary networks 137–8
internal locus of control, entrepreneurship 121
internal sabbaticals 102
international economics, idea activity 237–41
inter-organization relationships 198–9, 201–2,
    203–4
inter-person relationships 196–8, 200–1, 202–3
inter-team relationships 198–9, 201, 203
intrinsic benefits, economics 209, 211
intrinsic interest, entrepreneurship 122
intrinsic motivation 21, 133–4, 296, 300
introversion 251, 260, 268
intuition 17, 260, 268, 272–3
    entrepreneurship 124, 128
intuitional intelligence 334
investigative person, career interest type 261
investment theory, economics 206–7, 208

inward focus, leadership 279–91
Isaksen, S.G. 331

James, V. 71–87
James, W. 125
Jameson, F. 224
Jamison, K. 275
Janszen, F. 327
JAPE joke-writing program 184
Jeffcutt, P. 88–98, 365
joke programs 184
judgement-perception trait 260–1, 268
Jung, C. 260, 268

Kagan, J. 259
Kahn, R. 304, 308
Kahneman, D. 208
Kanter, R.M. 133
Kanungo, R.B. 307, 308
Katz, D. 304, 308
Katzenbach, J.R. 200
Kaufmann, G. 149–59, 328, 331, 365
Kempen, H.J.G. 167
Keynes, J.M. 210
Kickul, J. 281
Kirton Adaption-Innovation Inventory (KAI)
        71–2, 73–4, 75–85
Kirton, M.J. 259–60
Kirzner, I. 124
Knorr Cetina, K. 167
knowledge 295, 365–6
    brokering 321
    canned 152
    continuum 154
    conversion 160–1
    creation 155, 156, 160–76
    creative action 194–5
    creativity meta-theories 177–243
    cross-domain 137
    declarative-generative 150–1
    diversity 191
    economics 207–8, 215
    explicit 152, 156, 160–1
    as goal 150–1
    hidden 152
    idea activity 234
    implicit 152, 156
    interfaces 93
    management 6, 147–76
    as means 150–1
    relationships 88–98
    routine-procedural 150
    tacit 38, 150, 152, 156, 160–1
    task domain 215

knowledge-based economy 149–51
knowledge-creating firms 153
knowledge society 149
Koberg, C.S. 280
Kogut, B. 323
Kolb, D.A. 123
Korreman, D. 153–4
Kotler, P. 348
Kramer, R.M. 324
Kuhn, T.S. 206–7
Kutaragi, K. 335

Lacan, J. 29
Lacy, S. 16
Lakeoff, G. 296
Lamarck, J.B. de 110–11
language
    evolution 111, 116
    symbols 296
    theory 29
lateral thinking 8, 338–50, 366
    puzzles 348
leader cognition 280
leadership 7, 41, 44
    change-oriented behaviour 7, 302–13
    charismatic 309
    definitions 303–4
    genius 247–55
    idea activity 235
    outward focus, inward focus and integration
        279–91
    presidential 251
    transformational 307, 309
learning
    approach 257–8, 262
    idea activity 234
    style 256
Leonard-Barton, D. 39, 41
Leonardo da Vinci 27
leverage, buyers-suppliers 66
Levinthal, D.A. 196
Levitt, T. 105
liability of newness 119
liability of smallness 119
lifespan, creativity resources 207, 208
linear thinking 101
Livingston Lowes, J. 181
Lloyd Wright, F. 182
Locke, J. 154
Lonergan, D.C. 283–4
Long, W. 124
longevity, idea activity 235
Lord, A. 53, 54
Lubart, T. 206

McCaulley, M.H. 260
McClelland, D.C. 122, 208
McCrae, R.R. 268, 271–2, 274
McFazdean, E. 347
MacHale, D. 348
McKelvey, B. 123
MacKenzie, K.D. 319
McLuhan, M. 28, 29, 33
McMullan, W.E. 124
McPeck, J.E. 345
macro-level, knowledge management 156–7
Maeda, J. 225
Malthus, T. 111
Manimala, M. 119–31, 365
marginal utility, economics 209
Marine Consultants Group (MCG) 138–9
Marintek 138–9
market
    economics 209–10
    initiation 75
    initiators 75
    organizational economics 217
    revenue, business value 61
marketing
    consumer innovation 72, 75, 82–4
    lateral 348–9
    myopia 105
    vertical 348
Martensson, M. 153
Martindale, C. 109–18, 250
Marx, K. 226
Marxism 228
Matthew effect 210
Mayer, J.D. 275
Mead, G.H. 162–3, 164
meditation 334
memes 49, 50–1, 52–4, 112
memory, group 352–3
Mendel, G. 110
mental illness 274–5
mental self-government 260
mentors, geniuses 253
Mess-Finding step in CPS 331
meta-theories 177–243
Meyer, J.P. 297
Midgley-Dowling thesis 81–2
Miller, A. 318, 320
Miller, G. 116–17
mind style 256, 257–8, 261–2
missions, leadership 280–1, 282–4, 287–8, 289
mode 2 methods, knowledge economies 96–7
Moger, S. 3–9, 44, 238, 363–9
mood disorders, personality 274–5
Moran, S. 292–301, 365

motivation
    creative action 194–5
    individual creativity 133–4
    leadership 251
Muller, S.C. 356
Mumford, M.D. 133, 279–91, 366
Munkes, J. 354, 357
mutuality 62, 68
Myers, I.B. 260
Myers-Briggs Type Indicator (MBTI) 268, 272–3

Napoleon Bonaparte 247, 248–9, 250, 252–3
Narcissus 27–8
natural selection in evolution theory 110, 111
negative-sum outcomes see non-zero sum
        outcomes
nested multi-level networks 136–43
networks 44, 365
    complex innovations 5, 132–45
    creative industries 92, 93, 95
    entrepreneurship 125–6
    multi-level 6, 132–45, 364
    positive turbulence 102
neural networks 112, 114
    artificial 181
neuroticism, personality trait 268, 272, 274
neutrality, deconstructing creativity 227–9
new organizational knowledge (NOK) 160–76
Nijstad, B.A. 355–6
non-adversarial management 65
Nonaka, I. 153, 154, 155, 156, 160–1, 166, 168
non zero-sum outcomes, exchange relationships
        62, 64, 67–8
Noppe, L.D. 257
Norsk Hydro 142
Not Invented Here syndrome 133
novelty
    computers and creativity 179–80
    deconstructing creativity 223–6
    entrepreneurship 120
    improvisation 17–18, 19
    prototypes 323
Nussbaum, B. 336

objectivity
    knowledge creation 161
    positive turbulence 100
occupational profiles 269–71
O'Connor, G.C. 281, 282
Oedipus 27
Oetzel, J.G. 190
Ohio questionnaire, leadership 304–5
Oldenburg, C. 224
Oldham, G.R. 298

Open Innovation 41
openness
    personality trait 268, 271–3, 274
    to experience 251
opportunity
    costs 211
    identification 124
    improvisational creativity 14
Organisation for Economics Cooperation and
        Development (OECD) 237–41
organizational creativity 4, 8
    improvisation 13–24
    prototyping processes 317–26
organizations
    context 364
    creative industries 91, 92, 94, 95
    creative potential 37–45, 363
    ecologies 47–8
    economics 217–18
    effectiveness, CPE 308–9
    improvisation 18–21
    knowledge 156, 160–76
originality, deconstructing creativity 225–7
Osborn, A.F. 328, 336, 351
Osborne, A.A. 155
Osburn, H.K. 285
outsourcing 202
outward focus, leadership 279–91

Palladio, A. 26
paradigm-breaking techniques 347
paradigm-preserving techniques 347
paradigm-stretching techniques 347
Parnes, S. 155
Pasteur, L. 215
Paulus, P.B. 354, 355, 357
perception-judgement trait 260–1, 268
perceptual style 258
Perry-Smith, J.E. 137, 298
person, systems perspective 292–300
personal creativity 7
personality 365–6
    adaption-innovation theory 73–4
    consumer innovation 71, 72–3, 76–85
    entrepreneurship 119, 121–2, 125
    traits 215, 251–2, 267–78
    types 257–8, 260–1
person-environment interactions (PEI) 364, 365
Piaget, J. 157
Picasso, P. 294, 363–4
Plan for Action step in CPS 331
planning, leadership 284–5, 289
Plato 165
Poincaré, H. 25, 26, 113–15, 116, 117

Pélya, G. 347–8
Popper, K. 154
Porter, M.E. 235
positive turbulence 5, 39, 99–106
post-structuralism, memes 53
power 295
    buyers-suppliers 66, 67, 69
    leadership 303–4
    need 251
pragmatism 287
Prairie House program 182
praxis 222, 225, 228
predictive science 180
preparation
    creative process step 13, 15, 16, 109, 218
    idea generation 109
press, systems perspective 292–300
Price, I. 46–57, 365
problem presentation, creative process step 15, 16
problem solving 8, 248
    consumer innovation 83
    design 38, 42–3
    knowledge management 150–1
    past, present and future 327–37
procedural memory 21–2
process, systems perspective 292–300
Process Planning step in CPS 332
process view of creativity 318–20
product
    creativity 16
    development 40
    life cycle, consumer innovation 72, 82, 83
    systems perspective 292–300
production blocking 351, 352, 353–4
production dimension, CPE 307, 308
profitability, business value 61
prototypes 8, 39, 40, 41, 161, 167–8, 366
    organizational affects 317–26
Provocation, lateral thinking 343–4
psychoanalysis, self recognition 29
psychological creativity 179–80, 187, 366, 367
psychological differentiation 258
psychoticism, personality trait 268, 274
Puccio, G. 327–37, 366
punctuated equilibrium 49

quasi-dialogical exchanges 165–71, 172

Rabelais, F. 29–30
radical innovation 120–1, 133, 135, 138–43
Random Input, lateral thinking 343
random variation, evolution 111
realism 226
realistic person, career interest type 261

real-time information 21
reciprocal collaboration 66, 68
reflection, entrepreneurship 123
reflectivity-impulsivity, intellectual style 257–8, 259
Regressive Imagery Dictionary (RID) 250–1
Rehn, A. 222–31, 367
relationships
    collectives at multiple levels 189–205
    management 61–9
remote associations 100, 101, 214
resource activity, idea activity 235–6
resource allocation model 235
resources
    economics 207, 215
    entrepreneurship 119
response execution, creative process step 15, 16, 20
response generation, creative process step 15, 16, 20
Reversal, lateral thinking 344
RIASEC model 299
Richards, R. 274
Rickards, T. 3–9, 44, 124, 222, 238, 363–9
Ricoeur, P. 226
risk-taking
    change orientation 307
    economics 208
    entrepreneurship 121
    improvisation 21
Ritchie, G.D. 184
Roethlisberger, F.J. 303
role
    change, positive turbulence 103
    systems approach 298–300
role models
    geniuses 253
    intellectual styles 263
Romer, P.M. 212–14
Rose, N. 54
Rosenberg, N. 218
Rothberg, G. 232–43, 367
Rubenson, D.L. 158, 207–8, 209, 211, 212
Ruggiero, V.R. 332
Runco, M. A. 3–9, 149–59, 207–8, 209, 211, 212, 363–9
Ruskin, J. 25

Sapienza, H.J. 124
Sarasvathy, S.D. 322
Sartre, J.-P. 222
Sawyer, R.K. 295
scanning, leadership 280–1, 289
Schleicher, A. 111
Schoenfeldt, L.F. 134

Schön, D. 167, 169–71
Schrage, M. 167–8
Schubert 275
Schuldberg, D. 364
Schumpeter, J.A. 119, 121, 216, 224, 364
Schutte, N.S. 275
Scott, A. 92, 93, 94, 95
Scott, G.M. 283, 334
Second Life 335
selection, problem solving 328–30
self-confidence 157
self-consciousness 162
self-construal 190–1
self-control, personality trait 268
self-development 162–3
self-esteem, consumer innovation 73
self-recognition 29
self-reports 109, 269
sensation-seeking, consumer innovation 73
sensemaking 194–5, 286, 317, 320–1
senses, sound 25–36
sensing person 260
sensing trait 268
sensory experience 4
serious creativity 339–40
sexual selection 111–12, 116
Shalley, C.E. 133
shared vision 190, 191–3, 194, 200, 201–4
Shipman, A. 279–91, 366
Shissler, J. 271
signifiers, memes 53
Simon, H. 183
Simonton, D.K. 115–16, 208, 214, 215, 247–55, 299–300, 365
simplicity
    deconstructing creativity 225
    lateral thinking 341
Singh, R.P. 125–6
Sitkin, S.B. 319
situated creativity 4, 365
situatedness, creative industries 92, 95
Six Action Shoes, lateral thinking 341
Sixteen Personality Factor Questionnaire (16PF) 267–8, 270–1, 272
Six Thinking Hats, lateral thinking 341–2, 345
Six Value Medals, lateral thinking 341
Sloane, P. 348
Smith, A. 217
Smith, D.K. 200
Snodgrass, A. 30
social construction 33
social dimension, role theory 294, 295, 296–7, 300
social person, career interest type 261
socio-cultural evolution 111

So, K.-T. 334
Solow, R.M. 213, 214, 216
sound
    cuts 29–31
    sensory experience 4, 25–36
source traits 271–4
space to adapt 46–57
Spencer, H. 110–11
spiritual intelligence 334
Stacey, R.D. 296
Statoil 139, 142
Stepping Stone method of provocation 344
Steptoe, S. 327
Sternberg, R.J. 206, 209, 210, 211, 212, 256–66,
    366
Strange, J.M. 282–3
strategic alliances 134
strategic thinking 333
Stroebe, W. 351–2
structuralism, memes 53
structure dimension, CPE 307–8
structured interventions 8, 315–59
style/involvement model, consumer innovation 5,
    71–87
subconscious activity, entrepreneurship 124
subjectivity
    knowledge creation 161
    positive turbulence 100–1
Submerged Turret Loading (STL) 138–40, 142
Submerged Turret Production (STP) 138,
    139–40, 142
Sullivan, D.M. 323
superhuman-human fallacy 185
supplier dominance 66–7
surface personality traits 267–8, 272
sustainable development, creative industries 95
Sutcliffe, R. 347
Sutton, R.I. 321
symbolic dimension
    commitment 296–8
    lower visibility 295–6
    role 294, 295
    systems model 298–300
synergizing relationships 192–3, 195–6, 202–4
synesthesia 26
systems perspective 7, 292–301
systems theory 365
    leadership 304

Taalas, S. 228
tacit knowledge 38, 150, 152, 156, 160–1
tactical thinking 333
Takeuchi, H. 160, 161, 166, 168
Task Appraisal step in CPS 332

task domain, knowledge 215
task environment 122–3, 129
task facilitation, entrepreneurship 129
task motivation 15, 16
task orientation 300
teachers, intellectual styles 263
teams
    see also groups
    collaboration 363
    positive turbulence 103–4
technology
    see also artificial intelligence; computers
    complex, social networks 132–45
    creative industries 94
    entrepreneurship 121
    exogenous growth theory 212–13
    integration 335
    knowledge management 150, 152
    positive turbulence 101, 103–4
    push 121
    sound 28
temporally proximate stimuli 19, 20–1, 22
ten-year rule, career development 252–3
textuality 29
themes 238
Thermo Mechanical Pulping (TMP) 140–1
thinking
    see also divergent thinking
    brain dominance mode 257–8, 259
    contextual 333
    convergent 120, 126, 257–8, 261, 332, 336
    diagnostic 333
    evaluative 333
    ideational 333
    innovative 157–8
    lateral 8, 338–50, 366
    linear 101
    outside the box 338–50
    parallel 341–2, 347
    strategic 333
    style 256, 257–8, 260
    tactical 333
    visionary 333
    wishful 344
thinking person 260
Thinking Skills Model 330–4
thought experiments 318, 320–1, 322
Threefold Model of Intellectual Styles 256–66
Thrift, N. 93
Tierney, P. 279
time
    costs and benefits 211
    creative industries 92
    improvisation 17–18

pressure 22
timing 287
Timmons, J.A. 122
Torrance, E.P. 25
tough-mindedness, personality trait 268
trade shows 104
training, human capital 208–9
training and development programs, intellectual styles 263
transactional exchange, win-win collaboration 61–70
transaction costs, economics 211
transformational creativity 180
Transformation step in CPS 331
trans-governmental industries 89
trans-professional industries 89
trans-sectoral industries 89
travel assignments 102
Treffinger, D.J. 331
Trias de Bes, F. 348
trickle-down effects 211
Tsoukas, H. 160–76, 364, 366
turbulence 364
    positive 5, 39, 99–106
Tushman, M.L. 136
Tversky, A. 208

unconsciousness, idea generation 113–14
uniqueness, deconstruction 225–7
unity, sound 26
use-initiation 75, 85
use-innovativeness 74, 75

validation, creative process step 15, 218–19
value
    circuits, creative industries 93
    computers and creativity 180, 183, 185
    creation, win-win collaboration 61–70
    deconstruction 226
    markets 210
    screens 320
Van de Ven, A. 41–2, 319
variation and selective-retention (VSR) model, process view 319, 320, 321, 322
verification, creative process step 14, 109
vertical information transmission 51
vertical marketing 348
vertical relationships, business value 63, 64, 65–6, 67

Vesper, K.H. 124
virtual environments 335
vision
    change orientation 306, 307
    sound 25–33
visionary thinking 333
visualization, prototypes 317–18, 366
Vitruvius, P. 26
voice 164
Volosinov, V.N. 165
Vries, H. de 111
Vygotsky, L.S. 163, 292–3, 296, 300

Waddell, C. 275
Waddington, C. H. 54
Walberg, H. 207, 210
Wallace, A.R. 111
Wallas, G. 13–14, 109
Wallis, C. 327
Ward, T.B. 124
Watkins, M. 166
Web 2 358
Weick, K.E. 166, 317, 319, 320, 321
Weisberg, R.W. 134
Weitzman, M.L. 213
West, M.A. 279
Wiggins, G. 169–70
Williams, B. 228
win-lose outcomes 62
win-win collaboration 4–5, 61–70
Wishful Thinking 344
Wittgenstein 364
Woodman, R.W. 134, 189–205, 364
work experience, entrepreneurship 125
writing 29

Xiao, Y. 285

Yanow, D. 162, 164
Yeh, Y.-C. 133

Zander, U. 323
Zenger, T.R. 218
zero-sum outcomes, exchange relationships 62, 64, 67–8
Zhang, L.-F. 256–66, 366
Ziegler, R. 351–9, 366–7
Zizek, S. 224–5
zone of proximal development (ZPD) 292

eBooks – at www.eBookstore.tandf.co.uk

A library at your fingertips!

eBooks are electronic versions of printed books. You can store them on your PC/laptop or browse them online.

They have advantages for anyone needing rapid access to a wide variety of published, copyright information.

eBooks can help your research by enabling you to bookmark chapters, annotate text and use instant searches to find specific words or phrases. Several eBook files would fit on even a small laptop or PDA.

NEW: Save money by eSubscribing: cheap, online access to any eBook for as long as you need it.

Annual subscription packages

We now offer special low-cost bulk subscriptions to packages of eBooks in certain subject areas. These are available to libraries or to individuals.

For more information please contact webmaster.ebooks@tandf.co.uk

We're continually developing the eBook concept, so keep up to date by visiting the website.

www.eBookstore.tandf.co.uk